Washington DC

written and researched by

Jules Brown

this edition researched and updated by

Jeff Cranmer

D1465137

ROUGH
GUIDES

www.roughguides.com

The US Capitol at night

Introduction to

Washington DC

As a nation's capital, Washington DC – showtown USA and self-professed political arbiter of the Free World – takes some beating. Along its triumphant avenues stand historic buildings that define a world view, while on either side of the central Mall sit the various museum buildings of the planet's greatest cultural collection, the Smithsonian Institution. For an introduction to the United States or a crash course in politics, portraiture or paleontology look no further than the spacious, well-ordered, Neoclassical sweep that is downtown DC. With a population of less than 600,000 residents it comes way down the list of American cities, and is likewise outnumbered by just about every foreign capital you could think of. But though a small fry in terms of population, it's not small in scale at all. Everywhere Washington boasts the bold expanses and monumental architecture of a carefully planned capital.

Given that it would become the consummate political power center, it seems fitting that DC's very founding was the result of political wrangle. In the late eighteenth century, Congress acceded to the demands of the Northern states to assume their Revolutionary War debts, but squeezed a key concession for the South: rather than being sited in one of the big Northern cities, the new federal capital would be built from scratch

Fact file

- Washington DC is the **federal capital** of the United States of America, founded in 1791, named for George Washington and located in the District of Columbia.

- Every president except the first, George Washington, has **lived in the White House** in Washington DC. The first president to be inaugurated in DC was the third, Thomas Jefferson.

- DC's **population** is a modest 522,000 – down some 100,000 from a decade ago – 62 percent of whom are black, 34 percent white and 3 percent Asian. The population of the Greater Metropolitan Area, taking in parts of Virginia, West Virginia and Maryland – including the Baltimore area – is closer to 7.5 million.

- DC's **major employer** is the federal government (employing 185,000 people in the city alone); other primary industries include tourism and hospitality, the legal profession, trade associations, education, biomedical research, and publishing.

- The city covers approximately **70 square miles**. About 29 percent of the land is devoted to federal parks, making DC one of the greenest cities in the US.

- The DC area has the world's largest library (Library of Congress), largest office (Pentagon building), tallest masonry structure (Washington Monument) and most-visited museum (National Air and Space Museum), as well as the nation's biggest military cemetery (Arlington), oldest fish market (Fish Wharf), largest single-roofed interior space (Union Station) and first museum of modern art (Phillips Collection).

on the banks of the Potomac River, midway along the eastern seaboard. And while not actually *in* the Deep South, Washington in the Territory (later District) of Columbia was very definitely *of* the South. French architect Pierre L'Enfant planned the city on a hundred-square-mile diamond-shaped piece of land donated by the tobacco-rich states of Virginia and Maryland; Virginia later demanded its chunk of land back, which is why there's a bite out of the diamond shape across the Potomac River. Slave labor drained the floodlands and erected the public buildings, and Virginian high society frequented the townhouses and salons that flourished after the government moved in during 1800.

But to paint DC as a Southern city is to miss the point. John F. Kennedy famously pointed out its contradictions in his waspish comment that Washington was "a city of Southern efficiency and Northern charm." Even more important than its geographical location was its unique experimental nature – a modern, planned capital built for a disparate collection of states seeking security in unity. As a symbol of union, its finest hour came within a generation of its founding – the city that was built largely by slaves became the frontline headquarters of the fight against slavery, as Abraham Lincoln directed the Union troops from the capital's halls and offices. After the Civil War, thousands of Southern blacks arrived in search of a sanctuary from racist oppression and, initially, to some extent they found one. Racial segregation was banned in public places and Howard University, the first US institution of higher learning that enrolled black people, was set up in 1867. By the 1870s African-Americans made up over a third of the District's population, but as poverty and squalor worsened, official segregation was reintroduced in 1920, banning blacks from government buildings and the jobs they had come to find.

Since the 1930s, DC has been both a predominantly black city and a federal fortress. Shunned by the white political aristocracy, the city is run as a virtual colony of Congress, where residents have only nonvoting representation and couldn't even participate in presidential elections until the 1960s. Suffering an endless cycle of boom and bust, the city has one of the country's highest crime

Foods of the world

In a city where the world's politicians, bankers, diplomatic corps and press gather, it's hardly surprising that the traditional food of almost every nation is available at local restaurants. You can eat every-

thing from Argentinean to Vietnamese – the city's still waiting for its first Yemeni or Zambian eating houses – while for a quick bite you're never far from a taco, bagel, panino, wrap, sub, chili dog, muffin, blini, empanada, pizza or donut. Certain specialities are well worth seeking out: Vietnamese cafés and restaurants (especially across the river in Arlington) are always excellent; hands-on Ethiopian dining is big in Adams-Morgan and elsewhere; while gourmet Italian and suit-and-tie European places satisfy the expense-account crowd. And if you are in the mood for an all-American-style experience – perhaps some raw oysters and a grilled strip steak – clubby saloon-style restaurants pepper Georgetown, among other areas. For a run-down of the scene, plus our recommendations, turn to p.253.

DC for free

While London, Tokyo and Paris regularly figure as the world's most expensive capital cities, the cost of a visit to Washington DC can come as a hugely refreshing surprise. You can, of course, spend a fortune on five-star hotels and top-of-the-line restaurants, but so much of your day-to-day tourist itinerary is free it's hard to part with so much as a buck. It's all quality stuff, too. Virtually every museum and gallery – including the famous Smithsonian museums – has free entrance, and most have a free program of events too, from children's activities to evening concerts. The blockbuster tours of the White House, FBI, Congress, Supreme Court, Bureau of Engraving and Printing and Library of Congress – none costs a penny. The famous presidential memorials, historic houses, cemeteries, concerts on the Mall, Fourth of July fireworks, even the Zoo – you can't give your money away. You will need to spend five dollars a day on a transport pass if you're not to exhaust yourself completely, but that seems a small price to pay for accessing the biggest range of free attractions in the States. For city tranpsort details, see p.28; to start reading about the big attractions, turn to Chapter 1, "The Mall."

rates and appalling levels of unemployment, illiteracy and drug abuse. Federal government money props up the city, pays its administrators and affects virtually every aspect of local commerce and industry. That fact is galling in the extreme to the majority of American citizens, to whom "Washington" is a dirty word, a place inhabited only by self-seeking politicians isolated within the fabled Beltway, the ring road that circles the city and is used as a metaphor for all that's different about DC.

Meanwhile, twenty million visitors come to Washington each year for fun, making it one of the most visited tourist destinations in the country. Kept away from the city's peripheral dead zones, they tour a scrubbed, policed and largely safe downtown swathe where famous landmark –

White House, US Capitol, Washington Monument – follows world-class museum – National Air and Space Museum, National Gallery of Art – with unending and uplifting regularity. Even better, most of what you see in Washington is free, and getting around (on a subsidized transport system that has few equals in the United States) is easy. True, a sense of community, or even neighborhood, is rare – especially downtown, where the entire place falls strangely silent after 6pm and on weekends. But pockets of vitality do stand out, in historic

Pockets of vitality stand out in historic Georgetown, arty Dupont Circle and trendy Adams-Morgan, where what nightlife there is shakes its fist at the otherwise conservative surroundings

Georgetown, arty Dupont Circle and trendy Adams-Morgan, where what nightlife there is shakes its fist at the otherwise conservative surroundings. You'll eat well, from a bounty of different cuisines, and nowhere will you be better informed about what's happening in America. Pick up the paper, switch on the TV or radio, and tune in to the thousands of broadcasters, lobbyists, journalists and politicians who shape the views of the world from this city of glorious compromise.

What to see

There's no better way to come to grips with the city than by taking a two-mile stroll along the grassy reach of **The Mall**, the city's principal thoroughfare and major showpiece destination. You'll come back here time and again, to view the overpowering memorials and monuments to George Washington, Abraham Lincoln, Thomas Jefferson, Franklin Delano Roosevelt and the Vietnam and Korean War veterans, or to browse the collections of the peerless Smithsonian museums and galleries, or the National Gallery of Art. Whether you're interested in space rockets or fine art, American or natural history, African carvings or contemporary sculpture, there's an exhibit on the Mall to suit you.

The US Capitol, at the Mall's eastern end, marks the geographical center of the city, since all neighborhoods and quadrants radiate out from its familiar white dome. **Capitol Hill** is one of DC's oldest neighborhoods, rich in nineteenth-century row houses, and ripe for a stroll from the Capitol itself to other defining buildings such as the Supreme Court and Library of Congress. Immediately south of the Mall, two of the most popular attractions in DC – the Federal Bureau of Engraving and Printing and the Holocaust Memorial Museum – are the undisputed highlights of the **Southwest/Waterfront** area. Monolithic federal office buildings occupy the rest of the no-man's-land between the Mall and the Washington Channel, though a thriving fish market and several waterfront seafood restaurants pull visitors away from the museums. To the **Southeast**, hard against the Anacostia River, the neighborhood toughens: there are sporadic attractions at the Navy Yard and, across the river, in Anacostia itself, but these areas do not lend themselves to casual exploration – certainly not by tourists on foot. There are no such caveats about the heavily visited area around the **White House** and **Foggy Bottom**, a neighborhood that stretches off to the northwest of the Mall. Quite apart from the president's house, this compact block of streets holds heavyweight attractions such as the Corcoran Gallery of Art, the renowned Kennedy Center and the infamous Watergate building.

The city is run as a virtual colony of Congress, where residents have only nonvoting representation and couldn't even participate in presidential elections until the 1960s

See everything along and around the Mall and you've seen the greater part of monumental Washington, but you still won't have much impression of a living, working city. What's known as **Old Downtown** – north of the Mall between the White House and Union Station – was where nineteenth-century Washington first set out its shops and services along the spine of Pennsylvania Avenue, the country's most prominent parade route. After years of neglect, it's today undergoing spirited restoration and can count revitalized streets, plazas, galleries and restaurants alongside its traditional attractions: the FBI Building, the Old Post Office and the buildings associated with President Lincoln's assassination. North of Pennsylvania Avenue, another development zone centers on the MCI Center, a sports

Face-to-face with the president

It's unlikely you're going to bump into the president while you're in town (though you never know), but you'll come face-to-face with his distant predecessors at every turn. The major memorials on the Mall – to Washington, Jefferson and Lincoln – all feature their statues, Lincoln pops up again near Judiciary Square, while both Lincoln and Washington have likenesses in the National Cathedral. The only president honored near the White House itself is Andrew

Jackson, whose statue is in Lafayette Square, and there's one of Ulysses S. Grant by the Capitol Reflecting Pool, in front of the Capitol. More recent presidential statues are harder to come by, with FDR (at the FDR Memorial) and JFK (in the Kennedy Center) about the extent of it. Perhaps you have to be widely known by your initials before they'll consider erecting a statue in your honor – so Dubya (George W Bush) has made a good start.

and entertainment arena that sits between Chinatown and the fast-emerging 7th Street corridor. Wedged against the Mall, **Federal Triangle** siphons off downtown sightseers to the National Archives; fewer make the effort to tour the district's other splendid Neoclassical buildings.

It's in the business district of **New Downtown**, along and around K Street, that Washington most resembles any other modern American city. From here, long diagonal avenues march off through a number of neighborhoods that mark the end of the line for most tourists. The historic townhouses and mansions of chic **Dupont Circle** hide a gaggle of low-key museums and an expanding enclave of art galleries; the bar-and-restaurant zone of **Adams-Morgan** to the north gets trendier by the day at the same time as it squeezes out its Latino heritage; while, to the east, the historic black neighborhood of **Shaw** boasts the thriving nightlife corridor of U Street.

West of downtown, across Rock Creek, the historic neighborhood of **Georgetown** predates DC and was once a thriving town in its own right. It's now the quintessential hangout of the chattering classes and the students of Georgetown University, who make the shops, galleries, bars and restaurants very much their own. The first bona fide city suburbs were in the **Upper Northwest**, where the nineteenth-century wealthy created picket-fence paradises in areas like Woodley Park and Cleveland Park. The Metro brings visitors out here today for the hugely enjoyable National Zoological Park and the landmark National Cathedral, while with more time and your own transportation, you can get to the glades, dales and riverbanks of Rock Creek Park.

As a cursory glance at the map will tell you, that still leaves a lot of Washington to cover. Seventy percent of the city's population, predominantly black, lives outside the environs of the Mall and the affluent Northwest – what P.J. O'Rourke calls the "white pipeline" of the city. But there's little that tourists are encouraged to see in the disparate neighborhoods of Northeast and Southeast Washington – with just a few exceptions, these contain some of the poorest, most run-down areas in the city. Instead visitors are steered south and west across the Potomac into Virginia, to **Arlington**, easily accessible by Metro and holding the region's major military sights: Arlington National Cemetery (burial place of the Civil War dead and the Kennedys), the Marine Corps (Iwo Jima) Memorial and the Pentagon. Farther out from the city, day trips to historic **Alexandria** (fifty years older than Washington DC) and to **Mount Vernon**, the family estate and burial place of George Washington, are more than worth your time.

When to go

Before air conditioning Washington was deserted from mid-June to September... But [now] Congress sits and sits while the presidents – or at least their staffs – never stop making mischief.

Gore Vidal, *Armageddon: Essays 1983–1987*

The local **climate** isn't great, it has to be said – often unbearably hot and humid in summer and bitterly cold in winter. It's claimed, with some measure of truth, that such an inauspicious spot was picked precisely to discourage early elected leaders from making government a full-time job. The advent of widespread air-conditioning during the 1950s alleviated matters, though, and as long as you're suitably kitted out for venturing outdoors you'll encounter few periods when sight-seeing becomes unpleasant. **Best times to visit** are spring, early summer and fall, when the weather is at its most benign; there's usually snow (occasionally severe) in January and February, while late summer (July and August) is too hot and humid. Whenever you come, bring suitable, comfortable shoes – there's a lot of walking to be done.

	Jan	Feb	Mar	Apr	May	Jun	July	Aug	Sept	Oct	Nov	Dec
Av. daily max (°F)	42	44	53	64	75	83	87	84	78	67	55	45
Av. daily min (°F)	27	28	35	44	54	63	68	66	59	48	38	29
Av. rainfall (in)	3.4	3	3.6	3.3	3.7	3.9	4.4	4.3	3.7	2.9	2.6	3.1

things not to miss

It's not possible to see everything that Washington has to offer in one trip – and we don't suggest you try. What follows is a selective taste of the city's highlights: stirring memorials and savoury meals, street-level stimuli and tranquil urban retreats, all arranged in five colour-coded categories, which you can browse through to find the very best things to see and experience. All highlights have a page reference to take you straight into the guide, where you can find out more.

01 National Cathedral Page **208** • Come for a service, some inspiring music, or just to poke around this Gothic marvel, which wouldn't be out of place in medieval Europe.

02 Frederick Douglass National Historic Site

Page **129** • Well off the tourist track, the fairly humble home of former slave and abolitionist leader Frederick Douglass proves that not all DC's most affecting sights have to be monumental in scale.

03 Gospel brunch Page **144** • The city's most swinging date is the weekly Sunday song-and-food fest at the Corcoran Gallery of Art, when gospel numbers echo through the usually historic gallery.

04 **Rare bears** Page **211** • The National Zoological Park is much more than a mere animal display, with its re-created habitats and educational programs, but its star pandas (Mei Xiang and Tian Tian) still take center stage.

07 **Kayaking the Potomac River** Page **32** • Why walk when you can paddle? DC's most unusual sightseeing tour takes in the monuments and memorials from the river.

05 **Lincoln Memorial** Page **52** • The best-loved and most harmonious of all DC's presidential memorials – many come back here time and again to soak up the atmosphere.

06 **Adams-Morgan restaurants** Page **256** • DC's funkiest neighborhood has the city's most eclectic selection of restaurants, where you can eat anything from Ethiopian – the most ballyhoot local treat – to Salvadorean to Thai.

08 **The US Capitol** Page **98** • Highlight of the self-guided tour around the Capitol is the superbly embellished Old Senate Chamber, a rare survivor from the nineteenth century.

09 **Fourth of July celebrations** Page 316 • The city's biggest party erupts every Fourth of July, starting with a reading of the Declaration of Independence and ending with a stupendous fireworks display over the Mall.

10 **The Whistler collection** Page **64** • Whistler's works dominate the Freer Gallery of Art: some 1200 pieces, in addition to his glorious decoration of the Peacock Room, which occupies one corner of the museum.

11 **National Cherry Blossom Festival** Page **316** • When the cherry trees bloom in spring, DC celebrates with a parade, the crowning of a festival queen, lantern-lighting and dancing.

12 **The White House** Page **133** • You'll have to get up very early and wait in line if you want to tour the president's house at 1600 Pennsylvania Avenue NW, but it's a must-do if you want an inside glimpse of the most famous address in America.

13 **Ben's Chili Bowl** Page **272** • Chili dogs, cheese fries and shakes, at their very finest, in U Street's most venerable hangout.

14 **Sessions of the Supreme Court** Page **106** • Visitors are welcome when the Court is in session (October until June) to hear arguments presented at the nation's highest law court.

15 **Thomas Jefferson Building, Library of Congress** Page **112** • The Renaissance elegance of the building and its highly decorative interior is matched by the changing display of historical treasures inside.

16 **Chesepeake Bay seafood** Page **127** • The USA's oldest continuous fish market down on the Washington Channel still sells the daily catch from boats and trailers; a mess of some steamed crabs makes for a great picnic.

17 Rock Creek Park Page **213** • With its eponymous waterway at its center, DC's largest park has something for everyone – miles of trails and paths, ballparks, barbecues, picnic areas, Civil War remnants and summer concerts.

18 Starspangled banner Page **86** • The original tattered flag, now undergoing a massive preservation programme, is the highlight of the National Museum of American History.

19 National Air and Space Museum Page **68** • There's no better collection of air and space hardware in the world, with artifacts and machines from the earliest days of powered flight to missions to the moon.

20 Guided tours of the National Gallery Page **72** • It's impossible to take in the enormous scope of the country's National Gallery in just one visit, so the smartest option is to latch onto one of the excellent free guided tours, which concentrate on gallery highlights or particular periods and painters.

21 Eastern Market
Page **117** • Visit DC's longest-serving indoor market and then grab a coffee and a croissant in a nearby café; outside, on weekends, you can buy flowers, antiques and bric-a-brac.

22 Vietnam Veterans Memorial
Page **56** • There's no more poignant memorial in the city than that to the Vietnam vets, its somber granite walls etched with almost 60,000 names.

23 Mount Vernon
Page **236** • Best day trip from the city is to George Washington's Virginian country estate, his home for forty years and his burial place.

24 Arlington National Cemetery
Page **225** • The graves of the nation's finest, on landscaped grounds on the hillsides of Arlington, across the river from the city.

25 Biking along the C&O Canal
Page **218** • It's a lovely fourteen-mile bike ride along the canal towpath from Georgetown to the tumbling waters at Great Falls – a great way to escape the city for a while.

contents

Using the Rough Guide

We've tried to make this Rough Guide a good read and easy to use. The book is divided into seven main sections, and you should be able to find whatever you want in one of them.

front section

The front color section offers a quick tour of Washington DC. The **introduction** aims to give you a feel for the place, with suggestions on where to go. We also tell you what the weather is like and include a basic city fact file. Next, our author rounds up his favorite aspects of DC in the **things not to miss** section – whether it's great food, amazing sights or a special activity. Right after this comes the Rough Guide's full **contents** list.

basics

The basics section covers all the **pre-departure** nitty-gritty to help you plan your trip and the practicalities you'll want to know once there. This is where to find out about money and costs, internet access, transport, car rental, local media – in fact just about every piece of **general practical information** you might need.

the city

This is the heart of the Rough Guide, divided into user-friendly chapters, each of which covers a city district or day-trip destination. Every chapter starts with an **introduction** that helps you to decide where to go, followed by an extensive tour of the sights, all plotted on a neighborhood map.

listings

Listings contain all the consumer information needed to make the most of your stay, with chapters on **accommodation**, places to **eat** and **drink**, **nightlife** and **culture** venues, **shopping**, **sports** and **festivals**.

contexts

Read contexts to get a deeper understanding of how Washington DC ticks. We include a brief **history**, plus a look at the inner workings of the **US government**, along with a detailed further reading section that reviews dozens of **books** relating to the city.

index + small print

Apart from a **full index**, which covers maps as well as places, this section includes publishing information, credits and acknowledgments, and also has our contact details in case you want to send in updates and corrections to the book – or suggestions as to how we might improve it.

color maps

The back color section contains nine detailed maps and plans to help you explore the city up close and locate every place recommended in the guide.

contents ▶

basics ▶

guide ▶

listings ▶

contexts ▶

index ▶

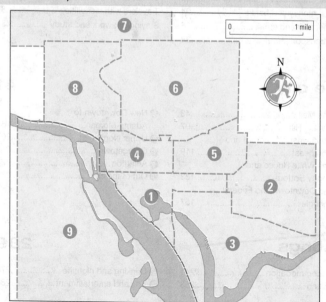

contents

contexts
321

index and small print
345

color maps at back of book

map symbols

maps are listed in the full index using colored text

Interstate		⊠	Post office
US Highway		🏛	Memorial
Other road		⊙	Statue
Footpath		⊞	Hospital
Tunnel		®	Restroom
Railway		⚲	Grave
Waterway			Building
Chapter division boundary			Church
Airport			Cemetery
Metro station			Park
Information office			

basics

basics

Getting there

The easiest way to get to Washington DC is to fly. Three airports serve the DC area — Reagan National (the city's domestic airport), Dulles International (the main international airport) and nearby Baltimore-Washington (BWI), just an hour from downtown DC. If the US capital is part of a longer trip, you may want to consider buying an open-jaw plane ticket, where you fly into one city (DC) and out of another (say New York). This is especially convenient for overseas visitors who want a fly-drive holiday.

If you don't want to fly, Amtrak rail services provide an alternate approach to DC within the US and Canada, though, apart from the high-speed route from New York City, this can be a fairly leisurely and expensive option. The Greyhound and Peter Pan bus companies cater to travelers on a budget. If you're planning on driving to DC, it's worth noting that you're unlikely to use the car much in the city itself (it has one of America's best and safest public transit systems).

Plenty of travel operators also offer **organized tours**, city breaks and other DC-centered holidays. Some of these specialist tours visit nearby Civil and Revolutionary War sites; others include two or three days in DC as part of a longer East Coast tour, **camping holiday or adventure trip**. Obviously, these are considerably more expensive than a mere city stay (and prices vary wildly according to what's being offered), but the DC element of the trip makes a suitably monumental start or finish to an all-American holiday.

Overseas visitors can buy air, train and bus passes for discounted travel throughout the United States; these normally have to be purchased in advance of your trip. All prices in this section are given in US dollars, unless otherwise stated.

Shopping for air tickets and passes

Competition on major routes keeps plane fares at a reasonable level, though prices do vary according to various factors. Within the US, prices for **domestic flights to Washington DC** are generally determined by the time of departure and seat availability, especially on the busy Northeastern commuter routes from New York and Boston.

From overseas, seasonal variations in price are common, with flights at their most expensive during the European high season, namely from June to August (actually the hottest and most humid time to visit DC); spring and autumn are slightly less pricey, while winter (excluding the Christmas and New Year holiday period) is the cheapest time to fly.

Whatever your departure point, if you want to travel during the **major American holiday periods** (around Fourth of July, Thanksgiving, and Christmas and New Year's Day), you should book well in advance.

Conditions and restrictions on the cheapest economy fares (given different names by different airlines) are fairly standard. Advance-purchase tickets must be bought between 7 and 28 days in advance, depending on the airline, and you must usually stay at least one Saturday night. Economy tickets are normally valid for between one and six months and are non-refundable, though you can usually change your return journey by paying an additional fee. Fares operate on a sliding scale, usually based on how far ahead you book – **flying during the week** always tends to be cheaper than on the weekend, while special seasonal deals or discount fares for students and anyone under 26 can bring the price down even more. Remember to allow for the extra cost of government **duty fees and airport taxes** whenever, and from wherever, you travel – you'll be quoted an all-inclusive price when you pay for your ticket, but not necessarily when you first make enquiries.

Rather than contacting all the separate airlines, you'll save yourself a lot of time, and possibly money, too, by checking out the various **discount travel and flight agents**.

They often advertise in the travel sections of the daily and weekend press. Some, such as Council Travel, STA, Travel Cuts and Usit Campus, specialize in **youth/student fares**, but even if you don't fit into that category, they'll do their best to find you the cheapest available flight. In addition to dealing with discounted flights, these agents may also offer a range of other travel-related services – from insurance to car rental. Finally, many airlines and discount travel websites offer you the opportunity to **book your tickets online**, often at a small discount. You'll need to be flexible about your departure and return dates to get the best prices from these sites. Make sure you read the small print before buying, as it can be difficult, if not impossible, to claim refunds or change your ticket, especially on last-minute deals.

If you're traveling from Europe or Australasia, and the US is only one stop on a longer journey, you might want to consider buying a **Round-the-World (RTW) ticket**. Some travel agents can sell you an "off-the-shelf" RTW ticket that will have you touching down in about half a dozen cities; others will have to assemble one for you. The latter type can be tailored to your needs but is apt to be more expensive. Washington DC does figure on some standard itineraries, though New York is a more usual US East Coast stopover.

Overseas travelers should also keep in mind that all the main American airlines offer **air passes** for flights within the US. These have to be bought in advance, and are usually sold with the proviso that you reach the US with the same airline. All the deals are broadly similar, involving the purchase of at least three coupons (costing around $450 for the first three coupons, $80 for each additional one), each valid for a flight of any duration within the US.

Online booking agents and general travel sites

www.cheapflights.com Flight deals and packages from the UK and Ireland, and good links to relevant destination sites.
www.cheaptickets.com American discount-flight specialists.
www.ebookers.com and
www.ebookers.com.ie Low fares on an extensive selection of scheduled flights from the UK and Ireland.

www.etn.nl/discount A US hub of discount agent web links.
www.expedia.co.uk and
www.expedia.com Discount airfares, all-airline search engine and daily deals.
www.flynow.com UK online resource for flights, plus US car rental.
www.hotwire.com Bookings from the US only. Last-minute savings of up to forty percent on regular published fares.
www.lastminute.com UK site offering good last-minute holiday package and flight-only deals.
www.priceline.co.uk and
www.priceline.com Name-your-own-price websites with deals at around forty percent off standard fares. You cannot specify flight times (although you do specify dates).
www.smilinjack.com/airlines.htm Lists an up-to-date compilation of airline website addresses.
www.travel.com.au and
www.travel.co.nz Discount fares and destination advice for Australian/New Zealand travelers.
http://travel.yahoo.com Incorporates Rough Guide material in its coverage of destination countries, with information about places to eat and sleep, etc.
www.travelocity.co.uk Destination guides along with deals for car rental, lodging and air fares.
www.travelshop.com.au Australian website offering discounted flights, packages, insurance and online bookings.
www.trip.com US site catering to the business traveler's air travel, lodging, and car rental needs.
www.unison.otc-uk.com Irish site with online flight bookings, car rental, insurance and more.

Flights and other approaches from the US and Canada

Unless you're on America's east coast (and perhaps even then too), you're most likely to fly into DC, which is unsurprisingly well connected to the rest of the country by air routes. Amtrak trains provide a viable option from places like New York and Boston, as do buses, from most anywhere really, if you're willing to put up with a bit more discomfort in exchange for value.

By plane

The most convenient airport for domestic arrivals into DC is Reagan National Airport. The main service is provided by Delta's and

US Airways' East Coast shuttles from New York La Guardia, with departures every 30–60mins between 6am and 8.30pm during the week, starting an hour later on weekends. US Airways also operates an hourly shuttle from Boston (Mon–Fri only). The following airlines also offer regular, daily service to Reagan National: Alaska Airlines (from Seattle), America West Airlines (Columbus, Phoenix), American Airlines (Boston, Chicago O'Hare, Dallas, Miami, St Louis), Continental (Houston, Newark), Delta (Atlanta, Dallas), United (Chicago O'Hare) and US Airways (Fort Lauderdale, Orlando, Philadelphia).

Some airlines – including American Airlines, Continental, Delta, United and US Airways – also provide nationwide service to **Dulles International**, which is probably where you'll fly to if you're coming from the West Coast.

If you don't mind flying into **Baltimore** (BWI), Southwest Airlines (from Chicago, Fort Lauderdale, and Los Angeles among others) and US Airways (from New York La Guardia) have some good deals.

Fares are lowest in the heavily trafficked Northeast corridor. **From New York**, you can pay as little as $90–100 round-trip, though $120–170 is the more usual price range; **from Boston**, you're looking at $150–180. Round-trip fares **from Chicago** range around $170–220 and **from Miami**, $200–250. The price of flights **from the West Coast** is more likely to fluctuate – round-trip fares from LA, San Francisco or Seattle sometimes fall as low as $350, but are more likely to be between $450 and $550.

If you're traveling **from Canada**, Air Canada has direct flights to DC from Toronto (to Reagan National) and Montréal (Reagan National and Dulles); from Vancouver, you'll have to change at Toronto. US Airways also flies from Toronto and Montréal, though some services are routed via other American cities. Special deals bring round-trip fares as low as C$300 from Montréal, though you're more likely to pay C$400–600, and the same from Toronto. From Vancouver, winter getaways start at C$700 round-trip, though the more usual price is around C$1200.

Airlines in the US and Canada

Air Canada US and Canada ☎1-888/247-2262, ⓦwww.aircanada.ca
Alaska Airlines ☎1-800/252-7522, ⓦwww.alaskaair.com

America West Airlines ☎1-800/235-9292, ⓦwww.americawest.com
American Airlines ☎1-800/433-7300, ⓦwww.aa.com
Canadian Airlines ☎1-888/247–2262, ⓦwww.aircanada.ca
Continental Airlines ☎1-800/523-3273, ⓦwww.continental.com
Delta ☎1-800/221-1212, ⓦwww.delta.com
Northwest/KLM Airlines ☎1-800/225-2525, ⓦwww.nwa.com
Southwest Airlines ☎1-800/435-9792, ⓦwww.southwest.com
United Airlines ☎1-800/241-6522, ⓦwww.ual.com
US Airways US and Canada ☎1-800/428-4322, ⓦwww.usairways.com

Discount travel and flight agents in the US and Canada

Airhitch ☎1-800/326-2009 or 212/864-2000, ⓦwww.airhitch.org. For a set price, they guarantee to get you on a flight to an airport as close to your preferred destination as possible, within a week.
Airtech ☎212/219-7000, ⓦwww.airtech.com. Standby seat broker.
Council Travel ☎1-800/226-8624 or 617/528-2091, ⓦwww.counciltravel.com. Nationwide organization that specializes in student/budget travel; flights and train passes.
Educational Travel Center ☎1-800/747-5551 or 608/256-5551, ⓦwww.edtrav.com. Student/youth discount agent.
Skylink US ☎1-800/AIR-ONLY or 212/573-8980, Canada ☎1-800/SKY-LINK. Discount fares.
STA Travel ☎1-800/777-0112 or ☎781-4040, ⓦwww.sta-travel.com. Specialists in independent travel; also student IDs, travel insurance, car rental, rail passes, etc.
Student Flights ☎1-800/255-8000 or 480/951-1177, ⓦwww.isecard.com. Student/youth fares, student IDs and other travel services.
Travac ☎1-800/872-8800, ⓦwww.thetravelsite.com. Discount fares and charter flights.
Travel Cuts Canada ☎1-800/667-2887, US ☎416/979-2406. Canadian student-travel organization; flights and rail passes.
Worldtek Travel ☎1-800/243-1723, ⓦwww.worldtek.com. Discount travel agency.
Worldwide Discount Travel Club ☎305/534-2642. Discount travel club.

Package tours

Booked **in the US**, a typical three-night jaunt to DC – including round-trip flight plus three-star room-only accommodation – starts at about $400 per person when flying from New York, or about $600 when flying from Los Angeles. Another $150–200 or so sees you upgraded to a room in a five-star or superior hotel.

AmeriCan Adventures/Roadrunner ☏1-800/873-5872, ⊛www.americanadventures.com. Camping and youth-hostel adventure trips featuring DC as part of longer tours. Huge variety of options, from 6-day East Coast Explorer ($359) to 39-day coast-to-coast round-trip ($1759).

American Express Vacations ☏1-800/241-1700, ⊛www.americanexpress.com/travel. Flights, hotels, last-minute specials, city-break packages and speciality tours.

Amtrak Vacations ☏1-800/321-8684, ⊛www.amtrak.com/services/amtrak-vacations/html. Train or Amtrak Air Rail trips through the Northeast, along with hotel reservations, car rental and sightseeing tours.

Collette Vacations ☏1-800/340-5158, ⊛www.collettevacations.com. DC figures in various escorted or independent tour permutations; from the four-night "Discover DC" option (from $419) to the "Heritage of America" tour, also covering New York, Pennsylvania and Virginia (from $1759); prices include meals but exclude airfares/travel to DC.

Contiki Holidays ☏1-888/CONTIKI, ⊛www.contiki.com. Trips for the 18–35-year-old crowd; the seven-day "Eastern Discovery" tour (from $769, land only) includes DC.

Globus and Cosmos ⊛www.globusandcosmos .com. Deluxe escorted tours. The "Historic East" (eight days, from $1099) and "Great Cities of the East" (ten days, from $2299) tours both include significant time in DC; the land-only prices include meals. Request brochures online or via a listed travel agent.

Suntrek ☏1-800/SUN-TREK, ⊛www.suntrek.com. Small (maximum thirteen people) whistle-stop camping tours, with the East Coast itineraries mixing city stays with the great outdoors. The most you get in DC, though, is two nights. A two-week "East Coast Adventure" costs around $799 (land only, meals and personal expenses extra).

Trek America US and Canada ☏1-800/221-0596, ⊛www.trekamerica.com. Fun, flexible, youth-oriented (18–38-year-olds) camping tours that include DC as part of larger tours of the region. The two-week "Best of the East," departing New York, costs from $759 (land only, meals and personal expenses extra).

United Vacations ☏1-888/854-3899, ⊛www.unitedvacations.com. Tailor-make your DC city break with United flights and a good choice of four- and five-star hotels. Car rental and other services can be arranged, too.

By train

The sprawling metropolitan area between Boston and Washington has the most dependable **Amtrak** service in the country (☏1-800/USA-RAIL, ⊛www.amtrak.com). The high-speed train, the 150mph Acela Express, has cut the travel time between New York City and Washington DC to just two hours and fifty minutes, and even the regular service only take around three and a half hours. If you're traveling from downtown New York or points south, this is probably the most convenient way of reaching Washington, not the least because it will drop you right in the middle of town, at Union Station. Amtrak has an arrangement with United Airlines that allows you to fly one leg of your trip to DC and travel the other by rail (**Air Rail** ☏1-800/437-3441).

Round-trip fares on the regular service **from New York** start at around $140, **from Boston** (9hr) around $160. Fares for the all-reserved express trains can be twice as high. These prices are for tickets purchased two weeks in advance of travel. Fares on services from cities outside the Northeast are comparable to or higher than the equivalent airfare, and if you want any extras (like a sleeping compartment) you'll have to pay a good deal more than the basic prices. To make the three-day rail journey **from Los Angeles** in relative comfort, for example, costs well over $1000 round-trip with an economy sleeper bed. In general, rail travel is not really a budget option, although some of the journeys are pleasant enough – the *Silver Star*, which travels from Miami through Georgia, the Carolinas and Virginia to DC, in particular, makes for a rewarding 22-hour trip.

From Canada, there is regular Amtrak service **from Toronto** (17hr; from C$300 round-trip) and **Montréal** (15hr; from C$276), both via New York City.

Seasonal special offers (for two or more people traveling together, etc) turn up quite often, while **seniors** and **students** get a fifteen percent discount on most rail journeys. Check for such offers on the Amtrak website – which also offers a booking service – or by phone. If Washington is part of a longer itinerary, Amtrak and VIA's (Canada's national rail company) **North American Rail**

Pass allows thirty days' unlimited travel for $674/C$1104 high season (June to mid-Oct) and $471/C$702 low season (mid-Oct to May); there's a ten percent discount for seniors and students.

Overseas visitors can buy a USA Rail Pass. The most suitable for visits to Washington DC is the **Northeast Rail Pass**, allowing travel between the Virginia coast and Montréal and Niagara Falls. There are two travel periods: peak (June to the beginning of September) and off-peak (rest of the year) and the pass is valid for five days ($149 either period), fifteen days ($205/$185) or thirty days ($240/$225). The passes aren't normally valid on the fastest express service, though you can purchase an add-on pass (five-day, $60; fifteen-day, $120; thirty-day, $150) that enables you to use the express trains on weekends only. Passes must be bought before you travel to North America and are available at equivalent rates of exchange from travel agents and specialist tour operators in your home country – see the listings in the relevant sections below for more details.

By bus

Buses are cheaper and more frequent than the train, but they do take forever, and in a worst-case scenario you may need to use one of those toilets. The chief operator to DC is **Greyhound** (☎1-800/229-9424, ⓦwww.greyhound.com); in addition, the **Peter Pan** company (☎1-800/343-9999, ⓦwww.peterpanbus.com) offers service to Washington DC from Boston, New York and Philadelphia. Standard midweek round-trip fares start at $84 for the five- to six-hour trip **from New York City**; you can expect to pay $132 **from Boston** (10hr), $175 **from Chicago** (18hr), and $220 **from Los Angeles** (3 days). On Greyhound Canada (☎1-800/661-8747, ⓦwww.greyhound.ca), round-trip fares from **Montréal** (14hr) or **Toronto** (16–20hr) are around C$200–230. On all routes, you'll pay a bit more if you travel between Friday and Sunday, though discounted seven-day advance-purchase tickets, and student, senior and "companion" (two-for-one) fares are often available.

Greyhound **Discovery Passes** buy unlimited travel on the entire Greyhound network, but are only really worthwhile for travelers including DC as part of a longer itinerary, or

for those coming from the West Coast. The **Domestic Ameripass**, for example, is valid across the entire country for periods of between seven days ($185) and sixty days ($509); there's fifty percent discount for accompanying children, ten percent off for seniors and students. The **Domestic Eastern CanAm Pass**, valid between Montréal or Toronto and DC, comes in fifteen-day ($319/C$507) and thirty-day ($429/C$682) versions. The same passes are available for **overseas visitors**, typically for about $50–60 less than the prices quoted here. However, passes for overseas visitors must be bought before leaving home: most travel agents can oblige, as can specialist agents like STA, Trailfinders and Usit Campus.

By car

Driving to DC gives you a certain amount of freedom and flexibility, but you'll probably never use the car once you reach the city since the public transit system is so good. The box overleaf gives an idea of the distances and times involved in driving to DC. Routes into the city are shown on color map 2 and explained in "Arrival," p.22 – where you'll also find some useful tips on the intricacies of driving in DC itself.

Car rental rates vary wildly, though in general you'll get better deals over the weekend than during the week. You can often realize **significant savings** by booking car rental in advance with a major firm that has representation in Washington DC – most agencies in the city have offices at Reagan National, Dulles International and BWI airports, and at Union Station. When booking, be sure to get free unlimited mileage and be aware that rates can go up by as much as $200 if you want to pick up the car in one location and leave it at another. If you choose not to pay until you arrive, take a written confirmation of the price with you. Always read the small print carefully for details on Collision Damage Waiver (sometimes called Liability Damage Waiver), a form of insurance that often isn't included in the initial rental charge but is well worth having. This specifically covers the car you are driving (you are in any case insured for damage to other vehicles). At $10–15 a day, Collision Damage Waiver can add substantially to the total rental cost, but without it you're liable for every scratch to the car – even those that aren't your fault. Then again, don't be suckered into insurance you already have – call your credit card company to see if they offer free insurance if you use your card to pay. If you are **under 25** be prepared for hefty surcharges on top of the usual rates.

Driving to DC

From Chicago: 16hr (710 miles)
From Miami: 24hr (1057 miles)
From Montréal: 14hr (610 miles)
From New York: 5hr 30min (240 miles)
From San Francisco: 3 days (2845 miles)
From Toronto: 12hr (570 miles)

Car rental companies

Alamo US ☏1-800/GO-ALAMO,
🖝www.alamo.com
Autos Abroad UK ☏0870/066 7788,
🖝www.autosabroad.co.uk
Avis Australia ☏13 6333, Canada ☏1-800/272-5871, New Zealand ☏0800/655 111, Republic of Ireland ☏01/605 7555, UK ☏0870/606 0100, US ☏1-800/331-1084, 🖝www.avis.com
Budget Australia ☏1300/362 848, New Zealand ☏0800/652 227, Republic of Ireland ☏01/878 7814, UK ☏0800/181181, US ☏1-800/527-0700, 🖝www.budgetrentacar.com
Dollar US ☏1-800/800-6000, 🖝www.dollar.com
Hertz Australia ☏1800/550 067, Canada ☏1-800/263 0600, New Zealand ☏0800/655 955, Republic of Ireland ☏0903/27711, UK ☏0870/844 8844, US ☏1-800/654-3001, 🖝www.hertz.com
Holiday Autos Republic of Ireland ☏01/872 9366, UK ☏0870/400 0099, US ☏1-800/422-7737, 🖝www.holidayautos.com
National Australia ☏13 1908, New Zealand ☏09/537 2582, UK ☏0870/536 5365, US ☏1-800/227-7368, 🖝www.nationalcar.com
Suncars UK ☏0870/533 5588,
🖝www.suncars.com
Thrifty Republic of Ireland ☏1-800/515800, UK ☏0800/973163, US and Canada ☏1-800/847-4389, 🖝www.thrifty.com

Flights from the UK and Ireland

There are daily **nonstop flights** to Washington DC **from London Heathrow** with British Airways, United Airlines and Virgin Atlantic; BMI British Midland flies nonstop **from Manchester** daily except Tuesday. These flights take about seven

hours, though following winds ensure that return flights are always an hour or so shorter than outward journeys. Flights out usually leave Britain mid-morning, while flights back from the US tend to arrive in Britain early in the morning. Most other airlines serving DC, including Air France, American Airlines, Continental, Delta, Icelandair, KLM/Northwest, Lufthansa and US Airways, fly **from London Gatwick** via their respective American or European hubs. These flights take an extra two to five hours each way, depending on how long you have to wait for the connection.

Return **fares** to Washington DC can cost more than £500 between June and August and at Christmas, though £350–400 is the more usual range. Prices in winter often fall to under £250. With BMI British Midland, you'll usually be able to add on a connecting domestic flight to Manchester from one of the other UK regional airports for no extra cost; with other airlines, add on fares from British regional airports to London cost around £80 return. More flexible tickets to DC, requiring less advance booking time or allowing changes or refunds, cost from £100 more whenever and from whomever you buy.

There are no nonstop flights from Ireland to Washington DC, though Delta and Aer Lingus offer service **from Dublin** via New York or Boston; the trip takes between nine and eleven hours all told. Other airlines (like BA and United) will route you through London, which takes about the same amount of time. Prices for either route are similar. Alternatively, you could arrange your own Dublin/Belfast–London flight with low-cost airlines like easyJet, Go or Ryanair and pick up an onward flight from there. Return fares from Dublin to DC start at around IR£450 in the low season, rising to IR£600–700 in high season.

Airlines in the UK and Ireland

Aer Lingus UK ☏0845/973 7747, Republic of Ireland ☏01/705 3333 or 01/844 4777, 🖝www.aerlingus.ie
Air Canada UK ☏08705/247 226, 🖝www.aircanada.ca
Air France UK ☏0845/0845 111, Republic of Ireland ☏01/605 0383, 🖝www.airfrance.co.uk
American Airlines UK ☏0845/778 9789, 🖝www.aa.com
BMI British Midland UK ☏0870/607 0555,

Republic of Ireland ☎ 01/407 3036,
ⓦ www.flybmi.com
British Airways UK ☎ 0845/773 3377, Republic
of Ireland ☎ 1800/626 747,
ⓦ www.britishairways.com
Continental UK ☎ 0800/776 464, Republic of
Ireland ☎ 1890/925 252,
ⓦ www.flycontinental.com
Delta UK ☎ 0800/414767, Republic of Ireland
☎ 01/407 3165, ⓦ www.delta.com
easyJet UK ☎ 0870/600 0000,
ⓦ www.easyjet.com
Go UK ☎ 0870/607 6543, ⓦ www.go-fly.com
Icelandair UK ☎ 020/7874 1000,
ⓦ www.icelandair.net
KLM/Northwest UK ☎ 08705/074 074,
ⓦ www.klmuk.com
Lufthansa UK ☎ 0845/773 7747, Republic of
Ireland ☎ 01/844 5544, ⓦ www.lufthansa.com
Ryanair UK ☎ 0870/156 9569, Republic of Ireland
☎ 01/609 7800, ⓦ www.ryanair.com
United Airlines UK ☎ 0845/844 4777, Republic
of Ireland ☎ 1800/535 300, ⓦ www.ual.com
US Airways UK ☎ 0845/600 3300, Republic of
Ireland ☎ 1890/925 065, ⓦ www.usairways.com
Virgin Atlantic UK ☎ 01293/747 747, Republic of
Ireland ☎ 01/873 3388, ⓦ www.virgin-atlantic.com

Discount travel and flight agents

UK

Bridge the World ☎ 020/7911 0900,
ⓦ www.bridgetheworld.com. Specializing in Round-
the-World tickets, with good deals aimed at the
backpacker market.
Destination Group ☎ 020/7400 7000,
ⓦ www.destination-group.com. Discount airfares,
as well as inclusive packages for US travel.
Dial A Flight ☎ 0870/333 4488,
ⓦ www.dialaflight.com. Discounts on airfares as
well as car rental, hotels and insurance.
Flightbookers ☎ 020/7757 2444,
ⓦ www.ebookers.com. Low fares on an extensive
selection of scheduled flights.
Flight Centre ☎ 08705/666677,
ⓦ www.flightcentre.co.uk. Large choice of
discounted flights.
Flynow ☎ 020/7835 2000, ⓦ www.flynow.com.
Wide range of discounted tickets.
London Flight Centre ☎ 020/7244 6411,
ⓦ www.topdecktravel.co.uk. Long-established
agent dealing in discount flights.
North South Travel ☎ 01245/608 291,
ⓦ www.northsouthtravel.co.uk. Discounted fares
worldwide – profits are used to support projects in

the developing world, especially the promotion of
sustainable tourism.
Quest Worldwide ☎ 020/8547 3322,
ⓦ www.questtravel.com. Specialists in Round-the-
World discount fares.
STA Travel ☎ 0870/160 6070,
ⓦ www.statravel.co.uk. Worldwide specialists in
low-cost flights and tours for students and under-26s
(other customers welcome); Amtrak passes available.
Trailfinders ☎ 020/7628 7628,
ⓦ www.trailfinders.com. One of the best-informed
and most efficient agents for independent travelers;
Amtrak passes available.
Travel Bag ☎ 0870/900 1350,
ⓦ www.travelbag.co.uk. Discount flights to the US.
Travel Cuts ☎ 020/7255 2082,
ⓦ www.travelcuts.co.uk. Budget, student and youth
travel, and Round-the-World tickets; Amtrak passes
available.
Usit Campus ☎ 0870/240 1010,
ⓦ www.usitcampus.co.uk. Student/youth-travel
specialists with an emphasis on North America;
offers discount flights and Amtrak passes.

Ireland

Apex Travel Dublin ☎ 01/671 5933,
ⓦ www.apextravel.ie. Specialists in flights to the
US.
CIE Tours International Dublin ☎ 01/703 1888,
ⓦ www.cietours.ie. General flight and tour agent.
Flightfinders Dublin ☎ 01/676 8326. Discount
flight specialists.
Joe Walsh Tours Dublin ☎ 01/872 2555 or 676
3053, Cork ☎ 021/427 7959,
ⓦ www.joewalshtours.ie. General budget fares agent.
McCarthy's Travel Cork ☎ 021/427 0127,
ⓦ www.mccarthystravel.ie. General flight agent.
Premier Travel Derry ☎ 028/7126 3333,
ⓦ www.premiertravel.uk.com. Discount flight
specialists.
Rosetta Travel Belfast ☎ 028/9064 4996,
ⓦ www.rosettatravel.com. Flight and holiday agent.
Trailfinders Dublin ☎ 01/677 7888,
ⓦ www.trailfinders.ie. One of the best-informed and
most efficient agents for independent travelers;
Amtrak passes available.
Twohigs Travel Dublin ☎ 01/677 2666. General
flight and travel agent.
Usit Now Belfast ☎ 028/9032 7111, Dublin
☎ 01/602 1777 or 677 8117, Cork ☎ 021/427
0900, Derry ☎ 028/7137 1888, ⓦ www.usitnow.ie.
Student and youth travel specialists offering flights
and Amtrak train passes.
World Travel Centre Dublin ☎ 01/671 7155,
ⓦ www.worldtravel.ie. Discount flights and other
travel services.

Package tours

There are plenty of companies running package deals **from the UK** to Washington DC, mostly short city breaks that span three to five days. For a three-day trip, typical rates will run to around £600 per person in summer, though prices drop to around £450 out of high season, and sometimes less than that. It's usually around £100 more for the five-star or superior-grade hotel package. If you plan to see more of the country than just DC, **fly-drive** deals – which include car rental when buying a transatlantic ticket from an airline or tour operator – are always cheaper than renting on the spot. Most of the specialist companies offer fly-drive packages, though watch out for hidden extras, such as local taxes, "drop-off" charges and extra insurance.

AmeriCan Adventures ☎01892/512 700,
Ⓦ www.americanadventures.com. Small group camping and youth hostel adventure trips throughout the US, with some tours including DC.

American Holidays Belfast ☎028/9023 8762, Dublin ☎01/679 8800 or 679 6611. Specialists in travel to the US.

British Airways Holidays ☎0870/242 4243, Ⓦ www.baholidays.co.uk. Superior DC city breaks with British Airways flights.

Contiki Tours ☎020/8290 6777, Ⓦ www.contiki.com. Trips for the 18–35-year-old crowd; their seven-day "Eastern Discovery" tour (from £519, excluding flights) includes DC.

Funway USA ☎020/8466 0222, Ⓦ www.funwayholidays.co.uk. DC city breaks, flight-only deals and car rental.

Kuoni Travel ☎01306/747 002, Ⓦ www.kuoni.co.uk. Build your own holiday package to DC, selecting hotels (three- to five-star), flights, car rental and other services.

North America Travel Service ☎020/7938 3737, Ⓦ www.americatravelservice.com. American vacation specialist offers tailor-made packages, flights and fly-drives; offices in Nottingham, Manchester, Barnsley and Leeds.

Thomas Cook Holidays ☎0870/0100 437, Ⓦ www.thomascook.com. City breaks in either three- or four-star accommodation.

Travel4less ☎020/7400 7075, Ⓦ www.travel4less.co.uk. Build-your-own holidays (flights, accommodation, car rental, tours) and last-minute bargains.

Travelscene ☎0870/777 4445, Ⓦ www.travelscene.co.uk. Good-value city breaks, with a choice of four hotels (two-star to four-star) in good locations.

TrekAmerica ☎01295/256 777, Ⓦ www.trekamerica.com. Youth-oriented (18–38-year-olds) camping tours including DC as part of larger tours of the region. The two-week "Best of the East" tour, departing New York, costs from £550 (flights, meals and personal expenses extra).

Unijet ☎0870/600 8009, Ⓦ www.unijet.com. City breaks, hotel reservations and car rental.

United Vacations ☎0870/606 2222, Ⓦ www.unitedvacations.co.uk. One-stop agent for tailor-made holidays, city breaks, fly-drive deals, pre-booked sightseeing tours, etc. Organized tours include a seven-night "Great American Cities" rail tour with Amtrak, from Boston to DC, from £553 (accommodation, transport and tours included, flights extra).

Virgin Holidays ☎0870/220 2788, Ⓦ www.virginholidays.co.uk. City breaks with hotels either in Arlington (near Metro stops) or the District. Flights are with Virgin Atlantic.

Flights from Australia and New Zealand

There are no direct scheduled flights to Washington DC from either Australia or New Zealand. The quickest way to reach DC is to fly via Los Angeles with Qantas or United Airlines. Alternatively, there are flights on a number of carriers (including Air New Zealand) to the West Coast of the US, from which onward travel to DC is easily arranged. The cheapest deals, though, are often to the East Coast – usually New York – but again you'll be looking at an extra fare to get you to DC. Specialist agents can help sort out all the routes and advise about US air passes, which are the cheapest way to fly on to DC from whichever American hub you've arrived at. Don't forget the overland options once in the States either – Amtrak and Greyhound passes can sometimes provide good value, especially if you're planning to see a bit of the country.

Return fares to the US East Coast often go for well under A$2000/NZ$2400, though ticketed through to DC it's more likely to cost around A$2200/NZ$2800. Unless you're specifically looking at a short-term city visit, it's going to be better value for most people to consider buying a **Round-the-World (RTW) ticket**. The most basic of these, which start at around A$2200/NZ$2800, buys you as many as five stopovers, often including New York. You may have to pick a ticket with more stopovers to get DC specifically included, but it's still unlikely to cost you more than A$2800/NZ$3500.

Airlines in Australia and New Zealand

Air New Zealand Australia ☎13 2476, New Zealand ☎0800/737 000, ⓦwww.airnz.com
American Airlines Australia ☎1300/650 747, New Zealand ☎0800/887 997, ⓦwww.aa.com
British Airways Australia ☎02/8904 8800, New Zealand ☎09/356 8690, ⓦwww.britishairways.com
Cathay Pacific Australia ☎13 1747, New Zealand ☎09/379 0861, ⓦwww.cathaypacific.com
Continental Airlines Australia ☎02/9244 2242, New Zealand ☎09/308 3350, ⓦwww.flycontinental.com
Delta Air Lines Australia ☎02/9251 3211, New Zealand ☎09/379 3370, ⓦwww.delta.com
Japan Airlines (JAL) Australia ☎02/9272 1111, New Zealand ☎09/379 9906, ⓦwww.japanair.com
KLM Australia ☎1300/303 747, New Zealand ☎09/309 1782, ⓦwww.klm.com
Korean Air Australia ☎02/9262 6000, New Zealand ☎09/307 3687, ⓦwww.koreanair.com
Malaysia Airlines (MAS) Australia ☎13 2627, New Zealand ☎0800/657 472, ⓦwww.mas.com.my
Northwest Airlines Australia ☎1300/303 747, New Zealand ☎09/302 1452, ⓦwww.nwa.com
Qantas Australia ☎13 1313, New Zealand ☎0800/808 767, ⓦwww.qantas.com.au
Thai Airways Australia ☎1300/651 960, New Zealand ☎09/377 3886, ⓦwww.thaiair.com
United Airlines Australia ☎13 1777, New Zealand ☎09/379 3800, ⓦwww.ual.com
Virgin Atlantic Australia ☎02/9244 2747, New Zealand ☎09/308 3377, ⓦwww.virgin-atlantic.com

Discount travel and flight agents in Australia and New Zealand

Anywhere Travel Australia ☎02/9663 0411 or 018/401 014. General fares agent.
Budget Travel New Zealand ☎09/366 0061 or 0800/808 040, ⓦwww.budgettravel.co.nz. Flights, RTW fares and tours.
Destinations Unlimited New Zealand ☎09/373 4033. RTW fares.
Flight Centres Australia ☎02/9235 3522 or for nearest branch 13 1600, New Zealand ☎09/358 4310, ⓦwww.flightcentre.com.au. Specialist agent for budget flights, especially RTW.
STA Travel Australia ☎13 1776 or 1300/360 960,

ⓦwww.statravel.com.au; New Zealand ☎09/309 0458 or 366 6673, ⓦwww.statravel.co.nz. Discount flights, travel passes and other services for youth/student travelers.
Student Uni Travel Australia ☎02/9232 8444. Good deals for students.
Thomas Cook Australia ☎13 1771 or 1800/801 002, ⓦwww.thomascook.com.au; New Zealand ☎09/379 3920, ⓦwww.thomascook.co.nz. General flight and holiday agent; Amtrak passes available.
Trailfinders Australia ☎02/9247 7666, ⓦwww.trailfinders.com.au. One of the best-informed and efficient agents for independent travelers; Amtrak passes available.
Usit Beyond New Zealand ☎09/379 4224 or 0800/874 823, ⓦwww.usitbeyond.co.nz. Youth/student travel specialist; also RTW tickets, train passes and other services.
Walshes World New Zealand ☎09/379 3708. Agent for Amtrak rail passes.

Specialist tour operators

Adventure World Australia ☎02/9956 7766 or 1300/363 055, ⓦwww.adventureworld.com.au; New Zealand ☎09/524 5118, ⓦwww.adventureworld.co.nz. DC hotel bookings, car rental and organized tours.
American Town and Country Holidays Australia ☎03/9877 3322. Tailor-made trips, accommodation, car rental and city breaks.
American Travel Centre/Journeys Worldwide Australia ☎07/3221 4788. All aspects of travel to the US.
Australian Pacific Tours Australia ☎03/9277 8444 or 1800/675 222, New Zealand ☎09/279 6077. Package tours and independent travel to the US.
Canada and America Travel Specialists Australia ☎02/9922 4600, ⓦwww.canada-americatravel.com.au. Can arrange flights and accommodation in North America, plus Greyhound Ameripasses and Amtrak passes.
Contiki Holidays Australia ☎02/9511 2200, New Zealand ☎09/309 8824, ⓦwww.contiki.com. Frenetic tours for 18–35-year-old party animals. Their seven-day "Eastern Explorer" tour includes DC (from A$1259, NZ$1649).
Creative Holidays Australia ☎02/9386 2111, ⓦwww.creativeholidays.com.au. City breaks and other packages.
Sydney International Travel Centre ☎02/9299 8000, ⓦwww.sydneytravel.com.au. US flights, accommodation, city stays and car rental.
United Vacations ☎02/9324 1000. Tailor-made city stays or wider American holidays, with departures available from several Australian airports.

Entry requirements

Under the Visa Waiver Scheme, if you're a citizen of the UK, Ireland, Australia, New Zealand or most Western European countries (check with your nearest US embassy or consulate) and visiting the United States for a period of less than ninety days, you only need an onward or return ticket, a full passport and a visa waiver form. The latter (an I-94W) will be provided either by your travel agency or by the airline during check-in or on the plane, and must be presented to immigration on arrival. The same form covers entry across the land borders with Canada and Mexico.

For a brief excursion into the US, Canadian citizens do not necessarily need even a passport, just some form of ID, though for a longer trip you should carry a passport, and if you plan to stay for more than ninety days you need a visa, too. If you cross into the States by car, your vehicle is subject to spot searches by US Customs personnel. Remember, too, that Canadians are legally barred from seeking gainful employment in the US.

Prospective visitors from other parts of the world not mentioned above require a valid passport and a **non-immigrant visitor's visa** for a maximum ninety-day stay. How you obtain a visa depends on what country you're in and your status on application, so contact your nearest US embassy or consulate. Most travelers do not require inoculations to enter the US, though you may need **certificates of vaccination** if you're en route from cholera- or typhoid-infected areas in Asia or Africa – check with your doctor before you leave.

On arrival, the date stamped on your passport is the latest you're legally allowed to stay. Leaving a few days later may not matter, especially if you're heading home, but more than a week or so can result in a protracted, rather unpleasant, interrogation from officials, which may cause you to miss your flight. **Overstaying** may also cause you to be turned away next time you try to enter the US.

To get an extension before your time is up, apply at the nearest **US Immigration and Naturalization Service** (INS) office, whose address will be under the Federal Government Offices listings at the front of the phone book. In DC the office is at 425 I St NW (☎202/514-4316, ⑩www.ins.gov). INS officials will assume that you're working in the US illegally, and it's up to you to convince them otherwise by providing evidence of ample finances. If you can, bring along an upstanding American citizen to vouch for you. You'll also have to explain why you didn't plan for the extra time initially.

US embassies

For details of foreign embassies and consulates in Washington DC, see "Directory," p.319.

Australia Moonah Place, Yarralumla, Canberra, ACT 2600 ☎02/6214 5600, ⑩www.usembassy-australia.state.gov/embassy
Britain 24 Grosvenor Square, London W1A 1AE ☎020/7499 9000, 24hr visa hotline ☎09068/200 290, ⑩www.usembassy.org.uk
Canada 490 Sussex Dr, Ottawa, ON K1P 5T1 ☎613/238 5335, ⑩www.usembassycanada.gov
Ireland 42 Elgin Rd, Ballsbridge, Dublin 4 ☎01/668 7122, ⑩www.usembassy.ie
New Zealand 29 Fitzherbert Terrace, Thorndon, Wellington ☎04/462 6000, ⑩www.usembassy.org.nz

Insurance

A typical travel insurance policy usually provides coverage for the loss of baggage, tickets and – up to a certain limit – cash or checks, as well as cancellation or curtailment of your journey. Most exclude so-called dangerous sports, so if you're visiting Washington DC as part of a wider trip and are also planning to do some water sports or other similar activity, you'll almost certainly have to pay an extra premium. For overseas visitors, travel insurance including medical coverage is essential in view of the high costs of health care in the US. If you need to make a claim, you should keep receipts for medicines and medical treatment. In the event you have anything stolen, you must obtain an official statement from the police.

Before paying for a travel insurance policy, it's worth checking whether you are already covered. Credit cards often have certain levels of medical or other insurance included; some all-risks home insurance policies may cover your possessions when overseas; and some private medical plans include coverage when abroad. If you do take medical coverage, ascertain whether benefits will be paid as treatment proceeds or only after you return home, and whether there is a 24-hour medical emergency number. When securing baggage insurance, make sure that the per-article limit – typically under $700/£500 – will cover your most valuable possession. Most travel agents and tour operators will offer you travel insurance, while any insurance broker, bank or specialist travel insurance company should also be able to help. Or consider the travel insurance deal offered by Rough Guides.

Rough Guides travel insurance

Rough Guides offers its own travel insurance, customized for our readers by a leading UK broker and backed by a Lloyds underwriter. It's available to anyone, of any nationality and any age, traveling anywhere in the world.

There are two main Rough Guide insurance plans: **Essential**, for basic, no-frills coverage, and **Premier**, with more generous and extensive benefits. Alternatively, you can take out **annual multi-trip insurance**, which covers you for any number of trips throughout the year (with a maximum of 60 days for any one trip). Unlike many policies, the Rough Guides plans are calculated by the day, so if you're traveling for 27 days rather than a month, that's all you pay for. If you intend to be away for the whole year, the Adventurer policy will cover you for 365 days. Each plan can be supplemented with a "Hazardous Activities Premium" if you plan to indulge in sports considered dangerous, such as skiing, scuba-diving or trekking.

For a policy quote, call the Rough Guide Insurance Line: US toll-free ☏1-866/220 5588, UK freefone ☏0800/015 09 06, or, if you're calling from elsewhere, ☏+44 1243/621 046. Alternatively, get an online quote or buy online at ⓦwww.roughguides.com/insurance.

Information, websites and maps

The main city information sources for tourists are the DC Chamber of Commerce and the Washington DC Convention and Tourism Corporation (see below for details). You can contact these organizations in advance of your trip for brochures, visitor guides, events calendars and maps, and both have telephone information services if you require specific help when in the city. However, only the Chamber of Commerce Visitor Center is set up for walk-in visits. There are also numerous DC-related websites, most with fully searchable databases. These let you read up on the hottest new restaurants and clubs and can help you plan your sightseeing itinerary around the capital.

Information

Before shoving off for Washington, you may wish to contact one of the organizations listed below under "Tourist offices" to help plan your sightseeing itinerary. Call ahead for information or visit their websites — WCTC in particular has reams of helpful information online, from an events calendar to hotel-and-tour packages.

On arrival, maps and information are available at desks in the airports, Union Station and in most hotels. The most useful item to pick up is the free *Washington DC Visitors Guide*, with listings, reviews and contact numbers. Once in the city, your first stop should be at the **DC Visitor Information Center**, Ronald Reagan Building, 1300 Pennsylvania Ave NW (℡202/328-4748, ＠www.dcvisit.com; Mon–Sat 8am–6pm), which can help with maps, tours and citywide information.

Out and about in DC, other useful information sources include the **White House Visitor Information Center** (see p.136), which has details on National Park sights all over DC; and the **Smithsonian Institution Building** (see p.94) on the Mall, which is the best stop for Smithsonian museum information. You'll also come across **National Park Service rangers** – in kiosks on the Mall, at the major memorials, etc – who should also be able to answer general queries. One of the most conveniently located ranger sites is the **Ellipse Visitor Pavilion** (daily 8am–3pm), on the east side of the Ellipse (in front of the White House) near the bleacher seats. The **National Park Service Information Office** (℡202/208-4747; Mon–Fri 9am–5pm), inside the Department of the Interior on C St NW, between 18th and 19th, has information about all the city's national monuments and memorials.

As far as the various **local newspapers and magazines** go, you can't go far wrong armed with a free copy of the weekly *CityPaper* (available in stores, bars and restaurants), the free monthly *Where: Washington* magazine (from major hotels and terminals), the glossy *Washingtonian* magazine ($2.95 at bookstores) and Friday's *Washington Post*. Many neighborhoods (Georgetown in particular) and all the universities also issue free weekly or monthly papers, full of news, reviews and listings peculiar to their area.

Tourist offices

DC Chamber of Commerce 1213 K St NW, Washington DC 20005 ℡202/347-7201, ℻202/638-6764, ＠www.dcchamber.org
National Park Service, National Capital Region 1100 Ohio Dr SW, Washington DC 20242 ℡202/619-7222, ℻202/619-7302, ＠www.nps.gov
Washington DC Convention and Tourism Corporation (WCTC), 1212 New York Ave NW, Suite 600, Washington DC 20005 ℡202/789-7000; in the UK ℡020/8877 4521 or 01235/824482 for information pack; ℻202/789-7037, ＠www.washington.org

Useful information numbers

DC Chamber of Commerce Visitor Center ℡202/328-4748. Main city information source.
Dial-A-Museum ℡202/357-2020. Smithsonian

Institution exhibits and special events.

Dial-A-Park ☎202/619-7275. Events at National Park Service attractions.

Post-Haste ☎202/334-9000. *Washington Post* information line for news, weather, sports, restaurants, events and festivals.

Washington DC Convention and Tourism Corporation ☎202/789-7000. City-wide information source.

White House Visitor Information Center ☎202/208-1631. Maps, brochures and information about major city sights.

Useful websites

It should go without saying that there is a bounty of helpful and informative websites dedicated to every aspect of life in DC; we've listed a few diverse favorites to help you get started.

Art and culture

Washington Art ⓦ www.washingtonart.com. DC-area visual artists display their work online. There's also exhibit information, art discussions and links to other local art sites. An associated poetry quarterly, *Beltway* (ⓦ www.washingtonart.com /beltway), publishes the work of local poets and lists relevant news and events.

Newspapers and magazines

City Paper ⓦ www.washingtoncitypaper.com. DC's alternative news weekly, strong on reviews (mainstream and off-the-wall), local events and classified ads. Searchable listings let you find a gig or get the latest local gossip.

Washingtonian ⓦ www.washingtonian.com. The online restaurant guide is the best part of the site; otherwise, plenty more information about living and working in DC.

Washington Post ⓦ www.washingtonpost.com. The online version of the city's best newspaper, with a full, searchable database, entertainment guide and visitor information.

Politics

American Politics Journal ⓦ www.americanpolitics.com. Online political magazine providing a "moderate and humorous look at Beltway shenanigans," with daily updates, articles and features by politicians, journalists, lobbyists, and party, federal and military insiders.

American Presidents ⓦ www.americanpresidents.org. Everything you ever wanted to know about every president, from George Washington to George Dubya, featuring biographies, portraits, inaugural addresses, links to reference material, quick facts and video clips.

The Onion ⓦ www.theonion.com. Scattershot satire. Read this first for the most ludicrous take on federal politics, presidential posturing and life in America.

Thomas ⓦ http://thomas.loc.gov. Library of Congress service that makes available legislative information on the internet. This sounds dry, but this is the one stop for biographies of every member of Congress since 1774; the full text of documents like the Constitution; committeee reports; roll calls of votes; and much, much more.

Tourism

DC Heritage Tourism Coalition ⓦ www.dcheritage.org. Good information on smaller museums, historic houses and neighborhood highlights to help you get off the beaten track. Also walking tours and an online itinerary planner that allows you to build a customized guide to the sites you want to see.

White House Historical Association ⓦ www.whitehousehistory.org. Online tours of the president's house, plus special presidential features, resources for children and teachers, and, of course, the chance to buy the annual White House Christmas ornament for your tree.

Maps

The maps in this guide, along with the free city plans you'll pick up from tourist offices, hotels and museums, will be sufficient to help you find your way around. If you want something more comprehensive, best is the small, shiny, fold-out *Streetwise Washington DC* map ($5.95, ⓦ www.streetwisemaps.com), available from book, travel and map stores in DC. Another useful map is Mapeasy's illustrated *Mini-Map to Washington DC* ($5.95, ⓦ www.mapeasy.com), with detailed maps of downtown, Dupont Circle, and Georgetown. For details on how to **orient** yourself in the city, see "Points of arrival,".

If you'll be traveling beyond DC, the **free road maps** issued by each state are usually fine for general driving and route planning. To get hold of one, either write to the state tourist office directly or stop by any state welcome center or visitor center. Rand McNally produces good commercial state maps. If you need something more detailed for hiking, ranger stations in national parks, state parks and wilderness areas sell good-quality local hiking maps for $1–3. Camping shops generally have a good selection as well.

The **American Automobile Association** (☎1-800/222-4357, ⊛www.aaa.com) provides free maps and assistance to its members, and to British members of the AA and RAC.

Arrival

Those traveling to Washington DC by train or bus arrive at the most central locations: Union Station and the downtown Greyhound terminal, respectively. From the airports, you can't count on being downtown much within the hour, though the various bus, train and Metro transfers are smooth enough; there's a Metro stop right outside National Airport. Taking a taxi from the airport won't save much time, especially if you arrive during rush hour, though filling a cab with three or four people may save a few dollars.

By air

The most convenient destination for domestic arrivals is **National Airport** (☎703/417-8000) – officially the Ronald Reagan Washington National Airport – four miles south of downtown. Driving or by bus it takes thirty minutes to an hour to reach the center from the airport, depending on traffic. National Airport Metro station is linked directly to Metro Center, L'Enfant Plaza and Gallery Place-Chinatown. A taxi downtown costs around $12–15 (including $1.25 airport surcharge). Another option is the **SuperShuttle** bus (24hr continuous service; one-way $13, round-trip $26), which drops you at your requested hotel.

The area's major airport, **Dulles International** (☎703/572-2700), 26 miles west in northern Virginia, handles most international and some domestic flights. The drive to or from downtown can take between forty minutes and an hour. Taxis downtown run $45–50. There's also a **SuperShuttle** bus from Dulles (24hr continuous service; one-way $22, round-trip $44), which will bring you to the hotel of your choice. It's cheaper, if a little more time-consuming, to take the **Washington Flyer Express** bus (every 30min, Mon–Fri 5.45am–10.15pm, Sat & Sun 7.45am–10.15pm; one-way $8, round-trip $14) to the **West Falls Church Metro** station, a thirty-minute ride; from there, the train ride

into downtown DC takes about twenty minutes. However, the most inexpensive option is to take public transport all the way into town: catch Metrobus #5A from the airport, which connects with the Metrorail system at the Rosslyn and L'Enfant Plaza Metro stations.

Other international and domestic arrivals land at **Baltimore-Washington International (BWI) Airport** (☎301/261-1000), 25 miles northeast of DC (and ten miles south of Baltimore). This, too, is up to an hour's drive from downtown DC, with taxis costing around $55 – agree on the price before setting off. **SuperShuttle** buses into Washington (daily 24hr; one-way $30, round-trip $60) will drop you off at your hotel. It's cheaper to take the train from BWI Airport: either the frequent peak-hour departures of the **MARC** commuter line (Mon–Fri only, 5.15am–9pm; one-way $5, round-trip $7.25), which takes 40-45 minutes, or the quicker, daily **Amtrak** trains (hourly; one-way $22), which take 30 minutes. Both trains arrive at Washington's Union Station (see "By train and bus," opposite). A free shuttle service connects the airport with the BWI rail terminal. If you have time to kill, you can also take **public transport** to the city center, riding express bus #B30 from BWI airport nonstop to Greenbelt Metro station and then catching the Green Line into town, though this route into DC will take you well over an hour.

Leaving DC: getting to the airports

Give yourself plenty of time to get to the airport, especially if you're driving: it can take up to thirty minutes to reach National, more like an hour to get to Dulles or BWI – and even more in rush hour.

SuperShuttle runs buses to all three airports from downtown, with pickup on request at your hotel; you'll need to make a reservation. Washington Flyer Express offers scheduled bus service to Dulles from West Falls Church Metro station as well as from National Airport. Alternatively, you can take a taxi or go on the cheap via public transport.

SuperShuttle ⓦ www.supershuttle.com, 24hr continuous service. To BWI (ⓣ1-888/826-2700) $30, round-trip $60. To Dulles (ⓣ703/416-7884 $22), round-trip $44. To National (ⓣ1-800/258-3826) $13, round-trip $26.

Washington Flyer Express ⓣ1-888/927-4359, ⓦ www.washfly.com. To Dulles from West Falls Church Metro: every 30min, Mon–Fri 6.15am–10.45pm, Sat & Sun 8.15am–10.45pm; $8, round-trip $14. To Dulles from National: hourly, Mon-Fri, 6am–11pm; every 1-2hr, Sat & Sun 6am-11pm; $16, round-trip $26.

Washington Flyer Taxi ⓣ703/661-6655. Offers 24hr metered service to Dulles airport; most cars accept credit cards.

Metro/bus ⓣ202/637-7000, ⓦ www.wmata.com. To BWI: Metro Green Line to Greenbelt station, where Metrobus #B30 (every 40min, Mon–Fri 6am–10pm, Sat & Sun 8.40am–10pm) continues on to the airport nonstop. To Dulles: Metrobus #5A from L'Enfant Plaza or Rosslyn Metro stations (hourly, Mon–Fri 5.30am–10.30pm, Sat & Sun 5.30–8.30am & noon–10.30pm). To National: Metro Blue or Yellow lines.

By train and bus

The gleaming malls of **Union Station**, 50 Massachusetts Ave NE, three blocks north of the Capitol, see arrivals from all over the country, including local **trains** from Baltimore, Richmond, Williamsburg and Virginia Beach, and major East Coast connections from Philadelphia, New York and Boston. Trains are operated either by Amtrak (ⓣ1-800/872-7245, ⓦ www.amtrak.com) – which has regular service to most destinations and quicker, more expensive Acela and Metroliner trains between DC and Boston – or the Maryland Rail Commuter Service (MARC; ⓣ1-800/325-7245, ⓦ www.mtamaryland.com), which connects DC to Baltimore, BWI Airport and suburban Maryland. Union Station has a connecting Metro station, and taxis line up outside. There are car rental desks here, too.

Greyhound (ⓣ1-800/231-2222, in DC ⓣ202/289-5154, ⓦ www.greyhound.com) and **Peter Pan** (ⓣ1-800/343-9999, ⓦ www.peterpanbus.com) buses – from Baltimore, Philadelphia, New York, Boston, Richmond and other cities – stop at the modern terminal at 1005 1st Street NE at L Street, in a fairly unsavory part of town, five long blocks north of Union Station. Take a cab at least as far as Union Station Metro (around $6), especially at night.

By car

Driving into DC is a sure way to experience some of the worst traffic on the East Coast. The six- to eight-lane freeway known as the **Capital Beltway** (due to be twelve-lane in parts within five years) circles the city at a ten-mile radius from the center and is busy eighteen hours a day. It's made up of two separate highways: I-495 on the western half and I-95/I-495 in the east. If it's the Beltway you want, follow signs for either.

Approaching the city **from the northeast** (New York/Philadelphia), you need I-95 (south), before turning west on Route 50; that will take you to New York Avenue, which heads directly to the White House. **From Baltimore** there's the direct Baltimore–Washington Parkway, which also joins Route 50. Route 50 itself is the main way in **from the east** (Annapolis, MD, and Chesapeake Bay). **From the south**, take I-95 to I-395, which crosses the river via the 14th Street (George Mason Memorial) Bridge to reach 14th Street. **From the northwest** (Frederick, MD, and beyond), come in on I-270 until you hit the Beltway, then follow I-495 (east) for

Connecticut Avenue south. **From the west** (Virginia) use I-66, which runs across the Theodore Roosevelt Bridge to Constitution Avenue. At peak periods inside the Beltway, high-occupancy vehicle restrictions apply on I-66 eastbound (6.30–9am) and westbound (4–6.30pm); at these times cars with fewer than three people face a small surcharge at the toll booths. See color map 2 for road routes into the city.

Costs, money and banks

DC may be the nation's capital, but it's a lot more affordable to vacation here than in most American cities: nearly all the major museums, monuments and sights are free, public transit is cheap and efficient, and the presence of so many students, interns and public service officials means that many establishments have great deals on drinks and food. That's not to say that you can't spend money in Washington – the city has some of the nation's finest and most expensive hotels and restaurants. But if you're sticking to a budget, you shouldn't have too hard a time.

Average costs

Accommodation will be your biggest single expense: the cheapest reasonable double hotel rooms go for $100–140 a night, though a few spartan hostels, dingy budget hotels and rather nicer B&Bs undercut that rate. However, within that price range you'll be able to cut some good deals on weekends and in the less popular summer months – see "Accommodation," Chapter 11, for more details. After you've paid for your room, count on spending a **minimum** of $35 a day, which will buy you breakfast, a fast-food lunch, a budget dinner and a beer, but not much else. Eating fancier meals, taking taxis, and drinking and socializing (especially drinking and socializing) will mean allowing for more like $60–70 a day. If you want to go regularly to the theater or major concerts, rent a car or take a tour, then double that figure.

What's good about DC is how much is **free**. Visiting the major national museums and art collections (and taking guided tours around them); tours of the US Capitol, FBI Building and Pentagon; spring and summer concerts, festivals, parades, gatherings, children's events – none costs a cent. The Metro and bus system gets you everywhere you want to go for a dollar or two at a time (or five bucks a day with a special ticket), taxis are inexpensive, and bars and restaurants routinely offer happy-hour drink and food discounts. Where there is an admission charge, **children** and (usually) **senior citizens** get in for half-price, and there are often discounts for full-time **students** (holding an International Student ID Card, or ISIC), anyone under 26 (with International Youth Travel Card) and teachers (with International Teacher Card). The ID cards are available from branches of youth/student/discount travel agencies.

Sales tax in Washington DC is 5.75 percent (and isn't part of the marked price on goods); **hotel tax** is 14.5 percent on top of the room rate.

Banks and ATMs

With an **ATM card** (and PIN number) you'll have access to cash from machines all over DC, though, as anywhere, you may be charged a fee for using a different bank's ATM network. Foreign cash-dispensing cards linked to international networks such as Cirrus and Plus are also very widely accepted – ask your home bank which branches you can use, as otherwise the machine may simply gobble up your plastic friend. To find the location of the nearest ATM in the capital region, call: **Amex** ☏1-800/CASH-NOW, **Plus** ☏1-800/843-7587 or **Cirrus** ☏1-800/424-7787.

Most **banks in Washington DC** are open Monday to Friday 9am–3pm; some stay open until 5pm or 6pm on Friday, a few open on Saturday 9am–noon. For banking services – particularly currency exchange – outside normal business hours and on weekends, try major hotels or the DC-area branches of Thomas Cook. See "Directory" (p.319) for the full addresses and contact details of downtown banks and Thomas Cook branches.

Travelers' checks

Travelers' checks should be brought in US dollars only – they are universally accepted as cash in stores and restaurants. The usual fee for travelers' check sales is one or two percent, though this fee may be waived if you buy the checks through a bank where you have an account. You can also **buy checks by phone or online** with Thomas Cook and American Express. It pays to get a selection of denominations. Make sure to keep the purchase agreement and a record of check serial numbers safe and separate from the checks themselves. In the event that checks are lost or stolen, the issuing company will expect you to report the loss forthwith; most companies claim to replace lost or stolen checks within 24 hours.

Credit cards

For many services, it's simply taken for granted that you'll be paying with plastic. When renting a car or checking into a hotel, you will be asked to show a credit card – even if you intend to settle the bill in cash. Most major credit cards issued by foreign banks are honored in the US. Visa, Mastercard, Diners Club and American Express are the most widely used. If you use your credit card in an ATM, remember that all cash advances are treated as loans, with interest accruing daily from the date of withdrawal; there may be a transaction fee on top of this.

Wiring money

Having money wired from home should be a last resort, since you (or, at least, the sender of the money) will pay for the privilege. The fee depends on the amount sent, where it's being sent from and to, and the speed of the service. The quickest way is to have someone take cash to the office of a money-wiring service and have it wired to the office nearest you: to the US, this process should take no longer than ten to fifteen minutes. You take along ID and pick up the money in cash. This service is offered by **Travelers' Express Moneygram** (also available at participating **Thomas Cook** branches) and **Western Union**: Travelers' Express only accepts cash, though with Western Union the person sending the money can use a credit card (from the UK only). Western Union's general rates are slightly higher, and if credit cards are involved, there'll probably be an extra charge too. Thomas Cook can also arrange to send money via its foreign-currency draft service, though it takes 48 hours for the funds to become available. See "Directory" (p.319) for the contact details of local

Money: a note for foreign travelers

Generally speaking, one pound sterling will buy $1.40–1.50; one Canadian dollar is worth 60-70¢; one Australian dollar is worth 50-60¢; and one New Zealand dollar is worth 40-50¢.

US currency comes in bills of $1, $5, $10, $20, $50 and $100. All are the same size and the same green color, so check bills carefully. The dollar is made up of 100 cents in coins of 1 cent (known as a penny), 5 cents (a nickel), 10 cents (a dime) and 25 cents (a quarter). Change (quarters are the most useful) is needed for buses, vending machines and telephones, though automatic machines are increasingly fitted with slots for dollar bills.

When working out your daily budget, allow for tipping, which is universally expected. You really shouldn't depart a bar or restaurant without leaving a tip of at least fifteen percent (unless the service is utterly disgusting); twenty percent is more like it in upmarket places. About the same amount should be added to taxi fares – and round them up to the nearest 50¢ or dollar. A hotel porter should get $1 a bag, $3–5 for lots of baggage; chambermaids $1–2 a day; valet parking attendants $1.

Western Union and Thomas Cook offices in Washington DC.

It's also possible to have money wired directly from a bank in your home country to a bank in DC. If you go this route, your home bank will need the address and telex number of the branch bank where you want to pick up the cash; money wired this way normally takes two working days to arrive. If you have a few days' leeway, sending a postal money order through the mail is cheaper; postal orders are exchangeable at any post office. The equivalent for foreign travelers is the **international money order**, but it may take up to seven days to arrive by mail. An ordinary check sent from overseas takes two to three weeks to clear.

Phone, mail and email

You should have little problem staying in touch while in DC. Every hotel room comes equipped with a phone (though these can be expensive to use), public pay phones are widespread, and there are enough places offering internet access to keep you up to date with your email. You can buy stamps at post offices throughout the downtown area, and mail boxes are easy to find.

Telephones

All telephone numbers in this guide have a ☏ 202 **area code** (for Washington DC), unless otherwise stated. You do not need to dial the area code within the District. Outside DC, dial 1 before the area code and number. Calls within the greater DC metropolitan area are counted as local even if they require a different code (☏ 703 for northern Virginia, or ☏ 301 for parts of Maryland, for example). Detailed information about calls, codes and rates in the DC area is listed at the front of the **telephone directory** in the *White Pages*.

In general telephoning from your **hotel room** is considerably more expensive than using a pay phone, costing up to $1 for a local call; that said, some budget hotels offer free local calls. **International calls** can be dialed direct from public phones; the lowest rates for calls to Europe are usually between 11pm and 8am (plus all day Sat and all day Sun except 5–11pm). Don't even think of

calling abroad from a hotel phone – you'll be charged a small fortune.

An increasing number of public phones accept **credit cards**, while all the major US phone companies issue their own **charge cards**. These allow you to make calls from most hotel, public and private phones – using access codes and a personal identification number (PIN) – that are then billed to your home account. For **overseas visitors,** the benefit of a telephone charge card is mainly one of convenience, as rates aren't necessarily cheaper than calling from a public phone while abroad and can't compete with discounted off-peak times many local phone companies offer. But since most major charge cards are free to obtain, it's certainly worth getting one at least for emergencies – contact your phone company for more details. In addition, various stores in Washington DC sell cheap phone cards offering cut-rate calls to virtually every country around the world; look for signs advertising rates in shop windows. Cards come is denominations of $5, $10, $20; calls are connected via a local or toll-free number.

If you want to use your **cell phone**, you'll need to check with your phone provider to find out whether it will work in DC and what the call charges are. Many phones only work within the region designated by the area code in the phone number.

If you are visiting from abroad, it is unlikely that your mobile will work inside the US, unless you have a tri-band phone, for example. If you do have a phone that works Stateside, you'll probably have to inform your service provider before you travel to get international access switched on. If you want to retrieve messages, you'll have to ask your provider for a new access code, as your home one is unlikely to work abroad. You are also likely to be charged extra for *incoming* calls when in the US. Tri-band phones will automatically switch to the US frequency, but these can be pricey, so you may want to consider renting a phone if you're traveling to the US.

For details of time differences between the US and the rest of the world, see "Time," p.320.

Useful telephone numbers

Emergencies ☎911 for fire, police or ambulance
Directory inquiries for toll-free numbers
☎1-800/555-1212
Local and long-distance directory
information ☎411
Operator ☎0
International calls to Washington DC:
Your country's international access code + 1 for the US + 202 for DC
International calls from Washington DC:
Australia ☎ 011 + 61 + number (minus the initial 0 of the area code)
Canada ☎ 011+ 1 + number (minus the initial 0 of the area code)
New Zealand ☎ 011+ 64 + number (minus the initial 0 of the area code)
Republic of Ireland ☎ 011+ 353 + number (minus the initial 0 of the area code)
UK and Northern Ireland ☎ 011+ 44 + number (minus the initial 0 of the area code)

US mail

Air mail between the US and Europe generally takes about a week. Letters that don't carry the **zip code** are liable to get lost or at least delayed; phone books carry a list for their service area, and post offices – even abroad – have directories. In this guide the zip code for addresses is given where it may be necessary to write in advance.

Letters sent to you c/o **General Delivery** (known elsewhere as **poste restante**) *must* include the post office zip code and will only be held for thirty days before being returned to sender – so make sure there's a return address on the envelope. In DC, a few post offices handle General Delivery, the most convenient of which is the Ben Franklin Post Office, 1200 Pennsylvania Ave NW, 20004 (Mon–Fri 9am–6pm, Sat 8.30–2pm; ☎202/523-2386). You can also ask to have mail held at a hotel or, if you're a cardholder, at an American Express office (see "Directory," p.319, for details on local offices).

Email

Email addicts will realize shortly after arrival in the District that the city lacks any real internet café culture. Unless you're fortunate enough to be staying somewhere that offers web access (cyber-friendly hotels are noted as such in the hotel listings in Chapter 11), you'll be forced to hunt down a Kinko's Copies branch or one of the handful of other spots offering internet service. As logging-on at the business center of a major hotel can get pricey fast, you're better off seeking out an alternative (see "Directory," p.319 for addresses and details); most places that offer internet access have fairly reasonable rates (usually around $6 for thirty minutes). Another option is to head to the Martin Luther King Memorial Library (see p.180) downtown, where you can log on for free for periods of fifteen minutes at a time. And if you're stuck waiting for a plane at Dulles or National, you're in luck: a handful of credit-card activated internet kiosks are scattered throughout each airport.

City transport

Most places downtown – including the Mall museums, the major monuments and the White House – are within walking distance of each other, while an excellent public transportation system connects downtown to outlying sites and neighborhoods. The Washington Metropolitan Area Transit Authority (WMATA, ⊛ www.wmata.com) operates a subway system (Metrorail) and a bus network (Metrobus); other options include using taxis or even renting a bike. Car rental (at least for driving around the city) is less appealing. For details on city tours, see p.31.

The Metro

Washington's subway – the **Metrorail**, or simply the **Metro** – is quick, cheap and easy to use. It currently runs on five lines that cover most of the downtown areas and suburbs (with the notable exception of Georgetown). Each line is color-coded and studded with various interchange stations: Metro Center, L'Enfant Plaza and Gallery Place-Chinatown are the most important downtown. Stations are identified outside by the letter "M" on top of a brown pylon; inside, the well-lit, uncluttered, vaulted halls make the Washington Metro one of the safest in the world. Nevertheless, you should take the usual precautions – the system itself may be substantially safe but a few of its stations are in fearsome neighborhoods.

Operating hours are Monday through Thursday 5.30am to midnight, Friday 5.30am to 2am, Saturday 8am to 2am and Sunday 8am to midnight. Trains run every five minutes on most lines during rush hours, and every ten to twelve minutes at other times. Pick up a

copy of the useful **Metro guide** (free, available in most stations), which spells out the bus and train routes to the city's various attractions. The entire system is shown on two **Metro System Route Maps** (one for DC/Virginia, one for DC/Maryland; $2 each), available from Metro sales offices (see below) and from ADC Map & Travel at 1636 I Street NW.

Each passenger needs a **farecard**, which must be bought from a machine before you pass through the turnstiles. Fares are based on when and how far you travel; maps and ticket prices are posted by the machines. **One-way fares** range from $1.10 (base rate, off-peak) to $3.25; the higher, **peak-rate** fares are charged Mon–Fri 5.30–9.30am and 3–7pm. Children under five ride free.

The farecards work like debit cards – you "put in" an amount of money when you purchase the card, and then the correct fare is subtracted from your total after each train ride. If you're going to use the Metro several times, it's worth putting in more money – an additional ten percent credit is added to the value of cards over $20. (Most stations have a

---

Washington Metropolitan Area Transit Authority

For route information and timetables for buses or the Metro call ☎202/637-7000 (Mon–Fri 6am–10.30pm, Sat & Sun 8am–10.30pm) or log onto ⊛ www.wmata.com.

Some helpful numbers
Transit Police ☎202/962-2121 (emergencies only).
Lost and Found ☎202/962-1195 (24hr message; office open Mon–Fri 11am–3pm).

Mobility Link ☎202/962-6464 (help line for people with disabilities).

Passes
For passes and other information, visit:
Metro Center Sales Office, 12th and F sts NW at Metro Center Station (Mon–Fri 7.30am–6.30pm).
Metro Headquarters (Lobby), 600 5th St NW (Mon–Fri 8am–1pm & 2–4pm).
Metro Pentagon Sales Office, Pentagon Concourse (Mon–Fri 7.30am–1pm & 2–3pm).

few machines that accept debit and credit cards.) Feed the card through the turnstile and retrieve it; when you do the same thing at the end of your journey, the machine prints out on the card how much fare remains. If you've paid the exact amount, the turnstile keeps the card; if you don't have enough money remaining on the card for the journey, insert it into one of the special exit-fare machines, deposit more money and try the turnstile again. If you plan on catching a bus after your Metro ride, get a **rail-to-bus transfer** pass at the station where you *enter* the rail system. The self-service transfer machines are on the mezzanine next to the escalator leading to the train platform.

The **Metrorail One Day Pass** ($5) buys unlimited travel after 9.30am on weekdays and all day on the weekend. There's also a **7-Day Fast Pass** ($25), for seven consecutive days' unlimited travel, and the **28-Day Pass** ($100) for 28 consecutive days. If you're also going to use buses (see below), you might consider the **Weekly Bus/Rail Fast Pass** ($30), valid for one week of unlimited bus and Metro travel. All passes are available at Metro Center station; at Metro Headquarters (see opposite); at most Safeway, Giant and SuperFresh stores; or online through the WMATA website.

Buses

WMATA is also responsible for DC's **buses**, which operate largely the same hours as the Metro (though some run until 2am on weekdays as well). We've listed the most useful routes below. The **base fare** for most bus journeys is $1.10, payable to the driver, though surcharges and zone crossings can increase this; the same peak-hour rates apply as on the Metro. If you're transferring from the Metro, give your pass to the driver and pay 25¢ on a regular route or $1.15 on an express route (rail transfers cover 85¢ of your bus fare). Tourists are unlikely to get full value out of a bus pass – the two most relevant are the Weekly Bus/Rail Fast Pass ($30; see "The Metro," above) and the **Weekly Pass** ($10), which buys seven days' unlimited base-fare bus trips. **Outside DC**, Maryland and Virginia have their own local bus systems. The only times you're likely to use these are in Alexandria (whose system is called DASH) and en route to Mount Vernon, which you can reach on a Fairfax Connector bus. Both systems link with the Metro: for timetable information contact **DASH** (☎703/370-3274, ⊛www.dashbus.com) or **Fairfax Connector** (☎703/339-7200, ⊛www.fairfaxconnector.com).

Taxis

Taxis are a useful adjunct to the public transportation system, especially in outposts like Georgetown and Adams-Morgan, which aren't on the Metro. If you know you're going to be out late in these neighborhoods, it's a good idea to book a taxi in advance.

Useful bus routes

Foggy Bottom to Woodley Park: #L1 via Virginia Ave, C St, 23rd St, Washington Circle, New Hampshire Ave, Dupont Circle, Connecticut Ave (National Zoological Park).

L'Enfant Plaza to McPherson Square: #52 via 6th St, Independence Ave, 14th St.

McPherson Square to Woodley Park: #L2 via K St, 20th St, Dupont Circle, 18th St (Adams-Morgan), Calvert St, Connecticut Ave (National Zoological Park).

Metro Center to Adams-Morgan: #42 via Metro Center (10th and F), H St, Connecticut Ave, Dupont Circle, Columbia Rd (Adams-Morgan).

Pennsylvania Ave to Georgetown:

#30, #32, #34, #35, #36 via Eastern Market, US Capitol, Independence Ave, 7th St, Pennsylvania Ave, 15th St, Pennsylvania Ave, Wisconsin Ave (Georgetown).

Pentagon–Mall Loop: #13A, #13B via 14th St Bridge (Jefferson Memorial), Bureau of Engraving & Printing/Holocaust Museum, Independence Ave, 7th St, Constitution Ave, Lincoln Memorial, Arlington.

Union Station to Georgetown: #D1, #D3, #D6 via E St, 13th St, K St, Dupont Circle, Q St (Georgetown).

Union Station to Kennedy Center: #80 via Massachusetts Ave, H St, 13th St, K St, 19th St, Virginia Ave, Watergate Complex.

Unlike cabs in most American cities, taxis in DC charge **fares** on a concentric zoned basis. Standard rates are posted in each cab; a ride at the basic rate within one zone costs $5. Most crosstown fares run from $5 to $15.60 (the maximum for any ride in the city limits) – Georgetown to Dupont Circle, say, costs about $6.50. During rush hours (Mon–Fri 7–9.30am & 4–6.30pm) there's a $1 surcharge, and groups may be asked to pay $1.50 for each extra passenger (in addition to the first one). Don't be surprised if the driver pulls over to pick up another passenger: this is perfectly legal, provided they don't have to go more than five blocks out of the way to reach your destination, and everybody pays the set amount for their journey. Once you get out of DC, into Maryland or Virginia, you'll be charged what's on the meter, which can prove expensive.

You can either flag cabs down on the street or use the ranks at hotels and transport terminals; there are always cabs available at Union Station. If you call a taxi in advance (see "Directory," p.320, for a list of cab companies) there's a $1.50 surcharge on the fare. For more information on DC cabs, zones and fares, call the **Taxicab Commission** at ☎202/645-6005.

Driving

It's not worth **driving** in the capital unless you have to. If you're heading out of the city by car, either pick up your vehicle at the end of your stay (there are rental desks at Union Station; you don't have to go back to the airports) or leave your own car at your hotel for the duration. For lists of **car rental agencies**, see p.14.

One-way streets can play havoc with the best-formulated driving routes, while the traffic-control system in place during the city's **rush hours** (Mon–Fri 6.30–9.30am & 4–7pm, plus lunchtime) means that many lanes, or even whole streets, **change direction** at particular times of the day, and left turns are often periodically forbidden. Read the signs carefully. To top it all off, the roads can be diabolical – even on major thoroughfares you'll want to keep a wary eye out for potholes and ridges.

Most mid- and upper-range hotels offer secure parking (from around $10 per night); **parking lots and garages** cost from $5 per hour to $15 a day. Looking for free **on-street parking** is not likely to pay for itself in terms of time and energy expended: there are free, limited-wait (2–3hr) parking spots around the Mall (Jefferson and Madison Drives, Independence Ave SW) and in West Potomac Park, but they're heavily subscribed. **Parking meters** tend to operate between 9.30am and 6.30pm, usually giving a maximum stay of two hours; stay longer and you'll get a $15 ticket.

At other times, just when you think you've found the perfect spot, it will almost certainly be reserved for local workers, or on a street that becomes one-way during rush hour, or temporarily illegal to park on because it *is* rush hour, or in a clearway reserved for snow plows, or rendered useless for a million and one other reasons. Naturally, the places you might want to drive to for an evening out, like Georgetown, Dupont Circle or Adams-Morgan, are, again, heavily cruised for parking spaces.

If you happen to be visiting a local resident, however, you can request an **on-street parking permit** from a local police station. You'll need to present your registration and your host will need to provide proof of residence. It's a quick and easy process that allows you to park in a specified zone in the vicinity of your host's address for up to two weeks. Sadly, it doesn't spare you the search for those elusive parking spots.

Should your car get towed away during your visit, call the **Brentwood Impoundment Lot** at ☎202/576-7217; expect to pay up to $100 to get it back. Vehicles towed away after 7pm on a Friday won't be returned until after 9am the following Monday.

Bikes

Given the traffic, few visitors will want to brave the DC streets on a **bicycle**, though several outfits can fix you up and provide maps and advice on traffic conditions. Bike rental costs around $30 a day, or $100 a week (slightly more for mountain bikes); you'll need to leave a deposit and/or a credit card or passport. It's worth noting that bikes are permitted on Metrorail except on weekdays from 7–10am and 4–7pm and on some major holidays, such as the Fourth of July.

If you want to find fellow bikers, you can join a cycling tour – see the next section for details – or follow the trails along the Potomac or the C&O Canal instead. For more ideas on where to bike, see "Sports and outdoor activities" (p.307).

Bike rental companies

Better Bikes ☎202/293-2080, ⓦwww.betterbikesinc.com. 24hr information line; will deliver anywhere in DC.
Big Wheel Bikes 1034 33rd St NW, Georgetown ☎202/337-0254; 2 Prince St, Alexandria, VA ☎703/739-2300; ⓦwww.bigwheelbikes.com.

Open Wed–Fri 11am–7pm & Sat–Sun 10am–6pm. Georgetown location convenient to C&O Canal and Capital Crescent trails; Old Town Alexandria location near Mount Vernon Trail.
Blazing Saddles 445 11th St NW, Old Downtown ☎202/544-0055, ⓦwww.blazingsaddles.com. Daily 9am–5pm; closed Nov–March.

City tours

There are any number of tour operators prepared to show you the sights of Washington DC, though even with just a couple of days it's easy to see most things on your own. However, some of the more popular tour-bus services, like the Tourmobile, are useful, since they allow you to get on and off the bus at will and shuttle you out to the more far-flung sights. River cruises, too, can be worth considering, especially in high summer when the offshore breeze comes as a welcome relief. Specialist tours show you a side of Washington you may not otherwise see; some of the best are described below. For more ideas on Washington tours, contact the DC Heritage Tourism Coalition (☎202/828-9255, ⓦwww.dcheritage.org); its website lists a variety of guided tours and provides a calendar of cultural events.

Building tours

For special, extended tours of the following buildings you must make reservations; see the relevant entries for details. American citizens should contact their Congressional representatives well in advance for special tours of government buildings. Tours arranged in this manner will be set for a specific day, usually outside opening hours; most last longer than the usual walk-in tours and show you areas or rooms not normally open to the public. Note that after the September 11, 2001, terrorist attacks, public tours were suspended at several of these buildings, including the Capitol, the FBI, the *Washington Post*, and the White House. We recommend calling ahead before heading off for a tour at any of these destinations:
Bureau of Engraving and Printing see p.125.
Department of State see p.150.
Federal Bureau of Investigation see p.162.
Federal Reserve Building see p.149.
National Archives, see p.166.
Old Executive Office Building see p.142.
Treasury Building see p.142.
US Capitol see p.98.

Washington Post see p.190.
White House see p.133.

Bicycle tours

Bike the Sites Inc ☎202/966-8662, ⓦwww.bikethesites.com. Three-hour guided bike tours of the city's major sights ($40, includes bike and helmet), plus tours of Mount Vernon and customized tours throughout the District. No fixed schedule; call for details. Reservations required.

Bus and trolley tours

Gray Line ☎202/289-1995 or 1-800/862-1400, ⓦwww.graylinedc.com. A variety of tours in and around DC, including a nine-hour tour of downtown sights and Mount Vernon ($48), a trolley tour ($28), an evening tour ($28) and trips to Colonial Williamsburg ($68) and Monticello ($68).
Old Town Trolley Tours ☎202/832-9800, ⓦwww.trolleytours.com. Motorized, board-at-will trolleys covering downtown, Georgetown and National Cathedral. Tickets ($24 a day) are available at trolley stops and downtown hotels.
Tourmobile ☎202/554-5100, ⓦwww.tourmobile.com. Narrated, open-sided

Tourmobile buses allow unlimited stops at numerous city locations (daily 9.30am–4.30pm). An $18 one-day ticket covers downtown and Arlington Cemetery. An extra $25 gets you to Mount Vernon and back, and it's another $7 to the Frederick Douglass Home (mid-June to Labor Day only). Two-day tickets for unlimited travel on both routes cost $45 (DC and Mount Vernon) or $34 (DC and Frederick Douglass). There's also a 3.5-hour "twilight tour" that departs every evening at 6.30pm from Union Station ($18). Tickets available at the office on the Ellipse, kiosks on the Mall (there's one at the Washington Monument) and on the bus itself.

Cruises and river trips

Atlantic Kayak Tours ⓣ703/838-9072, ⓦwww.atlantickayak.com. Kayak tours along the Potomac, including 2.5-hour sunset tours exploring the monuments and bridges of Georgetown or the Dyke Marsh Wildlife area ($39). Also moonlight tours, full-day trips and outings to view the Fourth of July fireworks. No experience is necessary and all equipment is included. Call for schedule; tours run April–Oct only.

Capitol River Cruises ⓣ301/460-7447 or 1-800/405-5511, ⓦwww.capitolrivercruises.com. Fifty-minute sight-seeing cruises leaving hourly throughout the day (April–Oct) from Georgetown's Washington Harbor, end of 31st St NW; $10 per person, reservations not necessary.

DC Ducks ⓣ202/832-9800, ⓦwww.dcducks.com. Converted amphibious carriers cruise the Mall and then splash into the Potomac (90min; $24). Hourly departures from Union Station (March–Oct daily 10am–4pm).

Spirit Cruises ⓣ202/554-8000 or 1-866/211-3811, ⓦwww.spiritcruises.com. Swish two-hour river cruises with bar and show bands for $30–40; three-hour dinner cruises for $50–80. Tickets and departures from Pier 4, 6th and Water sts SW (Waterfront Metro).

Specialist tours and activities

Anacostia: Different Voices … Different Views ⓣ202/347-7201. Monthly tour ($40) to little-visited Anacostia, one of DC's oldest neighborhoods, including a stop at the home of Frederick Douglass, a soul food lunch and entertainment at a local church (June–Sept only; call for schedule).

Capital Helicopters ⓣ703/417-2150. Twenty-minute helicopter tours ($125 per person; $65 for children under age 13) above the sights of central DC. A minimum of two people required; reservations necessary. Flights are out of National Airport.

Duke Ellington's DC ⓣ202/232-2915. A four-hour bus tour of the historic African-American U Street/Shaw neighborhood, boyhood home of the jazz legend. The tour ($40) includes visits to the Mary McLeod Bethune Council House and Lincoln Theatre, lunch in the Whitelaw Hotel ballroom and a play. Departures monthly May–Aug; call for schedule.

Goodwill Embassy Tour ⓣ202/636-4225, ⓦwww.dcgoodwill.org. Every May, some of DC's finest embassy buildings throw open their doors for one day (pre-booked $25; $30 on the day). Reserve well in advance. Many embassies also offer free guided tours provided you make reservations; for contact telephone numbers see p.319.

Kalorama House and Embassy Tour ⓣ202/387-4062. Various ambassadors' residences and private homes open to the public for one day every September; reserve in advance ($18).

SpyDrive ⓣ866/779-3748, ⓦwww.spydrive.com. Two-hour tours ($55) of spook sites in the "spy capital of the world," led by retired FBI, CIA and KGB officers. Call for schedule.

Walking tours

Anthony S. Pitch ⓣ301/294-9514, ⓦwww.dcsightseeing.com. Highly recommended historical walking tours of Adams-Morgan, Lafayette Square and Georgetown, led by the amiable Mr Pitch most Sunday mornings (call for schedules). They last two hours and cost $10.

DC Heritage Tours ⓣ202/828-9255. Ninety-minute walking tours of downtown DC, daily throughout the year ($7.50).

Lantern Lights: Ghost & Graveyard Tour ⓣ703/548-0100. Hour-long tours through Old Town Alexandria led by Colonial-costumed guides who spin ghoulish yarns by lantern light. Tours ($6; Fri, Sat & Sun evenings, March–Nov) depart from the Ramsay House Visitors Center at 221 King St.

Old Town Walking Tour ⓣ703/838-4200. Tour focusing on the history and architecture of Alexandria's historic district ($10; Apr–Nov Mon–Sat 10.30am, Sun 2pm), departing from the Ramsay House Visitors Center at 221 King St.

Washington Walks ⓣ202/484-1565, ⓦwww.washingtonwalks.com. Two-hour walks following various itineraries through downtown DC ($10).

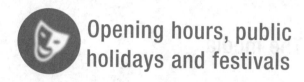

Opening hours, public holidays and festivals

The opening hours of specific visitor attractions, monuments, memorials, stores and offices are given in the relevant accounts throughout the guide. Telephone numbers are provided so that you can check current information with the places themselves.

Opening hours

As a general rule, **museums** are open daily 10am to 5.30pm, though some have extended summer hours; a few art galleries stay open until 9pm or so one night a week. Smaller, private museums close for one day a week, usually Monday or Tuesday. **Federal office buildings** (some of which incorporate museums) are open Monday through Friday 9am to 5.30pm. Most of the **national monuments** in the city are open daily 24 hours, though they tend to be staffed only between 8am and midnight. Finally, **stores** are usually open Monday through Saturday 10am to 7pm; some have extended Thursday night hours. In neighborhoods like Georgetown, Adams-Morgan and Dupont Circle, many stores open on Sunday, too (usually noon to 5pm). **Malls** tend to be open Monday through Saturday 10am to 7pm or later and Sunday noon to 6pm.

In the wake of the terrorist attacks of September 11, 2001, and subsequent security scares, many government buildings **suspended tours and prohibited access** to the general public as they reevaluated security measures. As a result, tours may not be up and running at some government sites. Throughout the guide we've noted buildings that may be affected by such changes and recommend calling ahead before heading off for a tour at any of these destinations.

Public holidays and festivals

On the **national public holidays** listed below, stores, banks and public and federal offices are liable to be closed all day. The Smithsonian museums and galleries, on the other hand, close only on Christmas Day. The traditional **summer tourism season**, when many attractions have extended opening hours, runs from **Memorial Day** to **Labor Day**.

Washington has a huge variety of **annual festivals and events**, many of them national in scope: America's Christmas Tree is lit each December on the Ellipse in front of the White House; the grandest Fourth of July Parade in the country takes place along and around the Mall; and every four years the new president takes part in a triumphal Inaugural Parade up Pennsylvania Avenue in January. Many of the national holidays listed are celebrated with special events and festivities in the city. Such is the range of festivals throughout the year, it's hard to turn up without coinciding with at least one; DC's full **festival calendar** is detailed in Chapter 18. Note, however, that during all major festival periods – particularly the spring Cherry Blossom Festival, Easter, Memorial Day and the Fourth of July– it can be very difficult to find accommodation in the city. Book well in advance if you plan to visit the capital at those times.

National holidays

January
1: New Year's Day
3rd Monday: Dr Martin Luther King Jr's Birthday
February
3rd Monday: President's Day
March/April
Easter Monday
May
Last Monday: Memorial Day
July
4: Independence Day
September
1st Monday: Labor Day
October
2nd Monday: Columbus Day
November
11: Veterans' Day
4th Thursday: Thanksgiving Day
December
25: Christmas Day

The media

DC is the most media-savvy city in the United States. Much of what makes the news around the world starts life in the capital's press briefings, and though you won't get into a White House press conference, you can watch matters unfold on C-SPAN (a no-frills public affairs channel that also broadcasts House and Senate sessions and congressional hearings) and then read about them first-hand in the *Washington Post*. For all that, overseas visitors will find news reporting – even in the nation's capital – fairly parochial. A small storm (no one injured) in Boise, Idaho, will get more coverage than a change of European government, so to keep in touch with day-to-day events back home you'll have to buy a foreign newspaper, easily done in DC.

Newspapers and magazines

DC's main newspaper, the relatively liberal *Washington Post,* is one of America's most respected dailies, routinely winning Pulitzer Prizes (the nation's highest news honor), most notably for its investigation of the Watergate scandal that led to the fall of President Nixon. That it lands each morning on the doorstep of some of the world's most powerful people – from ambassadors to leaders at the IMF and World Bank, not to mention President Bush – only serves to underscore its influence on the world stage. Top columnists on the paper's opinion pages include political commentator David Broder (Wednesday), noted conservative George F. Will (Thursday) and *Slate* editor Michael Kinsley, though DC-area residents hold a special place in their hearts for Dr Gridlock (Monday), who chronicles the Beltway blues felt by this traffic-troubled town. The *Post* is challenged in news coverage (though not style or balance) only by the conservative, Moonie-published, *Washington Times*. There's little reason to read it, unless you're looking to save a dime. The country's one truly national daily, the colorful *USA Today*, is published across the Potomac in Virginia, though overseas readers should only turn to this for anthropological, rather than news, purposes.

Free weeklies include the alternative *CityPaper* – a thick tabloid that hits the streets on Thursdays to provide the city's best source of arts and entertainment listings – and the gay *Washington Blade* and *Metro Weekly*. Glossy **monthly magazines** include the arts-and-leisure publications *Washingtonian* and *Where: Washington*, plus other local/neighborhood papers and magazines available in bars, restaurants, shops and hotels.

Newspapers from other US cities, as well as **foreign newspapers and magazines**, can be bought in Union Station, at major bookstores (like Barnes & Noble), and at The Newsroom, 1803 Connecticut Ave NW, Dupont Circle ☎202/332-1489.

TV and radio

For **television news**, the three major networks – NBC, ABC and CBS – broadcast news and talk shows all morning Monday to Friday until 10am and air their evening local news programs from 5pm to 6.30pm and again at 11pm, also on weekdays. National news is on at 6.30pm. The Murdoch empire's DC outpost, Fox 5, counters the major networks' news programs by airing episodes of *The Simpsons,* broadcasting its nightly news program daily at 10pm. Most hotels have cable TV, so you'll also be able to catch regular news updates on CNN or one of the other US cable news giants, Fox, MSNBC or CNBC, or possibly BBC World.

For quality news on the **radio**, tune into WAMU on 88.5 FM for National Public Radio broadcasts (Mon–Fri 5–10am & 4–8pm). On these you're likely to hear frequent reports by veteran Washington correspondent Cokie Roberts, also well known for her hour-long TV news program, *This Week*, which airs Sunday mornings at 9am on ABC.

TV stations

Channel 4 (WRC/NBC)
Channel 5 (WTTG/Fox)
Channel 7 (WJLA/ABC)
Channel 9 (WUSA/CBS)
Channel 26 (WETA/PBS)
Channel 50 (WBDC/WB)

Radio stations

Local AM stations

WMAL (630) for news, sports and talk (including Dr Laura and Rush Limbaugh)
WTEM (980) for sports talk
WOL (1450) for African-American talk

WTOP (1500) for news and Orioles games
WPGC (1580) for gospel

Local FM stations

WAMU (88.5) for talk, music and news (including National Public Radio programming)
WCSP (90.1) for Congress and public affairs coverage
WETA (90.9) for classical music and news
WHUR (96.3) for R&B
WMZQ (98.7) for country music
WHFS (99.1) for rock
WGMS (103.5) for classical music
WJFK (106.7) for talk (including Howard Stern in the morning)
WRQX (107.3) for contemporary pop and rock
WTOP (107.7) for news

Crime, security and personal safety

For many years Washington has had a poor reputation in terms of crime and personal safety. You'll be confidently told that it's the "Murder Capital" of the United States (even though, statistically, that's no longer true), and stories of drug dealers in business just blocks from the White House are in routine circulation amongst visitors and locals alike. Moreover, the terrorist attack on the Pentagon and anthrax scares on Capitol Hill and at city post offices have done little for Washington's confidence in its day-to-day security.

It's true, DC ain't Kansas: scan any copy of the *Washington Post* for a rundown of the latest daily drive-by shootings and drug-war escapades. However, to get things in perspective, almost all the crime that makes the newspaper headlines takes place in neighborhoods (most of NE, SE and distinct parts of upper NW) that tourists have no business venturing into – there's nothing there to see and certainly no "real" Washington that you'd want to experience. When neighborhoods are borderline in terms of personal security, this guide makes it clear where you should and shouldn't go; if there's a sight or museum you really want to see, take a cab there and back. However, in the places you will be spending most of your time – downtown, along the Mall, in Georgetown – all the major tourist sights, the Metro system and the main nightlife zones are invariably well guarded, well lit and well policed. Indeed, the Mall between the US Capitol, White House and Lincoln Memorial is probably the most heavily policed district in America, brimming with regular police officers, Secret Service operatives and park rangers.

ID and security issues

In the past, overseas visitors especially often commented on the ease of access to public buildings in the national capital. However, since the terrorist attacks on America you'll find that **security measures** have been stepped up, with more visual, physical and covert checks on anyone entering public and federal buildings — museums and galleries as well as obvious sites like the US Capitol and the White House. You can expect to have to wait in line and have your bags searched before entering many buildings, while metal detectors and other security devices are in place at federal sites throughout the city. The popular **tours of**

federal and national buildings – including the Pentagon (itself a target of the attacks), White House, FBI Building and US Capitol – are subject to cancellation or suspension at any time for security reasons; call ahead if you're making a special trip.

As far as your personal responsibility goes, you should **carry ID** at all times. Two pieces should suffice, one of which should have a photo: a passport or driver's license and credit card(s) are best. (Incidentally, not having your license with you while driving is an arrestable offense.) A university photo ID might be sufficient, but is not always easily recognizable. An International Student Identity Card (ISIC) is often not accepted as valid proof of age, for example in bars or liquor stores. Overseas visitors (often surprised to learn that the legal drinking age is 21) might want to carry their passport, unless they have a photo-style driving license.

Mugging and theft

Most people will have few problems, and if things do go wrong, foreign visitors tend to report that the **police** are helpful and obliging, although they'll be less sympathetic if they think you brought the trouble on yourself through carelessness.

You shouldn't be complacent. The fact that DC attracts so many tourists means that it has more than its share of **petty crime**, simply because there are plenty of unsuspecting holidaymakers to prey on. Even seemingly safe neighborhoods like Georgetown and Dupont Circle have their fair share of muggings. Keep your wits about you in crowds; know where your wallet or purse is; and, of course, avoid parks, parking lots and dark streets at night. Be careful when using ATMs in untouristed areas: try to use machines near downtown hotels, shops or offices, and during daylight. After the Metro has closed down, take taxis back from bars, restaurants and clubs. And if you have to ask directions, choose carefully who you ask (go into a store, if possible).

Should the worst happen, hand over your money, and afterwards find a phone and dial ☏**911**, or hail a cab and ask the driver to take you to the nearest police station. Here, report the theft and get a reference number on the report to claim insurance and travelers' check refunds. Ring the local Travelers Aid (see the "Directory," p.320) for

practical advice about hospitals and emergency services.

Another potential source of trouble is having your **hotel room burgled**. Always store valuables in the hotel safe when you go out. When inside, keep your door locked and don't open it to anyone you are suspicious of. If they claim to be hotel staff and you don't believe them, call reception to check. In hostels and budget hotels, you may want to keep your valuables on your person, unless you know the security measures to be reliable.

Needless to say, having bags that contain travel documents snatched can be a big headache, none more so for foreign travelers than **losing your passport**. Make photocopies of everything important before you go (including the business page of your passport) and keep them separate from the originals. If the worst happens, go to the nearest consulate and get them to issue you a **temporary passport**, basically a sheet of paper saying you've reported the loss, which will get you back home.

Keep a record of the numbers of your **travelers' checks** separately from the actual checks; if you lose them, call the issuing company on the toll-free number below. They'll ask you for the check numbers, the place you bought them, when and how you lost them and whether it's been reported to the police. All being well, you should get the missing checks reissued within a couple of days – and perhaps an emergency advance to tide you over.

Finally, it goes without saying that you should *never* **hitchhike** anywhere in DC, or indeed the entire US.

Emergency numbers for lost cards and checks

American Express Cards ☏1-800/528-4800
American Express Checks ☏1-800/221-7282
Citicorp ☏1-800/645-6556
Diners Club ☏1-800/234-6377
Mastercard ☏1-800/826-2181
Thomas Cook/Mastercard ☏1-800/223-9920
Visa Cards ☏1-800/847-2911
Visa Checks ☏1-800/227-6811

Car crime

Crimes committed against tourists driving **rented cars** have garnered headlines around the world in recent years, but there are certain precautions you can take to keep yourself safe. Not driving in DC itself would be a good first step: it's not necessary, since public transportation and cheap taxis can get you most places you'd want to go. On longer trips, pick up your rental car on the day you leave the city. Any car you do rent should have nothing on it – such as a particular license plate – that makes it easy to identify as a rental car. When driving, under no circumstances stop in any unlit or seemingly deserted urban area – and especially not if someone is waving you down and suggesting that there is something wrong with your car. Similarly, if you are "accidentally" rammed by the driver behind, do not stop but drive on to the nearest well-lit, busy area and phone the police at ☎**911**. Keep your doors locked and windows never more than slightly open. Do not open your door or window if someone approaches your car on the pretext of asking directions. Hide any valuables out of sight, preferably locked in the trunk or in the glove compartment (any valuables you don't need for your journey should be left in your hotel safe).

Outside the city, if your **vehicle breaks down** on an interstate or heavily traveled road, wait in the car for a patrol car to arrive. One option is to rent a mobile phone with your car, for a small additional charge – a potential lifesaver.

 # Travelers with disabilities

Washington DC is one of the most accessible cities in the world for travelers with special needs. All public buildings, including hotels and restaurants, have to be wheelchair-accessible and provide suitable toilet facilities. Almost all street corners have dropped curbs, and the public transit system has facilities such as subways with elevators, and buses that "kneel" to let people board.

Planning your trip

It's always a good idea for people with special needs to alert their travel agents when booking: things are far simpler when the various travel operators or carriers are expecting you. A **medical certificate** of your fitness to travel, provided by your doctor, is also useful; some airlines or insurance companies may insist on it. Most **airlines** do whatever they can to ease your journey and will usually let attendants of more seriously disabled people accompany them at no extra charge. Almost every **Amtrak train** includes one or more coaches with accommodation for passengers with disabilities. Guide dogs travel free and may accompany blind, deaf or disabled passengers in the carriage. Be sure to give 24 hours' notice. **Greyhound buses** are not equipped with lifts for wheelchairs, though staff will assist with boarding, and the "Helping Hand" scheme offers two-for-the-price-of-one tickets to passengers unable to travel alone (make sure to carry a doctor's certificate).

The American Automobile Association produces the *Handicapped Driver's Mobility Guide* for **disabled drivers** (available from Quantum-Precision Inc, 225 Broadway, Suite 3404, New York, NY 10007). The larger car rental companies provide cars with hand controls at no extra charge, though only on their full-size (which is to say most expensive) models; reserve well in advance.

Disabled access in the city

The **Washington Convention and Tourism Corporation** (see p.20) produces a free handout on accessibility in the city; call ☎202/789-7000. Each station on the **Metro** (subway) system has an elevator (with Braille controls) to the platforms. The wide train aisles can accommodate wheelchairs, and reduced fares and priority seating are available. Seventy percent of Metro buses are kneeling buses with lifts. The Metro website (www.wmata.com) outlines the system's accessibility features in some detail. Alternatively, seek out the free guide offering complete information on Metro access for the disabled at Metro stations or call ℡202/637-7000 or 638-3780 (TDD). Visually-impaired and wheelchair users can call Mobility Link at ℡202/962-6464 for further information.

Most of the **monuments and memorials** in DC have elevators to viewing platforms and special parking facilities, and at some sites large-print brochures and sign-language interpreters are available. The White House has a special entrance reserved for visitors in wheelchairs, who don't need to wait in line for a ticket. For more information on any site operated by the National Park Service, call ℡202/619-7222. All **Smithsonian museum** buildings are wheelchair-accessible, and with notice staff can serve as sign-language interpreters or produce large-print, Braille or taped material. The free *Smithsonian Access* is available in large print, Braille or audio cassette; call ℡202/357-2700 or 357-1729 (TTY). It's also available, as is an accessibility map, online at ⓦwww.si.edu. To receive a copy of the *Zoo Guide for Visitors with Disabilities* call ℡202/673-4989 or 673-4823.

In addition, most new downtown **shopping malls** have wheelchair ramps and elevators. **Union Station** (shops, trains and cinema) is fully accessible, as are the **Kennedy Center** (p.153) and **National Theatre** (p.292), both of which also have good facilities for visually- and hearing-impaired visitors.

Useful contacts

US and Canada

Access-Able ⓦwww.access-able.com. Online resource for travelers with disabilities.
Directions Unlimited ℡1-800/533-5343 or 914/241-1700. Tour operator specializing in customized tours for people with disabilities.
DisabilityGuide.org A free online source of information for the Washington metropolitan area; lists accessible hotels and shopping venues, rates restaurants in terms of accessibility and provides a referral service. The organization also publishes the *Access Entertainment Guide* ($7; order form available online or write 21618 Slidell Rd, Boyds MD 20841).
Mobility International USA ℡541/343-1284, ⓦwww.miusa.org. Information and referral services, access guides, tours and exchange programs. Annual membership ($35) includes quarterly newsletter.
Society for the Advancement of Travelers with Handicaps (SATH) ℡212/447-7284, ⓦwww.sath.org. Nonprofit educational organization that has actively represented travelers with disabilities since 1976.
Washington Ear, Inc ℡301/681-6636, ⓦwww.washear.org. Supplies large-print ($5) and tactile ($12) atlases of the DC area.
Wheels Up! ℡1-888/389-4335, ⓦwww.wheelsup.com. Provides discounted airfares and tour prices for disabled travelers; also publishes a free monthly newsletter.

UK and Ireland

Disability Action Group Northern Ireland ℡028/9049 1011. Provides information about access for disabled travelers abroad.
Holiday Care UK ℡01293/774 535, Minicom ℡01293/776 943, ⓦwww.holidaycare.org.uk. Provides free lists of accessible accommodation in the US and other destinations.
Irish Wheelchair Association Republic of Ireland ℡01/833 8241. Useful information provided about traveling abroad with a wheelchair.
RADAR (Royal Association for Disability and Rehabilitation) UK ℡020/7250 3222, Minicom ℡020/7250 4119, ⓦwww.radar.org.uk. A good source of general advice on holidays and travel.

Australia and New Zealand

ACROD (Australian Council for Rehabilitation of the Disabled) ℡02/6282 4333. Provides lists of travel agencies and tour operators for people with disabilities.
Disabled Persons Assembly New Zealand ℡04/801 9100. Resource center with lists of travel agencies and tour operators for people with disabilities.

Staying on: work and study

Anyone planning an extended stay in the United States should apply for a special working visa at any American embassy before setting off. Different types of visas are issued, depending on your skills and proprosed length of stay, but unless you've got parents or children over 21 in the US or a prospective employer to sponsor you, your chances of getting a working visa are at best slim.

Illegal work is nothing like as easy to find as it used to be, and the government has introduced hefty fines for companies caught employing anyone without the legal right to work in the US. Even in the traditionally more casual establishments, like restaurants and bars, things have really tightened up, and if you do find work it's likely to be of the less visible, poorly paid kind – dishwasher instead of waiter.

Another option for work is to acquire a place as an **intern**, basically a general administrative dogsbody serving someone connected, however tenuously, to the nation's political or corporate system. Senators, representatives, White House staff, federal agencies, lobbyists and other businesses all hire interns over the summer, and applications should be made early in the New Year to anyone you can think of who might be interested in your skills and experience. Large city bookstores carry guides to applying for internships such as the comprehensive annual publication,

Internships USA (published in the US and UK by Peterson's, Thomson Learning, Ⓦ www.petersons.com). Most posts are unpaid and filled by college students keen to get on in American politics and commerce, though foreign visitors with a special interest can try writing in the first instance to their local parliament members, who often have contacts or reciprocal arrangements with members of Congress.

Another option is to contact *City Paper*, which has an intern program (details on its website, Ⓦ www.washingtoncitypaper.com). Successful applicants are taken on three times a year (spring, summer and fall) for placements lasting three or four months. The internship pays minimum wage, and you'll be expected to have some journalistic experience and to know DC.

Foreign students wishing to **study** at an American university should apply to that institution directly; if they accept you, you're more or less entitled to unlimited visas so long as you remain enrolled in full-time education.

the city

the city

The Mall

Scrubbed, manicured and heavily policed, the showpiece greensward of **THE MALL** is quite unlike the center of any other American city, though European visitors, used to triumphal structures, royal parks and boulevards, will feel right at home. Laid out along two carefully tended miles between the US Capitol and the Potomac River are nine Smithsonian **museums**, unrivaled in their field; the two buildings of the National Gallery of Art; and the city's four most famous **monuments and memorials** – to George Washington, Abraham Lincoln, Franklin Delano Roosevelt and the Vietnam veterans. A fifth, to Thomas Jefferson, and the White House itself, stand perfectly aligned on either side.

The Mall is also where Washington comes to relax – Albert Camus talked fondly of "placid evenings on the vast lawns" during his visit in 1946 – and to party, not least at the annual Festival of American Folklife and on the Fourth of July. Yet its central role in a planned capital city also places it at the very heart of the country's **political** life. When there's a protest to be made, the National Mall – to give it its full title – is the place to make it. The 1963 March on Washington brought Dr Martin Luther King Jr to the steps of the Lincoln Memorial to deliver his "I have a dream" speech; in 1967, at the height of the anti-war protests, the notorious March on the Pentagon started from the same place; three decades later, in 1995, the controversial minister Louis Farrakhan of the Nation of Islam brought hundreds of thousands of black men here on the Million Man March. The sheer expanse of the Mall inspires grand gestures: on several occasions the AIDS Memorial Quilt – a patchwork of 40,000 individual squares remembering America's AIDS victims – has been laid in commemoration the full mile from the Capitol to the Washington Monument.

As a visitor, you'd have to concoct a fairly perverse **itinerary** to avoid setting foot on the Mall. Given a normal appetite for museums, galleries and monuments, and a fair constitution, you could get around most of the Mall's major sites in three days or so. But it's better to return at various times during your stay, if only to avoid complete cultural overload. Many of the attractions lend themselves to being seen with a combination of other city sights: the western monuments with the White House (Chapter 4); the Jefferson and Roosevelt memorials with the Holocaust Museum or Bureau of Engraving and Printing (Chapter 3); the museums on the Mall's north side interspersed with a stroll around Old Downtown (Chapter 5).

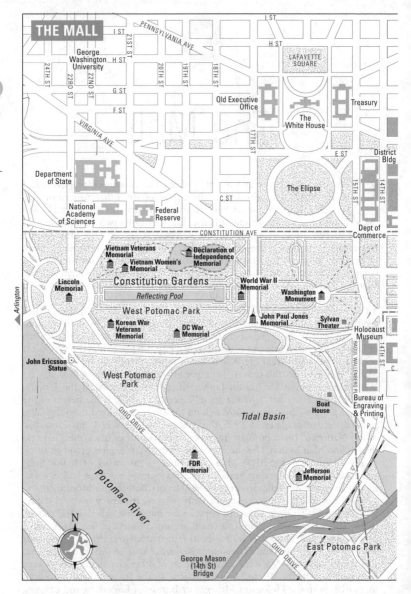

THE MALL

I ST
PENNSYLVANIA AVE
I ST
H ST
21ST ST
George
Washington
University
H ST
24TH ST
22ND ST
22ND ST
20TH ST
19TH ST
18TH ST
LAFAYETTE
SQUARE
G ST
Old Executive
Office
Treasury
F ST
The
White House
17TH ST
VIRGINIA AVE
E ST
District
Bldg
Department
of State
The Ellipse
15TH ST
14TH ST
National
Academy
of Sciences
Federal
Reserve
C ST
Dept of
Commerce
CONSTITUTION AVE
Vietnam Veterans
Memorial
Declaration of
Independence
Memorial
Constitution Gardens
Vietnam Women's
Memorial
World War II
Memorial
Lincoln
Memorial
Reflecting Pool
Washington
Monument
West Potomac Park
Arlington
Korean War
Veterans
Memorial
DC War
Memorial
John Paul Jones
Memorial
Sylvan
Theater
Holocaust
Museum
14TH ST
John Ericsson
Statue
West Potomac
Park
RAOUL WALLENBERG PL
C
Bureau of
Engraving
& Printing
Boat
House
Tidal Basin
Potomac River
FDR
Memorial
Jefferson
Memorial
East Potomac Park
N
OHIO DRIVE
George Mason
(14th St)
Bridge

Some history

French military engineer **Pierre Charles L'Enfant**'s plan for the new capital city had at its heart a 400-foot-wide Grand Avenue, leading west from the site of the Capitol. Along it he envisaged gardens and mansions for the political elite, and where a line drawn west from the Capitol met one drawn south from the President's Mansion (today's White House) was to stand a commemorative monument to George Washington. These were ambitious schemes indeed for

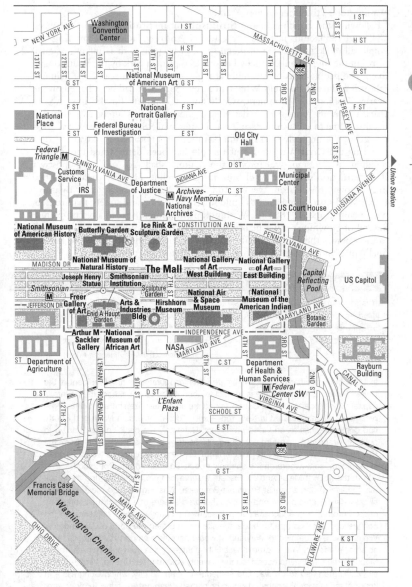

▶ Union Station

a piece of land that was, at the time, little more than a muddy, bug-infested swamp. Due to lack of funds, work didn't start on the Washington Monument until 1848, by which time any prospect of what had become known as "The Mall" transforming itself into a splendid avenue was laughable: cows, pigs and goats grazed on the open land, while along the north side ran the malodorous city canal (linking the C&O Canal in Georgetown with the Anacostia River), stinking with rotting refuse, spoiling fish, entrails and dead animals from

Washington's 7th Street Center Market.

Following the building of the **Smithsonian Institution** "Castle" between 1849 and 1855, eminent landscape gardener **Andrew Jackson Downing** was employed to design an elegant green space in keeping with L'Enfant's original plan, but the money only stretched to one tree-planted park by the Smithsonian. Even here people dared not venture at night, since it soon became the haunt of footpads and ne'er-do-wells. What's more, by 1855 work had been halted on the nearby Washington Monument, which stood incomplete for the next twenty years. The Mall continued to deteriorate and, as the city grew, its south side became home to meat markets and warehouses, while the avenue itself was criss-crossed by the ungainly tracks of the Baltimore and Potomac Railroad.

During the **Civil War**, President Lincoln had been determined to continue building as "a sign we intend the Union shall go on," and postwar Reconstruction saved the Mall from further decline. The city canal was filled in (it's now Constitution Avenue) and Center Market was closed; a Board of Public Works was established to build sewers, sidewalks and streets; mature trees were planted; and in 1884 the Washington Monument was finally completed. Several of Downing's other plans were resurrected, extending beyond the Mall to incorporate the Ellipse and the gardens on either side of the White House, finally placing the Mall at the ornamental heart of the city.

The planning of a capital city

It is sometimes called the City of Magnificent Distances, but it might with greater propriety be termed the City of Magnificent Intentions; for it is only on taking a bird's-eye view of it from the top of the Capitol that one can at all comprehend the vast designs of its projector, an aspiring Frenchman.

Charles Dickens, *American Notes*, 1842

In 1790, the year after George Washington was inaugurated as first President of the United States, it fell to Congress to decide upon a permanent site for the country's capital. Since Independence, Congress had met in a half-dozen different cities – the president was inaugurated in New York – and a dozen others, in North and South, had competing claims and loud promoters. Ultimately the decision came down to political wrangling: in return for Congress assuming the states' debts from the Revolutionary War (a key Northern demand), the new federal capital would be sited in the South, somewhere on the sparsely populated banks of the Potomac River.

With the help of Major Andrew Ellicott, a surveyor from Maryland, and the black mathematician and scientist Benjamin Banneker, Washington – no mean surveyor himself – suggested a diamond-shaped, hundred-square-mile site at the confluence of the Potomac and Anacostia rivers. It seemed a canny choice – centering on the confluence, and thus ripe for trade, the site incorporated the ports of Alexandria in Virginia and Georgetown in Maryland; it would have its own port in Anacostia, and, no small matter for Washington, it was only eighteen miles upriver from his home at Mount Vernon. Maryland ceded roughly seventy square miles of land, Virginia thirty; all Washington had to do was find someone to plan his city, which Congress – in honor of the president – decreed would be named **Washington**, in the Territory (later District) of Columbia (a reference to Christopher Columbus).

Washington found his "aspiring Frenchman," **Major Pierre Charles L'Enfant**, who had been a member of Washington's Continental Army staff. His reputation as an engineer stemmed from his successful redesign of New York's Federal Hall for the presidential inauguration; now the president gave him the chance to create an entire city. Within a year L'Enfant had come up with an ambitious plan to transform a

With the addition in 1881 of the **Arts and Industries Building** – America's first national museum – the Mall became seen as the natural site for grand public institutions (following L'Enfant's hope that it would be "attractive to the learned and afford diversion to the idle"). The Botanic Garden followed in 1902, the Museum of Natural History in 1911 and, eventually, the Smithsonian's first art gallery, the Freer, in 1923. Meanwhile, members of the **McMillan Commission** of 1901, under Senator James McMillan, charged with improving the Mall and the city's park system, returned from Europe fired up with plans to link the Mall with a series of gardens and memorials and to demolish the unsightly railroad station (later replaced by Union Station). Not everyone concurred: House Speaker Joseph Cannon railed that he "would rather see the Mall sown in oats than treated as an artistic composition." However, McMillan's proposals prevailed and, following the completion of the Lincoln Memorial in 1922, the Mall was extended west of the Washington Monument for the first time, reaching to the banks of the Potomac River and incorporating the grounds known today as West Potomac Park. More improvements came in the 1930s, under the auspices of Roosevelt's New Deal-era Works Progress Administration (WPA), including the planting of the now-famous elms. Meanwhile, the **National Park Service** was granted stewardship of the Mall and its monuments.

wilderness into gridded streets and diagonal avenues, radiating from ceremonial squares and elegant circles. A "Grand Avenue" (later known as the Mall) formed the centerpiece; government buildings were assigned their own plots; a central canal linked the city's ports; sculptures, fountains and parks punctuated the design. Its initial inspiration was the city of Paris and the seventeenth-century palace of Versailles, though L'Enfant did adopt suggestions made by others – including Secretary of State Thomas Jefferson, who proposed the sites of the US Capitol and the President's Mansion (later called the White House). The plan named avenues after the fifteen states that existed in 1791, placing avenues named after Northern states north of the Capitol, Southern ones to the south – the most populous states, Virginia, Pennsylvania and Massachusetts, were represented by the longest avenues.

Washington was delighted with the scheme, though the existing landowners were less than pleased with the injunction to donate any land needed for public thoroughfares. L'Enfant was planning avenues 100ft wide – whether he knew it or not, clearly following the Parisian model of making streets too broad for the public to barricade and big enough for troops to maneuver in during times of unrest. Disagreements with the landowners aside, L'Enfant found himself in constant dispute with the District Commissioners who had been appointed by Washington to oversee the construction. His obstinacy cost him his job in 1792, and the design of the Capitol and White House were both later thrown open to public competition. L'Enfant turned down the $2500 he was offered as payment for his services, sued Congress (unsuccessfully) for $100,000, harried the legislature with his grievances for the rest of his life and died in penury in 1825.

For decades L'Enfant's plan seemed full of empty pretensions as Washington DC struggled to make its mark. Any number of nineteenth-century observers commented upon the hilarious contrast between such "vast designs" and the less-than-impressive reality. But for all that, this unique attempt to create a capital city that could define a nation was a remarkable enterprise. Perhaps the last word should be with nineteenth-century abolitionist and orator Frederick Douglass, who said: "It is our national center. It belongs to us, and whether it is mean or majestic, whether arranged in glory or covered with shame, we cannot but share its character and its destiny."

The erection of the Jefferson Memorial in 1943 completed the Mall's initial triumvirate of presidential monuments. The same architect, John Russell Pope, designed the contemporaneous National Gallery of Art; the 1960s and 1970s contributed museums of American History and Air and Space, the Hirshhorn art gallery and an East Building of the National Gallery; the 1980s, the Sackler Gallery and African Art museum. The dedication of the Vietnam Veterans Memorial (1982) and the Korean War Veterans Memorial (1995) proved that there's still space, too, for further **additions**, the most popular of recent times being the FDR Memorial (1997). Meanwhile the National World War II Memorial is currently being built between the Lincoln Memorial and the Washington Monument, and the last free block in the eastern Mall, next to the Air and Space Museum, is reserved for the National Museum of the American Indian, scheduled to open in 2004.

Monuments and memorials

On the face of it, the Mall presents the easiest of choices to visitors: **monuments and memorials** to the west and **museums** to the east, with the Washington Monument standing sentinel between the two. Most people make a beeline for the Washington Monument, which is no bad thing. But there's an argument, too, for approaching the monument **on foot from the east**, keeping to the central paths and resisting the temptation to dive into the museums. This way you get a flavor of the piecemeal development of the Mall, the landscaped grounds and buildings reflecting 150 years of architectural styles, while at the same time coming to a fuller appreciation of the sheer scale of the Washington Monument itself.

Mall transportation

The **Metro stations** closest to the **eastern Mall** are Smithsonian (south side) and Federal Triangle or Archives–Navy Memorial (both north side); L'Enfant Plaza and Federal Center SW are both two blocks, or a ten-minute walk, from the south side. For **west** of the Washington Monument, the best bet is to take **Bus #13A/13B** (Pentagon–Mall Loop; see p.29), or the **Tourmobile** (see p.31), which both run along Constitution Avenue, though the Foggy Bottom–GWU Metro stop is within six blocks of the Mall.

Approaching the Washington Monument: the eastern Mall

From the eastern end of the Mall it's just under a mile to the Washington Monument, walking past the museums that lie on either side. Starting in the northeastern corner of the Mall lie the two buildings of the **National Gallery of Art** (p.72), along with its recently added Sculpture Garden. Built in 1941 by John Russell Pope, what is now known as the **West Building** (at 7th and Constitution) was DC's last great Neoclassical construction. With its domed rotunda and sweeping front steps, it's a veritable palace of pink Tennessee marble, though one that was not to everyone's taste; one critic complained it was "hollow and pompous . . . an outdated extravaganza." This is not a charge that could fairly be leveled at I.M. Pei's **East Building** of 1978, which lies across 4th Street, connected to the main building by underground tunnel. Using the same pink marble as the original building, Pei fashioned a thoroughly modern interlocking triangular design – his hand partly forced by the shape of the block of land on which the building stands.

A similar curtailment of space faced Douglas Cardinal, Canadian architect of the future **National Museum of the American Indian** (Ⓦ www.nmai .si.edu), which will face the East Building on a site bounded by Independence Avenue, Maryland Avenue and Jefferson Drive. Initial designs indicate that it will differ greatly from the Mall norm of lines and angles: influenced by Western landscapes (and by Cardinal's Native American ancestry), a curving, multilayered stone-and-glass building with terraced facade and forest and wet-land landscapes will rise from the awkward plot.

There are no such space restraints immediately to the west, where the 700-foot-long **National Air and Space Museum** (p.68) fills the land between 4th and 7th. All the adventure here is inside; the building itself, designed by Gyo Obata, is a rather dull spread of squat marble boxes split by glass frames. Farther along the south side of Independence Avenue is Gordon Bunshaft's cylindrical **Hirshhorn Museum** (p.66) of 1974, a neat counterweight to the angular gymnastics employed by Pei. Here, you're at possibly the single most rewarding stretch of the Mall, with an additional five museums and galleries imaginatively sited in the blocks between 9th and 12th streets. Most prominent of all is the **Smithsonian Institution Building** (p.94), the original home of the Smithsonian and known more widely as the "**Castle**." Completed in 1855 by James Renwick, its Gothic towers and battlements jut out into the Mall, halfway between the Capitol and the Washington Monument. It was mocked at the time by architect and sculptor Horatio Greenhough as a "medieval con-fusion"*, though today it's considered a triumph in red brick – one to which you're steadily drawn as you make your way down the Mall, since its central tower is the only structure other than the Washington Monument to rise above the trees. Between the Castle and the Hirshhorn Museum, the **Arts and Industries Building** (p.62) was the Mall's second public construction, built in 1881 to house exhibits from Philadelphia's 1876 Centennial Exhibition. Architects Cluss and Schulze clearly warmed to their brief, and it's positively jaunty in comparison with the Castle, featuring playful polychromatic brick-and-tile patterns.

There's a century between the Arts and Industries Building and its two near neighbors, the adjacent **National Museum of African Art** (p.84) and **Arthur M. Sackler Gallery** (p.60). Both designed by the same Boston archi-tectural firm and opened in 1987, the twin embellished, granite-and-limestone cubes complement each other in their interior and exterior thematic use of shapes (circles for the African Art museum, triangles for the Sackler). They're also connected by underground passage; indeed, all the gallery space at both museums is underground, a reflection of the shortage of room along this part of the Mall. Outside, between the two, sits the flower-filled **Enid A. Haupt**

---

*Greenhough was singularly ill-placed to criticize the work of others, having been on the end of a public lashing from Congress after he'd delivered his commissioned statue of George Washington in 1841, destined to be placed in the Capitol. It was too big to get through the door into the Rotunda, which had to be dismantled, and too heavy for the floor, into which it sank. When finally on display, according to Washington historian E.J. Applewhite, "The seated, half-naked figure . . . with a toga draped over his knees and right shoulder, provoked only derision and embarrassment." The statue was eventually donat-ed "in a gesture more desperate than generous" to the National Museum of American History, where it remains today.

Garden (daily: June–Sept 7am–8pm; Oct–May 7am–5.45pm), where you'll find several topiary bison – live animals were once kept here in pens so that nineteenth-century Smithsonian boffins could study their expressions and posture before stuffing the beasts destined for their natural history collection. The museum grouping on this side is completed by Charles A. Platt's **Freer Gallery of Art** (p.64), a granite-and-marble Italianate palazzo added to the corner plot at 12th and Independence in 1923. You can also reach this by underground passage from the Sackler Gallery.

Across the Mall from the Castle, the north side buildings finish in some style with Hornblower and Marshall's domed, Neoclassical **National Museum of Natural History** (p.92), built in 1911 (though with two additional wings added in the 1960s), and the symmetrical, Beaux-Arts **National Museum of American History** (p.86) of 1964. The two are divided by 12th Street as it tunnels under the Mall and by fifty years of architectural tradition, but both in their lofty, virtuous way find their echoes in the splendid Federal Triangle buildings of the Great Depression, located across Constitution Avenue. Indeed, like the Federal Triangle buildings, the American History Museum comes laden with exterior inscriptions, with the sheer Mall-facing facade etched with improving quotations by such luminaries as Smithsonian founder James Smithson and John Quincy Adams. The **Ice Rink**, ensconced amid the towering shapes of the National Gallery's Sculpture Garden, on the east side of the Museum of Natural History (between 7th and 9th), is a nice spot, with skates for rent in winter and shade, snacks and drinks in summer.

The Washington Monument

15th St NW at Constitution Ave ☎426-6841, ⊛www.nps.gov/wamo; Smithsonian Metro. Daily: April–Aug 8am–midnight; Sept–March 9am–5pm. Admission free.

If there's one structure that symbolizes Washington, it is surely the **Washington Monument**, an unadorned marble obelisk built in memory of the first US president. Simple, elegant, majestic and, above all, huge, it's immediately recognizable from all over the city (and from a fair distance beyond), providing the Mall and the capital with a striking central ornament.

There had been much early talk about honoring the achievements of George Washington with a commemorative monument. L'Enfant's original city plan proposed an equestrian statue at the intersection of the south axis of the White House with the west axis of the Capitol, an idea of which Washington himself approved. Yet even after Washington's death in 1799, virtually no progress was made save the placing of a small **stone marker** on the proposed spot by Thomas Jefferson in 1804; the "Jefferson Pier" is still visible today. Impatient at Congress's apparent lack of enthusiasm for the work, the **National Monument Sociey** was established in 1833 and fostered a design competition and subscription drive, from which emerged **Robert Mills'** hugely ambitious scheme to top a colonnaded base containing the tombs of Revolutionary heroes with a massive obelisk: L'Enfant's original idea received a nod with the addition of a statue of Washington driving a horse-drawn chariot.

The Society took one look at the meager collected subscriptions and settled for the obelisk on its own. In retrospect – given the trouble in getting even this built – it proved to be a wise decision. Early excavations revealed that L'Enfant's chosen spot was too marshy to build on, and when the cornerstone was finally laid on July 4, 1848, it was on a bare knoll 360ft east and 120ft south of the true intersection – which explains why the monument looks off-center on the map. By 1853, when funds ran out, the monument was just 152ft high, and stayed that way for almost 25 years – grievously truncated, bordered by the fetid Washington Canal, the site roamed by cattle awaiting slaughter at a nearby abattoir. Mark Twain likened it to a "factory chimney with the top broken off," while the *New York Tribune*, in a fairly universally held opinion, condemned it as a "wretched design, a wretched location."

After the Civil War, Congress finally authorized government funds to complete the monument and appointed **Lt Colonel Thomas Casey** of the Army Corps of Engineers to the work. He suffered his own tribulations, not least of which was the discovery that the original marble source in Maryland had dried up; you can still see the transition line at the 150-foot level, where work resumed with marble of a slightly different tone. At long last, by December 1884, the monument was finally ready and, at a shade over 555ft, stood unchallenged as the tallest building in the world; it's still the tallest all-masonry structure on the planet. Fifty-five feet wide at the base, tapering to 34ft at the top, where it's capped by a small aluminum pyramid, the structure was originally accessible by a steam-powered elevator, which took twenty minutes to reach the top. Women and children were forced to toil up the 897 steps because the elevator was considered too dangerous.

Today, the **elevator** up takes seventy seconds and deposits you at the 500-foot level from where the views, naturally, are tremendous, glimpsed through surprisingly narrow windows on all four sides. (If the lines at the monument are too long but you're still keen on getting a bird's-eye view of the city, you can head to the Old Post Office on Pennsylvania Avenue, where the views of the capital are, arguably, every bit as good; see p.162.)

The view aside, the only other diversion is provided by the bronze **statue of Washington** at ground level, which faces east towards the Capitol. Almost 7ft high, this is a faithful copy of the renowned statue by eighteenth-century French master sculptor Jean-Antoine Houdon,* which was commissioned for the Virginia State Capitol in Richmond and placed there in 1796. Washington, wearing the uniform of Commander-in-Chief of the Continental Army, holds a cane in one hand and is flanked on the other by a bundle of bound rods and a plowshare, signifying authority and peace respectively.

To visit the monument, you must pick up a free **ticket** from the 15th Street kiosk (on the Mall, south of Constitution Ave), which allows you to turn up at a fixed time later in the day. Or you can reserve with TicketMaster (☏1-800/505-5040; $1.50 per person). It's also worth calling the monument to ask about ranger-led **walk-down tours** of the interior steps – these were discontinued a couple of years ago but may have been restarted.

---

*Houdon was the first major European artist to visit America, traveling to George Washington's home at Mount Vernon in 1785, where he stayed long enough to make a life mask and other studies. Washington had to lie flat on his back while his face was covered with grease and then slapped with plaster of Paris. He breathed through tubes while the face mask set – at which point, so the story goes, his step-granddaughter, Eleanor, came into the room and fled in tears, thinking him dead.

George Washington

The Washington family, originally from the north of England, emigrated to America in 1656 after the English Civil War, during which they had been fierce loyalists. On February 22, 1732, George Washington was born on the wealthy family plantation in Westmoreland County, Virginia. Though most of what is known about his early life is almost entirely the product of various fawning and fictitious nineteenth-century biographies, it is clear that he received intermittent schooling, learned to ride and excelled in most outdoor pursuits. He also displayed a talent for surveying and in 1748 assisted in the surveying of the new town of Alexandria (see p.232).

At the age of 21, Washington was appointed by Virginia's governor to travel into the Ohio Valley to ascertain the strength of the French forces, which had been steadily encroaching on Crown British land. This experience led him to be appointed lieutenant-colonel in the Virginia Regiment and, later, aide-de-camp in the French and Indian War, in which he gained his first battle experience – a bad defeat, though Washington gained local respect for his leadership qualities. Finishing the war as regimental commander, he was subsequently elected to the Virginia House of Burgesses in Williamsburg. Giving up his commission, in January 1759 he married the equally wealthy Martha Dandridge Custis – who came with two children from a previous marriage – and settled at Mount Vernon (see p.236) into the agreeable life of a gentleman plantation owner, a lifestyle buttressed by the endeavor of a large number of slaves. George and Martha never had any children of their own, but later became guardians to the youngest two of Martha's grandchildren by her first marriage.

Washington continued to serve in the House of Burgesses throughout the 1760s, during the growing confrontation with Britain. Acquiring a reputation for honesty and good judgment, Washington was one of the Virginian delegates at the Continental Congress in 1774; the following year, when British soldiers clashed with American volunteers at Lexington and Concord, confrontation turned into revolution. At a second meeting of the Continental Congress in June 1775, the 43-year-old Washington was appointed commander-in-chief of the nascent American forces – as much for the fact that he was from Virginia (Congress wanted to combine the existing New England army with a general who would also attract Southern volunteers) as for his military experience, which was fairly modest.

Washington's achievements in the field during the Revolutionary War have been subsequently overplayed. He wasn't a great general: making early mistakes, his under-equipped Continental Army lost more battles than it won, and it took seven years to defeat a largely incompetently led British force fighting far from home. There was often insufficient money to pay, clothe or supply the American militiamen, who regularly deserted; the locals and often Congress, too, proved unsupportive; and to

The Lincoln Memorial

West Potomac Park at 23rd St NW ☎426-6841, ⓦwww.nps.gov/linc; Foggy Bottom–GWU Metro or #13A/B bus from Constitution Ave. Daily 24hr; staffed 8am–midnight. Admission free.

Proposals to erect a monument to the revered sixteenth president were raised as early as 1865, the year of his assassination (see pp.180–181): the problem was always to pinpoint a suitable structure and appropriate site. There was certainly no shortage of ideas: one early plan suggested building a Lincoln Highway between Washington and Gettysburg, while arch-Neoclassicist John Russell Pope submitted four designs (including a vast pyramid and a stone funeral pyre), all of which were rejected. In 1901 the McMillan Commission grasped the nettle and finally approved the construction of a Greek temple in the marshlands of the newly created West Potomac Park. This, the **Lincoln** top it all off, he was ill-served by traitors in his camp. But Washington was a dogged figure, determined to impose order and hierarchy onto the fledgling army. He also retained the respect of his forces during trying times, not least by sharing their hardships – throughout the war years, he stayed away from his Mount Vernon estate, Martha spending the winters encamped with George in his northern redoubts.

After Yorktown in 1781 and the winning of independence, Washington resisted military demands to assume an American "kingship," resigned his commission in 1783 and returned to Mount Vernon. However, four years later, at the Constitutional Convention in Philadelphia, Washington was back in the political frame. Called to safeguard the Revolution by devising a permanent system of government for the nation, the Convention unanimously elected Washington its presiding officer, as the only man able to command universal respect. Once the Constitution had been drawn up and ratified, there was only one realistic choice for the post of first President of the United States – indeed, there's evidence that the powers outlined in the Constitution concerning the presidency were specifically tailored with Washington's character and probity in mind. In February 1789, George Washington was unanimously elected president for the first time.

Washington defined the uncharted role of president, bestowing upon it an hauteur that became almost monarchical, while developing the relationship between the executive and the other branches of government. It's doubtful anyone else could have contained the subtle machinations of various members of his cabinet as the Federalists and Republicans skirmished for influence. Luckily, he presided over an early economic boom; skillfully, and despite severe provocation by both sides, he kept America out of the war between England and France. During his first term, he even negotiated the political minefield that was deciding upon the site of the new federal capital (see pp.46–47). The city was promptly named after him, and the president laid the cornerstone of the US Capitol in 1793. However, he never lived in Washington or the White House – which wasn't finished until 1800 – shuttling instead between New York, Philadelphia and other northeastern cities.

Washington was elected to a second term in 1793 and would undoubtedly have been granted a third, but in 1797 he was 65 and wanted nothing more than to retire to his farm. Delivering a farewell address to both houses of Congress, he went home to Mount Vernon, where he died two and a half years later on December 14, 1799, from a fever induced by being caught out in a snowstorm on his estate. Congress adjourned for the day, and even the British and French fleets lowered their flags in respect. Martha lived on until May 1802 (and on her death, Washington's will freed all their slaves); they're buried together on the grounds at Mount Vernon.

Memorial, has stood the test of time to become the best-loved of all DC's commemorative structures: solemn, inspirational, and providing a proportioned Classical counterpoint to the grandeur of both the Washington Monument and, beyond, the US Capitol.

Work began on the memorial in February 1914 under the aegis of New York architect **Henry Bacon**, who erected a bastardized Doric temple on a small rise in the park. Its 36 columns symbolize the number of states that made up the Union at the time of Lincoln's death, while bas-relief plaques on the attic parapet commemorate the 48 states of the Union that existed when the memorial was completed in 1922 (Alaska and Hawaii get a mere inscription on the terrace). But for all its restrained beauty, the temple is upstaged by what lies inside, the seated **statue of Lincoln** by Daniel Chester French (1850–1931), which faces out through the colonnade – one of America's most enduring images. French certainly succeeded in his intention to "convey the mental and physical strength of the great war President": full of resolve, a steely Lincoln clasps the armrests of a thronelike chair with determined hands, his unbuttoned coat falling to either side; the American flag is draped over the back of the chair. It's a phenomenal work, one which took French thirteen years to complete, fashioning the nineteen-foot-tall statue from 28 blocks of white Georgia marble.

Climbing the steps to the memorial is one of DC's more profound moments, as first you meet Lincoln's gaze and then turn to look out over the Reflecting Pool (see opposite) and down the length of the Mall. Turn back and you'll notice **murals** on the north and south walls, painted by Jules Guerin, representing Fraternity, Unity of North and South, and Charity (north wall) and Emancipation and Immortality (south wall), directly under which are carved inscriptions of Lincoln's two most celebrated **speeches**. On the north wall is the Gettysburg Address of November 19, 1863 (the speech that Lincoln himself thought a "flat failure"), while on the south is the measured eloquence of Lincoln's Second Inaugural Address of March 4, 1865, in which he strove "to bind up the nation's wounds" caused by the Civil War. The memorial's lower lobby exhibit fleshes out its history; there are also **restrooms** here.

The memorial wields an emotional influence far beyond its commemorative function. In many ways, it's as much a memorial to the preservation of the Union as to Lincoln himself, as the inscription behind the statue makes clear: "In this temple as in the hearts of the people for whom he saved the Union the memory of Abraham Lincoln is enshrined forever." Ironic, then, that on its dedication day in May 1922, while President Warren G. Harding and Lincoln's surviving son, Robert, could watch proceedings from the comfort of the speakers' platform, Dr Robert Moton, president of the Tuskegee Institute – who was to make the principal address – was forced to watch from a roped-off area since the crowds were segregated by color. From this point on, the memorial became a focus for demonstrations in the name of **civil rights**: Spanish Civil War veterans from the Abraham Lincoln Brigade marched here in 1938; a year later, on Easter Sunday 1939, black opera singer Marian Anderson performed from the steps to a crowd of 75,000, having been refused permission to appear at the nearby Constitution Hall – pointedly dedicating the event to "the ideals of freedom for which President Lincoln died." Groups

Lincoln and the Gettysburg Address

Four score and seven years ago our fathers brought forth on this continent, a new nation, conceived in Liberty, and dedicated to the proposition that all men are created equal . . .

Abraham Lincoln's Gettysburg Address astonished observers with its brevity – the official photographer hadn't even got his equipment ready before the president sat down again. At events such as the dedication of the war cemetery of Gettysburg, orators were expected to expound lengthily, as indeed did Edward Everett (former senator and one-time Secretary of State), who was first to speak at the ceremony. Everett later claimed he wished he had even come close in two and a half hours to what Lincoln had managed to encapsulate in two and a half minutes. Yet the president's speech was poorly received: Lincoln himself was convinced that the audience had failed to appreciate its fine nuances, while the *Chicago Times* lambasted its "silly, flat, and dish-watery utterances." Other newspapers had a keener sense of history – *Harper's Weekly* thought it "as simple and felicitous and earnest a word as was ever spoken."

Resurrection City

At the time of Dr Martin Luther King Jr's assassination, the Civil Rights leader was planning a second march on the capital, an idea that his successors saw to fruition. Under the auspices of the Southern Christian Leadership Conference, the Poor People's March of May 1968 converged on Washington from Mississippi, its organizers determined to force Congress to take a serious stand against poverty and unemployment. The 3000 marchers set up camp around the Reflecting Pool, in view of the US Capitol, and called their shantytown structures Resurrection City. Water and electricity were supplied, and churches and charities brought in food, but rain was heavy that June and the mud-caked camp soon lost its momentum. Many residents left early; those who stayed were joined at the Lincoln Memorial by a crowd of 50,000 on June 19, Solidarity Day, to listen to a Peter, Paul and Mary concert and to hear various fiery speeches. However, the turnout was much lower than expected, and with an ebbing of public support, the dispirited camp was dissolved a week later as city police cleared away the tents.

from the American Nazi Party to the Black Panthers have exercised their First Amendment rights at the memorial (as anyone can, provided they don't climb on the statue or hang banners from the building); but its brightest day saw the appearance of **Dr Martin Luther King Jr**, who chose the memorial to the Great Emancipator from which to make his "I have a dream" speech to the 200,000 people who gathered here on August 28, 1963, during the March on Washington for Jobs and Freedom. Five years later, in June 1968, after King's assassination, his successors brought the ill-fated Poor People's March to the memorial (see the "Resurrection City" box above); while Jesse Jackson addressed a 50,000-strong crowd here in 1988 on the 25th anniversary of King's celebrated speech.

The Reflecting Pool and Constitution Gardens

The view from the memorial would lose a significant part of its attraction were it not for the 2000-foot-long, 160-foot-wide **Reflecting Pool** that reaches out from the steps toward the Washington Monument. Supposedly inspired by the pools and canals at Versailles and by the landscaping at the Taj Mahal, the mirror images of memorial and monument captured in the water have the capacity to bring strollers up short with a gasp. It's particularly affecting at night, when both pool and memorial are lit. A National World War II Memorial has been allocated a site at the eastern end of the Reflecting Pool, though no completion date has yet been announced.

The pool was established at the same time as the Lincoln Memorial, in 1922. Though it was envisaged that the surrounding area – **West Potomac Park** – would be landscaped, "temporary" cement-board munitions and office buildings erected around the Reflecting Pool during both world wars proved hard to shift. Reconstruction was only considered seriously when President Nixon suggested the grounds might benefit from being turned into a Tivoli Gardens-style park in time for the Bicentennial. Money worries and aesthetic considerations produced the less flamboyant **Constitution Gardens** in 1976, a fifty-acre area of trees and dells surrounding a kidney-shaped lake. A plaque on the island in the center commemorates the 56 signatories of the Declaration of Independence.

Every September 17, Constitution Day, the signing of the Constitution is celebrated in the gardens by, among other things, an outdoor naturalization service for foreign-born DC residents.

The Vietnam Veterans Memorial

Constitution Gardens, Henry Bacon Dr and Constitution Ave at 21st St NW ☏634-1568, ⓦwww.nps.gov/vive; Foggy Bottom–GWU Metro or #13A/B bus from Constitution Ave. Daily 24hr, staffed 8am–midnight. Admission free.

The polished, black, V-shaped granite walls of the **Vietnam Veterans Memorial** cut straight into the green lawns of Constitution Gardens and straight into the psyche of a country scarred by a war it tried to forget. Here, the names of the 58,191 American casualties of the war in Vietnam are recorded in chronological order (1959–75), etched into an east and west wall that each run for 250ft, slicing deeper into the ground, until meeting at a vertex 10ft high. It's a sobering experience to walk past the ranks of names and the untold experiences they represent, not least for the friends and relatives who come here to take rubbings of the names and leave memorial tokens at the foot of the walls. Many of these artifacts – dog tags to teddy bears – end up at the National Museum of American History (see p.86). Directories list the names and their locations for anyone trying to find a particular person, and a ranger is on hand until midnight to answer questions. The annual Veterans Day ceremony held at the memorial on November 11 is one of the most emotional in the city, with the memorial walls decked in wreaths and overseen by military color-guards.

In so much as it commemorates human life rather than US involvement in the war, this extraordinary memorial serves its purpose with distinction. Indeed it coincides perfectly with the wishes of the Vietnam vets who first conceived the idea of a contemplative memorial in Washington: their sole intention was to record the sacrifice of every person killed or missing in action without making a political statement.

Once the grounds had been earmarked, a national competition was held in 1980, open to all US citizens, to determine the memorial's design; it was won by Maya Ying Lin, a 21-year-old Yale student from Ohio (whose original design is now held, and sometimes displayed by, the Library of Congress in its Jefferson Building). Determining that the names would become the memorial, she chose to record them on walls of reflective black granite that point to the city's lodestones, the Lincoln Memorial and Washington Monument, and that gradually draw visitors into a rift in the earth. Each **name** has appended the date of casualty and either a diamond (a confirmed death) or cross (missing in action and still unaccounted for – about 1100 names).

In the end, the memorial's nonpolitical stance came to be seen as a political act itself by some ex-soldiers. Concerned that these somber, dignified walls made no overt reference to military (as opposed to personal) sacrifice, successful lobbying led to the commissioning of a separate martial statue to be added to the site. This, the **sculpture** of three servicemen by Frederick Hart, stands at the west end, heralded by a sixty-foot flagpole flying the Stars and Stripes. These three young men, despite bulging with weaponry and ammunition, have an air of vulnerability all too easy to understand in the bewildering maelstrom that was Vietnam.

More lobbying – in particular by Diane Evans, a former army nurse – led to the establishment of the **Vietnam Women's Memorial** in 1993, which stands in a grove of trees at the eastern end of the main site. Few realize that 11,000 American women served in Vietnam (eight were killed), while almost a quarter of a million provided support services throughout the world during the conflict. The bronze sculpture, by Glenna Goodacre, shows one nurse on her knees, exhausted; one tending a wounded soldier; and a third raising her eyes to the sky in trepidation – none of the servicewomen bears insignia, emphasizing the universal intent of the sculpture.

The Korean War Veterans Memorial

West Potomac Park, south of Lincoln Memorial Reflecting Pool ☎619-7222,
ⓦwww.nps.gov/kwvm; Smithsonian Metro or #13A/B bus from Constitution Ave to Lincoln
Memorial. Daily 24hr, staffed 8am–midnight. Admission free.

The **Korean War Veterans Memorial** lies south of the Reflecting Pool, just
a few minutes' walk from the Lincoln Memorial. Dedicated in July 1995 (and,
again, largely funded by private contributions), its main component is a Field
of Remembrance in which nineteen life-size, heavily armed combat troops
sculpted from stainless steel advance across an open field toward the Stars and
Stripes. It's a moving ensemble, which rather overshadows the flanking, reflecting black granite wall, inscribed "Freedom is not free" and etched with a mural
depicting military support crew and medical staff. A plaque at the flagstand
proclaims "Our nation honors her sons and daughters who answered the call
to defend a country they never knew and a people they never met."

And what a call it was: between 1950 and 1953, when the war ended, almost
55,000 Americans were killed in Korea (with another 8000 missing in action
and more than 103,000 wounded), a harbinger of the slaughter to begin in
Vietnam a decade later. Unlike those who fought in Vietnam, however, the
American soldiers sent into battle by President Truman on behalf of the South
Korean government went, however tenuously, in the name of the United
Nations; the memorial lists the fifteen other countries who volunteered forces,
with Britain, France, Greece and Turkey in particular suffering significant casualties. Perhaps it's not the place, but the statistic the memorial signally fails to
record is that of the Korean civilian casualties. It's difficult to be certain but best
estimates are that about three million (North and South) Koreans died – quite
apart from half a million North Korean, 50,000 South Korean and possibly one
million Chinese soldiers.

The memorial has a CD-ROM database; relatives and friends can type in the
name of a fallen veteran and call up and print out their rank, serial number,
unit, casualty date and a photograph.

The Franklin Delano Roosevelt Memorial

West Potomac Park, Basin Dr, south bank of the Tidal Basin ☎376-6704 or 619-7222,
ⓦwww.nps.gov/fdrm; Smithsonian Metro or #13A/B bus from Constitution or
Independence avenues. Daily 24hr, staffed 8am–midnight. Admission free.

DC's most recent presidential memorial – that to **Franklin Delano
Roosevelt**, president from 1933 to 1945 – would never have seen the light of
day had it been up to FDR himself. Accepting that he would one day be so
honored, he favored only a small stone monument on Pennsylvania Avenue (see
p.161), but after his death, others insisted on a far more impressive memorial.
Designed by Lawrence Halprin, and dedicated in 1997, it spreads across a seven-acre site on the banks of the Tidal Basin and is made up of a series of inter-linking granite outdoor galleries punctuated by waterfalls, statuary, sculpted
reliefs, groves of trees and shaded alcoves and plazas. In its way it's among the
most successful of DC's memorials – and certainly one of the most popular –
with an almost Athenian quality to its open spaces, resting-places and benches,
and improving texts. On a bright spring or fall day, with the glistening basin
waters and emerging views of the Washington Monument and Jefferson
Memorial, it's one of the finest places in the city for a contemplative stroll.

As architect of the New Deal and wartime leader, Roosevelt's underlying
political spirit is captured in a series of carved quotations that defined his

presidency, perhaps most famously "The only thing we have to fear is fear itself." The four galleries of rustic stone (one for each of his terms of office) turn upon seminal periods: in the second gallery stand the sculpted figures of a city breadline and a man listening to one of Roosevelt's famous radio fireside chats; in the third room a tangle of broken granite blocks represents the war years, alongside a seated statue of FDR, his dog Fala and the heartfelt message "I have seen war . . . I hate war." The memorial ends in the fourth gallery with a timeline of dates and events inscribed in the steps and, perhaps more importantly, a recognition of Roosevelt's greatest ally in the shape of a statue of his wife, the redoubtable Eleanor.

There's great significance, too, in something most visitors don't notice about the memorial, namely that it is fully accessible to people in wheelchairs. At the age of 39, FDR contracted polio, which left him paralyzed from the waist down – a fact largely kept from the American people during his run for the governorship of New York and, later, the presidency. Believing, possibly correctly, that public knowledge of his disability would count against his political ambitions, he was almost always pictured standing while making speeches and only used his wheelchair when out of public view, a deception with which reporters and photographers colluded throughout his life. This led to a problem when it came to deciding how FDR should be portrayed in his statue at the memorial, the matter neatly sidestepped by having him seated, his wasted legs largely covered by the flowing cape he wore at the 1945 Yalta conference with Churchill and Stalin.

The Jefferson Memorial and the Tidal Basin

West Potomac Park, south bank of the Tidal Basin near 15th St SW and Ohio Dr ☏426-6841, ⓦwww.nps.gov/thje; Smithsonian Metro or #13A/B bus from Constitution or Independence avenues. Daily 8am–midnight. Admission free.

The last of the McMillan Commission's specific proposals was for a memorial to be erected to Thomas Jefferson, third President of the United States, prime drafter of the Declaration of Independence (see p.167) and the closest thing to Renaissance Man yet produced in America. When the **Jefferson Memorial** was finally completed in 1943 it was long overdue: Jefferson had died in 1826, yet was well beaten to national memorials by both Washington and Lincoln. It wasn't for the want of inspiration, for with Jefferson there was more than enough to honor. A speaker of six languages, he practiced law; studied science, mathematics and archeology; and was an accomplished musician and keen botanist as well as a lucid writer and self-taught architect of considerable prowess – the only surprise is that he didn't build the memorial himself.* With

---

* The genius Jefferson suffered a number of prejudices that put his achievements into perspective. The man who publicly strove to abolish slavery did nothing to free his own slaves, whose labor kept him in the luxurious style to which he was accustomed (DNA testing has also confirmed longstanding allegations that Jefferson fathered at least one child by his house slave, Sally Hemings). He was permanently in debt (spending $3000 on wine alone during his first year in the White House), fondly asserted that women should be kept in the home, and enjoyed a severely isolationist view in which immigrants were feared since they would dilute the virtues of the hardworking, independent farmers who formed his American Arcadia.

the US Capitol, Washington Monument, White House and Lincoln Memorial already in place, the obvious site lay on the southern axis, south of the Washington Monument, but it proved contentious. Many bemoaned the destruction of some of the city's famous cherry trees when the ground around the Tidal Basin was cleared (a few protesters even chained themselves to the trunks), while others argued that the memorial would block the view of the river from the White House. More practically, the site proved difficult to reach, since the basin blocked direct access from the north. This, in fact, provides much of its charm today, as the sinuous walk around the tree-lined basin makes for a fine approach.

If the site had its critics then so did the memorial, when John Russell Pope – architect of the National Gallery of Art – revealed his plans for a Neoclassical, circular, colonnaded structure with a shallow dome housing a nineteen-foot-high bronze statue. However, while for some it was too similar to the Lincoln Memorial, it was at least a design in keeping with Jefferson's own tastes. Not only was it influenced by the Neoclassical styles that he had helped popularize in the United States after his stint as ambassador to France in the 1780s, but also it echoes closely the style of Jefferson's own (self-designed) country home at Monticello, in Charlottesville, Virginia.

It's one of the most harmonious structures in the city: a white marble temple, reminiscent of the Pantheon, with steps down to the water's edge and framed by the cherry trees of the Tidal Basin. The standing bronze **statue of Jefferson** (by Rudulph Evans) gazes determinedly out of the memorial, while the inscription around the frieze sets the high moral tone, trumpeting "I have sworn upon the altar of God eternal hostility against every form of tyranny over the mind of man." Inside, on the walls, four more texts flank the statue, most notably the seminal words from the 1776 Declaration of Independence (for Jefferson's role in its creation, see p.167).

Around the Tidal Basin

The **Tidal Basin** fills most of the space between the Lincoln and Jefferson memorials. This large inlet, formerly part of the Potomac River, was created in 1882, primarily to prevent flooding, while the famous **cherry trees** – a gift from Japan – were planted around the edge in 1912; the annual Cherry Blossom Festival each spring (usually early April) celebrates their blooming with concerts, parades and displays of Japanese lanterns. To take it all in from the water, rent a **pedal boat** from the Tidal Basin Boat House (March–Sept Mon–Fri 10am–6pm & Sat–Sun 10am–7pm; two-seaters $8/hr, four-seaters $16/hr; ☏484-0206).

South of the Jefferson Memorial, the long spit of East Potomac Park has more cherry trees, while if you walk around the western side of the basin, following Ohio Drive, you pass the FDR Memorial (see p.57) before reaching the **statue of John Ericsson**, south of the Korean War Veterans and Lincoln memorials. Ericsson, the Swedish-born inventor of the screw-propellor, also designed the ironclad warship *Monitor* – known in its day as a "tin can on a raft" – which in 1862 held its own in battle against the Confederate vessel *Virginia* – the first naval conflict between iron ships. Nearby memorials on the north side of the basin include one to Revolutionary War naval hero **John Paul Jones**, marooned on a traffic island at the foot of 17th Street, and a colonnaded marble bandstand hidden in the trees to the west, which doubles as the **DC War Memorial**, honoring the city's World War I dead.

Museums and galleries

There are nine **museums and galleries** along the Mall, most of them national in name and scope and all but one (the National Gallery of Art) coming under the umbrella of the Smithsonian Institution. Quite apart from anything else, they're all free, so there's little excuse not to look around at least one. At the top of many lists are the **National Air and Space Museum** and the two buildings of the **National Gallery of Art**; followed by the **National Museum of American History** and the **Hirshhorn Museum** of modern art and sculpture. Lesser-known standouts include the **Arthur M. Sackler Gallery** of Asian art and the **Freer Gallery of Art**, a peerless matching of Asian and American art, specifically the finest single display of the works of James McNeill Whistler.

The museums and galleries are reviewed below in **alphabetical order**.

Arthur M. Sackler Gallery

1050 Independence Ave SW ☎357-4880 or 357-2700, ⊛www.asia.si.edu; Smithsonian Metro. Daily 10am–5.30pm. Admission free.

The angular, pyramidal **Arthur M. Sackler Gallery** conceals its artworks and devotional objects from Asia in comfortable, well-lit, underground galleries. About a thousand pieces were originally donated to the Smithsonian by research physician, publisher and art collector Dr Sackler, who also coughed up $4 million toward the museum's construction (the governments of Japan and Korea weighed in with $1 million apiece). We've covered the most permanent of the exhibitions below. However, **temporary exhibitions** taken from the gallery's collection might cover themes such as South Asian textiles and village arts; contemporary Japanese ceramics; early Islamic texts from Iran, gorgeously colored in gilt, silver, lapis lazuli and crushed stone pigments; or splendid fifteenth- to seventeenth-century illuminated Indian manuscripts. Of particular note is the Vever Collection, an unrivaled group of works related to the art of the Islamic book from the eleventh to the nineteenth centuries.

The Smithsonian Institution: practicalities

There are nine **museums** of the **Smithsonian Institution** on the Mall; the original building – known as the **Smithsonian Castle** – serves as the main information center (see p.94). Four more museums lie north of the Mall – the Smithsonian American Art Museum (p.175), the National Portrait Gallery (p.173), the Renwick Gallery (p.143) and the National Postal Museum (p.114), and one lies to the south, the Anacostia Museum (p.131); the National Zoological Park (p.211), a few miles north beyond Rock Creek, is also part of the Smithsonian. The Cooper-Hewitt National Design Museum and the National Museum of the American Indian, both also part of the Smithsonian, are in New York City; a Washington branch of the latter is due to open in 2004.

All Smithsonian museums and galleries are **open daily all year** (except Christmas Day) from 10am until 5.30pm; some have **extended spring and summer hours** – details are given in the text. **Admission** is free, though charges are levied for some special exhibitions. For details on **current exhibitions and events**, or a copy of the *Smithsonian Access* brochure for disabled visitors, call ☎357-2700 (Mon–Fri 9am–5pm, Sat & Sun 10am–4pm) or access the Smithsonian's homepage at ⊛www.si.edu; there's a 24-hour recorded announcement on ☎357-2020. To read about the history of the institution turn to p.94.

The **information desk** (daily 10am–4pm) at ground level should be your first stop. Ask about the highly informative free daily (except Wed) **guided tours**. The gallery also has a **shop**, with a fine range of prints, fabrics, ceramics and artistic gewgaws (see p.304), and an Asian art research **library**, shared with the Freer and open to the public (Mon–Fri 10am–5pm). The galleries connect the Sackler to the Freer Gallery of Art (p.64) and the National Museum of African Art (p.84).

The permanent exhibitions

The **permanent exhibitions** are located on the first level, most prominently "**The Arts of China**," which highlights the Sackler's noted group of 3000-year-old **Chinese bronzes**. As early as the fifteenth century BC, ritual wine containers were being fashioned from bronze and were showing decoration, such as the faces and tails of dragons, that would become ever more refined. By the time of the late Shang Dynasty (twelfth and eleventh centuries BC) the decorative motifs were outstanding, the artisans producing elegant bronze vessels with bold designs. All the decorated detail was produced using intricate clay molds — there was no carving of the surface after casting. The subsequent Western and Eastern Zhou dynasties (1050–221 BC) refined the vessels further, with the bird now appearing as the major motif – many of the pieces on display feature bird-shaped handles, or show wispy reliefs of plumage and feathers. **Jade pendants** also depicted birds and, more commonly, intricate dragon shapes. The technique used to create these items was just as impressive – since jade is too hard to be carved, the lapidaries would rub an abrasive paste across the surface with wood or bamboo to shape and polish the stone. The Sackler's collection of later Chinese art reveals other skills, notably of the ceramicists of the Tang Dynasty (618–907) who produced technicolored temple guard figures, designed to ward off evil spirits. The last Chinese dynasty, the Qing (1644–1911), witnessed the flourishing era of the imperial scholars, who would place so-called "scholar's rocks" (natural pieces of stone resembling mountains) on their desks to encourage lofty thoughts. From this period, too, date the Sackler's remarkably well-preserved carved wooden cabinets and book stands, showing a simple, understated decoration that English and Scandinavian craftsmen would later adopt as their own. By way of contrast, Qing imperial porcelain was richly embellished with symbolic figures and motifs – a plate depicting a young boy holding a pomegranate (full of seeds), a cockerel and ladies holding fans with painted butterflies, for instance, is an evocation of fertility.

"**Luxury Arts of the Silk Route Empires**" – taking up part of the underground walkway to the Freer – is designed to show the historic free flow of artistic ideas between Central, West and East Asia and the Mediterranean world. The decorative forms seen in medieval Western metalwork and ceramics are echoed in silver Syrian bowls, Persian plates and Central Asian swords and buckles. Dr Sackler's favorite piece from his entire collection shows these influences – a beautifully worked, fourth-century Iranian silver drinking vessel (called a *rhyton*) shaped in the form of a gazelle. Here, too, you'll find more Tang Dynasty ceramics, utilizing either simple white porcelain or vibrant tricolored glazes, as well as contemporaneous silverware – from everyday items like a ladle and stem cup to a fine mirror, inlaid with a winged horse and dragon motif. From the same period come the "Buddhist Heavenly Beings," floating angelic figurines of gold that once formed part of an altar set.

"**Sculpture of South and Southeast Asia**" traces the spread of devotional sculpture across the continent. The earliest piece here is from ancient Gandhara (now part of Pakistan and Afghanistan), a third-century carved head of the Buddha whose features were directly influenced by images from Greece and Rome, with which Gandhara traded. Later Hindu temple sculpture from India shows more pronounced Eastern traits: among the bronze, brass and granite representations of Brahma, Vishnu and Shiva, you'll find a superb thirteenth-century stone carving of the elephant-headed Ganesha (the remover of obstacles) – his trunk burnished by years of illicit, furtive touching by museum visitors. From India, Hinduism and Buddhism spread to the Khmer kingdom (Cambodia), which in addition to adopting classical Indian styles also developed its own naturalistic artistic style. On a thirteenth-century temple lintel, male figures are shown entwined with vines, alongside an unidentified female goddess with conical crown and sarong.

Also on the first level, "**Metalwork and Ceramics from Ancient Iran**" displays a collection of vessels, weapons and ornaments made between 2300 and 100 BC. Many of the ceramic vessels here are animal-shaped, or painted with animal motifs, while a ceramic trio from northern Persia resemble metal, such was the craftsman's skill in firing. There's great dexterity, too, displayed in the metalwork, particularly the bronze and copper finials (ornamental pole tops) depicting demons (denoting magical powers) or vegetation (fertility).

The Arts and Industries Building

900 Jefferson Dr SW ☎357-2700, ◍www.si.edu/ai; Smithsonian Metro. Daily 10am–5.30pm. Admission free.

America observed its centenary in 1876 by inviting its constituent states and forty foreign nations to display a panoply of inventions and exhibits that would celebrate contemporary human genius. The subsequent **Centennial Exhibition** in Philadelphia was a roaring success, though at its close the federal government was presented with an unforeseen problem when most of the exhibits were abandoned by their owners, who couldn't afford to take or ship them home. Congress made the Smithsonian responsible for the objects and voted funds for a new "National Museum" – now the **Arts and Industries Building** – to house them.

Opened in 1881 in time to host President Garfield's inaugural ball, the building soon became rooted in people's consciousness as the "nation's attic," since quite apart from the Centennial exhibits – which included an entire American steam locomotive and Samuel Morse's original telegraph – the Smithsonian came to acquire ever more bequests and purchases, not all of a strictly educational nature. Over the years, as the National Museum filled to bursting point, most of the Smithsonian holdings were farmed out to new, specialized museums, which rather diminished the quirky appeal of the Arts and Industries Building: as Bill Bryson laments, with tongue only slightly in cheek, "At the old Smithsonian it could have been absolutely anything – a petrified dog, Custer's scalp, human heads adrift in bottles."

The building was restored completely for the Bicentennial celebrations of 1976. Only the central rotunda and four of the original exhibit halls remain as first envisioned, but these show off the **Victorian interior** to splendid effect – the colorful tiled floor, high windows and abundant use of natural light signal the involvement of Montgomery C. Meigs, who went on to design the equally adventurous Pension Building (see p.170).

For twenty years after the Bicentennial, the Arts and Industries Building continued to house many of the items from the Philadelphia exhibition. Assorted bits and bobs of American Victoriana will probably remain on display for some time, but these days the building is used for **special exhibitions**, many of

△ Flanked by the US Capitol and Washington Monument

which are sponsored by the Anacostia Museum and by the nascent Museum of the American Indian. The Arts and Industries Building also hosts a regular children's program at its **Discovery Theater** (see p.291 or ⓦwww.discoverytheater .si.edu), while right outside you'll find the popular **Carousel**.

Freer Gallery of Art

Jefferson Dr at 12th St SW ⓣ357-4880 or 357-2700, ⓦwww.asia.si.edu; Smithsonian Metro. Daily 10am–5.30pm. Admission free.

Opened in 1923, the **Freer Gallery of Art** was the first Smithsonian museum devoted exclusively to art. The airy Italian Renaissance palazzo of granite and marble, designed by Beaux Arts architect Charles Adams Platt, has long been considered one of the city's most aesthetically pleasing museums, with small, elegant galleries encircling a herringbone-brick courtyard furnished with splashing fountain. Design appeal aside, the gallery's abiding interest lies in its unusual juxtaposition of Asian and American art, including more than 1200 prints, drawings and paintings by James McNeill Whistler – the largest collection of his works anywhere.

The original owner of the collection, and the impetus behind the gallery, was one **Charles Lang Freer**, an industrialist who made a fortune building railroad cars in Detroit and then spent it on what was then considered to be obscure Asian art. He bought his first piece, a Japanese fan, in 1887, and thirteen years later retired at the age of 44 to concentrate on his collection, adding Chinese jades and bronzes, Byzantine illuminated manuscripts, Buddhist wall sculptures and Persian metalwork during five trips to various Asian countries. Freer also began to put together a series of **paintings** by contemporary American artists whose work he thought complemented his Asian collection. Dwight William Tryon, Thomas Wilmer Dewing and Abbott Henderson Thayer benefited from Freer's patronage (indeed, the penurious Thayer was almost entirely dependent on him), though the most profitable relationship was with the London-based Whistler, practically all of whose works ended up in the hands of Freer. In 1912 Freer embarked upon a plan to endow and build a gallery to hold his collection. He was delighted with the plans drawn up by Platt but sadly never saw their fruition. Work began in 1916, but was interrupted by the outbreak of World War I; Freer died in 1919, and the gallery didn't open for another four years.

The **galleries** on the third level hold selections from the permanent collection, only a fraction of which is on display. It has grown since Freer's original bequest to around 28,000 works, but even when planning his gallery Freer wanted only to exhibit small samples of the works at any one time, though most of what's described in the following account is usually on display – pick up a current floor plan at the **information desk** by the Mall entrance. Here you can also inquire about the free, daily (except Wed) highlights **tour**. From the Freer, it's possible to reach the Sackler Gallery (p.60) via a shared underground gallery on the S level.

Whistler

Not unnaturally, it's **James Abbott McNeill Whistler** (1834–1903) who dominates proceedings at the Freer. Born in Lowell, Massachusetts, he moved first to Paris as an art student, from which time dates a *Self-Portrait* (1857) found here; the artist is shown wearing a flat-brimmed hat, looking very much the man at ease with Left Bank life. Moving to London in the early 1860s, Whistler not only began to collect modish Japanese prints and *objets* but embraced their influences wholeheartedly in a series of vibrant works, starting with *The Golden Screen* (1865), depicting a seated woman in Japanese dress in front of a fine painted screen. Freer, attracted by the Oriental flavor of Whistler's art, made a special journey to London to introduce himself, returning on several occasions over the years to buy more of the painter's work. There's an unfinished portrait of Freer (1902), started on his last visit just before Whistler's death. Other works include studies incorporating a red Oriental fan, a prop dear to Whistler's heart, and various examples of the tonal experiments that fascinated the artist, who constantly repeated and developed shades of color – purple and gold, blue and gold, rose and brown, red and pink – to harmonious effect. *Arrangement in White and Black* from 1873 contrasts the ghostly white dress and parasol of Whistler's mistress, Maud Franklin, with the dark shades of the background; *The Little Red Glove* harmonizes glove and bonnet with the subject's auburn hair. These and many other of Whistler's works in the Freer are signed with a butterfly monogram, a typically Japanese device (though one that the London *Times* of the day thought simply a "queer little label").

Besides these works, Whistler is also represented by the magnificent **Peacock Room** (permanently stationed in Room 12), which started life as a mere commissioned painting, *The Princess From the Land of Porcelain*. This hung above the fireplace in the London dining room of Frederick Leyland, a Liverpudlian shipowner (and patron of Whistler) who had commissioned interior designer Thomas Jeckyll to add a framework of latticework shelves and gilded leather panels to the room's walls so that he might display his fine collection of Chinese porcelain. Whistler happened to be working on another project in the house at the time and, taking advantage of Leyland's absence on business, took it upon himself to restyle Jeckyll's work. Using a technique similar to Japanese lacquerware, he covered the leather-clad walls, ceiling, shelving and furnishings with rich blue- and gold-painted peacock feathers, gilt relief decor and green glaze, while above the sideboard he placed two golden painted peacocks trailing a stream of feathers; his famous butterfly monogram is visible in the corner. The idea, according to Whistler, was to present his art as a harmonious whole (the room's full title incorporates the phrase *Harmony in Blue and Gold*), much as the Japanese did; the room was at once a framed picture and an object of applied art, like an Oriental lacquer box. This artistic hijack outraged Leyland, who refused to pay Whistler for the work (his overriding gripe was the cavalier way that Whistler had entertained visitors in the room without his permission). Completed in 1877, the room met a mixed critical reception, though Whistler's friend Oscar Wilde, for one, thought it "the finest thing in color and art decoration the world has known." After Leyland's death, the room and its contents passed into the hands of a London art gallery, which later sold it to Freer. Restoration has returned the iridescent colors to their nineteenth-century best, the framed shelves filled with blue-and-white porcelain to show what Leyland's original dining room might have looked like.

Other American artists

The other **American art** is less gripping, though it is interesting to trace what attracted Freer to many of the works. Note the Oriental-style calligraphic brush strokes of the trees in the foreground of *Winter Dawn on Monadnock*, just one of the Impressionist landscapes by **Abbot Handerson Thayer** (1849–1921), who was heavily influenced by Freer's Asian art collection, which he knew well. **Thomas Wilmer Dewing** comes closer to Whistler's mood with *The Four Sylvan Sounds* (1896), a folding painted screen clearly of Asian influence. Contemporaries considered Dewing to be elitist, and Freer didn't have much competition for his works, though he doubtless had to bid higher for paintings by the more popular John Singer Sargent, whose *Breakfast in the Loggia*, a scene in the arcaded courtyard of a Florentine villa, was bought to remind him of the gallery he planned to build in DC.

Asian art

Things pick up again with the Freer's collection of **Japanese art**, in particular the painted folding screens that so delighted Whistler. Called *byobu* (protection from the wind), these tend to depict the seasons or themes from Japanese literature and range from two to ten panels long. Other choice items include the nineteenth-century porcelain dish shaped like Mount Fuji and, one of the oldest pieces in the Japanese collection, a twelfth-century standing Buddha of wood and gold leaf. **Korean ceramics** – wine bottles, tea bowls, ewers – date mostly from the tenth to the fourteenth centuries and show a uniform jade-like glaze. They're remarkably well preserved, many having been retrieved from aristocratic tombs or having simply survived as venerated objects, handed down through the generations.

Other rooms are devoted to **Chinese art**, ranging from ancient jade burial goods to a series of ornate bronzes (1200–1000 BC), including ritual wine servers in the shape of tigers and elephants. There's also a stunning series of ink-on-paper hand scrolls, though the calligraphy (literally "beautiful writing") isn't just confined to paper – jars and tea bowls, even ceramic pillows, are painstakingly adorned. Freer also made three trips to **Egypt**, whose ancient sculpture he came to consider "the greatest art in the world." Many of the exhibits on display date from his last trip in 1909, when he bought a remarkable collection of richly colored glass vessels (used for scents and oils), bronze figurines and carved plaques, most around 4000 years old. Later Freer spread his net to incorporate pieces from **Buddhist, South Asian and Islamic art**. A remarkably well-preserved Pakistani stone frieze from the second century AD details the life of Buddha, while the South Asian art collection sports some of the most delicate pieces yet: temple sculpture, colorful devotional texts, and gold jewelry set with rubies and diamonds. Elsewhere, Turkish ceramics (many repeating garden motifs) are displayed alongside a fine inlaid Persian pen box (thirteenth century) emblazoned with animal heads and engraved with the name of the artist and the owner.

Hirshhorn Museum and Sculpture Garden

Independence Ave at 7th St SW ☎357-2700, ⊛www.hirshhorn.si.edu; L'Enfant Plaza or Smithsonian Metro. Museum daily 10am–5.30pm; Sculpture Garden daily 7.30am–dusk. Admission free.

Gordon Bunshaft's cylindrical **Hirshhorn Museum**, balanced on fifteen-foot stilts above a sculpture-littered concrete plaza, has been likened to everything from a monumental donut to a spaceship poised for takeoff. Inside – where, incidentally, you barely notice that the building is round – is contained the Smithsonian's extensive collection of late-nineteenth- and twentieth-century art, based on the mighty bequest of Joseph H. Hirshhorn, Latvian immigrant, stockbroker and uranium magnate. Hirshhorn's vast fortune enabled him to collect art on a positively excessive scale: the original bequest in 1966 was of 4000 paintings and 2600 sculptures; by the time of his death in 1981, the overall number had risen to more than 12,000 pieces, which Hirshhorn was happy to see go to the country ". . . as a small repayment for what this nation has done for me and others like me who arrived here as immigrants."

It's impossible for the museum to display more than a fraction of its collection at any one time – and for the visitor to get much impression of what is on display in just one visit. There are also changing **exhibitions** of contemporary art, thematic shows, and a **Sculpture Garden**, which together with the *Full Circle* outdoor **café** (summer lunch only) provides respite when it all gets too much. There are free **guided tours** of the permanent collection (Mon–Fri 10.30am & noon, Sat & Sun noon & 2pm), and highly rated art **films** shown a couple of evenings a week (☎357-1300 for details).

The museum

The Hirshhorn's two upper floors are split into inner and outer loops, with the museum's main galleries circling along the nearly windowless exterior wall, and sculpture from two centuries residing in the glass-enclosed inner exhibition halls overlooking the fountain. Modern art from the turn of the century to the 1960s and American and European sculpture (1910–70) occupy the third-floor galleries, while contemporary works and special exhibitions are featured on the second floor along with European sculpture spanning the period 1850 to 1935. The most contemporary works are found in the lower-level galleries, where the exhibits are frequently rotated.

As far as it's possible to generalize about the collection, quite simply, Hirshhorn bought what he liked. If the museum has a recognized strength it's in nineteenth-century **French sculpture**, considered the best selection of its kind outside France. With a bit of backtracking, it's possible to trace the transition from nineteenth-century naturalism to twentieth-century abstraction. Jean-Baptiste Carpeaux, principal French sculptor of the mid-nineteenth century, is represented, along with Auguste Rodin, whom he directly influenced; for sheer panache, however, seek out Honoré Daumier's raffish, crumpled, bewhiskered gent, *Ratapoi*. By the turn of the century, developments in sculpture and art were going hand in hand – often literally so, as painters became enamored of the possibilities of working in another medium. Of various bronzes by Henri Matisse, most notable is *The Serf*, a stumpy portrait of downtrodden spirit, while alongside Edgar Degas' usual muscular ballerinas are energetic studies of women washing, stretching and emerging from a bath. Masks and busts by Picasso trace his (and sculpture's) growing alliance with Cubism: contrast the almost jaunty bronze *Head of a Jester* (1905) with the severe *Head of a Woman*, produced just four years later. A similar exercise is possible with a series of five exemplary bronze heads by Matisse of his wife Jeanette (1910–13), which show clearly the journey from realism to Cubism.

Picasso and Matisse aside, you can spot Hirshhorn's other favorites a mile off. There's an abundance of 1950s Henry Moore, from the rather gentle *Seated Figure Against a Curved Wall* to the more imposing *King and Queen*, a regal pair of seated five-foot-high bronze figures whose curved laps and straight backs look as inviting as chairs. Look, too, for the nastiest piece by far, *General Nuke* (1984), Robert Arneson's snarling general's head with an erect missile for a nose, the neck sitting on a totem of entwined corpses. Nearby, it's hard to miss Nam June Paik's *Video Flag* (1985–96), which rounds out the sculpture section with a mind-bending flourish. Composed of seventy 13-inch monitors, Paik's mesmerizing flurry of images spans the presidents from Truman to Clinton, all the while managing to resemble a fluttering American flag. From here, turn and you'll find yourself at the start of the modern art galleries.

As with the sculpture, the Hirshhorn's **modern art collection** is a roll call of the twentieth century's great and good, with several strengths (de Kooning, Bacon) and some weaknesses (few women, no Kandinsky paintings and, despite his sculpture on display, no Matisse). The collection runs more or less chronologically through the third floor's outer loop, starting with figurative paintings from the late nineteenth and early twentieth century and winding its way toward Abstract Expressionism and Pop Art. Along the way, separate rooms showcase the various major currents of the past century, from the surrealism of Salvador Dalí, Max Ernst and Joan Miró to the organic abstractions of Alexander Calder.

American art makes a particularly good showing: there are portraits by John Singer Sargent, Mary Cassatt and Thomas Eakins (including a strong study of Eakins' wife), and representative works by Winslow Homer, Albert Bierstadt, William Merritt Chase, Marsden Hartley and Edward Hopper. In addition, Hirshhorn's collection of work by Abstract Expressionist Willem de Kooning is one of the most impressive anywhere, although changing displays, loans and special exhibitions play havoc with formal viewing plans. Two or three are usually on display, though, like the elaborate swatch of lines and color that reveals itself to be *Two Women in the Country*. In addition, there's a changing selection of paintings by Georgia O'Keeffe, Robert Motherwell, Robert Rauschenberg, Ellsworth Kelly, Louise Bourgeois, Clyfford Still, Piet Mondrian, Jasper Johns, Roy Lichtenstein, Andy Warhol, Gene Davis and Kenneth Noland – in short, just about anyone in the twentieth-century art world to whom Hirshhorn could hand over money. Other third-floor highlights include the Directions Gallery, where newer, often international, work is exhibited, and the Abram Lerner Room, which affords panoramic views of the Mall and a place to rest your feet.

Downstairs, the second level is given over to special exhibitions, with the remaining galleries featuring a thematically linked showing of selected works from the contemporary collection. There's more contemporary art on display on the lower level, where you're likely to catch works by artists currently setting the art periodicals abuzz as well as by widely known artists such as Warhol or Johns. Look out, too, for standout recent acquisitions such as Australian Ron Mueck's alarmingly lifelike and very unclassical nude *Untitled (Big Man)* of 2000, often found glowering in a corner amid the contemporary works.

The Sculpture Garden

Much of the Hirshhorn's monumental sculpture is contained in the **Sculpture Garden**, a sunken concrete arbor across Jefferson Drive on the Mall side of the museum. In May and October, there are special **free tours** (call for times). Masterpieces come thick and fast: casts of Rodin's *Monument to the Burghers of Calais* and of Matisse's four human *Backs* in relief (1919–30) attract regular admirers. Many of those artists represented inside the museum appear in the garden, too – Henry Moore, naturally, but also Aristide Maillol (in particular, a graceful *Nymph* of 1930) and Henri Laurens, Joan Miró and David Smith. Of the lesser-known works, several stand out: Gaston Lachaise's proud, bronze *Standing Woman (Heroic Woman)* from 1932 is particularly fine, and there's great humor in Jean Ipousteguy's *Man Pushing the Door*, not too far off. The pond is fronted by Alexander Calder's *Six Dots over a Mountain;* for a more impressive Calder, make for the museum entrance on Independence Avenue, where his *Two Disks* (1965) sit on five spidery legs, tall enough to walk under.

National Air and Space Museum

Independence Ave and 7th SW Ⓣ 357-2700, Ⓦ www.nasm.si.edu; L'Enfant Plaza Metro.
Daily: June–Aug 10am–6.30pm; Sept–May 10am–5.30pm. Admission free.

If there's one museum people have heard about in DC, and just one they want to visit, it's the **National Air and Space Museum**. Since it opened in 1976, it has captured the imagination of almost ten million people every year, making it easily the city's most popular attraction. The frisson of excitement begins in the entrance gallery, which flirtatiously throws together some of the most celebrated flying machines in history, prompting even the most steadfast Luddite to consider a brief technological romance. More than twenty monstrous galleries on two floors containing objects the size of, well, spaceships means that even on the busiest days it's not too much of a struggle to get close to the exhibits. You may have to wait a while to get into the Langley IMAX theater, but otherwise the worst lines are in the cafeteria.

However, there are disappointments. With some very honorable exceptions, many of the explanatory background displays are lackluster and too reliant on a photo-video-text storyboard approach, which palls somewhat after an hour or two. Many of the most frequented exhibits are also physically worn, giving parts of the museum a tired air. With children in tow, if you get no further than the huge lobbies, take in the "Apollo to the Moon" exhibit and catch a movie, you'll have seen the best of the museum in an afternoon.

Visiting the museum

The **information desk** is at the Independence Avenue entrance; **free tours** leave from here (daily 10.15am & 1pm). If you want to visit the Einstein Planetarium ($4) or see an IMAX **movie** in the Langley Theater ($6.50), buy tickets when you arrive or book in advance (☎357-1686). Come early to **eat** in the self-service cafeteria – which features the fast food of McDonald's, Boston Market (offering rotisserie chicken) and Donatos Pizzeria – since by noon it's a madhouse. Incidentally, the dining area has a great view of the Capitol dome. Finally, don't even think of entering the **museum shop** without wads of cash or the stamina to withstand repetitive demands from companions and kids for model spaceships, Klingon T-shirts and florid stunt kites.

The first floor

Hanging from the rafters in the "**Milestones of Flight**" gallery, which confronts you upon entry, is the machine that started it all – the *Wright Flyer*, the handmade plane in which the Wright Brothers made the first powered flight in December 1903 at Kitty Hawk, North Carolina. They were an unlikely pair of pioneers, church-going, bicycle shop-owning bachelors who just happened to make themselves aerodynamic experts. The first flight – 20ft above the ground – lasted twelve seconds and covered 120ft, and within two years they were flying over twenty miles at a time, but there was curiously little contemporary interest in their progress. In part this was snobbery: in the rush for the skies, the Smithsonian Institution itself was supporting the efforts of a noted engineer (and, completely coincidentally of course, its third Secretary), Samuel Pierpoint Langley, who conspicuously failed to fly any of his experimental planes. It was forty years before the churlish Institution formally recognized the brothers' singular achievement, while the original *Wright Flyer* was only accepted into the Smithsonian fold in 1985.

Powered flight quickly caught the public imagination and prompted individual daring: on May 20, 1927, the 25-year-old Charles Lindbergh made the first solo transatlantic crossing in the moth-like *Spirit of St Louis*, taking off from Long Island and landing near Paris almost 34 hours later. When he wanted to see where he was headed Lindbergh either had to use a periscope or bank the plane, since his gas reserve tank was mounted where the windscreen should have been. Just 59 years after the very first controlled, powered flight, John Glenn became the first American to orbit the earth with the launch of

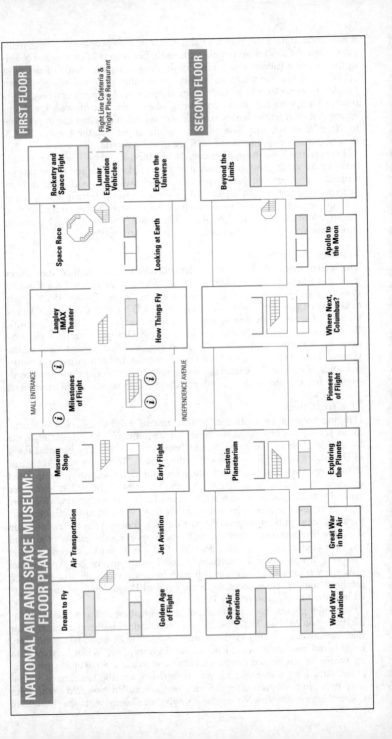

NATIONAL AIR AND SPACE MUSEUM: FLOOR PLAN

FIRST FLOOR

Dream to Fly

Air Transportation

Museum Shop

MALL ENTRANCE

Milestones of Flight

Langley IMAX Theater

Space Race

Rocketry and Space Flight

Flight Line Cafeteria & Wright Place Restaurant

Golden Age of Flight

Jet Aviation

Early Flight

INDEPENDENCE AVENUE

How Things Fly

Looking at Earth

Lunar Exploration Vehicles

Explore the Universe

SECOND FLOOR

Sea-Air Operations

Einstein Planetarium

Beyond the Limits

World War II Aviation

Great War in the Air

Exploring the Planets

Pioneers of Flight

Where Next, Columbus?

Apollo to the Moon

Friendship 7 in 1962. Glenn went around three times in five hours and saw four sunsets, in a craft barely big enough to swing an astronaut; his spacesuit is preserved upstairs in "**Apollo to the Moon**," as are the toothpaste tubes used to squeeze food into his mouth. Three years later, an American, Edward H. White, was walking in space for the first time, from the two-seater *Gemini 4*; while in July 1969, space travel came of age when the minuscule *Apollo 11* command module journeyed to the moon. The museum's first director was Michael Collins, the often-overlooked "third man" in Apollo 11: he got to orbit the moon while Armstrong and Aldrin made history by walking on it.

For more space bravado, head to the "**Space Race**" hall, which traces the development of space flight with machines as diverse as a V2 rocket — Hitler's secret weapon and the world's first ballistic missile system — and the pioneering Skylab Orbital Workshop. Just 120ft long, Skylab was home base during 1973–74 for three-person crews that stayed for as many as three months at a time; the confined space can be seen better from a platform on the second floor. For relaxation, the astronauts played with Velcro-covered darts and dartboard. With the thawing of relations between the Soviet Union and the US in the early 1970s came the Apollo-Soyuz Test Project, in which manned craft from the two countries docked in space for the first time (July 18, 1975). The docked craft are here, alongside various missiles, including an IBCM Minuteman whose sign, hardly comfortingly, states: "The Minuteman III displayed here has no nuclear warheads."

"**Lunar Exploration Vehicles**" displays the machines that in eight extraordinary years met President Kennedy's avowed aim of 1961 to land a man on the moon and return him safely. Unmanned probes – *Ranger*, *Lunar Orbitor* and *Surveyor* – finally gave way to the ludicrously flimsy lunar module *Eagle*, in which Neil Armstrong and Edwin "Buzz" Aldrin made their historic descent to the moon ("Houston . . . the *Eagle* has landed"). The *Eagle* itself isn't on display although the model that is, *LM-2*, was a backup, built for the moon-landing program but never used. If told it was made out of tin foil, cans and coat hangers, you could believe it. "**Rocketry and Space Flight**" traces the history of rocketry from the black-powder rockets used in thirteenth-century China to Robert Goddard's experiments with liquid fuel in 1926, which pointed the way to eventual space flight. Light relief is offered by coverage of sci-fi stalwarts Jules Verne and Buck Rogers, and examples of spacesuit development (including details of exactly where the bodily waste goes).

To see the museum chronologically, you'd need to start with the galleries on the other side of "Milestones of Flight." None is essential – if time is limited, the most engaging is perhaps "**Early Flight**," where you can see Otto Lilienthal's glider (1894), which first inspired the Wrights, whose success in turn provided the impetus for the resourceful Herman Ecker. Having taught himself to fly in 1911, a year later he built his *Flying Boat* using bits and pieces bought from hardware stores. The early technology explored by people like Ecker and the Wrights is covered in "**How Things Fly**," one of the museum's few interactive rooms. It's also worth a quick glance at "**Looking at Earth**," where aerial photographs include pictures of San Francisco after the 1906 earthquake (snapped from a kite camera), 1860 Boston photos taken from a balloon, and German castles recorded by camera-carrying pigeons.

The second floor

Upstairs, you can look down to the exhibits in "Milestones of Flight" below, before stepping back to view the complementary "**Pioneers of Flight**" gallery. The balloon basket of Captain Hawthorne Grey makes a suitable place to reflect on the early pioneers: in it, in May 1927, in a wonderfully heroic but pointless gesture, he reached a height of 42,470 feet – only to run out of oxygen and expire. More successfully, the *Fokker T-2* was the first airplane to make a nonstop American transcontinental flight in 1923, a journey that took 26 hours and 50 minutes. Just twelve years earlier – and after just twenty hours of flying lessons – one Cal Rogers had attempted to pick up the $50,000 prize offered by William Randolph Hearst to the first pilot to fly coast-to-coast in less than thirty days. He eventually managed the journey in a patched-up biplane, but it took him two months, seventy landings and several crashes. Perhaps the museum's most poignant airplane is the bright-red *Lockheed Vega* flown solo across the Atlantic in May 1932 by Amelia Earhart; she disappeared five years later over the Pacific attempting a round-the-world flight.

On either side of "Pioneers of Flight," fairly uninspired rooms deal with "**Exploring the Planets**" and, in "**Where Next, Columbus?**," the possibilities of future space travel. Most visitors make a beeline for "**Apollo to the Moon**," perhaps the most fascinating room in the museum (and usually the most crowded). The main gallery centers on the *Apollo 11* (1969) and *17* (1972) missions, the first and last flights to the moon. There are Neil Armstrong and Buzz Aldrin's spacesuits; a Lunar Roving Vehicle (basically a golf cart with a garden seat); *Apollo 17*'s flight-control deck, tools, navigation aids, space food, clothes and charts; and an astronaut's survival kit (complete with shark repellent). If you want to touch a bit of moonrock, however, you'll have to go back down to "Milestones of Flight," where a four-billion-year-old sample brought back by *Apollo 17* astronauts is displayed – just a small chunk of the 250 pounds of material they collected. In a side room, each American space mission is detailed, starting from May 1961, when in *Freedom 7* Alan B. Shepard Jr became the first American in space on a fifteen-minute flight to an altitude of 166 miles. A separate memorial commemorates the three men who died on the *Apollo* launchpad in 1967 – Virgil Grissom, Edward H. White II and Roger Chaffee. The other major US space disaster, the explosion of the space shuttle *Challenger*, is commemorated by a memorial plaque in Arlington cemetery (see p.227).

This is all stirring stuff and although there's heroism on display in other second-floor galleries – like "**Great War in the Air**," bursting with dog-fighting biplanes, and "**World War II Aviation**" – it's hard to see the "Apollo" gallery as anything but the high point of the museum. Only "**Beyond the Limits**" raises much interest. Detailing how computers have affected flight, this at least has the advantage of being as up to date as the museum gets, featuring touch-screen workstations and a cockpit simulator.

National Gallery of Art

Constitution Ave, between 3rd and 7th sts NW ☎737-4215, ⊛www.nga.gov; Archives–Navy Memorial Metro. Mon–Sat 10am–5pm, Sun 11am–6pm. Admission free.

The genesis of the **National Gallery of Art** lay in the vision of just one man, **Andrew Mellon**. An industrialist and financier, Mellon began to buy the works of European Old Masters in his late 20s, and his connection with central government in the 1930s – as Secretary to the Treasury and ambassador to Britain – persuaded him that there was means to create a national art gallery in Washington. His own collection certainly begged to be seen by a wider public: among the 121 paintings in Mellon's eventual bequest to the gallery were a score of masterpieces bought in 1931 from the government of the USSR, which plundered the works in the Hermitage to prop up its faltering economy.

NATIONAL GALLERY OF ART: WEST BUILDING MAIN FLOOR

Constitution Avenue (Ground Floor Entrance)

Rotunda

Coatroom

Micro Gallery

Mall Entrance

West Sculpture Hall

East Sculpture Hall

West Garden Court

East Garden Court

13th–15th c. Italian

16th c. Italian

17th & 18th c. Spanish, Italian & French

15th–16th c. German, Dutch & Flemish

17th c. Dutch & Flemish

19th c. French

18th & 19th c. Spanish & French

18th & 19th c. British

18th & 19th c. American

Special Exhibitions

⊠ Elevator
Ⓡ Restroom

The original National Gallery of Art, designed by John Russell Pope, was opened by President Franklin D. Roosevelt in March 1941. It wasn't (and still isn't) a government (or even Smithsonian) institution, despite its name, but the building and collection were at once perceived to be of national importance and scope. Now known as the **West Building**, Pope's symmetrical, Neoclassical gallery is positively overwhelming at first sight, especially when approached up the sweeping steps from the Mall. On the **main floor**, two wings without external windows stretch for 400ft on either side of a central **rotunda**, whose massive dome is supported by 24 black Ionic columns. The central vaulted corridor of each wing does duty as a sculpture hall, both wings ending at an internal, skylit, fountain-and-plant-filled **garden court**. The entire floor contains almost one hundred display rooms, full of masterpieces ranging from thirteenth-century Italian to nineteenth-century European and American art; down on the **ground floor** are changing exhibitions from the gallery's virtuoso collection of prints, drawings, sculpture and decorative art.

Remarkably, at its inauguration in 1941 the West Building was virtually empty, since Mellon's bequest – substantial though it was – filled only five of the rooms. But such was the influx of gifts and purchases that by the 1970s it was clear that the original building couldn't hope to hold them all. Consequently, I.M. Pei's thoroughly modernistic, triangular **East Building**, as it became known, was completed in 1978, utilizing a block of land between 3rd and 4th streets that Mellon had earmarked from the very beginning as the site of any future expansion. Pei's initial challenge was to deal with the awkwardly shaped block of land (truncated by Pennsylvania Ave), which he managed by making only the marble walls permanent; the rest of the internal structure can be shaped at will according to the dictates of the various temporary exhibitions. The East Building has a separate entrance on 4th Street, although an underground **Concourse**, with a moving walkway, connects the two

---

Visiting the National Gallery of Art

You can't hope to see the whole of the National Gallery in one visit, although it is surprisingly quick to move from West to East buildings using the Concourse, so visiting part of both collections in one go isn't out of the question. The most popular galleries (like the nineteenth-century French and American rooms) tend to be busiest in mid-afternoon and on weekends. To make best use of limited time, latch onto one of the informative daily **free tours and programs**; pick up a schedule from one of the gallery's **Art Information Desks**. They're located in the West Building on the main floor (Mall entrance) and on the ground floor (Constitution Ave at 6th St), and, in the East Building, at ground-level central court.

It's vital to note that even in the permanent galleries of the West Building, parts of the collection are **rotated or sent out on tour**, while some rooms may be **closed for renovation**. To track down the specific location of a particular work – including any of those mentioned in the account below – visit the **Micro Gallery** in the West Building (main floor, Mall entrance), in which an interactive computer system allows you to locate and view some 1700 works in the gallery. The system can also access biographies of more than 650 artists and provide the historical and cultural background of a work or artistic period – it can even print you a map of a self-selected tour. A CD-ROM version of the Micro Gallery is available for purchase in the gallery shops ($34.95). Alternatively, you can search the collection via the museum's excellent website (Ⓦ www.nga.gov).

Special **exhibitions and installations** are detailed in a monthly calendar, which also lists the **free classical music concerts** (Sept–June, usually Sun 7pm) held in the serene West Building West Garden Court. Ask for one at the information desks.

buildings. The Concourse also features more display space, a very good bookstore, an espresso bar and a large cafeteria – topped by pyramidal skylights and bordered by a glassed-in waterfall. The museum's most recent addition, the **Sculpture Garden**, can be found outside, situated between the gallery's West Building and the Museum of Natural History; here you'll also find the **Ice Rink**, where skaters circle well into the winter nights amid monumental sculptures of the post–World War II era.

Thirteenth- to fifteenth-century Italian art (Rooms 1–15)

The gallery's oldest works are the stylized thirteenth-century Byzantine **icons** (holy images) in which an enthroned Mary, Queen of Heaven, holds the Christ child who – as medieval art dictated – is a small adult figure. The Sienese artist **Duccio di Buoninsegna** was one of the first to move beyond strict Byzantine forms – there is genuine feeling in the faces of the subjects in his *Nativity*, a panel taken from the base of his masterpiece, the great *Maestà* altarpiece of Siena Cathedral. But while Duccio continued to work within flat Byzantine forms, his contemporary in Florence, **Giotto**, was producing works whose new spirit of humanism would lead eventually to the Renaissance. His *Madonna and Child* (completed by 1330) marks an extraordinary departure in its attempt to create believable human figures.

The emphasis then switches to fifteenth-century Florence, the city in which the ideas of the Renaissance were first and most lastingly expressed. In Europe's pre-eminent banking and trading center, rich families – like the Medicis – had sufficient money to sponsor a new band of innovative artists. The prominent *tondo* (circular painting) depicting the *Adoration of the Magi* (c.1445) was probably commissioned by the Medicis, and though started by the monk **Fra Angelico,** was substantially completed by **Fra Filippo Lippi**, who invested the biblical scene with his full range of emotive powers. **Domenico Veneziano**'s naked *St John in the Desert* (c.1445) would have been considered blasphemous before the Renaissance, when nudity was almost exclusively associated with the concept of sin. However, for dynamic realism there's nothing to compare with the decorative shield painted by **Andrea del Castagno** showing *The Youthful David* (c.1450) preparing to fling his sling. Goliath's decapitated head at his feet completed the story for Florentine viewers, who would have understood the picture as a warning to the city's squabbling neighboring states.

In the "Florentine Portraiture" section, all eyes are drawn to **Leonardo da Vinci**'s *Ginevra de' Benci* (c.1474), the only work by the artist in the United States. Painted when he was only 22, its subject is a 16-year-old Florentine beauty with alabaster skin sitting before a spiky juniper bush – not only symbolizing chastity (this was commissioned as an engagement portrait) but also a visual pun on her name, Ginevra, and the Italian word for juniper, *ginepro*. Masterpieces by **Sandro Botticelli** include his devout rendering of the *Adoration of the Magi* from the early 1480s – one of the paintings Mellon appropriated from the Hermitage. The scene here is set in the ruins of a Classical temple from which the frame of a new structure, representing Christianity, is rising.

Layout of the West Wing

The West Building's collection starts in Room 1 of the West Wing and proceeds chronologically, beginning with thirteenth- to fifteenth-century Italian art and wrapping up with nineteenth-century French art.

Other Renaissance developments come to light with **Andrea Mantegna**'s *Judith and Holofernes* – a calm Judith clutching the severed head of the Assyrian leader – less notable for its quality than for the obvious influence Mantegna had on his brother-in-law, Giovanni Bellini.

Sixteenth-century Italian art (Rooms 16–28)

By the beginning of the sixteenth century, new artistic ideas were being explored in other Italian cities, though not until the work of the accomplished Bellini family did Venetian art thoroughly shake off its erstwhile Gothic influences and produce its own Renaissance styles. Nowhere is this seen better than in *The Feast of the Gods*, started by the great **Giovanni Bellini** between 1511 and 1514. Virtually the artist's last work, it depicts deities feasting to bawdy excess in a bucolic setting. Bellini died in 1516 and in 1529 Titian, his former pupil, was engaged to restyle the painting, removing a grove of trees and adding the brooding mountain in the background. **Titian** would later become the finest Venetian painter of all, whose revealing portraits and visually seductive mythological scenes made him one of the most famous artists in Europe and eventually court painter to Charles V of Spain.

Back in Florence, painting of the Early and High Renaissance periods culminates in several works by **Raphael**. The prime piece here is the renowned *Alba Madonna* (1510), another of Mellon's purchases from the Hermitage. The Virgin and Child are seated on the ground, leaning against a tree stump, an unusual posture emphasizing their humility. The perspective is breathtakingly accurate, while the figures of Jesus and John the Baptist suggest that Raphael had studied the cherubic sculpture of Michelangelo.

Fifteenth to eighteenth-century Spanish art (Rooms 29-34, 36-37 and 52)

In the grip of the Counter-Reformation, **Spanish** art – its themes and parameters laid down by a zealous Catholic Church – remained deeply spiritual in character, with individual works designed to inspire devotion and piety. Paramount among these were the paintings of **El Greco**, "the Greek," the Cretan painter who moved to Spain in the mid-1570s (and is also said to have trained under Titian in Venice, which explains his often startling use of color). The National Gallery has the most important collection of his work outside of Spain. *Christ Clearing the Temple* (c.1570) portrays Jesus, leather whip in hand, laying into assorted traders and moneylenders. More typical, though, is the dour *Laocoön* (1610–14), in which the eponymous Trojan priest and his two sons are attacked by serpents sent by the Greek gods. From the same period, *St Jerome* – in retreat in the desert and about to beat his chest with a rock – expresses perfectly the emphasis the Spanish Church placed on the concept of penance.

Francisco de Zubarán, well known for his religious portraits, was responsible for *St Lucy*, a typical spiritual study, though one with an accompanying shock as your eyes are drawn to the saint's – which have been plucked out and laid on a dish that she holds in her hand. You'll also find work by Zubarán's contemporary, **Diego Velázquez**, the finest Spanish painter of the seventeenth century. So precocious was his talent, he was court painter to Phillip IV by the time he was 24 and spent the rest of his life executing powerful court and royal portraits for his patron. He did, however, return now and then to domestic scenes: *The Needlewoman* from 1640 is a fine (unfinished) example.

Spain's greatest eighteenth-century artist was the flamboyant **Francisco de Goya**, who after 1789 was court painter to Charles IV. The gallery owns several works, principally portraits, including the famous *Señora Sebasa García* in which the artist abandons background entirely to focus on the elegant *señora*.

The seventeenth and eighteenth centuries: French and Italian art (Rooms 29–34 and 36–37)

France's leading painters of the seventeenth century often set off for Rome, where the Counter-Reformation was playing out on the canvas in carefully observed paintings of the natural world. Popular landscapist **Claude Lorrain** was one such painter: French he may have been, but Claude's ideas of natural beauty, as represented in *Landscape with Merchants* (c.1630), were firmly Italian – he spent much of his life in and around Rome. One of the most significant paintings among the limited number of French works on display from this period is *The Repentant Magdalene* by **Georges de la Tour** (1640); its careful balance of form and light is typical of the early Baroque stirrings in France and Italy at this time.

Elsewhere in this section, the emphasis is strictly **Italian**. Notable is *River Landscape* (c.1590) by the Bolognese artist **Annibale Carracci**, an example of early Baroque art in which nature is the subject of the painting, rather than the backdrop. From here, the jump into the eighteenth century is fairly abrupt, ending with a stream of interiors and landscapes. Italian painters were still much in demand throughout Europe, and artists like **Bernardo Bellotto** could make a handsome living producing commissioned works like *The Fortress of Königstein*, executed for Augustus of Poland. Meanwhile, back in Venice, highly accomplished artists were producing *vedutas*, or view paintings, for sale to the traveling gentry who wanted a memento of their Grand Tour. **Giovanni Antonio Canaletto** was the first acknowledged master of this genre, and the gallery contains paintings by him of the entrance to the Grand Canal and of St Mark's Square.

Early German, and Dutch and Flemish: fifteenth- and sixteenth-century works (Rooms 35, 38–41)

Principal among early German masters of the Northern Renaissance is **Albrecht Dürer**. His visits to Italy had a direct influence on his art, something which can be seen in his *Madonna and Child* (1496–99), which grafts realistic Renaissance figures onto a landscape backdrop typical of Northern European religious paintings of the time. Dürer's contemporary, **Matthias Grünewald**, had less time for the Italian niceties of proportion and perspective, but there's no doubting the power behind his agonized *Crucifixion*, completed a decade or so later. It's the only painting by Grünewald in the US (indeed, there are only twenty left in the world). You'll also find portraits by **Hans Holbein the Younger**, who as an artist in Germany couldn't adapt to the religious turmoil of the Reformation and moved to England, where he became court painter to Henry VIII. In this role he executed the pudgy *Edward VI as a Child*, a portrait of Henry's heir and son of his third wife, Jane Seymour. Finished in 1538, the painting is thought to have been given to Henry as a present on New Year's Day 1539, complete with added Latin inscription judiciously encouraging Edward to emulate the myriad virtues of his father.

The gallery's early Flemish and Dutch works show the new techniques made possible by the revolutionary change from painting with quick-drying egg-based tempera to using slow-drying oil, which allowed artists to build up deep color tones. Acclaimed fifteenth-century artist **Jan van Eyck** was one of the first to adopt the new technique – his *Annunciation* (1434) shows a remarkable grasp of color and texture. Even more striking is the tiny panel by **Rogier van der Weyden** of *St George and the Dragon*, also executed in the mid-1430s. It followed the realism pioneered by van Eyck and applied it to a medieval subject with incredible attention to detail – the artist probably used a magnifying glass to paint individual tree branches and pinprick windows. Also notable is **Hieronymus Bosch**'s *Death and the Miser* (1485–90), a gloriously ghoulish tour de force.

Seventeenth-century Dutch and Flemish art (Rooms 42–50)

The mood changes with a swath of **Anthony van Dyck** portraits of assorted Italian, English and Flemish nobility, covering the period from 1618 to 1635. Van Dyck was an immensely popular portraitist, perhaps due in part to his flattery of his subjects – elongating their frames, painting them from below to enhance their stature, idealizing their features. He was duly knighted for his efforts in England by Charles I, but his inherent artistic skill shines through even the most overblown of his portraits; the earliest one here, *Portrait of a Flemish Lady* from 1618, was painted when he was just 19. Van Dyck's teacher, **Peter Paul Rubens**, is responsible for the one real masterpiece in this section, *Daniel in the Lions' Den* (1613–15), in which virtually life-sized lions bay and snap around an off-center Daniel.

Raffish gentlemen in white collars and tall hats were bread-and-butter work for a talented portrait-painter like **Frans Hals**. Not that, ultimately, it did him much good – in his dotage, Hals was virtually on the breadline, supported only by handouts from an almshouse whose governors liked the portrait he'd once painted of them. For portraiture there are few equals to **Rembrandt van Rijn**, amongst whose works the gallery numbers a prized painting of his wife, Saskia. After Saskia died in 1642, Rembrandt fell into debt and was eventually declared bankrupt; a second wife and his only son also died, though a mournful Rembrandt lived on until he was 63. *The Mill,* from 1650, is a typical later work, a brooding study of a cliff-top mill, backlit under black thunderclouds. It's a famous image, with its dark and light connotations of good and evil, and one that influenced nineteenth-century British artists such as J.M.W. Turner.

Most of Rembrandt's contemporaries settled for making a living from **genre painting**, depicting people in everyday social and work situations. These quickly became popular in seventeenth-century Holland, partly because the paintings allowed the newly independent Dutch to celebrate a nascent national identity. Each artist had his particular specialization: as Hals (a Flemish immigrant to Holland) produced portraits, so **Peter de Hooch** depicted quiet domestic households, such as those in *A Dutch Courtyard* and *The Bedroom*. With **Jan Steen**, the genre was typically festive, doubtless inspired by his experience as an innkeeper: witness his bacchanalian *The Dancing Couple*. Of all the genre artists, only **Johannes Vermeer** is still widely known. In his entire career he created just 45 paintings, only 35 of which survive. Of these, the gallery owns and displays in turn *The Girl with the Red Hat, Woman Holding a Balance* and *A Lady Writing*, contemplative scenes all set – like most of his works – in the artist's parents' house, which he later inherited. A fourth, *Young Girl with a Flute*, may not be by Vermeer; the jury is still out.

Eighteenth- and early nineteenth-century French art (Rooms 53–56)

Eighteenth-century **French** painting and sculpture is announced by the pair of marble busts of Voltaire by **Jean-Antoine Houdon**, sculptor of George Washington (see p.51). The main attraction, however, is the portrait of *Napoleon in his Study* (1812) by Neoclassicist **Jacques-Louis David**. Arch-imperial propagandist David meant the sword, crisp uniform, military papers and imperial emblems to bolster Napoleon's heroic image, while his slightly disheveled appearance, the dying candles and the time on the clock in the background point to the fact that he's been up all night working for the good of the country. Come the Battle of Waterloo in 1815, and the defeat of Napoleon, David's career was over and he was forced to flee to Switzerland.

By way of contrast, consider the still lifes and everyday scenes of **Jean-Siméon Chardin**, who worked directly from the subjects, hardly ever making the prior detailed studies that contemporaries considered essential. Works by **Antoine Watteau** include the delightfully absurd *Italian Comedians* (1720), a group portrait of clowns and players, whose characters and costumes he knew well, having once worked as a scene-painter. Watteau's highly decorative Rococo style is seen to best effect, however, in the oval panel depicting *Ceres*, the Roman goddess of the harvest, surrounded by the signs of the summer zodiac, Gemini, Cancer and Leo.

There's also a major showing of **Jean-Honoré Fragonard**, who knocked out his so-called "fantasy portraits" in as little as an hour. In *A Young Girl Reading*, a reflective study halfway between a sketch and a portrait, the neck ruff and bodice are etched in the paint using the wooden end of the brush, while the lines of the book are mere blurred traces of paint. *The Swing* (1765) is a more artful work, whose images of flounced dresses and petticoats had erotic connotations for contemporaneous viewers.

Eighteenth- and nineteenth-century British art (Rooms 57–59, 61, 63)

The gallery's few **British** works include individual pieces by William Hogarth, George Stubbs and George Romney, but the most interesting pieces are by contemporary eighteenth-century court rivals **Joshua Reynolds** and **Thomas Gainsborough**. Also usually on display are works by two American artists who enjoyed great popularity during their time in England: Benjamin West, the first American artist to study in Europe, and Gilbert Stuart, pictorial chronicler of the first American presidents. Stuart's *The Skater* (1782), produced during his time in London with West, depicts a nonchalant, black-clad ice-skating gent whose sheer cheek was beyond compare in Britain at the time.

Other works are firmly within the British tradition, particularly the harmonious landscapes by **John Constable** and the sea and river scenes of **J.M.W. Turner**, which run the gamut from a gentle, hazy *Approach to Venice* – which John Ruskin described as "the most perfectly beautiful piece of color of all that I have seen produced by human hands" – to *Keelmen Heaving in Coals by Moonlight* (1835), a light-drenched harbor scene set in the industrial north of England.

Eighteenth- and nineteenth-century American art (Rooms 60, 62, 64–71)

The enormously eclectic collection of eighteenth- and nineteenth-century **American art** is one of the most popular sections of the entire gallery. Pick of the collection for many is the line of portraits by **Gilbert Stuart** of the leading American men of his age. Born in Rhode Island, where he first studied painting, poverty forced Stuart to London, where he was taken on by fellow American Benjamin West. Stuart quickly became a success and set up his own studio, but later got into debt and returned after seventeen years abroad to a new United States, where he resolved to make his fortune by executing a portrait of the first president. In fact, he ended up painting the likeness of George Washington more than a hundred times during his career; the two examples here are the early *Vaughan Portrait* of 1795 and the more familiar *Athenaeum Portrait* (1810–15) – the latter eventually being used as the model for the portrait on the dollar bill. Following his success with Washington, Stuart became in effect the American court artist, painting the next four presidents – Adams, Jefferson, Madison and Monroe – and more than a thousand other portraits (the National Gallery alone has 41).

In contrast to the youthful Stuart, **John Singleton Copley** was already in his mid-30s when he decided to study painting in Europe. The outbreak of the American Revolution kept him in England longer than he had planned, and his family joined him instead in London – the *Copley Family* celebrates their reunion (the artist is in the rear left of the painting). Copley made his name internationally with *Watson and the Shark* (1778), which, with its depiction of a shark attack off the coast of Cuba, caused a stir in London at the time, as such dramatic scenes were usually reserved for the martyrdom of saints. The work was likely commissioned by Brook Watson, the subject of the work, who survived his youthful ordeal to become Lord Mayor of London later in life — though he apparently neglected to mention to Copley that sharks have neither lips nor ears. You'll also find work by **Benjamin West** who, though born in Pennsylvania, studied first in Rome in the 1760s before establishing himself as a history painter in England. There he succeeded Joshua Reynolds as President of the Royal Academy in 1792, an office he held for almost thirty years. Given this, it's debatable whether to consider him an American artist at all. Certainly in his splendid historical scenes, which he helped popularize as an art form, West took subtle side with the British – in *The Battle of La Hogue* (1778), which pits seventeenth-century English and French naval forces against each other, the heroic English admiral directs operations from close quarters while the French dandy is more concerned about losing his wig than with the hand-to-hand combat raging around him.

There's more portraiture by two of West's former pupils, John Trumbull (who was later responsible for the murals in the Capitol) and Thomas Sully. Both were highly regarded, although the one painting that most visitors are keen to see, *The Washington Family,* is by a much inferior artist, Edward Savage. His formal group portrait shows George, Martha and grandchildren sitting around a table at Mount Vernon in rather glum contemplation of a map of the new city of Washington DC.

By the nineteenth century, American artists were tackling the theme of territorial expansion head-on. *The Notch of the White Mountains* by **Thomas Cole** (1839) – leading light in the Hudson River School, in which human figures play second fiddle to their natural surroundings – is typical in its vibrant use of color. At around the same time, the German-born **Albert Bierstadt** brought his monumental eye to a grand study of a shimmering, turquoise *Lake Lucerne,* framed by mountains – the immediate progenitor of his startlingly successful American landscapes (the best are in the Smithsonian American Art Museum; p.175). Others, meanwhile, were recording the scale of human progress in the wilderness. *The Lackawanna Valley* (1855) by **George Inness** depicts a steam train puffing through a Pennsylvanian landscape of felled trees. The work was commissioned by a railroad company, and while Inness hadn't wanted the job, he needed the money. At the company's insistence he included the "roundhouse" building in which the trains were turned around, a technological innovation of which they were especially proud.

The late nineteenth century is ushered in with paintings by Philadelphia-based **Thomas Eakins**, whose light touch is atypical of the post–Civil War period, which tended to bring out a darker element in the works of his contemporaries. **Winslow Homer** is a case in point: trained as a graphic artist, he worked during the Civil War for *Harper's Weekly*, recording battlefield scenes

Taking a break in the National Gallery of Art

For food and drink, you need to head down a level from the main floor of the West Building or across to the East Building, noting as you go Salvador Dalí's *Last Supper*, which guards the escalators down to the Concourse.

Cascade Espresso and Gelato Bar, Concourse (Mon–Sat 10am–4.30pm, Sun 11am–5.30pm). Coffee, sandwiches, desserts, salads, ice cream and sorbets.

Concourse Buffet, Concourse (Mon–Sat 10am–3pm, Sun 11am–3pm). Self-service breakfast (10–11am), salads, burgers, sandwiches and hot meals.

Garden Café, West Building, ground floor (Mon–Sat 11.30am–3pm, Sun noon–6.30pm). Lunch daily; open later on Sunday for those attending the classical concerts in the Garden Court. For reservations call ☎216-2494.

Terrace Café, East Building, upper level (Mon–Sat 11.30am–3pm, Sun noon–4pm). Nicest lunch spot, with Mall views. For reservations call ☎216-2494.

that had a profound influence on his later work. **James Abbott McNeill Whistler** is dominant, too; his standout work here is *The White Girl*, subtitled *Symphony in White No. 1*. The full-length 1862 study of the artist's mistress is of secondary importance to his contrasting use of various shades of white, from dress to drapes to flowers, all subtly different in tone.

A more offbeat collection of works are those from the so-called Cartoon Collection by frontier artist **George Catlin** (for more on whom, see p.175), who certainly grabbed contemporary audiences' attention with his subject matter – notably himself sitting down to enjoy a feast of roast dog with his Sioux hosts.

The century turns with the last two rooms in the section, taking American art up to World War I. **Childe Hassam**'s *Allies Day, May 1917* is a packed New York streetscape of flags and crowds, while the gallery also displays works by leading Impressionist William Merritt Chase. **George Bellows**' assured *Portrait of Florence Davey* in no way prepares you for his other paintings, notably the brutal prizefight pictures *Club Night* (1907) and *Both Members of This Club* (1909), in which you can almost feel the heat as the crowd bays for blood. There's a similar energy in Bellows' brilliantly realized *Blue Morning* (1909), set on a New York construction site.

Nineteenth-century French art (Rooms 80–93)

The most popular rooms in the West Building are those containing the exceptional collection of nineteenth-century **French** paintings, with every Impressionist, post-Impressionist, Realist and Romantic artist of note represented.

There are always crowds before **Claude Monet**'s dappled European views, among them two facades of Rouen Cathedral. From 1892 onwards, he painted more than thirty of these, almost all from the same close-up viewpoint but at different times of the day and in varied conditions, forming an integral part of his experimentation with light and color. They were reworked in his studio, and a score of them finally exhibited in Paris in 1895. Significant, too, is *The Japanese Footbridge* (1899), whose water-lily theme he was to return to with spectacular success again and again until his death in 1926.

Other representatives of the Impressionist style are Monet's *Woman with a Parasol* (1875) – whose emphasis lies more on the vibrant summer light than its subjects, namely the artist's wife and child – and two of the dozens of studies he made of the town of Argenteuil, where he had a floating studio on the river in the 1870s. **Edouard Manet**'s *Gare Saint-Lazare* (1873), showing two contrasting figures before the station railings, is also here.

Works by **Vincent van Gogh** include his *The Olive Orchard* and the rich honey and yellow tones of the *Farmhouse in Provence*, both portraying an intensity – like all his Provençal paintings – that echoed his ever-present mental turmoil. Here too are female portraits by the American-in-Paris **Mary Cassatt**, whose work you can usually count on finding with the French Impressionists – a term she decried as not reflecting her own careful technique and observation. It's easy to agree after you study the flat blocks of color and naturalistic models in *Mother and Child* (c.1905) and especially the earlier *Woman with a Red Zinnia* (1891) and *The Boating Party* (1894).

Symbolism and post-Impressionism are explored in later rooms. The powerful *Self-Portrait* (1889) by **Paul Gauguin**, complete with halo, apple tree and serpent, resembles an early Salvador Dalí. Gauguin's declared aim to depict himself outside of Western society, as an "outlaw," was taken to its logical extreme with his move to Tahiti in 1891, where he completed dozens of paintings detailing its people, culture and religion. The gallery's collection of works by **Paul Cézanne** contains still lifes, portraits and landscapes from most periods of the artist's long life. Cézanne is often seen as the father of modern art, though he struggled to make an impression during his own lifetime, only ever selling around 50 of his 800 paintings. Hostile criticism forced him to stop exhibiting in 1877, and his first one-man show wasn't held for another eighteen years. The invective he inspired is now difficult to conceive: Evelyn Waugh thought him a "village idiot who had been given a box of paints to keep him quiet." Cézanne was 27 when he completed *The Artist's Father* (1866) – Cézanne *père* had no time for his son's desire to become an artist and opposed his move to Paris in the 1860s; Paul retaliated by perching his father uncomfortably in a high-backed chair in front of a representation of one of his own paintings.

The later rooms finish with a flourish, highlighting varied works by **Henri de Toulouse-Lautrec**, portraying the dancers, madames and café patrons he observed in his peregrinations around the fleshpots of Montmartre. The most famous piece here by **Edgar Degas** is the dreamlike *Four Dancers* (1899), one of his last large paintings. It's a swirl of motion which could be four young ballerinas in different poses, or one single dancer moving through a routine – rather like a flick-book of sketches laid flat on the canvas.

Twentieth-century art

Although the National Gallery's **East Building** was opened in 1978 to make room for the ever-expanding collection of **twentieth-century European and American art**, there still isn't anything like enough exhibition space to display the entire collection. This is partly due to I.M. Pei's audacious design, which places a generous premium on public areas. Since the exhibition spaces, squeezed in like an afterthought, are often taken up with special shows, it means that the gallery's own holdings may not be on display at all when you visit. If any of the artists or works below form part of your reason for visiting, be sure to call first.

Two or three items are always present, but that's only because they're too big to keep shifting around. Outside at the 4th Street entrance, **Henry Moore**'s bronze *Knife Edge Mirror Two Piece* is a male and female representation whose sensuous line and form contrast with the sharp angles of the building – Moore collaborated with Pei before deciding on its exact structure. Inside, dominating the atrium, a huge steel-and-aluminum mobile by **Alexander Calder** hangs from the ceiling, its red and black (and one blue) paddle-like wings moving slowly with the air currents. Also in the atrium, **Joan Miró**'s stunning tapestry *Woman* is usually on display.

When exhibitions from the twentieth-century collection *are* in place, they start chronologically on the upper level, which displays **pre-1945 art**, most of it European. The famous names are all here, none more so than **Pablo Picasso**, who is represented by several diverse works, including the Blue Period works *The Tragedy* (1903) and *Family of Saltimbanques* (1905), depicting itinerant circus performers captured in reflective mood in a stripped landscape. By 1910, when he completed *Nude Woman*, Picasso had turned fully to Cubism – this piece particularly challenged contemporary audiences with a dissection of anatomy reminiscent of X-ray photography.

There's a similar range in the gallery's collection of paintings by **Henri Matisse**, with restrained early works giving way to the exuberant *Pianist and Checker Players* (1924), pictured in Matisse's own apartment in Nice. Technically the most interesting pieces, however, are those kept behind light-sensitive doors down on the Concourse level (Mon–Sat 10am–2pm, Sun 11am–3pm), the so-called Matisse "Cut-Outs." To create these late works – completed during the 1940s and early 1950s when illness prevented him from gripping a paintbrush – Matisse cut painted primary-colored sheets into assorted shapes that were then attached to a white background to form vibrant patterns.

Post-1945 art (mostly American, though with several honorable exceptions) is usually shown downstairs in the Concourse-level galleries. **Andy Warhol**'s works are as familiar as they come, with classic examples of *32 Soup Cans, Let Us Now Praise Famous Men* and *Green Marilyn*. There's also usually art by **Roy Lichtenstein, Clyfford Still** and **Willem de Kooning**. Separate rooms are often set aside for the related works of those artists using huge color swatches: the gallery owns large, primeval canvases by **Mark Rothko**, as well as the thirteen hessian-colored *Stations of the Cross* by **Barnett Newman**, a series that took eight years to complete. There are various slabs of color, too, by **Robert Rauschenberg** and **Jasper Johns**, while other highlights include **Chuck Close**'s *Fanny/Fingerpainting* (1985), a mighty portrait of an elderly black woman realized from a brilliantly marshaled canvas of finger splodges.

Sculpture, decorative arts, prints and drawings

Changing exhibitions of sculpture, decorative arts, prints and drawings take place on the **ground floor** of the West Building; the information desks can point out current highlights. The gallery owns more than two thousand pieces of **sculpture**: many Italian and French pieces from the fourteenth to eighteenth centuries, as well as pieces from the excellent nineteenth-century French collection, with works by Rodin, Degas, Maillol, et al. Among the **decorative arts** are Flemish tapestries, eighteenth-century French furniture, Renaissance majolica, chalices and religious paraphernalia, Chinese porcelain, engraved medals, even stained-glass windows. Perhaps most impressive is the gallery's collection of **prints and drawings** – 65,000 works, from the eleventh to the twentieth centuries. Selections on display are necessarily limited and tend to be exhibited only for short periods, but if you're sufficiently clued up you can make an appointment to see particular works by calling ☏842-6380.

The Sculpture Garden and Ice Rink

Adjacent to the National Gallery's West Building, the **Sculpture Garden** (Mon–Sat 10am–5pm, Sun 11am–6pm) exhibits a small selection of contemporary sculpture around the popular **Ice Rink**. The garden is quite a bit livelier than its Hirshhorn counterpart, with floating cubes and eight-ton slabs of elegantly twisted steel scattered across a six-acre enclosure. Entering from the Mall, you'll soon arrive at yet another of Alexander Calder's stabiles; this time it's the bright, six-legged sheet metal *Cheval Rouge*. Nearby, Roy Lichtenstein's *House I* (1996/1998), with an illusory effect characteristic of the pop artist's later sculptures, routinely draws double takes from amused passers-by. Elsewhere, you'll find Barry Flanagan's pensive rabbit posing as the *Thinker on a Rock* (1997) in an irreverent ode to Rodin's nineteenth-century master-piece, as well as works by Joan Miró and Isamu Noguchi, the spiky blue mohawk of Claes Oldenburg, and Coosje van Bruggen's gargantuan *Typewriter Eraser* (1999), which guards the western gate along Constitution Avenue. Look, too, for Magdalena Abakanowicz's decidedly less frivolous gathering of thirty headless bronzes, *Puellae* (Girls), which recalls the story of a group of children who froze to death in cattle cars en route to Germany from the artist's native Poland in 1942.

At the center of it all is the Ice Rink, which doubles as a fountain in sum-mer (Mon–Thurs 10am–11pm, Fri–Sat 10am–midnight, Sun 11am–9pm). Two-hour skating sessions ($5.50) begin on the hour from November to March (weather permitting). Skates are available for rent ($2.50) and lockers are on hand to stow your valuables. Overlooking all the action, the **Pavilion Café** (Mon–Sat 10am–9pm, Sun 11am–7pm) is a pleasant spot to catch your breath and grab a bite: pastries, salads and sandwiches as well as beer, wine and coffee are all on offer.

National Museum of African Art

950 Independence Ave SW ☎357-4600, ⓦwww.nmafa.si.edu; Smithsonian Metro. Daily 10am–5.30pm. Admission free.

The **National Museum of African Art** – the nation's foremost collection of the traditional arts of sub-Saharan Africa – occupies the underground levels of one of the Mall's most appealing buildings. Its circular motifs and domes recall a traditional African dwelling while providing an architectural counterpoint to the triangular lines of the neighboring Sackler Gallery. These are fine sur-roundings in which to view the collection, which runs to some six thousand diverse sculptures and artifacts from a wide variety of tribal cultures, displayed in a series of permanent galleries and bolstered by special exhibitions.

In many ways, the museum is one of applied art, though the application of a particular piece is not always clear, not least to the curators. In part this is due to the techniques of early collectors, who tended not to concern themselves unduly with recording factual information about their loot. In most cases, even the artist's name isn't known, while dating a piece is fraught with difficulty, too. On the whole, most of the works are nineteenth or twentieth century – some are older, but because most African art is made from wood or clay, it tends not to survive for long.

For an overview of the collection, the free **guided tours** (daily except Fri) are an excellent introduction – pick up a schedule at the ground-floor **information desk**. It's also worth noting that the **gift shop** on the first level is one of DC's most intriguing, selling woven and dyed fabrics and clothes as well as the usual books and postcards. The permanent **galleries** are downstairs on the first level.

The Kerma and Benin collections

The Nubian trading city of **Kerma**, 180 miles south of the present

Egypt–Sudan border, flourished between 2500 and 1500 BC. Most of what is known about the city is derived from the excavations of royal tombs, discovered at huge cemeteries lost in the desert for centuries. On display are ceramic bowls (perfectly round, despite being hand-formed) and, more interestingly, carved legs and delicate ivory animal figures from the ceremonial beds used to carry the dead to the cemetery for burial. As in Egypt, Nubian royalty were buried with hundreds of what the museum likes to call "volunteers," who "allowed themselves to be buried alive" to serve their masters in the afterlife.

More coherent is the adjacent gallery's display of royal art from the **Kingdom of Benin**, home of Edo-speaking people in what is now Nigeria. It's a small collection of highly accomplished works relating to the rule of the *Oba*, or king, some dating back as far as the fifteenth century. Best pieces here are the copper alloy heads (made using the sophisticated lost-wax casting technique), some of which depict an erstwhile *Oba*, although one is of a defeated enemy – that he's not Edo is indicated by the four raised scars over each eye; the other heads have only three. There's a picture of the current *Oba* on the gallery wall, in resplendent orange, whose ceremonial headdress and neck-ruff echo those depicted on the copper heads – evidence that the same royal style has prevailed for more than five hundred years.

The other galleries

The other galleries make valiant efforts to contextualize the objects on display. In "**Images of Power and Identity**," the emphasis is on political, religious and ceremonial art – mostly from West and Central Africa – which by its nature includes some of the most elaborate of the museum's holdings. The exhibition contains the museum's two oldest pieces – rounded, stylized, terra-cotta equestrian and archer figures from Mali (thirteenth–fifteenth century) – and also includes the only work in the museum for which the artist is known. Olowe of Ise, an artist to royalty among the Yoruba people of Nigeria, was responsible for the carved wooden palace door, 6ft high and depicting in relief a king seated on a horse, his wives ranked above him, and soldiers and daughters below. Remarkably, the door was carved from a single piece of wood. Several works – fertility fetishes – represent a woman and child; note especially the worn wooden carving from Nigeria that would have sat at one end of a ceremonial drum. Unlike in the Western tradition, where Jesus is the dominant figure in any carving of Madonna and Child, here all the expressive power in the sculpture is with the woman – giver of life. In other cultures power is expressed in more abstract forms. From the Cameroon, a wooden sculpture of a regal male figure holds his chin in his hand (a sign of respect), his decorative bead clothing covered with symbolic representations of spiders (a wily opponent) and frogs (fecundity).

There's much to learn, too, about the varied African concepts of divinity or even beauty: a carved figure from the Ghanaian Asante people shows a seated male and female with disk-shaped heads, a form considered to be the aesthetic ideal. Not all the concepts reflected in this art are completely alien to Western tradition, however. One of the most engaging works – a headrest from the Luba people of the Congo – is supported by two caryatid figures who (if you look around the back) have their arms entwined.

The "**Art of the Personal Object**" displays precisely that: chairs, stools and more headrests, mostly carved from wood using an adze, as well as assorted ivory snuff containers (two from Angola with stoppers shaped like human heads), beer straws (from Uganda), carved drinking horns, combs, pipes, spoons, baskets and cups.

National Museum of American History

14th St NW and Constitution Ave ☎357-2700, ⊛www.americanhistory.si.edu; Smithsonian Metro. Daily: June–Aug 10am–6.30pm; Sept–May 10am–5.30pm. Admission free.

If there's one single museum in the United States that can begin to explain what it is to be American, it's the **National Museum of American History**. Behind a rather staid title hides a bizarre melange of artifacts that goes some way in recounting the lives and experiences of ordinary Americans by display-ing the very stuff of life – from eighteenth-century farming equipment to computer chips, jukeboxes to washing machines, harmonicas to train engines. Each floor is a serendipitous delight: George Washington's wooden teeth, Jackie's designer dresses and the ruby slippers Judy Garland wore in the *Wizard of Oz* are set among didactic displays tracing the country's development from colonial times. It's not so much a center for scholarly study as a sanctuary for vanishing Americana, though the museum looks forward, too, with its cover-age of the white heat of information technology – where its hands-on approach sets it apart from any other "history" museum.

The museum's roots lie in the prodigious bequests made to the original Smithsonian Institution (see p.62), starting with the exhibits left over from Philadelphia's 1876 Centennial Exhibition. Each item collected was destined for the "National Museum" (now the Arts and Industries Building), but since this meant displaying stuffed animals alongside portraits, postage stamps and patent models, the Smithsonian was soon forced to specialize. An attempt was made to direct part of the collection by founding a National Museum of History and Technology in 1954, for which this traditional Beaux Arts build-ing – the last such on the Mall – was purpose-built a decade later. The empha-sis proved important, since great parts of the museum are now devoted to the sweeping technological changes that helped mold modern America. But the final name change in 1980 was a belated acceptance of the constant underly-ing theme: that the museum of "American History" firmly relates its exhibits to the experiences of the American people. Not every item is domestic in ori-gin – indeed, huge swathes of the museum deal in imported products and ideas – but each in its application has had both a personal and national effect.

You could easily spend a full day here; three to four hours would be a rea-sonable compromise, though to stick to this time frame you'll have to be selec-tive. There's an extremely good **museum shop and bookstore** on the lower level – the biggest of the Smithsonian stores (see p.304) – as well as the main self-service **cafeteria**. The Ice Cream Parlor (11am–4pm) is on the first floor, in the **Palm Court**, where you'll also find a café serving coffee, fruit and snacks (next to a great 1950s-style Horn and Hardart automatic vending machine) and a functioning **post office** counter inside a transplanted nine-teenth-century general store (by the Constitution Avenue entrance). Ask at the information desks for details about free **tours, lectures and events**, includ-ing demonstrations of antique musical instruments, printing presses and machine tools. Located at both Mall (second-floor) and Constitution Avenue (first-floor) entrances, the desks are staffed from 10am to 4pm.

Second floor

Entering from the Mall puts you in the second-floor Flag Hall, permanent home of the battered red-white-and-blue flag that inspired the writing of the US national anthem – the **Star-Spangled Banner** itself, which survived the British bombing of Baltimore harbor during the War of 1812. With dimensions of about 30 by 34 feet, and (backed by heavy linen) weighing 150 pounds, it

NATIONAL MUSEUM OF AMERICAN HISTORY: FLOOR PLAN

⊠ Elevator
ℝ Restroom

FIRST FLOOR

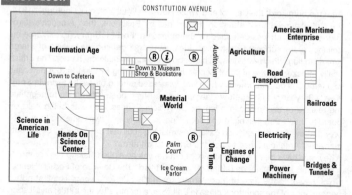

CONSTITUTION AVENUE

Information Age

ℝ ⓘ ℝ

← Down to Museum Shop & Bookstore

Down to Cafeteria

Auditorium

Agriculture

American Maritime Enterprise

Road Transportation

Material World

Science in American Life

Hands On Science Center

ℝ Palm Court ℝ

Ice Cream Parlor

On Time

Engines of Change

Railroads

Electricity

Power Machinery

Bridges & Tunnels

SECOND FLOOR

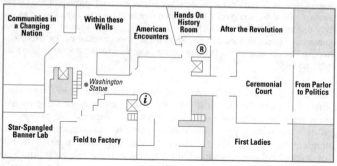

Communities in a Changing Nation

Within these Walls

American Encounters

Hands On History Room

ℝ

After the Revolution

Washington Statue

ⓘ

Star-Spangled Banner Lab

Field to Factory

Ceremonial Court

From Parlor to Politics

First Ladies

MALL

THIRD FLOOR

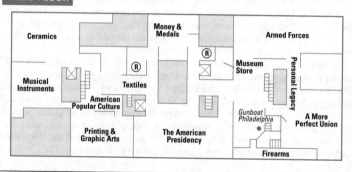

Ceramics

Money & Medals

Armed Forces

ℝ

ℝ

Museum Store

Musical Instruments

Textiles

American Popular Culture

Personal Legacy

Printing & Graphic Arts

The American Presidency

Gunboat Philadelphia

A More Perfect Union

Firearms

The Star-Spangled Banner

O say, can ye see by the dawn's early light
what so proudly we hail'd by the twilight's last gleaming?
Whose bright stars and broad stripes through the clouds of the fight,
o'er the ramparts we watch'd were so gallantly streaming?

After the burning of the Capitol and White House in Washington DC in August 1814, the British turned their attention toward nearby Baltimore, then America's third-largest city, which was defended by the garrison at **Fort McHenry**. To reinforce his defiance of the superior British force, the commander ordered the making of a large American flag, which was hoisted high above the fort in Baltimore harbor. The British finally attacked on the night of September 13, subjecting fort and harbor defenses to a ferocious bombardment, which was witnessed among others by **Francis Scott Key**, a 35-year-old Georgetown lawyer and part-time poet. Attempting to negotiate the release of an American prisoner, Dr William Beanes, Key was being held on board a British ship that night and come "dawn's early light" was amazed to see not only that the flag was still "so gallantly streaming" but that the cannons of the out-numbered Americans had forced the British to withdraw.

Key may have been a mediocre poet but he was no slouch. Taking the bombard-ment as his inspiration, he rattled off a poem titled "The Defense of Fort McHenry," which he set to the tune of a contemporary English drinking song. The first public performance of the song took place in Baltimore a month after the battle, and it soon became an immensely popular rallying cry: Union troops adopted it during the Civil War and it became the armed forces' anthem in 1916, though not until a decree by Herbert Hoover in 1931 did it become the official **national anthem** of the United States. Despite Key's original title, the song seems to have become known as the "Star-Spangled Banner" almost immediately – indeed, the idea of the felicitous phrase had already occurred to Key in an earlier poem celebrating the exploits of Stephen Decatur against the Barbary pirates, which contained the words "the star-spangled flag."

sports fifteen stars and fifteen stripes (eight red and seven white), representing the fifteen states in the Union at the time of the hostilities. In the early life of the new republic, there was no fixed design for the national flag, as arguments raged over the relative prominence to be given to existing and future states. Congress eventually settled on the more familiar thirteen stripes (for the num-ber of original colonies), while adding a new star to the flag each time a state joined the Union. Following decades of exposure to light and pollution, the flag is currently under long-term restoration, though it's still on view in the conservation lab behind the George Washington statue; it should move back into the Flag Hall inside a climate-controlled case in the near future. Hopefully, the Foucault Pendulum — a seventy-foot-long swinging pendulum named for the French physicist who used it in 1851 to demonstrate that the earth rotates on its axis — will also be reinstalled at that time.

It's difficult to miss Horatio Greenhough's much-ridiculed **statue of George Washington**, commissioned in 1832 during the centennial of Washington's birth. He was paid $5000 by Congress and in 1841 came up with an imperial, seated, toga-clad Washington with swept-back hair, bare torso and sandals – mothers reputedly covered their children's eyes at its public unveil-ing. Look past the ill-advised Classical Revivalism and the likeness actually isn't that bad; perhaps hardly surprising since Greenhough based it on the earlier sculpture by the far more talented Jean-Antoine Houdon (see p.51).

Beyond here in the West Wing, the first main gallery details "**Communities in a Changing Nation**," with nineteenth-century America showcased through various social environments – slave cabin from South Carolina, indigent peddler's cart and wealthy Gothic Revival bedroom interior. From here it's a quick move to "**Within These Walls**," where two hundred years of history are brought into focus through the stories of five families and their Ipswich, Massachusetts home. The history of African-American migration from 1915 to 1940 is recounted across the way in a display entitled "**Field to Factory**." The demand for unskilled labor stimulated by World War I saw an unprecedented move from the fields of the South to the factories of the North by hundreds of thousands of black Americans. The "Great Migration" proved a momentous change, establishing strong black communities in diverse Northern cities – in DC, the hub of settlement was the Shaw neighborhood – and setting the framework for modern demographic patterns. Most of the documents, photographs and exhibits recount the experiences of individuals, from the recorded voices of migrants as they traveled north on the (segregated) trains to the re-creations of the new domestic situations they encountered on a farm in southern Maryland or in a Philadelphian tenement row. "**American Encounters**" focuses on New Mexico, looking at how sixteenth- and seventeenth-century Hispanic invasions and, later, tourism have affected the native communities – in particular, the pueblo Indians of Santa Clara and Chimayo. Traditional and contemporary applied art, in the shape of ornate rugs, chests, figurines and ceramics, sit alongside photographs, videos and recordings of narrative stories, music and dance.

The museum's chief strength lies in creating compelling images of ordinary life for Americans of different backgrounds through the ages. Nowhere is this more apparent than in "**After the Revolution**," whose walk-through displays detail the lives of three eighteenth-century families (of a Delaware farmer, a Virginia planter and a Massachusetts merchant) as well as the wider concerns of three communities (African-Americans in Chesapeake, the Seneca people of New York State, and urban Philadelphia). Eager to efface difference and present a vision of consensus, the gallery tells of the same triumphs and difficulties in each community: the array of instruments and knives used for bleeding yellow fever victims in Philadelphia's 1793 epidemic is no more or less comforting than the brutal obstetrics equipment used on the Delaware farm.

The rest of the East Wing is devoted to presidential life in and beyond the White House. Its fulcrum is the walk-through **Ceremonial Court**, designed to resemble the Cross Hall of the White House as it appeared after its 1902 renovation; the Smithsonian managed to purloin some of the original architectural bits and pieces that are incorporated here into the design, as are displays of glass, porcelain, tinware and silver from the White House collections. More satisfying is the cabinet displaying personal items of the presidents: Washington's telescope*, Grant's leather cigar case, Nixon's gold pen, Wilson's golf clubs, Jefferson's eyeglasses and Theodore Roosevelt's toiletry set.

Off the Ceremonial Court, "**First Ladies**" begins with portraits of each one, from Martha (who liked to be known as Lady Washington) onwards. Though there's a game attempt to provide biographical padding, and exhibits exhort

---

*George Washington's wooden false teeth, also on display here, are in fact a facsimile: the originals, which he used to soak in wine to improve their taste, were stolen in the 1970s. Washington had several handmade denture sets, crafted from materials as diverse as elephant and walrus tusks, lead, and human teeth.

viewers to appreciate First Ladies as political partners (Eleanor), preservers of White House culture and history (Jackie), or advocates of social causes (Hillary), the real pleasure here is in the frocks. Helen Herron Taft was the first to present her inaugural ball gown to the Smithsonian for preservation, starting a tradition that allows the museum to display a backlit collection of considerable interest, if not always taste. Other outfits provide revealing historical snapshots: Jackie Kennedy's simple A-line brocaded dress and jacket raised hemlines in America almost overnight. There's access from the Ceremonial Court to "**From Parlor to Politics**," a worthy trawl through the history of women and political reform (1890–1925), with exhibits on women's clubs, the temperance movement and female suffrage.

First floor

Every technological change to affect America, from crop rotation to computers, is laid out with systematic and mind-bogglingly comprehensive clarity on the first floor. You know you're in for a treat when the central lobby, devoted to the "**Material World**," throws up a veritable bazaar of handcrafted and machine-made artifacts, designed to show what things are made of and why. There's a great half an hour or so to be spent here picking out favorite items: a steel slot machine from 1940, a brass US Army bugle, ornate nineteenth-century marble balusters from a Boston bank, a cast-iron toy train, an saluminum softball bat, even astroturf. Adjacent displays trace the development of items like washing machines, from the earliest wooden tub to the first electrically operated model of the 1960s; bicycles get the same treatment, with the oldest example (from 1869) made of hickory and wrought iron.

"**Science in American Life**" fills in the background to many of the discoveries that made the artifacts possible in the first place. There's coverage of every scientific development you could think of, and several you've never even heard of; the interactive **Hands On Science Center**, contained within the gallery, explains many of them by letting you conduct basic experiments. The similarly interactive "**Information Age**" traces communications from Morse's first telegraph to modern information technology by way of a phalanx of radios, phonograms, telephones and computers of every age, shape and size. Some of the most remarkable relics are the early models from Alexander Graham Bell's first experiments with the telephone, a device he exhibited to universal amazement at the 1876 Centennial Exhibition in Philadelphia; only thirteen years later, the first public pay phone, a bulky box of tricks, was installed in Hartford, Connecticut. Among other multifarious diversions, you can hear excerpts from early radio programs, deal with a 911 emergency call, check out the state of contemporary communications in a re-created 1939 street scene, or watch archival newsreel and movie footage in the Bijou Theater. The museum steps up a gear with its coverage of the development of computers: the thirty-ton ENIAC (Electronic Numerical Integrator and Computer) built for the US Army during World War II could compute a thousand times faster than any existing machine, but it takes up a thirty-by-fifty-foot room; by way of contrast, a dozen of its valves in a box are about the same size as the computer on which you can take part in an electronic opinion poll on recent government policies. There are up-to-the-minute computer-based presentations in the Multimedia Theater, and at the end of the section – if you can kick the kids off the consoles – you can explore the world of the "virtual Smithsonian."

For all the interactive goodies, it's the east side of the floor which, for many, is the most affecting, since here in glorious profusion are the artifacts and machines that have shaped America. Everyone will have their particular favorite, but the themes come thick and fast. "**American Maritime Enterprise**" is typical in its diversity, with the model boats and seafaring paraphernalia quite put in the shade by an entire ship's steam engine and a mock-up tattoo parlor; sea shanties warble away on tape in the background. The exhibits in "**Road Transportation**" are virtual icons of their various ages: a covered wagon from the mid-nineteenth century, a 1903 Oldsmobile (the first automobile to be built on an assembly line), a Ford Model T from 1913, Evel Knievel's Harley Davidson, and a solar-powered car that set a speed record of 75mph in 1988. In "**Railroads**," an enormous Pacific-type locomotive from 1926 had to be shunted in through the museum window on a specially laid track. Galleries like "**Civil Engineering: Bridges and Tunnels**" (self-explanatory), "**Power Machinery**" (big drills) or "**On Time**" (railroad pocket watches to the atomic clock) will have their particular devotees. Of wider interest, though, is "**Electricity**," which celebrates not only the peculiar genius of Thomas Edison, who invented the lightbulb among other luminous discoveries, but concentrates, too, on Ben Franklin's early research on static electricity.

Third floor

Up on the top floor is everything else that had to go somewhere, and while the exhibits are divided into various themes, some items are simply unclassifiable and have ended up in a section entitled "**American Popular Culture**," on display in cases at the top of the escalators in the West Wing. Many make a beeline straight for these, gawking in reverence at – among other things – Dorothy's slippers from the *Wizard of Oz* (silver, incidentally, in the original Frank Baum stories, but changed to red to utilize the new capabilities of Technicolor), Muhammed Ali's boxing gloves, Michael Jordan's NBA jersey, a Babe Ruth–autographed baseball, Dizzy Gillespie's trumpet and a Star Trek phaser.

The third-floor exhibits proper start with "**Printing and Graphic Arts**," which shows temporary exhibitions from the museum's large collection of original prints alongside paper-making machines and printing presses. The West Wing rooms then proceed thematically, covering musical instruments, textiles, ceramics, and money and medals. Amid the eighteenth-century grand pianos, the racks of English and American porcelain, and coins and notes from around the world is the odd offbeat treat: a display devoted to the life and work of DC native and jazz legend Duke Ellington (see p.202), for instance, and the exhibit of *fai*, or circular stone money of the West Pacific Yap Islands, which was up to 12ft in diameter and had to be carried around on poles. (There were, needless to say, no very rich Yap islanders.)

The East Wing is more consistently interesting, starting with "**The American Presidency: A Glorious Burden**," which has sections on various aspects of presidential life, revealing everything from the ways in which the chief executive has communicated with his public to how the office has fared under the gaze of Hollywood's lens. The exhibition displays a fascinating array of objects, including George Washington's general's uniform and Revolutionary sword, the "fireside chat" microphone through which Franklin Roosevelt soothed an America mired in the Great Depression, and a pair of Mao and Nixon table-tennis paddles, souvenirs from the days of "Ping Pong Diplomacy." In a section devoted to "**Assassinations and Mourning**," you'll find one of the Smithsonian's most prized relics, the top hat Abraham Lincoln wore to Ford's Theatre on the last night of his life. A stroke of luck and a fifty-page speech in just the right place spared Theodore Roosevelt's life as the former president was stumping to win another term; a display case contains the speech's first page, complete with bullet hole. Elsewhere on view is an object that may well be the Rough Rider's most cherished legacy: the teddy bear. An avid hunter, Roosevelt apparently inspired the creation of this children's toy when he refused to shoot a captured bear cub on a hunting trip.

Star piece of the various military-related collections is the oak gunboat **Philadelphia**, the oldest US man-of-war in existence. In 1776, in a campaign against the British on Lake Champlain, 63 men lived on this tiny ship for three months, suffering extraordinary privation – there was no upper or lower deck and only a canvas cover to protect them from the elements. Also on display near here is General Washington's linen tent, his campaign headquarters during the Revolutionary War, alongside his camp chest complete with tin plate and coffeepot. Adjacent "**Firearms**" is a romp through weapons from the colonial era to modern machine guns, after which you'd do best to cross to "**Armed Forces**," which combines model-ship displays and artillery pieces with a sympathetic look at the experiences of the American GI (named for their "Government Issue" gear) in World War II, from shipping out to homecoming.

Two final sections change the mood quickly and are the most moving parts of the whole museum. "**Personal Legacy: The Healing of a Nation**" brings together some of the 25,000 items left by relatives and friends at the Vietnam Veterans Memorial in DC (see p.56). These deeply personal mementoes tell of the strict human cost of a detached foreign policy: each child's letter, wedding band, dog tag or forage cap represents a host of other lives touched by the war.

After two decades, the Vietnam vets can stand up and recount their experiences without fear of rancor, but it took even longer to rehabilitate another group of Americans in the public's eye. Throughout the nineteenth century, racist laws were passed to restrict American citizenship for Asian immigrants, and there was little public opposition during World War II when Roosevelt agreed to the "evacuation" of Japanese-American citizens into "assembly centers" – basically concentration camps where people were interned solely on the basis of their race. FDR's Secretary of War, Henry L. Stimson, declared that "their racial characteristics are such that we cannot understand or even trust the citizen Japanese" – though no one ever suggested the containment of Italian- or German-Americans in the same period. "**A More Perfect Union**" deals with this shameful episode with commendable candor, pointing out for example that 25,000 Japanese-Americans served in the US forces, most of whom had family and friends in detention camps back home. Indeed, the largely Japanese 100th Infantry Battalion/42nd Regimental Combat Team was the most decorated military unit of its size at the end of the war. The displays contrast the dismal life in barracks at home with the valor of the combat units, who at the end of the war at least had their medals to prove their worth – the civilian Japanese-Americans, who had committed no crime other than to be born with the wrong "characteristics," got $25 and a ticket home.

National Museum of Natural History

10th St NW and Constitution Ave ☎357-2700, ⓦ www.nmnh.si.edu; Federal Triangle Metro. Daily: June–Aug 10am–6.30pm; Sept–May 10am–5.30pm. Admission free.

The imposing three-story entrance rotunda of the **National Museum of Natural History** feels like the busiest and most boisterous crossroads in all DC, with troops of screeching schoolkids chasing each other nonstop around a colossal African elephant. Hundreds of other stuffed animals, tracing evolution from fossilized four-billion-year-old plankton to dinosaurs' eggs and beyond, are displayed on all sides. It's one of the oldest of DC's museums, founded in 1911, with its early collection partly based on the specimens that the Smithsonian commissioned from the game-hunting Theodore Roosevelt on his African safaris of 1909–10. Roosevelt collected (ie shot) thousands, from lions and rhinos to gazelles and cheetahs, many of which are still on display.

You'll need to go early to avoid the worst of the crowds, especially in summer and during school holidays; pick up floor plans at the **information desk** at the elephant's feet, check on any **temporary exhibitions** and ask about the **free guided tours** (Mon–Fri at 10.30am and 1.30pm), which show you the highlights in around an hour. Schedules and information about the films at the museum's **IMAX theater** and programs at the multiscreened, interactive **Immersion Cinema** are also available at the desk. The soaring, glass-domed **Atrium Café** serves a variety of foods (10am–5pm) and offers live jazz on Friday evenings (5.30–10pm), along with a cash bar, buffet dinner and special IMAX screenings (call ☎633-7400 for schedule). There's also hands-on participation for children in the first-floor **Discovery Room** (Tues–Fri noon–2.30pm, Sat & Sun 10.30am–3.30pm): you need a free pass to get in (available at the door); arrive early at peak times, since the number of people admitted is limited.

The collection

Given that the museum owns more than 120 million specimens and artifacts, it can be forgiven for failing to exhibit some of them with sufficient gusto: there are only so many things you can do with a trayful of pinned butterflies and turning them into an attention-grabbing, interactive exhibit is not one of them. Much, then, is as you might imagine, with halls full of lifeless dioramas. To be fair, though, the museum has been breathing new life into its exhibits as a retooled triceratops and a new permanent exhibition exploring Africa's peoples and cultures attest. A new Mammals Hall is also in the works.

Naturally enough, the **Dinosaurs** section is the most popular part of the museum, with hulking skeletons reassembled in imaginative poses and accompanied by informative text, written with a light touch, accessible to children. The massive Diplodocus, the most imposing specimen, was discovered in Utah in 1923, at what is now Dinosaur National Monument. The museum's latest pride and joy, however, is the 65-million-year-old triceratops (lovingly dubbed "Hatcher"), which has returned in a more accurate form after a hi-tech face-lift. Stay in this section long enough to tour the related displays on the **Ice Age**, **Ancient Seas**, **Fossil Mammals** and **Fossil Plants** – each covering mollusks, lizards, giant turtles and early fish in exhaustive, engaging detail with the aid of diagrams, text and fossils.

Other highlights are upstairs on the second floor, where **Reptiles** and **Bones** give way to the splendid **Insect Zoo**, sponsored in a delicious irony by O. Orkin, the pest-control company. Here, many of the exhibits are actually alive, which may or may not be a recommendation. Behind screens – with notices pleading, unsuccessfully, "Please do not tap the glass" – are imprisoned tarantulas, roaches, crickets, bird-eating spiders, worms, termites, even a thriving bee colony. A member of staff with the most unenviable job in the world sits in one corner with assorted creepy-crawlies wandering up and down his arms; kids generally can't wait to grab a bug, while cowering adults try hard not to flinch. If you can stomach more of this sort of entertainment, stick around for one of the daily tarantula feedings (Tues–Fri 10.30am, 11.30am & 1.30pm, Sat & Sun 11.30am, 12.30pm & 1.30pm). Less scary insects are on display outside in the **Butterfly Garden**, on the 9th Street side of the museum building. There are wetland, wooded, meadow and urban habitats featuring – as the brochure has it – "plant-insect interaction"; it's on view at all times, though, as you might imagine, there's not much to see in the winter.

Since the museum's earliest days, "natural history" was deemed to embrace a broad remit, with the result that the museum's **Hall of Geology, Gems and Minerals**, also on the second floor, draws regular streams of wide-eyed visitors, many of whom would leave a little happier if they could only take home a few samples. Center of attention here are the astounding exhibits from the National Gem Collection, most importantly the legendary 45-carat **Hope Diamond**, once owned by Marie Antoinette – crowds also gather by a pair of her diamond earrings and a genuine crystal ball, the world's largest flawless quartz sphere, cut and polished in China in 1923. Farther on are explanations of matters as various as why diamonds sparkle to full investigations of related geological phenomena – from plate tectonics and meteors to earthquakes and volcanoes – culminating in the museum's extraordinary mineral collection. Scientists have identified around 4000 different minerals so far and it seems like every single one is represented here in glorious shape, texture and color. Hunt around and you'll even find an example of Smithsonite – a needle-like crystal mined for zinc – named after Smithsonian Institution benefactor James Smithson, who first recognized it as a distinct mineral. Before leaving the second floor, take a moment to puzzle over the rare **giant squid**; scientists don't know quite where it lives, but reckon it grows up to 50ft long. Also on hand is a second, smaller specimen, the taningia, another deep-sea squid, which possesses the largest light-producing organs of any known animal.

The museum has further to go before it deals successfully with its dated **ethnographical** collections; an early subtitle trumpeted it also as the "Museum of Man." There are moves to hive the ethnographical items off into their own museum, but for now entire galleries on the first and second floors continue to raise hackles with their 1950s-style attitudes and assumptions. Displays on "Native Cultures of the Americas" include the Lucayans, said to have "vanished" shortly after encountering Columbus, and static dioramas of the "primitive" pueblos of the Southwest stand alongside bison, bighorn sheep and other once-wild things. Occasionally, a token disclaimer notice, pointing out contemporaneous inaccuracies and prejudices, drags the exhibits into the late twentieth century. A few of the displays rise above the rest, however, such as that focusing on the Seminole native people of Florida, which portrays contemporary facets of tribal life, culture and activities alongside the museum's own historic objects. The way forward is perhaps shown by the much more imaginative "**African Voices**" exhibit on the opposite side of the first floor, where, bursting with colorful displays, films and funky Baaba Maal tunes, Africans from around the continent tell their stories in their own voices.

The Smithsonian Institution Building

1000 Jefferson Drive SW ☎357-2700 ⓦwww.si.edu; Smithsonian Metro. Daily 9.30am–5.30pm. Admission free.

Easily the most striking edifice on the Mall, the **Smithsonian Institution Building** resembles nothing so much as an English country seat, with its ruddy brown sandstone, nave windows and slender steeples – little surprise, then, that it's widely known as the **Smithsonian Castle**. It's the headquarters of the **Smithsonian Institution** (see p.60), an independent trust holding 140 million artifacts in sixteen museums (and one zoo), which, curiously, was endowed by an Englishman. **James Smithson**, gentleman scientist and illegitimate son of the first Duke of Northumberland, had never even visited the US and yet on his death in 1829 left half a million dollars "to found at Washington, under the name of the Smithsonian Institution, an establishment for the increase and diffusion of Knowledge" – provided, that is, his surviving nephew should die without an heir. Luckily for future generations he did (in 1835), though it took Congress until 1846 to decide, firstly, whether to accept the money and secondly, quite what establishment would fit the bill; John Quincy Adams, for one, favored an astronomical laboratory. In the end, the vote was for a multipurpose building that would encompass museum, art gallery and laboratory: the original Smithsonian Institution Building was duly completed in 1855.

For all its wealth, the **Smithsonian** had something of a shaky start, since it wasn't at all clear quite how it should diffuse the knowledge proposed by its benefactor. Even just a few years after its opening, the collections were too large and varied to be able to be displayed thematically in the Castle. Matters slowly improved under the stewardship of the Smithsonian's first Secretary, **Joseph Henry**, who tried to direct the institution primarily toward scientific research. Even the National Zoological Park had its origins here; a photograph inside shows buffalo grazing in the grounds in 1889.

As the Castle shed its collections and bequests to specific museums, it took up duty as the Smithsonian administrative headquarters and now houses the main **visitor center**, whose fine marble-pillared Great Hall offers a foretaste of the Smithsonian attractions. Here, too, are scale models of all the major city plans, from L'Enfant onwards; twenty-minute video shows highlighting the role of the institution; interactive touch-screen Smithsonian information displays and electronic wall maps. You can pick up the latest details on events at all the galleries at the information desk. The high-ceiling **Commons Restaurant**, a nineteenth-century beauty, may well be one of the nicest settings on the Mall to pause for a meal, but it's also likely the priciest, with buffet lunches (Mon–Sat 11am–2pm) running $14.95 (slightly less for a soup and salad) and a Sunday brunch (11am–3pm) that costs $24.95. Call ☎357-2957 for reservations.

Incidentally, Smithsonian founder James Smithson, who never visited America in life, found a place here in death: his ornate, Neoclassical **tomb** stands in an alcove just off the Mall entrance, placed here in 1904, 75 years after his death in Italy. In a neat counterpoint to the patent uncertainties of his life – which, not aware of his true parentage, he started as James Lewis Macie – the tomb records his age incorrectly, since he was 64 and not 75 when he died. Out on the Mall itself, in front of the entrance, the resplendent robed **statue** is not of Smithson, as you might suppose, but of first Smithsonian Secretary, Joseph Henry.

Capitol Hill

Everyone knows that Washington has a Capitol; but the misfortune is that the Capitol wants a city. There it stands, reminding you of a general without an army, only surrounded and followed by a parcel of ragged little dirty boys; for such is the appearance of the dirty, straggling, ill-built houses which lie at the foot of it.

Captain Frederick Marryat, 1839

Although there's more than one hill in Washington DC, when people talk about what's happening on "The Hill" they mean **CAPITOL HILL**, the shallow knoll at the eastern end of the Mall topped by the giant white dome of the US Capitol. Home of both the legislature – Congress – and the judiciary – the Supreme Court – city planner L'Enfant's "pedestal waiting for a monument" is still the place where the law of the land is made and refined.

Yet, as Marryat observed, the neighborhood faced a lengthy clamber to respectability. When L'Enfant and his surveyors first put pen to paper, the cross drawn on what was then Jenkins Hill was the focus of a grand, Baroque city plan. The **US Capitol** building was duly erected, and in 1800 Congress moved in. But this marshy outpost was slow to develop: it froze in the bitter winters and boiled in the harsh summers, and from their boarding houses around the Capitol legislators had to trudge the muddy length of Pennsylvania Avenue for an audience with the president in the White House. When the War of 1812 broke out, the British weren't exactly spoiled for targets in Washington, and the Capitol was the first to burn, prompting many at the time to suggest abandoning the city altogether and setting up somewhere more hospitable. Later, Marryat was only the first in a long line of critics to point out the incongruity of the splendid ideal of the Capitol building and its rather dismal surroundings – ironically, at the time of his visit the "dirty, straggling, ill-built houses" of Capitol Hill made up what was probably the most developed part of Washington.

However, as the capital and the federal government grew in stature, so did the Hill. Over the course of the nineteenth century appeared the rows of elegant townhouses that today form the keystone of Capitol Hill's status as a protect-

Eating, drinking and staying on Capitol Hill

For Capitol Hill listings, see the following pages: accommodation p.245; eating p.259; drinking and nightlife p.277.

ed historic district. One, the **Sewall–Belmont House**, is open to the public. Eventually the major federal institutions, housed since 1800 in the ever-expanding Capitol building, moved into homes of their own: first the **Library of Congress** in 1897, whose oldest building has been skillfully refurbished; then the **Supreme Court** in 1935, which – like all the Hill's federal institutions – remains open for public visits.

Today the federal buildings reach as far as the two C streets, on either side of the Capitol, and east to 2nd Street – for many, that is the extent of Capitol Hill. But beyond the buildings lie diverse residential neighborhoods, where politicians, aides, lawyers, lobbyists and even ordinary people live. The early stretches of **Pennsylvania Avenue**, around **Eastern Market**, provide a few distractions, not least of which is the market itself. **Lincoln Park**, with its memorial to the Great Emancipator, marks the eastern limit of the neighborhood, while to the north, the area around **Union Station** has been spruced up in the last decade or so.

The US Capitol

East end of the Mall, Capitol Hill ☎225-6827 for recorded tour information, ☎224-3121 general information, ⊛www.house.gov, www.senate.gov, www.aoc.gov; Capitol South or Union Station Metro, or Bus #30, #32, #34, #36 from Pennsylvania Ave. Daily: March–Aug 9am–6pm; Sept–Feb 9am–4.30pm. Admission free. Call ahead to check for changes in opening times and procedures.

It's not by chance that the dome of the **US Capitol** is visible from all over the city. Like the White House, it's both a workplace and a monument. This is where Congress – the nation's law-makers and tax-takers, made up of the **Senate** and the **House of Representatives** - meets. And it's from here that each president sets off on his inauguration parade, returning to give the annual State of the Union address. However, unlike the White House (where you get to see little more than museum-piece rooms), the US Capitol, with its grand halls and statues, committee rooms and ornate chambers, is one of the few places in the District where you get a tangible sense of the immense power wielded by the nation's elected officials.

Even if many visitors might be a touch too worldly to accept that the goings-on here truly represent democracy at work, the US Capitol has remained a powerful symbol for two centuries. As early as 1812, Thomas Jefferson was trumpeting it as "the first temple dedicated to the sovereignty of the people, embellishing with Athenian taste the course of a nation looking far beyond the range of Athenian destinies." The foot of the US Capitol has always been an obvious convergence point for **demonstrations**. In 1894, Jacob S. Coxey led an "army" of unemployed from Ohio and points west to demand a public works program; he was arrested for trespassing, and the few hundred men with him slunk off home. Unemployed soldiers set up camp outside the building after World War I, as did – fifty years later – the weary citizens of the Poor People's March of May 1968, whose makeshift tents and shelters they called "Resurrection City" (see p.55). More recently still, in 1995, Nation of Islam leader Louis Farrakhan harangued white America from the terrace steps while addressing the Million Man March. On occasion, the building itself has come **under attack**. Shots were first fired in the Capitol as early as 1835, while in

1915, 1971 and 1983 bombs were exploded by various aggrieved protestors, though no one was injured. The worst attack was in the summer of 1998, when a lone gunman stormed the building, killing two Capitol police officers and injuring several members of the public.

Yet, despite such attacks, modern security measures did not impinge upon the right of open access to the seat of government until terrorist strikes against New York and Washington put this tradition to the test in the fall of 2001. Anthrax mailed to Senate leader Tom Daschle – the first biological weapons attack on a government in history – heightened tensions on an already jittery Capitol Hill and forced the House to suspend its session for a week. Tours to the Capitol were canceled for several months, and many Hill staffers were left wondering when they could return to their offices, several of which were closed for decontamination. While it will likely be some time before a new balance between security and liberty is reached (as far as the public's access to government buildings goes), one can be fairly sure that the Capitol's open-door policy will be less freewheeling than in the past (see "Visiting the Capitol," p.101). When Congress is **in session** (every year, from January 3, as prescribed in the Constitution, until close of business, usually in the fall) the lantern above the dome is lit, and flags fly above Senate or House wings.

Some history

A chaste plan, sufficiently capacious and convenient for a period not too remote, but one to which we may reasonably look forward, would meet my idea in the Capitol.

George Washington, 1792

In the best democratic fashion, the **design** of the US Capitol was thrown open to public competition in 1792. It was won by a dabbling amateur, **Dr William Thornton**, whose plan, it was agreed, brought a certain pomp deemed appropriate for the meeting place of Congress. In particular, he dreamed up the domed rotunda, the feature that two centuries later grants the building its towering authority over the city skyline. The cornerstone was laid by George Washington on September 18, 1793, but by the time the government moved to the city from Philadelphia seven years later, work was nowhere near completion. Not only did President John Adams move into an unfinished White House (see p.135), but on November 22, 1800, Congress assembled for the first time in the half-built brick-and-sandstone Capitol, which still lacked its rotunda and most of its offices; only a small north wing was ready, housing the Senate Chamber, the House of Representatives, the Supreme Court and the Library of Congress. What ceilings there were leaked, and the furnaces installed to heat the building produced intolerable temperatures. Adams' successor, Jefferson (the first president to be inaugurated inside the Capitol), appointed the respected **Benjamin Latrobe** as Surveyor of Public Buildings in an attempt to speed up work, and by 1807 a south wing had been built for the House of Representatives. In addition, Latrobe added a second floor to the north wing, allowing separate chambers for the Supreme Court and the Senate.

In 1814 the Capitol suffered the same fate as the president's house, as British troops burned the seat of government virtually to the ground. Indeed, with President Madison having fled the city, it was touch and go whether Washington – never a hugely popular choice as capital – would again house executive and legislative arms of the government. But with Madison later installed in The Octagon (p.151), Congress met for four years in a quickly built "Brick Capitol" (see the box below) – on the site of today's Supreme Court.

The Brick Capitol

When the British marched into Washington in August 1814, they promptly burned down the Capitol and – in the words of Alistair Cooke – "the rest of the new public buildings that in those days were all that distinguished Washington from a fishing town on a marsh." It was a supreme humiliation, made more calamitous for the young republic in that it revived the often bitter debate about the suitability of Washington as the nation's capital. President Madison gave the Northern dissenters no chance to agitate: as well as returning to the city at the earliest opportunity, he also directed the building of a temporary **Brick Capitol** to forestall any talk of a move away from the city. Hastily designed by Benjamin Latrobe, it was erected on the site of today's Supreme Court – land then occupied by a tavern and vegetable allotment. Here, in 1817, Monroe became the first president to take the oath of office in an outdoor public ceremony in Washington. When the US Capitol was finally restored in 1819 and the government moved back in, the Brick Capitol became home to the Circuit Court of DC until the new City Hall was finished. From 1824 to 1861 the building was a lodging house, from 1861 until 1867 a prison, until finally it was replaced by three row houses – which were in turn demolished to make way for the Supreme Court in 1935.

Restoration work continued on what was left of the original Capitol. It wasn't much. Latrobe found the interior gutted and the surviving exterior walls blackened by smoke; the British soldiers, it seemed, had stacked up all the furniture they could find in one of the rooms and lit a bonfire. Commissioned to rebuild and expand the Capitol, Latrobe's rather grandiose ideas found few admirers, and in 1817 he was replaced by Charles Bulfinch. The reconstructed wings were reopened in 1819, and finally, in 1826, the Capitol appeared in a form that Thornton might have recognized, complete with central **rotunda**, topped by a low wooden dome wrapped in copper.

By the 1850s Congress had again run out of space and plans were laid to build magnificent, complementary wings on either side of the building and to replace the dome with something more substantial. The new south wing, ready in 1857, now contained the **House Chamber**; two years later, the **Senate Chamber** moved to the new north wing. The Civil War threatened to halt work on the dome, but Abraham Lincoln was determined that the Capitol should be completed, recognizing the building as an enduring symbol of the Union he was pledged to defend. A cast-iron **dome** was painstakingly assembled, though the work was hampered by the presence of Union troops stationed in the Capitol; a company made up of enlisted firefighters insisted on shinning up and down hundred-foot ropes draped from the Rotunda walls for amusement. But in December 1863 the splendid project came to fruition. Hoisted on top of the white-painted dome was a nineteen-foot-high **Statue of Freedom** by sculptor Thomas Crawford, resplendent in feathered helmet and clutching a sword and shield (which gives it its alternative name of "Armed Liberty").

Give or take a few minor additions, the US Capitol building today shows little external change from this last burst of construction. The surrounding **terraces** were added after the Civil War, and when extra office space was required in the last century, separate **House and Senate office buildings** were built in the streets on either side of the Capitol, with tunnels to connect the legislators with their places of work. The Capitol's East Front was extended in 1962 and faced in marble to prevent the original sandstone from deteriorating further; thus far, the West Front – now the oldest original part of the building – has avoided modern accretions, though it too was restored in the 1980s.

Visiting the Capitol

The Capitol is the only building in Washington DC without an address, since it stands foursquare at the center of the street plan: the city quadrants extend from the building, and the numbered and lettered streets count away from its central axis. For the same reason, the building doesn't have a front or a back, simply an "East Front" and a "West Front": the **public entrance** is at the East Front, where, from 1829 to 1977, all presidents were inaugurated.

Tours suspended in the fall of 2001 have since resumed on a limited basis, with no self-guided tours permitted; call ahead for an update at ☎225-6827. In the past, visitors could enjoy **free, walk-in access** all year to the Rotunda, Statuary Hall, the old Senate and Supreme Court chambers, and the Crypt. If you visit between April and September, expect to wait in line for maybe one or two hours; lines are much shorter (or nonexistent) in winter, and the place is generally less busy on Sundays and between noon and 1.30pm most other days. Once inside the Rotunda, you can join a **free guided tour** (every 15min 9am–4pm), though in the past there was nothing to stop you from wandering off on your own. That said, it's hard to find your way around, even with the information desks, signposts and the omnipresent Capitol police officers to keep you on the right track. Note that there's a split between the House side (to the south) and Senate side (north) inside the Capitol; for details on visiting the House and Senate chambers, see p.104. US citizens keen on climbing up to the dome can make arrangements through their representative or senator — this tour highlight is not available to walk-in visitors.

From Memorial Day to Labor Day, there are weekday evening brass band **concerts** on the east steps (Mon–Fri 8pm). And on those two holidays themselves, as well as July 4, the National Symphony Orchestra performs on the West Terrace.

The Rotunda and National Statuary Hall

Standing in the **Rotunda**, you're not only at the center of the US Capitol but at point zero of the entire city. It's a magnificent space: 180ft high and 96ft across, with the dome canopy decorated by Constantino Brumidi's mighty **fresco** depicting the *Apotheosis of Washington*. The painting took the 60-year-old Brumidi almost a year to complete – like the Renaissance masters, he was forced to work lying on his back in a wooden cradle – and shows George Washington surrounded by symbols representing American democracy, arts, science, industry, and the thirteen original states; though they look life-size from the floor, each of the figures is 15ft high. Brumidi had a hand, too, in the **frieze** celebrating American history that runs around the Rotunda wall, which starts with Columbus' arrival in the New World and continues (clockwise) through the ages, finishing with Civil War scenes.

From the floor, it's hard to see much detail of either frieze or fresco, and eyes are drawn instead to the eight large **oil paintings** that hang below the frieze. Four depict events associated with the "discovery" and settlement of the country – Columbus again, and the embarkation of the Pilgrims among them – though the most notable are the four of the Revolutionary War period by John Trumbull, who trained under the celebrated Benjamin West. George Washington is represented with a fair accuracy, and so he should be, since Trumbull once served as his aide-de-camp.

Consciously or not, William Thornton, the Capitol's first architect, took Rome's Pantheon as his model, and it's fitting that busts and statues of prominent American leaders fill in the gaps in the rest of the Rotunda. Washington, Jefferson, Lincoln and Jackson are all here, along with a modern bust of Dr Martin Luther King Jr and a gold-and-glass facsimile of the Magna Carta (the original was loaned to the Capitol during the 1976 Bicentennial). In such august surroundings, 29 prominent members of Congress, military leaders and eminent citizens (including nine presidents from Lincoln to Johnson) have been **laid in state** before burial; the most recently honored were the two Capitol police officers slain in the July 1998 gun attack.

From the Rotunda, you move south into one of the earliest extensions of the building, the section that once housed the chamber of the House of Representatives. The acoustics are such that, from his desk, John Quincy Adams was supposed to have been able to eavesdrop on opposition members on the other side of the room – something that is invariably demonstrated on the tour. When the House moved into its new wing in 1857, the chamber saw a variety of temporary uses – Anthony Trollope bought gingerbread from a market stall in here – until Congress decided to invite each state to contribute two statues of its most famous citizens for display in a **National Statuary Hall**. Around forty are still on show in the hall, with the others scattered around the corridors in the rest of the building; few are of any great distinction. That of suffragist Susan B. Anthony (one of just six statues of women in the entire building) was recently dusted off after years hidden in the Crypt to be placed in the Rotunda – Anthony is the only woman so honored.

The Old Senate Chamber, Supreme Court and the Crypt

North of the Rotunda, there's access to the **Old Senate Chamber**, built in 1810 and reconstructed from 1815 to 1819 after the British had done their worst. The Senate met in this splendid semicircular gallery, with its embossed rose ceiling, until 1859, when it moved into its current quarters. The chamber then housed the Supreme Court (see p.106) until 1935, when it, too, was given a new building. After that the Old Senate Chamber lay largely unused until restored to its mid-nineteenth-century glory in time for the Bicentennial. Its furnishings are redolent of that period, during which the Senate's membership increased from 46 to 64 (two senators for each state) in step with the number of states admitted to the Union. In its heyday, the chamber made a formidable impression upon visitors, like Anthony's pioneering mother, Fanny Trollope, whose travelog, *Domestic Manners of the Americans*, published in 1832, amused Europe but outraged America with its forthright observations. Sorely unimpressed with the goings-on in the House chamber, whose representatives were "sitting in the most unseemly attitudes, a large majority with their hats on," she was considerably more taken with the Senate, or at least the senators, who "generally speaking, look like gentlemen . . . and the activity of youth being happily past, they do not toss their heels above their heads." The members' desks today are reproductions, but the gilt eagle topping the vice president's chair is original, as is the portrait of George Washington by Rembrandt Peale.

Contemporary engravings helped restorers reproduce other features of the original Senate chamber, like the rich red carpet emblazoned with gold stars. As Charles Dickens noted when he visited, the original carpet received severe punishment from "tobacco-tinctured saliva" despite the provision of a cuspidor by every desk – the universal disregard of which led to "extraordinary improvements on the pattern which are squirted and dabbled upon it in every direction." If visitors dropped anything on the floor, they were enjoined "not to pick it up with an ungloved hand on any account." Yet, doubtless squelching underfoot as they stood to speak, members of this Senate chamber participated in some of the most celebrated debates of the era: in 1830 the great orator Daniel Webster of Massachusetts fiercely defended "Liberty and the Union" in a famous speech lasting several hours; over two days in 1850 Henry Clay pleaded his succession of compromises to preserve the Union (brandishing a fragment of Washington's coffin for emphasis); while in 1856, Senator Charles Sumner of Massachusetts – having, unwisely perhaps, talked too forthrightly against the Kansas-Nebraska Bill (extending slavery, which Sumner branded a "harlot," into the Great Plains) – was beaten senseless at his desk by an incensed congressman from South Carolina.

Before 1810, the Senate met on the floor below the Old Senate Chamber, in a room that architect Latrobe later revamped to house the Supreme Court. This sorely needed a permanent home: while the work was being carried out, Supreme Court sessions were often held in an inn opposite the Capitol, and once the British had delayed matters by burning the rest of the building, the nation's highest tribunal was forced to meet in rented townhouses on the Hill. However, by 1819 the Court was in residence in this chamber, where it remained until 1860, before moving again – confusingly, upstairs, to the chamber just vacated by the Senate. The **Old Supreme Court Chamber** served as a law library until 1950, after which it too was restored to its mid-nineteenth-century appearance. Its dark, comfortable recesses resemble a gentleman's club – which, in many ways, it was. Again, some of the furnishings are original, including the desks, tables and chairs, and the busts of the first five chief justices.

Having viewed the historic chambers, spare a moment for the **Crypt**, on the same level as the Old Supreme Court Chamber, underneath the Rotunda. Lined with Doric columns, it was designed to house a tomb containing George Washington's body, a plan that was never realized; he's buried with his wife, Martha, at Mount Vernon. The Crypt instead serves as an exhibition center, displaying details of the plans submitted for the 1792 architectural competition and snippets about the Capitol's construction.

The House and Senate chambers and office buildings

To gain entrance to the **visitors' galleries** of either the House or the Senate, **American citizens** must apply to their representative's or senator's office in advance for a pass valid for the entire (two-year) session of Congress. **Foreign citizens** need to present their passport either at the House or Senate appointments desk, both on the first floor; they'll be given a day pass for either body. As visiting procedures were in the process of being reviewed after the events of September 11, 2001, call ☎225-6827 for an update. To find out where a particular office or desk is, ask any Capitol police officer, or call Capitol **information** (☎224-3121), the House sergeant-at-arms (☎225-2456) or the Senate sergeant-at-arms (☎224-2341).

The **House and Senate chambers** may well be empty, or deep in torpor, when you show up, which is fine if all you want is a flavor of either place. Both chambers are suitably grand, and if you've already glimpsed the Old Senate Chamber you'll know what to expect. The **House chamber** is the most imposing, with its decorative frieze and oil paintings; from here the president addresses joint sessions of Congress, including making the annual State of the Union speech. If you're lucky, you may watch members introducing legislation or even voting on various bills or issues (or at least hear the bells and see the flashing lights summoning the members to vote). The **Senate chamber** is a little more widely recognized these days, as it was the setting for the final chapter of the impeachment trial of President Clinton.

Generally, most of the day-to-day fun and fireworks take place in committee rooms either in the Capitol or in the **House and Senate office buildings** on each side. The first of these six office buildings – named for past politicians – were built in 1908–09, the last in 1982, and they now house regular committee hearings, which have been open to the public since the 1970s. The buildings also contain the public and private offices of most representatives and senators. These follow the pattern of the Capitol in that the Senate office buildings (Russell, Dirksen and Hart) are to the north, the House office buildings (Cannon, Longworth and Rayburn) to the south: to reach them from the Capitol, head for the basement and ride the **Capitol subway** to the Senate offices or follow the pedestrian tunnels to the House offices. **Committee hearings** (usually held in the morning) are listed in the *Washington Post*'s "Today in Congress" section: unless you turn up early, you may not get in, especially to anything currently featured on the TV news.

Only in the Senate **Hart Building**, on Constitution Avenue NE at 2nd Street, is there anything to look at: dominating the atrium is Alexander Calder's monumental *Mountains and Clouds*. This was the artist's last work – and the only one to combine a separate mobile and stabile. In late 2001, the Hart Building attracted the public's attention for reasons more ominous than its artwork when an aide to Senate Majority Leader Tom Daschle opened a letter filled with anthrax spores. The building was closed for weeks as Environmental Protection Agency technicians fumigated the site – where more than half of the country's senators have offices – in an attempt to eradicate the lethal spores. It was too late, however, to spare the lives of the two District postal workers who died as a result of the bioterrorist attack.

In the past, there were security checkpoints at the street-level entrances to the Hart Building, but visitors were free to pass through to see the sculpture.

West of the Capitol

Although, technically, the Capitol has no front (or at least no back), the **West Front** facade – facing the Mall – gets most photo calls, and from the terrace steps the views down the Mall to the Washington Monument are rightly lauded. Presidential **inauguration ceremonies** have taken place in the plaza here since 1981; before that, they were consigned to the more confined space at the East Front.

Two low-key memorials – to Peace and to assassinated twentieth president James Garfield (shot only four months after his inauguration) – flank the **Capitol Reflecting Pool**, added in 1970, a stretch of water which mirrors in style that in front of the Lincoln Memorial, more than a mile away. But the most significant structure here is the 250-foot-long **Grant Memorial**, a group statue honoring **Ulysses S. Grant**, general-in-chief of the Union forces under President Lincoln (and the first since George Washington to hold the rank). Dedicated in 1922, it's an overbearing martial monument depicting a somber Grant on horseback, facing the Mall, guarded by lions and overseeing an artillery unit moving through thick mud into battle (south side) and a charging cavalry unit (north side). Sculptor Henry Merwin Shrady spent twenty years on the work, using uniformed soldiers in training as his models. The memorial is suitably single-tracked about Grant's achievements, focusing on his career as a soldier (as which he was formidable) rather than as twice-elected president (in which capacity he was undistinguished, verging on the corrupt; in the late nineteenth century, "Grantism" became a term synonymous with graft). In waging total war on the Confederate forces from 1864 to 1865, Grant secured final victory for Lincoln and the preservation of the Union, albeit at the cost of thousands of lives. Contemporaries talked of his personal short-comings (he was once described as "an ordinary scrubby-looking man with a slightly seedy look") and of his drinking habits (only Mrs Grant could keep him in check, and when the general went on a drinking bout too far, his aides would summon her to the front to sober him up). But Lincoln knocked back all complaints, recognizing his incalculable military worth: "You just tell me the brand of whiskey Grant drinks," thundered the President, "I would like to send a barrel of it to my other generals."

South of the Reflecting Pool, there's quiet relief in the **United States Botanic Garden**, 100 Maryland Ave SW at Independence Ave (daily 10am–5pm; free; ☎225-8333). Consisting primarily of a Conservatory crowned by the eighty-foot-tall Palm House, the garden recently reopened after a four-year renovation transformed the Victorian-style structure, built in 1933, into a state-of-the-art glasshouse. It's now possible to grow plants from almost everywhere in the world here. With 4000 plants now on display, the garden is a welcome retreat once you've maxed out on museums; wander around the colorful ranks of tropical, subtropical and desert plants or catch one of the popular tours (call for times).

While the garden's roots can be traced to early proponents such as George Washington and Thomas Jefferson, it was the 1838–42 expedition to the South Seas led by Lt Charles Wilkes that really got things going. The irascible Wilkes, said to be the model for the Captain Ahab character in Herman Melville's sea-faring epic *Moby Dick*, returned to America after four years and nearly 90,000 miles with a collection of ten thousand plants from around the world. These specimens formed the core of a revitalized garden — in fact, a cycad dating back to Wilkes' journey is still on view. On the Conservatory's western flank, construction on the new three-acre **National Garden**, which will feature a Rose Garden and a Water Garden as well as provide a showcase for plants native to the mid-Atlantic region, is scheduled for completion in mid-2004.

Across Independence Avenue, there's also a small demonstration garden on display next to the **Bartholdi Fountain** (at 1st St SW), a thirty-foot-high marine-style work by French sculptor Frédéric Auguste Bartholdi, who submitted it to the Centennial Exhibition in Philadelphia in 1876. There's no hint here that Bartholdi would go on to create, just a decade later, one of America's most enduring icons, the Statue of Liberty. Congress bought the fountain in 1877 for display on the Mall (it moved to this site in 1932), where its original gas lamps – illuminated at night – became a popular evening diversion.

If you walk north of the Reflecting Pool, toward Union Station, you'll pass through the small park bordered by Constitution and Louisiana avenues, site of the **Robert A. Taft Memorial**, a statue and sixty-foot-high, rectangular concrete bell tower erected in 1958 to commemorate the veteran Republican senator son of President William Howard Taft.

East of the Capitol

All the other notable buildings and institutions of Capitol Hill – like the Supreme Court and the Library of Congress – lie on the east side of the Capitol, within half a dozen blocks of each other. Unlike the Capitol, you have to choose your day to tour these places: the Supreme Court is closed on weekends, while other buildings are closed on all or part of Sunday.

The Supreme Court

1st St and Maryland Ave NE ☏479-3211, ⓦwww.supremecourtus.gov; Union Station or Capitol South Metro. Mon–Fri 9am–4.30pm. Admission free.

First stop after the Capitol for most visitors is the pseudo-Greek marble temple that houses the **Supreme Court of the United States**, the nation's final arbiter of what is and isn't legal. Since it was established at the Philadelphia Constitutional Convention of 1787, the Court has functioned as both the guardian and interpreter of the Constitution, flexing its muscular, judicial arm of government in favor of "Equal Justice For All" – the legend inscribed upon the architrave above the double row of eight columns facing 1st Street.

Oddly, for such a crucial pin in the American political system, the Supreme Court was forced to share quarters in the US Capitol until 1935, when on the prompting of William Howard Taft (then Chief Justice and formerly president – the only man to hold both offices) it was finally granted its own building.

△ The Conservatory and assorted flora at the US Botanic Garden

The architect, **Cass Gilbert**, 70 years old at the time, was perhaps an odd choice, known primarily for his tongue-in-cheek Gothic Woolworth Building in New York. But in Washington he behaved himself, creating in the Supreme Court – completed after his death – a work of dazzling Corinthian harmony. So well did it fit with the spirit of the age that Cass was unnerved by the compliments bestowed upon him – "It is receiving so much favorable praise [he wrote in 1933] that I am wondering what is wrong with it."

The answer is: absolutely nothing. Outside, the building positively glistens as natural light bounces back off the bright white marble, while the wide steps down to 1st Street are flanked by **sculptures** (by James Earle Fraser) of the Contemplation of Justice and the Guardian of Law. Solemn, if not pompous, their effect is lightened somewhat when you cast your eyes up to the sculpted **pediment** over the main entrance; here, among allegorical Greek figures, are relaxed representations of chief justices Taft (far left, portrayed as a Yale student)

The functioning of the Supreme Court

The duties of the Supreme Court are the simplest and best defined of any part of government. The Supreme Court justices have to do nothing but sit and let others make ugly fools of themselves in front of the Supreme Court bench.

P.J. O'Rourke, *Parliament of Whores*

The Constitution established the Supreme Court in an attempt to oversee the balance between the federal government and the states, and between the legislature and the executive; the Court itself (and the associated system of district courts) convened for the first time in February 1790. At the end of the following year, the ratification of the Bill of Rights in effect gave the Supreme Court an additional role – it was to defend the liberties enshrined in the Bill, directing the country as to what was and wasn't constitutional. However, it wasn't until 1803 and the case of *Marbury v Madison* that the Court's power of judicial review – the ability to declare a law or action of Congress or the president unconstitutional – was established. Since then, the Supreme Court has repeatedly directed the country's political debate by ruling on the constitutionality of subjects as diverse as slavery (as in the 1857 *Dred Scott* case), civil rights (1954 *Brown v Board of Education*, which outlawed school segregation), abortion (*Roe v Wade* in 1973) and political freedom (Pentagon papers and Watergate tapes cases in the early 1970s).

Because of the vagueness of parts of the Constitution, and the fact that the country relies on an eighteenth-century document as the basis of its twentieth-century political structure, the Supreme Court has its work cut out providing interpretive rulings. In practice, as O'Rourke points out, this leads to a great deal of arguing in front of the Supreme Court justices. That said, even though it's the country's final court of appeal, the Supreme Court takes only about five percent of the seven thousand cases a year it's asked to hear by lower courts. (Which ones is determined by the so-called "Rule of Four" – the agreement of four justices to hear a case.) These it grants *certiorari* – the prospect of making a case "more certain" – and then proceeds to hear written and oral arguments. After the deliberations, one justice is made responsible for writing the opinion, which then forms the latest interpretation of that particular constitutional issue. The justices don't all have to agree: they can concur in the majority decision even if they don't accept all the arguments; or they can produce a dissenting opinion, which might be cited in future challenges to particular laws.

Contributing to these opinions are nine judges, or justices, who are appointed by the president, though their positions have to be ratified by the Senate. One is named and Marshall (far right, reclining), while clad in togas are Gilbert (third from left) and sculptor Robert Aitken (second from right).

Inside, the main corridor – known as the **Great Hall** – features a superb carved and painted ceiling of floral plaques, while its echoing white walls are lined with marble columns, interspersed with busts of all the former chief justices. At the end of the corridor is the surprisingly compact **Court Chamber**, flanked by more marble columns and decorated with damask drapes and a molded plaster ceiling picked out in gold leaf. A frieze runs around all four sides, its relief panels depicting various legal themes, more allegorical figures and lawgivers ancient and modern. When in session, the Chief Justice sits in the center of the **bench** (below the clock), with the most senior justice on his right and the next in precedence on his left; the rest sit in similar alternating fashion so that the most junior justice sits on the far right (left as you face the bench); almost interestingly, the chairs for each justice are made in the Court's own carpentry shop.

Chief Justice, though the position is not necessarily reserved for the most senior figure on the bench (or even for a justice already on the Supreme Court – a Chief Justice can be appointed from outside). Once appointed, they're in for life ("during good behavior" as the Constitution has it) and can only be removed by impeachment. And, at $160,000 a year ($170,000 for the chief), the justices are pulling in a federal salary second only to the president's.

Given the system, it's obvious that the makeup of the Supreme Court is of the utmost relevance to the opinions it might produce. Not surprisingly, presidents down the years have thought it useful to have politically sympathetic justices on the bench and have made appointments accordingly. But the process is tinged with an element of luck, depending on the longevity of the existing incumbents: both Dwight D. Eisenhower and Richard Nixon, for example, got to appoint four justices, Jimmy Carter none. Controversial Supreme Court nominees can be rejected by the Senate – two of Nixon's were, as was Reagan's pet conservative judge, Robert Bork; Bush's second appointee, Clarence Thomas, only scraped through after the highly publicized hearings following allegations of sexual harassment against Anita Hill. And even when presidents do get the justices they want, they don't always want what they get: Earl Warren, appointed by the staunchly conservative Eisenhower, turned out to head the most liberal Court of the last century, his interpretation of the constitutional definition of "civil rights" aiding presidents Kennedy and Johnson in their radical domestic program. Despite the fact that seven out of the nine justices were Republican appointees, the current Court has proved to be more moderate than one might expect. (Concerns over the justices' political stripes were raised when the Court brought the controversial 2000 presidential election to a conclusion.)

Whichever way the Court leans, and despite its firm roots in the Constitution, it depends ultimately on the mood of the people for its authority. If it produces opinions that are overwhelmingly opposed by inferior courts, or by the president or Congress, there's not much it can do to enforce them. Indeed, Congress actually has the constitutional right (Article 3, Section 2) to restrict the Court's jurisdiction – a notion proposed by FDR when he tired of the Court's constant interference with his New Deal legislation. Strangely perhaps, and virtually unique among federal institutions, the Court has retained the respect of most of the population, not necessarily for the decisions of its justices (which are often viewed as confused or conflicting) but for its perceived impartiality in defending the Constitution against encroachment by that most hated of species: the politicians.

Visiting the Supreme Court

The Court is **in session** from October through June. Between the beginning of October and the end of April, oral arguments are heard every Monday, Tuesday and Wednesday from 10am to noon and 1pm to 3pm for two weeks each month. The cases to be heard are listed in the day's *Washington Post* (or call the Supreme Court for information), and the sessions, which last one hour per case, are open to the public on a first-come, first-served basis. They are rarely particularly illuminating for lay persons, but if you really want to witness an entire session you'll need to arrive by 8.30am to be sure of getting one of the 150 seats. Most casual visitors simply join the separate line, happy to settle for a three-minute stroll through the standing gallery. On Mondays in May and June, fifteen- to thirty-minute public sessions deal with the rather less interesting reading of orders and opinions. When Court is not in session, guides give informative **lectures** in the Court Chamber (Mon–Fri 9.30am–3.30pm; hourly on the half-hour).

On the **ground floor**, which has its own Great Hall overseen by a mighty statue of Chief Justice John Marshall lounging in his chair, there's a permanent **exhibition** about the Court: a free, short movie fills you in on the political and legal background while architectural notes, sketches and photos trace the history of the building itself. You'll also find restrooms, a gift shop, a snack bar (10.30am–3.30pm) and a cafeteria (7.30–10.30am & 11.30am–2pm) on this level.

Sewall-Belmont House

144 Constitution Ave NE ☎546-1210, ⦿www.natwomanparty.org; Union Station Metro. Tues–Fri 11am–3pm, Sat noon–4pm. Suggested donation $3.

North of the Supreme Court, across Constitution Avenue at 2nd Street, the red-brick townhouse known as the **Sewall–Belmont House** is among the oldest private residences in the city. Overwhelmed by the surrounding Senate Office monoliths, the dainty building dates back, in part, an astonishing – for Washington – 300 years. However, like most of historical Capitol Hill its aspect is firmly early nineteenth century, dating from the restructuring carried out in 1800 by its owner Robert Sewall. The house's next owner was Albert Gallatin, Secretary of the Treasury under Jefferson. Gallatin took part in the negotiations for the Louisiana Purchase (1803), which was signed in one of the front rooms – and which, acquiring all land west of the Mississippi to the Rockies, at a stroke roughly doubled the size of the country for a mere $12 million. In 1814, while the Capitol was burning, a group of soldiers under Commander Joshua Barney retreated to the house and fired upon the British. It was virtually the sole act of resistance in Washington itself, but only stirred the British to have a go at setting the house ablaze too. Unlike the Capitol, it wasn't too badly damaged; enough survived, in fact, for Gallatin to negotiate the Treaty of Ghent – which ended the war – here. The treaty was signed, however, in The Octagon (see p.151).

In 1929, the house was sold to the **National Woman's Party** and was home for many years to Alice Paul, the party's founder and author of the 1923 Equal Rights Amendment. The house is still the party headquarters, and maintains a museum and gallery dedicated to the country's women's and suffrage movements. A short film fills in some of the background, and then you'll be escorted around on a short tour that makes much of the period furnishings; the carriage house, one of the oldest parts of the building, contains the country's earliest feminist library. There are portraits, busts and photographs of all the best-known activists, starting in the lobby with suffragist sculptor Adelaide Johnson's formidable busts of Susan B. Anthony, Elizabeth Cady Stanton,

Lucretia Mott and Alice Paul. Other mementoes of the famous include the desks of both Alice Paul and Susan B. Anthony, while over the staircase hangs the banner used to picket the White House during World War I as the clamor for universal suffrage reached its loudest pitch. The women jailed for protesting were later presented with "jail-house pins" by Alice Paul – the one mounted on the wall here once belonged to Betsey Graves Reyneau.

Folger Shakespeare Library

201 E Capitol St SE ☏544-7077, ⊛www.folger.edu; Union Station or Capitol South Metro. Mon–Sat 10am–4pm. Admission free.

On the south side of the Supreme Court, the renowned **Folger Shakespeare Library** provides an unexpected burst of Art Deco architecture, with a sparkling white marble facade split by geometric window grilles and panel reliefs depicting scenes from the Bard's plays. Inside, however, the expansive 1930s mood is immediately transformed by a dark oak-paneled Elizabethan Great Hall, featuring carved lintels, stained glass, Tudor roses and a fine, sculpted ceiling. Founded in 1932, the Folger now holds more than 300,000 books, manuscripts, paintings and engravings, accessible to scholars, and has also evolved over the decades into a celebration of Shakespeareana. The Great Hall displays changing exhibitions about the playwright and Elizabethan themes; the reproduction Elizabethan Theater hosts lectures and readings as well as medieval and Renaissance music concerts by the Folger Consort (see p.289); there's even an Elizabethan garden outside on the east lawn, growing herbs and flowers common in gardens of the sixteenth century.

For more background, plan your visit to coincide with one of the free ninety-minute **guided tours** (Mon–Fri 11am, Sat 11am & 1pm); every third Saturday, from April through October, a guide also expounds upon the intricacies of the garden. You should be able to take a quick look inside the theater on most days; the library itself – another masterfully reproduced sixteenth-century room – is open to the public only during the Folger's annual celebration of Shakespeare's birthday (usually the Saturday nearest April 23). Finally, as you'd expect, the **gift shop** sells everything from the Stratford lad's books to jokey T-shirts based on Shakespearean quotations, Elizabethan garden seeds, prints and postcards.

The Library of Congress

Jefferson Building, 10 1st St SE; Madison Building, 101 Independence Ave SE ☏707-8000, ⊛www.loc.gov; Capitol South Metro. Mon–Sat 10am–5.30pm. Admission free.

With Congress established in Washington in 1800 in its new, if incomplete, Capitol building, it was considered imperative to fund a library for the use of the members. Five thousand dollars was made available to buy books for a **Library of Congress**, which was housed in a small room in the original north wing. Calamitously, the carefully chosen reference works were all lost when the British burned the Capitol in 1814, an act that prompted Thomas Jefferson to offer his considerable personal library as a replacement. This was no empty gesture – at his retirement home at Monticello Jefferson was surrounded by more than six thousand volumes, which he had accumulated during fifty years of service at home and abroad, picking up, he said, "everything which related to America." But neither was it an act of selfless charity: Jefferson's extravagant lifestyle always left him short of money, so he was doubtless delighted when, in 1815, Congress voted to buy this stupendous private collection for almost $24,000, a massive sum at the time.

Jefferson's sale laid the foundation for a well-rounded collection, but another fire in 1851, this time accidental, caused severe damage. From that point, the library was forced to rely on donations and select purchases until it received two major boosts. In 1866, it acquired the thousands of books hitherto held by the Smithsonian Institution, and in 1870 it was declared the national copyright library – adding to its shelves a copy of every book published and registered in the United States. Almost overnight, the Library of Congress was transformed into the world's largest library, and with time and technological progress books became the least part of its unimaginably large collection. Today, 110 million items (from books, maps and manuscripts to movies, musical instruments and photographs) are kept on 600 miles of shelving; it's said that on average ten items a minute are added to the library's holdings.

Hardly surprisingly, the library soon outgrew its original home, and in 1897 the exuberantly eclectic **Thomas Jefferson Building** opened across from the Capitol, complete with domed octagonal Reading Room and adorned with hundreds of mosaics, murals and sculptures. This was projected to have enough space to house the library until 1975, but by the 1930s it, too, was full, and in the surrounding blocks the **John Adams Building** was erected in 1939, followed by the **James Madison Memorial Building** in 1980. These three buildings today comprise the Library of Congress, which is open to the public as readers, researchers or visitors.

Visiting the library

Visitors are directed toward the magnificent **Jefferson Building**, whose visitor center (ground-level entrance on 1st St SE) can point you to the library highlights and give you a calendar of events detailing forthcoming concerts and lectures. You're free to wander around inside, but you'd do well to catch one of the free library **tours** (Mon–Sat 10.30am, 11.30am, 1.30pm, 2.30pm & 3.30pm; last tour Saturday is at 2.30pm) or catch the continuously running twelve-minute **film** on the history of the library. Taking the buildings of the Italian Renaissance as their model, the Jefferson Building architects John L. Smithmeyer and Paul J. Pelz produced a peach, centered on a domed Reading Room and flaunting a **Great Hall** that, after a decade of restoration, is again looking its best: marble walls and floors that were once blackened by the smoke from coal fires and the cinders from Union Station are now pristine, with the medallions, inscriptions, murals and inlaid mosaics as clear as the day they were fashioned. A treasured copy of the **Gutenberg Bible** is on display, while upstairs the visitor's gallery overlooks the octagonal marble-and-stained-glass **Main Reading Room**, a beautiful galleried space whose columns support a dome 125ft high. The mural in the dome canopy, the *Progress of Civilization*, represents the twelve nations supposed to have contributed most to world knowledge.

The library's huge collection is showcased on the second floor in the "**American Treasures**" gallery, where themed cabinets – "Civil Society," "Mapping," "Invention and Film," "Technology," and so on – display some of the nation's most significant documents. The exhibits are periodically rotated, but you'll encounter such diverse pieces as Walt Whitman's Civil War notebooks, the original typescript of Martin Luther King Jr's "I have a dream" speech, a copy of Francis Scott Key's "Star-Spangled Banner" and a multitude of music scores, historic photographs, early recordings, magazines and baseball cards. Changing exhibitions of especially significant documents, such as those associated with Washington, Lincoln and Jefferson, receive central billing (and are shown in an environmentally-controlled cabinet). Other exhibit areas are downstairs on the ground floor, where a **Gershwin Room** preserves George's Steinway and Ira's typing table and typewriter, and the **Swann Gallery** puts on temporary shows extracted from the library's unrivaled collection of American caricature and cartoon art.

There's no real need to walk over to the massive marble **Madison Building** (Independence Ave between 1st and 2nd), though there is an information desk in the lobby, an exhibition about the **Copyright Office** on the fourth floor, a **snack bar** on the ground floor and, on the sixth floor, a **cafeteria** (Mon–Fri 9–10.30am & 12.30–3pm) with river views.

Using the library

Anyone over high-school age carrying photo ID can **use the library**, and some one million readers and visitors do so each year. To find out what's where, head for the information desks or touch-screen computers in the Jefferson or Madison buildings. The Main Reading Room in the Jefferson Building is just one of 22 reading rooms, and the rules are the same in each. It's a research library, which means you can't take books out; in some reading rooms you have to order what you want from the stacks. You can also access papers, maps and musical scores, and the advent of the **National Digital Library** means that many now come in machine-readable format – the desks in the Main Reading Room are wired for laptops and there are CD-ROM indexes. Major exhibitions, as well as prints, photographs, films and speeches, are also available online. To check out the Library of Congress online, access Ⓦwww.loc.gov. For research advice, call ☏707-6500; for reading room hours and locations, call ☏707-6400.

Union Station and around

At Capitol Hill's northern limit, **Union Station** stands at the center of a re-development plan designed to revitalize a formerly neglected part of the city. In addition to the station, a sight in its own right, you should try to make time for the Smithsonian's **National Postal Museum**, located just opposite. Those looking for a day away from the monuments also might want to pay a visit to the **National Arboretum**; although not in Capitol Hill, the grounds are a short ride away via a direct shuttle from Union Station.

Union Station

The city's main railroad station, **Union Station**, at 50 Massachusetts Avenue NE, was built here in 1908 after the McMillan Commission decreed an end to the chaos caused by the separate lines and stations that crisscrossed the city. Its architect, Daniel H. Burnham, a member of the commission, produced a classic Beaux Arts building of monumental proportions to house the train sheds and waiting rooms, alive with skylights, marble detail and statuary, culminating in a 96-foot-high coffered ceiling covered in gold leaf. The model was no less than the Baths of Diocletian, the relaxation spot of the militarily bold and resolute third-century Roman emperor; the immense main waiting room is certainly imperial in scale if not in bathing appointments. For five decades, Union

Union Station amenities and services

For Union Station listings, see the following pages: accommodation p.250; cafés and restaurants p.272; nightlife p.281. For Union Station services, see: arrivals p.23; car rental agencies p.14; departures p.23.

Station sat at the head of an expanding railroad network that linked the country to its capital: hundreds of thousands of people arrived in the city by train, catching their first glimpse of the Capitol dome through the station's great arched doors – just as the wide-eyed James Stewart does at the beginning of Frank Capra's *Mr Smith Goes to Washington*. Incoming presidents arrived at Union Station by train for their inaugurations (Truman was the last) and were met in the specially installed Presidential Waiting Room; some, like FDR and Eisenhower, left in a casket after lying in state at the Capitol.

Come the 1960s, though, and with the gradual depletion of train services, Union Station was left unkempt and underfunded. An ill-conceived scheme turned it into a visitor's center during the Bicentennial in 1976, and it wasn't fully **restored** until 1988. The exterior is of a piece with much of monumental Washington, the facade studded with allegorical statuary and etched with prolix texts extolling the virtues of trade, travel and technology. Enter through the main, triple-arched portico and you're immediately confronted by the soaring vastness of its dimensions – the only other single-roofed space in America to touch it is New York's Grand Central Terminal, which is some 20,000 square feet smaller.

Although you can still catch **trains** at Union Station – there's a Metro station on the east side of the building as well as Amtrak and MARC departures – the renovation project wouldn't have succeeded without its commercial adjuncts: the lower-gallery food court and movie theater, and upper-floor stores, restaurants, money-exchange offices, car rental agencies, ticket counters and parking garage. Take a look at the statue near Gate D honoring **A. Phillip Randolph**, founder of the Brotherhood of Sleeping Car Porters union and one of the prime movers in the 1963 March on Washington for Jobs and Freedom.

It's also worth taking a turn outside in **Union Station Plaza**, the landscaped approach to the station that stretches all the way down to the Capitol grounds. In the middle, slam-bang in front of the station (and destroying the sight lines to the Capitol), the **Columbus Memorial Fountain**, dedicated in 1912, features a statue of the old mercenary standing on the prow of a ship, between two lions and male and female figures representing Old World and New. A replica of Philadelphia's Liberty Bell stands nearby.

City Post Office: the National Postal Museum

Having unwrapped the design for Union Station, Burnham turned his attention to a new **City Post Office** opposite the station (at Massachusetts Ave and N Capitol St). Built between 1911 and 1914, it was a working post office until 1986, when it was renovated at a cost of $200 million, in part to house a fascinating new National Postal Museum. A research library and a brew-pub are also in the renovated structure. Before you descend to the lower-level galleries, take time for a quick look at the **building** itself, whose white Italian marble reaches are some of the most impressive in the city. In the style of the day, it is adorned with improving texts for the edification of the public: look up and read how the postal service is "Messenger of Sympathy and Love . . . Consoler of the Lonely . . . Enlarger of the Common Life" and "Carrier of News and Knowledge" among other treacly attributes. **Inside**, the main lobby has been restored to its 1914 appearance, full of burnished marble, though the bulk of the building on this level has been taken over by the *Capitol City Brewing Company* (see p.281).

The museum

The **National Postal Museum** (daily 10am–5.30pm; free; ☎357-2700, ⓦwww.si.edu/postal) is one of the Smithsonian's quiet triumphs. The collection, from the National Museum of American History, includes sixteen million artifacts. But since many of these are stamps, only a few of which are displayed at any one time, it's not that daunting a show. Indeed, the museum's strength is its selectivity, judiciously placing the history of the mail service within the context of the history of the United States itself.

Escalators down to the galleries dump you in "**Moving the Mail**," basically an excuse to stack up some rattling pieces of machinery, from a Concord mail coach to a biplane. Beyond here you follow the first postal route, the seventeenth-century King's Best Highway between New York and Boston, while tracing the development of the postal system. Interactive video panels allow you to create your own route between two towns in the 1850s, your choices determining whether the mail gets through or not. It was soon clear that established overland mail routes helped attract commerce and settlers, with President Buchanan envisaging a "chain of living Americans" along the roads from east to west. Yet some of the most famous of the pioneering stories turn out to be more hype than substance. The relay-rider system of the famed Pony Express lasted for only two years (1860–61), and although it cut mail delivery times in half – from San Francisco to New York in thirteen days – the founding partners lost $30 on every letter carried; in the end, without government backing, the private enterprise collapsed.

It was seventh president Andrew Jackson who first realized the political importance of being able to rely on the mail, which could disseminate information – and propaganda – quickly and efficiently to even the most isolated communities; for a century after him, whenever the party in power lost a presidential election, the employment patronage system led to a huge turnover in postal workers. In the museum, photos and text trace the early racial makeup of the service, from the opportunities offered to blacks during Reconstruction to the segregation measures introduced in 1913, which in DC led to the establishment of a post office on T Street in Shaw staffed only by black workers.

Elsewhere in the museum, there are examples of weird and wonderful rural mailboxes, including one made from car mufflers in the shape of a tin man; a paddle punch used to fumigate letters during Philadelphia's yellow fever outbreak of 1890; and the uniform of the supremely annoying Cliff Clavin, barfly and postie in *Cheers*. Only in "**Stamps and Stories**" does the philatelic collection finally get a look-in – up until this point, there's barely a stamp to be seen. Here you'll find some splendid rarities as well as frequently rotated exhibitions drawing on artifacts from the museum's collection.

Before leaving (allow ninety minutes or so), print out your free personalized postcard at the machines in the lobby and buy a stamp from the stamp store in order to mail it home.

National Arboretum

3501 New York Ave, ☎245-2726, ⓦwww.usna.usda.gov; on weekends #X6 bus from
Union Station, on weekdays Stadium-Armory Metro, then #B2 bus. Daily 8am–5pm.
Admission free. Check the website or call for updates on what's in bloom.

Nestling along the Anacostia River roughly two miles northeast of the Capitol
Building, the sprawling **National Arboretum** is an oasis of green amid an
otherwise grim part of the district. While the arboretum probably won't rank
high on your must-see list, a weekend visit can make for a relaxing alternative
to the tried-and-true destinations downtown. The best time to visit is on a
weekend from mid-April to October, when plenty of plants are in bloom and
park access is made easier by direct bus service from Union Station and on-site
open-air **tram tours** (10.30am–4pm; $3). The forty-minute tours meander
along the park's 9.5 miles of roadways past ponds, gardens and plant collections,
taking in everything from colorful bursts of azaleas to the woodlands of Japan.
You can catch the tram near the administration building, located by the 24th
and R streets entrance. Inside you'll find the **visitor's center** (daily
8am–4.30pm), where you can pick up a visitor's guide, which includes a map,
seasonal plant information and descriptions of the gardens. It's also possible to
drive, hike or bike through the park — although biking *to* the park might be
more adventure than you're after.

  It's well worth a visit to the surreal gathering of "**Capitol Columns**," which
stand in a meadow at the heart of the grounds, supporting open sky. Once part
of the Capitol Building, the sandstone pillars, crafted in Corinthian style,
presided over every presidential inauguration from Jackson to Eisenhower.
They were effectively put out to pasture in the 1950s in order to correct a flaw
in the Capitol's design, which caused the columns to appear mismatched relative to the size of the dome. Other Arboretum highlights include the
Dogwood Collection, best seen in bloom on a late spring afternoon, and the
National Grove of State Trees, a thirty-acre site where trees native to each state
(plus the District of Columbia) grow on individual plots. Those preferring a
short **walking tour** can take in a selection of sights closest to the administration building. Here, in addition to the National Herb Garden, you'll find the
arboretum's most popular destination, the renowned **National Bonsai and
Penjing Museum** (daily 10am–3.30pm), which celebrates the ancient
Chinese and Japanese art form of growing tiny trees.

  It's easiest to get to the arboretum on weekends, when the #X6 **Metrobus**
makes the twenty-minute trip from Union Station every forty minutes. On
weekdays, it's a bit more complicated. You'll need to take the Metro to the
Stadium-Armory stop then transfer to the #B2 bus, disembarking on
Bladensburg Road, from which it's a four-block walk. Given the multiple transfers and a walk through dodgy turf, you're best off simply hailing a cab instead.

East to Lincoln Park

East Capitol Street, one of the city's four axes, runs off between the
Supreme Court and the Library of Congress' Jefferson Building. One of the
first streets on the Hill to be settled, its wide tree-lined reach presents a fine
aspect for the first ten blocks or so, studded with frame and brick townhouses, some dating from before the Civil War, others sporting the trademark

turrets and "rusticated" (roughened) stonework so beloved of DC's turn-of-the-century builders.

Close to the Supreme Court, the typical row house at 316 A Street NE was home to black orator and writer **Frederick Douglass** when he first moved to the capital in 1870 to take up the editorship of the *New National Era*, a newspaper championing the rights of African-Americans. His family owned No. 318, too, and Douglass lived here with his first wife, Anna, until 1877, when they moved to the rather grander Cedar Hill in Anacostia, which is where you'll have to go to discover more about his life (see p.130).

From here, it's just a few blocks north to **Stanton Park**, centered on its equestrian statue of Revolutionary General Nathanial Greene, though there's more interest in **Lincoln Park,** farther east along East Capitol Street between 11th and 13th streets. In 1876, on the eleventh anniversary of Lincoln's assassination and in the presence of President Grant, Frederick Douglass read out the Emancipation Proclamation to the assembled thousands as the "Freedom Memorial" was unveiled in the center of the specially designed park. It was paid for by funds collected from freed men and women; the first contributor, Charlotte Scott of Virginia, gave $5, "being her first earnings in freedom." To contemporary eyes it seems a paternalistic work, the bronze statue portraying Lincoln – proclamation in one hand – standing over a kneeling slave, exhorting him to rise. But it was considered rather daring in its day: working from a photograph, sculptor Thomas Ball re-created in the slave the features of one Archer Alexander, the last man to be seized under the Fugitive Slave Act, which empowered slaveowners to recapture escaped slaves. Under Lincoln's gaze Alexander is breaking his own shackles.

It was a century, however, before any monument was erected in DC specifically to honor the achievements of a black American, or, indeed, a woman. Facing Lincoln, across the park, a second memorial – dedicated in 1974 – remembers **Mary McLeod Bethune**, educator, black women's leader and special advisor to Franklin Delano Roosevelt. Just as significant as the Lincoln statue, it is possibly even more striking: Robert Berks (responsible for the head of JFK in the Kennedy Center) provides an inimitable study of a stout Bethune, leaning on her cane, reaching out to two children, passing on, as the inscription says, her legacy to youth. Across town near Logan Circle stands another memorial to Bethune, the Bethune Council House (see p.204).

East of the park the neighborhood degenerates. Come here in daylight and peer up East Capitol Street to the **RFK Stadium** in the distance (home of DC United, see p.313), but don't head there on foot.

Along and around Pennsylvania Avenue

Along the first few blocks of **Pennsylvania Avenue**, between 2nd Street and Eastern Market (at 7th), lie a score of bars and restaurants, including some notable Hill institutions: they're reviewed on p.277 (bars) and p.259 (restaurants). **Eastern Market** itself (7th and C, south of N Carolina Ave SE; Tues–Sat 7am–6pm, Sun 9am–4pm) makes a grand target, a red-brick edifice constructed in 1873 by Adolph Cluss, with rather less flamboyance than his Arts and Industries Building on the Mall. What it lacks in visual stimulus outside, though, it makes up for inside, where the traders continue to do roaring business: on the weekend, the stalls spill onto the sidewalk, when you can buy produce and flowers (Sat), or antiques and junk (Sun). On either side, along 7th Street, delis, coffee shops with outdoor seating, antique stores and clothes shops make it one of the more appealing hangouts on the Hill.

There are more restored townhouses in the vicinity of Pennsylvania Avenue, and green splashes at places like Folger Park, Seward Square and Marion Park, but on the whole, the district south of E Street is not one to wander around on your own. Two churches stand out, though, and in daylight at least there should be no problem in visiting them. The utilitarian red-brick **Ebenezer United Methodist Church** at 420 D Street SE (Mon–Fri 8.30am–3pm, Sun service 11am; ☏544-1415) is the oldest black congregation in the neighborhood. Founded in 1805, the church was the site of DC's first public school for black people; it was a short-lived affair (1864–65), but a pioneering one, since the teachers were paid out of federal funds. The current building dates from 1897, and if you call in advance someone will be on hand to show you around. On the 4th Street side stands a wooden model of "Little Ebenezer," the original frame church that stood on this site. Farther south, but unlikely to be open, **Christ Church** at 620 G Street SE is an early work (1806) by Capitol architect Benjamin Latrobe.

3

Southwest, Waterfront and Southeast

The **Southwest** quadrant, cut into by the encroaching curve of the river and East Potomac Park, is the most compact in the city: it's easy to loop through on your way from the Capitol to the Jefferson Memorial. This is the least distinguished of the city's areas – locals know it as the home of various federal agencies, while most visitors are hardly aware of its existence. Indeed, the district's two principal sights, the **Holocaust Memorial Museum** and the **Bureau of Engraving and Printing**, sit just off the Mall itself, necessitating only the briefest diversion.

Museums aside, the bright spots are all down at the district's southwestern edge, by the restored **Waterfront**, which runs along Water Street on the north side of the Washington Channel. Modern waterside apartment buildings have replaced nineteenth-century slum housing, and the area today is defined by its smart marina, promenades and seafood restaurants – useful lunch stops before walking back to the Mall or on to the monuments and memorials. The original fish market still survives at the Fish Wharf on Washington Channel, though in a much more regulated and less offensively smelly fashion than its eighteenth-century predecessor.

It's more of an effort (involving Metro, bus or taxi rides) to explore the limited attractions contained in the blighted neighborhoods of Washington's **Southeast**. Visitors are advised to head directly to the three individual sights – the Navy Museum, the former home of black orator and writer Frederick Douglass, and the neighborhood Anacostia Museum – and then come straight back again. To attempt any further exploration would be fruitless and possibly dangerous.

Southwest

In the early nineteenth century, **SOUTHWEST** was a fashionable residential area, thriving on its proximity to the Capitol. But in the 1870s the arrival of the railroad, whose tracks cut right through the district – and still do – diminished its social cachet, and the wealthy moved north of the Mall. Those left behind were mostly poor blacks, an additional influx of whom soon turned Southwest into the largest black neighborhood in the city, its inhabitants working at the briefly flourishing goods yards, storage depots and wharves. As the work dried up, the swamp-ridden housing became ever more dilapidated, and by the 1920s the district had degenerated into a notorious slum.

However, the federal government, looking for centralized office space, saw underutilized potential in the Southwest. The low-rent housing was demolished and families displaced to make room for federal **agencies**, including the Department of Agriculture and the Bureau of Engraving and Printing, both of which remain in situ. More buildings were added in the 1930s (to complement the work being undertaken across the Mall in Federal Triangle) and the 1960s. While these developments undoubtedly rescued Southwest from neglect, they also firmly stamped "federal" across its streets – there's little life here after 6pm on weekday evenings, even less on weekends, and few places to grab a coffee or sandwich that aren't brimming with office workers. There's a lack of architectural cohesion within the northern part of the quadrant too, certainly when compared to the public-works grandeur of Federal Triangle, just four blocks north.

Almost all the agencies are contained within a rectangle of land bounded by Independence Avenue, 3rd Street, E Street and 14th Street, and are served by two **Metro stations**, Federal Center SW and, further west, L'Enfant Plaza.

Federal buildings

Heading west from the Capitol, you're not missing anything by sticking to **Independence Avenue** as far as 4th Street. The block between 3rd and 4th is taken up by the **Department of Health and Human Services**, whose imposing bulk makes it one of the few buildings in Southwest to stand comparison with the Classical entities of Federal Triangle; it dates from the same (late 1930s) period. It's the only federal building hereabouts open for public visits; part of the building houses the offices of the **Voice of America** (free 40min tours Mon–Fri 10.30am & 2.30pm, reservations required; ☎619-3919, Ⓦ www.voa.gov). The entrance is around the back, on C Street between 3rd and 4th.

Along with the BBC, the VOA is one of the world's two biggest international broadcasters, established in 1942 as part of the war effort and given its own charter in 1960 (as part of the US Information Agency) to transmit programs overseas giving a flavor of US life and values. In theory, the VOA Charter is as admirable as they come: "VOA will serve as a consistently reliable and authoritative source of news . . . [which] will be accurate, objective, and comprehensive." But, whichever way you cut it, its intention to "present the policies of the United States clearly and effectively" makes it a valuable propaganda tool for the government – which is why the VOA's broadcasts have often been on the receiving end of jamming by various disaffected foreign powers. This, of course, is not something you hear too much about on the tour, in which you're walked through the corridors and studios from which broadcasts are made in 53 different languages to 91 million listeners in 120 countries. It's only really of interest if you've never been in a radio studio before, in which case you'll be happy to get up close to broadcasters and journalists at work (or at least reading the *Washington Post* and eating donuts). The two most interesting discoveries are that you can call collect to the *Talk to America* talkshow from anywhere in the world, a fact that (unsurprisingly) isn't widely advertised, and that,

SOUTHWEST AND WATERFRONT

▲ US Capitol

▲ Virginia Avenue

▲ National Archives

▲ The Mall

▲ Washington Monument

▲ Lincoln Memorial

▲ 14th St Bridge

Arena Stage & Waterfront Metro ▶

Cruise boat pier ▶

Capitol Reflecting Pool

Botanic Garden

MARYLAND AVE

CANAL ST

2ND ST

3RD ST

4TH ST

6TH ST

7TH ST

9TH ST

12TH ST

14TH ST

Voice of America

Department of Health & Human Services

Food & Drug Administration

Federal Center SW M

Department of Education

Department of Transportation

NASA

L'Enfant Plaza M

Department of Housing & Urban Development

Loews L'Enfant Plaza Hotel

L'Enfant Plaza

Federal Aviation Administration

Energy Department

Forrestal Building

Smithsonian Institution Arts & Industries Building

Hirshhorn Museum

Freer Gallery

National Air & Space Museum

Smithsonian M

JEFFERSON DRIVE

INDEPENDENCE AVE

MARYLAND AVE

L'ENFANT PROMENADE (10TH ST)

Department of Agriculture

Bureau of Engraving & Printing

Holocaust Memorial Museum

RAOUL WALLENBERG PL

VIRGINIA AVE

DELAWARE AVE

D ST

E ST

G ST

I ST

SCHOOL ST

395

Benjamin Banneker Memorial Circle

MAINE AVE

WATER ST

16TH ST

Fish Wharf

Washington Channel

Francis Case Memorial Bridge

14TH ST

OHIO DRIVE

OHIO DR

Tidal Basin

Jefferson Memorial

East Potomac Park

N

0   200 yds

as evidenced by the photograph gallery of the personalities who've appeared on VOA over the years, Telly Savalas once had a fine head of hair.

The other federal buildings – large, and largely unappealing structures – occupy a no-man's-land between 4th and 14th streets. Presumably it wasn't for want of trying that the area appears so dreary: the **Department of Transportation** building (between D and E at 7th) was designed by Edward Durrell Stone, who managed to make the Kennedy Center (see p.153) stand out in similarly unpromising surroundings, and even I.M. Pei has had a hand in the regeneration of the various plazas and streetscapes. The closest thing here to modern swagger, though, is the curving double-Y-shaped concrete structure from the late 1960s that holds the **Department of Housing and Urban Development** (D St between 7th and 9th), whose architect, Marcel Breuer, gave more than a nod to his Bauhaus origins. The only semblance of style, however, comes with the oldest (and westernmost) agency, the **Department of Agriculture** (Independence Ave between 12th and 14th): sited here since 1905, the original building on the north side of Independence Avenue is connected by slender arches to the much larger, 1930s Classical structure across the avenue.

L'Enfant Plaza to Benjamin Banneker Memorial Circle

The main focus of development in Southwest in the 1960s and 1970s was **L'Enfant Plaza**, at D Street between 9th and 10th, where there's now also a useful Metro station. The buildings surrounding the plaza are no more gripping than their neighbors, but from the Metro station there's direct access into a huge underground shopping mall and up into the luxurious **Loews L'Enfant Plaza Hotel**, which occupies the entire east block of the plaza. Quite apart from being the one decent place in the district where you can get a cup of coffee, the outdoor terrace that wraps around the hotel has great views. Nonetheless, it's easy to feel a twinge of sympathy for Pierre L'Enfant – alone of the city's spiritual founders, he gets not a monument but a windswept 1960s concrete square and Metro station as his memorial.

From the plaza, 10th Street is immediately accessible, forming a landscaped mall (known as L'Enfant Promenade) that heads south to the **Benjamin Banneker Memorial Circle**, where there's a viewpoint over the Washington Channel and Waterfront. The African-American Banneker, born in Maryland in 1731 to a former slave and a servant girl, was a remarkable figure. Almost entirely self-taught, he distinguished himself as a mathematician, astronomer (he accurately predicted a solar eclipse) and inventor (of, among other things, a striking clock with every part made of wood) before being invited, at the age of 60, to assist in the surveying of the land for the new capital. He followed this coup, extraordinarily for the time, by publishing several editions of a successful almanac and spent his last years (he died in 1806) in correspondence with Thomas Jefferson, whom he hoped would abandon his "narrow prejudices" against the native intelligence of African-Americans.

United States Holocaust Memorial Museum

100 Raoul Wallenberg Place SW; entrance on 14th St ☎488-0400, ⓦ www.ushmm.org; Smithsonian Metro. Daily 10am–5.30pm; closed on Yom Kippur and Christmas Day. Admission free.

Nothing in DC is more disturbingly unforgettable than the large and symbolically sited **United States Holocaust Memorial Museum**. Just a step from the Mall, and within the triangle formed by the Washington, Lincoln and

Jefferson memorials, the museum commemorates in a uniquely provocative fashion the persecution and murder of six million Jews by the Nazis. Upon entry, each visitor is given the ID card, containing biographical notes, of a real Holocaust victim, whose fortunes are followed as the museum unfolds. This approach personalizes the fate of the affected individuals, while never losing sight of the wider historical machinations that allowed Hitler to assume power in the first place. The detail throughout is perfectly pitched – highly informative and pulling no punches, without being overly emotive. No knowledge of the events of the Holocaust is assumed, and this, too, is deliberate. Indeed, however much you already know, nothing prepares you for this relentless, remorseless documentation of systematic brutality. The solemn mood throughout is reflected by the museum's design, overseen in part by noted Holocaust survivors. Half-lit chambers, a floor of ghetto cobblestones, an obscenely cramped barracks building, and an external roofline that resembles the guard towers of a concentration camp – all add to the overwhelming feeling of oppression. The themed displays are a mix of personal possessions and photographs alongside historical montages and video presentations, before which visitors stand visibly moved. And on this level, certainly, the museum passes the acid test: personal remembrance of an international horror.

The museum

Crowding can be a problem. To control the flow of people, **tickets** for fixed entry times are available free (limited to four per person) from 10am each day at the 14th Street entrance. You can also book in advance through Tickets.com (☎1-800/400-9373; fee charged). If you arrive without a ticket any later than mid-morning, you're unlikely to get into the permanent exhibition that day, but a certain number of temporary displays are usually open to all. Note that the main exhibitions are not considered suitable for **children** under the age of 11, though the less forbidding gallery, "Daniel's Story: Remember the Children," is designed for those over the age of 8.

The **permanent exhibitions** are on the second, third and fourth floors; you start at the top and work your way down. The 14th Street entrance is at first-floor level, where you'll find the information desk, children's exhibit and museum **shop**; stairs lead down to the auditoriums and **special exhibition** area at concourse level.

The first rooms on the fourth floor chronicle the **Nazi rise to power** from 1933 to 1939 through storyboards, newspapers and film clips. The point that prejudice soon sweeps all before it is forcefully made: what started with the boycott of Jewish businesses and book-burning was swiftly followed by the organized looting of Jewish shops and the parading of German women who had "defiled" their race by associating with Jews. From there, anyone who didn't fit the Nazi ideal, like homosexuals (who were forced to wear a pink triangle), gypsies and even Freemasons were persecuted and imprisoned. Beyond a glass wall etched with the names of the hundreds of Eastern European Jewish communities wiped off the map forever, a towering stack of photographs records the breadth of life in just one of them. Domestic life in the *shtetl* (community) of Eishishok, in what's now Lithuania, is vividly shown in photographs of street scenes, ceremonies, parties, family groups and individuals taken between 1890 and 1941.

The third floor covers the era of Hitler's **Final Solution**, beginning with the first gassing of Jews to take place at a death camp in Poland in December 1941. The Jews were transported to the camps from the ghettos in which they'd been incarcerated, most infamously at Warsaw. Even in the ghettos, there was resistance – although it's clear from the displays just how ultimately futile that proved to be. Some 33,000 Jews were slaughtered at Babi Yar in Kiev in 1941 in retaliation after Soviet saboteurs had blown up buildings in the city; in the Warsaw uprising of 1943, the resistance held out, remarkably, for a month but had no real weapons, no supplies and no hope. In the end, all the surviving ghetto Jews were taken to the camps in packed rail freight cars; the one that you can walk through in this section stands on railroad tracks taken from the camp at Treblinka.

The most harrowing part of the exhibition deals with life and death in the **concentration camps** themselves. There's an overwhelming poignancy in the pile of blankets, umbrellas, scissors, cutlery and other personal effects taken from the hundreds of thousands who arrived at the various camps expecting to be forced to work – most were gassed within hours. A re-created barracks building from Auschwitz provides the backdrop for the oral memories of some survivors, as well as truly shocking film of gruesome medical experiments carried out on selected prisoners.

Many histories claim that it was only after the war had ended that the full scale of these atrocities became apparent, but as the museum clearly – and uncomfortably – shows, the Americans knew of the existence of Auschwitz as early as May 1944 and yet refused to bomb it; Assistant Secretary of War John J. McCloy argued that its destruction "might provoke even more vindictive action by the Germans." It's a moot point now, though it's instructive that contemporary American Jewish organizations repeatedly demanded that the camps be bombed, while survivors later testified that they would have welcomed such terminal liberation – "Every bomb that exploded . . . gave us new confidence in life," records one witness. The third floor also ends with photographic coverage of the Eishishok *shtetl*, this time relating it to the Final Solution. The pictures show a town and community that had existed for more than nine hundred years completely destroyed, and its inhabitants (including two of the photographers) shot, in just two days.

As the Nazi front collapsed across Europe during 1945, many different groups became involved in efforts to save the Jews. The **Last Chapter** on the second floor recounts the heroism of particular individuals and the response of governments (the Danish government in particular has the most reason to feel that it did all it could to save its Jewish citizens). Much of the floor is taken up with details of the **liberation of the camps** by the Allied forces: film reels show German guards being forced to bury mountains of bodies in mass graves, while locals were made to tour the camps to witness the extent of the horror. If people later looked to the **war trials** in Nuremberg to draw a line under this evil, little comfort was offered there either. Despite the imprisonment and execution of various high-profile Nazis, and a continuing trickle of prosecutions over the years, most people responsible for the planning, maintenance and administration of the camps were never tried; thousands of others were treated leniently or acquitted altogether.

The sheer amount on display requires most visitors to spend at least three hours in the museum. There are rest areas throughout, and a contemplative **Hall of Remembrance** on the second floor. The **Wexner Learning Center**, on the same floor, has computer stations that allow you to access text, photographs, film and other source materials. There's also a **café** in the Administrative Center, around at the Raoul Wallenberg Place (15th St) entrance, open 8.30am–4.30pm.

The Bureau of Engraving and Printing

14th and C streets SW ☎622-2000, ⊛www.moneyfactory.com; Smithsonian Metro.
Mon–Fri 9am–2pm (with extended evening hours from 5–7pm in summer); closed
Christmas to New Year's Day. Admission free. Call ahead to check for changes to tour
schedule due to security concerns.

Half a million visitors a year wait patiently in line at the **Bureau of
Engraving and Printing** before being led through narrow corridors for a
tantalizing glimpse of the nation's money-making process. It must be the avaricious
thrill of being close to so much money that drags in the crowds, because
it certainly isn't the twenty-minute tour of what is, effectively, a large printing
plant. The difference is that the presses here crank out millions of dollars in
currency every day, $120 billion a year (95 percent of which is replacement
currency for money already in circulation).

The Bureau is the federal agency for designing and printing all US currency,
government securities and postage stamps (of which it produces 30 billion a
year). It was established in 1862, when Abraham Lincoln empowered six

△ Seafood offerings at the Fish Wharf

3

employees to start up business in the attic of the Treasury Building, sealing up blocks of $1 and $2 bills that had been printed by private banks. By 1877, all US currency was produced by the Bureau, which finally moved into this building in 1914. Nowadays, almost three thousand employees work either here or at a second plant in Fort Worth, Texas.

So much for the history, much of which is served up on video as you wait in line in the main corridor. What everyone wants to see is the cash, which is quickly revealed during the march through claustrophobic viewing galleries looking down upon the printing presses. It's a surprisingly low-tech operation: hand-engraved dyes are used to create intaglio steel plates, from which the bills are printed in sheets of 32, checked for defects and loaded into large barrows. On a separate press, they're then over-printed with serial numbers and seals, sliced up into single bills by ordinary paper cutters, and stacked into "bricks" of four thousand notes before being sent out to the twelve Federal Reserve Districts, which issue the notes to local banks. Star facts, fired out amid lame jokes by the guides, include the Trivial Pursuit-winning tidbit that the bills aren't made from paper at all, but from a more durable fabric that's three-quarters cotton. Even so, the most used note, the dollar bill, lasts only eighteen months on average. Those whose job it is to spot flaws in the currency get short shrift from federal-employee-baiting visitors, who see only a line of people with their heads in their hands gazing at bundles of notes. What you don't see in the two-minute gaze through the window is the rigor of the two-year apprenticeship that all undergo, or the eight-hour daily shift worked staring at one sheet a second, with just two twenty-minute breaks and a thirty-minute lunch. Yet they catch all but one in a thousand of misprinted bills. As a finale, guides deftly usher you into the **visitor center** (Mon–Fri 8.30am–3.30pm), which sells souvenirs like small bags of shredded currency – it's cheaper to provide yourself with two dollar bills and a pair of scissors from WalMart.

Despite the relative ordinariness of the process, the tour is immensely popular and between Easter and Memorial Day you must pick up **tickets** in advance; note that these are often all gone by 11.30am. At other times, you can simply show up, though you'll still have to wait in line.

The Waterfront

Downtown Washington has always been rather removed from the rivers (Potomac and Anacostia) on which the city stands. They meet at a Y-junction some considerable way from the Mall and the other central axes, and for a century after the city was founded, the nearest accessible riverbanks (in today's West Potomac Park) were too marshy and malarial to develop anyway. The only practicable wharves and piers were those built along the Washington Channel, the thin finger of water that sheers off from the Potomac. But this too had a tendency to stagnate – at least until the Tidal Basin was created this century. The opening of the basin's gates now serves to flush the channel clean after every tide. The rather haphazardly developed commercial buildings and piers that lined the north bank of the Washington Channel were finally redeveloped during the 1960s as the **WATERFRONT**, a project designed to convince Washingtonians that they didn't have to go to Georgetown when they wanted a riverside stroll. Despite lacking Georgetown's natural advantages, the development has succeeded admirably, in part due to the proximity of so many office workers. Most people come here to eat seafood at one of the restaurants (see pp.271) that line the waters of the Channel, along Maine Avenue or the parallel Water Street SW, west of 7th; all have terraces and patios with views across to East Potomac Park. The district even has its own Metro stop, at 4th and M.

The two main Waterfront attractions are next to each other, near the bridge that crosses the Channel to East Potomac Park. The **Washington Marina** is the usual tangle of pricey nautical hardware and provides a backdrop for various summer fairs and events. Adjacent lies the **Fish Wharf** (daily 7.30am–8pm), the oldest continuous fish market in America, conducted from permanently docked boats and trailers. This puts on a great spread, with huge trays of Chesapeake Bay fish, shrimp, clams, oysters and, especially, crabs, which you can buy live or steamed. There's nowhere to sit and eat, but there's nothing to stop you from heading down the waterside promenade for a picnic.

Further down Maine Avenue, east of 7th Street, the **Waterfront Metro** station is closest if you're heading for the Arena Stage (see p.291). There's little specific to venture farther south for, but it's a nice walk along the Channel past the cruise boat docks (see p.32 for tour details) and DC harbor patrol as far as the Titanic Memorial. Set back, opposite the Spirit Cruises dock, the **Thomas Law House** (built 1794–96) is one of DC's oldest surviving federal townhouses, and if you cut through past here to 4th Street, you can see another row of federal houses, called **Wheat Row** (1315–1321 4th St SW), maintained within the **Harbor Square** development at 4th Street between N and O.

Channel and river collide just to the south of here, with the strategic spit of land occupied by the military (and subsequently off-limits) since the city's earliest days. Now known as **Fort McNair**, the base – originally fortified in 1791 – became home to the **Washington Arsenal** in 1804, though its buildings were blown up by the British in 1814 and later destroyed by an explosion that killed 21 people in 1864. At the US Penitentiary, built in the 1820s on the arsenal grounds, the conspirators in the Lincoln assassination (see pp.180–181) were imprisoned, tried and executed.

Southeast

Run-down, impoverished **SOUTHEAST** Washington makes its presence felt just a few blocks south of the US Capitol; visitors shouldn't stroll around too far south of Eastern Market Metro or east of Waterfront Metro. Not that you'd have cause to: the only attraction hereabouts is the enclosed military campus of **Washington Navy Yard**, which can be reached directly by Metro or by bus (#90 or #92 down 8th St SE from Eastern Market Metro, #V6 along M St SE from Waterfront Metro). There's parking inside the compound.

Washington Navy Yard

The **NAVY YARD** is the US Navy's oldest shore establishment, building ships and producing weaponry for the fleet continuously from 1799 until 1961 – interrupted only in 1812 when the commander was ordered to burn the base to prevent the British capturing it. Since the 1960s the base has acted as a naval supply and administrative center, and would be of no interest whatsoever were it not for its splendid Navy Museum. While you're within the confines of the Yard you'll probably also look into the Marine Corps Historical Center and

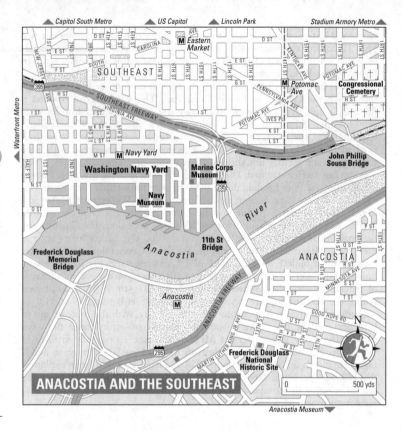

ANACOSTIA AND THE SOUTHEAST

0   500 yds

Anacostia Museum ▼

the Navy Art Gallery, though both are very much an afterthought. You'll need **photo ID** to show the guard at the main gate at 9th and M – and, as with all government sites, you should call ahead to check for any changes to opening hours due to security concerns.

Navy Museum

Housed in the Navy Yard's former gun factory is the **Navy Museum** (Mon–Fri 9am–4pm, June–Aug until 5pm, Sat & Sun all year 10am–5pm; admission free; ☏433-4882). This focused and illuminating collection traces the history of the US Navy from its foundation in 1794 in response to attacks on American ships by Barbary pirates. Dress uniforms, ship figureheads, vicious cat-o'-nine-tail whips, and a walk-through frigate gun-deck, illustrate the gradual development of the Navy as a fighting force, while separate galleries deal with every conflict the US Navy has taken part in – from the War of 1812 to the Gulf War. A painting illustrates the exploits of early naval hero Stephen Decatur (see p.141), who captured three boats during hand-to-hand fighting at Tripoli in 1804. The World War II displays are particularly affecting, featuring anti-aircraft guns in which you can sit, crackly archive film footage and an account of the sinking by a Japanese destroyer of a PT109 patrol boat on August 2, 1943. (The PT109's commander, one John Fitzgerald Kennedy, his back badly injured, swam ashore towing the boat's badly burned engineer, an act for which he was later decorated.)

The museum gets the balance just right, mixing informative text and glass-case displays with huge pieces of hardware that you're encouraged to explore – not least of which is the USS *Barry*, a destroyer docked outside the museum, whose mess room, bridge and quarters are open to the public.

Anacostia

Washington's most notorious neighborhood, **ANACOSTIA**, is also one of its oldest, the name deriving from that of the area's original Native American inhabitants, the tobacco-growing Nacotchtanks. They were supplanted by nineteenth-century merchants seeking homes close to the Capitol, who in turn were displaced in the 1850s by a white working and middle class encouraged to settle in what the developers called Uniontown. Post–Civil War Reconstruction saw the neighborhood thrive, boosted by the building of the 11th Street Bridge, which connected Anacostia with the rest of DC. But the white flight to the suburbs gathered pace in the 1950s, and by 1970 over 95 percent of Anacostia's residents were black – and largely abandoned by the city authorities. The 1968 riots did as much damage to infrastructure and confidence here as in Shaw, and it's been a long clamber back for the embattled community, which still suffers grievously from underfunding, poor housing, unemployment and crime – the last fueled by the city's spiraling drug problem.

None of which makes for a neighborhood you should visit lightly. There are, of course, handsome pockets of old houses, revitalized commercial areas and worthy community projects in Anacostia – people, after all, *do* manage to live perfectly ordinary lives here – but there's no reason to come as a tourist. Much of it is dangerous to outsiders who don't know where they're going; the two attractions reviewed below are best reached by cab from Anacostia Metro station. A good way to see the neighborhood is to sign up for the DC Heritage Coalition's "Anacostia: Different Voices...Different Views" tour, which runs once a month during summer (see pp.32 for details).

Frederick Douglass National Historic Site

Frederick Douglass – former slave, abolitionist leader and blistering orator – was 60 when in 1877 he moved to the white brick house in Anacostia he knew and loved as **Cedar Hill**. Its mixed Gothic Revival–Italianate appearance, 21 rooms and 15 acres were typical of the high-quality homes built in Uniontown twenty years earlier, though at that time they were restricted to whites. Douglass, newly appointed US marshal in DC, was the first to break the racial ban, paying $6700 for the property and living out the last eighteen years of his life here.

The house is now known, rather cumbersomely, as the **Frederick Douglass National Historic Site**, 1411 W St SE (daily May–Sept 9am–5pm, Oct–April 9am–4pm; ☎426-5961, ⓦwww.nps.gov/frdo). Reserve a place on one of the free hourly **tours** by calling ☎1-800/967-2283; a handling fee of $2 is charged. In summer you can see the site as part of a Tourmobile excursion (see p.31 for details). The tours begin in the visitor center below the house, where a short docudrama and a few static exhibits fill you in on Douglass' life. You're then led up the steep green hill for a rather dry tour around the house. It was a substantial property for the time, and Douglass entertained all the leading abolitionist and suffragist lights of the day here, talking in the parlors or eating in the dining room. Many brought him mementoes, which are now on display – there's President Lincoln's cane, given to Douglass by Mary Lincoln, and a

Frederick Douglass (1818–95)

Frederick Douglass was born into slavery as Frederick Bailey on a Maryland estate in 1818; the exact date of his birth is unknown, as is the identity of his father (Bailey was his mother's name), though it was rumored to be a white man, perhaps his owner. At the age of 8, he was sent to work as a house servant in Baltimore, where, although it was illegal to educate slaves, the owner's wife taught him to read, and he secretly taught himself to write. By 1834 he had been hired out to a nearby plantation, where he was cruelly treated; his first attempt to escape, in 1836, failed. Later, apprenticed as a ship caulker in Baltimore docks, Frederick attended an educational association run by free blacks, where he met his first wife, Anna Murray. With money borrowed from her and equipped with a friend's passbook, he fled to New York in 1838 disguised as a free seaman. Anna followed him and they were married later that year, moving to Massachusetts where Bailey – now working as a laborer – became Douglass (after a character from Sir Walter Scott's *Lady of the Lake*) so as to confound the slave-catchers.

Douglass became active in the **abolition movement**, lecturing about his life for the Massachusetts Anti-Slavery Society during the 1840s and risking capture when, at just 27 years old, he published his early autobiography, *Narrative of the Life of Frederick Douglass, an American Slave*, in 1845. It was a resounding success, forcing the increasingly famous Douglass to leave for England (which had a strong abolitionist movement) for fear he'd be recaptured. After two years on the lecture circuit, friends raised the money to buy his freedom and Douglass returned home. His views were slowly changing, and in a break with pacifist white abolitionists (particularly William Lloyd Garrison), he founded his own newspaper, the *North Star* (later renamed *Frederick Douglass' Paper*), in Rochester, New York, in 1847. In it, Douglass began increasingly to explore the idea of political rather than moral reform as a means of ending slavery. His reputation grew as a compelling orator and writer; another autobiography, *My Bondage and My Freedom*, appeared in 1855.

desk and chair from Harriet Beecher Stowe. Family portraits loom large: his first wife, Anna, who died in 1882; his second wife, Helen, much younger and – far more shocking for hidebound DC – white; and his five children, two of whom served with distinction in the black Massachusetts 54th regiment during the Civil War.

Most of the fixtures and fittings are original and give a fair idea of middle-class life in late nineteenth-century Washington. Douglass kept chickens and goats outside in the gardens, and the only water source was a rainwater pump, but inside the kitchen the domestic staff had access to all the latest technology, like the cranky Universal clothes wringer ("giving universal satisfaction"). Frederick himself worked either in his study, surrounded by hundreds of books, or in the outdoor "Growlery" – a rudimentary stone cabin he used for solitary contemplation.

The **#B2 bus**, which drops you right outside the Frederick Douglass house door on the way *from* Anacostia Metro, heads back *to* the Metro from Good Hope Road SE, three blocks down 14th Street from the house; cross Good Hope Road and wait for the bus (every 15min) on the other side, outside the grocery-deli. It's much less hassle to arrange for a taxi to pick you up from the house.

Meanwhile, he extended his interests to women's suffrage (a bold move at the time), debating issues with such luminaries as Susan B. Anthony, Lucretia Mott and Elizabeth Cady Stanton.

When Lincoln issued the Emancipation Proclamation during the Civil War, the country's most respected black leader turned his attention to urging "men of color" to join the war effort, which backfired somewhat when it became clear that his fiery recruitment speeches promised black soldiers an equality in service and conditions that the Union Army didn't offer. With **slavery abolished** in 1865, and Reconstruction set in place, Douglass turned to pressing for black suffrage. He campaigned for Ulysses S. Grant and the Republicans in 1868 and played a major role in pushing through the Fifteenth Amendment (granting all "citizens" the right to vote) – though this caused a temporary rift with his suffragist colleagues since "citizens" still didn't include women. Frederick and Anna moved to DC in 1870, buying a house on Capitol Hill, where Douglass continued to earn his living lecturing, writing and, for a while, editing the progressive *New National Era* newspaper. In 1877 he was appointed to the largely ceremonial position of marshal of Washington DC and moved to Cedar Hill in Anacostia the same year.

He was made recorder of deeds for the city in 1880 and in 1881 published his third autobiographical work, the *Life and Times of Frederick Douglass*. Anna died a year later, but Douglass was quickly remarried – to Helen Pitts, a quick-witted white secretary almost twenty years his junior, whom he had met in the records office. More controversy followed as Douglass was accused of cozying up to successive political administrations that had been deemed to have betrayed the aspirations of black Americans ever since Emancipation. Quitting his post as recorder, Douglass regained his reputation with a series of searing attacks on injustice. In 1889, at a time when others might have considered retirement, he accepted the post of consul-general in Haiti, where he served for two years. Back at Cedar Hill, but by now in ill health, he continued to write and speak publicly until his death from a heart attack on February 20, 1895, at the age of 77. His funeral, effectively a state occasion, was held at the Metropolitan AME Church in downtown DC; his writings continued to inspire a new generation of black leaders who took his fight into the twentieth century.

Anacostia Museum

The Smithsonian's least-known outpost, the **Anacostia Museum**, 1901 Fort Place SE (daily 10am–5pm; admission free; ☎287-2061, ⓦwww.si.edu/anacostia), devotes itself to recording African-American history and culture, with particular reference to the life of blacks in the upper South (DC, Maryland, Virginia and the Carolinas). The museum's permanent collection is mostly historical in nature, holding documents, photographs, books and objects such as the fur coat opera singer Marian Anderson wore to her famed 1939 concert on the steps of the Lincoln Memorial. There's also a small art collection — a sampling of paintings and prints by local artists like Samella Lewis, John Robinson and Elena Bland; works by folk artist Leslie Payne; and a contemporary quilt collection. The museum is perhaps best known for its renowned temporary exhibitions on themed topics (held here and at the Arts and Industries Building on the Mall). Call or check the website to see what's on, or ask for details at the Smithsonian Castle on the Mall. The museum is well worth an hour or two of your time, but don't even think about walking here from the Metro; buses #W2 or #W3 from Howard Road (outside the Metro) stop at the museum, though it's less unnerving by far to come by taxi. As it's not far from the Frederick Douglass home, you could even get the same taxi to take you to both.

The White House
and Foggy Bottom

Few residences in the world are as recognizable as the patrician outline of the **White House**. With an impeccable lineage – oldest public building in Washington DC, home of the US president since 1800, and, with the Capitol, one of the two original cornerstones of L'Enfant's master plan for the city – it stands as perhaps the most enduring symbol of democracy in the nation, a symbol bolstered by the extraordinary public access granted since the time of Thomas Jefferson.

Around the White House are genteel squares and streets fashionable since the early nineteenth century. To the west, in the high ground of **Foggy Bottom** – basically, the leafy area north of Constitution Avenue and west from the White House to the river – the chattering classes entertained the political elite in houses like **The Octagon**. Washington's first art gallery opened just a block from the White House in what is now the Smithsonian's **Renwick Gallery** of decorative arts and crafts; later, the art collection was moved into the larger **Corcoran Gallery of Art**, still one of the most respected art institutions in the country.

Today Foggy Bottom is best known for the federal institutions that have their headquarters here. However, the students of **George Washington University**, set bang in the heart of Foggy Bottom, add a certain life to the otherwise nine-to-five flavor of the streets, and there are a handful of minor museums and galleries. The biggest draws, however, are the **Kennedy Center**, the city's major cultural complex, and – though there's little actually to see – the nearby **Watergate Complex,** scene of the infamous burglary that led eventually to the toppling of President Nixon.

The White House

1600 Pennsylvania Ave NW ☏456-7041, ⊛www.whitehouse.gov; McPherson Square or Farragut West Metro. Continuous tours Tues–Sat 10am–noon; additional tours at other hours in summer; closed some holidays and official functions. Admission free. Call ahead to check for changes in tour schedule.

For two centuries, the **White House**, 1600 Pennsylvania Avenue NW, has been the most famous house at the most famous address in America. For

THE WHITE HOUSE AND FOGGY BOTTOM

▲ Pennsylvania Avenue

N

◀ Georgetown

◀ Dupont Circle

NEW HAMPSHIRE AVE

WASHINGTON CIRCLE

PENNSYLVANIA AVE

L ST

K ST

I ST

H ST

G ST

F ST

E ST

Farragut West M

McPherson Square M

St John's Church

Hay-Adams Hotel

Decatur House

New Executive Office

Renwick Gallery

Blair House

LAFAYETTE SQUARE

Andrew Jackson Statue

Treasury

National Place

District Building

ICC

15TH ST

14TH ST

NEW YORK AVE

EAST EXECUTIVE AVE

WEST EXECUTIVE AVE

The White House

Sherman Statue

1st Division Monument

Zero Milestone

White House Visitor Center

Dept of Commerce

Boy Scout Memorial

Original Patentees Monument

The Ellipse

Jefferson Memorial ▶

Old Executive Office

AIA

The Octagon

World Bank

IMF

2000 Pennsylvania Avenue

United Church

Corcoran Gallery of Art

Rawlins Park

American Red Cross

DAR Continental/Constitution Hall

OAS

Art Museum of the Americas

Bolivar Statue

CONSTITUTION AVE

Department of the Interior

VIRGINIA AVE

Federal Reserve

National Academy of Sciences

Einstein Statue

Vietnam Veterans Memorial

Lincoln Memorial ▶

Lisner Auditorium

George Washington University

GWU Hospital H

Foggy Bottom-GWU Metro M

Academic Center

St Mary's Church

Snow Court

Juarez Statue

Department of State

American Pharmaceutical Association

John F Kennedy Center for the Performing Arts

Watergate Complex

Theodore Roosevelt Memorial Bridge

ROCK CREEK AND POTOMAC PKWY

Rossfyn ▶

29TH ST

25TH ST

24TH ST

23RD ST

22ND ST

21ST ST

20TH ST

19TH ST

18TH ST

17TH ST

16TH ST

15TH ST

17TH ST

C ST

E ST

F ST

G ST

H ST

I ST

K ST

PENNSYLVANIA AVE

NEW HAMPSHIRE AVE

0   200 yds

millions, the notion of touring the White House, residence and office of the **President of the United States**, has an almost totemic quality. Quite apart from relishing the freedom to stand in the same building, for a moment at least, as the chief executive of the nation, the person with his finger on the button, there's the undeniable thrill of nosing around the home of the closest the country has to royalty.

In the end, however, if it's domestic curiosity that brings you to the White House, you're likely to go away disappointed. Many are surprised by how small it is – "I think I may say that we have private houses in London considerably larger," sniffed Anthony Trollope in 1862 – while tours tend to consist of a lot of waiting around followed by a quick shuffle past railed-off rooms filled with portraits of ex-presidents.

Public access (see "Visiting the White House," overleaf) can be affected by official functions and security concerns. And **security** is every bit as tight as you'd imagine. In 1995 the stretch of Pennsylvania Avenue immediately outside the White House was permanently closed to vehicles, following two incidents in which shots were fired at the house and a light aircraft crashed into one of the outer walls. The Oklahoma City bombing shortly afterwards and the events of September 11, 2001—the White House was presumably the target of the fourth plane, which crashed in a Pennsylvania field—served to heighten the fear of terrorist attack.

Balancing security requirements with the historic right of access is not a new problem: in the nineteenth century, though there were armed sentries at every door and plainclothes policemen mingling with the visitors, virtually anyone could turn up at the president's house without an introduction. In his diary, naval novelist Captain Frederick Marryat deplored the way a visitor might "walk into the saloon in all his dirt, and force his way to the President, that he might shake him by the one hand while he flourished the whip in the other." As late as the 1920s, the general public was allowed to saunter across the White House lawns and picnic on the grounds. President Warren Harding even used to answer the door himself.

Some history

From the outset, the White House – or **President's Mansion**, as it was first known – was to be the focal point of the executive branch of government, connected to the proposed Capitol building by the broad diagonal sweep of Pennsylvania Avenue. L'Enfant was fired before he could make a start on the house, however, and its design was thrown open to an architectural competition in 1792. The winner, Irish immigrant and professional builder **James Hoban**, picked up a $500 prize for his Neoclassical design, which was influenced by the Georgian manor houses of Dublin. It coincided exactly with President Washington's requirement for a mansion that would command respect without being extravagant and monarchical – attributes the leader of the new republic was keen to avoid. A stone house, moreover, would give the crucial impression of permanence and stability, though unfortunately for Hoban the city had few skilled masons and no quarries. Advertisements were even placed in European newspapers before Scottish masons from the Potomac region and local slaves were recruited for the work. Progress was slow: the masons downed tools in 1794 in the city's first pay strike, and the house of gray Virginia sandstone wasn't completed in time to house George Washington, whose second term in office ended in 1797.

John Adams was the first presidential occupant, moving into the unfinished structure on November 1, 1800; the family was reduced to hanging its laundry

Visiting the White House

We entered a large hall, and, having twice or thrice rung a bell which nobody answered, walked without further ceremony through the rooms on the ground-floor, as diverse other gentlemen (mostly with their hats on, and their hands in their pockets) were doing very leisurely. Some of these had ladies with them, to whom they were showing the premises; others were lounging on the chairs and sofas; others, in a perfect state of exhaustion from listlessness, were yawning drearily. The greater portion of this assemblage were rather asserting their supremacy than doing anything else, as they had no particular business there, that anybody knew of. A few were closely eyeing the movables, as if to make quite sure that the President . . . had not made away with any of the furniture, or sold the fixtures for his private benefit.

Charles Dickens, *American Notes* (1842)

Long gone are the days when you could simply stroll into the White House. Indeed, for months after the September 11, 2001 terrorists attacks, the country's most famous home was closed to the public. The following information reflects past tour procedures and schedules, but additional security measures and restrictions may be in place at the time of your visit. We recommend calling for current details on public access and tours.

If you want to take a White House tour between **April and September** (or the two weeks before Christmas), you must first go to the **White House Visitor Center**, 1450 Pennsylvania Ave NW (daily 7.30am–4pm; ☎208-1631), housed in the Department of Commerce, a couple of hundred yards southeast of the White House. There you can pick up free tickets (maximum of four per person) for entrance to the White House at a fixed time later that morning. Arrive at the visitor center as early as possible – in high season, the ticket line snakes right around the outside of the building by 7am; from the 15th Street edge the wait averages thirty to forty minutes. The 4500 tickets available each day are usually all gone by 8.30am; on some days they're all spoken for as early as 6.30am (although you'll be informed if you have no chance of getting tickets). The first group of visitors is admitted to the White House at 10am: assemble in good time at the bleacher seats on the Ellipse and wait for your number to be called, at which point park rangers will lead your group to the East Executive Avenue gate.

From **October to March** (apart from the two weeks before Christmas), when there are fewer visitors, advance tickets are not required. Simply join the line at the gate – though you'll still need to get there early.

American citizens can arrange special tours by writing to their congressperson at least six months in advance. If you get a ticket this way, you'll be given a more in-depth VIP tour. Other parts of the White House are accessible on occasion throughout the year. In April and October the **gardens** are opened for afternoon tours; at **Christmas** there are special evening tours of the festively decorated interior; and on **Easter Monday**, the traditional Easter Egg Roll takes place on the South Lawn, a ceremony introduced during the nineteenth-century administration of Rutherford B. Hayes.

The visitor center also is worth a visit in its own right – preferably after the lines have disappeared. It displays photos and film footage of First Families and their distinguished guests, and the inaugural portraits, in which a succession of drawn and exhausted presidents hand over power to their beaming successors.

White House recorded information lines:
Special events ☎456-2200
Tours ☎456-7041
The president's daily schedule ☎456-2343

in the grand East Room while final touches were put on the mansion. East and west terraces were built during the administration of Thomas Jefferson, who, incidentally, had entered the original design competition under an assumed name; he also installed the first water closets and (true to extravagant form) introduced a French chef to the house. Under James Madison, the interior was redecorated by Capitol architect Benjamin Latrobe, who copied parts of Jefferson's earlier competition design with the defense that Jefferson's ideas were lifted in turn from "old French books, out of which he fishes everything." Occupying British forces burned down the mansion in August 1814, forcing Madison and his wife to flee; when the troops entered, they found the dining table set for forty, the wine poured in the decanters and the food cooked in the kitchen – they tucked in and then torched the building. Hoban was put in charge of its reconstruction after the war and the mansion was again ready for occupation in 1817, but with one significant change: to conceal fire damage to the exterior, the house was painted white. This was fitting, as – for obscure reasons – the mansion was already commonly known as the "White House."

Throughout the nineteenth century, the White House was decorated, added to and improved with each new occupant, though occasionally there were unforeseen setbacks. To celebrate his inauguration in 1829, the populist Andrew Jackson invited back the rowdier campaigning elements of his fledgling Democratic Party, who, in overexuberant mood, wrecked the place. Jackson was forced to spend the first night of his presidency in a hotel. He atoned by having the first indoor bathroom installed, in 1833; later improvements included gaslights in 1848, central heating and a steam laundry in 1853, the telephone in 1877 and electric lighting in 1891. During the Civil War, troops were briefly stationed in the East Room, cooking their dinner in the ornate fireplace, while the South Lawn was used as a field hospital. At the end of the war in 1865, following his assassination, Lincoln's coffin lay in state in the East Room (the first of seven presidents to be so honored). When a second president, James A. Garfield, lay dying from an assassin's bullet in 1881, enterprising naval engineers cooled his White House bedroom by concocting a prototype air-conditioner from a fan and a box of ice; full air-conditioning didn't follow until 1909.

Many of the house improvements were piecemeal, and not until Theodore Roosevelt's administration (1901–09) was any serious attempt made to coordinate structural repairs and the expansion necessary for family and staff. Elevators were added for convenience (Teddy once had a pony called Algonquin brought up in one to delight his sick son*) and an executive West Wing built, which incorporated the president's personal **Oval Office**. The famous **Rose Garden** was planted outside the Oval Office in 1913 on the orders of Ellen Wilson, and became used for ceremonial purposes. An entire residential third floor was added in 1927, an East Wing followed in the 1940s, while World War II saw additions as diverse as an air-raid shelter, swimming pool (which the lame FDR

---

* Theodore Roosevelt's children were the last presidential kids permitted to impose themselves on the often stifling formality of the White House, sliding down the banisters, chasing their pet rat and flying squirrel, and interrupting state dinners. They were encouraged by the prank-loving Teddy himself – "the very embodiment of noise," according to Henry James – who was happy to join in most of the rowdy pastimes, whatever the occasion. As the British ambassador at the time wrote home, rather wearily, "We must never forget that the President is seven years old." But even Roosevelt couldn't keep up with his eldest, wildest daughter Alice, later to be a famous Washington socialite. Asked if anything could be done to curb her high spirits, he allegedly replied: "I can be President of the United States, or I can control Alice. I cannot possibly do both."

The executive Power shall be vested in a President of the United States of America.

Article 2, Section 1, Constitution of the United States

The President is simply chief enforcer of American financial interests.

Gore Vidal

When they created the role of **President of the United States**, the delegates at the Constitutional Convention in Philadelphia in 1787 had no intention of replacing a discredited but all-powerful British monarchy with an American version. The federal system of government they devised separated executive, legislative and judicial powers (see p.331 for more) and prescribed precisely the limits of their authority. The president was made chief executive, though one whose role was within, rather than above, the uniquely balanced federal system. Indeed, the relative importance the Founding Fathers placed upon the position is clear from its place in the Constitution – presidential powers were detailed in Article 2, after full discussion of the more fundamental role of Congress in Article 1. At first, the president wasn't even directly **elected**, but chosen instead by an electoral college appointed by the states, the idea being to free the presidency from factional influence. The 12th Amendment (1804) opened up the ballot for president (and vice president) to popular election.

The president's place within the Constitution may be strictly defined, but the Constitution has very little to say about the presidency itself. Specific, enumerated **powers** are few – to make treaties, appoint federal officers, act as commander-in-chief, etc – and this may have reflected the fact that the Constitution's authors couldn't agree themselves exactly what the president's role should be. The subsequent elevation of the role is due in part to the succession of extraordinarily able leaders who occupied and enhanced the post in the late eighteenth and nineteenth centuries, from George Washington to Abraham Lincoln. The presidency has subsequently been molded beyond recognition as incumbents have thrust themselves forward as head of state, leader of their particular party and even national symbol – in fact, the almost monarchical figure the Constitution's authors desperately tried to avoid creating.

No longer simply chief executive, the US president is the embodiment of American power. Although the president's constitutional powers have barely expanded since the eighteenth century, the real influence available to him has. For example, under the president, the government's work is carried out by fourteen **executive departments**, whose appointed secretaries form the **Cabinet**. This is less a collective policy-making body than an advisory forum. Constitutionally, the president has sole executive responsibility, albeit he is assisted by special advisors, private White House staff and co-opted experts. Incoming presidents routinely change the staff at scores of federal agencies and advisory bodies, from the Post Office to the National Security Council, to ensure political consistency within the new administration (and also, in a more deep-seated practice, to reward loyal camp followers). These days, something approaching two thousand people work directly or indirectly for the Executive Office of the President, providing great scope for presidential patronage, while another 100,000 nonstrategic federal posts are technically within the presidential gift.

Additional information on the presidency can be found in Contexts, where there's a roll call of US presidents (p.336) and a description of the role of the president within the American political system (p.333).

used for exercise) and movie theater. Roosevelt, though, refused to entertain the idea of painting the White House black in order to foil enemy bombers.

All these renovation projects were completed while the presidential family of the day was in residence. This meant that additions and expansions tended to be finished too quickly, so that by 1948 the entire building was on the verge of collapse. Harry Truman – who had already added a poorly received balcony ("Truman's folly") to the familiar south side portico – had to move into nearby Blair House (see p.141) for four years while the structure was stabilized; new foundations were laid, all the rooms were dismantled and a modern steel frame inserted. The Trumans moved back in 1952, and since then there have been no significant alterations – unless you count Nixon's bowling alley, Ford's outdoor pool and Clinton's jogging track. Jimmy Carter contented himself with converting part of the house to solar energy.

The interior

Pick up a leaflet at the visitor center and you're set to steer yourself around the **self-guided tour**, which concentrates on the core of rooms on the ground and state (principal) floors. The Oval Office, family apartments and private offices on the second and third floors are off-limits; posted guards make sure you don't stray from the designated route. Once inside, your group is allowed to wander one-way through or past a half-dozen furnished rooms. Though guards will answer questions if they can, the tour is not exactly conducive to taking your time, and in many rooms you can't get close enough to appreciate the paintings or the furniture. Caught up in the flow of the crowd, most people are outside again well within thirty minutes. As if this weren't bad enough, there's a paucity of quality fixtures and fittings on display, and not just because much of the best stuff is kept in private quarters. Until Jackie Kennedy and her Fine Arts Committee put a stop to the practice, each incoming presidential family changed, sold or scrapped the furniture according to individual taste, while outgoing presidents took favorite pieces with them – you're just as likely to come across White House furniture and valuables in places like Dumbarton House or the Woodrow Wilson House.

Visitors enter the East Wing from the ground floor and traipse first past the Federal-style **Library**, paneled in timbers rescued from a mid-nineteenth-century refit and housing 2700 books by American authors. Opposite is the **Vermeil Room**, once a billiard room but now named for its extensive collection of silver gilt; the portraits are of recent First Ladies. Regular tours don't go any further on this floor, while VIP tours head next to the **China Room** – used to display china and glass since Wilson's presidency, and the spot where Annette Bening and Michael Douglas first kiss in the movie *The American President*. Beyond, in the oval **Diplomatic Reception Room**, where panoramic wallpaper depicts American landscapes, new ambassadors present themselves to the president. Eight days after his inauguration in 1933, this was the room from which Franklin D. Roosevelt broadcast the first of his so-called "Fireside Chats," popularizing the New Deal. The adjacent **Map Room** was FDR's private retreat during World War II, where he and Winston Churchill sank into the Chippendale chairs to chart the progress of the war. It's now used as a private reception room for the president; in 1998, Bill Clinton testified from here by video link during the Grand Jury hearings into the Lewinsky affair.

The regular tour moves upstairs to the State Floor, where the first stop is the **East Room.** The largest in the White House, the East Room has been open to the public since the days of Andrew Jackson. Used in the past for weddings, various lyings-in-state and other major ceremonies, it's on a suitably grand scale for once, with long, yellow drapes, a brown marble fireplace and turn-of-the-century glass chandeliers. Between the fireplaces hangs the one major artwork on general display: Gilbert Stuart's celebrated 1797 portrait of a steely George Washington, rescued from the flames by Dolley Madison when the British burned the White House.

The last rooms on the tour are more intimate in scale. The **Green Room**, its walls lined in silk, was Jefferson's dining room and JFK's favorite in the entire house. Portraits line the walls, Dolley Madison's French candlesticks are on the mantelpiece, and a fine matching green dinner service occupies the cabinet. The room is now often called upon to host receptions, as is the adjacent, oval **Blue Room**, whose ornate French furniture was bought by President Monroe after the 1814 fire. In 1886, Grover Cleveland was married in here, the only time a president has been married in the White House. The **Red Room** is the smallest of the lot, decorated in early nineteenth-century Empire style and sporting attractive inlaid oak doors. Finally, the painted-oak-paneled **State Dining Room** harks back to the East Room in scale and style and hosts banquets for important guests. At one time Theodore Roosevelt used to stick his big game trophies in here, though the most enduring item is the inscription engraved on the mantelpiece, part of a quotation from a letter by John Adams to his wife – "May none but honest and wise men ever rule under this roof." Some hope. You then loop back through the cross halls and exit on the north side of the White House, opposite Lafayette Square.

The Ellipse

The Ellipse – the large grassy expanse south of the White House – forms an integral part of the city plan's symmetry: due north is the rounded portico and porch of the White House, with the axis of 16th Street beyond; south, the Washington Monument and Jefferson Memorial.

In summer you'll probably have considerable time to kill here waiting for your White House tour. Bleacher seats and occasional concerts help maintain the spirits, though the same can't be said of the group of nearby sights. On the northern edge of the Ellipse, at E Street opposite the South Lawn, the **Zero Milestone** marks the point from which all distances on US highways are measured. Here, too, is the rather stumpy **National Christmas Tree**, lit by the president every year to mark the start of the holiday season. If you can stand the excitement, keep to the east (15th St) side of the Ellipse and walk south to where a bronze boy scout marks the site of the **Boy Scout Memorial** – the flanking figures entirely unsuited to moral guardianship, at least until they put some clothes on. Nearby, the simple granite **Monument to the Original Patentees** commemorates the eighteenth-century landowners who ceded land so that the city could be built. At the southeastern corner of the Ellipse, the stone **Bulfinch Gatehouse** at Constitution and 15th was one of a pair that once stood at the western entrance to the Capitol grounds. Its partner stands across the Ellipse at Constitution and 17th.

Lafayette Square and around

Originally part of the White House gardens, spick-and-span **Lafayette Square** was known until 1824 as President's Square and lined with the houses of cabinet members and other prominent citizens. Jefferson later turned it into a public park, at the same time as the White House was opened to visitors; since then it's remained the most attractive approach to the president's house beyond. **Redevelopment** threatened the surrounding houses on several occasions, until the Kennedys took a keen interest in their preservation in the 1960s, saving them from further interference. However, cosmetic changes are imminent in "America's Town Square," as it's referred to rather self-importantly. The banning of traffic on Pennsylvania Avenue outside the White House has prompted proposals to extend the square's parameters, introducing shops, galleries and cafés as part of a fully pedestrianized zone between H Street and the White House. In the meantime, in-line skaters take advantage of the lack of traffic by organizing scratch games of street hockey in front of the president's house.

The square

Regularly patrolled by the police, **Lafayette Square** is one of the safest places to stretch out on the grass in downtown DC. It's also the closest that protesters are allowed to get to the White House; there's a knot of banner-clutching citizens in place most days with various points to make.

For many decades in the nineteenth century, the only statue here was the central figure of **Andrew Jackson**, astride a rearing horse and doffing his hat – soldiers encamped on the square during the Civil War used to hang their washing from it – though this was framed in the twentieth century by the addition of four corner statues, all of foreign-born Revolutionary generals. Most famous of all, in the southeast corner, is the Frenchman, the **Marquis de Lafayette**, who – inspired by the Declaration of Independence and his friendship with Benjamin Franklin, American minister in Paris – raised an army on behalf of the American colonists and was made a US general at the age of 19. Later imprisoned in France as a "traitor," he was never abandoned by America. He returned to the States an old man in 1824, a triumphal visit during which he was feted on the Mall and received various honors, including the naming of this square. His statue shows him flanked by French admirals and being handed a sword by a female nude, symbolizing America.

Built by the first surgeon-general in 1826, **Blair House**, in the southwestern corner of Lafayette Square, was where Robert E. Lee was offered – and refused – the command of the Union Army. It has served as the presidential guest house since the 1940s, hosting foreign dignitaries, while both the Truman and Clinton families used it while White House renovations were in progress.

Oldest house on the square is **Decatur House** at 748 Jackson Place NW, at the corner with H Street (Tues–Fri 10am–3pm, Sat & Sun noon–4pm; free; ⊺842-0920, ⊚www.decaturhouse.org). Dating from 1819, this red-brick house was built by Benjamin Latrobe (who had already worked on the White House) for Stephen Decatur, another precociously young American hero who performed with distinction as a navy captain in the War of 1812. As things turned out, Decatur lived here for little more than a year, since he was killed in a duel with one Commodore Barron; the Federal-style first floor, studded with naval memorabilia, is decorated in the fashion of the day. Most of the other period rooms owe their inlaid floors, furnishings and decorative arts to the successive owners' penchant for heavy-handed Victorian style. Short guided tours run throughout the day.

Walking east along the top of the square, you pass the Renaissance splendor of the **Hay-Adams Hotel** (at H and 16th; see p.246 for details), fashioned from the former townhouses of statesman John Hay (once President Lincoln's private secretary) and his friend, historian and author Henry Adams. Their adjacent homes were the site of glittering soirées, attended by Theodore Roosevelt and his circle, an association that appealed to hotshot society hotel developer Harry Wardman, who jumped at the chance to buy the properties in 1927. Since then, the hotel (which boasted the first air-conditioned dining room in the city) has been at the heart of Washington politicking – Henry Kissinger lunched here regularly, Oliver North did much of his clandestine Iran-Contra fundraising here, while the Clintons stayed over before Bill's first inauguration.

Immediately across 16th Street, the tiny, yellow **St John's Church** (Mon–Sat 8am–4pm; free tours after 11am Sun service; ☎347-8766) dates from 1816. Latrobe again did the honors, providing the neighborhood with a handsome domed church in the form of a Greek cross, with appealing half-moon windows in the upper gallery of the intimately proportioned interior. Unsurprisingly, St John's is commonly known as the "Church of the Presidents"; all since Madison have visited – sitting in the special pew (No. 54) reserved for them (the kneeling cushions are embroidered with their names) – and when an incumbent dies in office the bells of St John's ring out across the city.

Old Executive Office and Treasury buildings

The highly ornate, granite **Old Executive Office Building** at 17th Street and Pennsylvania Avenue NW (free tours Sat 9–11.30am; reservation required ☎395-5895) was built (1871–88) to house the State, War and Navy departments. Its architect, Alfred B. Mullet, claiming to be inspired by the Louvre in Paris, produced an ill-conceived French Empire-style building with hundreds of free-standing columns, extraordinarily tall and thin chimneys, a copper mansard roof, pediments, porticos, and various pedantic stone flourishes. It was never terribly popular – Truman thought it a monstrosity – but schemes to renovate or rebuild came to nothing, mainly because of the expense involved in tackling such a behemoth. These days its gracefully aging facade is loved a little more, and the roomy interior provides office space for government and White House staff. Notoriously, the building was the base of the White House "Plumbers," Nixon's dirty-tricks campaign team, and hosted several of the infamous tape-recorded Watergate meetings; it was also where the zealously patriotic Colonel Oliver North shredded documents central to the Iran-Contra affair. You need to call well in advance to tour the public rooms, ornate with marble and gilt, stained glass, tiled floors and wrought-iron balconies.

It's a similar story if you want to see inside the **Treasury Building,** whose long facade interrupts the line of Pennsylvania Avenue on the other side of the White House. Call at least a week in advance (☎622-0896, ⓦwww.ustreas

.gov/curator) to reserve a spot on a free guided tour (Sat only). Built – or at least started – in 1836 by Robert Mills (of Washington Monument fame), this is commonly judged to be the finest Greek Revival building in the city. Its thirty-column colonnade facing 15th Street is particularly impressive. During the Civil War, the basement was strengthened and food and arms stored in the building, since Lincoln and his aides were determined to hole up here if the city was ever attacked. The **statue** at the southern entrance, facing Hamilton Place, is of **Alexander Hamilton**, first Secretary of the Treasury (and the man on the front of the $10 bill; the Treasury Building itself is on the back). One of the most highly respected members of Washington's first administration, Hamilton later died in a duel with Aaron Burr, Jefferson's vice president and scheming Northern Confederalist, to whom Hamilton was implacably opposed.

The Renwick Gallery

Pennsylvania Ave at 17th St NW ☎357-2531, ⓦ www.nmaa.si.edu; Farragut West Metro. Daily 10am–5.30pm. Admission free.

The Second Empire flourishes of the Old Executive Office Building were directly influenced by the earlier, smaller and much more harmonious **Renwick Gallery** of American arts and crafts, which lies directly opposite across Pennsylvania Avenue. Built by James Renwick (architect of the Smithsonian Castle) in 1859, the red-brick building was originally destined to house the private art collection of financier William Wilson Corcoran. Work was interrupted by the Civil War, during which the building was requisitioned for use by the Union Army's quartermaster-general; Corcoran, a man with Southern sympathies, had left for Europe in 1862, where he stayed for the entire war. On his return, Corcoran finally got his gallery back (and, having sued, $125,000 from the government as back rent) and opened it to the public, but within twenty years his burgeoning collection had outgrown the site – which led to the building of the new Corcoran Gallery, just a couple of blocks south (see overleaf). After several decades as the US Court of Claims, the by then decrepit building was saved and restored in the 1960s by the Smithsonian, which uses it to display selections from the National Museum of American Art.

The building itself is a treat: an inscription above the entrance announces it to be "Dedicated to Art," and the ornate design reaches its apogee in the deep-red **Grand Salon** on the upper floor, a soaring parlor preserved in the style of the 1860s and 1870s – featuring windows draped in striped damask, period portraits (including one of Corcoran), velvet-covered benches, marble-topped cabinets and splendid wood-and-glass display cases taken from the Smithsonian Castle. This was the main picture gallery in Corcoran's time; its lofty dimensions meant that there was no difficulty in converting it into a courtroom and judge's chambers during the Court of Claims' tenure. Opposite, the smaller **Octagon Room** was specifically designed to hold Hiram Powers' notorious nude statue *The Greek Slave* (now in the Corcoran Gallery itself).

Between the two rooms on the same floor are galleries devoted to American crafts, mostly modern jewelry and furniture but also sculpture, ceramics, abstracts and applied art in all its manifestations. The first floor hosts **temporary exhibitions** of contemporary crafts (weekday walk-in tours at noon).

South along 17th Street

Having seen the major sights around the White House, you can stroll south down **17th Street** toward Constitution Avenue, calling in at a clutch of buildings along the way. Main port of call is the **Corcoran Gallery of Art**, the city's earliest art gallery, and still among its finest, though there are smaller, more offbeat collections nearby. Keep an eye out, too, for a couple of other notable structures: the five-story, iron-framed **Winder Building** (604 17th St NW), housing federal government offices, was in 1848 the tallest building in Washington and the first to incorporate central heating; the white marble headquarters of the **American Red Cross** (between D and E streets) sports Tiffany stained glass in its second-floor assembly rooms.

The Corcoran Gallery of Art

500 17th St NW ☏639-1700, ⓦwww.corcoran.org; Farragut West Metro. Mon, Wed & Fri–Sun 10am–5pm, Thurs 10am–9pm; tours daily (except Tues) at noon, additional tours Thurs at 7.30pm and Sat & Sun at 2.30pm. Admission $5 ($8 for family groups); free Monday all day and Thursday after 5pm.

When the **Corcoran Gallery of Art** shifted premises at the end of the nineteenth century, moving from what is now the Renwick Gallery, it took its collection and ideals with it. Ernest Flagg's Beaux Arts design is a beautiful construction of curving white marble with a green copper roof, the light and airy interior enhanced by a superb double atrium. When an extension was required in the late 1920s, the trustees, seeking continuity, looked to Charles A. Platt, who had done such a good job with the Freer Gallery of Art.

The Corcoran Gallery's American holdings are mighty: more than three thousand paintings, from colonial to contemporary, alongside American Neoclassical sculpture and forays into modern photography, prints and drawings. Over the years, the permanent collection has expanded considerably to include European works (particularly seventeenth-century Dutch and nineteenth-century French), Greek antiquities and even medieval tapestries. Benefactors continue to bestow impressive gifts: in recent years Dr Armand Hammer has donated a large collection of Daumier lithographs, and there's been an important bequest by Olga Hirshhorn (wife of Joseph of the eponymous gallery) of seven hundred works by two hundred nineteenth- and twentieth-century artists and sculptors, from Picasso to Calder.

A 140,000-square-foot new wing, already in the works, will go a long way toward accommodating the museum's burgeoning collection — and, given that it's been designed by renowned architect Frank Gehry, the flowing, sculptural addition is also sure to stand out amid Foggy Bottom's venerable old buildings.

Works from the permanent collection are rotated throughout the year, and other pieces are sent out on tour; not everything mentioned below will be on display at any one time – especially given the space constraints caused by the new wing's construction. Details of changing exhibitions are available at the **information desk**, inside the main entrance, which is also where you sign up for the **guided tours** of the permanent collection. The **gallery shop** has one of the city's better collections of posters, cards and books. The **café** (daily except Tues 11am–2pm, Thurs until 8pm) is decent too, especially during the gospel brunch (Sun 11am–2pm; $19), when the songs ring out through the gallery.

THE WHITE HOUSE AND FOGGY BOTTOM | The Corcoran Gallery of Art

European art

The gallery's collection of **European art** is a very mixed bag, mainly composed of the 1925 bequest of Senator William A. Clark, an industrialist with more money than discretion. That's not to say there aren't some splendid pieces on display; rather that there's little overall cohesion, certainly in a gallery otherwise devoted to American art. Corcoran himself, though, had already blurred the edges of his collection by commissioning 120 animal bronzes by French sculptor **Antoine-Louis Barye** (1796–1875), a selection of which are usually on display. These are graphic representations, often of snarling, fighting animals: a horse attacked by a lion, a python crushing a gazelle.

Some of the most familiar names hang in the **Clark Landing**, a two-tier, wood-paneled gallery accessed from the Rotunda on the second floor. Here you're likely to find paintings by Degas, Renoir, Monet and Pissarro. Perhaps the most prominent of the earlier **French and English** paintings of the seventeenth to nineteenth centuries are the sympathetic Thomas Gainsborough portraits of Lord and Lady Dunstanville. The only other European exhibits of real interest are the selection of sixteenth-century **French and Italian** works, including some outstanding Italian majolica plates depicting mythological scenes, and two large, allegorical wool-and-silk French tapestries (1506) representing contemporaneous political and historical events.

However, the gallery's main European holding is not painting, but the corner room on the first floor known as the **Salon Doré** (Gilded Room), which originally formed part of an eighteenth-century Parisian home, the Hôtel de Clermont. Clark bought the entire room, intending to install it in his New York mansion; it came to the Corcoran after his death, where it now stands as a supreme example of French design. Framed mirrors (flanked by medallion-holding cherubs) make it seem larger than it actually is; the floor-to-ceiling hand-carved wood paneling, gold-leaf decor and ceiling murals are perfectly judged.

American art

The bulk of the **American art** is usually displayed on the second floor. Approach through the Rotunda and Clark Landing and you'll be presented with a preliminary burst of minor paintings by early American artists such as Gilbert Stuart, Thomas Cole, George Inness and Benjamin West. One piece with real spark is Rembrandt Peale's imperious, equestrian *Washington Before Yorktown* (1824), showing the general in the hours before the decisive battle for independence.

The gallery possesses a fine collection of **landscapes**, starting with the expansive *Niagara* (1857) by Frederic Edwin Church and Albert Bierstadt's splendid *The Last of the Buffalo* (1889), both masterpieces of immense scale. While Church concerned himself with the power of nature, Bierstadt here celebrates human endeavor in the natural world, portraying the Native American braves pursuing buffalo so numerous they darken the plain in their thousands. In marked contrast, Thomas Cole's *The Return* (1837), a mythical medieval scene of an injured knight returning to a priory glowing in the evening light, has little to do with America, though it does display the Hudson River School theme of ethereal natural beauty. An interesting historical note is provided by artist-cum-inventor Samuel F.B. Morse's *The Old House of Representatives* (1822), which the artist finished in a studio at the US Capitol so that he could observe his subjects at work. For all his efforts, he failed to convey any sense of the urgency of debate. Morse lost money when he exhibited the painting – which led him to conclude he'd be better off sticking with inventing.

△ Major General Andrew Jackson statue, Lafayette Square

One room is usually devoted to nineteenth-century portraiture, with formal studies by renowned artists like John Trumbull (who painted the Capitol murals) and Charles Bird King. Most prominent, though, are the presidential portraits by **George Peter Alexander Healy**, commissioned by Congress in 1857 for display in the White House: van Buren, Tyler, Polk, Taylor, Arthur and a highly sympathetic Lincoln. This seems an odd room in which to display the gallery's most notorious piece of sculpture, **Hiram Powers'** *The Greek Slave* (1846), originally on show in the Renwick Gallery. Her manacled hands and simple nudity so outraged the sensibilities of contemporary critics that women visitors were prevented from viewing the statue while there were men in the room.

Moving into **late nineteenth-century** art, the gallery holds works by John Singer Sargent, Thomas Eakins and Mary Cassatt among others. Society portraitist Sargent also produced one of the gallery's most loved pieces – the startling landscape of crags and boulders of *Simplon Pass* (1911). Few works, however, are as robust as Winslow Homer's depiction of sea folk: the brawny arms of the woman swathed in fishing nets in *A Light on the Sea* (1897) suggest the realities of her life better than any storm-tossed fishing scene. Working women are rare subjects indeed in works of this period, while American blacks were hardly ever considered an enlightening contemporary subject – exceptions include Richard Norris Brooke's beautifully lit family on the receiving end of *A Pastoral Visit* (1881). At the other end of the social scale, genre scenes of genteel domesticity, seen in works by Edmund Charles Tarbell, Frank Weston Benson, William Paxton and others, are a common in the Corcoran collection.

Pre-World War II paintings include works by Childe Hassam, George Bellows, Rockwell Kent, Thomas Hart Benton and, of course, Edward Hopper, whose yachting picture *Ground Swell* (1939) adds a real splash of color while providing a mere hint of menace. Meanwhile, realists Raphael Soyer (*Waiting Room*, 1940) and Ross Moffett (*Provincetown Wharf*, 1935) show an interest instead in the more mundane minutiae of daily working life. The remainder of the second-floor rooms are devoted to changing selections of prints, drawings and photographs from the permanent collection, as well as special exhibitions. Depending on space, **postwar and contemporary** American art gets a glance too, and you can expect examples from all the big names, including Lichtenstein, Warhol and de Kooning.

DAR Museum

1776 D St NW ☎879-3241, ✆www.dar.org/museum; Farragut West Metro. Mon–Fri 8.30am–4pm, Sun 1–5pm; tours Mon–Fri 10am–2.30pm, Sun 1–4.30pm; closed two weeks in April. Admission free.

The **National Society of the Daughters of the American Revolution** (DAR) has had its headquarters in Washington for more than a century. Founded in 1890, this thoroughly patriotic (if unswervingly conservative) organization is open to women who can prove descent from an ancestor (male or female) who served the American cause during the Revolution. Fueled by the motto "God, Home and Country," it busies itself with earnestly nonpolitical good-citizen and educational programs, including one designed to promote "correct flag usage" throughout America: the Stars and Stripes adorning the rostrums in the Senate and the House in the US Capitol are gifts from the DAR, just two of more than 100,000 given away since 1909.

The organization's original meeting place was the 1905 Beaux Arts **Memorial Continental Hall**, facing 17th Street, whose main chamber hosted the world's first disarmament conference in 1921. Delegates now meet for their annual congress (the week of April 19, anniversary of the Battle of Lexington) in the massive adjoining **Constitution Hall** on 18th Street, designed with typical exuberance by John Russell Pope in 1929, but which you're unlikely to see unless your visit coincides with a concert (see p.288). It's one of the finest auditoriums in the city (indeed, until the Kennedy Center was built, the hall was the home of the National Symphony Orchestra), so it came as no surprise that when the peerless black contralto **Marian Anderson** (1902–93) was invited to sing in Washington in 1939, she was originally booked to appear here. What was shocking was that a racially hidebound DAR refused to allow her to perform at the hall: Eleanor Roosevelt resigned from the organization in outrage, and Anderson gave her concert instead on Easter Sunday at the Lincoln Memorial to a rapt crowd of 75,000.

Visitors to the DAR Museum (entrance on D St) are shown first into the **gallery**, a hodgepodge of embroidered samplers and quilts, silverware, toys, kitchenware, glass, crockery and earthenware – in fact just about anything the Daughters have managed to lay their hands on over the years. Although exhibits change, there's usually a particularly fine selection of ceramics, popular in the Revolutionary and Federal periods (from which most of the collection dates). On request, one of the docents will lead you through the rest of the building, starting off in the 125,000-volume genealogical **library** – once the main meeting hall, but now open to DAR members and the public ($5 a day) keen to bone up on such topics as *The History of Milwaukee* (in eight alarmingly large volumes) or *The Genealogy of the Witherspoon Family*.

What they're most proud of, however, are the **State Rooms**, a collection of no fewer than 33 period salons, mainly decorated with pre-1850 furnishings, each representing a different state. Few are of any historical or architectural merit, though occasionally there's a glimmer of relief: the New England room, containing a supposedly original lacquered wooden tea chest retrieved from Boston Harbor after the Tea Party in 1773; the Californian adobe house interior; and the New Jersey room whose entire furnishings, paneling and furniture were fashioned from the wreck of a British frigate sunk off the coast during the Revolutionary War – the overly elaborate chandelier was made from the melted-down anchor.

Organization of American States Building

17th St at Constitution Ave NW ☎458-3000, ⓦwww.oas.org; Farragut West Metro. Mon–Fri 9am–5.30pm. Admission free.

Founded in 1890 "to strengthen the peace and security of the continent," the **Organization of American States** (OAS) is the world's oldest regional organization, with 35 member states from Antigua to Venezuela. Its headquarters occupy one of the more charming buildings in the city, a squat, white Spanish Colonial mansion built in 1910 and facing onto the Ellipse. From the main entrance on 17th Street – fronted by a gaunt statue of Queen Isabella of Spain, who sent Columbus on his New World voyage – you pass through fanciful iron gates to a cloistered lobby. The decor here turns almost to whimsy, with a fountain and tropical trees reaching to the wooden eaves and stone frieze above. Beyond the lobby, it's usually possible to catch temporary exhibitions of Latin American art; check in at the reception desk. Then climb upstairs, walk through the gallery of national flags and busts of OAS founder members, and take a peek in the grand Hall of the Americas.

A path leads from the Constitution Avenue side of the building through the so-called **Aztec Garden** to the smaller building behind. The **Art Museum of the Americas** – officially at 201 18th Street NW (Tues–Sun 10am–5pm; free; ☎458-6016) – shows changing exhibits of Central and South American art, but again it's the interior that catches the eye. In the main brick-floored gallery, the walls are lined with lively Latin American ceramics reaching to a wood-beamed roof.

Foggy Bottom

Together with Georgetown, **FOGGY BOTTOM** – south of Pennsylvania Avenue to Constitution Avenue, between 17th and 25th streets – forms one of the oldest parts of DC. Settled as early as the mid-eighteenth century, the thriving town on the shores of the Potomac (which reached further north in those days) was known variously as Hamburg or Funkstown, after its German land-

Eating, drinking and staying in Foggy Bottom

For Foggy Bottom listings, see the following pages: accommodation p.249; eating p.268; drinking and nightlife p.280.

lord Jacob Funk. Fashionable houses were built on the higher ground above today's E Street, though down by the river, in what is now West Potomac Park, it was a different story: filthy industries emptied effluents into the Potomac and the city canal, while workers' housing was erected on the low-lying malarial marshlands, blighted by plagues of rats, rampant poison ivy and winter mud and fog. It's not hard to see how the popular name originated.

The poor, predominantly black, neighborhood changed radically once the marshlands were drained in the late 1800s. Families and industries were displaced by the new West Potomac Park; the neighborhood's southern limit was now defined by the grand Constitution Avenue, which replaced the filled-in city canal. The smarter streets to the north formed the backdrop for a series of **federal and institutional organizations** that moved in during the years on either side of World War II, as the federal workforce rapidly expanded. Early city plans had made little provision for an influx of government support staff. In 1802, there were only 291 federal employees; by the 1970s the total number of civilians employed by the US government had risen to over two million, and entire districts like Foggy Bottom were appropriated to house DC's burgeoning share.

The cultural activities at the **Kennedy Center** and the various offices and institutions rather set the white-collar tone, but you can visit enough of the buildings to make a walk through the neighborhood worthwhile. The nearest Metro is **Foggy Bottom–GWU**, which is handy for George Washington University, Washington Circle and the Kennedy Center but is half a dozen blocks and fifteen minutes from Constitution Avenue. Consider, instead, approaching from the east, after touring the White House. The Tourmobile bus runs along Constitution Avenue and up 23rd Street to the Kennedy Center.

Constitution Avenue

From the OAS Building (see opposite) at the corner of 17th Street, **Constitution Avenue** – known as B Street until the 1930s – presents an attractive line of buildings framed by the greenery of Constitution Gardens across the way. The first of any distinction is the enormous, eagle-fronted **Federal Reserve Building** of 1937, between 20th and 21st streets (Mon–Fri 11am–2pm; ☎452-3326), designed by Paul Cret, who was also responsible for the OAS and the Folger Shakespeare Library on Capitol Hill. It's the headquarters of the Federal Reserve System – the organization that controls the money supply, issues government securities and is responsible for the country's gold reserves. If you want to know any more than that, weekly tours of the building are available, though you can walk in during the week to check out the special art exhibitions.

The **National Academy of Sciences** (Mon–Fri 8am–5pm; free; ☎334-2000) is next, created by Congress in 1863 to provide the nation with independent, objective scientific advice. Again, there's exhibition space inside, and the academy also hosts chamber recitals (see p.289). The style here is Neoclassical, the facade adorned with Greek inscriptions, but its cold lines are tempered by a grove of elm and holly trees at the southwest (22nd St) corner, in which sits a large bronze **statue of Albert Einstein**, by Robert Berks, erected to commemorate the centennial of the scientist's birth. The rumpled Einstein lounges on a granite bench with the universe (in the shape of a galaxy map) at his feet; in his hand is a piece of paper inscribed with the famous formula ($E=mc^2$) from his Theory of Relativity. Finally, the corner plot of the avenue, at 23rd Street, is occupied by the building of the **American Pharmaceutical Association**, a severe Beaux Arts construction by John Russell Pope, completed in 1933.

Department of State

Between 21st and 23rd streets NW, at C St ☎647-3241, ⊕www.state.gov; Farragut West Metro. Tours by appointment only Mon–Fri 9.30am, 10.30am & 2.45pm. Reserve several weeks in advance. Admission free.

The **Department of State** received its own headquarters in 1960, following its move out of the Old Executive Office Building, and handsome they are too – a long, white, unblemished building occupying two entire blocks in the southwest corner of Foggy Bottom. The nation's oldest and most senior cabinet agency, established as early as 1789, the State Department is effectively the federal foreign office. It's also notoriously circumspect, and it's a wonder that visitors were ever allowed in at all. In fact, after the September 11, 2001 terrorist attacks, the Department suspended tours indefinitely. If and when such visits resume, it will still likely be all but impossible for foreign tourists to visit, as in the past the hour-long tours had to be booked several weeks in advance. But if you are able to visit, your effort is rewarded by a glimpse of one of the capital's more overblown interiors. During the 1960s, many of the rooms were redecorated and refurnished to provide a series of chambers suitable for the reception of diplomats and visiting heads of state. In came a wealth of eighteenth- and nineteenth-century paintings and furniture – including the desk on which the Treaty of Paris, which ended the War of Independence, was signed.

Department of the Interior

C St NW, between 18th and 19th streets ☎208-4743, ⊕www.doi.gov; Foggy Bottom–GWU Metro. Mon–Fri 8.30am–4.30pm; call in advance for tours of the building and murals. Admission free.

For a walk-in tour of a government department, head further east down C Street to the **Department of the Interior**, the nation's principal conservation agency. One of the earliest federal departments to take up residence in Foggy Bottom, the Interior Department moved into Waddy Butler Wood's granite, square-columned building in 1937. Inside, grand WPA-era murals enliven the walls, including one commemorating Marian Anderson's 1939 concert at the Lincoln Memorial (see p.147).

Present ID at the reception desk and you'll be directed to the **Department of the Interior Museum**, a little-visited nook that throws some light on the various agencies that come under the Department's auspices – such as the Bureau of Land Management, the National Park Service and the Bureau of Indian Affairs. The wood-paneled museum, opened in 1938, is very much of its time: then more than 100,000 people a year toured its dioramas and exhibits; now you'll be on your own as you puzzle over fossil and mineral samples and examine stuffed bison heads, old saddles and paintings by nineteenth-century surveyors of the West. With so much else to see in Washington, you'll probably want to give the museum a miss, unless you're keen on seeing one of the regularly changing special exhibitions of photography, paintings or sculpture – often on a theme broadly related to the Department's mandate. Around the corner from the museum, a **gift shop** sells Native American crafts.

Elsewhere inside the Department, the **National Park Service informa-tion office** (Mon–Fri 9am–5pm) has free leaflets about every NPS park, museum and monument in the country – in DC, that includes all the major memorials along the Mall.

The Octagon

1799 New York Ave NW ☎638-3105, ⊛www.archfoundation.org; Farragut West Metro. Tues–Sun 10am–4pm. Admission $5.

When Virginian plantation owner John Tayloe had his Washington townhouse built in 1800, he picked a prime corner plot just two blocks away from the new President's Mansion. In those days **the Octagon**, as it became known, was set amid fields and flanked by a line of fir trees. Today, dwarfed by the office build-ings behind it, it still serves as a fine example of the type of private mansion that once characterized the neighborhood. Tayloe, a friend of George Washington, was so rich and well connected that he could afford to spend the colossal sum of $35,000 on his house, engaging the services of William Thornton, winner of the competition to design the US Capitol.

The **War of 1812** guaranteed the house its place in history. Spared the bon-fire that destroyed the White House – possibly because the French ambassador was in residence at the time – the Octagon was offered to the Madisons, who had been forced to flee the city. For six months in 1814–15, President Madison conducted the business of government from its rooms; on February 17, 1815, the Treaty of Ghent, making peace with Britain, was signed in the study (on a table still kept in the house). For much of the latter part of the nineteenth cen-tury, the Octagon was left to deteriorate, but at the turn of the last century it was bought by the American Institute of Architects (AIA), which used it as its headquarters until 1973. The AIA – now ensconced in modern premises to the rear – still maintains the Octagon, which is open as both a historic house and **museum of architecture**, with changing exhibitions devoted to architecture, decorative arts and city history.

The **building** itself is not, in fact, an octagon – forced into an acute street corner, it has only six sides; the name was mis-assigned by the Tayloes when it was built. A rather simple brick exterior hides an example of period American Federal architecture unsurpassed in the city. The circular entry hall sports its original marble floor, while beyond, a swirling, oval staircase climbs up three stories. The house had two master bedrooms and five more for the Tayloe's fif-teen children; most of the rooms are now used as gallery space. In the dining and drawing rooms, period furnishings reveal how the house would have looked – light, with high ceilings, delicate plaster cornicing and Chippendale accompaniments. The two portraits in the dining room are of the architect and the owner; the beautifully carved stone mantel in the drawing room is an ori-ginal, signed and dated 1799.

GWU to Washington Circle

The L'Enfant city plan allowed for the building of a university in the Foggy Bottom district, and it was certainly a development that Washington himself was keen on; he even left money in his will to endow an educational institu-tion. Baptist college founded by an Act of Congress in 1821 was the precursor of today's **George Washington University** (GWU), which moved into the neighborhood in 1912. Since then it has played a crucial role in the city's development, buying up townhouses and erecting new buildings on such a scale as to make it the second-biggest landholder in DC after the federal government. Famous alumni include Jacqueline Kennedy Onassis (who gets a building named after her), J. Edgar Hoover, General Colin Powell and crime author (and Harry's daughter) Margaret Truman. The main campus spreads over several city blocks between F, 20th and 24th streets and Pennsylvania Avenue; there's an information desk in the **Academic Center** at 801 22nd Street NW (Jan–April & Aug–Oct Mon–Fri 9am–5pm, Sat 10am–3pm; T 994-6602), on the H Street side. You can pick up a map of the campus here and ask about the occasional student-led historic **walking tours** of the neighborhood. GWU's main entertainment hall is the Lisner Auditorium (see p.287 and p.289 for details).

Although the student presence certainly enlivens the district, few of the university buildings are worth more than a passing glance; some people have kind words for the **Law Library** (716 20th St NW), which at least makes an attempt to fit in with its surroundings. This backs onto perhaps the nicest part of the campus, **University Yard** (between G and H, and 20th and 21st), a green, rose-planted park surrounded by Colonial Revival buildings; the statue of George Washington here is yet another copy of the famous Houdon image.

Nearby, on the southeast corner of 20th and G, the red-brick Gothic, Lutheran **United Church**, built in 1889 for the descendants of the neighborhood's Germanic immigrants, provides a solitary reminder of Foggy Bottom's antecedents. If you're heading back toward the White House, you may as well stick with G Street, which passes the concrete chicken-coop buildings of the twin peaks of international capitalism – the **International Monetary Fund** and, in the next block, the **World Bank**. For a glimpse of how modern development has encroached completely upon the remaining nineteenth-century pockets of Foggy Bottom, head instead up 20th Street to Pennsylvania Avenue. Between 20th and 21st, the **2000 Pennsylvania Avenue** complex of offices, shops and cafés preserves the original pastel-colored facades of a row of townhouses.

West of the university, en route to Foggy Bottom–GWU Metro station, you can swing by **St Mary's Church**, at 730 23rd Street, between G and H (daily 9.30am–3pm), the first black Episcopal church in DC. Established in 1886, the church was paid for by a wealthy band of local citizens who stumped up $15,000 to hire the services of none other than James Renwick (of the Smithsonian Castle and Renwick Gallery), whose hand is clear in the church's careful Gothic proportions. Two blocks west, **25th Street** (north of H) gives a hint of Foggy Bottom's historic charms with a carefully preserved run of attractive nineteenth-century brick houses picked out in pastels. The most interesting are those in **Snow Court** (off 25th, between I and K), the district's only surviving interior alley, where the houses are a bare twelve feet wide – in the 1880s each one probably housed ten people; nowadays they change hands for a fortune.

One block north of the Metro, the northern limit of Foggy Bottom is marked by **Washington Circle**, L'Enfant's radial point for the major thoroughfares of Pennsylvania and New Hampshire avenues and K Street. In its center sits Clark Mills' equestrian statue of George Washington, erected at the outbreak of the Civil War and looking toward the White House and Capitol; not a thing of great splendor it's true, but quite how it aroused the particular ire of Anthony Trollope is a mystery. He thought it "by far the worst" equestrian statue he had ever seen, claiming "the horse is most absurd, but the man sitting on the horse is manifestly drunk."

Watergate

If there's a building that defines modern, political Washington, it's not the White House or the Capitol but the **Watergate Complex**, at 25th Street NW by Virginia Avenue, which gave its name to the most noxious political scandal ever to rock the country. This unassuming curving, Italian-designed mid-1960s residential and commercial complex – named for the flight of steps behind the Lincoln Memorial that lead down to the Potomac – has always been a much sought-after address, both for various foreign ambassadors and for city top brass. The Doles and Caspar Weinberger have maintained apartments here for years, while a young White House intern called Monica Lewinsky also lived here before scandal forced her from DC. In 1972, its sixth floor housed the headquarters of the Democratic National Committee, the burglary of which led, two years later, to the resignation of a president.

The Kennedy Center

2700 F St NW, at Rock Creek Parkway ☎467-4600, ⓦwww.kennedy-center.org; Foggy Bottom–GWU Metro. Daily 10am–midnight; box office Mon–Sat 10am–9pm, Sun noon–9pm; tours daily 10am–1pm. Admission free. For details of performances at the Kennedy Center, see Chapter 14.

Although government departments have been based in the capital for two centuries, it wasn't until 1971 that Washington got its national cultural center, a $78-million white marble monster designed by Edward Durrell Stone. Though the building has its detractors – travel writer Jan Morris dismissed it as "a cross between a Nazi exhibition and a more than usually ambitious hairdresser" – the **John F. Kennedy Center for the Performing Arts**, to give it its full title, continues to be the city's foremost cultural outlet. The National Symphony Orchestra, Washington Opera and the American Film Institute have their homes here, and there are four main auditoriums, various exhibition halls, and a clutch of restaurants and bars.

There's an **information desk** on your way in, and you're free to wander around. Provided there's no performance or rehearsal taking place, you should also be able to take a look inside the theaters and concert halls (most are open to visitors 10am–1pm). Free 45-minute **guided tours** depart daily from Level A (beneath the Opera House).

The **Grand Foyer** itself is some sight: 630ft long and 60ft high, it's lit by gargantuan crystal chandeliers and features a seven-foot-high bronze bust of JFK in the moon-rock-pimple style favored by sculptor Robert Berks. You can also drop by the **Hall of States** (flags of the states hung in the order they entered the Union) and **Hall of Nations** (flags of nations recognized by the US). In addition, each of the theaters and concert halls also has its own catalog of artwork, from the Matisse tapestries outside the Opera House and the Barbara Hepworth sculpture in the Concert Hall to the Felix de Welden bronze bust of Eisenhower above the lobby of the Eisenhower Theatre.

The **Roof Terrace Level** holds the **Performing Arts Library** of scripts, performance information and recordings (Tues–Fri 11am–8.30pm, Sat 10am–6pm) and the center's eating places: the *KC Café* and the much pricier *Roof Terrace Restaurant*. While you're up here, step out onto the terrace itself for scintillating **views** across the Potomac to Theodore Roosevelt Island, and north to Georgetown and the National Cathedral.

I lied to protect the Presidency – until it became clear that the President was frantically trying to preserve himself, not his high office.

Howard Hunt, Watergate burglar

The burglars who broke into the headquarters of the Democratic National Committee at the Watergate were in effect breaking into the home of every citizen of the United States. And . . . what they were seeking to steal was . . . their most precious heritage, the right to vote in a free election.

Sam Ervin, chairman of Senate Investigating Committee

4

The 1972 presidential election campaign was well under way when five men were arrested at the Watergate Complex on June 17. Richard Nixon, running for re-election against the Democratic challenger Governor George McGovern, was determined to win a second term, elevating the election race into a moral, almost personal, struggle against encroaching liberal forces, who, crucially, were pushing the anti-Vietnam War message to the top of the political agenda.

After being spotted by a security guard on his rounds, the five men were apprehended in the offices of the Democratic National Committee in the act of tapping the phone of Lawrence O'Brien, the national party chairman. Once arraigned in court, it became clear that these were no ordinary burglars: one, **James McCord**, worked directly for the Committee to Re-Elect the President (known, delightfully, as **CREEP**), all had CIA connections, and some were later linked to documents which suggested that their escapade had been sanctioned by White House staffer **Howard Hunt** and election campaign attorney **Gordon Liddy**. To anyone who cared to look, the connections went further still: at the White House, Hunt worked for Charles Colson, Nixon's special counsel, while McCord's direct superior was the head of CREEP, John Mitchell, who also happened to be Attorney General of the United States.

Amazingly, at least in retrospect, hardly anyone looked further. The burglars, together with Hunt and Liddy, were indicted in September 1972 but continued to refuse to provide any collaborative detail. The Democrats, none more so than McGovern, complained loudly about dirty tricks, but the White House officially denied any knowledge. In the election in November, Nixon won a **landslide**, carrying 49 out of the 50 states (only Massachusetts and, ironically, the District of Columbia, went for McGovern).

From such commanding heights, it was remarkable how quickly things unraveled. Initially the only people asking questions were *Washington Post* reporters **Bob Woodward** and **Carl Bernstein**. As the months went by, and aided by a source known to Woodward only as "Deep Throat," the pair uncovered irregularities in the Republican campaign, many of which had tantalizingly close, but unprovable, links with the Watergate burglary. To the FBI's annoyance, the stories often relied on verbatim accounts of the FBI's own investigations – someone, somewhere, was leaking information. However, it still proved difficult to generate much interest outside Washington in the matter, and the story would probably have been forgotten but for the impetus provided by the trial of the defendants. All pleaded guilty to burglary, but before sentencing in January 1973 the judge made it clear that he didn't believe that the men acted alone; long sentences were threatened. Rather than face jail, some defendants began to talk, including James McCord, who not only implicated senior officials like John Mitchell for the first time but also claimed that secret CREEP funds had been used to finance an anti-Democrat smear campaign, which employed so-called "plumbers" – like the burglars – to work against domestic "enemies." This was precisely what Woodward and Bernstein had been trying to prove for months.

As pressure on the administration for answers grew, the Senate established a **special investigating committee** under Sam Ervin and appointed a special prosecutor, Archibald Cox. The trail led ever closer to the White House. In a desperate damage-control exercise, Nixon's own counsel, John Dean, was sacked, and the resignations of White House Chief of Staff Robert Haldeman and domestic affairs advisor John Erlichman were accepted; all, it seemed, were involved in planning the burglary.

In June 1973, the **Watergate hearings**, now broadcast on national television, began to undermine Nixon's steadfast denial of any involvement. The Watergate burglars had been promised clemency and cash by the White House if they remained silent, it transpired; the CIA had leaned on the FBI to prevent any further investigations; illegal wiretaps, dirty tricks campaigns and unlawful campaign contributions appeared to be commonplace.

The President continued to stand aloof from the charges, but was finally dragged down by the revelation that he himself had routinely bugged offices in the White House and elsewhere, taping conversations that pertained to Watergate. It quickly became a matter of what the President knew and when he knew it. The tapes were subpoenaed as evidence by Cox and the Senate committee, but Nixon refused to release them, citing his presidential duty to protect executive privilege. Soon after, he engineered the sacking of Cox, a move that led to the convening of the House Judiciary Committee, the body charged with preparing bills of impeachment – in this case, against the President for refusing to comply with a subpoena. To deflect mounting suspicion, Nixon finally handed over edited transcripts of the tapes in April 1974; despite the erasure of eighteen minutes of conversation, the "smoking gun" transcripts, rather than clearing Nixon of any involvement, simply dragged him further in. The President, it seemed, at least knew about the cover-up, and there was clear evidence of wrongdoing by key government and White House personnel. A grand jury indicted Mitchell, Haldeman, Erlichman, Dean and others for specific offenses, while the House Judiciary Committee drew up a bill of **impeachment** against Nixon for committing "high crimes and misdemeanors."

On August 5, 1974, the Supreme Court ordered Nixon to hand over the tapes themselves. These proved conclusively that he and his advisors had known about the Watergate burglary within days and had devised a strategy of bribes and the destruction of evidence to cover up White House and CREEP involvement. The President, despite his protestations, had lied to the people, and it was inevitable that he should face impeachment. Urged on by senior Republican senators, on August 8, 1974, Richard Milhous Nixon became the first president to **resign**. Combative to the end, he made no acknowledgment of guilt, suggesting instead that he had simply made errors of judgment.

Nixon was replaced by his vice president, **Gerald Ford**, but though the president changed, little else did. Secretary of State Henry Kissinger – architect of the bombing of Laos and Cambodia and the My Lai massacre, campaigns hidden from the American public – kept his job, while Alexander Haig, a key figure in withholding and doctoring the Watergate tapes, was promoted to become head of NATO. To top it all off, Ford formally pardoned Nixon with unseemly haste, allowing him to live out his retirement without controversy in California. In a bizarre twist, Richard Nixon slowly rehabilitated himself in the eyes of the political establishment and even in the eyes of the press; when he died in 1995 there was a full turn-out at his funeral by leaders of all political hues.

Old Downtown and Federal Triangle

The land between the Capitol and the White House, north of the Mall, was the only part of nineteenth-century Washington that resembled anything like a city. A convenient **downtown** developed in the diamond formed by Pennsylvania, New York, Massachusetts and Indiana avenues, where just a few blocks' walk from the seats of legislative or executive power, fashionable stores and restaurants existed alongside printing presses and shoeshine stalls, oyster sellers and market traders. Entertainment was provided by a series of popular theaters – not least Ford's Theatre, where President Lincoln was shot dead as he relaxed just days after the end of the Civil War (see pp.180–181).

By the 1960s, downtown was a shambling, low-rent neighborhood, later to be badly affected by the riots of 1968 following the assassination of Dr Martin Luther King Jr. As established businesses fled to the developing area north of the White House, the old neighborhood eventually became known, rather infelicitously, as **Old Downtown** (to distinguish it from the mushrooming buildings of New Downtown – see p.185).

In the nineteenth century, **Pennsylvania Avenue** marked the southern limits of civilized Washington society; the shops on its north side were as far as those of genteel sensibilities would venture. The area was given a new lease of life in the 1930s with the construction of the majestic buildings of **Federal Triangle**, though it wasn't until the 1980s that the avenue itself was finally rescued from years of neglect. An enormous amount of money has been pumped into renovation, especially in the easternmost area (south of G St, between 3rd and 12th), now being trumpeted by the authorities as the **Penn Quarter** – grafting a Left-Bank-like swatch of delis, restaurants, galleries and landscaping onto the existing historic buildings and cleaned-up streets. Just to the north of here, the opening of the **MCI Center** (at 7th and F) has sparked another revitalization – at present, this part of downtown DC is changing faster than any other.

Tours of Old Downtown start quite properly with the grand length of Pennsylvania Avenue and its landmark sights – the **Navy Memorial**, **FBI Building**, **Old Post Office** and **Willard Hotel**. Adjacent Federal Triangle

Eating, drinking and staying in Old Downtown

For Old Downtown listings, see the following pages: accommodation p.247; eating p.263; drinking and nightlife p.278.

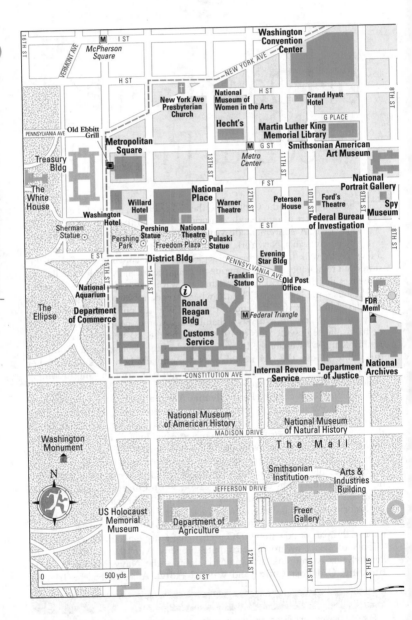

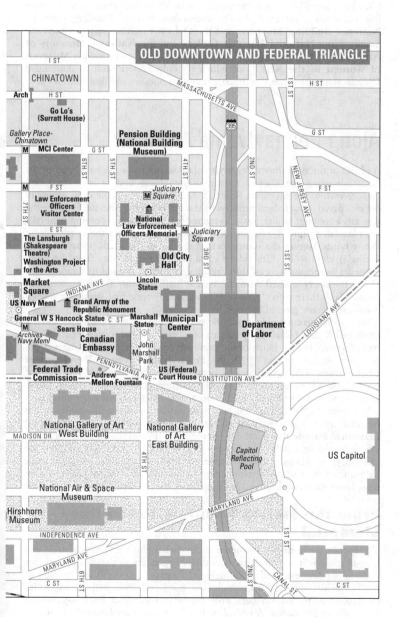

OLD DOWNTOWN AND FEDERAL TRIANGLE

I ST

CHINATOWN

H ST

Arch

MASSACHUSETTS AVE

1ST ST

H ST

395

**Go Lo's
(Surratt House)**

G ST

*Gallery Place-
Chinatown*

M MCI Center

6TH ST

5TH ST

**Pension Building
(National Building
Museum)**

4TH ST

2ND ST

NEW JERSEY AVE

G ST

F ST

*Judiciary
M Square*

F ST

**Law Enforcement
Officers
Visitor Center**

7TH ST

E ST

**National
Law Enforcement
Officers Memorial**

M *Judiciary
Square*

**The Lansburgh
(Shakespeare
Theatre)**

**Washington Project
for the Arts**

**Old City
Hall**

3RD ST

1ST ST

**Lincoln
Statue**

D ST

**Market
Square**

INDIANA AVE

US Navy Meml

**Grand Army of the
Republic Monument**

General W S Hancock Statue   C ST

**Marshall
Statue**

**Municipal
Center**

**Department
of Labor**

LOUISIANA AVE

M

*Archives-
Navy Meml*

Sears House

**Canadian
Embassy**

**John
Marshall
Park**

**Federal Trade
Commission**

PENNSYLVANIA AVE

**Andrew
Mellon Fountain**

**US (Federal)
Court House** CONSTITUTION AVE

**National Gallery of Art
West Building**

MADISON DR

**National Gallery
of Art
East Building**

4TH ST

*Capitol
Reflecting
Pool*

US Capitol

**National Air & Space
Museum**

**Hirshhorn
Museum**

INDEPENDENCE AVE

MARYLAND AVE

MARYLAND AVE

1ST ST

6TH ST

C ST

2ND ST

CANAL ST

C ST

has less to show, since so many of the buildings are closed to the public, save for the outstanding collection of manuscripts in the **National Archives**. Elsewhere, many of the grander municipal buildings have been converted into fine museums – for example, the exceptional Pension Building, now the **National Building Museum**, and the Old Patent Office, split between the Smithsonian's **National Portrait Gallery** and the **National Museum of American Art**. Other sights include **Ford's Theatre** and a unique **Museum of Women in the Arts**, from which it's only a short stroll to diminutive **Chinatown**, where you can lunch cheaply on noodles and dim sum.

Along Pennsylvania Avenue

A glance at the map shows **Pennsylvania Avenue** to be the backbone of the city, connecting the Capitol to the White House and, at its extremities, Georgetown to the Anacostia River. In its early days it was the only avenue in the city paved using federal funds, yet although it was the obvious focus for the new city's commercial life, it was hampered by the piecemeal development taking place all around. While fashionable shops traded along the north side of Pennsylvania Avenue, the swamp-ridden reaches to the south (today's Federal Triangle), close to the filth-ridden canal that isolated the city from the Mall, housed a notorious stew of slum housing, bordellos and cheap liquor joints. Often, the slurry washed onto the avenue itself; Anthony Trollope noted that in the 1860s there were "parts of Pennsylvania Avenue that would have been considered heavy ground by most hunting-men."

Turn-of-the-century additions to the avenue – notably the Post Office and the renowned Willard Hotel – formed part of an early attempt to transform the district's fortunes, but for much of the twentieth century Pennsylvania Avenue was in severe decline. In the 1970s the **Pennsylvania Avenue Development Corporation** (PADC) came into being, with whose assistance the area has become much livelier, dotted with small plazas, memorials framed by newly planted trees and with Victorian flourishes decorating lampposts and street furniture.

As a result, for the first time in years the avenue provides a suitable backdrop for that most Washingtonian of ceremonial processions – the triumphal **Inaugural Parade** that takes each new president from the Capitol to his residence for the next four years. Thomas Jefferson led the first impromptu parade in 1805; James Madison made the ceremony official; and every president since has trundled up in some form of conveyance or another – except Jimmy Carter who, famously, walked the sixteen long blocks to the White House.

From the Mellon Fountain to the Navy Memorial

The bronze, triple-decker **fountain** in the corner plot between 6th Street and Constitution Avenue commemorates former Secretary of the Treasury and art connoisseur Andrew Mellon, fittingly sited across from the West Building of the National Gallery of Art, which he funded and filled with paintings. It's overlooked by the ultramodern stone-and-glass **Canadian Embassy**, on the north side of the avenue. A typical piece of contemporary braggadocio, it cuts a neat bite out of its lower story and then props up the overhang on a circle of columns to form a covered piazza. Next door, the embassy will be getting a new neighbor in 2005, when the Newseum finally relocates from its former home in Arlington.

A little farther up on the same side, the turreted, pink-stone **Sears House**, at 633 Pennsylvania Avenue, once contained the studio of nineteenth-century photographer Matthew Brady, whose graphic photographs of the slaughter at Antietam in 1862 first brought home the full horror of the Civil War to the American public. Small Indiana Plaza, at 7th Street, is taken up by the monument to the victorious **Grand Army of the Republic**, a triangular obelisk adorned with figures representing Fraternity, Loyalty and Charity. Across 7th Street, the gruff equestrian statue is of **General Winfield Scott Hancock**, commander-in-chief of the Union forces – aged 74 at the outbreak of war and ridden with gout, he barely left the War Department offices close to the White House.

Across Pennsylvania Avenue from here, in the green plot in front of the National Archives at 9th Street, a small marble memorial commemorates another war leader, **Franklin Delano Roosevelt**. It was FDR's wish that any memorial to him erected after his death be "plain, without any ornamentation," and that's what he got, at least at first. Placed here in 1965 on the twentieth anniversary of his death, this monument is inscribed simply "In Memory of Franklin Delano Roosevelt 1882–1945." But despite his request, FDR's supporters couldn't help themselves – the Mall's newer FDR Memorial (p.57) is a grander affair altogether.

Market Square

In 1801 the city's biggest outdoor market opened for business at the foot of 7th Street. Known as **Center Market**, it backed onto the canal along the Mall where goods barges could be unloaded; out front, top-heavy carts and drays spilled across Pennsylvania Avenue and up 7th Street on the way out of the city. It was a notoriously noxious spot – presidential secretary John Hay in Gore Vidal's novel, *Lincoln*, "was haunted by the ghosts of the millions of cats who had given their lives that the nearby canal might exude its distinctive odor" – and there was little clamor when it was demolished in 1870. The National Archives (see p.166) were erected on the site in 1935. The concave, colonnaded buildings of the development opposite, known as **Market Square**, frame the view up 8th Street to the Old Patent Office Building. The ground floors are given over to café-restaurants and outdoor seating, while upper-floor apartments provide sweeping views over the revitalized Penn Quarter.

The US Navy Memorial

Market Square's circular plaza is entirely covered by an etched representation of the world, circled by low, tiered, granite walls lapped by running water. These together make up the **US Navy Memorial**, complemented by the statue of a lone sailor, kit bag by his side, and inscribed naval quotations from the historic (Themistocles, architect of the Greek naval victory during the Persian Wars) to the tenuous (naval aviator Neil Armstrong's "That's one small step for man . . ."). In summer, the Navy Band holds a regular series of **concerts** at the memorial. Directly behind the memorial, in the easternmost Market Square building at 701 Pennsylvania Avenue NW, the **Naval Heritage Center** (Mon–Sat 9.30am–5pm; ☎737-2300) can tell you more about the service with its changing exhibits and daily showing of the tub-thumping *At Sea* movie (11am & 1pm; $4). Portraits honor the various presidents who have served in the US Navy: JFK famously commanded a motor torpedo boat and was awarded the Navy and Marine Corps Medal for heroism (see p.128), but

Johnson, Nixon, Ford and Carter all served with distinction, too, while George Bush, the Navy's youngest bomber pilot, received the Distinguished Flying Cross and three Air Medals for his endeavors.

The Federal Bureau of Investigation

9th St and Pennsylvania Ave NW ☏324-3447, ⊛www.fbi.gov; Federal Triangle Metro. Mon–Fri 8.45am–4.15pm. Admission free.

Disappointingly, the lightweight, partisan and ultimately tedious hour-long tour of the **Federal Bureau of Investigation** does not deserve its status as one of Washington's most popular attractions. The building itself sets the tone: a 1970s concrete excrescence ponderously named for the organization's most notorious Red-baiting, cross-dressing chief, J. Edgar Hoover, it's hardly the most inspiring structure in the city, and not one that provides any distraction for visitors who can expect to wait an hour (more in summer) before being ushered into what is effectively a PR job for America's most mythologized law-enforcement agency.

Established in 1908 (motto: Fidelity, Bravery, Integrity) under the auspices of the Department of Justice, the FBI owed its early investigative techniques to those pioneered by the Pinkerton Detective Agency in the 1870s, and made its reputation in the 1920s and 1930s by battling gangsters and attempting to enforce Prohibition. Today, ten thousand Special Agents are employed to fight organized and white-collar crime, pursue drug traffickers and terrorists and lurk in the shadowy world of counter-intelligence.

After an introductory video, the walk-through tour continues with stilted presentations about FBI training and duties, led by guides who have swallowed the textbook whole. After a brief exposition about drugs (bad) and FBI agents (good) – note that the phials are filled with make-believe marijuana and crack, so as not to offend – it's off to the next exhibit. The whole set-up is rife with contradictions: while being led to condemn crimes of violence and their per-petrators, visitors are titillated with casefuls of confiscated, historic weaponry – "Pretty Boy" Floyd's Colt .45, John Dillinger's Winchester rifle – in a retro-spective glorification of an age of cartoon villains. The tour is, if anything, even more problematic when looking to the future: systematic DNA sampling and the concept of a national fingerprint bank are championed as developments in the fight against crime, with not a mention of the encroachment upon civil lib-erties that each might bring.

The tour finishes down in the shooting range, where an FBI agent fires semi-automatic handguns and assault rifles at a paper human target to approving gasps and whistles from the audience. The question-and-answer session after-wards tends to run, worryingly, along the lines of "how can I get one of those?" To be fair, the agent, when prompted, will point out that most FBI agents don't discharge their weapons during the entire course of their careers. Neither, it turns out, do they have much contact with aliens, despite the high-profile exploits of the *X-Files'* special agents, who are often filmed running in and out of the building pursuing matters of life and death.

The Old Post Office

Built in 1899, the fanciful Romanesque **Old Post Office**, 1100 Pennsylvania Ave NW, at the junction with 12th Street, has survived various attempts to demolish it to become one of the most recognizable of downtown's monu-ments. For years it served as federal offices, but since the mid-1980s it's been turned over to business. It's one of the city's great indoor spaces, with a glorious galleried interior, known as the **Pavilion** (mid-April to mid-Sept Mon–Sat 10am–9pm, Sun noon–8pm; mid-Sept to mid-April Mon–Sat 10am–7pm, Sun noon–8pm; ☎289-4224, ⓦwww.oldpostofficedc.com), whose glass roof throws light down onto the restored iron support beams, brass rails, balconies and burnished wood paneling. There's a large food court in the first-floor courtyard (where clerks once sorted mail), and gift shops and stalls on the second. Check out the period **post office counter** (Mon–Fri 9am–5pm), still in use at the Pennsylvania Avenue entrance.

Signs point the way to the **clock tower** (mid-April to mid-Sept daily 8am–11pm, closed Thurs 6.30–9.30pm; mid-Sept to mid-April daily 10am–5.45pm; free; ☎606-8691), where park rangers oversee short tours up to the observation deck, 270ft above Pennsylvania Avenue. The glass-elevator ride allows you to see the interior in all its glory, and the viewing platform itself, three flights of stairs beyond the elevator, boasts a stunning city panorama. On the way back down to the elevator, you can see the Congress Bells, replicas of those in Westminster Abbey. A Bicentennial gift from London, they were installed here in 1983.

Back outside on the avenue, **Benjamin Franklin** – "Philosopher, Printer, Philanthropist, Patriot," as his statue has it – gives a cheery little wave. You can park yourself on a bench and look across to the Neoclassical facade of the **Evening Star Building** (1898), whose attractive balconies, pediments and carvings provide virtually the only exterior relief on any building on the north side of the avenue as far down as Sears House.

Freedom Plaza to the Willard Hotel

Where Pennsylvania Avenue kinks into E Street (at 13th) is the large open space of **Freedom Plaza**, site of various festivals and open-air concerts. Lined in marble, it's inlaid with a large-scale representation of L'Enfant's city plan, picked out in bronze and colored stone, and etched with various laudatory inscriptions. The view down the avenue to the Capitol dome is splendid from here, but it's a scalding place to hang around in summer. The only shade is provided by the statue of General Casimir Pulaski, Polish hero of the Revolutionary War, at the eastern end.

Freedom Plaza also offers a first-hand view of the development going on along Pennsylvania Avenue. On the south side, the sculpted capitals and pediments of the Beaux Arts District Building (see p.165) offer a sharp rebuke to the faceless behemoth that lines the plaza's entire north side. The *Marriott* hotel and the restored facade of the **National Theatre** (see p.292) – on this site since 1835, though the current building dates from 1922 – both form part of the **National Place** complex, whose unexciting exterior hides a three-level shopping mall. There's access to The Shops at National Place (Mon–Sat 10am–7pm, Thurs until 8pm, Sun noon–5pm; ☎662-1250) through the hotel, as well as on 14th and F streets. At the northeastern corner of the plaza, the historic **Warner Theatre Building** (at 13th and E) forms part of the 1299 Pennsylvania Avenue development, whose carved stone latticework facade shines pink in the sun.

This section of the avenue ends at **Pershing Park**, named for the commander of the American forces during World War I, whose statue stands alongside a sunken terrace that becomes a skating rink in winter. Just to the west, Hamilton Place marks the spot at which an earlier general, William Tecumseh Sherman (also honored by a statue), presided over the **Grand Review of the**

Union Armies in May 1865; six weeks after Lee's surrender, the victorious troops marched proudly up Pennsylvania Avenue in the most stirring military parade ever seen in the capital. It was a show of Union strength tinged with sadness, since many at the time didn't think it appropriate to celebrate so soon after the assassination of Lincoln.

The Willard Hotel

Peering over the north side of Pershing Park at 14th Street stands one of the grand old ladies among Washington hotels, the **Willard**, a Washington landmark for 150 years. Though a hotel has existed on the site since the capital's earliest days, it was after 1850, when Henry Willard gave his name to the place, that it became a haunt of statesmen, politicians and top brass – not the least of whom was Abraham Lincoln, who was smuggled in before his first inauguration (during which snipers were placed on the roof). The hotel's opulent public rooms attracted placemen and profit-seekers anxious to press their suit on political leaders; it's claimed, with a bare smidgen of proof, that this is whence the word "lobbyist" derives. Somewhat less apocryphal is the story that Julia Ward Howe wrote *The Battle Hymn of the Republic* while closeted in her *Willard* room during the Civil War – supposedly inspired by Union soldiers marching under her window belting out their favorite song, *John Brown's Body*.

In 1901, Henry Hardenbergh – architect of some of New York's finest period hotels – was engaged to update the *Willard* and produced the splendid Beaux Arts building that stands today. It went out of business after the riots of 1968, but a thorough restoration in 1986 has recaptured its early style. Drop by the galleried lobby and tread the plush carpets of the grand main corridor for a coffee in the Art Nouveau *Café 1401*; other refreshment spots are the *Round Robin* bar – a great spot for a proper drink – and *Willard Room* restaurant.

While you're here, you may as well slip into the **Washington Hotel**, a little farther along at 15th Street. The attraction here is not so much the architecture (though it's a decent enough building of 1917, with a fine lobby and handsome brown-and-white facade) as the **rooftop bar** (May–Sept only; see p.279), from which there are splendid views across to the White House grounds.

Federal Triangle

The wedge of land east of the White House between Pennsylvania and Constitution avenues, **FEDERAL TRIANGLE** makes one of the most coherent architectural statements in the city. Grand Neoclassical government buildings follow the lines of the avenues, presenting imposing facades to the Mall on one side and Pennsylvania Avenue on the other; all were erected in the 1930s in an attempt to graft an instant "imperial" look upon the capital city of the Free World. The district's nineteenth-century origins, however, were distinctly humble, as a canal-side slum known, graphically, as Murder Bay. Hoodlums frequented its brothels and taverns, while on hot days the stench from Center Market drifted through the ill-fitting windows of the district's cheap boardinghouses. Few improvements were effected until the mid-1920s, when an increasing shortage of office space forced the federal government's hand. The triangle of land was bought and redeveloped in its entirety between 6th and 15th streets, following a Neoclassical plan that featured buildings opening onto quiet interior courtyards. Although never fully realized – the Old Post

Office and the District Building intruded into the Triangle but were saved from successive attempts to knock them down – it's a remarkably uniform area, even today. Different architects worked on the buildings, but they all have the same characteristics: granite facades, stone reliefs, columns and worthy inscriptions.

Department of Commerce to the Federal Trade Commission

One of the first Federal Triangle buildings completed, in 1931, was the thousand-foot-long **Department of Commerce**, which forms the western base of the Triangle, at 14th Street between E and Constitution. Its main interest today is as site of the White House Visitor Center (on the north side of the building; see p.136) and home of the **National Aquarium** (daily 9am–5pm; $3; ☎482-2825, ⓦwww.nationalaquarium.com), tucked into the basement; the entrance is on the 14th Street side. Founded in 1873, it's the oldest aquarium in America, and even though it's had a home here since 1932, the gray federal corridors seem a strange environment for the fish. More surreal still are the dulcet tones of Dudley Moore drifting past the tanks from the aquarium theater, where he narrates an introductory video. There are 1700 creatures of 260 species kept down here, forced to listen to Dud day in, day out; the sharks (Mon, Wed & Sat), gar (Tues, Thurs & Sun) and alligators (Fri) get fed at 2pm.

Also at 14th Street, with a facade fronting Pennsylvania Avenue, the Beaux Arts **District Building** predates the other Triangle edifices; walk down 14th for a view of its mighty caryatids and bold corner shield emblems. Erected as city council offices in 1908, it escaped demolition during the decade of Federal Triangle construction and clung on until 1992, when the mayor's office was shifted to Judiciary Square. Since then, the District Building has been restored as part of the massive adjacent development, which stretches right down 14th Street. This, the **Ronald Reagan Building**, 1300 Pennsylvania Ave/14th St NW – despite being the US's second-largest federal building after the Pentagon – hides its bulk well behind a facade that's broadly sympathetic to its neighbors. Walk in to look at the immense barrel-vaulted atrium: inside, along with the International Trade Center and other offices, is a basement food court, restaurant, exhibition space and the **DC Chamber of Commerce Visitor Center** (Mon–Sat 8am–6pm; ☎328-4748, ⓦwww.dcvisit.com), which can help with maps, tours and citywide information.

East along Constitution Avenue, between 14th and 12th streets, the large complex housing the **Customs Service Building** is as fussy as a building could be, its long colonnade and entablature of lazing nudes a stark contrast to the stripped facade of the National Museum of American History over the road. Across 12th Street is the **Internal Revenue Service Building**, the earliest (1930) federal building to grace the area; while across 10th Street stands the **Department of Justice Building**, in whose (enclosed) courtyard stands a bust of former Attorney General Robert Kennedy fashioned by Robert Berks – who was also responsible for the mighty bust of older Kennedy brother, John Fitzgerald, in the Kennedy Center (see p.153). The National Archives (see overleaf) are next, across 9th Street, and the Triangle is completed by the suitably triangular **Federal Trade Commission Building**, between 7th and 6th streets, where friezes over the Constitution Avenue doors depict agriculture and trade – and the control of trade, as shown by the twin exterior statues of a muscular man wrestling a wild horse (at the rounded 6th Street side).

The National Archives

7th St and Pennsylvania Ave NW ☎501-5000, ⊛www.archives.gov; for guided tours call ☎501-5205; Archives–Navy Memorial Metro. Daily 10am–5.30pm, April–Labor Day until 9pm. Admission free. Exhibitions closed for renovation through 2003.

As if bored with the restrictions of his brief, John Russell Pope's **National Archives** building completely subverts the tenets of the Federal Triangle plan. This is Neoclassical with knobs on, with 72 highly ornate Corinthian columns, each 50ft high, plain walls supporting a dome 75ft above floor level, and a sculpted pediment (facing Constitution Ave) topped by eagles. But then, unlike the other buildings, it was destined to hold a collection of national significance, namely the country's federal records dating back to the 1700s. When opened in 1935, the roll call of the National Archives' holdings already made impressive reading; today the collection is of an almost unfathomable quantity. What everyone comes to see is the Holy Trinity of American historical record – the Declaration of Independence, the Constitution and the Bill of Rights – but the National Archives also encompass hundreds of millions of pages of paper documents, from war treaties to slave-ship manifests; seven million pictures; 120,000 reels of movie film; almost 200,000 sound recordings; eleven million maps and charts; and a quarter of a million other artifacts.

The Archives' exhibition areas closed for renovation in July 2001; the project is scheduled for completion in 2003, at which point America's "Charters of Freedom" will once again be on permanent display, encased in state-of-the-art airtight containers made of aluminum, titanium and glass and filled with argon gas. The documents will return to the magnificent marble Rotunda, where you'll be able to examine the **Declaration of Independence** – rather faded now, but with its opening words and signatures still clear – and the **US Constitution**. The copy of the Constitution is the one signed at the Constitutional Convention in Philadelphia in September 1787 by twelve of the original thirteen states (Rhode Island signed three years later). All four pages of the document, rather than only the first and last pages, will be on display. The first ten amendments to the Constitution became the articles of the **Bill of Rights**, of which this is the federal government's official copy. For more on the Constitution, see "The American system of government," p.331.

Murals on the Rotunda's side walls – also under renovation – bang home the significance of the documents, with pictures of Thomas Jefferson handing the Declaration to John Hancock, and James Madison presenting the Constitution to George Washington (who chaired the Constitutional Convention).

Another historic document that will once again be on display is one of the few extant copies of the English **Magna Carta**, this one a specimen revised in 1297 after its initial agreement by King John in 1215. Written in Latin, it seems out of place here, but the privileges and freedoms it guaranteed (trial by jury, equality before the law, etc) were a precursor of those enshrined in the Bill of Rights. Incidentally, it's owned (and permanently loaned to the National Archives) by businessman and failed presidential candidate Ross Perot, who liked democracy so much he tried to buy it.

Given that the Archives hold items as diverse as Napoleon Bonaparte's signature on the Louisiana Purchase, the World War II Japanese surrender document, the Strategic Arms Limitation Treaty of 1972 and President Nixon's resignation letter, it's always worth checking the **temporary exhibitions**. A shuttle bus will take you to the Maryland depository, where you can hear selections from the Watergate tapes (see pp.154–155), which led to Nixon's downfall (call the Archives for details).

The Declaration of Independence

We hold these truths to be self-evident: that all men are created equal, that they are endowed by their Creator with certain unalienable rights, that among these are life, liberty, and the pursuit of happiness . . .

Declaration of Independence, Second Continental Congress, 1776

We are the only nation in the world based on happiness. Search as you will the sacred creeds of other nations and peoples, read the Magna Carta, the Communist Manifesto, the Ten Commandments, the Analects of Confucius, Plato's Republic, the New Testament or the UN Charter, and find me any happiness at all. America is the Happy Kingdom.

P.J. O'Rourke, *Parliament of Whores*

Revolutionary fervor was gaining pace in the American colonies in the early months of 1776, whipped up in part by the publication of Tom Paine's widely read, coruscating pamphlet, *Common Sense*, which castigated monarchical government in general and George III of England in particular. In May, the sitting **Second Continental Congress** in Philadelphia advised the colonies to establish their own governments, whose delegates in turn increasingly harried Congress to declare independence. The die was cast on June 7 when **Richard Henry Lee** of Virginia moved in Congress that "these United Colonies are, and of right ought to be, Free and Independent States." Four days later, while debate raged among the delegates, Congress authorized a committee to draft a formal declaration of independence.

Five men assembled to begin the task: **Thomas Jefferson, Benjamin Franklin, John Adams, Roger Sherman** and **Robert Livingston**. Jefferson, an accomplished writer, was charged by the others to produce a draft, which was ready to be presented to Congress by June 28. Despite the evidence of most history books, though, Jefferson didn't simply rattle off the ringing declaration that empowered a nation. For a start, he lifted phrases and ideas from other writers – the "pursuit of happiness" was a common contemporary rhetorical flourish, while the concept of "unalienable rights" had appeared in George Mason's recent Declaration of Rights for Virginia. Moreover, his own words were tweaked by the rest of the committee and other changes were ordered after debate in Congress, notably the dropping of a passage condemning the slave trade in an attempt to keep some of the Southern colonies on board. However, by the end of June, Congress had a document that spelled out exactly why Americans wanted independence, who they blamed for the state of affairs (George III, in 27 separate charges) and what they proposed to do about it. Read today, it's still a model of perfect clarity of political thought.

At this point, myths start to obfuscate the real chain of events. After a month of argument – not every delegate agreed with the proposed declaration – Congress finally **approved Lee's motion** on July 2, 1776. Technically, this was the day that America declared independence from Great Britain, though two days later, on **July 4, 1776**, Congress, representing the "thirteen United States of America," also approved Jefferson's explanatory declaration – and within a couple of years, and ever since, celebrations were held on the anniversary of the later date. The only man to sign the Declaration itself on July 4 was John Hancock (president of the Continental Congress) – hence the use of the colloquialism "John Hancock" for someone's signature; other signatures weren't added until August 2 and beyond, since many of the delegates had gone home as soon as the Declaration was drawn up.

Excellent **guided tours**, which allow you to see many more of the holdings, should resume once renovation is complete, though you'll need to call well in advance. Visitors keen on tracing their family history will be able to do so in a new **genealogy center** – the Archives' resources were of great help to Alex Haley, author of *Roots*, who spent many hours tracing his ancestry here.

Washington DC has always had an anomalous place in the Union. It's a **federal district** rather than a state, with no official constitution of its own, and its citizens are denied full representation under the American political system: they have no senator to pursue their interests and only a nonvoting representative in the House (a position the capital city shares, ingloriously, with Samoa, Guam and the Virgin Islands). Perhaps most incongruously, only since 1961, by virtue of the 23rd Amendment, have they been able to vote in presidential elections; the first they participated in was that of 1964.

Local powers have been similarly disregarded. There's been a city mayor and some sort of elected council since 1802, but in the early days so many inhabitants were temporary visitors – politicians, lobbyists, lawyers and appointed civil servants – that there was no question of granting local tax-raising powers. Congress simply appropriated money piecemeal for necessary improvements. The District was given **territorial status** in 1871. President Grant appointed a governor and council, under whom worked an elected house of delegates and boards of public works and health; all adult males (black and white) were eligible to vote. Many of the most significant improvements to the city infrastructure date from this period of limited self-government, with the head of the Board of Public Works, **Alexander "Boss" Shepherd**, instrumental in sinking sewers, paving and lighting streets and planting thousands of trees. However, Shepherd's improvements and a string of corruption scandals put the city $16 million in debt. Direct control of DC's affairs passed back to Congress in 1874, which later appointed three commissioners to replace the locally elected officials.

And that was the way matters stood for a century, until Congress passed the **Home Rule Act** in 1973. Small improvements had already been effected – the first black commissioner (for a city now predominantly black) was appointed in 1961; later, an elected school board was established. But only in 1974, when the District's first elected **mayor** for more than a century, Walter E. Washington (who is black), took office, supported by a fully elected thirteen-member council, did the city wrest back some measure of autonomy. However, Congress still retained a legislative veto over any proposed local laws, as well as keeping a close watch on spending limits.

Washington was succeeded as mayor in 1978 by **Marion S. Barry**, former civil rights activist and as picaresque a political leader as any city could wish for. At first, he was markedly successful in attracting much-needed investment; he also significantly increased the number of local government workers, which gave him a firm support base among the majority black population. But longstanding whispers about Barry's turbulent private life – charges of drug addiction in particular – exploded in early 1990, when he was surreptitiously filmed in an FBI sting operation, buying and using crack cocaine. Barry spent six months in prison, being replaced as mayor by the Democrat **Sharon Pratt Kelly**, a former corporate manager who, despite her undoubted expertise, signally failed to improve the city's worsening finances. Nor did she endear herself to the city's employees, and in the mayoral

Judiciary Square

East of 5th Street, between E and F streets, **Judiciary Square** has been the focus of the city's judiciary and local government since 1800, when storehouses here served as rank jails for runaway slaves. Today, the mayor's new offices are at One Judiciary Square, while the unobtrusive **Old City Hall** on D Street, dating from the early nineteenth century, now houses courts and other offices – in 1881 it saw the trial for murder of Charles Guiteau, who shot President James Garfield in the back just four months after his inauguration. There's a rare outdoor **statue of Abraham Lincoln** in front of the building on D Street. Within a few election of 1994, Barry made an astounding **comeback**, after admitting to voters the error of his ways. But a year later, Congress – influenced by the sweeping Republican gains in the previous year's general election – finally tired of the embarrassment of DC's massive budget deficit and **revoked the city's home rule charter**. A congressionally appointed **financial control board** was subsequently given jurisdiction over the city's finances, personnel and various work departments, stripping away what little responsibility the mayor had left.

Barry didn't stand in the 1998 mayoral elections and was succeeded by Democrat **Anthony A. Williams**, a former chief financial officer of the control board, who won a resounding two-thirds share of the vote in his first political foray. Perhaps even more significantly, the election results produced for the first time a white majority on the District council. This result, together with the election of an avowed technocrat as mayor, signaled a shift away from the confrontation of the later Barry years (as well as an increase in the political clout of DC's white residents).

Washington rebounded under the control board, as deficits became surpluses and city residents could once again afford to be optimistic about their trash being collected. By virtue of its success, the control board put itself out of business in October 2001, and full executive power returned to the mayor and the council ahead of schedule, with Congress (which subsidizes the District) less fearful than before that the federal capital will simply collapse. The city once again seems a worthy place to live: the population appears to have stabilized at last after decades of decline – in part due to an influx of white and Hispanic residents – thanks to lower crime rates, tax credits and the optimism generated by Mayor Williams' leadership and reformist agenda.

But although the District's financial management has improved, a daunting fiscal challenge remains. DC's **tax base** is too narrow to support the level of services the city requires: two-thirds of the city's workers live (and pay local taxes) in Virginia and Maryland; roughly forty percent of the land is owned by the government (which excuses itself from taxes); and years of middle-class flight to the suburbs have left the population at its lowest level since the 1930s. The obvious solution to this problem – a commuter tax – is a nonstarter for political reasons, while past attempts to raise the income tax have only led to further flight to the suburbs.

Granting **statehood**, with all the political, tax and jurisdictional rights that would entail, is another option, though there's no real enthusiasm at the local level, at least when it comes to voting – in the 1998 elections, the DC Statehood Party's mayoral candidate received just two percent of the vote. But the crux of the whole matter of granting statehood to DC lies in the realm of national politics: as statehood would likely mean that the District's voters, who are overwhelmingly Democratic, would send one Democrat to the House and two to the Senate term after term, the chances of garnering enough Republican support for DC's statehood are extremely slim.

---

blocks of here stand the US Tax Court, the District of Columbia Court House, the Municipal Center and the US (Federal) Court House, all without exception uniformly bland – nineteenth-century workers in the nearby Pension Building (see overleaf) had a vastly superior working environment. All the courthouse galleries are open to members of the public interested in watching proceedings: the **US (Federal) Court House** (main entrance on Constitution Ave) sees the most high-profile action, from the trial of various Watergate and Iran-Contra defendants to that of former mayor Marion Barry. This was also where the 1998 grand jury hearings on the Clinton–Lewinsky affair were played out, with all the main players appearing to give evidence in person save for the President, who testified via closed-circuit TV from the White House.

National Law Enforcement Officers Memorial

Davis Buckley's impressive **National Law Enforcement Officers Memorial** occupies the whole of the center of Judiciary Square; one of the Metro entrances emerges right by it. Dedicated in 1991, the walls lining the circular pathways around a reflecting pool are inscribed with the names of more than 14,000 police officers killed in the line of duty, starting with US Marshall Robert Forsyth, shot dead in 1794. With symbolic bronze lions overseeing their cubs at the end of the memorial walls, it's a poignant spot in the oft-claimed Murder Capital of the nation (though the state with the highest number of police, as opposed to civilian, deaths is actually California). Each May new names are added to the memorial, which has space for 29,000 – at the present rate (a murdered police officer every other day on average), it will be full by the year 2100. There are directories at the site if you want to trace a particular name, or call in at the nearby **visitor center**, two blocks west at 605 E Street NW (Mon–Fri 9am–5pm, Sat 10am–5pm, Sun noon–5pm; free; ⊕737-3400, Ⓦwww.nleomf.com).

The Pension Building and National Building Museum

In the late 1860s the sheer number of Civil War casualties put a huge strain on the government's pension system. New offices were required in which to process claims and payments to veterans and dependents; subsequently, in the 1880s, what became known as the **Pension Building** was erected between 4th and 5th streets, framing the entire north side of today's Judiciary Square. Emerging from the Metro up the escalators brings you face-to-face with its imposing red-brick facade.

Architect Montgomery C. Meigs' concern was to honor veterans of both sides with a building of distinction, and in this he succeeded admirably. The Renaissance-style palazzo is handsome in the extreme, its exterior enhanced by a three-foot-high terra-cotta **frieze** that runs around the entire building (between the first and second floors) and depicts the Union Army in all its manifestations: drilling soldiers and the walking wounded, horses pulling wagons, marines rowing in a storm-tossed sea, charging cavalry and thunderous artillery.

Inside, Meigs maximized the use of natural light and freely circulating air to produce a majestic **Great Hall**, inspired by the generous proportions of Rome's Palazzo Farnese, a stadium-sized interior centering on a working fountain. The eight supporting columns are 8ft across at the base and more than 75ft high; each is made up of 70,000 bricks, plastered and painted to resemble Siena marble. Above the ground-floor Doric arcade, the three open-plan galleried levels, 160ft high, were aired by vents and clerestory windows – opened each day by a young boy employed to walk around on the roof. In the upper-floor niches Meigs planned to put busts of prominent Americans, though this plan never came to fruition; today, the 244 busts are a repeated series of eight figures (architect, construction worker, landscape gardener, etc) representing the building arts. Hardly surprisingly, such a vast, sympathetic space has been in regular demand. Grover Cleveland held the first of many presidential inaugural balls here in 1885 (when there was still no roof on the building); a century later, it hosted President Reagan's second inaugural and then President Clinton's first; while every year the *Christmas in Washington* special is filmed here.

171

△ The FBI Building

The Pension Bureau moved out in 1926, and for a time the building served as a courthouse and housed various federal offices. It's now preserved as the **National Building Museum**, 401 F Street NW (Mon–Sat 10am–5pm, Sun noon–5pm; free but donation suggested; ℡272-2448, Ⓦwww.nbm.org), presenting changing exhibitions on all aspects of architecture and building history. The permanent exhibition on the second floor, "Washington: Symbol and City," usefully concentrates on the construction of the city itself. Free **tours** (Mon–Wed 12.30pm; Thurs–Sat 11.30am, 12.30pm & 1.30pm; Sun 12.30pm & 1.30pm) give you access to the otherwise restricted third floor (the best spot to view the towering column's curlicued capitals) and to the former Pension Commissioner's Suite on the second floor. Sandwiches, salads and snacks are served at **Blueprints Café** (Mon–Sat 9am–5pm, Sun noon–5pm) just off the Great Hall – one of the most jaw-dropping spots in DC to take a break.

Old Patent Office Building

Three blocks west of the Pension Building, the older **Patent Office Building** houses two of the city's major art displays, the **National Portrait Gallery** and the **American Art Museum**, both of which come under the aegis of the Smithsonian.

The Greek Revival building, begun in 1836 by Robert Mills, is among the oldest in the city, though it wasn't completed for thirty years. It was designed to hold offices of the Interior Department and the **Commissioners of Patents**, displaying models of all patents taken out in nineteenth-century America. Thus it became one of the city's earliest museums, featuring models of inventions by Thomas Edison, Benjamin Franklin and Alexander Graham Bell as well as Whitney's cotton gin, Colt's pistol and Fulton's steam engine. Charles Dickens remarked that it was "an extraordinary example of American enterprise and ingenuity," although Anthony Trollope, hard to please as usual, was put out that he couldn't see what many of the inventions were supposed to be and thought the building "no better than a large toy shop." During the Civil War the echoing halls were pressed into emergency service as a **hospital** with over two thousand beds. One of the clerks in the Patent Office, a certain Clara Barton, abandoned her clerical duties to work in the hospital, going on to found the American Red Cross in 1881. The poet Walt Whitman worked here, too, as an untrained volunteer, dressing wounds and comforting injured soldiers, an experience that led directly to the long series of poems known as *Drum-Taps*, which was included in the fourth edition (1867) of *Leaves of Grass*. In March 1865, just before the end of the war, Whitman's "noblest of Washington buildings" hosted **Lincoln's second inaugural ball,** with four thousand people in attendance for a night of dancing and feasting. "Tonight," wrote Whitman later, "beautiful women, perfumes, the violins' sweetness . . . then, the amputation, the blue face, the groan, the glassy eye of the dying."

Despite its heritage, the building was scheduled for demolition in the 1950s, before the Smithsonian stepped into the breach; the double museum, which opened in 1968, is now in the throes of a major renovation, scheduled for completion some time in 2004. The galleries occupy separate wings: the American Art Museum on the G Street side; the Portrait Gallery on F Street. There are separate main entrances, but since you can cross into either museum from the other once you're inside, it can occasionally get a little confusing.

National Portrait Gallery

8th and F streets NW ☎357-2700, 🌐www.nmaa.si.edu; Gallery place–Chinatown Metro. Daily 10am–5.30pm. Admission free. Closed for renovation through 2004.

Portraits of prominent citizens formed the basis of many early American art collections – Congress itself commissioned a series of presidential portraits for the White House in 1857 – but the country wasn't provided with a **National Portrait Gallery** until the 1960s, when the Old Patent Office Building was converted for artistic use. The permanent collection contains more than four thousand images of notables from every walk of life, and there are some excellent paintings on show – Gilbert Stuart's celebrated "Lansdowne" portrait of George Washington being the best-known. But the strength of the collection is in the people it honors, from politicians, novelists and inventors to sports heroes, civil rights leaders and industrialists. The collection isn't restricted to paintings, either: there's a wealth of **sculptures** and **photographs**, including more than five thousand plate-glass negatives of the Civil War era alone by Matthew Brady.

Although you won't be able to view the gallery's collection until it reopens late in 2004, you may be able to catch some of its artwork elsewhere in the meantime. The museum has organized four touring exhibitions, which will make stops nationally and internationally (check 🌐www.nmaa.si.edu for details).

The **main entrance** is on F Street at 8th; the **information desk** is here, as is the gallery **shop**. Ask at the desk about **guided tours** of the permanent collection (usually on request Mon–Fri 10am–3pm, Sat & Sun 11am–2pm); you can also pick up a schedule of events.

The collection

Portraits of figures from the **performing arts** comprise the most popular part of the collection. The starburst of works includes Paul Robeson as Othello by Betsy Graves Reyneau; a regal portrait of singer Marian Anderson; photographs of Gloria Swanson and Boris Karloff; a bronze bust of Grace Kelly; and an almost three-dimensional metallic study of Ethel Merman as Annie Oakley by Rosemary Sloat. Perhaps most striking, though, is Harry Jackson's terrific polychrome bronze sculpture of a *True Grit*–era John Wayne. The spot-the-celebrity games continue with the **champions of American sports**, with studies varying from a pugnacious Joe Louis (again by Betsy Graves Reyneau) to a poignant Arthur Ashe (Louis Briel), painted in the last few months of his life. There are action paintings, too – Mickey Mantle watching as Roger Maris hits another homer in the 1961 season, and best of all, James Montgomery Flagg's depiction of the Jack Dempsey–Jess Willard heavyweight championship fight of 1919. With Willard (in black shorts) in trouble, the eager reporter seated to the right of his knee is Damon Runyon, who was a sports reporter before embarking on his humorous stories.

As you might expect, the museum possesses an impressive array of **presidential portraits**, with paintings of every American president. Gilbert Stuart's portrait of George Washington (1796), an imperial study of an implacable man, is one of the star attractions. The museum recently purchased the work, which had been on long-term loan, for $20 million. It's known as the "Lansdowne" portrait after the person for whom it was commissioned: the Marquis of Lansdowne, who had earned American respect by defending the rebellious colonies in the British Houses of Parliament. Stuart (see p.79) based this full-length work on the portrait-head of Washington he had completed from life in April 1796, when he also took the opportunity to paint his only known likeness of Martha Washington – these so-called "Athenaeum" portraits of George and Martha are usually hung in the Rotunda.

Some of the studies of the chief executive are most notable for the artists who created them: Norman Rockwell's overly flattering portrait of Richard Nixon is the most striking, while one of the more recent acquisitions is a bust of a relatively carefree, first-term Bill Clinton by Jan Wood, a sculptor otherwise best known for her depictions of horses. Other portraits illuminate the characters of the various presidents, starting with the work of George Peter Alexander Healy, who was first commissioned to produce presidential portraits in the 1850s. His pensive study of Abraham Lincoln manages to make the Great Emancipator rather more handsome than in virtually any other portrait of the time. Civil War painter Ole Peter Hansen Balling also managed portraits of presidents Chester A. Arthur and, in what must have been a rush job, James Garfield, who was inaugurated in March 1881, shot in July and died in September. Other artists faced different problems. Edmund Tarbell's Woodrow Wilson had to be painted entirely from photographs since Wilson was always too ill to pose, while one critic noted of Joseph Burgess' stern portrait of Calvin Coolidge that the subject looked as if, "without further provocation, he would bite the person . . . who, obviously, had been annoying him." English portraitist Douglas Chandor's rather raffish Franklin Delano Roosevelt has FDR in a chic fur-lined cape and sporting his trademark cigarette holder. This was to form part of a (never-completed) study of FDR with Churchill and Stalin at Yalta – which explains the alternative sketches of Roosevelt's hands, holding cigarettes, glasses and pens.

The gallery's "**notable Americans**" collection includes portraits of colonial Americans and Native Americans, with several studies of braves and chiefs by George Catlin (see opposite), and a painting of Pocahontas in English dress. There's a lithograph of Sitting Bull and a bust of Geronimo, sculpted by his distant relative, the Apache artist Allan Houser. Industrialists, inventors and businessmen are pictured alongside churchmen and feminists, so together with Bell, Edison and Carnegie there's Belva Ann Lockwood, the first woman to run for president (in 1884; she got 4149 votes), a bust of Susan B. Anthony by Adelaide Johnson (who sculpted many other suffrage leaders of the day) and a rather stuffy portrait of early feminist Elizabeth Cady Stanton.

Studies of personalities from **literature and the arts** include such gems as a touching early photograph by Man Ray of Ernest Hemingway and his young son, and the extraordinary, bulky terra-cotta figure of Gertrude Stein, depicted by Jo Davidson as a tranquil, seated Buddha. Honors, too, for Edward Biberman's creepy study of Dashiell Hammett in a horrible wool coat, and to the staring Samuel Clemens (better known as Mark Twain) portrayed by John White Alexander in 1902; in 1889 the same artist painted Walt Whitman as a seated sage, with light streaming through his bushy beard. The most prized piece, however, is Edgar Degas' severe portrait (1880–84) of his friend, Impressionist Mary Cassatt, hunched over a chair with a sneer on her face – the subject hated it so much she had it sold on the expressed understanding that it wouldn't be allowed to go to an American collection where her family and friends might see it.

Other highlights include Marshall D. Rumbaugh's sculpture of Rosa Parks manacled between two law-enforcement officers after she had taken her seat on the bus in Montgomery, Alabama – their small heads and shaded eyes contrasting with the seamstress' defiant gaze as her handbag dangles beneath her handcuffs – and the striking copy of the notorious portrait of Lincoln taken in February 1865 by war photographer Alexander Gardner. A crack in the plate runs right across Lincoln's forehead – after the President's assassination, many observers saw this, in retrospect, as a terrible omen.

Smithsonian American Art Museum

8th and G streets NW ☎357-2700, ⓦwww.nmaa.si.edu; Gallery place–Chinatown Metro. Daily 10am–5.30pm. Admission free. Closed for renovation through 2004.

The **American Art Museum** holds one of the more enduring of the city's art collections. Even before the founding of the Smithsonian, the federal government had its own art collection which, together with pieces loaned by prominent Washington citizens, was displayed for a time in the 1840s in the Patent Office Building. These works were later transferred to the Smithsonian, which had yet to find premises for a planned "National Gallery" based on its expanding art collection. In the end the Smithsonian resorted to displaying its paintings in the Natural History Museum, receiving a second blow when Andrew Mellon's bequest to the nation resulted in the founding of a quite separate National Gallery of Art. Not until the Patent Office Building became available did the Smithsonian finally find a home for its 38,000 paintings, prints, drawings and sculpture, photographs, folk art and crafts – the largest collection of American art, colonial to contemporary, in the world.

The museum is closed through 2004 for renovation, although you may be able to catch parts of the collection on tour (see ⓦwww.nmaa.si.edu for details). You can, of course, always visit the museum's excellent **Renwick Gallery** (see p.143), which showcases the collection's decorative arts and crafts.

The **main entrance** is on G Street, marked by Luis Jiménez's bucking, multicolored fiberglass *Vaquero* sculpture. There's an **information desk**, which has floor plans and details of the free daily **guided tours** (Mon–Fri noon, Sat & Sun 2pm) and free **lectures**, and a gallery **shop** (daily 10am–5.15pm) just across the corridor.

The collection

The museum scores an early success with its nineteenth-century **art of the American West**. The collection includes almost four hundred paintings by George Catlin, who spent six years touring the Great Plains, painting portraits and scenes of Native American life that he later displayed as part of his "Indian Gallery." Catlin received no formal training, and certainly had his critics as an artist, but as an early anthropologist his work was invaluable. His paintings were the first contact many white settlers had with the aboriginal peoples of America, and viewers were fascinated by his lush landscapes showing buffalo herds crossing the Missouri, or those featuring tribes at work and play. The contrast between cultures is best seen in Catlin's 1832 painting of a warrior named Pigeon's Egg Head arriving in Washington DC in full traditional dress, only to return to his tepee encampment in frock coat and top hat, sporting an umbrella and smoking a cigarette. Perhaps Catlin is most interesting for recording civilizations and habitats that survived only briefly after the onslaught of the pioneers – soon after he visited and painted the Plains Mandan tribes, they were wiped out by a smallpox epidemic introduced by white settlers. Not all the scenes are of warriors or hunts: Catlin also produced many keenly observed domestic studies, like that of the woman with child in an elaborately decorated cradle, while Joseph Henry Sharp has a later picture (1920) of Blackfoot Indians making medicine by burning feathers over an open fire. One of Catlin's contemporaries, John Mix Stanley, concentrated on depicting Apache warriors, though he's also represented by the graphic *Buffalo Hunt* (1845). There's a remarkable bronze statue, too, of an *Indian Ghost Dancer* by Paul Wayland Bartlett (1888), the dancer clearly near total exhaustion after hours of trancelike dancing.

The museum's **folk art** includes some traditional pieces, notably Native American ceramics, but it's the contemporary art that stands out. Malcah Zeldis' *Miss Liberty Celebration* is typically exuberant – the work, which depicts the Statue of Liberty surrounded by a family group of Elvis, Einstein, Lincoln, Marilyn and Chaplin, was completed to celebrate the artist's recovery from cancer. The most extraordinary piece is perhaps the so-called **Hampton Throne**, a mystic, cryptic cluster of foil- and gilt-covered lightbulbs, boxes, plaques, wings, altars and furniture capped by the text "Fear Not." The work of James Hampton, a solitary figure who referred to himself as "Saint James" and worked in a garage on N Street NW between 1950 and his death in 1964, it's full of obscure religious significance. It's also thought that it was unfinished at the time of his death, though quite how anyone could tell is a mystery. Incidentally, the Hampton Throne's full title is *The Throne of the Third Heaven of the Nations' Millennium General Assembly.*

The heavyweights of **nineteenth- and early twentieth-century** American art supply some of the museum's most enjoyable art. There are significant chunks of work by Albert Pinkham Ryder, whose dark, often nightmarish paintings are full of symbolism, though there's more general appeal in those of Winslow Homer, whether it's the rural studies of his *Bean Picker* or *A Country Lad,* or the leisurely antics of female models in his dappled *Sunlight and Shadow* and *Summer Afternoon,* all executed in the same prolific period during the 1870s. Other works by renowned artists include Mary Cassatt's *Spanish Dancer* (1873), showing little of her later Impressionist flair; accomplished society portraitist John Singer Sargent's direct study of the beautiful, taffeta-clad *Elizabeth Winthrop Chanler* (1893) and his later, jauntier *Betty Wertheimer* (1908); and colonial master John Singleton Copley's striking portrait of *Mrs George Watson* (1765). Among the sculpture from this period is Daniel Chester French's *The Spirit of Life* (1914), a winged sprite with laurel wreath fashioned by the man who produced the powerful statue in the Lincoln Memorial. There are also examples from the noted collection of sculptures and models by **Hiram Powers**. The surface of *America* (1848), a plaster model of crowned Liberty, is punctured by the tips of a series of metal rods, inserted to act as a guide for carving the eventual marble version. *Thomas Jefferson* (1860) shows the same technique, unfortunately making it look as if the frock-coated president has a severe case of acne.

The museum excels in American **landscapes**. *Among the Sierra Nevada Mountains* (1868) is a superb example of the dramatic power of **Albert Bierstadt**, whose three long trips to the American West between 1858 and 1873 provided him with enough material for the rest of his career – the detail is typical, with the ethereal light picking out distant waterfalls, ducks in flight and high snow-capped peaks. People rarely intruded into these romanticized scenes. There is no hint of human presence, for example, in the enormous, startlingly colored **Thomas Moran** landscapes at the top of the main staircase – two sweeping studies of Yellowstone Canyon, fully 12ft across, and *Chasm of the Colorado,* alive with multifarious reds. There are similar, though smaller, expressions of grandeur in scenes from Lake Placid, the Colorado River and Niagara Falls, painted by Hudson River School artists (see p.80) such as Jasper Francis Cropsey and John Frederick Kensett, who cast their sensuous eye across what Americans soon came to regard as their own backyard. **Charles Bird King** portrays the original inhabitants of these landscapes in the powerful picture of five Pawnee braves sporting red face-paint and ceremonial bead earrings. King studied in London under Benjamin West (see p.80) before moving to Washington DC, where he earned a comfortable living painting society portraits. The steady flow of Native

Americans through the capital in the 1820s – there to sign away their land in a series of ultimately worthless treaties – prompted him to divert his attentions to recording their likenesses instead. Also rather extraordinary, though in quite a different fashion, is Charles Bird King's contemporaneous portrait of *Mrs John Quincy Adams*, obviously uncomfortable with the artist's suggestion that she sit at a harp in an ill-advised crown of feathers.

The museum's **twentieth-century** art is usually displayed in the spectacular 260-foot-long **Lincoln Gallery**, which runs down the east side of the building. It was here, amid the white marble pillars, that Abraham Lincoln and his entourage enjoyed his second inaugural ball. High-profile names among the modern and contemporary collection include Robert Motherwell, Willem de Kooning, Robert Rauschenberg, Clyfford Still, Ellsworth Kelly and Jasper Johns. But there are noteworthy pieces from less well-known names, too, like Leon Golub's red, raw *Napalm Head*, which is painted onto a torn canvas sack, and Marisol's comical *Charles de Gaulle* (1967), which depicts the great French president as a rectangular wooden box and head atop a small cart. The museum also owns a decent selection of abstract works by the artists of the **Washington Color School** – primarily Gene Davis, Morris Louis, Kenneth Noland, Thomas Downing, Paul Reed and Howard Mehring. All tended to stain their canvases with acrylic paint to give greater impact to color and form, methods that first came to public attention in 1965 at a groundbreaking Washington exhibition of modern art.

Around the MCI Center and Chinatown

The biggest engine of downtown change has been the construction of the **MCI Center**, a 20,000-seater sports, concert and entertainment arena located opposite the Old Patent Office Building, on the fringes of Washington's skimpy **Chinatown**. This has underpinned the ongoing redevelopment around **7th and F streets**, part of a concerted effort to breathe sustainable commercial life back into DC's original downtown. By 2003 the main arteries of 7th, 9th and F streets – largely abandoned since the 1970s – will host a plethora of new office complexes, arts and leisure facilities, stores and apartments. The city hopes that a new **Spy Museum** will also draw visitors to the resurgent area. The MCI Center has already succeeded in channeling sports fans and concertgoers into a series of new bars and restaurants that are currently among the city's most fashionable. The Gallery place-Chinatown Metro gives direct access to the MCI Center, from which it's an easy eight-block walk back toward the White House, past historic Ford's Theatre, where President Lincoln met his end.

The MCI Center

With the opening of the $200-million **MCI Center**, 601 F St NW, at the end of 1997, professional sports came back to downtown DC – and with it, on game nights, the crowds and the buzz. The center is the home of the NBA's Washington Wizards (formerly Bullets), the Women's NBA Washington Mystics and the Washington Capitals NHL team – suddenly there's a bit more to DC sports than not being able to get a ticket to a Redskins game. To serve the crowds, and to encourage extra visits, the center hosts several other attractions, including a restaurant, *Nick and Stef's Steakhouse*, where a private room overlooks the Wizards' practice court. There's also a huge, four-floor **Discovery Channel** showcase store (daily 10am–10pm), which, while introducing you to the wonderful interactive, scientific world of Discovery Channel, also just happens to sell every conceivable gift on the planet.

For sports fans, though, there's only one stop, and that's the **MCI National Sports Gallery** on the third floor (daily 10am–6pm; $5; ☏661-5133), which displays a veritable pantheon of the greatest sports stars alongside historic mementoes, photographs and sports gear. There's some attempt to present the history, so if you didn't know that baseball's first professional team was the 1869 Cincinnati Red Stockings or that football's "huddle" was invented by DC's own Gallaudet University team of deaf players (who didn't want opponents who could sign to steal their plays), this is where you'll find out. But most visitors are just along for the vicarious thrill of touching Babe Ruth's bat, checking out the story of the great home-run race of 1998, and seeing Joe Montana's last touchdown ball, Ali's boxing robe from the "Thrilla in Manila," Sonny Liston's trunks, and more autographed baseballs and football jerseys than you can count. Foreign visitors are going to find it all a bit bewildering, and even English soccer fans will be puzzled to read the American take on their greatest moment in 1966 when "regulation time ended with a 2-2 tie . . . [but] eleven minutes into overtime a shot by Geoffrey [sic] Hurst bounced from the crossbar to the grass and away." *Sir* Geoffrey, please. Charge up your entrance card with extra dollar-credits and you can play on the forty or more interactive games in the gallery – shooting hoops, throwing a World Series-winning strike, or speeding down a tricky downhill ski run.

Along 7th and F streets

The downtown transformation is taking place rapidly along **7th Street**, between F and D, whose spruced-up buildings form the focus of a nascent arts district studded with galleries. New cafés, bars and restaurants contribute to the area's growing appeal, perhaps best exemplified by the residents of 7th Street's finest building, **The Lansburgh**, at No. 420 (between D and E). Once a department store, the building's soaring Neoclassical facade now provides a grand frame for the **Shakespeare Theatre** (see p.292) and the swish apartments above it – home to (or at least Washington mailing address of) various celebs including Betty Friedan. Major improvements are also under way along **F Street**, between 7th and 10th, though it still has a way to go before it resembles its thriving turn-of-the-century commercial self. The street lost its heart after the 1968 riots, when its core businesses moved west; these included Hecht's (see p.182) department store, whose once-forlorn old building at 7th and F, with its beautifully carved facade, is at last being rescued. Nearby, other elegant facades are likewise in the process of getting a makeover, starting with the Greek Revival **Tariff Commission Building** (7th between E and F) opposite the old Hecht's; used by the Post Office Department for many years, the building will be reborn as the five-star *Hotel Monaco*. In 1814, following the burning of the Capitol by the British, Congress convened here briefly before moving into the temporary Brick Capitol (see p.100). Two blocks west, at 9th Street, the elegant former **Riggs National Bank Building** has been rescued by *Marriott* hotels and now also features a trendy brew-pub (see p.278), while there are more stirring facades on F Street at No. 918 (the rustic National Union Building) and No. 930 (Atlantic Building).

The International Spy Museum

800 F St NW ☎393-7798, ⓦ www.spymuseum.org; Gallery place-Chinatown Metro. Daily 10am–8pm. Admission $10. (Hours and admission fee may vary.)

The Penn Quarter's newest major attraction, the **International Spy Museum,** will deign to uncloak the history, craft and practice of espionage when it opens its doors in mid-2002. Across the street from the National Portrait Gallery, the museum is very much a part of F Street's revival: it resides in five nineteenth-century buildings, including the Atlas Building, which, fittingly enough, was home to the US Communist Party from 1941 to 1948. Experts in the field, ranging from former FBI, CIA and KGB chiefs to specialists in cryptology, disguise and clandestine photography, helped create the $30-million museum, whose exhibits aim to illuminate the impact of espionage on various historic events and to showcase dozens of nifty gizmos that would earn Q's grudging respect.

The role of code-making and code-breaking operations is investigated in "**Spies Among Us**," where you'll find Germany's World War II Enigma cipher machine. (The United States, meanwhile, capitalized on the talents of its American Indian population: the native language of "Navajo codetalkers" provided an unbreakable code for the Allies during the war.) Interactive exhibits allow budding spymasters to create, break and hide coded messages. Elsewhere, "**The Secret History of History**" explores the institutionalization of spying in the Soviet Union and traces the development of espionage technology, while the "**War of the Spies**" takes a closer look at the cloak-and-dagger techniques employed during the Cold War.

Among the numerous artifacts on view are such goodies as a Soviet shoe transmitter, a listening device that would have done well on an episode of *Get Smart;* the East German Robot T1340 camera, designed to photograph through walls; and the "escape boots" crafted for British pilots in World War II. Also highlighted are the many personalities, real and imagined, that make up the colorful world of espionage: James Bond is here, of course, as is the great Mata Hari as well as so-called celebrity spies such as singer Josephine Baker and – drop that cookie – Julia Child, the matronly television chef.

Chinatown and around

Washington's **Chinatown** isn't a patch on those in San Francisco, New York or even London, stretching no more than a few undistinguished city blocks along G and H streets NW, between 6th and 8th. The vibrant **triumphal arch** over H Street (at 7th), paid for by Beijing in the 1980s, is hopelessly at odds with the neighborhood, since it heralds little more than a dozen restaurants (see p.260) and a few grocery stores. Come here to eat, by all means – restaurants are particularly thick on H Street – but don't expect much else, other than dodging the attentions of panhandling drunks at night. Washington DC's first Chinese immigrants, in the early nineteenth century, didn't live in today's Chinatown (which only became such at the beginning of the last century) but in the gloriously named slums of Swampoodle, north of the Capitol. At that time, H Street and its environs were home to small businesses and modest but respectable rooming houses. In one of these, during the 1860s, Mary Surratt presided over the comings and goings of her son John and his colleagues, including a certain John Wilkes Booth – all subsequently implicated in the assassination of Abraham Lincoln (see overleaf). A plaque marks the **site of the house** (then No. 541 H St), now *Go-Lo's* restaurant at 604 H Street NW.

At present, full-scale development encroaches Chinatown on either side, slowly reviving the area – or rather tearing it down and starting again. The first moves were made in the 1980s, which saw the construction of the colossal **Washington Convention Center** (H St, between 9th and 11th) and the multistory **Grand Hyatt**, 1000 H St NW– the latter is worth popping into in order to experience its soaring atrium. The area's latest large-scale development project is on view just north of Mount Vernon Square, where a sprawling new convention center is in the works. The occasional remnant of former days survives: walk past the Convention Center up to **1100 New York Avenue**, where the sprightly Art Deco facade of the avenue's former bus terminal is now preserved within an office complex.

Southeast, heading back toward the Gallery place-Chinatown Metro station, a stroll along the pedestrians-only section of G Street at 9th brings you up hard against the **Martin Luther King Memorial Library**, at 901 G Street NW (Mon–Thurs 10am–9pm, Fri & Sat 10am–5.30pm, Sun 1–5pm; ☎727-1186), whose sleek lines of brick, steel and glass announce it immediately as the work of Mies van der Rohe. Opened in 1972, it's the city's main public library, and you can walk in to see the large mural of the life of the assassinated civil rights leader, painted by Don Miller.

The assassination of President Lincoln

Five days after General Ulysses Grant received Robert E. Lee's sword and surrender at Appomattox, effectively ending the Civil War, President Abraham Lincoln went to the theater. There was a celebratory mood in the city and on the evening of Good Friday, **April 14, 1865**, President and Mrs Lincoln opted to go to Ford's Theatre to see top actress Laura Keene perform in the comedy *Our American Cousin,* a play about a yokel who travels to England to claim his inheritance. The president's advisors were never very keen on him appearing in public, but Lincoln, as on several previous occasions, overrode their objections. The Lincolns were accompanied by their acquaintances Major Henry Rathbone and his fiancée, Clara Harris; the four took their seats upstairs in the presidential box, just after the play had started.

The conspirators had been planning for weeks. **John Wilkes Booth**, a 26-year-old actor with Southern sympathies and delusions of grandeur, had first conceived of a plan to kidnap Lincoln during the war and use him as a bargaining chip for the release of Confederate prisoners. Booth drew others into the conspiracy, notably John Surratt, whose mother owned a rooming house on H Street, where the conspiracy was hatched; John Surratt was already acting as a low-level courier for the secessionist cause. George Atzerodt from Maryland was recruited because he knew the surrounding countryside and its hiding places, as was David Herold, a pharmacist's clerk in DC; Lewis Powell (or Paine, as he was sometimes known) was hired as muscle. With Lee's surrender in April, Booth decided to assassinate the president instead; Herold, Atzerodt and Powell were to kill Secretary of State William Seward and Vice President Andrew Johnson. Surratt had already left the group when the talk turned to murder, and the other attacks came to naught: Johnson was left alone by a fearful Atzerodt while Seward, although injured by Powell, later recovered.

At about 10.15pm, during the third act, when only one actor was on stage and the audience was laughing as a joke, the assassin struck. Lincoln's bodyguard had left the box unattended, and Booth took the opportunity to step inside and shoot Lincoln in the back of the head. Major Rathbone grappled with Booth but was stabbed in the arm with a hunting knife and severely wounded. Booth then jumped the 12ft down onto the stage, catching one of his spurs and fracturing a bone in his left leg as he fell. But he was on his feet immediately – most of the audience still thought it was part of the play – and shouted "Sic semper tyrannis!" ("Thus ever to tyrants": the motto of the state of Virginia) before running off backstage, where in the alley he had a horse waiting for him.

Ford's Theatre and the Petersen House

The district north of Pennsylvania Avenue has been home to several theaters since the founding of the city, being little more than a stroll from the White House and mansions of Lafayette Square for Washington notables who fancied a night's entertainment. In 1861, the National Theatre (see p.292) was joined by **Ford's Theatre**, at 511 10th Street NW (☎347-4833, ⓦwww.fordstheatre .org), opened in a converted church by theatrical entrepreneur John T. Ford. It proved just as popular as its near neighbor, until on April 14, 1865 – during a performance of *Our American Cousin* – it witnessed the dramatic **assassination of Abraham Lincoln** by John Wilkes Booth, actor and Southern sympathizer. During the play, which Lincoln was watching with his wife from the presidential box, Booth shot the president once in the head before escaping; pandemonium broke out and Ford lost his theater in one fell swoop. Initially draped in black as a mark of respect, it was closed while the conspirators were pursued, caught and tried; Ford later abandoned attempts to reopen the theater after he received death threats. The theater was converted into offices and only in the 1960s was restored to its previous condition.

First into the box was Charles Augustus Leale, a young army doctor. Lincoln was unconscious and laboring badly, and it was decided to carry him to the nearest house to care for him better. Once inside the Petersen House, Lincoln was placed in the small back bedroom, where Leale and the other doctors strived to save him. Soon the house was bulging at the seams, as Mrs Lincoln, her son Robert, Secretary of War Edwin Stanton, various politicians and army officers and, eventually, Lincoln's pastor, all arrived to do what they could. Lincoln never regained consciousness and died at 7.22am the next morning, April 15; Stanton spoke for all, declaiming "Now he belongs to the ages" (or, as some historians assert, to the "angels"). Lincoln's body was taken back to the White House, where it lay in state for three days before the funeral.

Booth, meanwhile, had fled on horseback through Maryland with David Herold, stopping at a certain Doctor Mudd's to have his injured leg treated. The pair hid out for several days, but after crossing into Virginia were eventually surrounded by Union troops at a farm. Herold surrendered, and on the same day, April 26, Booth was shot dead while holed up inside. All the other alleged conspirators were soon captured and sent for trial on May 10 in a military court at Fort McNair (see p.127). They were kept chained and hooded and, after six weeks of evidence, Herold, Powell, Atzerodt and Mary Surratt were sentenced to hang, the punishment being carried out on July 7, 1865. A last-minute reprieve for Mary Surratt – who, although she housed the conspirators, probably knew nothing of the conspiracy – was refused, and she became the first woman to be executed by the US government. Dr Mudd received a life sentence, while the stagehand who held Booth's horse at the theater got six years, though both were pardoned in 1869 by Andrew Johnson, Lincoln's successor. John Surratt, who had fled America, was recaptured in 1867 and also stood trial, but was freed when the jury couldn't agree on a verdict.

Much has been written about the effect of the assassination of Lincoln on the country and its future. He was at the start of his second term as president when he died, and many have held that the slavery question would have been settled with more skill and grace under his leadership. It's impossible to say, though it is interesting to note the personal effect that the close-quarters assassination may have had on the three other occupants of the presidential box that night: ten years later Mary Lincoln – never the most stable of people – was judged insane and committed; in 1883 Clara Harris (by now Clara Harris Rathbone) was herself shot, by her husband, Henry Rathbone, who died in an asylum in 1911.

Today it's a rather heavy-handed period piece, furnished in the style of 1865. Although it still serves as a working theater, it's more notable as a museum dedicated to the night that Lincoln died. Provided rehearsals or matinées aren't in progress (usually Thurs, Sat & Sun), the theater hosts entertaining **talks** (hourly 9.15am–4.15pm; free) recounting the events of the fateful night. You can then file up to the circle for a view through glass of the damask-furnished presidential box in which Lincoln sat in his rocking chair; most of the items inside are reproductions. In the basement, the **Lincoln Museum** (daily 9am–5pm; free; ☎426-6924, ⓦwww.nps.gov/foth) puts more flesh on the story. The actual weapon – a .44 Derringer – is on display, alongside a bloodstained piece of Lincoln's overcoat, and Booth's knife, keys, and diary, in which he wrote "I hoped for no gain. I knew no private wrong. I struck for my country and that alone."

The Petersen House

Having been shot, President Lincoln – now unconscious – was carried across the street and placed in the back bedroom of a house belonging to a local tailor, William Petersen. Lincoln never regained consciousness and died the next morning. Built of the same red brick as the theater, the **Petersen House**, at 516 10th Street (daily 9am–5pm; free; ☎426-6924, ⓦwww.nps.gov/foth), has also been sympathetically restored, and you can troop through its gloomy parlor rooms to the small bedroom to see a replica of the bed on which Lincoln died (laid diagonally, since he was too tall to lie straight). Period furniture aside, there's little to see – in a concession to taste, the original bloodstained pillow that used to be laid on the bed has been moved to the theater museum. However, it's interesting to note just how small the room is: Lincoln's immediate family and colleagues were present in the house during his last night, but not all could cram into the room at the same time – something ignored by contemporaneous artists who, in a series of mawkish deathbed scenes popular at the time, often portrayed up to thirty people crowded around the ailing president's bed.

Around Metro Center

The downtown hub of the Metro system is **Metro Center**, with separate exits along G and 12th streets. From either you emerge by the **Hecht Company Department Store**, in a stunning modern structure on G Street (between 12th and 13th), but with decades of tradition behind it. Other aged department stores in the area haven't done quite so well: a block east, at 11th and F, the venerable Woodward and Lothrop closed in 1995 – if the Washington Opera ever raises the money, the empty store is slated to be its future home – while Garfinkel's lost its fight for survival in 1990, though its location at 14th and F forms part of the **Metropolitan Square** and **Hamilton Square** development. This development retains various historic Beaux Arts facades along 15th Street (facing the Treasury Building), notably the turn-of-the-century B.F. Keith's Theatre and the National Metropolitan Bank; there's also access to the historic **Old Ebbitt Grill** (see p.264).

Around the corner on the south side of F Street, there's an entrance to The Shops at National Place (see p.163); the facade incorporates the original, highly decorative half-rotunda entrance of the **National Press Club**.

National Museum of Women in the Arts

1250 New York Ave NW ☏783-5000, ⊕www.nmwa.org; Metro Center Metro. Mon–Sat 10am–5pm, Sun noon–5pm. Admission $5.

The **National Museum of Women in the Arts** houses the world's most important collection of art of its kind – more than 2500 works by some 600 artists, from the sixteenth century to the present day. Incorporating silverware, ceramics, photographs and decorative items as well as paintings, the museum opened in 1987 and proved an instant hit. This is partly due to the building itself, converted from – of all things – a former masonic lodge built by Waddy Butler Wood.

The **permanent collection** is on the third floor. Rotating selections of contemporary works are displayed in the mezzanine level, and there are temporary exhibitions on the ground, second and fourth floors. The **information desk** and **shop** are on the ground floor as you enter; you can book ahead for group tours (☏783-7996; $7). The museum's airy **Mezzanine Café** (Mon–Sat 11.30am–2.30pm) is one of the most appealing lunch spots in the city.

The collection

The collection runs chronologically, starting with works from the **Renaissance**, like those of Sofonisba Anguissola (1532–1625), who was considered the most important woman artist of her day. From a noble family, she achieved fame as an accomplished portraitist before becoming court painter to Phillip II of Spain; her well-judged *Double Portrait of a Lady and Her Daughter* is on display, along with the energetic *Holy Family with St John* by her contemporary, Lavinia Fontana (who had a head start by being the daughter of a successful Bolognese artist). A century or so later, **Dutch and Flemish** women like Clara Peeters, Judith Leyster and Rachel Ruysch were producing still lives and genre scenes that were the equal of their more famous male colleagues – witness the vivacity of Peeters' *Still Life of Fish and Cat*. Women broke out of their restricted environment on occasion too, as demonstrated by the superbly crafted natural-science engravings of German-born Maria Sybilla Merian, the result of her intrepid explorations in Surinam in 1699. Meanwhile, in France, women like Elisabeth-Louise Vigé-Lebrun (1755–1842) held sway as court painters, depicting the royalty fluttering around Marie Antoinette. But as a woman artist she was marginalized, her paintings denied the respect accorded those of her male contemporaries – who kept her out of the Académie des Beaux-Arts until the 1780s.

In the **nineteenth century**, American women artists began to enter the fray. Lilly Martin Spencer was inordinately popular as a producer of genre scenes: *The Artist and Her Family at a Fourth of July Picnic* (1864) is typically vibrant. As Impressionism widened the parameters of art, painters like Berthe Morisot (1841–95) and particularly **Mary Cassatt** (1844–1926) produced daring (for the time) scenes of nursing mothers, young girls and mewling babies. Cassatt, like many of her contemporaries, was intrigued by the forms and colors of Oriental art; *The Bath* (1898), an etching of mother and baby using crisp swatches of pale color, was influenced by an exhibition of Japanese woodblocks she had seen in Paris, where she lived from an early age. Cecilia Beaux (1863–1942), also inspired by her stay in Paris, was sought after for her rich, expressive portraits – so much so that she was honored with a commission to paint Theodore and Mrs Roosevelt in 1903.

Twentieth-century artists and works include the Neoclassical sculpture of Camille Claudel (1864–1943), the occasional painting by Georgia O'Keeffe and, most boldly, a cycle of prints depicting the hardships of working-class life by the socialist and feminist **Käthe Kollwitz** (1867–1945), part of her powerful *A Weaver's Rebellion* (1893–98). Self-portraits add some interesting insights into character: Kollwitz appears drained by her work in an etching of 1921, while **Frida Kahlo** (1907–54), dressed in a peasant's outfit and clutching a note to Trotsky, dedicates herself to the Revolution. The last gallery brings you into modern times, with contemporary pieces by sculptor Dorothy Dehner, minimalist Dorothea Rockburne and Abstract Expressionists Helen Frankenthaler and Elaine de Kooning, among others. Should these appeal, you'll need to set off for the Hirshhorn, National Gallery East Wing and Smithsonian American Art Museum, whose contemporary art holdings are all more substantial.

The New York Avenue Presbyterian Church

Half a block west of the museum, at 1313 New York Avenue at H Street, the red-brick **New York Avenue Presbyterian Church** (daily 9am–1pm; guided tours Sun after 9am & 11am services; ☎393-3700, ⓦwww.nyapc.org) is a clever 1950s facsimile of the mid-nineteenth-century church in which the Lincoln family worshipped. The pastor at that time, Dr Gurley, was at Lincoln's bedside at the Petersen House (see p.182) when he died and conducted the funeral service four days later at the White House. Ask in the office on the New York Avenue side and someone should be on hand to show you the president's second-row pew, while downstairs in the "Lincoln Parlor" you can see an early draft of his Emancipation Proclamation and portraits of Lincoln and Dr Gurley.

New Downtown to Adams-Morgan

While the tourists zigzag back and forth through the cultural triangle formed by the Mall, White House and US Capitol, the business brain and artistic heart of the city tick away in the very different neighborhoods to the north. Not all will be high on everyone's vacation agenda – many locals visit parts infrequently if at all, and some districts probably shouldn't be investigated by anyone with a desire to live a long and fruitful life. But to go home without sampling any of downtown Washington beyond the Mall would be a mistake.

Closest to the center, **New Downtown** – for the want of a better label – has the least to recommend it, though visitors, perversely, often end up seeing more of these few blocks between K Street and Scott Circle than any others, since they contain most of the city's central mid-range hotels. Here, L'Enfant's grid contains some of the city's least inspiring architecture, and although as many political and economic decisions are made in these white-collar offices as in Congress, a stately hotel, a church or two and a couple of offbeat museums are about the limit of New Downtown's interest. Things pick up at nearby **Dupont Circle**, DC's major arts corridor, with a score or more of private galleries and the **Phillips Collection**, the first modern art museum in America. There's enough to keep you in the neighborhood for a day at least: avenues of imposing turn-of-the-century mansions (several open to the public), the buildings of **Embassy Row**, the townhouse museums of neighboring **Kalorama**, and some of the city's best shopping and nightlife. To the north, ethnically mixed **Adams-Morgan** has more soul and less pretension, and is one of the few areas in the city with a safe, democratic and inexpensive nightlife; dine out at least once here, since the area's range of ethnic restaurants is unbeaten in the city. Only in **Shaw**, to the east, do you have to pick your spots carefully. Once *the* thriving black neighborhood, and home of a vibrant music scene in the 1920s and 1930s, the area is still feeling the effects of its rapid postwar decline, though pockets are slowly being dragged back toward respectability. The odd museum, a fringe theater scene and booming bar-life on **U Street** offer rare diversions.

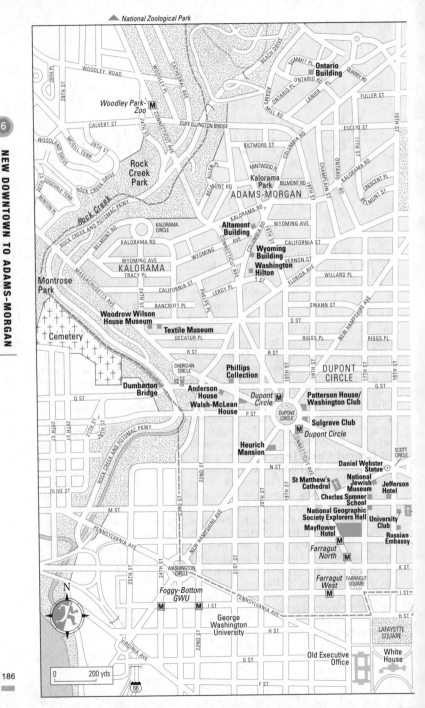

▲ National Zoological Park

Woodley Park-Zoo

Rock Creek Park

Rock Creek

Montrose Park

Cemetery

NEW DOWNTOWN TO ADAMS-MORGAN

6

Ontario Building

Kalorama Park

ADAMS-MORGAN

Altamont Building

Wyoming Building

Washington Hilton

KALORAMA

Woodrow Wilson House Museum

Textile Museum

Phillips Collection

DUPONT CIRCLE

Dumbarton Bridge

Anderson House

Walsh-McLean House

Dupont Circle

Patterson House/ Washington Club

Sulgrave Club

Dupont Circle

SCOTT CIRCLE

Heurich Mansion

Daniel Webster Statue

St Matthew's Cathedral

National Jewish Museum

Jefferson Hotel

Charles Sumner School

National Geographic Society Explorers Hall

University Club

Mayflower Hotel

Russian Embassy

Farragut North

Foggy-Bottom GWU

Farragut West

FARRAGUT SQUARE

George Washington University

Old Executive Office

LAFAYETTE SQUARE

White House

N

186

0   200 yds

66

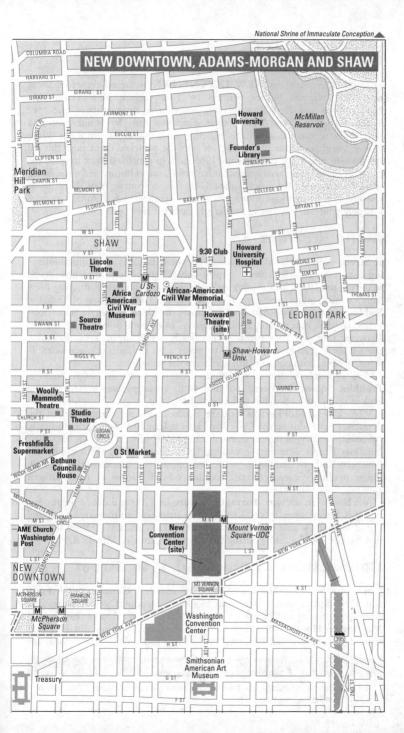

NEW DOWNTOWN, ADAMS-MORGAN AND SHAW

COLUMBIA ROAD

HARVARD ST

GIRARD ST

GIRARD ST

FAIRMONT ST

EUCLID ST

Howard University

McMillan Reservoir

Founder's Library

HOWARD PL

CLIFTON ST

Meridian Hill Park

CHAPIN ST

BELMONT ST

BELMONT ST

FLORIDA AVE

BARRY PL

COLLEGE ST

GEORGIA AVE

BRYANT ST

W ST

SHAW

V ST

W ST

V ST

9:30 Club

Howard University Hospital

OAKDALE ST

ELM ST

THOMAS ST

Lincoln Theatre

U ST

U St-Cardozo

U ST

Africa American Civil War Museum

African-American Civil War Memorial

T ST

T ST

LEDROIT PARK

SWANN ST

Source Theatre

Howard Theatre (site)

WILTBERGER ST

FLORIDA AVE

S ST

S ST

RIGGS PL

FRENCH ST

Shaw-Howard Univ.

RHODE ISLAND AVE

R ST

R ST

Woolly Mammoth Theatre

WARNER ST

Studio Theatre

LOGAN CIRCLE

O ST

MARION ST

P ST

CHURCH ST

P ST

Freshfields Supermarket

RHODE ISLAND AVE

O St Market

Bethune Council House

MASSACHUSETTS AVE

N ST

NEW JERSEY AVE

AME Church Washington Post

THOMAS CIRCLE

M ST

M ST

New Convention Center (site)

Mount Vernon Square-UDC

NEW YORK AVE

NEW DOWNTOWN

L ST

L ST

MT. VERNON SQUARE

K ST

MCPHERSON SQUARE

FRANKLIN SQUARE

McPherson Square

NEW YORK AVE

Washington Convention Center

MASSACHUSETTS AVE

395

H ST

Treasury

Smithsonian American Art Museum

G ST

F ST

New Downtown

DC's business district, or **NEW DOWNTOWN**, is the off-center diamond north of Lafayette Square formed by Pennsylvania, New Hampshire, Massachusetts and New York avenues. Some of its thoroughfares, like 16th Street and Connecticut Avenue, were developed early by businessmen and hoteliers who saw the advantage in being just a few blocks from the White House, but these streets really took off after the panicked flight from the old downtown areas to the east after the 1968 riots. In part the district has paid the price for this shotgun arrangement: it has little sense of history and virtually no sense of a meaningful neighborhood. In this, of course, New Downtown resembles the anonymous downtown ghettos of other modern American cities – largely white, largely sterile and largely deserted after 6pm.

Along K Street

K Street – spine of New Downtown's corporate business and political lobbying district – is DC's Wall Street in spirit only. When the companies first moved in during the 1970s, local zoning ordinances prevented them from aping New York's soaring urban streetscape. Restricted to a maximum height of 130ft, the buildings are generally production-line boxes of little distinction in which lobbyists, lawyers, brokers and bankers beaver away from dawn 'til after dusk. Between 13th and 20th streets there's barely a building to raise the pulse, though street traders do their best to inject a bit of life, hustling jewelry, T-shirts, silk ties, hot dogs and bath salts from the wide sidewalks.

Most agreeable of the trio of squares on the south side of K Street is **Franklin Square** (between 13th and 14th), its large, tree-covered expanse broken up by paths, benches and a central fountain.

A block west, **McPherson Square** is named for the commander of the Tennessee Army during the Civil War. Here, at least, late nineteenth- and early twentieth-century architects injected a modicum of style and wit into their buildings' facades, as in the Neoclassical Investment Building (15th and K), the Southern Railway Building (1500 K St, opposite the square) and, best of all, the scrupulously carved capitals and lion's head plaques of the Southern Building (805 15th St).

Two blocks farther west, **Farragut Square** (at 17th) is the least prepossessing of K Street's open spaces, a small green stain beneath the gaze of Admiral David Farragut, whose statue celebrates his reckless heroism ("Damn the torpedoes. Full speed ahead") during the Civil War Battle of Mobile Bay.

Connecticut Avenue and 17th Street

North of K Street the business-oriented boulevards of **Connecticut Avenue** and **17th Street** march four long blocks to Dupont Circle. Connecticut Avenue is the grander, graced since 1925 by the double bay-fronted **Mayflower Hotel** (No. 1127), whose first official function was President Coolidge's inaugural ball. Designed by the New York architects responsible for

Eating, drinking and staying in New Downtown

For New Downtown listings, see the following pages: accommodation p.246; eating p.261; drinking and nightlife p.278.

Grand Central Terminal, it has the same glorious height and space: inside, the remarkable 500-foot-long Promenade – effectively a lobby connecting Connecticut Avenue to 17th Street – could comfortably accommodate an army division or two. It's rich in rugs, oils, sofas, gilt and mirrors, as is the hotel's Grand Ballroom, in which a dozen incoming presidents have swirled around the dance floor over the years. FDR even lived in the *Mayflower* for a while after his inauguration; J. Edgar Hoover lunched here every day during his tenure at the FBI; and Monica Lewinsky was interviewed in her suite by House prosecutors during the Clinton impeachment proceedings.

Cut through to 17th Street, then head north for one block to M Street, where the **National Geographic Society** maintains its **Explorers Hall** at 1145 17th Street NW (Mon–Sat 9am–5pm, Sun 10am–5pm; free; ☎857-7588, ⓦ www.nationalgeographic.com/explorer). Founded in 1888, the Society started off by funding important expeditions to various uncharted territories, but its greatest asset was Gilbert Hovey Grosvenor, founding editor of *National Geographic* magazine, who first conceived that geography could be presented in an exciting fashion, primarily by commissioning spectacular illustrations. The yellow-bordered magazine is now recognized the world over. The Explorers Hall presents excellent special exhibitions in the tradition of the magazine's globe-trotting coverage as well as child-friendly geography exhibits; there are also frequent **events** featuring explorers, photographers, scientists and filmmakers as well as occasional concerts (call for details and ticket information). Also on hand is the National Geographic **store**, which has a wide selection of maps, globes, videos, photography books and souvenirs for sale.

Across M Street, the **Charles Sumner School**, at 1201 17th Street (Mon–Sat 9am–6pm; free; ☎442-6060), was named for the nineteenth-century senator beaten up in the Old Senate Chamber by pro-slavery Congressman Preston Brooks of South Carolina, who violently objected to Sumner's more enlightened views (see p.103). To improve the education offered to black children, a separate public high school – the first in the country – was established in the city in 1870; for a period it was located here at 17th Street. A harmonious redbrick structure with a handsome central clock tower, the 1872 school building is today largely used for conferences, but sign in at the desk and check the list of current exhibits, which range from temporary shows by African-American artists to displays relating to the city's school system.

Half a block farther north, turn left down Rhode Island Avenue to see princely **St Matthew's Cathedral**, 1725 Rhode Island Avenue NW (Mon–Fri & Sun 6.30am–6.30pm, Sat 7.30am–6.30pm; ☎347-3215, ⓦ www.stmatthewscathedral.org), where JFK's funeral mass was held in 1963; there's a memorial in front of the altar (JFK was, of course, buried at Arlington National Cemetery; see p.225). Call ahead to inquire about the free tours, usually scheduled for Sunday at 4.30pm.

B'nai B'rith Klutznick National Jewish Museum

1640 Rhode Island Ave NW ☎857-6583, ⓦbbi.koz.com; Farragut North Metro. Daily (except Sat) 10am–5pm; closes at 3pm on Fri Nov–March. Suggested donation $3.

On the corner of Rhode Island Avenue and 17th Street, the exemplary **B'nai B'rith Klutznick National Jewish Museum** presents a captivating look at Jewish life through historical, ceremonial and folk art objects. The galleries cover every aspect of the Jewish experience, from birth to Bar Mitzvah, marriage and death – eighteenth-century circumcision instruments and tax permits, painted Italian marriage contracts and linen Torah (liturgical scroll) binders are all on display. The oldest items are 2000-year-old incantation bowls, whose Hebrew inscriptions were believed to cast a protective spell over whoever the words were dedicated to. Other pieces show extraordinary workmanship; note the silver spice containers adorned with turrets, and the micrographic writing on miniature Bibles. Enthusiastic docents point out the significance of silver amulets, Torah crowns and various parchment scrolls; slender metal Torah pointers in the shape of a hand, for example, are designed to avoid having a human hand touch the sacred scroll itself. The museum also displays changing exhibits of Jewish art and has a hall of fame celebrating Jewish-American contributions to sports. There's also an excellent museum shop.

Along and around 16th Street

If New Downtown has a street to match the grandiloquence of Pennsylvania Avenue it's **16th Street**, the wide boulevard that starts at Lafayette Square and runs north to the Maryland border, six miles away. Most of the area above K Street was scantily populated until well into the nineteenth century, but post–Civil War expansion changed 16th Street completely, replacing a ramshackle black neighborhood with large mansions, gentlemen's clubs and patrician hotels, all reveling in their proximity to the White House.

The best of the buildings in the lower reaches are between K Street and Scott Circle, starting with the imposing **Russian Embassy** (1125 16th St NW); across the street from here, the original mansion facade of the **National Geographic Society** is far more appealing than its modern 17th Street addition. Farther up come the equally grand **University Club** and, opposite, the stately **Jefferson Hotel** (1220 16th St NW), before you reach Scott Circle itself.

There was a time, at the end of the nineteenth century, when **Scott Circle** was a fashionable park at the center of a residential neighborhood. Now the traffic is thick and the park is nonexistent – the only diversion being provided by the statue of Union commander General Winfield Scott astride a prancing horse. The views, though, are majestic, particularly those south to the White House.

Off 16th: Metropolitan AME Church and the Washington Post
Half a block to the east at 1518 M Street, the large Gothic red-brick **Metropolitan African Methodist Episcopal (AME) Church** – built and paid for in 1886 by former slaves – saw the funeral of Frederick Douglass in February 1895. The statesman and orator was brought to lie in state in the church where he had often preached. On the day of the funeral, crowds swamped the street outside, black schools closed for the day and flags in the city flew at half-mast. The church isn't open for visits, though you may be able to take a look around after a service or at other times if the doors are open. (For more on Frederick Douglass, see pp.130–131).

Walk around the block onto 15th Street to see the offices of the **Washington Post**, at 1150 15th Street NW. Together with the *New York Times*, the *Post* likes to imagine that it informs the informed in America. The daily newspaper's reputation is based squarely on the investigative coup of its reporters Bob Woodward and Carl Bernstein, who brought to light the Watergate scandal that led ultimately to the resignation of President Nixon (see pp.154–155). Free tours of the offices were suspended indefinitely in 2001 due to a spate of anthrax attacks on various media organizations around the country; call ☎334-7969 to see if tours have resumed. In the past, you could see how the paper is produced – not, it has to be said, a deeply exciting experience, and unless you're hot on the Watergate trail, it's one you can probably live without.

Dupont Circle, Embassy Row and Kalorama

Until the Civil War, Pacific Circle – as **Dupont Circle** was first known – marked the western edge of the city, beyond which the nation's capital petered out into a series of farms, slaughterhouses and barns. With the postwar boom, however, came something of a transformation, as streets were paved and a bridge was built across Rock Creek to nearby Georgetown. The British Embassy was built here in the mid-1870s, and subsequently lawyers and businessmen installed their families in substantial brick Victorian houses here. By the turn of the century, Dupont Circle was where all self-respecting industrial barons and high-flying diplomats built their city mansions, often in the favored Beaux Arts style of the time. Massachusetts Avenue, northwest of the Circle, became so popular with foreign legations that it acquired the tag **Embassy Row**, while the even more secluded residences north of S Street developed into the exclusive neighborhood of **Kalorama** – named (in Greek) for the "beautiful view" it afforded of the Rock Creek Valley.

Dupont Circle's golden age of soirées, socialites and selectivity ended at roughly the same time as World War II. Many of the wealthy residents had already been hard hit by the 1929 stock market crash and had sold up; other mansions were torn down or, the ultimate ignominy, turned into rooming houses for the postwar influx of federal workers. The Circle became solidly middle-class and, during the 1970s, even vaguely radical, as a younger crowd moved in, attracted by a dilapidated housing stock in which they could strip pine, throw down weave rugs and demonstrate against Vietnam.

Rampant gentrification has long seen off the Dupont Circle hippies, and it's once more an upmarket address, but the neighborhood has managed to retain something of a cultural edge. There's a thriving **gallery district** (around Q and R streets, between 20th and 22nd), while Dupont Circle is also the center of the city's **gay scene**, with bars and clubs along 17th Street (east of the Circle) and P Street (west). Washington's influx of designer coffee shops began here, and there are more impressive restaurants and bookshops than in any other part of DC. One of the best times to visit is the first weekend in June, when a consortium of ten area museums sponsors the **Dupont–Kalorama Museums Walk Weekend** (Ⓦ www.dkmuseums.com/walk), featuring free concerts, historic-house tours and various craft activities. Another popular Dupont happening is May's Goodwill Embassy Tour (Ⓣ 636-4225, Ⓦ www.dcgoodwill.org), which offers the public a rare opportunity to go inside DC's embassies – see p.32.

Dupont Circle

Dupont Circle itself is one of the city's major intersections, with New Hampshire, Massachusetts and Connecticut avenues converging at a large traffic island centered on an allegorical **fountain** whose frolicking nude figures – representing sea, stars and wind – were designed to honor the Civil War naval

Eating, drinking and staying in Dupont Circle

For Dupont Circle listings, see the following pages: accommodation p.248; cafés and restaurants p.264; nightlife p.279.

△ Souvenir T-shirts

exploits of Admiral Samuel Dupont. In modern times the Circle itself has always looked a little ragged at the edges – hip thriller writer George P. Pelecanos, writing about the 1970s, pictured it full of "girl-watching business-men, stoners, cruising homosexuals, short-skirted secretaries, doe-faced chick-en hawks eyeing little boys, the whole Dupont stew," a tableau that's not entire-ly outdated today. But on the whole it's an easygoing hangout with chess-play-ers hogging the permanent tables in the center of the circle, and a multitude of cafés, bookstores and restaurants within a few minutes' walk. There are **Metro** entrances to the north and south.

It's hard to imagine Dupont Circle in its prime, since most of the surround-ing mansions were razed by developers in the 1950s and 1960s. Two survivors are the Beaux Arts specimen at the corner with Massachusetts Avenue (now the **Sulgrave Club**), and the Neoclassical building at No. 15 – now the Washington Club but once the **Patterson House** where, famously, the Coolidges, camping out while White House renovations took place, enter-tained Charles Lindbergh, fresh from his solo transatlantic crossing.

The Heurich House Museum

Built in 1894 for German-born brewing magnate Christian Heurich, the Romanesque **Heurich House Museum**, a block south of the Circle at 1307 New Hampshire Avenue NW, announces its owner's origins and wealth loud and clear with its turret, castellations and richly carved wood-and-plaster inte-rior. The building is now occupied by the **Historical Society of Washington DC** (Mon–Sat 10am–4pm; $3; ☎785-2068, ⓦ www.hswdc.org), which allows visitors to take a self-guided tour through many of the restored rooms, dwelling on the mansion's lavish decor and the lifestyle of its occupants. On display are the formal parlor, drawing room and dining room, a music room with a mahogany musicians' balcony, and the basement *Bierstube* (beer room), carved with clunky Teutonic drinking mottos ("He who has never been drunk is not a good man"), where the family had breakfast. Temporary exhibitions highlight aspects of city history and architecture, and there's a good bookstore, devoted to works about the city.

Embassy Row

Embassy Row – as it still likes to think of itself – starts in earnest a few paces northwest up Massachusetts Avenue, where the Indonesian Embassy at No. 2020 (opposite the *Embassy Row Hilton*) occupies the magnificent Art Nouveau **Walsh-McLean House**, built in 1903 for gold baron Thomas Walsh. It's a superb building, with colonnaded loggia and intricate, carved windows, and saw regular service as one of Washington society's most fashionable venues, with soirées presided over by Walsh's daughter Evalyn, the last private owner of the Hope Diamond (now in the National Museum of Natural History).

A block further up – past the stately red-brick *Westin Fairfax* hotel (former-ly the *Ritz-Carlton*) – the **Anderson House** at 2118 Massachusetts Avenue NW is a similarly impressive pile, a veritable palace built between 1902 and 1905 as the winter residence of Larz Anderson, who served as ambassador to Belgium and Japan. As a Beaux Arts residence it has no equal in the city, its gray-stone exterior sporting twin arched entrances with heavy wooden doors and colonnaded portico. Inside, original furnishings – cavernous fireplaces, inlaid marble floors, Flemish tapestries, diverse murals and a grand ballroom – provide a suitably lavish backdrop for ambassadorial receptions. Some of this you'll be able to see for yourself, since the house was bequeathed in Anderson's will to the **Society of the Cincinnati** (Tues–Sat 1–4pm; free; ☎785-2040), which maintains a small museum of Revolutionary memorabilia. Anderson's great-grandfather was a founder-member of the Society; established in 1783, it's the oldest patriotic organization in the country. All its members are direct descendants of Revolutionary War officers. George Washington was the first President-General of the Society; there's a white marble bust of him in the entrance hall by Thomas Crawford, who sculpted the Freedom figure on top of the Capitol. Probably the best time to come to the Anderson House is for one of the regular **free concerts** (see p.289).

This far up the avenue, virtually every building flies a national flag outside its front door, and security is discreet but tight. With time on your hands, you may as well stroll the block or so farther northwest to **Sheridan Circle**, whose equestrian statue of Union General Phillip H. Sheridan was erected in 1909. It's quite a dainty representation of the general astride a boisterous horse – restrained in the extreme compared to the sixty-foot-high heads of Washington, Jefferson, Lincoln and Roosevelt that its sculptor Gutzon Borglum went on to carve at Mount Rushmore. On the south side of the Circle, the **Residence of the Turkish Ambassador** (1606 23rd St) is awash with Near Eastern motifs – oddly, it wasn't commissioned by the Turks at all but by one Edward Everett, the man who patented the fluted bottle-top. Finally, from the Circle, duck briefly down 23rd Street to see **Dumbarton Bridge**, guarded on either side by enormous bronze bison. The bridge provides the quickest route into northern Georgetown, emerging on Q Street by Dumbarton House, about twenty minutes from Dupont Circle.

The Phillips Collection

1600 21st St NW ☎387-2151, ⓦ www.phillipscollection.org; Dupont Circle Metro. Tues & Wed 10am–5pm, Thurs 10am–8.30pm, Fri & Sat 10am–5pm, Sun noon–7pm (summer hours may vary); tours Wed & Sat 2pm (reservations required). Admission Mon–Fri free (suggested donation $7.50), Sat & Sun $7.50; tours free.

The **Phillips Collection**'s much trumpeted claim to be "America's first museum of modern art" is based on its opening eight years before New York's Museum of Modern Art. It's one of the most congenial galleries in Washington: the oldest part of the brownstone Georgian Revival building was the family home of founder Duncan Phillips, who lost his father and brother in little over a year and established a memorial gallery in the house in 1921 in their honor. Financed by the family's steel fortune, Phillips bought nearly 2400 works over the years; during the 1920s, he and his artist wife, Marjorie, became patrons of young painters such as Georgia O'Keeffe and Marsden Hartley, while there are works by everyone from Renoir to Rothko (and several by distinctly non-modern artists like Giorgione and El Greco, in whose work Phillips saw the sources of modern art). Highlights are picked out below, but note that not everything can be displayed at any one time: changes of paintings and temporary exhibitions are common, which can frustrate particular viewing plans but can also present unexpected delights.

The **main entrance** is in the Goh Annex, on 21st Street. The permanent collection is exhibited on the first two floors of the annex and on the first and second floor of the original building; annex and original building are connected by an enclosed "skywalk." The annex's third floor is used for **special exhibitions**, while the ground level of the main building also holds the **museum shop**. There's a full program of cultural events: in particular, **classical**

music recitals (Sept–May Sun 5pm; free with admission), and "**Artful Evenings**" (Thurs 5–8.30pm; $5), with live music, lectures and a bar.

The Goh Annex

The permanent collection on the **first floor** of the Goh Annex makes for a rather low-key introduction, usually featuring a handful of Abstract Expressionist works from the 1950s, including a characteristically gloomy set of paintings by Rothko. Things cheer up no end once you climb the stairs to the **second floor,** where there's a wistful Blue Period Picasso, Matisse's *Studio, Quai St-Michel*, a Cézanne still life and no fewer than four van Goghs, including the powerful *Road Menders* (1889). Pierre Bonnard gets a good showing – you have to stand well back to take in the expansive and assertive *The Terrace* (1918) and *The Palm* (1926). Top billing generally goes to *The Luncheon of the Boating Party* (1891) by Renoir, where straw-boatered dandies linger over a long and bibulous feast. Phillips bought the painting in 1923 for $125,000 as part of a two-year burst of acquisition that also yielded Cézanne's *Mont Saint-Victoire* and Honoré Daumier's *The Uprising*. There's an interesting spread of works by Degas, too, from early scenes like *Women Combing Their Hair* (1875) to a late ballet picture, *Dancers at the Bar* (c. 1900), in which the background and hair of the subjects collide in an orange frenzy.

The English landscapes of John Constable include the fine *On the River Stour* (c. 1834-37), where a fisherman battles against the elements, alongside other nineteenth-century works by artists including Gustave Courbet and Eugène Delacroix – the latter responsible for a wonderful picture of the violinist Paganini in full fiddle, with the light falling only on his white hands and expressive face. Phillips' catholic taste comes to the fore with the juxtaposition of two paintings of the *Repentant Peter*: one, fat and bluff, by Goya, the second – two centuries older – a more familiar, biblical study by El Greco. An odd pictorial choice on the face of it, this last was bought by Phillips for his modern art museum for the very good reason that he considered El Greco "the first impassioned expressionist."

Main building

Across the skywalk and down the stairs to the **first floor** of the main building brings you into the oak-paneled "**Music Room,**" where Cubist paintings by Georges Braque (a particular favorite of Phillips, who owned thirteen of his works) vie for attention. *Round Table* (1929) is the most famous, piled high with guitar, dagger, apples, books, clay pipe and wallet – the sort of stuff lying around the average Cubist's kitchen. Beyond here the collection begins to concentrate more on late nineteenth-century American artists, with Winslow Homer's bleak *To The Rescue*, James McNeill Whistler's gentle *Miss Lilian Woakes* and moody Albert Pinkham Ryder landscapes to the fore.

The **second floor** features artists championed by Phillips in the 1920s and 1930s, including Milton Avery (who influenced the young Rothko) and Jacob Lawrence – the latter represented by extracts from a powerful series known as *The Migration of the Negro*. Better-known names abound, too, notably Edward Hopper, whose works here include the faintly menacing *Sunday* (1926) and the much later *Approaching a City*, viewed from the vantage point of sunken train tracks. A separate **Klee Room** displays a stunning collection of paintings by the Bauhaus teacher and artist, from the stick figures embellishing *Arrival of the Jugglers* (1926) to the abstract *The Way to the Citadel* (1937), where red arrows point the way through a kaleidoscopic maze of rectangles, triangles and trapezoidal shapes.

Kalorama

North of Sheridan Circle, in the exclusive district of **Kalorama**, quiet, crisp, lawned streets stretch out to meet Rock Creek Park. Here the city's diplomatic community sits behind lace curtains and bulletproof glass in row after row of multimillion-dollar townhouse embassies, private homes and hibiscus-clad gardens. If you wanted an immediate object lesson in the inequalities of life in downtown DC, just ten blocks to the east you can buy crack on the street in Shaw.

As in all rich American ghettos, there is very little to see (the only similarity they have, in fact, with poor American ghettos). But for an agreeable stroll in quite the nicest neighborhood this side of Georgetown, head up 24th Street toward **Kalorama Circle**, from where there are splendid views across Rock Creek Park. Just to the east, the **Residence of the French Ambassador** at 2221 Kalorama Road NW is the most ambitious building hereabouts, a Tudor-style country manor built originally for a mining magnate and sold to the French in 1936 for the then ludicrously expensive sum of almost half a million dollars.

Woodrow Wilson House

2340 S Street NW ☎387-4062, ⊛www.woodrowwilsonhouse.org; Dupont Circle Metro. Tues–Sun 10am–4pm. Admission $5.

Woodrow Wilson (1856–1924)

He was the perfect prototype of the seventeenth-century Puritan reincarnated.

Alistair Cooke, *America*, 1973

Born **Thomas Woodrow Wilson** in Stanton, Virginia, to a plain-living Presbyterian family, the future president dropped the "Thomas" at a very early age, convinced that the new version would sound better when he was famous. He attended law school and, though he didn't take his final exams, practiced law in Georgia for a year, only to discover that it wasn't his métier. Wilson returned to graduate school to take his doctorate (making him the only American president to have earned a PhD) and taught law and political economics for twelve years, eventually rising to become a reforming president of Princeton. Known and respected as an academic writer on political science and a stern critic of government corruption, there he might have stayed but for the Democratic Party's need for progressive candidates to run against the splintering Republicans. In 1910 Wilson won election as the **Governor of New Jersey** and two years later received the Democratic nomination for president. The split in the Republican Party – with Theodore Roosevelt running against the incumbent William Howard Taft – gave the Democrats both houses in Congress and let Wilson into power.

In his two terms of office, Wilson – a stirring orator (and the last president to write his own speeches) – saw through a batch of **reforming legislation** that wouldn't be matched until the days of FDR. The Federal Reserve Bank was established to better regulate the banking system, anti-trust laws were strengthened, the 19th Amendment (for women's suffrage) passed, and labor laws were enacted that at least gave a nod to workers' rights. But, with Congress dominated at least at first by Southern Democrats, Wilson also presided over rather darker deeds – not least the violent breaking of the Colorado coal strike, leaving 66 people dead, and the entrenchment of segregation in the federal system. Indeed, it's misleading to see Wilson as any kind of liberal; his reforms made capitalism safe in a period of con-

Many presidents-to-be have lived in Washington DC before their stint in the White House; all but one of them left the moment they had passed on the presidential baton. Only Woodrow Wilson, the 28th President, stayed on in the city, moving into a fine Waddy Butler Wood–designed Georgian Revival house on S Street that is now open to the public as the **Woodrow Wilson House**. It's a comfortable home – light and airy, with high ceilings, wood floors, a wide staircase and solarium – which, despite his incapacitating stroke in 1919, Wilson aimed to use as a workplace where he could write political science books and practice law. That his second wife, Edith, a rich jeweler's widow, wanted to stay in DC near her family and friends probably had something to do with the decision to remain; she lived in the house for more than 35 years after Wilson's death.

Visitors are first ushered into the front parlor, where Wilson liked to receive guests, to watch a hagiographical film narrated by Walter Cronkite. There's plenty to see in the house itself, not least of which is the elevator – powered from the nearby streetcar supply – installed to help the enfeebled ex-president move between floors, and the bedroom, furnished by Edith as it had been in the White House. The canvas-walled **library** of this most scholarly of presidents once contained eight thousand books (they were donated to the Library of Congress after his death); those that remain are the 69 volumes of Wilson's own writings. (The only president to have written more was Theodore Roosevelt – who, incidentally, Wilson used to impersonate, unflat-

siderable turmoil and were very much part of the turn-of-the-century strengthening of federal power at the expense of individual freedom. It's no coincidence that the 18th Amendment sanctioning Prohibition was passed during his presidency.

If Wilson was blind to the narrow concerns of workers and minorities, he had a keen political eye for the wider picture, mixed with a high moral tone that brooked no argument. Inspired by his sound analysis of the mood of the American people, and perhaps also by a gut pacifism, he managed to keep America out of **World War I** until 1917 – the politician in him happy to win re-election on the pacifist ticket. Within four months, however, the country was at war, prompted ostensibly by unprovoked German attacks on American shipping, though later critics would claim that the government wanted Allied war orders to stimulate the economy. Abandoning his pacifist stance, Wilson instead declared a war "for democracy" and devoted his considerable energies to ending it quickly and imposing a new moral order on the world. This manifested itself in his championing of a **League of Nations**, an idea he took to the peace conference in Paris, seeing it as a "matter of life or death for civilization." Returning in June 1919 to sell the idea to the American people (and more importantly to the Senate, which has to ratify any treaty by a two-thirds majority), Wilson undertook a draining speaking tour. After a series of blinding headaches he had to cut it short, returning to DC where, on October 2, 1919, he suffered a huge stroke that half-paralyzed him.

His cherished treaty was finally rejected by the Senate in March 1920, but by then Wilson was almost completely incapacitated. Few people outside government were informed of this, and in what today looks suspiciously like a cover-up, his wife Edith – sixteen years his junior – took on many of the day-to-day decisions in the White House, prompting critics to complain of a "**petticoat presidency**." As inflation rose and the economy slumped, Warren Harding was swept into power in the 1920 presidential elections. Wilson, old and infirm, and his wife left the White House for S Street, where crowds greeted him on the steps. There he died three years later on February 3, 1924, and was buried in Washington National Cathedral.

teringly, to amuse his children.) The silent-movie projector and screen were given to him after his stroke by Douglas Fairbanks Sr. Frozen in the 1920s, the fully equipped **kitchen** is a beauty, with blacklead range and provisions stacked in the walk-in pantry.

Textile Museum

2320 S St NW ☎667-0441, ⊛www.textilemuseum.org; Dupont Circle Metro. Mon–Sat 10am–5pm, Sun 1–5pm. Suggested donation $5.

Next door to the Woodrow Wilson House, in two equally grand converted residences, the **Textile Museum** presents temporary exhibitions drawn from its 15,000-strong collection of textiles and carpets. The museum had its roots in the collection of George Hewitt Myers, who bought his first Oriental rug as a student and opened the museum with three hundred other rugs and textile pieces in 1925. Based in his family home, designed by no less an architect than John Russell Pope, the museum soon expanded into the house next door; today both buildings, and the lovely gardens, are open to the public. Displays – in some of the most pleasingly presented galleries in town – might take in pre-Columbian Peruvian textiles, Near and Far Eastern exhibits (some dating back to 3000 BC) and rugs and carpets from Spain, South America and the American Southwest.

It's best to call for a schedule of exhibitions; better still, plan your visit to coincide with a free **tour** (Sept–May Wed, Sat & Sun 1.30pm) or the weekly **rug/textile appreciation** mornings (Sat 10.30am; free). The museum **shop** (see p.304) is an excellent place to buy textiles and fabrics.

Adams-Morgan

Nowhere is gentrification faster undermining the original, ethnic character of a Washington neighborhood than in **ADAMS-MORGAN**, DC's trendiest district. With every passing month new designer restaurants, stylish bars and hip stores march farther into the area, if not – for the time being – displacing, then at least beginning to outnumber the traditional Hispanic businesses that have thrived here since the 1950s. Spanish signs and notices are still much in evidence, and the neighborhood certainly celebrates its heritage fulsomely at the annual Latin American Festival (July) and Adams-Morgan Day (Sept) shindigs. But these days the area's character is better defined by the burgeoning number of cafés where asking for a latte frappé won't be met by a blank stare. For a night out largely free from the braying collegiate antics of Georgetown, you'll find Adams-Morgan's 18th Street strip a refreshing change – laid-back, open-to-the-sidewalk bars, restaurants, cafés and clubs with an ethnically and socio-economically mixed clientele.

Ironically, this middle-class influx into the neighborhood is simply turning Adams-Morgan full-circle. In the last decades of the **nineteenth century**, its hilly, rural reaches were colonized by wealthy Washingtonians looking for a select address near the power-housing of Dupont Circle. Impressive apartment buildings were erected in the streets off Columbia Road, boasting fine views and connected to downtown by streetcar. Until World War II some of the city's most prominent politicians and business people lived here, and many of their mansions survive intact. After the war, the city's housing shortage meant that

Eating, drinking and staying in Adams-Morgan

For Adams-Morgan listings, see the following pages: accommodation p.244; cafés and restaurants p.256; nightlife p.276.

many buildings were converted into rooming houses and small apartments; well-to-do families moved farther out into the suburbs and were replaced by a growing blue-collar population, black and white, and, crucially, by an increasing number of Latin American and Caribbean **immigrants**, whose numbers grew rapidly in the 1960s. Concerned that the area was becoming too segregated, a local group fashioned a symbolic name from two local schools: one all-white (Adams), one all-black (Morgan).

Today, Adams-Morgan is regarded as the most racially mixed neighborhood in the city, and for the most part there's a good-natured atmosphere in the streets, where grocery stores and corner cafés rub shoulders with arty boutiques and sharp bars. Adams-Morgan frequently pops up in establishing shots in the movies – *In the Line of Fire, Dave, A Few Good Men* and *Enemy of the State* all feature scenes shot in the neighborhood.

Undoubtedly, the yuppies have "discovered" Adams-Morgan, or at least discovered that it's a relatively cheap, fairly groovy, reasonably central place to live; but they're not the only recent immigrants. As any quick glance at the storefronts will tell you, Adams-Morgan's **restaurant scene** is the most eclectic in the city – Ethiopian arrivals are responsible for some of the neighborhood's most highly rated places, but you can eat anything from Argentinian to Vietnamese.

Some orientation

Adams-Morgan is generally thought of as being bounded by Connecticut and Florida avenues and 16th and Harvard streets, although in practice most visitors see little more than the few blocks on either side of the central **Columbia Road/18th Street intersection**, where most of the bars and restaurants are situated. The eastern boundary of the neighborhood is marked by 16th Street and **Meridian Hill Park** – don't stray further east than 16th Street into Shaw. To the west, the boundary is formed by the National Zoological Park and Connecticut Avenue NW, which is where you'll find the nearest **Metro**: from Woodley Park–Zoo Metro on Connecticut Avenue, it's a fifteen-minute walk across the Duke Ellington Bridge to the Columbia Road/18th Street junction. From Dupont Circle Metro it's a steep twenty-minute hike up 19th Street to Columbia Road. By **bus**, take the #L2 from McPherson Square, which travels up 18th Street to Calvert Street.

Along and around Columbia Road

Adams-Morgan's Hispanic legacy is at its strongest in the stretch of Columbia Road northeast of 18th Street, a good place to check out the street stalls, jewelry sellers and thrift stores; 18th Street south of the intersection with Columbia Road is lined with the best of the bars, clubs and restaurants. A Saturday market occupies the southwestern plaza where the two meet. For most visitors that's more than enough, though the streets east and west of the two main drags contain a fair amount of interest – Anthony Pitch's walking tours of the district (see p.32) can show you more.

The **Wyoming Building**, 2022 Columbia Road NW, is a classic example of the marvelous apartment houses built early in the twentieth century, its mosaic floor, molded ceilings and marble reception room forming one of DC's loveliest private interiors. The Eisenhowers lived here between 1927 and 1935. Up the street the Italian-Renaissance-style **Altamont Building**, 1901 Wyoming Avenue NW, at 20th, is similarly well endowed, with a baronial reception room and a top floor that once incorporated its own roof-terrace restaurant.

Often, the historical associations and **former occupants** are more diverting than a building itself: Admiral Robert Peary, first to reach the North Pole in 1909, lived at 1831 Wyoming Avenue; Tallulah Bankhead spent her teenage years in the Norwood building, 1868 Columbia Road (her father was Speaker of the House of Representatives); while Lyndon Baines and Ladybird Johnson spent the early years of their marriage at the Woburn building, 1910 Kalorama Road. Ronald Reagan was shot in Adams-Morgan, surviving an assassination attempt in 1981 as he left the *Washington Hilton*, at the southern end of Columbia Road. Most glamorous of all the Adams-Morgan buildings is the cupola-topped **Ontario** building, 2853 Ontario Road (at 18th), built between 1903 and 1906, whose roll call of famous residents has included five-star generals Douglas MacArthur and Chester Nimitz; journalist Janet Cooke, whose Pulitzer Prize-winning story about youth and drugs was later discredited; and Bob Woodward, who could afford to live here once Watergate had made his reputation. At the time of Watergate, his partner Carl Bernstein lived in Adams-Morgan too, in a much less grandiose apartment in the Biltmore apartment building, 1940 Biltmore Street, off 19th Street, just a couple of blocks south.

U Street and Shaw

East of Adams-Morgan, the historic district of **SHAW** has an upbeat past and the stirrings of a future, but is in the meantime still sorely affected by three intervening decades of neglect. The neighborhood – roughly north of M Street between North Capitol and 15th streets – is one of the oldest residential areas in DC; its first settlers were immigrant whites who built shanty housing along **7th Street** after the Civil War. The district was one of the booming city's main commercial arteries and remained busy during the Depression, when the low-rent housing in the alleys on either side began to attract countless black immigrants from the rural Southern states in search of work. Pool halls, churches, cafés, theaters and social clubs sprang up; a shopping strip developed across on **14th Street**; while **U Street** evolved into the "Black Broadway." For years the neighborhood was known simply as "14th and U," eventually taking the name "Shaw" after Colonel Robert Gould Shaw, the (white) commander of the first black regiment (the Massachusetts 54th) in the Union Army – the unit featured in the film *Glory*. With the all-black **Howard University** at 6th Street, and **Griffith Stadium** (now Howard University Hospital) at 2401 Georgia Avenue attracting massive crowds to its black baseball games, there was a rare vibrancy to this corner of DC.

Eating and drinking in U Street/Shaw

For U Street/Shaw listings, see the following pages: eating p.272; drinking and nightlife p.282.

Segregation – entrenched in Washington since the late nineteenth century – only secured Shaw's prosperity, since the local blacks stayed within the neighborhood to shop and socialize. Conversely, **desegregation** (starting with the Supreme Court's overturning of the "separate but equal" schools policy in 1954) opened up the varied attractions of downtown Washington to Shaw's black inhabitants, and the ensuing decline of the neighborhood was swift. Black middle-class flight to the periphery had been taking place since the turn of the century, with larger Victorian properties bought from suburb-bound whites in fringe neighborhoods such as LeDroit Park, Logan Circle and the so-called "Striver's Section" of U Street (between 15th and 18th).

By the 1960s, the older black streets in Shaw were feeling the pinch, while the **riots** of 1968 finished them off. News of the assassination of Dr Martin Luther King Jr sparked three days of arson, rioting and looting that destroyed businesses and lives along 7th, 14th and H streets. A dozen people were killed, millions of dollars of property lost and the confidence of nearby businesses in Old Downtown jolted so severely that within a decade that area, too, was virtually abandoned.*

The three decades since have done little for Shaw, much of which has become indistinguishable from the drug-infested neighborhoods to the northeast and southeast. Signs of **revival** are now evident, however – revitalized U Street has a Metro station and once again features on the city's nightlife scene, while 14th Street has blossomed as an alternative theater district.

There's no harm in a night out on U Street or a stroll around some of the peripheral historic sights and landmarks covered below, but heed the fact that you're away from the safer parts of Northwest. Drugs (and the crime that goes with them) are still very prevalent, many buildings are run-down, and the atmosphere is often oppressive. Don't wander aimlessly and alone in the neighborhood, which can change from borderline to downright threatening in a block or two; head straight for your destination, take cabs when necessary, and keep your wits about you. A good way to see the neighborhood is to take a **walking tour** (call ☎828-WALK) or sign up for "Duke Ellington's DC," a summer bus tour taking in a play and several local sites (see p.32).

U Street and around

The only part of Shaw most visitors see – and the safest to visit – is the thriving section of **U Street** in the blocks near **U Street–Cardozo Metro**, where more trendy bars and clubs move in with every passing year. Between the wars, U Street – known locally as "You" Street – ranked second only to New York's Harlem as the center of black entertainment in America. At the splendid **Lincoln Theatre**, built at 1215 U Street in 1921, vaudeville shows and movies were bolstered by appearances from the most celebrated jazz performers of the day: Count Basie, Billie Holiday, Cab Calloway, Ella Fitzgerald and DC's own Duke Ellington among them. The theater now serves as a performing arts center (see p.292). Next door, *Ben's Chili Bowl* (see p.272) is a 40-year-old institution frequented by the likes of Bill Cosby and Denzel Washington.

---

*The 1968 riots weren't the first to tear Shaw apart. Immediately after World War I, returning black servicemen were dismayed to find segregation forcefully applied in DC. In the summer of 1919, prompted by the violent antics of vigilante white ex-soldiers, five days of racial rioting – including fierce fighting on U, 7th and T streets as well as in areas of southwest Washington – left thirty people dead.

Duke Ellington (1899–1974)

Edward Kennedy Ellington was born in Washington DC (on 22nd St NW), and grew up in Shaw at 1212 T Street (not open to the public). A precocious child, nicknamed "Duke," at fifteen he was playing ragtime in scratch bands at local cafés; he wrote his first composition, *Soda Fountain Rag*, in 1914. Also an accomplished young artist, Ellington turned down a scholarship to New York's Pratt Institute to form instead "The Washingtonians," a trio with which he played extensively in DC before making the big move to New York in 1923. By 1927, his trio had expanded to become **The Duke Ellington Orchestra**; a year later, it was a permanent fixture at Harlem's Cotton Club, where Ellington made his reputation in five tumultuous years, writing early, atmospheric classics like *Mood Indigo* and *Creole Love Call*. Composer and band appeared in their first feature film, *Check and Double Check*, in 1930; by 1932, the Duke Ellington Orchestra had made more than 200 recordings.

Established as one of America's finest jazz composers and bandleaders, Ellington set off on his first European tour in 1933, where he took the Continent by storm. The following decade saw the penning of his most celebrated works – from *Sophisticated Lady* and *Take the A Train* to *Don't Get Around Much Anymore*.

The Ellington style was unmistakeable: melodious ballads and stomping swing pieces alike employed inventive rhythmic devices and novel key changes to devastating, creative effect. In 1943, he was the first popular musician to perform at Carnegie Hall (where he premiered the ambitious *Black, Brown and Beige*) and, despite a decline in Big Band popularity after World War II, managed to keep both his band and personal following largely intact. He spent much of the 1950s and 1960s touring and diversifying his output – writing soundtracks for (and appearing in) movies, and composing extended pieces that mixed jazz with classical music. In 1969 he received the Presidential Medal of Freedom for his services to music and the arts.

By the time of his death in 1974, Duke Ellington had arranged or composed more than six thousand works. Duke married Edna Thompson in 1918 and they had one son, Mercer, though the couple later separated. Mercer went on to play trumpet in his father's band and, after Duke's death, led the Duke Ellington Orchestra.

In DC, the city remembers its favorite son with a week-long festival of his music each year around April 20: the **Duke Ellington Birthday Celebration**. The Calvert Street Bridge between Woodley Park and Adams-Morgan was renamed Duke Ellington Bridge in his honor, while the city established the **Duke Ellington School of the Arts** in Georgetown (35th and R streets NW; ☏337-4022). The public high school offers a four-year course of study for artistically talented youths; free tours are available once a month (except June–Sept) – call for details.

The once-elegant **Howard Theatre**, several blocks east of the U Street scene at 624 T Street, was the neighborhood theater with the proudest pedigree. Opened in 1910, it was the first theater in DC built strictly for black patrons, though that didn't stop hip whites from flocking here to see the shows. An unknown Ella Fitzgerald won an open-mike contest here; 1940s Big Bands filled the place; and later artists such as James Brown, Smokey Robinson, Gladys Knight, and Martha and the Vandellas were lining up to appear; in 1962 the Supremes played their first headlining gig here. The theater survived the riots in one piece but closed soon after and still stands abandoned today. There's not much to see now, and for safety you're advised to come in a taxi, if at all.

African-American Civil War Memorial and Museum

1200 U St NW ☏667-2667, ⊛www.afroamcivilwar.org; U Street–Cardozo Metro. Mon–Fri 10am–5pm, Sat 10am–2pm. Admission free.

202

Leave the Metro by the 10th Street exit and you'll emerge right by the **African-American Civil War Memorial**, the country's only monument honoring the African-American soldiers who fought for the Union. *The Spirit of Freedom* sculpture stands in the center of a granite-paved plaza, partially encircled by a Wall of Honor, along which you'll find the names of the 209,145 United States Colored Troops (and their 7000 white officers) who served in the war. President Lincoln sanctioned the creation of the African-American regiments in 1862, and slaves, former slaves and freedmen joined the fight. The rush to enlist was best summed up by Frederick Douglass, whose words "Who would be free themselves must strike the blow. Better even die free than to live slaves" are inscribed at the site. Sadly, these brave troops were not included in the celebratory Grand Review of the Union Armies along Pennsylvania Avenue after the war's end, an early sign that the battle for equality had only begun.

Three blocks west of the memorial, in the five-story Italianate True Reformer Building, the **museum** tells the soldiers' largely unknown story as part of its small permanent exhibition, "**Slavery to Freedom: Civil War to Civil Rights**." Composed largely of photographs and documents, the collection wastes little time in cutting to the chase, beginning its rendering of African-American history with the original bill of sale for an 11-year-old girl. Other features include a "Descendents Registry," where visitors can look up relatives who may have served with the United States Colored Troops, and a "Computer Search For Your Soldier," which employs the Civil War Soldiers and Sailors Names Index to identify troops along with the history of their regiments.

The building housing the museum is an attraction in its own right: erected in 1903, it was among the finest structures of its time to be designed, built and financed by African-Americans. Its designer, John A. Lankford, DC's first registered African-American architect, saw the building as an example "to the civilized world ... of what the Negro can do and has done with his brain, skill, and money."

Howard University and LeDroit Park

Perhaps the most prestigious black university in the country, **Howard University** – named for General Otis Howard, commissioner of the Freedmen's Bureau – was established in 1867 by a church missionary society to provide a school for blacks freed after the Civil War. Its first faculties were in law, music, medicine and theology, though nowadays hundreds of subjects are taken by almost 13,000 students from over a hundred countries. Famous Howard alumni include Toni Morrison, Jessye Norman, Thurgood Marshall, David Dinkins, Andrew Young and Shaka Hislop. Sadly, none of the original campus buildings remains; the earliest structure was replaced by the **Founder's Library** in the 1930s. The library now maintains the Moorland-Spingarn Research Center (Mon–Thurs 9am–4.45pm, Fri 9am–4.30pm; ☎806-7240), housing the country's largest selection of literature relating to black history and culture. This is open to the public, but as a casual visitor, you're more likely to come for a campus **tour** (contact ☎806-2755 or ✉campustour@howard.edu in advance). The **main entrance** is at 2400 6th Street NW; nearest **Metro** is Shaw-Howard University, half a dozen blocks south down Georgia Avenue – don't walk, take a taxi to the gates.

Short of money just a decade after its inauguration, the university sold a plot of land to the south (in the shallow angle formed by Florida and Rhode Island avenues) to developers who built an exclusive parkland suburb of sixty detached houses. White university staff were the first to take up residence in

LeDroit Park, as it was known, though the addition of brick row houses in the 1880s and 1890s signaled the advance of well-to-do black families. By 1920 LeDroit Park was established as a fashionable black neighborhood, and though much of it has decayed over the decades, the area has been declared a historic district, with the best surviving group of original houses along the 400 block of U Street. Prominent black citizens continue to be associated with the area – the family of DC's first black mayor, Walter Washington, has owned a house here for years, while Jesse Jackson also maintains a property in the district. Perhaps it was LeDroit Park that blues musician Leadbelly had in mind when he wrote his *Bourgeois Blues* in the 1930s; to an ex-jailbird, these rarefied streets must have seemed miles away from the basement jazz and blues clubs on U:

> Look a here people, listen to me,
> Don't try to find no home in Washington DC
> Lord, it's a bourgeois town, it's a bourgeois town.

Logan Circle and 14th Street

At the same time that LeDroit Park saw a black middle-class influx, so too did the roomy Victorian houses around **Logan Circle**, at the southern edge of Shaw. Nearby 14th Street was the black community's swankiest shopping thoroughfare; in the 1930s, the blocks between P and U streets were known as "Auto Row" after the rash of car showrooms that opened up, eager to sell vehicles to the upwardly mobile residents. Fashionable Iowa Circle, as it was then known, became Logan Circle in 1930, named for the Civil War general whose impressive equestrian statue still lords over it. The surrounding Victorian houses have miraculously survived the neighborhood's slow decline since the 1950s – turrets, terraces, balconies and pediments in various states of repair signal the fact that this, too, is a protected historic district.

Fourteenth Street, half a block west, was almost completely lost to the 1968 riots, but its rough edges have been tamed by the arrival of various fringe **theater companies** and **bars** that have set up shop here and in the surrounding streets. It's still a bit risky at night – don't wander around alone – but the fact that it's already known to some as "Dupont East" is probably symptomatic of the way the neighborhood's going.

The Bethune Council House

Based in one of the district's restored Victorian townhouses just off Logan Circle, the **Bethune Council House** at 1318 Vermont Avenue NW (Mon–Sat 10am–4.30pm; free; ☎673-2402, ⊛www.nps.gov/mamc/) serves as a memorial to one of DC's most prominent African-American inhabitants. **Mary McLeod Bethune** was born on a cotton farm in South Carolina in 1875, one of seventeen children of poor parents, both ex-slaves. A bright, inquiring child, she was sent to a local school and later entertained thoughts of becoming a missionary in Africa (she was turned down on account of her race), before moving to Florida in 1904 to found the Daytona Educational and Industrial School for Negro Girls (later the Bethune-Cookman College). Starting in a rented room and using homemade materials, Bethune persevered with her intention to train teachers who would serve the African-American community. In 1935, recognition came with the award of a prize by the National Association for the Advancement of Colored People (NAACP), swiftly followed by a call from President Roosevelt to serve as special advisor on minority affairs. Later, as the director of the Division of Negro Affairs in the

National Youth Administration, Bethune became the first African-American woman to head a federal office, and was the only woman to work in the ad-hoc "Black Cabinet" that advised FDR on the implications for blacks of his New Deal policies. In 1945, under the aegis of the NAACP, Bethune was invited to San Francisco to attend the conference that established the concept of the United Nations.

The house on Vermont Avenue was bought by Bethune in 1942 to serve both as her home (she lived there for seven years) and as headquarters for the National Council for Negro Women, which she had founded in 1935, bringing together various organizations in order to fight discrimination more effectively. Her work here formed the basis of her "Legacy," finished just before her death in 1955, in which she encapsulated the meaning of her life's work in a stirring series of messages for those who would follow: "I leave you a thirst for education. I leave you a respect for the use of power. I leave you faith. I leave you racial dignity." Now administered by the National Park Service, the house still serves as a research center and archive, though you're welcome to tour the restored rooms, which contain a few mementoes of Bethune alongside period photographs and changing exhibitions. The memorial to Mary McLeod Bethune in Lincoln Park (see p.117) records more of the "Legacy."

The best way to the house is the fifteen-minute walk straight up Vermont Avenue from McPherson Square Metro, past Thomas Circle.

Upper Northwest

N one of the fluctuating fortunes that have afflicted DC's other neighborhoods has ever ruffled the well-to-do feathers of the districts of the **Upper Northwest**. The upper- and middle-class flight up Connecticut, Wisconsin and Massachusetts avenues began with a series of nineteenth-century presidents who made the cool reaches of rural **Woodley Park** – across Duke Ellington Bridge from Adams-Morgan – their summer home. Grover Cleveland later bought his own stone cottage a little farther north in an area which, as a consequence, became known as **Cleveland Park**. Few others could afford the time and expense involved in living a four-mile carriage-ride from the city center until the arrival in the 1890s of the streetcar; within three decades both Woodley Park and Cleveland Park had become bywords for fashionable, out-of-town living, replete with apartment buildings designed by the era's top architects. The tone is no less swanky today, with a series of ritzy suburbs stretching into Maryland. Politicians and media people choose to live in the safe streets of Cleveland Park; while the gleaming malls and power shoppers of Friendship Heights, on the DC/Maryland boundary, are second only to those of New York's Fifth Avenue.

For all its pedigree, however, this part of town has relatively little to offer visitors. You can only view the most celebrated mansions from the outside, while the surrounding streets, though pleasing, are hardly exciting. The three major tourist targets are the excellent **National Zoological Park**, the farthest-flung of the Smithsonian attractions; **Washington National Cathedral**; and the expanses of **Rock Creek Park**, largest and most enjoyable of the city's green spaces.

The area is most easily reached using the **Metro** Red Line. Alternatives are bus #L2, which runs up Connecticut Avenue from McPherson Square via Adams-Morgan (18th St) to Chevy Chase, and buses #30, #32, #34, #35 and #36, which travel up Wisconsin Avenue from Georgetown to Friendship Heights.

Eating, drinking and staying in the Upper Northwest

For Upper Northwest listings, see the following pages: accommodation p.251; eating p.272; drinking and nightlife p.281.

Woodley Park and Cleveland Park

Architect Harry L. Wardman designed many of the apartment buildings and townhouses in **WOODLEY PARK**. His most adventurous project was the massive **Wardman Park Hotel** (Connecticut Ave NW and Woodley Rd), built in 1918, whose tower still dominates the local skyline (it's now part of the 1500-room *Marriott Wardham Park*). It proved a resounding success, attracting high-profile politicians and social gadflys who entertained guests in the grand public rooms and rented apartments for themselves. Within a decade a second landmark followed, the hybrid Art Deco–Renaissance-style **Shoreham** on Calvert Street (now the *Omni Shoreham*), designed by Joseph Abel for owner-builder Harry Bralove. Built in 1930 at a cost of $4 million, this has held an inaugural ball or gala for every president from FDR to George W. Bush; here Truman played poker, JFK courted Jackie, Nixon announced his first cabinet and, in the hotel's celebrated *Blue Room*, Judy Garland, Marlene Dietrich, Bob Hope and Frank Sinatra entertained the great and the good. The *Marriott*, for its part, keeps up with the times and the political players, too, and in 2001 hosted "Dubya's" Texas Black Tie & Boots inaugural ball.

For a view of where the generally more staid nineteenth-century presidents passed their summers, head up Connecticut Avenue to Cathedral Avenue and walk west past 29th Street to the white stucco Georgian **Woodley Mansion**. This was built in 1800 for Philip Barton Key, whose nephew Francis was later to pen the "Star-Spangled Banner." Its elevation meant it was a full ten degrees cooler in the summer than downtown, and presidents Van Buren, Tyler and Buchanan needed no second invitation to spend their summers here; it's now a private school.

Back on Connecticut Avenue and heading north past the zoo you're soon, and imperceptibly, in **CLEVELAND PARK**. For sheer exuberance, the **Kennedy-Warren** apartment building (3133 Connecticut Ave NW) on the east side takes the local honors – this soaring Art Deco evocation of 1930s wealth is home today to P.J. O'Rourke, among others. Slightly farther north, just before Cleveland Park Metro station, the Art Deco movie house, the **Uptown** (3426 Connecticut Ave NW), now part of the Cineplex Odeon chain, has been showing movies since 1936.

Backtracking from Cleveland Park Metro down Connecticut Avenue you can make your way to the cathedral along **Newark Street** and **Highland Place**. These hold the area's highest concentration of upper-class residences, dating from its great turn-of-the-century expansion: Robert Head, Waddy Butler Wood and Paul Pelz all built houses here, and it was on Newark Street that Grover Cleveland's (long-demolished) summer house – the one that prompted the whole influx – once stood.

Washington National Cathedral

Massachusetts and Wisconsin aves NW ☎537-6200 or 537-5596 (for weekly listing of special events), ⊕www.cathedral.org/cathedral; Bus #30, #32, #34, #35 or #36 from Pennsylvania Ave (downtown) or Wisconsin Ave (Georgetown), or Bus #N2, #N4 or #N6 from Farragut Square; Woodley Park-Zoo Metro. May–Sept Mon–Fri 10am–9pm, Sat 10am–4.30pm, Sun 8am–5pm; Oct–April Mon–Fri 10am–5pm, Sat 10am–4.30pm, Sun 8am–5pm. Suggested donation $3.

The twin towers of **Washington National Cathedral** – the sixth-largest cathedral in the world – are visible long before you reach the church itself.

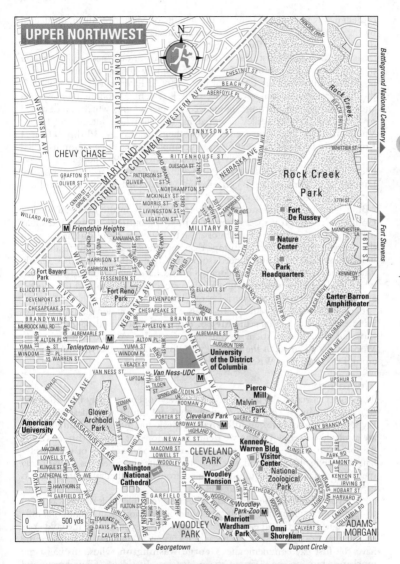

Cathedral services

The Cathedral's daily worship schedule is: Mon–Fri 7.30am, noon & 4.30pm; Sat 4pm; Sun 8am, 9am (10am Sept–June), 11am, 4pm & 6.30pm.

Turn the final corner and you're confronted by one of the city's most surprising edifices, a monumental building so medieval in spirit it should surely rise from a dusty European old town plaza rather than from a two-car, two-kid suburb. It comes as no surprise in this planned city, however, that the siting of the cathedral was intentional: here, on the heights of Mount St Alban, unaffected by the District's zoning restrictions, the architects could have free rein to produce their anachronistic Gothic masterpiece.

George Washington first proposed the establishment of a "national" church in the city, but it was a century before Congress finally granted a charter for what is officially known as the Cathedral Church of St Peter and St Paul. In 1907, the foundation ceremony was held, with President Theodore Roosevelt in attendance, and construction commenced on the building, which was designed by architects George Bodley (a noted English church architect) and Henry Vaughan. They were succeeded after their deaths by **Philip Hubert Frohman**, who spent the next fifty years completing the design. Frohman died in 1972; the cathedral was finally completed only in 1990, though parts have been in use since the 1920s. It's a Protestant church, the seat of the Episcopal Diocese of Washington, yet is conceived of as a national church, and also hosts services for other denominations.*

Built from Indiana limestone and modeled entirely in the medieval English Gothic style – its great spaces supported by flying buttresses, bosses and vaults – it's a supreme achievement. Unfortunately, there are more similarities with the hoary, crumbling relics of Europe than appearances alone suggest: although it looks brand-new – and indeed, some parts are – the cathedral is already undergoing restoration. The decorative bosses have been attacked by lichen, while Washington's freezing winters have cracked the gutters and the roofing and damaged some of the exterior gargoyles.

It's easiest to reach the cathedral by bus (see above); if you don't mind a twenty-minute walk, you can take the **Metro.** From the Woodley Park–Zoo station, turn left from Connecticut Avenue into Cathedral Avenue and right into Woodley Road to reach the lower-level information center; the west door is around the corner on Wisconsin Avenue.

The interior

The center portal in the west facade isn't always open; you may have to **enter** from the northwest cloister. For a floor plan and information, descend to the crypt floor, where there's an **information desk** and gift shop. **Guided tours** are available on request at the west entrance (Mon–Sat 10–11.30am & 12.45-3.15pm, Sun 12.30–2.30pm; suggested donation $3); ask one of the purple-hatted docents. Phone ahead or check the website for schedules of the many speciality tours, which feature everything from the cathedral's gardens to its gargoyles — there's even a "Tour and Tea."

Place yourself first at the west end of the **nave** (completed as recently as 1976) to appreciate the immense scale of the building; it's more than a tenth of a mile to the high altar at the other end, and the only reason you can see the gold cross on the altar from this distance is because it's 6ft tall. Along the south side of the nave, the first bay commemorates **George Washington**, whose marble statue proclaims him to be "First Citizen, Patriot, President, Churchman and Freemason," while five bays down is the sarcophagus of **Woodrow Wilson** – the only president to be buried in the District (although Eisenhower's funeral was also held in the cathedral). Much of the work on the building took place

---

*Thoroughly Roman Catholic but similarly immense in scale is DC's other major church, the Basilica of the National Shrine of the Immaculate Conception (4th St and Michigan Ave NE), a striking hilltop Marian shrine in NE, three blocks west of Brookland-CUA Metro. It's an architectural hodgepodge compared to the National Cathedral, but the majolica-tiled dome and mosaics are spectacular.

during Wilson's presidency, a process which so fascinated him he used to visit the construction site in his chauffeur-driven limousine. In the adjacent bay, look up to the **Space Window**, whose stained glass incorporating a sliver of moon rock commemorates the flight of Apollo II, and resembles nothing so much as the cover of a Robert A. Heinlein paperback. On the north side, across from Washington, the **Abraham Lincoln Bay** is marked by a bronze statue of Abe with Lincoln-head pennies set into the floor. The next berth down is for cathedral architect **Philip Hubert Frohman**, a Catholic whose family received special dispensation to have him buried in this Protestant church. Last bay before the North Transept features a small likeness of **Dr Martin Luther King Jr** above the arch, inscribed "I Have A Dream": on Sunday March 31, 1968, the reverend preached his last sermon here before heading for Memphis where he was due to lead a march of striking black workers; four days later he was dead, assassinated by a bullet fired by James Earl Ray.

At the **High Altar** there's a splendid view back down along the carved vault to the west rose window. The beautifully intricate reredos features 110 figures surrounding Christ in Benediction. An elevator from the south porch at the west end of the nave (near the Washington statue) ascends to the **Pilgrim Observation Gallery**, which affords stupendous city views.

The 57-acre grounds, or **Cathedral Close** – virtually a small fiefdom – hold cathedral offices, three schools, a college, sports fields and a swimming pool, not to mention a **Herb Cottage** selling dried herbs and teas, a **Greenhouse** and the attractive **Bishop's Garden**, a walled rose-and-herb garden laid out in medieval style.

National Zoological Park

3001 Connecticut Ave NW ☎673-4800, 🌐www.natzoo.si.edu; Cleveland Park or Woodley Park-Zoo Metro, or Bus #L2 from McPherson Square or 18th St (Adams-Morgan). Grounds daily: May–mid-Sept 6am–8pm; mid-Sept–April 6am–6pm. Buildings daily: May–mid-Sept 10am–6pm; mid-Sept–April 10am–4.30pm. Admission free.

The enormously entertaining **National Zoological Park** forms part of the Smithsonian ensemble – which apart from anything else means that admission is free. Sitting between Woodley Park and Adams-Morgan, it sprawls down the steep slopes of the gorge cut by Rock Creek, with trails through lush vegetation leading past comparatively humane simulations of the home environments of more than three thousand creatures. Although founded in 1889 as a traditional zoo, it likes to think of itself these days as a "BioPark," combining the usual menagerie of giraffes, elephants, lions and tigers with botanic gardens, a prairie and a wetlands zone, "Amazonia" (a re-creation of a tropical river and rainforest habitat), as well as aquariums and natural history displays.

The **main entrance** on Connecticut Avenue is a ten-minute walk from either of the Metro stations noted above, but it's easiest to arrive at the Cleveland Park station; from there the zoo is a level stroll south along Connecticut Avenue – from Woodley Park you'll have to hike uphill. Just inside the gates, the **visitor center** has a map and list of the day's events, including feeding times. From here, two trails loop downhill through the park to Rock Creek itself: the **Olmsted Walk**, passing most of the indoor exhibits, and the steeper **Valley Trail**, with the major aquatic exhibits, birds and "Amazonia." Head down one and back up the other, visiting the side exhibits on the way, and you'll walk more than two miles – allow a minimum of three hours to do the park justice. On your way, you'll find a café, restaurant, concession stands, paid parking, police post and restrooms scattered throughout the park.

Park highlights

The scales outside the **Cheetah Conservation Station** provide the first interaction between visitor and captive. Weigh yourself, check the chart to see with which animal your weight corresponds – and then read just how quickly the apparently somnolent cheetahs in the paddock beyond would take to kill and eat you. A little farther on you'll have your first zoo celebrity sighting: the **pandas** Mei Xiang and Tian Tian, who arrived from the People's Republic of China in December 2000. The two fill the absence created by the 1990s deaths of Ling Ling and Hsing Hsing, the famous pair presented by Beijing during Richard Nixon's 1972 visit. Although the pandas are on exhibit daily from 9am to 4.30pm, the best time to catch the duo is first thing in the morning, when the lines are shorter and the animals tend to be more active.

The path winds down past elephants, giraffes, hippos and rhinos to perhaps the saddest relic in the zoo. Before the European settlement of America, millions of **bison** roamed the country; now, along with the couple here, just 140,000 or so survive in scattered parks, refuges and private ranches, their numbers boosted by the modern success in breeding bison for its low-calorie and minimum-cholesterol meat. An **American Prairie** exhibit puts the beasts in context, providing some explanation of the natural and cultural histories of the nation's grasslands. The first of the zoo's garden areas, the **American Indian Heritage Garden**, celebrates the natural history knowledge of the Native Americans, whose lives were sustained by the bison herds before they and the animals became surplus to white American requirements. Here you learn about the healing properties of herbs and plants like the coneflower (used to treat insect bites, venereal disease and rabies) and the gloriously emetic Indian tobacco plant: should you ever be tempted to make cigarettes out of this, bear in mind that it's also known as vomitweed, pukeweed and gagroot.

Some of the zoo's most adventurous work is taking place with its primates. The orangutans are encouraged to leave the confines of the **Great Ape House** and commute to the "**Think Tank**" and back down the "**O Line**" – overhead cables strung from towers across public areas of the zoo, with only the depth of the fall (and some low-amperage electric wires on the towers) to deter them from leaping off. At the Think Tank, scientists and orangutans come together to hone their communications skills and discuss world events in the fascinating Orangutan Language Project. If in any doubt about the relative intelligence of ape and human, take a look at the glass case in the Great Ape House, which displays the ludicrous items visitors have thrown into the enclosures over the years – from cans of soda to plastic crocodiles.

Between Ape House and Think Tank is the **Reptile Discovery Center,** with a full complement of snakes, turtles, crocs, alligators, lizards and frogs, and some enterprising interactive displays, though quite how interactive you want to be with said beasts is open to question. Ponder here on the remarkable komodo dragons, one of which was the first to be born in captivity outside Indonesia. Since her celebrated birth in 1992, Kraken has grown to a length of seven feet, all thanks to a steady diet of rats. The adjacent **Invertebrate Exhibit** covers the lives and loves of everything from ants to coral and octopus – admission to these two popular centers can be restricted at busy times; check first at the visitor center. Beyond here, the special moated island with the **lions and tigers** marks the end of the big animals, though you might want to duck in and out of the thoroughly unpleasant **bat cave** before heading back up the Valley Trail.

The best thing on the Valley Trail is undoubtedly "**Amazonia**," the indoor tropical river and forest habitat. A cleverly constructed undulating aquarium gets you close to the fish – piranhas included – while bombarding you with informative notes. You then climb up a level into the humid, creeper-clad rain forest, above the water you've just walked along, familiarizing yourself with roots, leaf mold, forest parasites and birdcalls.

Outside again, seals and sea lions splash in an outdoor pool, and then it's a slow pull uphill, past beaver dams, an impressive **bird house**, an artificial wetland replete with cranes and herons, and assorted eagles, bongo antelope and tapirs. If there's some jiggery-pokery in the bushes as you go, it'll be the golden lion tamarins, or South American marmosets, the successful breeding of which is one of the zoo's quiet triumphs – more than one thousand now roam the wild in Brazil, the majority of which were reintroduced by the zoo or descend from this group of Washingtonians.

Rock Creek Park

Most visitors and many Washingtonians overlook the attractions of the city's major park, **Rock Creek Park** (Ⓦwww.nps.gov/rocr), the bulk of which stretches between the quiet suburbs of the Upper Northwest. Established by mandate of Congress in 1890, its 1800 acres cut a generous six-mile-long swath, tracing the line of the eponymous creek from its early meanderings through Georgetown and Woodley Park to the northernmost DC–Maryland border. Little more than a narrow gorge in its southern reaches, the park spreads out above the National Zoo to become a mile-wide tranche of woodland west of 16th Street.

A road shadows the creek for much of its length, called the **Rock Creek Parkway** until it reaches the zoo, north of which it's known as **Beach Drive**. A car is the easiest way to get in and around the park; by **public transit**, your only real choices are the Metro to Cleveland Park, which provides access to the section of the park just north of the zoo, or the Metro to Friendship Heights, from which Buses #E2, #E3 and #E4 run up Western Avenue and McKinley Street before cruising along Military Road through the middle of the park. To reach the east side of the park, take Bus #S2 or #S4; both run straight up 16th Street from anywhere north of K Street NW. Alternatively, you can hop on a bike in Georgetown and simply ride north along Rock Creek.

The park is open during **daylight hours**, which in practice means from around 7.30am. It's not a wise idea to come on foot, on your own, at night, though traffic is permitted 24 hours a day.

Inside the park

There are fifteen miles of **trails and paths** in the park, along both sides of the creek. They include tracks and workout stations, bridleways (in the wooded, northern section) and a **cycle route** that runs from the Lincoln Memorial, north through the park and into Maryland; to the south, Arlington Memorial Bridge links the route to the Mount Vernon Trail in Virginia (see p.231). On weekends (from 7am Sat to 7pm Sun), Beach Drive between Military and Broad Branch roads is closed to cars, and the **rollerblading** crowd comes out to primp and preen. The park also features ballparks, thirty **picnic areas** and the Carter Barron Amphitheater (16th St and Colorado Ave NW; see p.287), which hosts a variety of summer concerts.

The sights start at the southern end of the park, a mile above the zoo, where the serene, granite **Pierce Mill** (Wed–Sun noon–4pm; free; ☎426-6908) stands in a beautiful riverside hollow on Tilden Street, near Beach Drive. One of eight nineteenth-century gristmills in the valley, and the last to shut down (in 1897), it has been restored by the National Park Service and today produces cornmeal and wheat flour for sale to visitors. You can observe the process, and even have a go yourself with small hand grinders and sifters. Just across the way, the old carriage house serves as the **Rock Creek Gallery** (Thurs–Sun noon–6pm; ☎244-2482), which displays local art.

The **Nature Center** on Glover Road, just south of Military Road (Wed–Sun 9am–5pm; free; ☎426-6828), acts as the park visitor center, with natural history exhibits and details of weekend guided walks and self-guided nature trails. Finally, just on the other side of Military Road, the remains of **Fort De Russey** stand as a reminder of the network of defenses that ringed the city during the Civil War. Guarding against Confederate attack from the north, this was just one of 68 forts erected around the city. The sites of others – notably forts Reno, Bayard, and Stevens (see below) – have been appropriated as small parks on either side of Rock Creek Park proper.

Fort Stevens and Battleground National Cemetery

Drive east on Military Road from the park to 13th Street NW, where **Fort Stevens** marks the spot at which the city came closest to falling to Confederate troops during the Civil War. An army of 15,000 men crossed the Potomac in July 1864 and got within 150 yards of the fort before the hastily reinforced Union defense drove them back under a barrage of artillery fire. President Lincoln was in the fort during the attack and mounted the parapet for a better look at the Confederate line, drawing a stinging rebuke from a nearby soldier, who is said to have shouted "Get down you damned fool!" at his commander-in-chief. Lincoln, to his credit, heeded the advice, but not all his troops were so lucky. Seven blocks farther north on Georgia Avenue is **Battleground National Cemetery** (sunrise–sunset), in whose restricted confines lie the remains of the Union soldiers killed in the battle to defend the fort. Buses #70 and #71 run here, up 7th Street (which becomes Georgia Ave NW) from the Mall, but given Georgia Avenue's rather fearsome reputation you're advised to come and go by taxi.

8

Georgetown

S ocially, politically and culturally, **GEORGETOWN** sits at the center of Washington high life. Geographically, of course, it's out on a limb, way to the west of downtown, off the Metro line and beyond the divide of Rock Creek. This relative isolation has engendered an elitism that isn't entirely imagined: to stroll around the area's steep, leafy streets, past rows of million-dollar chocolate-box houses, is to step inside what Jan Morris has called "the most obsessively political residential enclave in the world." The Kennedys moved here before Jack made it to the White House and were followed by a cocktail party full of establishment figures who have adopted Georgetown as their home (or, more usually, one of their homes): Bob Woodward, Katherine Graham (the late *Washington Post* publisher), Ben Bradlee (executive editor of the *Post* during Watergate), art collector and philanthropist Paul (son of Andrew) Mellon, biographer Kitty Kelley, novelist Herman Wouk, Elizabeth Taylor (during her marriage to Senator John Warner) – the list goes on and on.

There is, of course, more to Georgetown than its upper-crust inhabitants. The area is at its vibrant best along the spine of **Wisconsin Avenue** and **M Street**, with their enjoyable saloons, coffee shops, fashionable restaurants and antique bookstores in which students of Georgetown University rub shoulders with staid old power brokers. Its history is diverting too, and many of the district's buildings date back to the early eighteenth century, making it older than the capital itself. Genteel Federal-era and shuttered Victorian townhouses hung with flower baskets stud the streets, while **north of Q Street** lies a series of stately mansions and handsome parks, gardens and cemeteries. Down on the **C&O Canal**, below M Street, horse-drawn boats fill the waterway, while the tree-shaded towpaths have been turned over to cyclists and walkers; to the east, the boardwalk, cafés and restaurants of the **Washington Harbour** development provide views down the Potomac to the Kennedy Center.

Georgetown's most annoying anomaly is that it's not on the **Metro** (Rock Creek and its valley are in the way). And don't even think about driving here: there's nowhere to park. The nearest Metro station is **Foggy Bottom–GWU**, from which it's a fifteen- to twenty-minute walk up Pennsylvania Avenue and along M Street to the junction with Wisconsin Avenue. Alternatively, approach from Dupont Circle, a similar-length walk west along P Street (or over the Dumbarton Bridge and along Q St; see p.194), which puts you first in the ritzier, upper part of Georgetown – in which case you might want to start your

---

Eating, drinking and staying in Georgetown

For Georgetown listings, see the following pages: accommodation p.249; eating p.269; drinking and nightlife p.280.

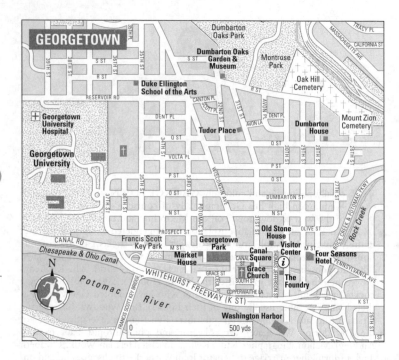

tour with the mansions, parks and gardens of northern Georgetown (see p.221). **Buses** #30, #32, #34, #35 and #36 run up Pennsylvania Avenue from Washington Circle (and other points downtown), along M Street and Wisconsin Avenue; #D5 runs from Farragut West to M Street; and #G2 runs from Dupont Circle to P and Dumbarton streets. At night you'll find **taxis** relatively easy to come by on the main drags; it's a $7–8 ride to and from most downtown DC locations.

Some history

In the early eighteenth century, when this area was part of Maryland, **Scottish merchants** began to form a permanent settlement around shoreside warehouses on the higher reaches of the Potomac River (or "Patowmack," as it was then known). Here they oversaw a thriving trade, exporting the plentiful tobacco from nearby farms and importing foreign materials and luxuries for colonial settlers. In 1751 the Maryland Assembly granted a **town charter** to the merchants, who named their flourishing port after their royal protector, George II. Within a decade, "George Towne" was a runaway success, attracting other merchants who built large mansions on estates to the north of the river, and by the 1780s it was America's largest tobacco port.

Once George Washington had pinpointed the Potomac region as the site of the new federal capital, it seemed logical that such a thriving port be included in the plans. In 1791, together with Alexandria in Virginia, the town was incorporated within the federal district. And while for many years the new city of Washington remained little more than an idea, Georgetown itself continued to prosper – by 1830 it had a population of nine thousand, and boasted streets of Federal-style brick houses, fashionable stores, well-tended gardens and even a university (founded in 1789). By the time of the **Civil War**, Georgetown was still separate enough from Washington to be considered suspect in Union eyes. Many of the town's early landowners came from the South, and during the war there was strong support (by the "Sessesh" – or secessionists – as they termed themselves) for the Confederate cause. But Georgetown's proximity to the capital (and the Union troops stationed in the town) kept the lid on any overt secessionist feeling.

The war and Georgetown's commercial prospects flickered and died at about the same time. The tobacco trade had already faltered due to soil exhaustion, while the steady growth of Baltimore and Washington itself badly affected the town's prosperity. The **Chesapeake and Ohio (C&O) Canal**, completed in 1850, represented an attempt to revive trade with the interior, and for a time Georgetown became a regional center for wheat, coal and timber shipment. But the canal was soon obsolete: the coming of the railroads was swiftly followed by the development of larger steamboats, which couldn't be accommodated by Georgetown's canal or harbor. Relegated to a mere neighborhood in the District of Columbia after losing its charter in 1871, Georgetown was delivered another insult in 1895 when most of its old **street names** – some in use for more than 150 years – were abandoned by order of Congress in favor of the numbers and letters of the federal city plan. There was even a suggestion that Georgetown become known as "West Washington."

For much of the late nineteenth and early twentieth centuries, Georgetown was anything but a fashionable place to live. Water-powered foundries and mills provided employment for a growing, predominantly black population, based in the neighborhood of Herring Hill, south of P Street and close to Rock Creek. Gardens were lost to speculative row housing and many larger mansions were subdivided; a noisy streetcar system was installed; and M Street became a workaday run of cheap stores and saloons owned by immigrant families. However, a mass influx of white-collar workers to DC during the New Deal era and World War II reversed Georgetown's rather down-at-heel image. Black and immigrant families were slowly pushed out of the Victorian streets, apartments were knocked back into houses and Federal mansions renovated. Part of the charm for newcomers was that Georgetown's natural boundaries – southern river, eastern creek, western university grounds and northern estates – had prevented wholesale, indiscriminate development. Despite the disruption, a certain small-town character had survived the years.

Now, of course, this character is zealously preserved by Georgetown residents who, since the 1950s and 1960s, have included ever-increasing numbers of DC's most fashionable and politically well-connected inhabitants. Certain historic houses have been lost to developers and some of the streets are overwhelmed by traffic, but since 1967 Georgetown has been registered as a **national historic landmark** – new buildings and renovations have to be sympathetic to their surroundings, house facades are color-coordinated, and the canal has been landscaped and preserved as a national historic park.

Along the C&O Canal

On a summer's day there's no finer part of Georgetown than the **Chesapeake and Ohio (C&O) Canal,** whose eastern extremity feeds into Rock Creek at 28th Street NW. The canal is overlooked on both sides by restored red-brick warehouses, spanned by small bridges, lined with trees and punctuated by occasional candy-colored towpath houses. The prettiest central stretch starts at 30th Street, where the adjacent **locks** once opened to allow through boatloads of coal, iron, timber and corn from the Maryland estates upriver.

The Potomac River had been used by traders since the earliest days of settlement in the region, but a series of rapids and waterfalls – like those at Great Falls, just fourteen miles from Georgetown – made large-scale commercial navigation all but impossible. A canal was proposed (George Washington was one of the shareholders) that would follow the line of the river and open up trade as far as the Ohio Valley, but when construction finally finished in 1850, the C&O reached only as far as Cumberland in Maryland, 184 miles and 74

Canal boats and other C&O activities

It is 184 miles from Georgetown to the canal terminus at Cumberland, MD. Along the way, the canal travels through highly varied scenery: past waterfalls, through forests, and skirting the ridges and valleys of the Appalachian Mountains.

Canal boats

To sign up for trips on the ninety-foot, mule-drawn **canal boats** – accompanied by park rangers in nineteenth-century costume who work the locks – stop in at the Georgetown **C&O Canal Visitor Center**, 1057 Thomas Jefferson Street NW (April–Oct daily 10am–4pm; ☎653-5190, ⊛www.nps.gov/choh). Tickets cost $8, and there are usually three or four departures on Wednesday through Sunday from mid-June to early September, with reduced service from April to mid-June and mid-September to late October.

Along the canal

A number of outlets along the canal rent boats, canoes and bikes, including several in the first twenty-mile stretch from Georgetown (see p.307). For a day trip by **bike**, Great Falls (see below) – an easy, flat fourteen miles away – is a reasonable destination. You'll need to observe a 15mph speed limit on the towpath, wear a helmet and give way to all pedestrians and horses. It takes most people a couple of hours to bike to Great Falls from Georgetown, and the only slightly tricky bit is just before Lock 15, where you'll have to carry the bike for a couple hundred yards. **Canoes** and **boats** are limited to specific areas (visitor centers and rental outlets can advise) and should not venture onto the Potomac River, which can be very dangerous. You also shouldn't **swim** in the canal or river due to unpredictable currents. You can **picnic** anywhere you like, but only light fires in authorized fireplaces. First-come, first-served basic campsites are dotted along the entire length of the canal; the one closest to the city is at Swain's Lock, twenty miles from Georgetown.

Great Falls

At **Great Falls**, fourteen miles from Georgetown, the Great Falls Tavern Visitor Center, 11710 MacArthur Boulevard, Potomac, MD (daily 9am–4pm; ☎301/299-3613, ⊛www.nps.gov/choh), has a museum covering the history of the canal. This is the starting point for guided local tours, walks and canal boat trips (same prices and schedules as in Georgetown). Nearby, a boardwalk offers terrific views of the falls themselves. There's a snack bar but no other eating or rental facilities. By car, take MacArthur Boulevard, signposted from Georgetown, or Exit 41W off the Beltway; outside rush hour, it's a twenty-minute drive. Parking is $4 per vehicle. There's also a visitor center on the Virginia side of the falls (☎703/285-2965) – though no access between the two sides of the canal and the Potomac River – featuring more tours and trails, though no boat trips. Get there by following Route 193 West, also known as Georgetown Pike (Exit 44 off the Beltway); turn right on Old Dominion Drive, from where it's a mile to the entrance station (parking $4).

locks away. Confederate raiding parties found the barges and locks easy targets during the Civil War and much of the traffic dried up for the duration – doubtless to the satisfaction of the Union troops stationed in Georgetown, who used to swim naked in the canal, offending local sensibilities. Even after the war the canal never attracted sufficient trade, mainly because of competition from the railroads; the last mule-drawn cargo boat was pulled through in the 1920s, after which severe flooding from the Potomac destroyed much of the canal infrastructure. The C&O's historical importance was recognized in 1971 when its entire length was declared a national historic park, and today scores of visitors hike, cycle and horseride along the restored towpaths; canoeing and boating are allowed in certain sections, too, and the National Park Service offers passenger **canal boat** services (see opposite).

One of the most appealing stretches of the canal is the short section between Thomas Jefferson Street and 31st Street, where artisans' houses dating from the building boom of the mid-nineteenth century have been handsomely restored as shops, offices and, occasionally, private homes. Thomas Jefferson Street itself is lined with attractive brick houses, some in the **Federal style**, featuring rustic stone lintels, arched doorways with fanlights and narrow top-floor dormers. On the south side of the canal, **The Foundry**, 1050 30th Street, is just one of the many brick warehouses that line the canal, originally built as a machine-shop and later serving as a veterinary hospital to care for the mules that worked the boats. It's been sympathetically restored and expanded, and now houses shops as well as the Odeon Foundry cinema (see p.284). Other warehouses have received similar treatment – like the shops and offices at **Canal Square**, 1054 31st Street – and frame either side of the waterway as far up as Francis Scott Key Bridge, five blocks west. Various steps and paths from the towpath connect with the backstreets off M Street, and there's also direct access to Georgetown Park shopping mall (see p.301).

At **Wisconsin Avenue**, south of the canal, you're at the oldest part of Georgetown. This was the first road built from the river into Maryland during colonial times, and was a major route for farmers and traders who used the slope of the hill to roll their barrels down to riverside warehouses. Later, canal boatmen would be enticed into the Gothic Revival **Grace Church** on South Street, just off Wisconsin Avenue, by promises of salvation from the earth-bound drudgery of hauling heavy goods from barge to warehouse. Others sought solace in nearby Suter's Tavern, where, it's claimed, George Washington met Maryland landowners to discuss the purchase of property so that work could start on the federal city; the inn was knocked down long ago, but there's a plaque marking its approximate site at 31st and K streets.

K Street itself was once known as Water Street for the very good reason that it fronted the Potomac River, though land reclamation has now pushed the water a hundred yards or so farther south. Its most noticeable feature is what's above it, namely the **Whitehurst Freeway**, the elevated road built in the 1950s to relieve traffic congestion on M Street. Cross the road under the freeway and you reach the riverside development of **Washington Harbor** (east of 31st), its interlocking towers and capsules set around a circular, terraced plaza with spurting fountains. The waterfront on either side is due to be landscaped as part of a new Georgetown Waterfront Park, and there are views upriver to the Francis Scott Key Bridge, and downriver to Theodore Roosevelt Island and Bridge as well as of the backs of the Watergate Complex and Kennedy Center. The restaurants and bars in the harbor complex are all fairly expensive, but there's nothing more relaxing than a summer evening on the terrace, sipping drinks and watching the boats sculling by.

Along and around M Street

The central artery of Georgetown for two centuries, **M Street** cuts through the lower town before crossing Rock Creek into the city of Washington. As elsewhere in Georgetown, the street retains many of its original Federal-style and later Victorian buildings, though the ground floors have all long since been converted to retail use. Where new buildings have filled in any gaps they've tended to follow the prevailing red-brick style, none more noticeably than the elegant and supremely luxurious **Four Seasons Hotel** between 28th and 29th streets. Built in 1979, it regularly garners awards as one of the most exclusive hotels in the US.

The **Old Stone House**, facing Thomas Jefferson Street at 3051 M Street (Wed–Sun noon–5pm; free; ☎426-6851), has the very real claim to fame of being the only surviving pre-Revolutionary house in DC – it was built in 1765 by a Pennsylvania carpenter, Christopher Layman. Nonetheless, the only thing that saved it from demolition in the 1950s was the fanciful suggestion that L'Enfant used it as a base while designing the federal city. Today it has been restored to the state it probably resembled in the late eighteenth century, and short guided tours lead you through the kitchen and carpenter's workshop downstairs, paneled parlors and bedrooms upstairs.

Shops, restaurants and bars proliferate around the main M Street/Wisconsin Avenue junction, whose useful landmark is the gold dome of the Riggs National Bank. Just beyond, the late twentieth century imposes upon the late nineteenth in the shape of **Georgetown Park**, a high-profile shopping mall at 3222 M Street (Mon–Sat 10am–9pm, Sun noon–6pm). As a deskbound designer's idea of what a Victorian architect might have come up with given the money, material and tools, it's just about a success – wrought-iron fencing and balconies, glass lanterns and skylights, potted ferns and polished brass all add to the period ambience, though no Victorian marketplace was ever this clean. There's a food court inside, too, and one exit from the mall leads directly to the canal towpath. A block west, at Potomac Street, the triple-arched, red-brick **Market House** has been the site of a public market since the 1860s, even if today the butchered carcasses and patent medicines have made way for a celebrated Dean & Deluca deli.

Potomac Street is as good a point as any to detour north to **N Street** – known as Gay Street until the late nineteenth century – which contains some of Georgetown's finest Federal-era buildings. None is open to the public, but there are several particularly attractive facades between 29th and 34th streets. At 3014 N Street, Robert Todd Lincoln (President Lincoln's son) lived out the last decade of his life – the house is now owned by *Washington Post* stalwart Ben Bradlee. Four blocks along, JFK and Jackie owned No. 3307 from 1957 to 1961; Jackie also moved briefly into No. 3017 after the assassination. Other historic houses cluster on **Prospect Street**, one block south, where late eighteenth-century merchants built mansions like those at nos. 3425 and 3508; as the street name suggests, they once possessed splendid views down to the river from which they derived their wealth.

Back on M Street, aim for the junction with 34th Street, from which the **Francis Scott Key Bridge** (better known as just "Key Bridge") shoots off across the river to Rosslyn. Francis Scott Key, author of the "Star-Spangled Banner," moved to Washington in 1805 and lived in a house here at M Street. His home was later demolished to make way for the Whitehurst Freeway – an act of sacrilege only belatedly acknowledged by the establishment of **Francis Scott Key Park**, just off the street. There's a bronze bust of the man, a sixty-foot flagpole flying the Stars and Stripes, a wisteria-covered arbor and a few benches from which to peer through the break in the buildings to the river. Walk down the steps here and you're standing on the point at which, in September 1781, General Washington and his ally Jean-Baptiste de Rochambeau, Commander-in-Chief of the French Army in America, prepared to cross the Potomac en route to Mount Vernon and, ultimately, Yorktown, where a decisive victory against the British the following month turned the course of the Revolutionary War.

Before you leave lower Georgetown you may as well swing by **Georgetown University**, splendidly sited on the heights above the river; the main gate is at 37th and O streets. Founded in 1789 as the Jesuit Georgetown College, it's the oldest Catholic university in the US. The university and its six thousand students are what give the neighborhood much of its buzz. No one will mind if you pop in for a look around, though apart from treading in the footsteps of exorcized priests and excitable college grads (see "Georgetown in the Movies," opposite), there's little incentive to do so. The architecture is a bit of a hybrid, ranging from the plain facade of the building known as Old North, which dates from 1795, to the Romanesque niceties of Healy Hall, finished ninety years later.

Northern Georgetown

Set above the rest of Georgetown on "The Heights" (above Q St), the grand mansions and estates of **northern Georgetown** sat out the nineteenth- and twentieth-century upheavals taking place below. Owned by the richest merchants, the land here was never exploited for new building when Georgetown was in the throes of expansion. Today several of the fine mansions are open to the public, their grounds and nearby cemeteries forming a pleasing backdrop.

From the middle of Georgetown, the easiest access is straight up Wisconsin Avenue (Bus #30, #32, #34, #35 or #36 from M St). Alternatively, if you approach from Washington, crossing Dumbarton Bridge from Massachusetts Avenue NW (Dupont Circle Metro) puts you directly on Q Street.

Mount Zion Cemetery

Five minutes from Dumbarton Bridge, hidden away down an offshoot of 27th Street (northern side of Q St), is **Mount Zion Cemetery**, the oldest burial ground in the city. Formerly the Old Methodist Burying Ground, the land was bought in 1842 by a women's association known as the Female Union Band for the burial of members of the Mount Zion Methodist Church (whose fine red-brick church building still stands at 1334 29th St, at Dumbarton St). The cemetery has been neglected over the years, with headstones scattered through the tangled undergrowth, but a start has been made in tidying up the grounds and restoring some of the monumental gravestones. There's still a long way to go, though, before it matches the pristine grounds of the adjacent (white) Oak Hill Cemetery (see below), whose tiered gravestones you can glimpse through the trees beyond.

Dumbarton House

Past 27th Street, **Dumbarton House**, one of the oldest houses in Georgetown, built between 1799 and 1804, comes into view at 2715 Q Street NW (hourly tours Tues–Sat 10.15am–12.15pm; closed Aug & last week of Dec; small donation requested; ☎337-2288, ⓦwww.dumbartonhouse.org). Known for a century as "Bellevue," the elegantly proportioned Georgian mansion housed Georgetown's first salon, as political leaders of the day came to call on Joseph Nourse, registrar of the US Treasury, who lived here until 1813. The following year, as the British overran Washington, Dolley Madison watched the White House burning from Bellevue's windows – the house was the first sanctuary for the fleeing presidential couple. It's a period that the guides from the National Society of Colonial Dames of America (now headquartered at Dumbarton House) make much of, and you'll be escorted slowly through period rooms, filled with Federal furniture, early prints of Washington DC and less-than-accomplished portraits. If you don't have an hour to spare, or an insatiable interest in decorative porcelain that once, possibly, adorned the White House, content yourself instead with a seat in the restful garden and contemplate perhaps the most remarkable fact about the place: that the building of the bridge over Rock Creek in 1915 necessitated the house's removal, brick by brick, from farther down Q Street to its present position.

Oak Hill Cemetery

Endowed by banker and art collector William Wilson Corcoran, the exclusive **Oak Hill Cemetery** (Mon–Fri 10am–4pm; free; ☎337-2835) began receiving the wealthy dead of Georgetown in 1849. Dating from that time is the brick gatehouse at 30th and R streets, where you enter the lovingly kept grounds that spill down the hillside to Rock Creek. Within the grounds, the diminutive brick-and-sandstone Gothic chapel is the sprightly work of James Renwick (architect of the Smithsonian Castle, among other structures), while to the west stands a marble plinth with a bust of John Howard Payne – author of the treacly "Home Sweet Home." Ask at the gatehouse for directions to the cemetery's other notable inmates, among them Corcoran himself; Edwin Stanton, Secretary of War under President Lincoln; and former Secretary of State Dean Acheson.

Dumbarton Oaks

If one estate typifies both the success of the early Georgetown merchants and the durability of their property, it's **Dumbarton Oaks**. In 1703, Scottish pioneer Ninian Beall was granted almost 800 acres of land, stretching from the river to Rock Creek, and proceeded to make himself a fortune from the tobacco trade. Although much of the land was later sold by his descendants, more than enough of the coveted northern reaches remained for incomer William H. Dorsey to build a grand red-brick mansion, surrounded by gardens and woods, in 1800. This was added to and renovated over the years before being acquired by diplomat Robert Woods Bliss in 1920 to house his significant collection of Byzantine and pre-Columbian art. In 1940 the house was handed on to Harvard University (the current owners), and in 1944 its commodious Music Room saw a meeting of American, Russian, British and Chinese delegates whose deliberations led directly to the founding of the United Nations the following year.

The house (entrance at 1703 32nd St), restored to its Federal glory, contains a beautifully presented **museum** (Tues–Sun 2–5pm; suggested donation $1; ☏339-6401, ⊚www.doaks.org;) featuring the Bliss collection. Eight connected circular glass pavilions, added in 1963, display selected carvings, sculpture, jewelry and textiles of Olmec, Inca, Aztec and Mayan provenance – ceremonial axes, polychrome vases depicting palace scenes, jade pendants, goldwork recovered from graves and bluff stone masks of unknown significance. Bliss was equally fascinated by the Byzantine Empire; the silver Eucharist vessels, decorated ivory boxes and various painted icons stand out. Perhaps most extraordinary is the celebrated miniature fourteenth-century mosaic icon of the Forty Martyrs, so called because it depicts – in cubes of enamel paste and semiprecious stone – forty Roman soldiers left to freeze to death because they refused to recant their Christian beliefs.

Outside, the ten acres of formal **gardens** (entrance at 3101 R St; daily 2–5pm; closed in bad weather; free), with their beech terrace, evergreens, rose garden, brick paths, pools and fountains, provide one of DC's quietest retreats.

Tudor Place

The area's final mansion is stately **Tudor Place**, 1644 31st Street NW, between Q and R streets, designed by William Thornton, who won the competition to design the US Capitol. Commissioned by Thomas Peter (descendant of one of the original Scottish tobacco merchants and son of Georgetown's first mayor) and his wife Martha Custis (granddaughter of Martha Washington), the house displays a pleasing incongruity, rare for the period – Thornton embellished the fundamentally Federal-style structure with a Classical domed portico on the south side. The exterior has remained virtually untouched since and, as the house stayed in the same family for over 150 years, the interior is considered rather fine, too, being saved from the constant "improvements" wrought in other period Georgetown houses by successive owners.

Tours (Tues–Fri 10am, 11.30am, 1pm & 2.30pm, Sat on the hour 10am–3pm; $6; ☎965-0400, ⊛www.tudorplace.org) point out highlights including furnishings lifted from the Washington's family seat at Mount Vernon. You're supposed to reserve in advance for the tours, but ringing the bell at the front gate gives you access to the **gardens** during the day (Mon–Sat 10am–4pm; free). Walk up the path and bear to the right where a white box holds detailed maps ($2 donation) of the paths, greens, box hedges, arbors and fountains.

9

Arlington

A cross the Potomac River from DC lies the Virginian county of **Arlington**, which formed part of Washington itself until 1846, when Virginia demanded back the thirty square miles it had contributed to the capital city. The river here was always more than a geographical boundary: for many people in the nineteenth century, Arlington was where the South started, and it was to prove significant that Confederate commander Robert E. Lee had his home for many years on the Arlington heights, over-looking the Potomac and the capital city beyond. In the 1930s, as a final act of reconciliation, **Arlington Memorial Bridge** was dedicated – symbolically connecting the Lincoln Memorial with the dead of both sides buried in Arlington National Cemetery.

It might be in Virginia, but modern Arlington is still effectively part of Washington DC, with easy access from the capital via four bridges and the Metro to the commuter and shopping belt that stretches from Rosslyn and Clarendon to Crystal City. Planes land at **National Airport**, the closest airport to downtown DC, while locals descend on the **mega-malls** at Pentagon City and Crystal City, refueling on Southeast Asian food in the **restaurants** that proliferate along Wilson Boulevard in Clarendon. For most visitors, though, the area is defined by two high-profile attractions: **Arlington National Cemetery**, burial place of John, Jackie and Robert Kennedy, and the **Pentagon**, the country's military headquarters.

Arlington National Cemetery

Across Arlington Memorial Bridge, Arlington, VA ☎703/695-3250, ⓦwww.arlingtoncemetery .org; Arlington Cemetery Metro. Daily: April–Sept 8am–7pm; Oct–March 8am–5pm. Admission free.

The grand monuments of the capital across the river are placed into sharp per-spective by the vast sea of identical white headstones that spreads across the hill-sides of **Arlington National Cemetery**. The city's celebration of the lives of a few prominent Americans – Lincoln, Washington and Jefferson – gives way at

Eating and drinking in Arlington

For Arlington listings, see the following pages: eating p.259; drinking and nightlife p.277. We've not given any accommodation listings; you're unlikely to be staying out here.

Arlington to the commemoration of the deaths of many thousands of others, including the assassinated Kennedy brothers, the presence of whose graves here elevates the cemetery to the status of a pilgrimage site. Primarily a military burial ground – the largest in the country – Arlington's 600 landscaped acres contain the graves of almost a quarter of a million war dead and their dependents, as well as those of a panoply of other national heroes with military connections, from boxer (and ex-GI) Joe Louis to the crew of the doomed space shuttle *Challenger*. In some ways it's America's pantheon, a fact that partly excuses the constant stream of visitors on sightseeing tours, which elsewhere might be considered unseemly in a cemetery. What saves it is not only its size – far too large to take in every plot on a single visit – but also the dignity inherent in the democratically similar lines of simple markers and unadorned headstones. Paris's Père Lachaise it's emphatically not; there's a restrained, understated ambience here that honors presidents, generals and enlisted personnel alike.

The **Metro** takes you right to the main gates on Memorial Drive. The **visitor center** by the entrance issues sketch maps indicating some of the more prominent graves, while various guidebooks on sale at the center offer more thorough coverage; call the gravesite office (☎703/607-8052) for information about particular graves. The cemetery is absolutely enormous, so if you simply want to see the major sites without doing too much walking, board a **Tourmobile** for a narrated tour – you can get on and off these shuttle buses as many times as you like. Tourmobile tickets ($5.25) are sold at the booth inside the visitor center; combined Tourmobile tickets, including sights in DC and transportation to Arlington, are also available; see p.31.

The cemetery

In good weather the cemetery is busy by 9am. A good portion of the crowds heads straight for the Kennedy gravesites, though few realize they're bypassing Arlington's only other presidential occupant. Through Memorial Gate, just to the right, lies **William Howard Taft**, the poorly regarded 27th president (1909–13) who, in a heartfelt outburst toward the end of his administration, said "the nearer I get to the inauguration of my successor [Woodrow Wilson], the greater the relief I feel." Taft – uniquely – enjoyed a second, much more personally rewarding, career as Chief Justice of the Supreme Court between 1921 and 1930.

The focus of attention, though, is the marble terrace farther up the hillside where simple name plaques mark the graves of **John F. Kennedy**, 35th US president, his wife Jacqueline Kennedy Onassis (laid to rest here in 1994), and two of their children – a son, Patrick, and an unnamed daughter – who both died shortly after birth. The eternal flame was lit at JFK's funeral by Jackie, who ordered the funeral decor to be copied from that of Lincoln's, held a century earlier in the White House. When it's crowded here, as it often is, the majesty of the view across to the Washington Monument and the poignancy of the inscribed extracts from JFK's inaugural address – "Ask not what your country can do for you . . ." – are sometimes obscured; come early or late in the day if possible. In the plot behind Jack's, a plain white cross picks out the gravesite of his brother Robert, assassinated in 1968 during the presidential primaries.

The **Tomb of the Unknowns**, a white marble block dedicated to the unknown dead of two world wars and the Korean and Vietnam conflicts, is guarded 24 hours a day by impeccably uniformed soldiers, who carry out a somber **Changing of the Guard** (April–Sept every half-hour, otherwise on the hour) on the sweeping steps; the circular, colonnaded Memorial

Amphitheater behind is the site of special remembrance services. DNA testing in June 1998 provided positive identification of the remains of the previously unknown soldier in the Vietnam War tomb, which – for now – stands empty.

The cemetery began as a burial ground for Union soldiers, though as a national cemetery it was subsequently deemed politic to honor the dead of both sides in the Civil War. The **Confederate Section**, with its own memorial, lies to the west of the Tomb of the Unknowns; other sections and memorials commemorate conflicts from the Revolutionary War to the Gulf War. Presumably, a section memorializing those who served in Afghanistan will soon be created; casualties from the conflict are already buried here.

The highest concentration of notable individual graves is found in the myriad plots surrounding the Tomb of the Unknowns: with a map, and an eye for knots of camera-toting tourists, you'll find the graves of **Audie Murphy**, most decorated soldier in World War II, and boxer **Joe Louis** (born, and buried here, as Joe Louis Barrow), world heavyweight champion from 1937 to 1949. Elsewhere, among others and in no particular order, are buried Robert Todd Lincoln, Abraham's son; John J. Pershing, commander of the American forces during World War I; Arctic explorer Robert Peary; civil rights leader Medgar Evers, shot in 1963; astronauts Virgil Grissom and Roger Chaffee of the ill-fated 1967 *Apollo* flight; actor Lee Marvin; thriller-writer Dashiell Hammett; and William Colby, former director of the CIA.

The most photographed of the many memorials is the one dedicated to those who died aboard the **Space Shuttle Challenger**, located immediately behind the amphitheater; adjacent is the memorial to the **Iran Rescue Mission**, whose failure doomed Jimmy Carter at the polls. Both stand close to the **mast of the USS Maine**, whose mysterious destruction in Havana harbor in 1898 prompted the short-lived Spanish–American War – the war itself is commemorated by both a memorial and a monument to the **Rough Riders**, a devil-may-care cavalry outfit in which a young Theodore Roosevelt made his reputation. More controversial is the memorial inscribed with the names of those killed over **Lockerbie**, Scotland, in the 1988 terrorist explosion; some felt its siting in a military cemetery inappropriate. One of the most recent memorials to be dedicated, situated at the main gateway, honors **Women in Military Service** – the country's first national monument to American servicewomen.

Arlington House

The entire cemetery stands on land that formerly belonged to George Washington Parke Custis, the grandson of Martha Washington by her first marriage. Custis built an imposing Georgian Revival mansion known as **Arlington House** on the high ground above the Potomac, which passed to his daughter, Mary, after his death. Her marriage in 1830 to Lieutenant **Robert E. Lee** (1807–70) of the US Army was later of enormous consequence: in 1861, Lee was at home at Arlington House when he heard the news of the secession of Virginia from the Union. Coming from a proud Virginian family, whose number included two signatories of the Declaration of Independence, the West Point-trained Lee was torn between loyalty to his native state and to the preservation of the Union that he served. His decision was made more acute when he was also offered command of the Union Army by Lincoln, who greatly respected his ability. But familial loyalty held out, and Lee resigned his US Army commission and left Arlington for Richmond, where he took command of Virginia's military forces. Mary fled Arlington a month later as Union soldiers consolidated their hold on DC, and the estate was eventually confiscated by the federal government. The Lees never returned to Arlington (though the family was later compensated for the estate's seizure), and as early as 1864 a cemetery for the Union dead of the Civil War was established on the grounds of the house. A year later, Lee – now general-in-chief of the Confederate armies – surrendered to General Grant at Appomattox.

Since the 1950s Arlington House has stood as a memorial to the Lee family. The house is immediately above the Kennedy gravesites and you can look around during cemetery opening hours on a self-guided **tour** (information ☎703/557-0613, ⓦwww.nps.gov/arho). Highlights include the principal bedroom, where Robert E. Lee wrote his resignation letter, and the family parlor below, in which he was married. A fair proportion of the furnishings are original.

Outside, the views across the river to the Mall are exemplary. Fittingly, the grave of city designer **Pierre Charles L'Enfant** was belatedly sited here in 1909 after the city forgave his feuding about low pay for his services. No less a man than the Marquis de Lafayette, a guest at Arlington House in 1824, thought the aspect "the finest view in the world," and who's to say that's still not the case.

The Marine Corps Memorial and Netherlands Carillon

Lying to the north, just outside the cemetery walls, the hugely impressive, 78-foot-high, bronze **Marine Corps Memorial** (open 24hr; free; ☎703/289-2500, ⓦwww.nps.gov/gwmp/usmc.htm;) shouldn't be missed. It's a twenty-minute walk north of the cemetery's main section, through the Ord–Weitzel Gate, though the easiest approach is actually from Rosslyn Metro, from which it's a ten-minute, signposted walk. The affecting memorial commemorates the marine dead of all wars – from the first casualties of the Revolutionary War to the fallen in more recent times – but it's more popularly known as the **Iwo Jima Statue**, after the "uncommon valor" shown by US troops in the bloody World War II battle for the small Pacific island, a battle that took 6800 lives. In a famous image – inspired by a contemporaneous photograph by Robert Rosenthal – half a dozen marines raise the Stars and Stripes on Mount Suribachi in February 1945; three of the survivors of the actual flag-raising posed for sculptor Felix W. de Weldon. In summer (June–Aug), the US Marine Corps presents a parade and concert at the memorial every Tuesday at 7pm, and the annual Marine Corps Marathon starts here each October.

Nearby, to the south, rises the **Netherlands Carillon**, a 130-foot-high steel monument dedicated to the Netherlands' liberation from the Nazis in 1945. Given by the Dutch in thanks for American aid, the tower is set in landscaped grounds featuring thousands of tulips, which bloom each spring. The fifty bells of the carillon are rung on Saturdays and holidays from May through September (call ☎703/289-2552 for times or log onto ⓦwww.nps .gov/gwmp/events); at those times visitors can climb the tower for superlative city views.

The Pentagon

Along I-395, Arlington, VA ☎703/695-1776, ⊛www.defenselink.mil; Pentagon Metro. Call ahead to determine whether or not tours have resumed.

The headquarters of the US military establishment, the **Pentagon** is one of the largest chunks of architecture in the world, with a total floor area of 6.5 million square feet (three times that of the Empire State Building) and five 900-foot-long sides enclosing 17.5 miles of corridors. Terrorists left their mark on this massive structure in a shocking fashion on September 11, 2001, when they crashed American Airlines Flight 77 into its western flank, killing nearly two hundred people and tearing a hole almost two hundred feet wide in the building.

In the wake of the attack, the Department of Defense suspended all Pentagon tours as the country's military leaders launched a "war on terrorism" and began to rebuild their severely damaged home, a process that may take up to three years. Even when the Pentagon does reopen its doors to tourists, however, you'd be better off coming here simply to catch a glimpse of the building's famous outline and, perhaps, to reflect on the attack than to sign up for one of the tours, which have never been particularly interesting or enlightening. Rather than lending any insight into the inner workings of the Department of Defense, the resumed tours, like those in the past, will most likely focus on such irrelevant statistics as the Pentagon's 284 restrooms and the 1700 pints of milk used every day by the 25,000 employees.

Indeed, the most interesting thing about the Pentagon is the structure itself, which was thrown together in just sixteen months during World War II to consolidate seventeen different buildings of what in those days was known less euphemistically as the War Department. Efficiency dictated the five-story pentagonal design: with so many employees, it was imperative to maintain quick contact between separate offices and departments – for someone versed in the arcane numbering system, it takes just seven minutes to walk between any two points in the building. Built on swamp- and waste-land, the building was constructed entirely of concrete (fashioned from Potomac sand and gravel) rather than the marble that brightens the rest of Washington; President Roosevelt thus neatly avoided boosting the Axis war effort since Italy was then the world's foremost supplier of marble.

Crossing the Potomac by bridge, the Metro Yellow Line affords great views of the Pentagon. The **Pentagon Metro station** debouches right into the Pentagon lobby area, where you'll be able to sign up for the tours, once they resume. In the meantime, you can satisfy yourself with the 24-minute virtual tour available on the Pentagon's website (see above).

Out of the city

Arlington aside, the other forays into northern Virginia made by virtually every visitor to Washington DC are to the historic port town of **Old Town Alexandria**, six miles south of the capital, and to **Mount Vernon**, country seat of George Washington, another ten miles beyond. Virginia was the first and biggest British colony on the continent, generating the bulk of its wealth through a tobacco industry that relied on the forced labor of thousands of imported slaves. When the Civil War came, Virginia declared for the Confederacy, its forces led by Robert E. Lee, scion of one of the state's most venerable families. Alexandria – a solidly Southern town – was occupied by federal forces.

A generation earlier, before the great divide, Alexandria had been a typical town in the heartland of Virginia. The state had a habit of producing great leaders and here the Lee family socialized with the Washingtons in the local churches and parlors. Tours of northern Virginia provide fascinating glimpses of their private lives: especially at Mount Vernon, where the daily experiences of George Washington, farmer, are laid bare.

Access to both places is easy, by public transportation, car or the Mount Vernon Trail (see below). You could see the best of either in half a day, though at Alexandria, in particular, you'll probably want to spend more time.

Old Town Alexandria

ALEXANDRIA, six miles south of Washington DC, predates the capital considerably, and its preserved old town district gives a good idea of what eighteenth-century life was like for the rich tobacco farmers who lived here. First

Mount Vernon Trail

The 18.5-mile **Mount Vernon Trail** – a biking-and-hiking route – runs parallel to the George Washington Memorial Parkway, from Arlington Memorial Bridge south via Alexandria (7 miles) to Mount Vernon in Virginia. In DC, you can pick up the trail near the Lincoln Memorial, from which an offshoot also runs north to Rock Creek Park. The trail sticks close to the Potomac for its entire length (diverting around the west side of National Airport) and runs past a number of sites of historic or natural interest. There are picnic areas en route. For more **information**, and a free trail guide, contact the National Park Service in Washington (☏202/619-7222).

Alexandria has a full calendar of **festivals**, many of them linked either to the Scottish connections of the town's original settlers or to the Washington and Lee families. Call the visitor center (℡703/838-4200) or log onto ⊛www.funside.com for exact dates.

January (3rd Sun): music, house tours and other entertainment to celebrate the birthday of Robert E. Lee.

February (3rd weekend): George Washington's birthday, with a ball at *Gadsby's Tavern*, a parade, and a mock battle at nearby Fort Ward.

March St Patrick's Day parade.

April Special homes and gardens tours in Old Town.

June Waterfront festival, with music, fireworks, tours, cruises and entertainment.

July (last weekend): Virginia Scottish Games, featuring highland dancing and Celtic games, sports and pastimes.

December (1st Sat): Scottish Christmas Walk with more dancing and parades. (2nd Sat): candlelit tours of museums and historic houses, accompanied by traditional music.

settled by Scotsman John Alexander in 1699, Alexandria was granted town status fifty years later – according to tradition, a 17-year-old George Washington assisted in the preliminary survey (a claim bolstered by the existence of a contemporaneous parchment map with his name on it in the Library of Congress). By the time of the Revolution, Alexandria was a booming port and trading center, exporting wheat and flour to the West Indies, with a thriving social and political scene. With the establishment of the new capital in 1791, the town was incorporated into the District of Columbia very much against the wishes of its estate- and slave-owning Southern inhabitants, and few were sorry when in 1846 Virginia demanded its land back from the federal government. Alexandria's Confederate sympathies led to it being occupied by Union troops during the Civil War. The war, in turn, led to the town's decline: the new railroad tracks used to move troops and supplies throughout northern Virginia were later employed to carry freight, destroying Alexandria's shipping business in one fell swoop.

What's now known as **Old Town Alexandria** – the compact downtown grid by the Potomac – was left to rot for a generation. Many of the warehouses and wharves were abandoned, while other buildings became munitions factories during both world wars. Today, after twenty years of spirited renovation, the preserved colonial-era streets and converted warehouses are hugely popular tourist attractions, and although the gift shops, costumed guides and endless insistence on "authenticity" can become wearing, there are still plenty of fascinating buildings, museums and tours. Nor is it all preserved in theme-park isolation, since the Old Town forms part of the booming commuter town of greater Alexandria. Consequently, you can get here easily on the Metro, and there's more than a fair share of decent **cafés** and **restaurants** (p.258), not to mention some attractive **accommodation** (p.245).

Arrival, orientation and information

The **Metro** station for the Old Town is King Street (Yellow and Blue Lines; 25min from downtown DC), a mile or so from most of the sights. Outside the station, pick up local DASH Bus #2 or #5, which runs down King Street, and get off at Fairfax Street – alternatively, it's about a twenty-minute walk. **Drivers** should follow the George Washington Memorial Parkway south from Arlington and take the East King Street exit. Metered **parking** in the Old

OLD TOWN ALEXANDRIA

Robert E. Lee House

Lee-Fendall House

ORONOCO ST

PRINCESS ST

QUEEN ST

CAMERON ST

KING ST

PRINCE ST

DUKE ST

WOLFE ST

WILKES ST

NORTH ALFRED ST

NORTH COLUMBUS ST

NORTH WASHINGTON ST

NORTH ST ASAPH ST

NORTH PITT ST

NORTH ROYAL ST

NORTH FAIRFAX ST

NORTH LEE ST

NORTH UNION ST

QUAY ST

Founders Park

Christ Church

Gadsby's Tavern

City Hall

MARKET SQUARE

Carlyle House

Cruises

Torpedo Factory Arts Center

Potomac River

The Lyceum

Apothecary Shop

The Athenaeum

Waterfront Park

THE STRAND

SOUTH FAIRFAX ST

SOUTH ROYAL ST

SOUTH PITT ST

SOUTH LEE ST

SOUTH UNION ST

Old Presbyterian Meeting House

King Street Metro, Washington Memorial (0.5 mile)

N

HOTELS
Holiday Inn Select 1
Morrison House 2

RESTAURANTS AND BARS
Bayou Room D
Ecco A
Fish Market E
Las Tapas F
Murphy's Grand Irish Pub C
Santa Fe East H
South Austin Grill B
Union St Public House G

0   200 yds

Town is hard to come by and limited to two hours, though a free 24-hour parking pass is available by taking ID and car registration to the visitor's center (see below). Cyclists or walkers can get here using the **Mount Vernon Trail** (see p.231); in Old Town Alexandria, **Big Wheel Bikes**, 2 Prince Street (☎703/739-2300, ⓦwww.bigwheelbikes.com) can rent you a bike to ride to Mount Vernon, ten miles away, and back.

The Old Town is laid out on a grid plan and most of the sights lie within the same ten blocks. A good first stop is the **Ramsay House Visitor's Center**, 221 King Street, at Fairfax Street (daily 9am–5pm; ☎703/838-4200 or 1-800/388-9119, ⓦwww.funside.com), where you can pick up dozens of leaflets and brochures and book various **tours.** Guided walks and ghost tours (see p.32) as well as river cruises (from $8) all operate from the end of March to the end of November. There's a **combination-museum** ticket available at the visitor's center for some of the most visited attractions ($9; valid indefinitely), or you can pay as you go. Note that many sights are **closed on Monday**, and that opening hours are limited on Sunday.

Around the town

It's a relief, after the expansive boulevards and monuments of DC, to walk around a town built on a more human scale. Although the main drags – particularly King Street – are top-heavy with traffic, it's not hard to find eighteenth-century peace and quiet. Cobbled, tree-lined streets with herringbone brick sidewalks are lined with pastel-washed houses featuring boot-scrapers and horse-mounting blocks outside the front door, and cast-iron drainpipes stamped "Alexandria, DC." The angled second-floor mirrors allowed the occupants to see who was calling.

A convenient place to start your tour is the visitor center on King Street (see above); it occupies **Ramsay House**, the oldest in town, built (though not originally on this site) in 1724 for William Ramsay, one of Alexandria's founding merchants and later its first mayor. Ramsay had the house transported upriver from Dumfries, Virginia, and placed facing the river, where his ships loaded up with tobacco. The water is now three blocks away: the bluff that the town was built on was excavated after the Revolution, and the earth was used to extend the harbor into the shallow bay. This is why Ramsay House stands so high above the street, its foundations exposed.

Ramsay's fellow merchant, John Carlyle, bought two of the most expensive land plots when the town was established and built Alexandria's finest colonial-era house. In the 1750s, when all the town's other buildings were constructed of wood, the white sandstone **Carlyle House**, 121 North Fairfax Street (Tues–Sat 10am–4.30pm, Sun noon–4.30pm; $4; ☎703/549-2997, ⓦwww.carlylehouse.org), made an ostentatious statement about its owner's wealth. Accounts of Carlyle's business dealings – he ran three plantations and traded slaves – inform the half-hour guided tours of the restored house. Contrast the family's draped beds, expensively painted rooms and fine Georgian furniture with the bare servants' hall, which has actually been over-restored – in the eighteenth century it would have had an earthen floor and no glass in the windows. In August 1755, the house was used as General Braddock's headquarters during the planning of the French and Indian War. George Washington was on Braddock's staff, and later he frequently visited Carlyle's house from Mount Vernon.

Braddock's troops paraded across the way in **Market Square**, off King Street, the heart of Alexandria since its founding. The modern brick terrace around the square sounds one of the few discordant notes in the Old Town, and the restored eighteenth-century **City Hall** that faces the square also fails to look its age, though a weekly **farmers' market** still sets up in the City Hall arcades (Sat 5–10am), as it has for more than two hundred years.

Follow Cameron Street past City Hall to **Gadsby's Museum Tavern**, 134 North Royal Street (April–Sept Tues–Sat 10am–5pm, Sun 1–5pm; Oct–March Tues–Sat 11am–4pm, Sun 1–4pm; $4; ☎703/838-4242, ⓦww.ci.alexandria .va.us/oha/gadsby), occupying two (supposedly haunted) Georgian buildings in a prime spot close to the market. Downstairs, *Gadsby's Tavern* is still a working restaurant (complete with "authentic" colonial food and costumed staff). Short tours by a knowledgeable guide lead you through the old tavern rooms upstairs – in the galleried ballroom, George Washington used to cut a rug at parties thrown for his birthday. Three blocks west up Cameron Street, the English-style **Christ Church** (Mon–Sat 9am–4pm, Sun 2–4.30pm; free), set in a beautiful churchyard, retains the Washington family pew.

The Washingtons weren't the only notable family with ties to Alexandria. A descendant of the Lees of Virginia, Phillip Fendall built his splendid clapboard mansion in 1785. In the **Lee-Fendall House**, 614 Oronoco Street (Tues–Sat 10am–4pm, Sun 1–4pm; $4; ☎703/548-1789, ⓦwww.leefendallhouse.org), distinguished Revolutionary War general Henry "Light Horse Harry" Lee composed Washington's funeral oration (in which, famously, he declared him "first in war, first in peace, and first in the hearts of his countrymen"). Henry Lee bought his own house across the road just before the War of 1812 and installed his wife and five children there. This, the boyhood home of Robert E. Lee, at 607 Oronoco Street, is a beauty, a red-brick Federal-era property first owned by a Virginia tobacco planter who entertained George Washington at dinner on occasion. Unfortunately, the house, once open for tours, is now a private home. For more on Robert E. Lee, see p.227.

South of King Street, the **Lyceum**, 201 South Washington Street (Mon–Sat 10am–5pm, Sun 1–5pm; free; ☎703/838-4994, Ⓦwww.ci.alexandria.va.us/oha/lyceum), houses the town's history museum in a Greek Revival building of 1839. The changing displays, film shows and associated art gallery can put some flesh on the town's history; varied exhibits range from old photographs and Civil War documents to locally produced furniture and silverware (the latter an Alexandrian speciality in the nineteenth century). Four blocks east you'll find the **Old Presbyterian Meeting House**, 321 South Fairfax Street (Mon–Fri 9am–3pm; free; ☎703/549-6670), in whose quiet graveyard lies the tomb of John Carlyle. The Scottish town founders met here regularly, most prominently in December 1799, when they gathered in the cool, white pews for the memorial service for George Washington, who had recently died on his estate at Mount Vernon. Patent medicines for Washington were made up at the nearby **Stabler-Leadbeater Apothecary Shop**, whose yellow bay windows jut out at 105–107 South Fairfax Street (Mon–Sat 10am–4pm, Sun 1–5pm; $2.50; ☎703/836-3713, Ⓦwww.apothecary.org). The shop was founded in 1792 and still displays its original furnishings, herbs, potions and medical paraphernalia.

The waterfront

Eighteenth-century Alexandria wouldn't recognize its twentieth-century **waterfront** beyond North Union Street, not the least because the riverbank is several blocks farther east, following centuries of landfill. Where there were once wooden warehouses and wharves heaving with barrels of tobacco, there's now a smart marina and boardwalk, framed by the green stretches of **Founders Park** to the north and **Waterfront Park** to the south. In front of the *Food Pavilion,* forty-minute sightseeing **cruises** depart (several daily April–Oct; $8); longer trips run to DC or Mount Vernon and back. For information, contact the Potomac Riverboat Company (☎703/548-9000, Ⓦwww.potomacriverboatco.com).

Before this whole area was cleaned up, the US government built a torpedo factory on the river, which operated until the end of World War II. Restyled as the diverting **Torpedo Factory Arts Center** (daily 10am–5pm; free; ☎703/838-4565, Ⓦwww.torpedofactory.org), its three floors contain the studios of more than two hundred artists. All the studios are open to the public, displaying sculpture, ceramics, jewelry, glassware and textiles in regularly changing exhibitions. Take a look, too, inside the center's **Alexandria Archaeology Museum** (Tues–Fri 10am–3pm, Sat 10am–5pm, Sun 1–5pm; free; ☎703/838-4399, Ⓦwww.ci.alexandria.va.us/oha/archaeology), where much of the town's restoration work was carried out.

George Washington Masonic Memorial

In a town bursting with Washington mementoes, nothing is more prominent than the **George Washington Masonic Memorial** (daily 9am–5pm; free; ☏703/683-2007, 🌐www.gwmemorial.org), whose 333-foot tower – built on top of a Greek temple – looms over town behind the King Street Metro station. Washington was considered a "deserving brother" by the Virginian Freemasons, who built this memorial in his honor in 1932. Inside, there's a tall bronze statue of the man, sundry memorabilia, and dioramas depicting events from his life. To see this, and – more pertinently – the superb views from the observation platform, you'll have to wait for a forty-minute **tour**, which leaves from the hall (on the half-hour in the morning, on the hour in the afternoon, last tour 4pm). But even from the steps outside, the views are magnificent, across the Potomac to the Washington Monument and Capitol dome in the distance.

Mount Vernon

George Washington Pkwy, Mount Vernon, VA ☏703/780-2000, 🌐www.mountvernon.org; Huntington Metro, then Fairfax Connector Bus #101. Daily: March 9am–5pm; April–Aug 8am–5pm; Sept & Oct 9am–5pm; Nov–Feb 9am–4pm. Admission $9.

Set on a shallow bluff overlooking the broad Potomac River, sixteen miles south of Washington DC, **MOUNT VERNON** is among the most attractive historic houses in America. The beloved **country estate of George Washington**, it was his home for forty years, during which he ran it as a thriving and progressive farm, anticipating the decline in Virginia's tobacco cultivation and planting instead grains and food crops with great success. When he died, it seemed only natural that he be buried in the grounds, as his will directed; America's first president lies next to his wife, Martha, in the simple family tomb.

His father, Augustine, first built a house on the Washington estate in 1735. When he died, the house and lands passed first to George's elder brother, Lawrence, and, after the death of Lawrence in 1752 and his widow in 1761, to George. Not that he had much early opportunity to spend time here, since for much of the 1750s he was away on service with the Virginia militia, later fighting in the French and Indian War. He married in 1759, and it was during the years before 1775 – when he was next called away on service, as commander-in-chief of the Continental Army – that Washington came to know his estate. He tripled its size to eight thousand acres, divided it into five separate working farms, and landscaped the mansion grounds – rolling meadows, copses, riverside walks, parks and even vineyards were all laid out for the family's amusement.

Just five hundred acres of the estate remain today, the rest having been split and sold off by the terms of successive wills, but there's more than enough to provide an idea of the whole. The lifestyle of an eighteenth-century **gentleman farmer** was an agreeable one, in Washington's case supported by the labor of more than two hundred slaves who lived and worked on the outlying farms. The modest house he inherited was enlarged and redecorated with imported materials; formal gardens and a bowling green were added; and the general bred stallions, hunted in his woods, fished in the river and entertained visitors. But it would be unfair to view Washington as a dilettante. Daily at dawn he made a personal tour of inspection on horseback, sometimes riding twenty miles around the grounds. He studied the latest scientific works on farming, corresponded with experts, and, introducing new techniques, expanded the farms' output to include the production of flour, textiles and even whiskey. His experimental methods often cost him financially, and once he was away fighting the Revolutionary War, he was forced to turn over the day-to-day operation of his estate to others – who were doubtless thrilled to receive his sixteen-page letters from the front directing the latest farm improvements.

Washington spent eight years away from Mount Vernon during the war, but still wasn't allowed to retire there for good, as was his wish, at the end of the fighting. By 1787 he was back at the head of the Constitutional Convention in Philadelphia, and two years later was elected to his first term as president – news he heard first at Mount Vernon from a messenger who had ridden all the way from Philadelphia. He only visited his house another dozen or so times during his presidency, often for just a few days. When he finally moved back in 1797, at the end of his second term in office, he and Martha had just two and a half years together before his death on December 14, 1799. Out on one of his long estate inspections, he got caught in the snow and succumbed to a fever that killed him (for more on Washington's life see pp.52–53).

Practicalities

To reach Mount Vernon, go first to **Huntington Metro** (Yellow Line) then take Fairfax Connector **Bus #101** (hourly; call ☏703/339-7200 for schedules). It's an easy enough route, though it takes over an hour – more if you miss the bus. A **cab** from the station costs around $15 to $20 (call White Top Cab at ☏703/644-4500). **Drivers** should follow the George Washington Parkway from DC; there's free parking. The **Mount Vernon Trail** (see p.231) ends here, too.

Spirit **cruises** depart from Pier 4, 6th and Water streets SW in DC (mid-March through Sept; $30 round-trip, reservations recommended; ☏202/554-8000, ⍇www.spiritcruises.com); it take ninety minutes to reach Mount Vernon. It's only fifty minutes by water to Mount Vernon from Old Town Alexandria on cruises offered by the Potomac Riverboat Company (April–Oct; $26; ☏703/548-9000, ⍇www.potomacriverboatco.com). The **Tourmobile** bus (see p.31) also runs out here – a four-hour trip. The prices of both cruise and Tourmobile trips include admission to the house and grounds.

Mount Vernon is an extremely popular day trip, and summer weekends, especially, can be very busy. Come early or midweek, if you can, and allow at least two hours to see the house and grounds. You can't eat or drink on the estate, but just outside the gate is a snack bar (daily 9.30am–5.30pm) and a more refined **restaurant**, the *Mount Vernon Inn* (☏703/780-0011; Mon–Sat 11am–3.30pm & 5–9pm, Sun 11am–3.30pm), specializing in colonial food. Visitors are allowed to leave the estate to eat and then return without paying a second admission fee.

Events at Mount Vernon

Throughout the year, Mount Vernon hosts a range of festivals and special events, from a presidential birthday bash to candlelight tours. Around the third weekend in February, Washington's birthday is celebrated with a wreath-laying ceremony and fife and drum parades; admission to Mount Vernon is free at that time. Each May a three-day festival toasts local winemakers in a series of evening events, featuring live jazz and visits to the cellar vaults. In December, special Christmas tours re-create the Washingtons' yuletide celebrations and allow visitors access to the third floor of the mansion, which is usually closed. On winter evenings (late Nov to mid-Dec Fri–Sun 5–8pm), there are also special "Mount Vernon by Candlelight" tours. Book ahead for a candlelight visit or for the wine festival through Ticketmaster (☏202/432-SEAT, ⍇www.ticketmaster.com); a special admission price applies. For further information, call or visit the Mount Vernon website.

The house and grounds

Pick up a map of the grounds at the entrance gate and, if you need historical background, watch a few minutes of the saccharine video, which ends with the treacly commendation, "Thank you, George Washington, for being there when we needed you."

The path up to the mansion passes various outbuildings, including a renovated set of former **slave quarters**. Ninety slaves lived and worked in the mansion grounds alone, and though there's evidence that Washington was a kinder master than most – for instance, refusing to sell children away from their parents, allowing slaves to raise their own crops, and engaging the services of a doctor for them – they still lived lives of deprivation and overwork. His overseers were continually enjoined to watch the slaves like hawks and guard against theft and slacking. Washington was quick to realize that the move away from tobacco cultivation to more skilled farming made slavery increasingly unprofitable. He stopped buying slaves in the late 1770s, allowing those he owned to learn occupations such as carpentry, bricklaying and spinning, and to be maintained once they had reached the end of their working lives. His will freed his remaining slaves a year after his death, making provision for them all.

Nearby, a small **museum** traces Washington's ancestry and displays porcelain from the house, medals, weapons, silver and a series of striking miniatures, by Charles Willson Peale and his brother James, of Martha and her two children by her first marriage. The clay bust of Washington was produced by French sculptor Jean-Antoine Houdon, who worked on it at Mount Vernon in 1785 prior to completing his famous statue for the Richmond Capitol.

Around the corner, fronting the circular courtyard, stands the **mansion** itself, with the bowling green stretching before it. Join the line and walk through the wings and connecting colonnades into the house, where guides answer questions. It's a handsome, harmonious wooden structure, reasonably modest, but sporting stunning views from the East Lawn. The wooden exterior was painted white, beveled and sand-blasted to resemble stone; inside, the Palladian windows and brightly painted and papered rooms follow the fashion of the day, while the contents are based on an inventory prepared after Washington's death. Fourteen rooms are open to the public: portrait-filled parlors and cramped bedrooms, and the chamber where Washington breathed his last on a four-poster bed still in situ – his body was later laid out downstairs in the striking green dining room. Curiosities in his study offer insights into his character – a wooden reading chair with built-in fan, and a globe he ordered from London – while in the central hall hangs a key to the destroyed Bastille, presented to Washington by Thomas Paine in 1790 on behalf of Lafayette.

After touring the mansion there's plenty more to see on the **grounds**, including the kitchen (set apart from the house because of the risk of fire), cluttered storehouse, stables, smokehouse, wash house, overseer's quarters, kitchen garden and shrubberies. There's also a **forest trail** nature walk, and you can take a stroll down to the **tomb**, where two marble sarcophagi for George and Martha are set behind iron gates, "interred here in a private manner, without parade or funeral oration," as Washington's will stipulated. The will also directed that a new brick vault be erected after his death, since the original family vault on the grounds was in poor shape; the current structure was built in 1831. Nearby lies a slave burial ground, while beyond there's a site where demonstrations of the crop-growing and farming techniques used by Washington are occasionally held.

listings

listings

Accommodation

A s you might expect, Washington DC possesses some of the most exclusive hotels in America: Georgetown's *Four Seasons* is top of the scale, while rates at the *Willard Inter-Continental, Omni Shoreham, Hay-Adams* and *Jefferson* reflect their standing as historic landmarks. There are also plenty of reasonably priced, centrally located accommodations options, though you'll need to plan ahead if you want to be guaranteed a certain room at a particular time. For a full list of vacancies, contact one of the city information offices listed on p.20 or one of the free **reservation services** listed below. All hotels reviewed here are marked on the **map** overleaf.

There are hotels in all the main downtown **areas**, though those near the White House, on Capitol Hill and in Georgetown tend to be business-oriented and pricey. The occasional budget option exists in Foggy Bottom and Old Downtown (where you'll find the city's youth hostel), while most of the chain hotels and mid-range places are in New Downtown – particularly on the streets around Scott and Thomas circles. Outer neighborhoods tend to have a wider selection of smaller, cheaper hotels and B&B-style guest houses, and it's no hardship at all to be staying in Dupont Circle, Adams-Morgan or Upper Northwest – you'll probably be eating and drinking in these places anyway. We've also listed a few options in Alexandria, VA, though it's easy to see that city on a day trip from the capital. For lodging places that cater to gay and lesbian travelers, see p.294.

You're more likely to be able to **park** for free in the outer neighborhoods; garage parking is available at most downtown hotels, but you'll be charged $10–20 a night for the privilege. Very occasionally, an inn or hotel we list is on the cusp of a slightly iffy neighborhood; where **safety** is an issue, we've said so, and you're advised to take taxis back to your hotel at night in these areas.

Standard **room rates** throughout the city start at around $100–120 a night, but there's plenty of scope for negotiation for canny travelers. Most hotels **discount** their rates on weekends (some by up to fifty percent), while prices are low throughout July and August, when Congress is in recess, and again in December and January. Always ask if the rate you've been quoted is the best available; often, discount information has to be ferreted out of desk clerks. Where places offer particularly good discount deals, we've said so in the review. Also, since hotels charge by the room, three people can often stay in a double

Hotel reservation services

Capitol Reservations ☏202/452-1270 or 1-800/847-4832, ℱ452-0537, wwww.capitolreservations.com

Washington DC Accommodations ☏202/289-2220 or 1-800/554-2220, ℱ338-4517, ⓦwww .washingtondcaccommodations.com

ACCOMMODATION

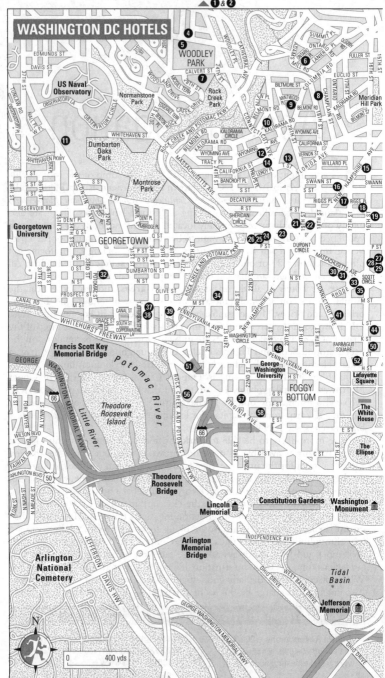

WASHINGTON DC HOTELS

ACCOMMODATION

Adams Inn	6	India House Too	3
Allen Lee Hotel	57	Jefferson Hotel	35
The Brenton	18	JW Marriott	61
Brickskeller Inn	26	Kalorama Guest House at Kalorama Park	9
Bull Moose B & B	67	Kalorama Guest House at Woodley Park	1
Capital Hilton	44	Latham Hotel	37
Capitol Hill Suites	68	Loews L'Enfant Plaza	70
Carlyle Suites	17	Marriott at Metro Center	55
Channel Inn Hotel	72	Marriott Wardham Park	5
Crowne Plaza Washington	45	Morrison-Clark Inn	43
Days Inn Connecticut Avenue	2	Normandy Inn	12
Days Inn Premier	46	Omni Shoreham	7
Doubletree Hotel Park Terrace	29	Phoenix Park	63
Dupont at the Circle	21	Radisson Barceló	25
Embassy Inn	19	Red Roof Inn	54
Embassy Row Hilton	23	Renaissance Mayflower	41
Four Seasons Hotel	39	St Regis Washington	50
Georgetown Inn	32	Simpkins' B & B	22
Governor's House	33	State Plaza	58
Grand Hyatt	53	Swann House	16
Hay-Adams Hotel	52	Swiss Inn	42
Henley Park Hotel	48	Swissotel Washington, The Watergate	56
Hereford House	71	Tabard Inn	30
HI-Washington DC	47	Topaz	31
Holiday Inn Capitol	69	Washington Courtyard by Marriott	14
Holiday Inn Central	27	Washington Hilton and Towers	13
Holiday Inn Georgetown	11	Washington International Student Center	8
Holiday Inn on the Hill	66	Washington Monarch Hotel	34
Hotel George	62	Washington Plaza	36
Hotel Harrington	64	Westin Fairfax	24
Hotel Lombardy	49	Willard Inter-Continental	60
Hotel Monticello	38	William Lewis House	20
Hotel Rouge	28	Windsor Inn	15
Hotel Washington	59	Windsor Park Hotel	10
Howard Johnson Premier Hotel	51	Woodley Park Guest House	4
Hyatt Regency Washington	65	Wyndham Washington	40

11

ACCOMMODATION

243

Accommodation price codes

① Under $50   **③** $70–100   **⑤** $140–200   **⑦** $250–300
② $50–70   **④** $100–140   **⑥** $200–250   **⑧** Over $300

The price codes given in the reviews below reflect the **average price for a standard double room in peak season** (late March to early July), excluding room tax. Unless otherwise stated all rooms come with bathroom; breakfast is not normally included.

for the same (or a slightly higher) price as two. Although **breakfast** usually isn't included in the room rate at most hotels, it often *is* as part of the special weekend packages.

The **price codes** are explained in the box above; keep in mind in the off-season you'll often be paying less than what's indicated in our reviews. Groups and families should consider the city's **suite hotels**, where you'll get a kitchen and possibly a separate living room, too. One other thing to keep in mind: DC in summer is hot and humid, and **air-conditioning** is essential for getting a good night's rest.

A number of **B&B agencies** (see box below) offer rooms in small inns, private homes or apartments, starting from around $55–65 per night; a luxury B&B, though, can be every bit as pricey as a hotel, with rates reaching as high as $150–250 a night. For rock-bottom alternatives, there's the official international **youth hostel** (which is very central, but at its busiest in July and August) and a couple of similar places, one in Adams–Morgan, the other out in Takoma Park. **Students** can try contacting one of the educational establishments listed in the box opposite.

Note that all DC hotels add **14.5 percent room tax** to your bill.

Adams-Morgan

Adams Inn 1744 Lanier Place NW ☎745-3600 or 1-800/578-6807, ℻319-7958, ⊛www.adamsinn.com; Woodley Park–Zoo Metro. Clean, simple B&B rooms, with and without bath, in three adjoining Victorian townhouses on a quiet residential street (just north of Calvert St). No TVs, but free breakfast, coffee all day, garden patio and laundry facilities. **②–③**

Kalorama Guest House at Kalorama Park 1854 Mintwood Place NW, ☎667-6369, ℻319-1262; Woodley Park–Zoo Metro. Victorian guest house, near Adams-Morgan restaurants. Spacious rooms (31; 12 en-suite) in four spotless houses filled with period *objets*, plants and handsome furniture (no TVs). Free breakfast, papers,

B&B agencies

Bed & Breakfast Accommodations Ltd ☎202/328-3510, ℻332-3885, wwww.bedandbreakfastdc.com
Bed & Breakfast League ☎202/363-7767, ℻368-8396

coffee and evening sherry, plus washing machines. Booking essential. **②–③**

Normandy Inn 2118 Wyoming Ave NW ☎483-1350 or 1-800/424-3729, ℻387-8241, ⊛www.jurys.com; Dupont Circle or Woodley Park–Zoo Metro. Quiet hotel in upscale neighborhood, with comfortable rooms (each with private bath, fridge and coffeemaker). Continental breakfast is $6, taken in the garden in summer. Coffee and cookies are served daily, and there's a weekly wine and cheese reception. **④**

Washington Courtyard by Marriott 1900 Connecticut Ave NW ☎332-9300 or 1-800/321-3211, ℻328-7039, ⊛www.courtyard.com/wasnw; Dupont Circle Metro. The top-floor rooms of this well-located hillside hotel have splendid views. Outdoor pool and very keen prices (even better on the weekend) for this area, which is a short walk from the heart of both Dupont and Adams-Morgan. **⑤**

Washington Hilton and Towers 1919 Connecticut Ave NW ☎483-3000 or 1-800/445-8667, ℻265-8221, ⊛www.hilton.com; Dupont Circle Metro. Massive 1960s convention hotel midway between Dupont Circle (downhill) and Adams-Morgan (uphill). The quiet, well-equipped rooms are decked out in the usual chain style and are a bit on the small side (there are over 1100 of them after all), but most have very good views. Facilities include pool, health club, tennis courts and bike rental. ❼

Washington International Student Center 2451 18th St NW ☎667-7681 or 1-800/567-4150, ⒺDCStudentCentr@aol.com; Dupont Circle or Woodley Park–Zoo Metro. Backpackers' accommodation in plain multi-bedded dorm rooms in the heart of Adams-Morgan (not particularly close to either Metro station), with internet access, lockers for personal belongings, and free pickup from bus and train stations. At $17 a night (coffee-and-toast breakfast included) it's downtown DC's cheapest bed, but you may find the cramped surroundings, shared bathrooms and "traveling" crowd tiresome after a while. Book at least two weeks in advance. ❶

Windsor Park Hotel 2116 Kalorama Rd NW ☎483-7700 or 1-800/247-3064, Ⓕ332-4547, ⓌEwww.windsorparkhotel.com; Dupont Circle or Woodley Park–Zoo Metro. Pleasant little Victorian-style rooms, outfitted with cable TV, in a quiet neighborhood, just off Connecticut Avenue. Continental breakfast included. ❸

Alexandria, VA

Bed & Breakfast Ltd ☎1-800/470-5588, ⓌEwww.alexandriabandb.com. Call Mon–Fri 10am–6pm for hosted B&B accommodation in historic Old Town homes. All rooms have air-conditioning and private bath, and breakfast is included. Minimum stay two nights at peak times. ❸–❹

Holiday Inn Select 480 King St, Old Town ☎703/549-6080 or 1-800/368-5047, ⓌEwww.oldtownhis.com. Alexandria's best-situated hotel, just off Market Square, makes a great base for exploring. There's an indoor pool, and many rooms have balconies overlooking a quiet internal courtyard. The hotel is pet-friendly, too. ❺–❼

Morrison House 116 S Alfred St, Old Town ☎703/838-8000 or 1-800/367-0800, Ⓕ684-6283, ⓌEwww.morrisonhouse.com. Stunning re-creation of a Federal-era townhouse (built 1985, looks like 1795) complete with butlers, parlor, parquet floors and crystal chandeliers, yet with all modern comforts. Rooms are well appointed, and there's an acclaimed restaurant. ❻

Capitol Hill

Bull Moose B&B 101 Fifth St NE ☎547-1050 or 1-800/261-2768, Ⓕ548-9741, ⓌEwww.bullmoose-b-and-b.com; Union Station or Capitol South Metro. In keeping with its new name, this turreted brick Victorian (formerly the *Capitol Hill Guest House*) evokes themes from the life and times of legendary US president and Bull Moose Party founder Teddy Roosevelt — from tropical Panama to the charge up San Juan Hill. The ten guest rooms (some en-suite) lack phones, but phone, fax and internet access are all available. Other extras include free continental breakfast, evening sherry and use of a kitchen. Special rates for long-term stays ($350/week). ❸–❺

Capitol Hill Suites 200 C St SE ☎543-6000 or 1-800/424-9165, Ⓕ547-2608; Capitol South Metro. Popular converted apartments whose units are all equipped with kitchenettes or proper kitchens; free

Student accommodation

Georgetown University (☎687-4560), **George Washington University** (☎994-6688), **Catholic University** (☎319-5277) and **American University** (☎885-3370) all offer a variety of dorms, doubles and apartments at budget rates in summer (June–Aug). Arrangements must be made well in advance; you may find there's a minimum stay requirement (as much as thirty days), since the service is intended for interns or students in summer educational programs.

ⓐ

ACCOMMODATION

morning coffee, muffins and juice, and daily paper are included. Busy when Congress is in session – on weekends and in August the price drops a category. ⑤

Hereford House 604 South Carolina Ave SE ⓣ543-0102, ⓦwww.bbonline.com/dc/hereford; Eastern Market Metro. Attractive brick townhouse with hardwood floors, small garden and bright, reasonably sized rooms (no TVs) in residential Capitol Hill, just a block from the Metro. Offering B&B accommodation in the "true British tradition" – which means a hearty welcome from its English owner and a cooked breakfast. Just four rooms (sharing two bathrooms), and three more (no breakfast) in a separate house five minutes away. ③

Downtown: New

Capital Hilton 1001 16th St NW ⓣ393-1000 or 1-800/445-8667, ⓕ639-5742, ⓦwww.hilton.com; Farragut North, Farragut West or McPherson Square Metro. Art Deco trappings, great location three blocks from the White House, buzzing lobby-bar and spacious rooms. Facilities include health club and a good sports bar-restaurant. Weekend rates are among the lowest for quality downtown rooms. ⑤–⑦

Crowne Plaza Washington 14th and K St NW ⓣ682-0111 or 1-800/227-6963, ⓕ682-9525, ⓦwww.crowneplazawashington.com; Metro Center Metro. Resurrected Beaux Arts–style hotel with fine city views from its sought-after Franklin Square location. Elegant rooms, lobby espresso bar, health club and sauna. ⑥

Doubletree Hotel Park Terrace 1515 Rhode Island Ave NW ⓣ232-7000 or 1-800/222-8733, ⓕ232-7152, ⓦwww.doubletree.com; Dupont Circle or Farragut North Metro. Comfortable rooms, marble bathrooms, outdoor terrace for summer dining and good-value buffet breakfasts. You're near the Dupont Circle nightlife, too. ④

The Governor's House 1615 Rhode Island Ave NW ⓣ296-2100 or 1-800/821-4367, ⓕ331-0227; Dupont Circle or Farragut North Metro. Although the exterior is unpromising, it is calm and comfortable inside, with decent-size rooms, some with sofa beds and kitchenettes. Plus there's a popular bar and grill, and a pool, and guests can use the nearby YMCA fitness center. Weekend rates are a good deal. ④–⑤

Hay-Adams Hotel 1 Lafayette Square NW ⓣ638-6600 or 1-800/424-5054, ⓕ638-2716, ⓦwww.hayadams.com; Farragut West or McPherson Square Metro. One of DC's finest hotels, fashioned from two historic townhouses in 1928 and ever since a byword for indulgence, from the gold-leaf and walnut lobby to the ornate, airy rooms and suites with fireplaces and original cornicing, marble bathrooms, balconies and high ceilings. Splash out (a lot) for views of St John's Church or (from upper floors) the White House; 8th-floor rooms are best of all. Breakfast in the stylish park-facing restaurant. ⑦–⑧

Henley Park Hotel 926 Massachusetts Ave NW ⓣ638-5200 or 1-800/222-8474, ⓕ638-6740, ⓦwww.henleypark.com; Mount Vernon Square–UDC or Metro Center Metro. Former apartment building north of the Convention Center turned into a cozy English country house-style hotel. It's rather at odds with the borderline neighborhood; take your after-dinner stroll somewhere else. ⑤

HI-Washington DC 1009 11th St NW ⓣ737-2333, ⓕ737-1508, ⓦwww.hiwashingtondc.org; Metro Center Metro. Large (270 beds), clean and very central hostel, just three blocks north of the Metro. Single-sex dorms ($25), kitchen, lounge, laundry, luggage storage, enthusiastic staff and organized activities. Guests who are not HI members pay $3 more per night (and may be refused in busy spring and summer months). Open 24hr, but take care at night around here. Book well in advance, especially in summer; six-night maximum stay. ①

Holiday Inn Central 1501 Rhode Island Ave NW ⓣ483-2000 or 1-800/248-0016, ⓕ797-1078, ⓦwww.inn-dc.com, ⓔholiday@inn-dc.com; Dupont Circle or Farragut North Metro. One of downtown's better mid-range options, with pleasant, modern rooms, rooftop pool, bar, and breakfast included. It's at Scott Circle. ⑤

Jefferson Hotel 1200 16th St NW ⓣ347-2200 or 1-800/365-5966, ⓕ331-7982, ⓦwww.thejeffersonhotel.com; Farragut North Metro. Patrician landmark on 16th Street, a favorite with politicians since the 1920s. Antique-strewn interior, with busts, oils and porcelain at every turn, fine restaurant, personal service and all the modern conveniences in the superb rooms. Weekend rates can fall to under $200 a night. ⑧

Morrison-Clark Inn 1015 L St NW ☏898-1200 or 1-800/332-7898, ℻289-8576, ⓦwww.morrisonclark.com; Mount Vernon Square-UDC or Metro Center Metro. Antique-and-lace accommodation in a historic Victorian mansion complete with veranda. Fifty-odd rooms in overblown styles, balconies overlooking a courtyard, a comfortable lounge and a good restaurant. Weekend rates, when available, come down to the $100 mark. Watch your step at night – the neighborhood is a trifle edgy. ➎

Renaissance Mayflower 1127 Connecticut Ave NW ☏347-3000 or 1-800/228-7697, ℻776-9182, ⓦwww.renaissancehotels.com/WASSH; Farragut North Metro. Restoration has left the *Mayflower* better than ever, with the Promenade – a vast, imperially decorated hall – one of DC's great public spaces. Rooms, facilities and service are all top-notch, the bars, café and restaurant much in demand by power diners. ➑

St Regis Washington 923 16th St NW ☏638-2626 or 1-800/562-5661, ℻638-4231, ⓦwww.starwood.com/stregis; Farragut North, Farragut West or McPherson Square Metro. President Calvin Coolidge cut the ribbon opening this 1920s Italian Renaissance palace. A couple of blocks north of the White House, it offers elegant rooms (complete with marble bathrooms), the highly rated *Timothy Dean* restaurant and perfect service. ➐

Swiss Inn 1204 Massachusetts Ave NW ☏371-1816 or 1-800/955-7947, ℻371-1138, ⓦwww.theswissinn.com; Metro Center Metro. Friendly townhouse accommodation with eight "efficiencies" (air-conditioned rooms with kitchenettes, TV and bath), multilingual hosts and parking (free on weekends) outside. Book well in advance since prices don't get much better downtown – in winter you may score a small discount for being a Rough Guide reader. ➌

Tabard Inn 1739 N St NW ☏785-1277, ℻785-6173, ⓦwww.tabardinn.com; Dupont Circle Metro. Three converted Victorian townhouses, two blocks from Dupont Circle, with forty individually decorated, antique-stocked rooms (some with shared bath). Laid-back staff, comfortable if aging lounges with romantic fireplaces, courtyard and an excellent restaurant. Rates include breakfast and a pass to the fully equipped YMCA nearby. ➍–➎

Topaz 1733 N St NW ☏393-3000, ⓦwww.topazhotel.com; Dupont Circle Metro. Boutique hotel brings West Coast pizzazz to quiet N Street. Padded headboards with polka dots, lime-green striped wallpaper and funky furniture liven up the 99 rooms, several of which also have space for exercise or yoga, complete with workout gear and exercise videos. ➏–➐

Washington Plaza 10 Thomas Circle NW ☏842-1300 or 1-800/424-1140, ℻371-9602, ⓦwww.washingtonplazahotel.com; McPherson Square Metro. Convenient location three blocks from the Metro, seasonal outdoor pool and deck and great views across the Circle from the large rooms. Tourists mingle with convention and business guests in the lobby bar. Good weekend discounts. ➏

Wyndham Washington 1400 M St NW ☏429-1700 or 1-800/996-3426, ℻785-0786, ⓦwww.wyndham.com/Washington_DC; McPherson Square Metro. Contemporary comfort near Thomas Circle, with soaring atrium, bars, coffee shop and fitness club. Formerly the notorious *Washington Vista*, where ex-Mayor Marion Barry was arrested in a drug sting. Weekend rates often include breakfast and parking. ➏

Downtown: Old

Grand Hyatt 1000 H St NW ☏582-1234 or 1-800/233-1234, ℻628-1641, ⓦwww.washington.hyatt.com; Metro Center Metro. Nearly 900 rooms, but its location opposite the Convention Center keeps it busy. Rooms are fine but not as flash as the twelve-story atrium, lagoon, waterfalls and glass elevators. There's also a deli-café, restaurant and sports bar. ➏

Hotel Harrington 1100 E St NW ☏628-8140 or 1-800/424-8532, ℻347-3924, ⓦwww.hotel-harrington.com; Metro Center Metro. Large, simple, welcoming, family-owned hotel off Pennsylvania Ave, offering adequate air-conditioned rooms (singles to quads) with TV and cheap parking ($8.50). It's a bit worn around the edges, but the prices are tough to beat for the area. ➌

Hotel Washington 515 15th St NW ☏638-5900 or 1-800/424-9540, ℻638-1595, ⓦwww.hotelwashington.com; Metro Center Metro. Historic hotel next to the *Willard* with a popular rooftop restaurant-bar that boasts one of the city's best views and

ACCOMMODATION

heavily decorated Edwardian rooms; some look across to the White House. It rarely needs to offer discount rates, but off-season weekends can see price reductions. **⑤–⑥**

JW Marriott 1331 Pennsylvania Ave NW ☎393-2000 or 1-800/228-9290, ℻626-6991, ⓦwww.marriott.com; Metro Center or Federal Triangle Metro. Flagship *Marriott* property in one of the best locations in the city, part of the National Place development and overlooking Freedom Plaza (ask for a room facing the avenue). Rooms are a notch or two above the standard, plus there are several restaurants, a sports bar and a health club with indoor pool. Weekend rates include breakfast. **⑥**

Marriott at Metro Center 775 12th St NW ☎737-2200 or 1-800/228-9290, ℻347-5886, ⓦwww.marriott.com; Metro Center Metro. Downtown hotel close to the Convention Center with popular bar and grill, and sizeable rooms. Weekends can be a real bargain, often including free breakfast and parking. **④–⑤**

Red Roof Inn 500 H St NW ☎289-5959 or 1-800/733-7663, ℻289-0754, ⓦwww.redroof.com; Gallery Place–Chinatown Metro. Reasonable rates for this location, with Chinatown and the MCI Center on the doorstep. The café serves a buffet breakfast (not included in the room rate), and there's an exercise room with sauna. Rooms are merely standard, but there are good weekend and off-season discounts, and kids under 18 stay free. **④**

Willard Inter-Continental 1401 Pennsylvania Ave NW ☎628-9100 or 1-800/327-0200, ℻637-7326, ⓦwww.washington.interconti.com; Metro Center Metro. Few hotels have the style of the *Willard*, in business on and off since the 1850s. It's a Beaux Arts beauty with acres of marble, mosaics and glass; slick service; finely furnished rooms; and a top-drawer clientele. **⑧**

Dupont Circle

Brickskeller Inn 1523 22nd St NW ☎293-1885, ℻293-0996, ⓦwww.brickskeller.net; Dupont Circle Metro. A converted apartment house with clean and simple rooms, most with sinks and a couple with bath and TV; the top floor has a view of Rock Creek Park. It's above one of the Circle's oldest bars. Good weekly rates. **②–③**

Carlyle Suites 1731 New Hampshire Ave NW ☎234-3200 or 1-866/468-3532, ℻387-0085, ⓦwww.carlylesuites.com; Dupont Circle Metro. Art Deco beauty in a surprisingly tranquil street near Dupont Circle. Furnishings have been upgraded, though the Deco tone prevails throughout the comfortable self-catering suites, which have dining areas and small kitchens. Other pluses are a café, parking, laundry and weekend discounts. **⑤**

The Dupont at the Circle 1604 19th St NW ☎332-5251 or 1-888/412-0100, ℻332-3244, ⓦwww.dupontatthecircle.com; Dupont Circle Metro. Eight beautifully appointed rooms – high ceilings, kitchenettes, marble bathrooms – in a Victorian townhouse virtually on the Circle (at Q St). Free continental breakfast and morning paper included; parking available ($15); smoking prohibited. **④–⑤**

Embassy Inn 1627 16th St NW ☎234-7800 or 1-800/423-9111, ℻234-3309; Dupont Circle Metro. Welcoming inn, popular with Europeans, on a residential street in northeastern Dupont Circle, well placed for bars and restaurants. Attractive, good-value rooms, free continental breakfast, coffee and papers available all day, plus an early-evening sherry to speed you on your way. **③–④**

Embassy Row Hilton 2015 Massachusetts Ave NW ☎265-1600 or 1-800/774-1500, ℻328-7526, ⓦwww.hilton.com; Dupont Circle Metro. Smart Embassy Row standard, with marble bathrooms, cable TV, complimentary newspaper, lobby bar, health center and seasonal rooftop pool. **⑥**

Hotel Rouge 1315 16th St NW ☎232-8000; ℻332-6257, ⓦwww.rouge-dc.com; Dupont Circle Metro. Doormen in black leather jackets and a café-bar throbbing with house music set the tone for Dupont's hippest hotel, where the 137 sleek rooms are outfitted with crimson velvet drapes, floor-to-ceiling red leatherette headboards, Aveda toiletries, flatscreen TVs and minibars stuffed with, among other things, Redi-Whip and condoms. The hotel's check-your-guilt-at-the-door mentality is perhaps best expressed in the complimentary "last call" bar where you can start your day with cold pizza and Bloody Marys. In case you do want to leave your room, you'll find yourself a quick walk from Dupont Circle scene. **⑥–⑦**

Radisson Barceló 2121 P St NW ☎293-3100
Or 1-800/333-3333, ℱ857-0134,
ⓦwww.radisson.com; Dupont Circle Metro.
European-style hotel (with great Spanish
restaurant, the *Gabriel,* see p.266) in the
heart of the Dupont Circle nightlife scene.
Rooms are spacious, and there's a pool
and sundeck. ❺

Simpkins' B&B 1601 19th St NW ☎387-1328;
Dupont Circle Metro. Victorian townhouse
with six rooms just a minute from the Metro
– unbeatable rates for such a good
location. Décor is plain and facilities simple
– guests (mostly foreign) share two
bathrooms, a small kitchen (and free tea
and toast), and the cable TV in the lounge;
there's also free high-speed internet
access. Call at least two weeks in advance
and have your passport handy – it's
required of all guests at check-in. ❶–❷

Swann House 1808 New Hampshire Ave NW
☎265-4414, ℱ265-6755, ⓦwww.swannhouse
.com; Dupont Circle Metro. Elegant B&B set
in a Romanesque-style mansion built in
1883 on a tree-lined residential street, a ten-
minute walk from both Dupont Circle and
Adams-Morgan. There are nine individually
decorated rooms – some with working
fireplaces – as well as an array of porches
and decks for reclining, and a private
garden with fountain. Free continental
breakfast, afternoon refreshments and an
early-evening sherry to round out the day.
Parking is available ($12). ❺–❼

Westin Fairfax 2100 Massachusetts Ave NW
☎293-2100 or 1-800/WESTIN-1, ℱ293-0641,
ⓦwww.starwood.com/westin; Dupont Circle
Metro. Embassy Row highlight (formerly the
Ritz-Carlton), once owned by Al Gore's
family, and still catering to clubby politicos,
media types and business people who
frequent its *Jockey Club* restaurant. Anglo-
French country-house chic, with
impeccable facilities and service. ❼

Windsor Inn 1842 16th St NW ☎667-0300 or
1-800/423-9111, ℱ667-4503; Dupont Circle
Metro. Under the same welcoming
management as the *Embassy Inn*, the
Windsor is a few blocks farther north, its
rooms (in twin brick 1920s houses) a
shade larger. The spacious suites are a real
steal. Ground-floor rooms look onto a
terrace. Free continental breakfast, coffee
and sherry served in the attractive lobby.
❸–❹

Foggy Bottom

Allen Lee Hotel 2224 F St NW ☎331-1224 or
1-800/462-0186, ⓦwww.allenleehotel.com;
Foggy Bottom–GWU Metro. Misleadingly
attractive exterior hides musty rooms (with
and without private bath), with clunky air-
conditioning – check a couple before
checking in. The place has seen much
better days, but is in a reasonable location
and is certainly cheap for DC. ❸

Hotel Lombardy 2019 Pennsylvania Ave NW
☎828-2600 or 1-800/424-5486, ℱ872-0503,
ⓦwww.hotellombardy.com; Foggy
Bottom–GWU Metro or Farragut West
Metro. Red-brick apartment-style hotel in
favored Pennsylvania Avenue location (it's
equally close to both Metro stations).
Spacious rooms, most with kitchenettes
and coffeemakers; the café has outdoor
seating and is good for breakfast. ❹

State Plaza 2117 E St NW ☎861-8200 or 1-
800/424-2859, ℱ659-8601, ⓦwww.stateplaza
.com; Foggy Bottom–GWU Metro. Spacious
suites with fully equipped kitchens and
dining area, plus a rooftop sundeck, health
club and good café. Great weekend rates,
and there's often room here when other
places are full. ❺

Swissotel Washington, The Watergate 2650
Virginia Ave NW ☎965-2300 or 1-800/424-
2736, ℱ965-1173, ⓦwww.swissotel.com;
Foggy Bottom–GWU Metro. Sniffy hotel
with comfortable rooms and suites (some
with kitchen, and balconies with river views)
in the now notorious complex near the
Kennedy Center. It's a bit of a hike from
most bars and restaurants, though there is
a small pool, and the complex offers shops
and services as well as *Jeffrey's* restaurant
(see p.269), whose Texas counterpart is a
presidential favorite. ❼

Washington Monarch Hotel 2401 M St NW
☎429-2400 or 1-800/505-9042, ℱ457-5010,
ⓦwww.washingtonmonarch.com; Foggy
Bottom–GWU Metro. High-class West End
oasis with extremely comfortable rooms,
pool, excellent health club and internal
garden courtyard. It's just north of
Washington Circle, midway between Foggy
Bottom and Georgetown. ❼

Georgetown

Four Seasons Hotel 2800 Pennsylvania Ave NW
☎342-0444 or 1-800/332-3442, ℱ944-2076,
ⓦwww.fourseasons.com. DC's most

expensive and luxurious hotel – a sympathetic red-brick at the eastern end of Georgetown – is also its most sought-after. Stars, royalty and business high-rollers hanker after the lavish rooms and suites with views of Rock Creek Park or the C&O Canal. Service is superb, the *Seasons* restaurant impeccable; there's also a pool, fitness center and *Garden Terrace* bar-lounge. ❽

Georgetown Inn 1310 Wisconsin Ave NW ☏333-8900 or 1-800/424-2979, ☏333-8308, ⊛www.georgetowninn.com. Stylish, hi-tech red-brick hotel in the heart of Georgetown offering tastefully appointed rooms (those off the avenue tend to be quieter) with marble bathrooms and high-speed internet hook-ups. Downstairs, there's a buzzing *Daily Grill* outpost serving spruced-up American standards. ❻

Holiday Inn Georgetown 2101 Wisconsin Ave NW ☏338-4600 or 1-800/465-4329, ☏338-4458, ⊛www.holiday-inn.com. The only relative cheapie in Georgetown – a bit far up Wisconsin Avenue, though buses and cabs get you down to M Street pretty quickly. Newish rooms, parking, outdoor pool, fitness room and good discount rates. ❺

Hotel Monticello 1075 Thomas Jefferson St NW ☏337-0900 or 1-800/388-2410, ☏333-6526, ⊛www.hotelmonticello.com. All-suite hotel nicely located off M Street, near the canal towpath, with spacious standard suites and some two-level penthouse units that sleep up to six. Free internet access in the business center. Summers (June–Aug) see a small saving, as do some weekends. ❺

Latham Hotel 3000 M St NW ☏726-5000 or 1-800/368-5922, ☏342-1800, ⊛www.thelatham.com. Well-sited hotel insulated from the Georgetown noise, with a rooftop pool, sundeck and – in *Citronelle* – one of the city's finest dining experiences; lesser mortals breakfast in *La Madeleine*. Some rooms have canal and river views. There are also some superb split-level executive suites with business facilities such as high-speed internet access and fax/copy machines. Rooms ❺, suites ❼

Southwest

Channel Inn Hotel 650 Water St SW ☏554-2400 or 1-800/368-5668, ☏863-1164, ⊛www.channelinn.com; Waterfront Metro. The city's first (and, thus far, only) waterfront hotel, a 1970s development down at the Washington Channel, with some rooms looking across to East Potomac Park. There's free parking, an outdoor pool and sundeck and a choice of seafood restaurants nearby. ❹

Holiday Inn Capitol 550 C St SW ☏479-4000 or 1-800/465-4329, ☏479-4353, ⊛www.holidayinncapitol.com; L'Enfant Plaza or Federal Center SW Metro. Variously sized rooms within walking distance of the Capitol and the Smithsonian museums; there's a bar, restaurant, deli and a seasonal rooftop pool. As with all the city's *Holiday Inns*, weekend rates are attractive. ❺

Loews L'Enfant Plaza 480 L'Enfant Plaza SW ☏484-1000 or 1-800/235-6397, ☏646-4456, ⊛www.loewshotels.com; L'Enfant Plaza Metro. Superbly appointed modern hotel, a couple blocks south of the Mall and with direct access to the Metro. Spacious rooms in nineteenth-century French style, most with river or city views, plus health club and rooftop pool. Special winter and weekend rates apply – ask about special deals. The hotel is kid- and pet-friendly. ❻

Union Station

Holiday Inn on the Hill 415 New Jersey Ave NW ☏638-1616 or 1-800/638-1116, ☏638-0707, ⊛www.holiday-inn.com; Union Station Metro. Rooms are nothing special, though you get a coffeemaker, hair dryer and iron in the pricier ones. There's a pool, exercise room, and sports bar and grill dedicated to the Washington Senators, DC's one-time pro baseball team. Weekend rates here can be a bargain. ❺

Hotel George 15 E St NW ☏347-4200 or 1-800/576-8331, ☏347-4213, ⊛www.hotelgeorge.com; Union Station Metro. A modern makeover for the old *Bellevue*, bringing New York style to DC: sleek lines, contemporary furnishings, hip staff, great marble bathrooms and a very trendy bar-bistro called *Bis*. Weekend rates, when available, typically knock around $50 off the price. ❻

Hyatt Regency Washington on Capitol Hill 400 New Jersey Ave NW ☏737-1234 or 1-800/233-1234, ☏737-5773, ⊛www.hyatt.com; Union Station Metro. Two blocks from Union Station, this 800-room luxury monster features a multistory garden atrium, pool and health club. ❻

Phoenix Park 520 N Capitol St NW ☏638-6900 or 1-800/824-5419, ☏638-4025,

@www.pparkhotel.com; Union Station Metro. Pleasing, well-equipped rooms in an Irish-owned hotel conveniently located across from Union Station. Popular with politicos and an after-work crowd, who frequent the associated *Dubliner* pub. There's a good restaurant, too, serving hearty breakfasts. ❺

Upper Northwest

Days Inn Connecticut Avenue 4400 Connecticut Ave NW ☎244-5600 or 1-800/329-7466, ⓕ244-6794, @www.daysinn.com; Van Ness–UDC Metro. A couple of stops beyond the zoo (and just two blocks from the Metro), in a residential/university neighborhood, the hotel has reasonable, if smallish, rooms plus all the modern conveniences. Call ahead for weekend and other special rates. ❸–❹

India House Too 300 Carroll St NW ☎291-1195, @www.dchostel.com; Takoma Metro. Rambling Victorian red-brick in a safe neighborhood, ten minutes from Union Station by Metro – it's on the hill, fifty yards up from the station, on the right. An international backpacking crowd loves this free-and-easy hostel with bunk-bed dorms (plus two plain doubles) and shared bathrooms. A kitchen, cable TV, lockers, parking, a rec room, and a deck and garden for summer parties complete the picture. And at $14 a night, it's the cheapest option in DC. ❶

Kalorama Guest House at Woodley Park 2700 Cathedral Ave NW ☎328-0860, ⓕ328-8730; Woodley Park–Zoo Metro. More friendly Victorian charm from the *Kalorama* people (see p.244), here much nearer the Metro in Woodley Park. Two houses (19

rooms, 12 en-suite), and the same good service and facilities – comfortable brass beds, free continental breakfast, aperitifs, papers and coffee. Book well in advance. ❷–❸

Marriott Wardham Park 2660 Woodley Rd NW ☎328-2000 or 1-800/228-9290, ⓕ234-0015, @www.marriott.com; Woodley Park–Zoo Metro. Second of Woodley Park's historic, celeb-filled hotel-palaces (formerly the *Sheraton*), it's the largest hotel in DC, with two pools, health club and restaurants bristling with attentive staff. Very good weekend and off-season discounts make this more affordable than you might think, though convention business keeps rooms full most of the year. ❻–❼

Omni Shoreham 2500 Calvert St NW ☎234-0700 or 1-800/843-6664, ⓕ756-5145, @www.omnihotels.com; Woodley Park–Zoo Metro. Plush, grand, Washington institution bursting with history. Features include tasteful, comfortable rooms, many overlooking Rock Creek Park, outdoor pool and tennis courts, the foliage-filled *Garden Court* for drinks and, when available, bargain weekend rates. ❻

Woodley Park Guest House 2647 Woodley Rd NW ☎667-0218 or 1-866/667-0218, ⓕ667-1080, @www.woodleyparkguesthouse.com; Woodley Park–Zoo Metro. Pleasant guest house on residential Woodley Park side street (opposite the massive *Marriott*) offering a quiet refuge, with 16 newly renovated rooms (most en-suite), ample parking ($10), and free continental breakfast. It's well located near the Metro, the zoo and a swath of good restaurants along Connecticut Avenue. Reservations essential. ❷–❹

⑪

ACCOMMODATION

Eating

Washington's dining scene has thrived in recent years, fueled in part by the various downtown developments and reflecting the amount of disposable income in the country's political and legal capital currently at hand. But shifting economic fortunes and a jittery tourism industry may mean a shakeout is around the corner.

That said, the city keeps up with the times (though it's generally a few steps behind New York and San Francisco), which means that current **trends** are favoring the opening of Asian-fusion restaurants, steak houses, casual bistros and brew-pub restaurants. Successful chefs and restaurateurs – Roberto Donna, Bob Kinkead, Gerard Pangaud, the Clyde's group, even Vietnamese families from Arlington – are not above cloning their successes, so you can expect new offshoots of the most popular of DC's eating houses, both in the city and in the suburbs.

As for specific **cuisines**, good Southern and Southwestern **American** food isn't hard to find, while Georgetown, in particular, has a rash of renowned New York-style saloon-restaurants serving everything from oysters to strip steaks. **European** restaurants tend to be pricey, but there are some good bistros (Georgetown again), while tapas, tortilla wraps and comfort food like meat loaf and mac and cheese are creeping onto menus everywhere. On the whole, the **Chinese** restaurants in Chinatown don't hold a candle to their counterparts in other cities – you'll do better eating **Thai** or **Vietnamese** (the best of these eateries are across the river, in Arlington). The city's other dining bonus is its comparatively large number of **Ethiopian** restaurants (especially in Adams-Morgan). Fans will also be able to track down places serving food from countries as diverse as Argentina, Burma, Greece and El Salvador.

For visitors, it can often prove exasperating to try to find exactly the kind of food you want, when you want it. Certain **neighborhoods** tend to attract similar kinds of restaurants: homey downtown trattorias are as scarce as staid power-dining spots in Adams-Morgan. Perhaps the most annoying discovery is that the areas in which visitors spend much of their time – the Mall, around

Chains

The main **chains** can be found throughout the city – you're never very far from a *Starbuck's* coffee, an *Au Bon Pain* sandwich or a *Baja Fresh* fish taco. But quirkier independent coffee shops are spreading like wildfire, and there are a couple of smaller local chains with just a few outlets that are worth keeping an eye out for: *Chesapeake Bagel Bakery* and *Whatsa Bagel* for great stuffed bagels, *Julia's Empanadas* for the eponymous Mexican filler, and *La Prima/Via Cucina* for Italian deli sandwiches and provisions. And whenever you're in the mood for coffee or tea, drop by *Firehook Bakery & Coffeehouse* or *Teaism*, two very good local chains that have outposts around the city.

the White House and Federal Triangle – have a positive dearth of good–value cafés and restaurants.

Happily, the Metro system and the sheer number of taxis means that nowhere is really off–limits when it comes to choosing a restaurant. Downtown, **Chinatown** is the only central ethnic enclave with its own swatch of restaurants, though the **7th Street** corridor, near the MCI Center, has recently emerged as a food street. But it's only really in the outer neighborhoods that

Cuisines

Our restaurant reviews are grouped by neighborhood. To track down a particular cuisine, consult the lists below.

African (also see Ethiopian)
Bukom Café p.256
Harambe Café p.257

American
America p.272
Ardeo p.273
Art Gallery Bar & Grille p.269
Capitol City Brewing Company p.263
Cashion's Eat Place p.257
Clyde's p.270
District Chophouse & Brewery p.264
Fran O'Brien's p.262
Hard Times Café p.259
J. Paul's p.271
The Mark p.264
Martin's Tavern p.271
The Monocle p.260
Morton's of Chicago p.271
Mr Henry's p.260
New Heights p.273
Nora's p.268
Old Ebbitt Grill p.264
Perry's p.258
Sign of the Whale p.263
Stoney's p.263
Tabard Inn p.263
Two Quail p.260
U-topia p.272
Woodley Café p.273

Asian (also see specific cuisines)
Café Asia p.261
Malaysia Kopitiam p.262
Oodles Noodles p.261
Perry's p.258
Spices p.273
Yanyu p.273

Burmese
Burma p.260

Cajun
Cajun Bangkok p.259
Rocky's Café p.258

Caribbean
Red Ginger p.271

Chinese
City Lights of China p.266
Go-Lo's p.260
Hunan Chinatown p.260
Mr Yung's p.261
Tony Cheng's p.261

Diners and cafeterias
Ben's Chili Bowl p.272
The Diner p.256
Duplex Diner p.256
Five Guys p.258
Furin's p.269
Luna Grill & Diner p.268
Reeve's Restaurant and Bakery p.263

Ethiopian
Fasika's p.257
Meskerem p.257
Red Sea p.258
Zed's p.271

French
Au Pied de Cochon p.269
Bistro du Coin p.266
Bistro Français p.270
Café la Ruche p.270
Gerard's Place p.262
La Fourchette p.257

German
Café Berlin p.260

Greek
Taverna The Greek Islands p.260
Yanni's Greek Taverna p.273
Zorba's Café p.268

Indian
Amma Vegetarian Kitchen p.269
The Bombay Club p.261

Italian
Ecco Café p.259

you can saunter up and down, checking out the options. There are also lots of opportunities to sit outside when the weather's clement; patios, sidewalk tables, and opening front windows are all de rigueur in DC.

Georgetown has the most varied selection of dining places – rowdy saloons, diners, ethnic restaurants of all shades and some rather more sniffy establishments – most of them in the few blocks on either side of the M Street/Wisconsin Avenue intersection. **Dupont Circle** (chiefly P St and Connecticut Ave) rivals

Georgetown for sheer choice, with a recent influx of flash new eateries reinvigorating a neighborhood already known for its designer Italian restaurants and coffee shops. The most down-to-earth spot to dine out is **Adams–Morgan**, a multicultural neighborhood with the city's best bargains. Though prices are moving up slowly, 18th Street at Columbia Road is lined with scores of choices, all still offering pretty good value.

The **listings** in this chapter are arranged **geographically** (in alphabetical order) and correspond largely to the city chapters in the guide. Each neighborhood section is in turn split into two divisions: "**Cafés, snacks and light meals**," detailing spots good for a quick bite or a coffee, and "**Restaurants**." These two categories are not necessarily mutually exclusive; you can, of course, eat lunch or dinner at many of the diners, cafés and coffee shops we've listed, and also perhaps get a light meal at many of the restaurants. The bigger distinction made is whether or not it's the type of establishment at which you can make a night of it. If it's essential (and possible) to **reserve a table**, we've said so. You'll need to book well in advance to eat at the most renowned restaurants.

For **listings by cuisine**, turn to the box on pp.254–255. For restaurants popular with a gay and lesbian clientele, see p.294. We've given each restaurant a **price category** (see box opposite), which reflects the cost of a three-course meal per person, *excluding drinks, tax and service*. These are only a guideline: most people will be hard-pressed to get through three courses in many restaurants, and often you'll be able to eat for less than we suggest; on the other hand, don't forget you have to add the price of **drinks** to your bill and (in most places) at least fifteen percent for **service**. To keep the price of meals at a minimum, look for **set lunches** (from as little as $5) and **early-bird dinners** (usually served before 7pm); these are not just a feature of budget restaurants, with many fancier establishments maintaining sensible pricing policies in the face of a volatile restaurant market.

Adams-Morgan

All the places listed in Adams–Morgan are within a few blocks of the junction of 18th Street and Columbia Road; the nearest Metro stops (noted below) are a good fifteen-minute walk away.

Cafés, snacks and light meals

The Diner 2453 18th St NW ☏232-8800; Dupont Circle or Woodley Park–Zoo Metro. A high ceiling and weathered tile floor make this Adams-Morgan oasis more stylish café than down-at-the-heels Jersey-style diner; but with greasy classics adorning the eggs-and-sandwich-filled menu, a coffee counter with chrome-and-red-leather stools, and round-the-clock service, it's a winner. Daily 24hrs.

Duplex Diner 2004 18th St NW ☏234-7890; Dupont Circle Metro. Classic comfort foods such as mac and cheese and meat loaf go toe-to-toe with spruced-up favorites such as salmon quesadillas. Mon 6–11pm, Tues–Sat 6pm–12.30am, Sun 11am–3pm & 6–11pm.

Pizza Mart 2445 18th St NW ☏234-9700; Dupont Circle or Woodley Park–Zoo Metro. Clubgoers mop up an evening's worth of drinks with the elephantine slices on offer at this hole-in-the-wall pizzeria. Sun–Thurs 11am–3am, Fri & Sat 11am–4am.

Tryst 2459 18th St NW ☏232-5500; Dupont Circle or Woodley Park–Zoo Metro. It's not quite Central Perk but it's just as Friendly – no one minds if you hang out all day on the great squishy sofas and tuck into coffee, wine, soup and sandwiches, or just read the paper. Mon–Thurs 7am–2am, Fri & Sat 7am–3am, Sun 8am–2am.

Restaurants

Bukom Café 2442 18th St NW ☏265-4600; Dupont Circle or Woodley Park–Zoo Metro. Laid-back restaurant-bar serving delicious African dishes like *egusi*, a broth of goat

Each restaurant has been given one of the following price categories:

Budget: under $10	Expensive: $25–40
Inexpensive: $10–15	Very expensive: over $40
Moderate: $15–25	

These are per-person prices for a three-course meal or equivalent, excluding drinks, tax and service.

meat with ground melon seeds and spinach, and chicken *yassa*, baked with onions and spices, for around $10. All washed down with African beers (try the Ngoma) and African music (live Tues–Sat). Mon, Tues & Sun 4pm–1am, Wed & Thurs 4pm–2am, Fri & Sat 4pm–3am. Moderate.

Cashion's Eat Place 1819 Columbia Rd NW ☎797-1819; Dupont Circle or Woodley Park–Zoo Metro. A real chef's restaurant serving fabulous New American cuisine in a vibrant atmosphere. Book ahead or sip a proper cocktail while you wait at the chic elevated bar and take in the buzz. If you can't stomach the prices – high for the neighborhood – try the more reasonable and very good Sunday brunch. Tues 5–10pm, Wed–Sat 5–11pm, Sun 11.30am–2.30pm & 5–10pm. Expensive.

Fasika's 2477 18th St NW ☎797-7673; Dupont Circle or Woodley Park–Zoo Metro. Most upmarket of the local Ethiopian places, with sidewalk seating, live music three nights a week and spicy stews for $10 to $12 or so. Mon–Thurs 5pm–midnight, Fri–Sun noon–midnight. Moderate.

The Grill from Ipanema 1858 Columbia Rd NW ☎986-0757; Woodley Park–Zoo Metro. Worth visiting for the name alone, though the *feijoada* (Brazilian meat stew) and the shrimp dishes are great, and the Sunday brunch sees off most appetites. Try the baked clams to start and watch your caipirinha (rum cocktail) intake. Mon–Thurs 5–11pm, Fri 5pm–midnight, Sat noon–midnight, Sun noon–11pm. Moderate.

Harambe Café 1771 U St NW, at Florida Ave and 18th ☎332-6435; Dupont Circle Metro. Simple, family-run African dining room with some of the cheapest food in town – filling chicken, beef and lamb *wot* (spicy stew) served on *injera* bread, plus vegetarian platters – all accompanied by some great music. Mon–Thurs & Sun noon–1am, Fri & Sat noon–2am. Budget.

I Matti 2436 18th St NW ☎462-8844; Dupont Circle or Woodley Park–Zoo Metro. Roberto Donna's trendy trattoria-pizzeria finds favor with bargain-seekers after accomplished Italian cooking at less than stratospheric prices. Classic pastas, gnocchi and pizzas, a great antipasto selection, and grilled meat and fish specials. Dishes like braised rabbit, seared lamb and grilled sea bass push the price up a notch. Daily noon–11pm. Moderate.

La Fourchette 2429 18th St NW ☎332-3077; Dupont Circle or Woodley Park–Zoo Metro. The brasserie's been here forever and the food – French classics served at closely packed tables – is reliable. Main bonus is the sidewalk patio. Mon–Fri 11.30am–10.30pm, Sat 4–11pm, Sun 4–10pm. Moderate.

Las Placitas 1828 Columbia Rd NW ☎745-3751; Woodley Park–Zoo Metro. Not much more sophisticated than shack-dining, but for calorific refueling and friendly service it's hard to beat. All the Mexican standards, plus Salvadorean specials like *churrasco a caballo* (basically steak, eggs, rice and beans), *pupusas* (stuffed fried tortillas) and plantains. Mon–Thurs & Sun noon–2am, Fri & Sat noon–3am. Inexpensive.

Meskerem 2434 18th St NW ☎462-4100; Dupont Circle or Woodley Park–Zoo Metro. The district's favorite Ethiopian hangout, with funky décor and cheery staff. Eat with your hands, scooping food up with the sourdough *injera* bread. There are lots of vegetarian and seafood choices, and the *messob* platter gives you a taste of everything. Daily noon–11pm. Moderate.

Meze 2437 18th St NW ☎797-0017; Dupont Circle or Woodley Park–Zoo Metro. A wide array of delicious Turkish meze (the Middle East's answer to tapas), both hot and cold, is served in a fashionable restaurant-lounge setting. The kitchen closes around 10.30pm or so but continues to serve a smattering of dishes after midnight for

⑫

EATING

257

At all the places listed below, you'll be able to order a meal after midnight on at least one night of the week (usually Fri and/or Sat).

America, Union Station, p.272
Au Pied de Cochon (24hr), Georgetown, p.269
Ben's Chili Bowl, Shaw, p.272
Bistro Français, Georgetown, p.270
Bukom Café, Adams-Morgan, p.256
Café la Ruche, Georgetown, p.270
Clyde's, Georgetown, p.270
Coppi's, Shaw, p.272
The Diner (24hr), Adams-Morgan, p.256
Fasika's, Adams-Morgan, p.257
Go-Lo's, Chinatown, p.260

Harambe Café, Adams-Morgan, p.257
J. Paul's, Georgetown, p.271
Jaleo, Downtown: Old, p.264
Las Placitas, Adams-Morgan, p.257
Martin's Tavern, Georgetown, p.271
Meze, Adams-Morgan, p.257
Mr Henry's, Capitol Hill, p.260
Old Glory, Georgetown, p.271
Paolo's, Georgetown, p.271
Pizza Mart, Adams-Morgan, p.256
Stoney's, Downtown: New, p.263

hungry clubbers looking to snack in style. Mon–Thurs 5.30pm–2am, Fri 5.30pm–3am, Sat 11.30am–3am, Sun 11.30am–2am. Inexpensive (meze) to Moderate (meals).
Mixtec 1792 Columbia Rd NW ☎332-1011; Woodley Park–Zoo Metro. You're unlikely to linger, but when you want great-tasting, low-priced Mexican food – tacos and tortillas, plus spit-roasted chicken and mussels steamed with chilis – this is where to come. Mon–Thurs & Sun 11am–10pm, Fri & Sat 11am–1am. Inexpensive.
Pasta Mia 1790 Columbia Rd NW ☎328-9114; Woodley Park–Zoo Metro. Expect long lines at this no-frills, family-run pasteria – it piles on the pasta at prices so low it's worth the wait. Mon–Sat 6.30–11pm. Inexpensive.
Perry's 1811 Columbia Rd NW ☎234-6218; Woodley Park–Zoo Metro. The exclusive-o-meter is turned up high at this in-crowd restaurant serving sushi and Asian-influenced American entrées. Rooftop tables are always at a premium and the drag queen brunch (Sun 11am–3pm) is a blast. Mon–Thurs & Sun 5–11pm, Fri & Sat 5pm–midnight; bar stays open 1hr later. Moderate.
Red Sea 2463 18th St NW ☎483-5000; Dupont Circle or Woodley Park–Zoo Metro. Plentiful portions of spicy food (including vegetarian specials) keep diners coming back to the oldest Ethiopian place in the neighborhood – the *yetsom wat* provides a taste of six veggie dishes. There's a good beer list, too. Daily noon–midnight. Moderate.
Rocky's Cafe 1817 Columbia Rd NW ☎387-2580; Woodley Park–Zoo Metro. Easygoing bistro serving tasty Creole-Cajun and

Caribbean eats is a solid choice on the Adams-Morgan scene – especially if you're in the mood for a laid-back Saturday brunch. Mon–Wed 5.30–10pm, Thurs&Fri 5.30–11.30pm, Sat 11am–3pm & 5.30–11.30pm. Inexpensive–Moderate.
Saigonnais 2307 18th St NW ☎232-5300; Dupont Circle Metro. Gourmet Vietnamese food in a cozy townhouse – splash out on the whole steamed fish. Prices are cheaper at lunch. Daily 11.30am–3pm & 5.30–11pm. Moderate.

Alexandria, VA

Cafés, snacks and light meals

Five Guys 107 N Fayette St ☎703/549-7991. This Old Town greasy spoon cooks its juicy, handmade hamburger patties to order, piles on the fixings and tucks 'em between a heavenly bun. The result? The best burger in the Washington area, if not the whole Eastern Seaboard, hands down. And don't forget the fries – the fresh, hand-cut boardwalk-style chips boast their own loyal following. Daily 11am–10pm.

Restaurants

Blue Point Grill 600 Franklin St ☎703/739-0404. It's the fresh seafood that's earned this Old Town jewel its reputation as one of Alexandria's very best restaurants. In warmer weather pass up sitting in the elegant dining room for a spot on the veranda. Daily 11am–3pm & 5.30–10pm. Expensive.

Cajun Bangkok 907 King St ☏703/836-0038.
The Thai chef presiding over the incendiary
blend of Thai and Cajun fare served here
pulls no punches when it comes to spicing
up his tasty Thai jerk chicken. While Thai
dishes dominate the appetizers (try the full-
flavor Crying Tiger, grilled steak with a spicy
sauce), Cajun dishes with Asian accents –
such as the zesty Cajun Bangkok Gumbo –
make up the bulk of the entrées. Mon–Fri
11am–10.30pm, Sat 5–11pm, Sun
5–10.30pm. Moderate.
Ecco Café 220 N Lee St ☏703/684-0321.
Gourmet pizza and pasta joint with a
neighborhood feel, good lunch specials and
jazz brunch on Sunday. Mon–Thurs
11am–11pm, Fri & Sat 11am–midnight,
Sun noon–10pm. Inexpensive–Moderate.
Fish Market 105 King St ☏703/836-5676.
Brick-walled restaurant with terrace,
serving oysters and chowder at the bar and
fried-fish platters, pastas and fish entrées.
Daily 11am–midnight; bar until 2am.
Moderate.
Hard Times Café 1404 King St ☏703/638-
5340. Three styles of chili; wings, rings and
fries; country music; and microbrews add
up to one of Alexandria's better American
restaurants. It's up toward the Metro
station. Mon–Thurs 11am–10pm, Fri & Sat
11am–11pm, Sun noon–10pm.
Inexpensive.
Las Tapas 710 King St ☏703/836-4000. Best
of the local tapas bars, with a wide
selection, plus paella and regular (free)
flamenco sessions. Mon–Thurs & Sun
11.30am–11.30pm, Fri & Sat 11am–1am.
Moderate.
Santa Fe East 110 S Pitt St ☏703/548-6900.
Contemporary Southwestern cooking – lots
of exotic chili seasoning, freshly made
salsas, hickory-smoked meats and grilled
fish – in one of Alexandria's nicest
restaurant interiors. Mon–Thurs
11.30am–2pm & 5.30–10.30pm, Fri & Sat
11.30am–midnight, Sun 11.30am–2pm &
5.30–10.30pm. Moderate.
South Austin Grill 801 King St ☏703/684-
8969. Quality Tex-Mex fare packs lively
crowds into this Old Town institution. The
Cadillac-sized fajitas, stacked nachos and
zesty margaritas make the long waits
worthwhile. Mon 11.30am–10.30pm,
Tues–Thurs 11.30am–11pm, Fri
11.30am–midnight, Sat 11am–midnight,
Sun 11am–10.30pm. Moderate.

Arlington, VA

Restaurants

Café Dalat 3143 Wilson Blvd, at Highland St
☏703/276-0935; Clarendon Metro. Brisk,
Formica-tabled Vietnamese joint with a
popular lunch buffet and some tasty menu
specials such as grilled lemon chicken and
five-spice pork. Most dishes come with
noodles and greens, making for pretty
cheap eats. There's also a good selection
of vegetarian dishes. Mon–Thurs & Sun
11am–9.30pm, Fri & Sat 11am–10.30pm.
Inexpensive.
Il Radicchio 1801 Clarendon Blvd, at Rhodes St
☏703/276-2627; Court House Metro. The
cross-river branch of Roberto Donna's
pizza-and-pasta empire offers great-value
wood-fired pizzas and mix-and-match
spaghetti-and-sauce combos. Mon–Sat
11.30am–10pm, Sun 5–10pm.
Inexpensive–Moderate.
Queen Bee 3181 Wilson Blvd, at Highland St
☏703/527-3444; Clarendon Metro. No
question – the best Vietnamese food in
town, with renowned crunchy spring rolls,
seafood over crispy noodles, grilled pork,
huge bowls of noodle soup, Saigon
pancakes and grilled shrimp. Expect to wait
in line. Daily 11am–10pm. Inexpensive.
Red Hot & Blue 1600 Wilson Blvd, at Pierce St
☏703/276-7427; Court House Metro. Also
3014 Wilson Blvd, at Highland St
☏703/243-1510; Clarendon Metro.
Memphis barbecue joint that spawned a
chain, serving the best ribs in the district. A
rack, with coleslaw and beans, costs just
ten bucks. Mon–Thurs 11am–10pm, Fri &
Sat 11am–11pm, Sun noon–10pm.
Inexpensive–Moderate.

Capitol Hill

Cafés, snacks and light meals

Bread and Chocolate 666 Pennsylvania Ave SE
☏547-2875; Eastern Market Metro. Popular
bakery-cum-coffeehouse with street-view
seating and tip-top sandwiches. Mon–Sat
7am–7pm, Sun 8am–6pm.
Le Bon Café 210 2nd St SE ☏547-7200;
Capitol South Metro. Close to the Library of
Congress and good for a wholesome lunch
of soup, salad or sandwich. Mon–Fri
7.30am–5pm, Sat & Sun 8.30am–3.30pm.

The Market Lunch Eastern Market, 7th Ave SE
☎547-8444; Eastern Market Metro. Eat-and-go market-hall-counter meals – sandwiches and fries, salads, crab cakes and fish platters – served to a loyal band of local shoppers and suit-and-tie staffers. Tues–Sat 7.30am–3pm, Sun 11am–3.30pm.

Stompin' Grounds 666 Pennsylvania Ave SE
☎546-5228; Eastern Market Metro. Coffee in a million guises, along with muffins and other munchies. Mon–Sat 7am–7pm, Sun 8am–5.30pm.

Restaurants

Café Berlin 322 Massachusetts Ave NE ☎543-7656; Union Station Metro. Schnitzel, huge *Wurst* platters and German beer. Soup-and-sandwich deals keep prices low at lunch. Mon–Thurs 11am–10pm, Fri & Sat noon–11pm, Sun 4–10pm. Moderate.

Las Placitas 517 8th St SE ☎543-3700; Eastern Market Metro. Great value Mexican standards and Salvadorean specials pack the tables nightly at this no-nonsense eatery. Mon–Thurs 11.30am–3pm & 5–10.30pm, Fri 11.30am–3pm & 5–11pm, Sat & Sun 4–11pm. Moderate.

The Monocle 107 D St NE ☎546-4488; Union Station Metro. Elegant saloon-bar-restaurant with a congressional clientele tucking into crab cakes, steaks and the like in between votes. Mon–Fri 11.30am–midnight, Sat 6–11pm. Expensive.

Mr Henry's 601 Pennsylvania Ave SE ☎546-8412; Eastern Market Metro. Saloon-bar-restaurant, with outside patio, charcoal grill and loyal gay crowd. Even the most expensive choices – the steak and shrimp plates – don't exceed $10; burgers are half-price on Mon, and jazz trios play weekly. Mon–Thurs & Sun 11am–12.30am, Fri & Sat 11am–2am. Inexpensive.

Taverna The Greek Islands 305 Pennsylvania Ave SE ☎547-8360; Capitol South Metro. Unsophisticated, rustic, friendly Greek joint. Order something from the grill (all meat) and you won't need appetizers. Also pricier fish specialties, wine by the carafe and a carryout section in the basement. Mon–Sat 11am–11pm, Sun 5–11pm. Moderate.

Thai Roma 313 Pennsylvania Ave SE ☎544-2338; Capitol South Metro. Thai sauces over Italian pasta are not always as successful as you'd hope, but there's a full Thai menu – good on noodles and for vegetarians – in this saloon-style Thai place. You can sink a beer before or after in the cozy attached *Conrad Pub*. Daily 11am–11pm. Moderate.

Two Quail 320 Massachusetts Ave NE ☎543-8030; Union Station Metro. Romantic little townhouse bistro serving changing menus of modern American food. Set lunches are a great value at $10–12, while dinner sees entrées such as grilled fish or lamb chops over wild rice. Reservations recommended. Mon–Fri 11.30am–2.30pm & 5.30–10pm, Sat & Sun 5.30–10.30pm. Expensive.

Chinatown

Restaurants

Burma 740 6th St NW ☎638-1280; Gallery Place–Chinatown Metro. Plain second-floor dining room with Burmese art, approachable staff and very filling food. The noodles are great (try the pork in black bean sauce), and the beer is Thai or Chinese. Mon–Thurs 11am–3pm & 6–10pm, Fri 11am–3pm & 6–10.30pm, Sat 6–10.30pm, Sun 6–10pm. Inexpensive.

Coco Loco 810 7th St NW ☎289-2626; Gallery Place–Chinatown Metro. Large but relaxed in-crowd restaurant, where you can choose from new-wave Mexican tapas or all-you-can-eat Brazilian grills. The tapas ($5–10 a plate) are the way to go, a mile away in quality from most tired Spanish offerings. Mon–Thurs 11.30am–2.30pm & 5.30–10pm, Fri 11.30am–2.30pm & 5.30–11pm, Sat noon–2pm & 5.30–11pm, Sun noon–3pm. Moderate–Expensive.

Go-Lo's 604 H St NW ☎347-4656; Gallery Place–Chinatown Metro. Friendly spot where local office workers are greeted by name. Rice/noodle lunch plates are great value, while meals mix Cantonese and Szechuan influences. Mon–Thurs & Sun 11am–10.30pm, Fri & Sat 11am–2am. Inexpensive.

Hunan Chinatown 624 H St NW ☎783-5858; Gallery Place–Chinatown Metro. Sleekly furnished, Western-friendly restaurant (you'll have to ask for chopsticks) where spiciness replaces taste on occasion. You probably won't need appetizers, though the wonton in chili sauce are good. Mon–Thurs & Sun 11am–11pm, Fri & Sat 11am–midnight. Moderate.

Mr Yung's **740 6th St NW** ☎628-1098; Gallery Place–Chinatown Metro. Extremely amiable Cantonese restaurant, good for a dim-sum or rice-plate lunch. Some unusual seasonal dishes are served – ask for recommendations. Daily 11am–11pm. Inexpensive–Moderate.

Tony Cheng's **619 H St NW** ☎842-8669 **(Mongolian)**, ☎371-8669 **(seafood)**; Gallery Place–Chinatown Metro. Good-value, fun, do-it-yourself, all-you-can-eat Mongolian barbecues downstairs; upstairs, a Cantonese seafood restaurant with daily dim sum (11am–3pm). The upstairs dining room has been visited by every president since Carter, and sundry sporting stars besides. Mon–Thurs & Sun 11am–11pm, Fri & Sat 11am–midnight. Inexpensive (barbecue/dim sum); Moderate (meals).

Downtown: New

Cafés, snacks and light meals

Café Promenade *Renaissance Mayflower*, **1127 Connecticut Ave NW** ☎347-2233; Farragut North Metro. A serenading harpist and pricey Mediterranean menu set the tone in this elegant hotel coffee shop-restaurant. Daily 6.30am–11pm.

Julia's Empanadas **1221 Connecticut Ave NW** ☎861-8828; Dupont Circle Metro. "Made by Hand, Baked with Love" – the motto just about says it all, except for the price of these savory Mexican turnovers, which is so cheap you'll barely notice the money leaving your wallet. Mon–Wed 10.30am–9pm, Thurs & Fri 10.30am–midnight, Sat & Sun 10.30am–6pm.

The Mudd House **1724 M St NW** ☎822-8455; Farragut North Metro. Good downtown coffee stop, specializing in organic blends. Mon–Fri 8am–6pm.

Naan and Beyond **1710 L St NW** ☎466-6404; Farragut North Metro. Mildly spiced but flavorful Indian dishes, wrapped in freshly baked *naan*, are tasty alternatives to traditional sandwiches for the Farragut lunch crowd and Friday night clubgoers. Vegetarian options available. Mon–Thurs 11am–9pm, Fri 11am–4am.

Oodles Noodles **1120 19th St NW** ☎293-3138; Farragut North Metro. Noodle lovers looking for a cheap and hearty bowl should sample the full-flavor offerings at this New Downtown lunch favorite. Mon–Thurs 11.30am–3pm & 5–10pm, Fri & Sat 11.30am–3pm & 5–10.30pm.

Teaism **800 Connecticut Ave NW** ☎835-2233; Farragut West or Farragut North Metro. Pleasant spot for a pick-me-up chai or a dose of Pan-Asian cuisine after a White House tour. Food – salads, sandwiches and bento boxes – is served until 2.30pm; only munchies are available thereafter. Mon–Fri 7.30am–5.30pm.

Restaurants

The Bombay Club **815 Connecticut Ave NW** ☎659-3727; Farragut North or West Metro. Sleek Indian restaurant a block from the White House (and a favorite of former president Clinton), with Raj-style surroundings, piano accompaniment and dishes that are a little out of the ordinary. Mon–Sat 11.30am–2.30pm & 6–11pm. Moderate.

Café Asia **1134 19th St NW** ☎659-2696; Farragut North Metro. Breezy Pan-Asian restaurant in an old townhouse. This is the place for budget sushi and sashimi, or try the big plates of lemongrass-grilled chicken, seafood *bakar* (in banana leaf with spicy prawn sauce), satay or Thai noodles. Be sure to check out the sushi happy hour

⑫

EATING

Monument, museum and gallery cafés and restaurants

Most of Washington's major sight-seeing attractions have their own cafés and fast-food restaurants, and often they're the only local option for lunch, especially on and around the Mall. Those listed below are particularly good; follow the page numbers for more details.

Corcoran Gallery of Art (*Café des Artistes*), p.268
Library of Congress Cafeteria, p.113
National Gallery of Art, p.81
National Museum of American History, p.86

National Museum of Women in the Arts, p.183
Supreme Court Cafeteria, p.110

(Mon–Sat 5.30–7.30pm) – it's a real bargain. Mon–Fri 11.30am–10pm, Sat noon–10pm, Sun 5–10pm. Inexpensive–Moderate.

Fran O'Brien's *Capital Hilton*, 1001 16th St NW ☎783-2599; McPherson Square Metro. Former Redskins player's steak house-saloon in the *Hilton* basement. Check out the Hall of Fame, munch on a bountiful steak or chop and watch the game on TV. Mon–Fri 11.30am–3pm & 5–10.30pm, Sat & Sun 5–10.30pm. Moderate–Expensive.

Galileo 1110 21st St NW ☎293-7191; Foggy Bottom or Farragut West Metro. Superb Northern Italian cuisine from wonderchef Roberto Donna. Risotto makes a regular appearance on the ever-changing menu. Service is snappy, and the wine list impressive. Book well in advance. Mon–Fri 11.30am–2pm & 5.30–10pm (Fri until 10.30pm), Sat & Sun 5.30–10.30pm. Very expensive.

Gerard's Place 915 15th St NW ☎737-4445; McPherson Square Metro. Accomplished Michelin-starred French cuisine by Gerard Pangaud. The $60 five-course fixed menu is a good choice; add on $35 if you want a different wine with every course. Reservations essential. Mon–Fri 11.30am–2pm & 5.30–10pm (Fri until 10.30pm), Sat 5.30–10.30pm. Very expensive.

Grillfish 1200 New Hampshire Ave NW ☎331-7310; Dupont Circle or Foggy Bottom–GWU Metro. One of the best finds in DC – imperial in size and décor, but offering casual dining and perfectly cooked fish and seafood. The daily catch options might include sea bass, tuna, snapper, trout, mahi-mahi, shark or calamari; grilled, over pasta or served in a sauté pan – it's all terrific. Mon–Fri noon–2.30pm & 5.30–10.30pm, Sat & Sun 5.30–11pm. Moderate.

Malaysia Kopitiam 1827 M St NW ☎833-6232; Dupont Circle or Farragut North Metro. Although the décor in this basement eatery is decidedly no-frills, the extensive selection of Indian, Malay and Chinese fare is a first-class ticket to Southeast Asia. Tuck into a bowl of noodles or, for heartier fare, try the spicy beef *rendang* or black pepper lamb. Mon–Thurs 11.30am–10pm, Fri & Sat 11.30am–11pm, Sun noon–10pm. Inexpensive–Moderate.

McCormick & Schmick's 1652 K St NW ☎861-2233; McPherson Square Metro. Hugely popular seafood grill and raw bar, complete with booths, Victorian stained glass and lamps, and a buzzing bar. Best food deals are weekdays between 3.30pm and 6.30pm, and from 10.30pm to midnight Monday through Saturday, when clams, chowders, fajitas and other plate-sized snacks are just a couple bucks apiece. Mon–Fri 11am–11pm, Sat 5pm–midnight, Sun 5–10pm; bar open until midnight. Moderate–Expensive.

The Palm 1225 19th St NW ☎293-9091; Dupont Circle or Farragut North Metro. This "power meatery," is renowned for its New York strip and lobster – and for the power players and celebrities who wine and dine here. The DC outpost of the famous New York steak-house chain was the first *Palm* to open outside of Manhattan and has earned a reputation in its own right. Reservations required. Mon–Fri 11.45am–10.30pm, Sat

Hotel restaurants

Some of DC's best power-dining restaurants are in its glitzier hotels. The pick of the bunch are listed below: expect first-rate food and service and high ($60–100 a head) prices. Always call ahead for reservations.

Four Seasons Hotel (*Seasons*), 2800 Pennsylvania Ave NW ☎944-2000. Contemporary American.

Hay-Adams Hotel (*Lafayette*), 1 Lafayette Square NW ☎638-2570. Contemporary American.

Jefferson Hotel (*Jefferson*), 1200 16th St NW ☎833-6206. Contemporary American.

Latham Hotel (*Citronelle*), 3000 M St NW ☎625-2150. Contemporary French-American.

Morrison-Clark Inn, 1015 L St NW ☎898-1200. Contemporary American.

Willard Inter-Continental (*Willard Room*), 1401 Pennsylvania Ave NW ☎637-7440. Contemporary American-European.

5.30–10.30pm, Sun 5.30–9.30pm.
Expensive–Very expensive.

Sign of the Whale 1825 M St NW ☎785-1110;
Dupont Circle or Farragut North Metro.
Downtown saloon best known for its
supreme burgers (half-price on Monday),
grilled to perfection, though there's also
famous jerk chicken, pasta, fish and other
entrées, most around $10. On Sundays
(11am–4pm) DC's largest make-your-own
Bloody Mary bar opens up to cure the
weekend hangovers. Daily 11.30am–
10.30pm; bar open until 1.30am
(Mon–Thurs & Sun), 2.30am (Fri & Sat).
Inexpensive–Moderate.

Stoney's 1307 L St NW ☎347-9163;
McPherson Square Metro. Down-to-earth
saloon and bar, 30 years old and reveling in
its big servings of burgers, fries, chili and
country fare. Two-buck margaritas on
Fridays. Daily 9am–1am.
Budget–Inexpensive.

Tabard Inn 1739 N St NW ☎785-1277; Dupont
Circle Metro. The restaurant hidden within
this mellow Victorian inn serves creative
New American fare in dining rooms rich
with Old World ambience. There's also a
very pleasant garden that's the perfect spot
for brunch when the weather's right.
Mon–Fri 7–10am, 11.30am–2.30pm &
6–10.30pm, Sat & Sun 8–10am, 11am–
2.30pm & 6–10.30pm. Expensive–Very
expensive.

Vidalia 1990 M St NW ☎659-1990; Dupont
Circle or Farragut North Metro. The New
American cuisine turned out at this
celebrated Dupont South restaurant is
dished up with a decidedly Southern twang
and has garnered the eatery a reputation as
one of the District's best. But despite the
warm, classy ambience, the basement digs
are a turn-off for some. Mon–Thurs
11.30am–10pm, Fri 11.30am–10.30pm,
Sat & Sun 5.30–10.30pm. Expensive.

Downtown: Old

Cafés, snacks and light meals

Corner Bakery The Shops at National Place,
529 14th St NW ☎662-7400; Metro Center
Metro. Self-serve bakery-café, handy to the
White House and with a full range of
ciabatta sandwiches, cookies, salads and
pizza slices. Mon–Fri 7am–8pm, Sat
8am–8pm, Sun 11am–6pm.

Dean & Deluca 1299 Pennsylvania Ave NW
☎628-8155; Metro Center Metro. Gourmet
sandwiches, great homemade soups, hot
dishes and an appetizing salad bar in a
boiler room turned café-carryout. Try to
avoid the lunchtime crush. Mon–Fri
8am–5pm.

Ebbitt Express 675 15th St NW ☎347-8881;
Metro Center Metro. Carryout adjunct to
the infinitely pricier *Old Ebbitt Grill* (see
overleaf). Superior salads, sandwiches and
snacks to go. Mon–Thurs 7.30am–8pm,
Fri 7.30am–6pm.

Harry's *Hotel Harrington*, 436 11th St NW
☎624-0053; Metro Center Metro. Down-to-
earth meals (meat loaf, spaghetti and
meatballs); the adjacent self-service
Harrington Café is even cheaper. Daily
8am–1am; bar open 1hr later; café Mon–Fri
7am–2.30pm & 5–9pm, Sat & Sun 7–11am
& 5–9pm.

Reeve's Restaurant and Bakery 1306 G St
NW ☎628-6350; Metro Center Metro.
Classic diner, in business since 1886, with
an all-you-can-eat breakfast and fruit bar,
crisp-coated chicken at lunchtime, and
famous pies. Mon–Sat 7am–6pm.

Restaurants

Capitol City Brewing Company 1100 New
York Ave NW, entrance at 11th and H ☎628-
2222; Metro Center Metro. It's better known

Food courts

There are food courts in the following locations, usually open Monday through
Saturday from 10am to 9pm, Sunday noon to 6pm.

Georgetown Park Food Court, Level
One, 3222 M St NW, Georgetown.
Old Post Office Pavilion, 1100
Pennsylvania Ave NW, Old Downtown.
Ronald Reagan Building, 1300

Pennsylvania Ave NW, Federal Triangle.
The Shops at National Place, 1331
Pennsylvania Ave NW, Old Downtown.
Union Station Food Court, 50
Massachusetts Ave NE.

as a brew-pub, but the kitchen serves up burgers, grilled sausages, pasta, salads and other bar standards. Reservations advised for weekends. Mon–Thurs & Sun 11am–11pm, Fri & Sat 11am–midnight. Inexpensive–Moderate.

Casa Juanita's 908 11th St NW ☏**737-2520**; Metro Center Metro. Family-run Salvadorean-Mexican restaurant with histrionic Latin American music, excellent-value combo dishes and bargain house wine. Mon–Thurs & Sun 11am–10.30pm, Fri & Sat 11am–11pm. Inexpensive.

District Chophouse & Brewery 509 7th St NW ☏**347-3434**; Gallery Place–Chinatown Metro. Classy Swing-era joint with great music and a grill-house menu. Portions are huge, which softens the prices a bit, and you could order a burger, which comes with the house salad, and soak up the atmosphere for just ten bucks. Reservations advised. Mon 11am–10pm, Tues–Thurs 11am–11pm, Fri 11am–midnight, Sat 4pm–midnight, Sun 4–10pm. Expensive.

Haad Thai 1100 New York Ave NW, entrance on 11th St ☏**682-1111**; Metro Center Metro. Opposite the Convention Center, this classy, business-oriented Thai restaurant features coconut-milk curries, tasty steamed fish and shrimp, and spicy soups. Mon–Fri 11.30am–2.30pm & 5–10.30pm, Sat noon–10.30pm, Sun 5–10.30pm. Moderate.

Jaleo 480 7th St NW ☏**628-7949**; Gallery Place–Chinatown Metro. Renowned upscale tapas bar-restaurant with fashionable young things draped across the tables. As the limited reservation policy and long waits can put a crimp on an otherwise fun evening, call in early for a glass of good house wine and some of the fabulous tapas or consider dining at the snazzy bar. Mon & Sun 11.30am–10pm, Tues–Thurs 11.30am–11.30pm, Fri & Sat 11.30am–midnight. Moderate (tapas); Expensive (restaurant).

The Mark 401 7th St NW ☏**783-3133**; Gallery Place–Chinatown Metro. Fashionable dining on now happening 7th, with seasonally changing, Modern American interpretations of dishes like roast chicken, strip steak, salmon and ravioli; vegetarians should do well, too (wild mushrooms are a favorite). There's a select choice of wines by the glass. Mon 11.30am–3pm &

5–9.30pm, Tues–Thurs 11.30am–3pm & 5–10.30pm, Fri & Sat 11.30am–3pm & 5–11pm, Sun 11am–3pm & 5–9pm. Expensive.

Old Ebbitt Grill 675 15th St NW ☏**347-4801**; Metro Center Metro. In business in various locations since 1856, this plush re-creation of a nineteenth-century tavern is a joy, with mahogany bar (serving microbrews), gas chandeliers, leather booths and gilt mirrors. Professional/politico clientele feasts on everything from burgers to oysters, breakfasts to late dinners. Mon–Fri 7.30am–midnight, Sat 8am–midnight, Sun 9.30am–midnight; bar open Mon–Thurs & Sun until 1.30am, Fri & Sat until 2.30am. Expensive.

Red Sage 605 14th St NW ☏**638-4444**; Metro Center Metro. Landmark Southwestern restaurant, owned by Mark Miller and dripping with Santa Fe chic, featuring rotisserie-grilled meat, fish and vegetarian specials. The funkily decorated café-bar is less exclusive, though the menu is more mainstream (but still miles better than any of the Southwestern pretenders). Reservations essential for the restaurant. Restaurant Mon–Sat 11.30am–10pm, Sun 5–10pm; café Mon–Sat 11.30am–11.30pm, Sun 5–10pm. Moderate (café); Very expensive (restaurant).

Sky Terrace Hotel Washington, 515 15th St NW ☏**638-5900**; Metro Center Metro. When the weather warms, take a break from pounding the tourist beat to enjoy a sweeping view of the city and a simple sandwich. While the food is nothing special, it's a bargain considering the outdoor perch above the White House. Daily 11am–1am (May–Oct only). Inexpensive–Moderate.

Dupont Circle

Cafés, snacks and light meals

Afterwords Café 1517 Connecticut Ave NW ☏**387-1462**; Dupont Circle Metro. In the back of Kramerbooks, this spot serves breakfast and brunch, great cappuccino and full meals – salad, pastas, grills and sandwiches, with plenty of vegetarian choices. Live blues and jazz Wednesday through Saturday. Mon–Thurs & Sun 7.30am–1am, Fri & Sat 24hr.

Cyberstop Café 1513 17th St NW ☏**234-2470**; Dupont Circle Metro. One of DC's very few

12

EATING

RESTAURANTS & CAFÉS
Afterwords Café	23	Cyberstop Café	26	Jolt 'n' Bolt	8	Skewers	32
Annie's Paramount Steakhouse	21	Duplex Diner	1	Lauriol Plaza	9	SoHo Tea & Coffee	34
Ben's Chili Bowl	3	Firehook Bakery & Coffeehouse	19	Luna Grill & Diner	41	Sushi Taro	31
Bistro du Coin	12	Franklin's Coffeehouse Café	2	Marvelous Market	23	Tabard Inn	42
Café Citron	40			Newsroom	10	Teaism	14
Café Luna	33	Gabriel	29	Nora's	15	Thai Chef	13
City Lights of China	11	Java House	22	Pizzeria Paradiso	30	U-topia	5
Coppi's	6	Johnny's Half Shell	35	Prego Again	20	Zorba's Café	16

cybercafés, this laid-back neighborhood coffee shop serves good java, cakes and bagels, with seating inside the arty townhouse or out front on the sidewalk patio. Daily 7am–midnight.

Firehook Bakery & Coffeehouse 1909 Q St NW ☎588-9296; Dupont Circle Metro. The renowned bakery-café serves up daily sandwich specials and a huge range of breads (also pies, desserts and cookies) – plus good coffee at reasonable prices. There's not much in the way of comfortable seating at this branch, though. Mon–Fri 7am–9pm, Sat & Sun 8am–9pm.

Java House 1645 Q St NW ☎387-6622; Dupont Circle Metro. This Dupont favorite arguably serves the neighborhood's best coffee – grab a cup to go or scramble for a sunny seat on the packed patio, a good

spot to read a book or have an afternoon chat. Muesli, bagels and breakfast sandwiches are on offer throughout the day. Daily 7am–midnight.

Marvelous Market 1511 Connecticut Ave NW ☎332-3690; Dupont Circle Metro. Superb carryout deli with ready-made sandwiches, a selection of cheeses and olives, fresh produce and very good brownies and bread. Mon–Sat 8am–9pm, Sun 8.30am–7pm.

The Newsroom 1803 Connecticut Ave NW ☎332-1489; Dupont Circle Metro. Coffee, snacks and pastries are served at this newsstand, which carries one of DC's best selections of hipster magazines, British and French imports and hard-to-find newspapers. There's internet access upstairs. Daily 7am–9pm.

Prego Again 1617 17th St NW ☎745-7007; Dupont Circle Metro. Popular spot for locals looking to recharge with a refreshing fresh-squeezed juice or smoothie. If it's something more substantial you're after, grab a salad, some sushi or a sandwich – the Maryland crab roll is sublime – and hit the sidewalk patio. Mon–Sat 7.30am–8.30pm, Sun 8.30am–8.30pm.

Teaism 2009 R St NW ☎667-3827; Dupont Circle Metro. This serene Asian-inspired teahouse serves Japanese bento boxes, Thai curries, yummy ginger scones and, of course, tea. If you're looking to stock up on tea leaves, you'll find three dozen types on offer here as well as assorted teapots and mugs. Mon–Thurs 8am–10pm, Fri 8am–11pm, Sat 9am–11pm, Sun 9am–10pm.

Restaurants

Bistro du Coin 1738 Connecticut Ave NW ☎234-6969; Dupont Circle Metro. Classic bistro with a superb bar, boisterous atmosphere and genuine French food that actually tastes like French food – a rare treat in DC. All at prices that won't cost you your Armani shirt. Tues & Wed 11.30am–11pm, Thurs–Sat 11.30am–1am, Sun 11.30am–11pm. Moderate–Expensive.

Café Citron 1343 Connecticut Ave NW ☎530-8844; Dupont Circle Metro. Hip Dupont South restaurant serving tasty Caribbean-influenced Latin food – try the ceviche or fill up on one of their popular fajitas. By ten, the dining crowd makes way for smartly dressed thirtysomethings to groove to tunes provided by DJs or live Brazilian or salsa/merengue bands – and to fuel up on some of the best mojitos in town. Mon–Sat 11am–midnight; bar stays open until 1.30am. Moderate.

Café Luna 1633 P St NW ☎387-4005; Dupont Circle Metro. Italian coffee, breakfast, weekend brunches and substantial sandwiches, pasta and pizza in a laid-back hangout with a handful of sunny sidewalk tables. One of Dupont's best. Mon–Thurs 8am–11pm, Fri 8am–1am, Sat 10am–1am, Sun 10am–11pm. Inexpensive.

City Lights of China 1731 Connecticut Ave NW ☎265-6688; Dupont Circle Metro. Above-average, well-priced Chinese restaurant, with spicy Szechuan and Hunan specialties and a strong emphasis on seafood – try the Hunan shrimp. It's also one of the few Chinese spots that does vegetarian food right – standouts include the steamed dumplings and garlic eggplant. Mon–Thurs 11.30am–10.30pm, Fri 11.30am–11pm, Sat noon–11pm, Sun noon–10.30pm. Moderate.

Gabriel 2121 P St NW ☎956-6690; Dupont Circle Metro. New-wave Spanish restaurant at the *Radisson Barceló* hotel that has gathered plaudits for its inventive tapas and sherry list, great Sunday brunch, and a full range of delicately flavored, lightly spiced, grilled and seared meat and fish entrées. Reservations recommended. Mon–Thurs & Sun 11.30am–10pm, Fri & Sat 11.30am– 11pm. Moderate (tapas); Expensive (restaurant).

Johnny's Half Shell 2002 P St NW ☎296-2021; Dupont Circle Metro. Retro 1920s décor and a swank marble bar sit well with this bistro's down-to-earth menu. It features local seafood specialties like crabs and rockfish – go for the very good gumbo or, in summer, the soft-shell crabs. Mon–Sat 11.30am–11pm; bar open past midnight. Moderate–Expensive.

Ten great places for brunch

Weekend brunch – mostly Sunday, but Saturday too at some places – is a Washington institution. The city's most prestigious hotels offer the best spreads (like that at Georgetown's *Four Seasons*) and provide visitors and locals with a relatively inexpensive way to experience their dining rooms. But many restaurants pride themselves on their brunches, too. The places listed below may not all offer the swanky surroundings and free champagne refills of the hotels (though some do), but all in their way are excellent. Follow the page references for full reviews.

△ Comings and goings at the *Old Ebbitt Grill*, Old Downtown

Lauriol Plaza 1801 18th St NW ☎ 387-0035; Dupont Circle Metro. Lines form early at this packed, family-run restaurant for the excellent Mexican, Spanish and Latin American food – the fajitas are stunning. Eat on the sidewalk patio or the rooftop terrace in summer, although it's easier to score a table in the industrial-chic interior. Mon–Thurs & Sun 11.30am–11pm, Fri & Sat noon–midnight. Moderate.

Luna Grill & Diner 1301 Connecticut Ave NW ☎ 835-2280; Dupont Circle Metro. "Not your usual diner" by virtue of its bright décor, planetary murals and mosaics, and wholesome blue-plate specials, "green plate" (vegetarian) dishes, and organic coffees and teas. Also makes for an excellent weekend brunch spot; try the "Eggs Neptune" – eggs Benedict with a Maryland twist, crab cakes. Outdoor patio, too. Mon–Fri 11am–10pm, Sat & Sun 10.30am–11pm. Inexpensive.

Nora's 2132 Florida Ave NW ☎ 462-5143; Dupont Circle Metro. Set in a converted corner store with walls tastefully decorated with Amish and Mennonite quilts, this New American gem is considered one of DC's best, setting itself apart with down-home elegance and a personal touch. What's more, it's the nation's first certified all-organic restaurant. Book ahead. Mon–Thurs 5.30–10pm. Fri & Sat 5.30–10.30pm. Very expensive.

Pizzeria Paradiso 2029 P St NW ☎ 223-1245; Dupont Circle Metro. Arguably DC's best pizzeria, with lines forming nightly on the steps outside. Thunderingly good food and affordable house wine. Mon–Thurs 11am–11pm, Fri & Sat 11am–midnight, Sun noon–10pm. Inexpensive.

Skewers 1633 P St NW ☎ 387-7400; Dupont Circle Metro. It has Dupont Circle's funkiest interior, but the food doesn't take a backseat to the décor. The restaurant (above *Café Luna*) is tops for grilled spits of meat or seafood with delicately flavored rice. Or put together a meal of Middle Eastern appetizers. Mon–Thurs 11.30am–11pm, Fri 11.30am–midnight, Sat 5pm–midnight, Sun 5–11pm. Moderate.

Sushi Taro 1507 17th St NW ☎ 462-8999; Dupont Circle Metro. While one wouldn't expect sushi the spot sliced above a Dupont East CVS, the steady stream of Japanese suits seeking a taste of home testifies that this is indeed one of DC's very best

Japanese restaurants. If raw fish isn't your thing, choose from the selection of tasty curries and noodles. When the cherry blossoms start to bloom, keep an eye out for the annual all-you-can-eat sushi-fest. Mon–Fri 11.30am–2pm & 5.30–10pm, Sat & Sun 5.30–10pm. Moderate-Expensive.

Thai Chef 1712 Connecticut Ave NW ☎ 234-5698; Dupont Circle Metro. While you'd have to journey far into the wilds of Virginia to find the area's best Thai joints, ex-pat Thais stranded in Dupont settle for this easy going hangout, where they praise the pad thai, squid salad and, when in season, the *bu nim* (soft-shell crabs). Mon–Thurs 11.30am–3.30pm & 4.30–10.45pm, Fri 11.30am–11pm, Sat noon–11pm, Sun noon–10.45pm. Moderate.

Zorba's Café 1612 20th St NW ☎ 387-8555; Dupont Circle Metro. Filling Greek combo platters, kebabs and pita-bread sandwiches, as well as daily specials and traditional dishes like bean casserole and spinach pie. Wash down one of the very good gyro sandwiches or tasty pizzas with pitchers of draft beer. Everything comes on plastic plates – it's self-service, with hard-to-get sidewalk seating in summer. Mon–Sat 11am–11.30pm, Sun noon–10.30pm. Budget.

Foggy Bottom

Cafés, snacks and light meals

The Breadline 1751 Pennsylvania Ave NW ☎ 822-8900; Farragut West Metro. DC's best sandwiches made with DC's best bread. This superb open bakery (with seats inside and out) also turns out pizza, empanadas, flatbreads, salads, smoothies, coffee and tea, using (pricey) organic ingredients where possible. Mon–Fri 7am–6pm.

Café des Artistes 500 17th St NW ☎ 639-1700; Farragut West or Farragut North Metro. This Corcoran Gallery café serves coffee, tea and lunches. Go for the shrimp salad on a croissant or the grilled chicken Caesar salad. Book for the elaborate $19 gospel brunch (Sun 11am–2pm). Mon, Wed & Fri–Sun 11am–2pm, Thurs 11am–8pm.

Capitol Grounds 2100 Pennsylvania Ave NW ☎ 293-2057; Foggy Bottom–GWU Metro. Breakfast, gourmet sandwiches, salads and good coffee, also a handy GWU location and seats inside and out. Mon–Fri 7am–6pm, Sat 8.30am–4pm, Sun 9am–3pm.

Cosi Sandwich Bar 1700 Pennsylvania Ave NW
☎638-6366; Farragut West Metro. Just a
short hop from both the White House and
Corcoran, this franchise lunch spot is good
for a quick bite while on the tour circuit –
although you'd be wise to avoid the midday
crush. An assortment of tasty, if pricey,
sandwiches on freshly baked flatbread is
served. Mon–Fri 7am–7pm, Sat & Sun
9am–6pm.

Restaurants

Art Gallery Bar & Grille 1712 I St NW ☎298-
6658; Farragut West Metro. Play the
Wurlitzer jukebox and soak up the Art Deco
ambience or sit on the outdoor patio as you
tuck into breakfast, salads, burgers,
sandwiches, omelets, pizza and grills.
Mon–Fri 7.30am–10pm. Moderate.
Jeffrey's at the Watergate 2650 Virginia Ave
NW ☎965-2300; Foggy Bottom–GWU Metro.
A Texas favorite of the First Family, this
upscale New American–Southwestern
hybrid was ushered into DC on the coattails
of President Bush. Sample the Texas Crispy
Gulf Oysters, a specialty. Daily 7–10.30am,
11.30am–2pm & 5–10pm. Expensive–Very
expensive.
Kinkead's 2000 Pennsylvania Ave NW ☎296-
7700; Foggy Bottom–GWU Metro. One of
DC's favorite restaurants, with a
contemporary American menu specializing
in fish and seafood. It's pricey, but worth
every cent. You'll need to book ahead.
Mon–Wed & Sun 11.30am–2.30pm &
5.30–10pm, Thurs–Sat 11.30am–2.30pm &
5.30–11pm. Very expensive.
Zuki Moon 824 New Hampshire Ave NW ☎333-
3312; Foggy Bottom–GWU Metro. Spiffy
Japanese-style noodle bar where diners
hunker down over big, lip-smacking bowls
of soba or udon noodle soups. Before and
after, try the tempura appetizer and the
green-tea ice cream. It's all great value and
a good choice if you're heading on to the
Kennedy Center. Mon–Fri
11.30am–2.30pm & 5–11pm, Sat & Sun
5–11pm. Inexpensive–Moderate.

Georgetown

Cafés, snacks and light meals

Booeymonger 3265 Prospect St NW ☎333-
4810. Crowded deli-coffee shop at the

corner of Prospect and Potomac streets,
popular with students. Daily 8am–midnight.
Ching Ching Cha 1063 Wisconsin Ave NW,
☎333-8288. Bright and pleasant tearoom
transports teetotalers to Old Asia with a tidy
menu of appetizers and mains and an array
of snazzy collectibles for sale. Tues–Sat
11.30am–9pm.
Dean & Deluca 3276 M St NW ☎342-2500.
Superior self-service conservatory-style
café (and fantastic attached deli-market
with sushi stand) in one of M Street's most
handsome red-brick buildings. Croissants
and cappuccino, designer salads, pasta
and sandwiches. Café Mon–Thurs & Sun
8am–8pm, Fri & Sat 8am–7pm; market
Mon–Thurs & Sun 10am–8pm, Fri & Sat
10am–9pm.
Furin's 2805 M St NW ☎965-1000.
Georgetown's best bet for a home-cooked
eggs-and-fries breakfast, blue-plate lunch,
or soup, salad and sandwich. Mon–Fri
7.30am–7pm, Sat 8am–5pm.

Restaurants

Amma Vegetarian Kitchen 3291 M St NW
☎625-6625. A scrumptious safe haven for
strict vegetarians, this South Indian joint
specializes in *dosa* – lentil and rice flour
wraps – but also has very good curries and
yummy breads, including hard-to-find
bathura. Mon–Thurs 11.30am–2.30pm &
5.30–10pm, Fri 11.30am–2.30pm &
5.30–10.30pm, Sat 11.30am–3.30pm &
5.30–10.30pm, Sun noon–3.30pm &
5.30–10pm. Inexpensive.
Au Pied de Cochon 1335 Wisconsin Ave NW
☎337-6400. So the food isn't the best
French you've ever had – you can't fault the
availability or the prices. The 24hr bistro-
bar serves breakfast (until noon), $10 early-
bird dinners (3–8pm), and a *carte* of eggs,
fish, coq au vin, steaks and the like. Daily
24hr. Inexpensive–Moderate.
Bangkok Bistro 3251 Prospect St NW ☎337-
2424. Pitches some style into Thai dining
with a sleek dining room that's often full.
The old favorites (tom yum, pad thai,
shrimp cakes and satay) sit alongside new
takes on mussels (steamed in lemongrass
broth), grilled chicken, vegetarian noodles,
grilled fish and curries. Mon–Thurs
11.30am–11pm, Fri 11.30am–midnight, Sat
noon–midnight, Sun noon–11pm.
Moderate.

12

EATING

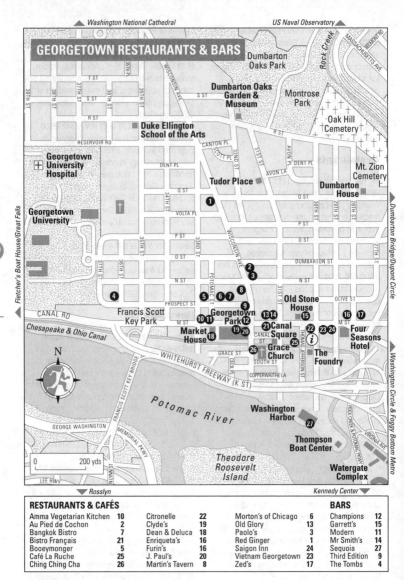

Fletcher's Boat House/Great Falls ◄

Chesapeake & Ohio Canal

Dumbarton Bridge/Dupont Circle ►

Washington Circle & Foggy Bottom Metro ►

Rock Creek & Potomac Pkwy ►

▲ *Washington National Cathedral*   *US Naval Observatory* ▲

GEORGETOWN RESTAURANTS & BARS

▼ *Rosslyn*   *Kennedy Center* ▼

RESTAURANTS & CAFÉS				BARS	
Amma Vegetarian Kitchen	10	Citronelle	22	Morton's of Chicago	6	Champions	12
Au Pied de Cochon	2	Clyde's	19	Old Glory	13	Garrett's	15
Bangkok Bistro	7	Dean & Deluca	18	Paolo's	3	Modern	11
Bistro Français	21	Enriqueta's	16	Red Ginger	1	Mr Smith's	14
Booeymonger	5	Furin's	16	Saigon Inn	24	Sequoia	27
Café La Ruche	25	J. Paul's	20	Vietnam Georgetown	23	Third Edition	9
Ching Ching Cha	26	Martin's Tavern	8	Zed's	17	The Tombs	4

Bistro Français 3128 M St NW ☎338-3830.
Renowned for its French cooking, from a
simple steak-frites, rotisserie chicken and
roast pigeon to more complex, traditional
dishes, this bistro stays open late. There
are early-bird (5–7pm) and late-night
(10.30pm–1am) set dinners for under $20,
but check the specials board for what the
kitchen does best. Mon–Thurs & Sun

11am–3am, Fri & Sat 11am–4am.
Moderate.

Café la Ruche 1039 31st St NW ☎965-2684.
Relaxing bistro away from M Street's
madding crowds, with patio seating ideal
for dining alone or in twos in warmer
weather. Count on the onion soup, quiches
and croques or drop by for a pastry and an
espresso. Mon–Thurs 11.30am–10pm, Fri

11.30am–midnight, Sat 10am–2am, Sun 10am–midnight. Budget–Inexpensive.

Clyde's 3236 M St NW ☎333-9180. Classic New York-style saloon-restaurant featuring the obligatory checked tablecloths, Art Deco lampshades and burnished wood interior. It's a Georgetown institution, which makes weekend dinner reservations essential. Book ahead for the great Sunday brunch, too. Mon–Thurs 11.30am–2am, Fri 11.30am–3pm, Sat 10am–3am, Sun 9am–2am. Moderate.

Enriqueta's 2811 M St NW ☎338-7772. Perhaps the best genuine Mexican restaurant in DC. Not a fancy place, but one offering fine, flavorful servings of pork, chicken, beef and shrimp. Be guided by your waiter, but don't miss the mussels appetizer and the excellent margaritas. Mon–Thurs 11.30am–2.30pm & 5–10pm, Fri 11.30am–2.30pm & 5–11pm, Sat 5–11pm, Sun 5–10pm. Inexpensive–Moderate.

J. Paul's 3218 M St NW ☎333-3450. Rivaling *Clyde's* in clientele, style and popularity. Distinctive points are a great raw bar and its own-brewed Amber Ale; otherwise, it's the standard grill/barbecue menu, all of it usually excellent. Try the famous crab cakes. Last orders for food are taken around midnight. Mon–Thurs 11.30am–1.30am, Fri & Sat 11.30am–2.30am, Sun 10.30am–1.30am. Moderate.

Martin's Tavern 1264 Wisconsin Ave NW ☎333-7370. Four generations of the Martin family (the first including a professional baseball player) have run front-of-house here and counted politicos from JFK to Nixon among their regulars. The old-fashioned, clubby saloon serves up famous steaks and chops, great burgers, linguine with clam sauce, and oyster platters – or come for the popular brunch (Sun 10am–3pm). Mon–Thurs 10am–11pm, Fri 10am–1am, Sat 8am–1am, Sun 8am–11pm. Moderate–Expensive.

Morton's of Chicago 3251 Prospect St NW ☎342-6258. Premium steak-house chain's Georgetown branch makes a fabulous porterhouse. Pick your cut – and make sure you've come with a *huge* appetite – or go for entrées ($20 and up) from chicken to swordfish. Mon–Sat 5.30–11pm, Sun 5–10pm. Very expensive.

Old Glory 3139 M St NW ☎337-3406. Rollicking barbecue restaurant with hickory smoke rising in earnest from the kitchen. Accompany your huge portions of ribs and chicken with one of the half-dozen sauces on every table and a shot of great bourbon. Mon–Thurs & Sun 11.30am–11.30pm, Fri & Sat 11.30am–12.30am. Moderate.

Paolo's 1303 Wisconsin Ave NW, at M St ☎333-7353. Designer Italian dining with a few, hotly contested, tables open to the sidewalk. Gourmet pizza (with such toppings as feta cheese, grappa-cured salmon, goat's cheese, spinach and sun-dried tomato) and even better pasta are specialties; save room for dessert. Mon–Thurs & Sun 11.30am–12.30am, Fri & Sat 11.30am–1.30am. Moderate.

Red Ginger 1564 Wisconsin Ave NW ☎965-7009. Colorful Caribbean bistro brings a splash of the islands to Georgetown, with plenty of rum for everyone. Mon–Thurs 6–10.30pm, Fri & Sat 6pm–midnight, Sun 6–11pm. Moderate.

Saigon Inn 2928 M St NW ☎337-5588. The food served in this eager-to-please Vietnamese restaurant makes a few concessions to Western tastes, but is still eminently enjoyable. The lunch deal (four dishes for under $5, Mon–Fri 11am–3pm) is a real steal. Mon–Thurs 11am–11pm, Fri & Sat 11am–midnight, Sun noon–11pm. Inexpensive.

Vietnam Georgetown 2934 M St NW ☎337-4536. The best Vietnamese restaurant in Georgetown, with a touch more flair than the adjacent *Saigon Inn*. Specials include terrific grilled lemon chicken, stuffed crepes, and shrimp curry to warm the heart. Mon–Thurs 11am–11pm, Fri & Sat 11am–11.30pm, Sun noon–11pm. Moderate.

Zed's 1201 28St NW ☎333-4710. *The* spot for Ethiopian food in Georgetown, and an intimate one at that. The set lunch is cheap but eating from the menu won't ever break the bank. The *doro wot* (chicken stew in a red pepper sauce) is a good, spicy choice. Mon–Thurs & Sun 11am–11pm, Fri & Sat 11am–1am. Inexpensive.

Southwest

Cafés, snacks and light meals

Custis & Brown 12th St and Maine Ave SW ☎484-0168; L'Enfant Plaza Metro. Fish Wharf seafood stand serving humongous fried-fish sandwiches, steamed spiced shrimp, crab and lobster, clam chowder and oyster platters to go – all at giveaway prices. Great for a lunch or sundowner picnic overlooking the Washington Channel. Daily 8am–8pm.

Restaurants

Hogate's 800 Water St SW ☎484-6300; L'Enfant Plaza Metro. Marina restaurant with zealous nautical interior, air-conditioned bar and patio. The river view is the main attraction, for which hundreds pack in to sample the spiced-shrimp lunch buffet and uninspired seafood à la carte menu. Mon–Thurs 11am–11pm, Fri 11am–midnight, Sat noon–midnight, Sun 10.30am–10pm. Moderate–Expensive.

Phillips 900 Water St SW ☎488-8515; L'Enfant Plaza Metro. The second major Waterfront seafoodery is also firmly on the tour-bus circuit, and only those looking for quantity from the lunch, dinner and weekend brunch buffets are going to get much from the menu. Daily 11am–11pm. Moderate–Expensive.

U Street and Shaw

Cafés, snacks and light meals

Ben's Chili Bowl 1213 U St NW ☎667-0909; U Street–Cardozo Metro. Venerable U Street hangout across from the Metro, serving renowned chili dogs, burgers, milk shakes and cheese fries at booths and counter stools. A scene in *The Pelican Brief* was shot here, as photos on the wall attest. Mon–Thurs 6am–2am, Fri & Sat 6am–4am, Sun noon–8pm.

Restaurants

Coppi's 1414 U St NW ☎319-7773; U Street–Cardozo Metro. For an indication of how much the neighborhood has changed, look no further than this trendy little pizza palace with its brick oven, cycling-photo fetish and yuppie-collegiate clientele. The menu offers plenty of choice at decent prices. Mon–Thurs 5pm–midnight, Fri & Sat 5pm–1am, Sun 5–11pm. Inexpensive–Moderate.

Florida Avenue Grill 1100 Florida Ave NW ☎265-1586; U Street–Cardozo Metro. Southern-style diner serving hearty meals

for almost half a century to locals and stray celebs. Tues–Sat 6.30am–9pm. Inexpensive.

U-topia 1418 U St NW ☎483-7669; U Street–Cardozo Metro. Arty, romantic bar-restaurant with regular live blues and jazz, art exhibits, good veggie dishes and a popular weekend brunch. Mon–Thurs & Sun 11am–2am, Fri & Sat 11am–3am. Inexpensive–Moderate.

Union Station

Cafés, snacks and light meals

Center Café Union Station, 50 Massachusetts Ave NE ☎682-0143; Union Station Metro. Split-level café-restaurant in the main hall. Also breakfast (8–11am) or coffee – served in large French-style cups – and cake. Daily 8am–10pm.

Restaurants

America Union Station, 50 Massachusetts Ave NE ☎682-9555; Union Station Metro. Bustling restaurant-bar with a huge menu culled from all corners of the US, but the people-watching is far better than the food. Double-decker restaurant inside, concourse or gallery seating outside. Mon–Thurs & Sun 11.30am–11.30pm, Fri & Sat 11.30am–1am. Moderate.

B. Smith's Union Station, 50 Massachusetts Ave NE ☎289-6188; Union Station Metro. Cooking from the American South brings in folks hankering after fried-green tomatoes, Cajun paella, catfish, and red beans 'n' rice, though just as many come for the glorious restaurant space – this was once the station's presidential waiting room. Mon–Thurs 11.30am–4pm & 5–11pm, Fri & Sat 11.30am–4pm & 5pm–midnight, Sun 11.30am–4pm & 5–9pm. Expensive.

Upper Northwest

Cafés, snacks and light meals

Firehook 3411 Connecticut Ave NW ☎362-2253; Cleveland Park Metro. Breads, cakes, cookies and very good coffee are all on offer at this DC institution's Cleveland Park outpost; seating in the wonderful garden completes the scene. Mon 7am–8pm, Tues–Thurs 7am–10pm, Fri 7am–11pm,

Sat 8am–11pm, Sun 8am–9pm.

Krupin's 4620 Wisconsin Ave NW ☎686-1989;
Tenleytown Metro. Jewish deli-diner with
attitude – it's a long way from anywhere,
but devotees consider the trek worth it for
the true tastes of hot corned beef, lox and
bagel platters, stuffed cabbage, pastrami
and the rest. Daily 8am–10pm.

Vace 3315 Connecticut Ave NW ☎363-1999;
Cleveland Park Metro. Grab a slice of the
excellent pizza or pack a picnic from this
deli's selection of sausage, tortellini salad
and olives and head for the zoo. Mon–Fri
9am–9pm, Sat 9am–8pm, Sun 10am–5pm.

Restaurants

Ardeo 3311 Connecticut Ave NW ☎244-6750;
Cleveland Park Metro. This chic New
American bistro is a favorite haunt of media
celebrities. The equally flash *Bardeo*, a wine
bar with a tasting menu, is attached.
Mon–Thurs 5.30–10.30pm, Fri & Sat
5.30–11.30pm, Sun 11am–2.30pm &
5–10pm. Expensive.

Cactus Cantina 3300 Wisconsin Ave NW
☎686-7222; no nearby Metro stop. *Lauriol
Plaza*'s Cleveland Park sibling makes for a
festive Tex-Mex treat for Cathedral-goers.
Although it lacks the chic décor of its
Dupont counterpart (see p.268), it has a
great veranda and the food can be every bit
as good. Mon–Thurs 11.30am–11pm, Fri &
Sat 11.30am–midnight, Sun 11am–11pm.
Inexpensive–Moderate.

Lebanese Taverna 2641 Connecticut Ave NW
☎265-8681; Woodley Park–Zoo Metro.
Delicious Middle Eastern joint with
soothingly dark, authentic décor inside and
ample sidewalk tables under shady
umbrellas outside. Sample something from
the assortment of kebobs and platters, or
go straight for the leg of lamb. Mon–Fri
11.30am–2.30pm & 5.30–10.30pm, Sat
11.30am–3pm & 5.30–10.30pm, Sun
5–10pm. Moderate–Expensive.

Nam Viet 3419 Connecticut Ave NW ☎237-
1015; Cleveland Park Metro. No-frills
Vietnamese eatery frequented by Senator
John McCain. The soups are good, as are
the grilled chicken and fish, the caramel
pork, the Vietnamese steak – really, you
can't go wrong. Mon–Thurs 11am–3pm &
5–10pm, Fri & Sat 11am–11pm, Sun

11am–10pm. Inexpensive–Moderate.

New Heights 2317 Calvert St NW ☎234-4110;
Woodley Park–Zoo Metro. Fashionable,
new-wave American restaurant serving an
inventive, seasonal menu that culls its
influences from many cuisines. Book ahead
in summer to sit outside, especially for
Sunday brunch. Mon–Thurs & Sun
5.30–10.30pm, Fri & Sat 5.30–11pm; bar
open until 12.30am. Expensive.

Spices 3333 Connecticut Ave NW ☎686-3833;
Cleveland Park Metro. Stylish Pan-Asian
place serving spicy bowls of *laksa*, stir-fried
basil chicken and sushi in a spacious, high-
ceilinged dining room, complete with sushi
bar. Mon–Fri 11.30am–3pm & 5–11pm, Sat
noon–11pm, Sun 5–10.30pm.
Inexpensive–Moderate.

Woodley Café 2619 Connecticut Ave NW
☎332-5773; Woodley Park–Zoo Metro.
Roomy neighborhood café-bar attracting a
laid-back crowd. Breakfast and Sunday
brunch are good, there's a full menu for
lunch and dinner, and late-night pizza, too.
Daily 9am–10pm; later pizza and bar
service. Inexpensive.

Yanni's Greek Taverna 3500 Connecticut Ave
NW ☎362-8871; Cleveland Park Metro.
Popular pit stop before hitting the
Cleveland Park bars. Bargain grilled meat
platters, a tasty *tzatsiki* and pricier house
specials like squid and octopus. Daily
11.30am–11.30pm. Inexpensive.

Yanyu 3433 Connecticut Ave NW ☎686-6968;
Cleveland Park Metro. Celebrated for its
inventive Asian cuisine and elegant décor,
this Cleveland Park enclave ranks high on
the list of DC's upscale Asian restaurants.
Tues–Thurs & Sun 5.30–10.30pm, Fri & Sat
5.30–11pm. Expensive.

⑫

EATING

Drinking and nightlife

Bars, **clubs and pubs** congregate in distinct Washington DC neighborhoods, notably Capitol Hill (near Union Station and along Pennsylvania Ave SE), Georgetown (M and Wisconsin), Dupont Circle (along 17th and along Connecticut Ave), along U Street (near the Metro) and in Adams-Morgan, where a wide range of dining, drinking and dancing spots sit side by side at 18th and Columbia. The few bars downtown tend to cater to an after-work crowd, though there's a burgeoning bar district along 7th Street, near the MCI Center. There's also a thriving – if relatively small-scale – **gay scene**, with most of the action in Dupont Circle, especially on P Street (between 21st and 22nd) and 17th Street (between P and R); for more on these spots turn to Chapter 15.

Most bars are **open** daily from around noon until 2am, often later on the weekends. Virtually all have **happy hours** during which drinks are two-for-one or at least heavily discounted; the optimum time for these is weekdays between 4pm and 8pm. Some bars also offer free snacks to happy-hour drinkers.

DC's **club scene** moves at a frenetic pace – *CityPaper*, the *Washington Post*'s "Weekend" section, and the gay-oriented *Metro Weekly* and *Washington Blade* each carry schedules, reviews and ads. Clubs come and go in all of the above neighborhoods, but the trendiest area is in New Downtown, near the intersection of Connecticut Avenue and 18th Street (just north of M St), a section known as "Dupont South" due to its proximity to the Circle. The places listed below are some of the better-established venues in a city where clubs open and close with alarming regularity; you're sure to find others that are new or some that have changed hands and style. At many venues the music and clientele may change radically on different nights; call to check before setting out for a specific spot. If it's live music you're after, flip to Chapter 14 for more ideas.

Plenty of clubs have low or no **cover charges** – where they exist, they're generally between $5 and $15 (highest on weekends). Swanky lounges and clubs are most likely to charge a steeper cover, and more often than not they have vague and at times completely arbitrary **dress codes**; if you avoid athletic gear, sneakers and sandals, and baseball caps you'll greatly enhance your standing with the guardians of the velvet ropes. **Opening hours** vary wildly at DC clubs, though most places don't get going until well after 11pm and stay open until at least 3am, with some continuing (especially on weekends) until 5am. If you're going to be out this late, make sure you have a taxi number with you, since some clubs are in

All telephone numbers in this chapter are area code ☎202, unless otherwise stated.

dubious parts of town where walking around in the small hours invites trouble. Also remember to take **photo ID** or your passport with you; you won't get into many places without one. You must be at least 21 to drink alcohol in DC.

Adams-Morgan

All places listed in Adams-Morgan are within a few blocks of 18th Street, Columbia Road and Calvert Street. The closest Metro stations are Woodley Park–Zoo, a fifteen-minute walk away, and Dupont Circle, a twenty-minute walk.

Bedrock Billards 1841 Columbia Rd NW ☎667-7665. A lively if low-key subterranean setting, quality bartenders and loyal clientele set this funky pool hall apart from Adams-Morgan's more frenzied club scene. Mon–Thurs 4pm–2am, Fri 4pm–3am, Sat 1pm–3am, Sun 1pm–2am.

Blue Room 2321 18th St NW ☎332-0800. Classier than the typical Adams-Morgan fare, this swank venue, which boasts a bar worthy of Bogart's elbows, enforces a dress code with just enough attitude to set the scene without spoiling it. Wed, Thurs & Sun 9.30pm–2am, Fri & Sat 9.30pm–3am.

Café Toulouse 2431 18th St ☎238-9018. Eat out on the patio or cozy up inside in the dark old barroom for a beer or coffee. There's live jazz or blues most nights after 9pm. Mon–Thurs & Sun 6pm–2am, Fri & Sat 6pm–3am.

Chief Ike's Mambo Room 1725 Columbia Rd NW ☎332-2211. Ramshackle mural-clad bar (featured, briefly, in *Enemy of the State*) with live bands or DJs hosting theme nights. It all makes for an unpretentious, fun spot to dance. The *Chaos* bar upstairs has indie music and a pool table. Mon–Thurs & Sun 4pm–2am, Fri 4pm–3am, Sat noon–3am.

Cities 2424 18th St NW ☎328-7194. Periodically changing (cities-of-the-world) décor and menu brings in the high-fashion Eurocrowd. The outdoor terrace overlooks the Adams-Morgan streetlife parade; dance upstairs to world music or, in chilly weather, enjoy a bottle of wine on a comfy fireside couch. Mon–Thurs 5–11pm, Fri & Sat 5pm–3am, Sun 11am–11pm.

Columbia Station 2325 18th St NW ☎462-6040. Live jazz and blues nightly in a sophisticated supper-club setting. Mon–Thurs & Sun 11.30am–1.45am, Fri & Sat 11.30am–5am.

The Common Share 2003 18th St NW ☎588-7180. One of the district's cheapest watering holes, this welcoming and boisterous (if a bit grimy) dive attracts what is perhaps the neighborhood's most diverse crowd. They're reeled in by pints and rail drinks that cost a mere $2 and premium spirits that clock in at a kind $3. Mon–Thurs 5.30pm–2am, Fri & Sat 5.30pm–3am.

Habana Village 1834 Columbia Rd NW ☎462-6310. Intoxicating Latin dance joint infused with the eclectic spirit of the Adams-Morgan of old. Tango and salsa lessons are available (call for a schedule), and a good downstairs lounge/bar serves a fine mojito. Daily 7.30pm–3am.

Heaven & Hell 2327 18th St NW ☎667-4355. While *Hell* downstairs would have trouble making Dante's hit list, *Heaven* features techno, dance and live indie, reaching its cheesy best on 1980s night. On most evenings there's no real action until after 10.30pm, when the student/Goth crowd takes the floor. Occasional cover. Mon–Thurs & Sun 6pm–2am, Fri & Sat 6pm–3am.

Beer talk

Don't want another Bud? **Microbrews** are big business these days, and you'll be able to get a decent selection of beers in many bars. For the best choice, hit one of the city's brew-pubs – *Capitol City Brewing Company* (see Downtown: Old, p.278 & Union Station, p.281), *District Chophouse & Brewery* (Downtown: Old, p.278), *Gordon Biersch Brewery* (Downtown: Old, p.279), *John Harvard's* (Downtown: Old, p.279) – or the beer specialist *Brickskeller* (Dupont Circle, p.280). Elsewhere, keep an eye out for the following local brews: Foggy Bottom Ale (from DC), Virginia's Rock Creek, Potomac River or Dominion; and from Maryland, Blue Ridge, Clipper City and Wild Goose.

Millie and Al's 2440 18th St NW ☎387-8131. Crusty neighborhood tavern of a type all too rare in Adams-Morgan – food, beer and shots for local wastrels. Mon–Thurs 4pm–2am, Fri & Sat noon–3am, Sun noon–2am.

Rumba Cafe 2443 18th St NW ☎588-5501. A Latin oasis, this sliver of a café-bar, its walls rich with paintings and photographs, is a good bet for a night of sipping caipirinhas and grooving to live Brazilian bossa nova and Afro-Cuban rhythms. Tues–Sat 5pm–2am.

Toledo Lounge 2435 18th St NW ☎986-5416. Barebones café-bar with attitude, featuring windows looking out on the local streetlife. The patio seats, best spot for hanging out, are like gold dust in summer. Mon–Thurs 6pm–2am, Fri 6pm–3am, Sat noon–3am, Sun noon–2am.

Alexandria, VA

For details on how to get to Alexandria, see p.232.

Bayou Room. 219 King St ☎703/549-1141. Not your typical King Street spot, this stone-walled dungeon makes for a low-key local pub, with cheap, simple and tasty Cajun eats, TVs tuned to sports, and classic rock blaring over the sound system. Above, in *Two Nineteen*, there's a jazz lounge that serves Creole food in a more stylish setting. Daily 11.30am–1.30am.

Murphy's Grand Irish Pub 713 King St ☎703/548-1717. Old Town's nightlife revolves around this boisterous pub, where the city's best pint of Guinness is on tap. Local solo acts take to a small stage upstairs, urging packed weekend crowds on to drunken heights with their "Irish drinking songs." Mon–Sat 11am–2am, Sun 9am–midnight.

Union Street Public House 121 S Union St ☎703/548-1785. Old Town inn that's just as nice for eating as drinking, though it gets chock-full on weekends. Daily 11.30am–1.30am.

Virginia Beverage Company 607 King St ☎703/684-5397. Brew-pub in the traditional style with copper vats to the fore and half a dozen ales on tap. Mon–Thurs & Sun 11am–midnight, Fri & Sat 11am–1am.

Arlington, VA

Dr Dremo's Taphouse 2001 Clarendon Blvd ☎703/528-4660; Court House Metro. Drink the tasty beer brewed in nearby Rappahannock County, relax and shoot pool in this converted car showroom. Mon–Thurs & Sun 5pm–midnight, Fri & Sat 5pm–2am.

Ireland's Four Courts 2051 Wilson Blvd, at N Courthouse Rd ☎703/525-3600; Court House Metro. One of the nicest of the area's Irish bars, drawing a cheery Arlington crowd for the live music (Tues–Sat), dozen beers on tap, whiskey selection and filling food. Mon–Sat 11am–2am, Sun 10am–2am.

Whitlow's on Wilson 2854 Wilson Blvd ☎703/276-9693; Clarendon Metro. Neighborhood retro bar on Wilson with something going on most nights: happy hour drinks and food, live music, pool, or just hanging out in the booths or at the wraparound bar. Daily noon–2am.

Capitol Hill

Bullfeathers 410 First St SE ☎543-5005; Capitol South Metro. Pol watchers just may catch a sighting at this old-time Hill favorite, named for Teddy Roosevelt's favorite stand-in swear during his White House days. Mon–Sat 11am–10.30pm, Sun 10.30am–9pm.

Capitol Lounge 229 Pennsylvania Ave SE ☎547-2098; Capitol South Metro. More sophisticated than most of the Hill bars – cigars and martinis are de rigueur in the downstairs bar – but there's still plenty of life up in the brick-walled saloon thanks to happy hours (Wednesdays are a big hit), NFL on the TVs and DJs who whip up the weekend action. Mon–Thurs & Sun 11am–2am, Fri & Sat 11am–3am.

Hawk 'n' Dove 329 Pennsylvania Ave SE ☎543-3300; Capitol South Metro. Famous old pub, a bit tatty at the edges now, hung with football pennants, bottles and bric-a-brac. The young, loud crowd comes (depending on the night) for the cheap beer, half-price food or football on TV. Mon–Thurs & Sun 10am–2am, Fri & Sat 10am–3am.

Politiki and the Penn Ave Pourhouse 319 Pennsylvania Ave SE ☎546-1001; Capitol South Metro. Hill staffers and interns pour into this three-bars-in-one Hill hangout for the daily food and drink specials. There's a kitschy tiki bar with pool tables downstairs, a Swing-era/World War II-themed bar upstairs and, oddly enough, a gloriously down-to-earth ode to Pittsburgh in the middle, complete with Penn State pennants, kielbasa sandwiches and Iron City beer on tap. Mon–Fri 4pm–2am, Sat & Sun 11am–3am.

Tune Inn 331 Pennsylvania Ave SE ☎543-2725; Capitol South Metro. Crusty neighborhood dive bar that – next to the preppie *Hawk 'n' Dove* – seems to be in the wrong neighborhood. Settle down in a booth, munch on the burgers and feed the jukebox. Mon–Thurs & Sun 8am–2am, Fri & Sat 8am–3am.

Downtown: New

Dragonfly 1215 Connecticut Ave NW ☎331-1775; Dupont Circle Metro. This *Wallpaper*-hip sushi-and-cocktail bar, with its Jetsons décor and steady stream of japanimation, feels slightly out of sync with DC's nightlife. But, less snobbish than its neighbors, it's a good alternative on the Dupont South scene. Mon–Wed 5.30pm–1am, Thurs–Sat 5.30pm–2am, Sun 6pm–1am.

Eighteenth Street Lounge 1212 18th St ☎466-3922; Dupont Circle Metro. One of the District's best nights out, the ESL manages to be ultrastylish and yet very DC. Housed discreetly in Teddy Roosevelt's former mansion, the space – all hardwood floors and high ceilings – is now home to Thievery Corporation, whose members sometimes take a turn on the decks. While the attitude can be a bit thick at times, especially on the weekends, the beats – mostly acid jazz, dub and trip-hop – are always smooth. Look for the unmarked door next to the mattress shop and dress smart. Come early to beat the cover and line. Tues & Wed 9.30pm–2am, Thurs 5.30pm–2am, Fri 5.30pm–3am, Sat 9.30pm–3am.

Lucky Bar 1221 Connecticut Ave NW ☎331-3733; Farragut North or Dupont Circle Metro. Everybody-knows-your-name kind of place, with plenty of room and booths at the back to hang out and shoot pool. Dance nights, cheap drinks and English soccer on TV – it all makes for a home-from-home for some. Mon–Fri noon–2am, Sat & Sun 4pm–2am.

Lulu's Club Mardis Gras 1217 22nd St NW ☎861-5858; Foggy Bottom–GWU Metro. There's DJ rock and pop and a wild party scene every night at this good-natured club. Small cover on the weekend, when lines form early. Mon–Thurs 4pm–2am, Fri & Sat 4pm–3am.

The Madhatter 1831 M St NW ☎833-1495; Farragut North or West Metro. Homey saloon where the after-office crowd – in for the 4pm to 8pm happy hour – gives way later to a free-and-easy student set. DJ music Tuesday through Friday from 9pm. Mon–Fri 1.30pm–1.30am, Sat 11.30am–2am, Sun 10.30am–midnight.

Ozio 1813 M St NW ☎822-6000; Farragut North or Dupont Circle Metro. Ritzy cigar bar and lounge popular with the District's beautiful types. Treat yourself to a cocktail. Mon–Thurs 11.30am–2am, Fri 11.30am–3am, Sat 6pm–3am.

Red 1802 Jefferson Place NW ☎466-3475; Dupont Circle Metro. A diverse crowd shows up well past midnight at this hip underground hideout to get down to deep house beats, often until dawn. With sparse seating and a tiny bar, there's little space for anything but dancing. Mon–Thurs 10pm–3am, Fri & Sat 10pm–5am.

Tequila Grill, 1990 K St NW ☎833-3640; Farragut West Metro. No one really comes to eat the Tex-Mex food; instead a young, after-work mob packs in for the very good happy-hour specials. Mon–Thurs & Sun 11.30am–1.30am, Fri & Sat 11.30am–2.30am.

Downtown: Old

Capitol City Brewing Company 1100 New York Ave NW, entrance at 11th and H ☎628-2222; Metro Center Metro. Copper vats, pipes and gantries adorn this techno-microbrewery, serving a changing menu of home-brewed beers to an excitable bunch of drinkers. In September, the Mid-Atlantic Beer and Food Festival kicks off here. Daily 11am–2am.

DC Live 932 F St NW ☎347-7200; Gallery Place–Chinatown Metro. Huge downtown space (once a department store) attracts a mainly African-American crowd, though Thursday club nights see more of a mix. The music is reggae, world, salsa, Top 40, hip-hop, or jazz, depending on the night; call for schedule. Wed & Fri–Sun 9pm–3am.

District Chophouse & Brewery, 509 7th St NW ☎347-3434; Gallery Place–Chinatown Metro. This stunning conversion of an old downtown banking hall lends Swing-era class to the emerging neighborhood. Come to eat or just stop by for a drink – the busy

Some of DC's restaurants have very funky bars in their own right – you'll be welcome to stay for just a drink in any of the following.

America, Union Station, p.272
B. Smith's, Union Station, p.272
Bukom Café, Adams-Morgan, p.256
Café Citron, New Downtown, p.266
Cashion's Eat Place, Adams-Morgan, p.257
Gabriel, Dupont Circle, p.266

Grillfish, New Downtown, p.262
Jaleo, Old Downtown, p.264
Johnny's Half Shell, Dupont Circle p.266
Old Ebbitt Grill, Old Downtown, p.264
Perry's, Adams-Morgan, p.258
Red Sage, Old Downtown, p.264

bar serves five or six of its own brews. Mon–Thurs & Sun 11am–12.30am, Fri & Sat 11am–1.30am.

ESPN Zone 555 12th St NW ☎783-3776; Metro Center Metro. Sports fanatics will delight in the sports empire's DC branch, with hundreds of TVs – even above the urinals – showing every sporting event under the sun, plus tables outfitted with individual audio feeds and, oh yes, beer. The uninitiated will find this a noisy orgy of frattish mayhem and should stay far, far away. Mon–Thurs & Sun 11.30am–11pm, Fri & Sat 11.30am–midnight.

Fadó 808 7th St NW ☎789-0066; Gallery Place–Chinatown Metro. The buzzing DC outpost of this growing Irish pub chain – complete with expensively designed Victorian, faux-rural and ancient Celtic drinking areas – is a good spot for a Guinness and a bite to eat, especially if you're off to the MCI Center for a game. Mon–Thurs & Sun 11.30am–2am, Fri & Sat 11.30am–3am.

Gordon Biersch Brewery 900 F St NW ☎783-5454; Gallery Place–Chinatown Metro. This classy brew-pub, a California export, makes its various lagers on site in accordance with the *Reinheitsgebot*, the German purity law of 1516. But it's the extravagant setting that steals the show – a restored nineteenth-century bank that is a historic downtown landmark. Mon–Thurs & Sun 11.30am–midnight, Fri & Sat 11.30am–2am.

John Harvard's Warner Building, 1299 Pennsylvania Ave NW ☎783-2739; Metro Center Metro. Upscale basement brewhouse and restaurant, with half a dozen beers on tap. Mon–Thurs 11.30am–11pm, Fri 11.30am–midnight, Sat noon–midnight, Sun 3–10pm.

Platinum 915 F St NW ☎393-3555; Gallery Place–Chinatown Metro. Set in a converted

bank, this stylish, multilevel dance club sees its share of high rollers. Three DJs spin house and techno. Thurs–Sat 10pm–3am, Sun 9pm–2.30am.

Polly Esther's 605 12th St NW ☎737-1970; Metro Center Metro. The DC outpost of the enthusiastic Seventies, Eighties and Nineties dance-club chain is the place for a good-time night of getting down. No cover before 9pm. Thurs 9pm–2am, Fri 5pm–4am, Sat 8pm–4am.

The Ritz 919 E St NW ☎638-2582; Gallery Place–Chinatown Metro. Five music bars in one club where fashionable power-dressers wallow in everything from pop and reggae to soul, go-go and house. Mainly black crowd, who wait patiently in line after midnight; Friday is the big night. Wed 9pm–2am, Fri 9pm–3.30am, Sat 10pm–3.30am, Sun 10pm–2am.

The Rock 717 6th Street NW ☎842-7625; Gallery Place–Chinatown Metro. One of DC's better places to catch the game, this expansive sports bar is a bit rough around the edges but has big-screen action, a rooftop terrace and a handful of pool tables. It's steps from the MCI Center. Mon–Thurs & Sun 11am–2am, Fri & Sat 11am–3am.

Sky Terrace *Washington Hotel*, 515 15th St NW ☎638-5900; Metro Center Metro. Superb rooftop views from the ninth-floor bar-terrace. It's usually very busy – go early or late or expect to wait. Daily 11am–1am (May–Oct only).

The Big Hunt 1345 Connecticut Ave NW ☎785-2333; Dupont Circle Metro. As well known for its eccentric décor – including the tarantula candelabra – as for its beer. More than 25 brews on tap, good jukebox and a groovy crowd. It's always busy during happy hour, which segues right into dinnertime with excellent nightly food specials (Monday is half-price pizza night). Mon–Thurs 4pm–2am, Fri 4pm–3am, Sat noon–3am, Sun 5.30pm–2am.

The Brickskeller 1523 22nd St NW ☏ 293-1885; Dupont Circle Metro. Renowned brick-lined basement saloon serving "the world's largest selection of beer" – as many as 800 different types, including dozens from US microbreweries. Knowledgeable bar staff can advise. Mon–Thurs 11.30am–2am, Fri 11.30am–3am, Sat 6pm–3am, Sun 6pm–2am.

Buffalo Billiards 1330 19th St NW ☏ 331-7665; Dupont Circle Metro. Classy basement hangout with a seemingly endless sea of pool tables, plus darts, a good selection of tap beers and tasty pub grub. There's even a lone snooker table. Mon–Thurs 4pm–2am, Fri 4pm–3am, Sat 1pm–3am, Sun 1pm–1am.

The Childe Harold 1610 20th St NW ☏ 483-6700; Dupont Circle Metro. Friendly old red-brick pub with an outdoor patio; it draws a mixed crew that comes to chew the fat and watch TV sports. There's a good restaurant, too. Mon–Thurs 11.30am–2am, Fri & Sat 11.30am–3am, Sun 10.30am–2am.

Fox and Hounds 1537 17th St NW ☏ 232-6307; Dupont Circle Metro. Smack in the middle of the 17th Street action, this easygoing bar draws a diverse crowd, here mostly to kick back and enjoy the very stiff and very cheap rail drinks. Choose between the packed patio and the soothingly dim interior, wherein lies the District's best jukebox. Mon–Thurs 11am–2am, Fri 11am–3am, Sat 10am–3am, Sun 10am–2am.

Gazuza 1629 Connecticut Ave NW ☏ 667-5500; Dupont Circle Metro. See and be seen at this upscale lounge, whose perch above Connecticut Avenue attracts an eclectic mix for cocktails, electronica and house. Mon–Thurs & Sun 5pm–2am, Fri & Sat 5pm–3am.

Foggy Bottom

Red Lion 2040 I St NW ☏ 785-2766; Foggy Bottom–GWU Metro. No gimmicks, few frills – just a GWU student hangout doing a roaring trade in cheap food and drinks. Mon–Thurs 11am–1.30am, Fri & Sat 11am–2.30am.

Georgetown

Champions 1206 Wisconsin Ave NW; ☏ 965-4005. Full-on sports bar awash with memorabilia, with big games on the TV and high-calorie food to help the beer down. DJ after 11pm. Mon–Thurs 5pm–2am, Fri 5pm–3am, Sat 11.30am–3am, Sun 11.30am–2am.

Garrett's 3003 M St NW ☏ 333-1033. With the usual brick-and-wood interior so beloved of DC bars, *Garrett's* stands out by virtue of the damn big rhino head by the door, and a pumping jukebox that keeps the student crowd in party mood. Mon–Thurs 11.30am–2am, Fri 11.30am–3am, Sat noon–3am, Sun noon–2am.

Modern 3287 M St NW ☏ 338-7027. A welcome respite from the area's usual saloon-and-frat fare, this upscale lounge boasts a stylish bar and fittingly mod décor. Tues–Thurs 8.30pm–2am, Fri & Sat 8.30pm–3am.

Mr Smith's 3104 M St NW ☏ 333-3104. Most welcoming of Georgetown's saloons, with a splendid garden drinking-and-eating area, cheap beer-and-burger nights, and live

Saloons

DC has a wealth of traditional saloon-restaurants, bristling with checked tablecloths, paneled wood, good-value food and sharpshooting waiters. The list below picks out those where the bar action is pretty good, too.

Clyde's, Georgetown, p.270
Fran O'Brien's, New Downtown, p.262
J. Paul's, Georgetown, p.271
McCormick & Schmick's, New Downtown, p.262
The Monocle, Capitol Hill, p.260

Mr Henry's, Capitol Hill, p.260
Old Glory, Georgetown, p.271
Sign of the Whale, New Downtown, p.263
Stoney's, New Downtown, p.263

bands on weekends. Mon–Thurs & Sun 11am–1.30am, Fri & Sat 11am–2.30am.

Sequoia 3000 K St NW ☎944-4200. Popular restaurant-bar at the eastern end of Washington Harbor, with outdoor terrace seating overlooking the river. Arrive early on weekends. Mon–Thurs & Sun 11.30am–1am, Fri & Sat 11.30am–2am.

Third Edition 1218 Wisconsin Ave NW, near M St ☎333-3700. Gung-ho college bar on several floors. It's a cattle-market on weekends (when you'll probably have to wait in line and pay cover after 10pm). Mon–Thurs 4pm–2am, Fri 4pm–3am, Sat 11.30am–3am, Sun 11.30am–2am.

The Tombs 1226 36th St NW, at Prospect St ☎337-6668. Busy, basement student haunt, adorned with rowing blades. It's good for catching college football games on Saturday afternoons in fall or just soaking up the Georgetown vibe. Occasional live bands and club nights (small cover). Mon–Thurs 11.30am–2am, Fri & Sat 11.30am–3am, Sun 9.30am–2am.

Southeast

Buzz 1015 Half St SE ☎554-1500; Navy Yard Metro. Recently hailed as the country's top club by *URB Magazine,* this weekly 18-and-over dance party happens on Friday nights at *Nation*, with superstar DJs drawing hordes of ravers here to groove on trance, house, drum 'n' bass and techno until dawn. Take a cab there and back. Fri 10pm–6am.

Southwest

Zanzibar on the Waterfront 700 Water St SW ☎554-9100; L'Enfant Plaza Metro. Waterfront club with a view draws the international crowd with live bands and DJs who kick out music spanning salsa, R&B, reggae and jazz. Also not a bad spot to watch a sunset. Mon–Sat 11am–10.30pm.

U Street and Shaw

Exercise caution at night around all the places listed below – and take a cab home.

2:K:9 2009 8th St NW ☎667-7750; U Street–Cardozo Metro. Close to Howard University and the *9:30 Club* (see p.290), this flashy multilevel nightclub draws a

diverse crowd of twentysomethings with its hip-hop and house beats, velvet ropes and dancers in cages. Thurs–Sat 9pm–2am.

Chi-Cha Lounge 1624 U St NW ☎234-8400; U Street–Cardozo Metro. Swank candlelit lounge oozing atmosphere, with live Latin music and regulars toking on fruit-cured tobacco from Middle Eastern-style hookahs. Sink into a sofa and sample the excellent Andean tapas. Mon–Thurs & Sun 6pm–2am, Fri & Sat 6pm–3am.

Polly's Café 1342 U St NW ☎265-8385; U Street–Cardozo Metro. Neat little brick-and-board café-bar with a few outdoor tables, good food, tap beers and bottled microbrews. Live music on Wednesdays. Mon–Thurs 6pm–midnight, Fri 6pm–2am, Sat 10am–2am, Sun 10am–midnight.

Red Room Bar *Black Cat*, 1811 14th St NW ☎667-7960; U Street–Cardozo Metro. Independent, no-cover bar attached to the *Black Cat* music club, with pool, pinball, draft beers and amiable, punky clientele. Mon–Thurs & Sun 8pm–2am, Fri & Sat 8pm–3am.

Republic Gardens 1355 U St NW ☎323-2730; U Street–Cardozo Metro. One of U Street's hottest nights out, with DJs spinning hip-hop, soul and jazz in a converted townhouse heavy on the décor. Live music some nights; cover charge. Wed & Thurs 5pm–2am, Fri 5pm–3am, Sat 9pm–3am.

State of the Union 1357 U St NW ☎588-8810; U Street–Cardozo Metro. Long, red, and dimly lit, festooned with hammer-and-sickles and sporting a fearsome vodka list. DJ's music ebbs gently from funk, Latin and jazz to acid jazz and hip-hop; occasional small cover. Mon–Fri 5pm–2am, Sat 6pm–3am, Sun 11am–2am.

Velvet Lounge 915 U St NW ☎462-3213; U Street–Cardozo Metro. Schmooze-and-booze in a relaxed bar, with laid-back live music five nights a week (small cover) and an open-mike session every Tuesday. Mon–Thurs & Sun 11am–2am, Fri & Sat 11am–3am.

Union Station

**Capitol City Brewing Company
2 Massachusetts Ave NE** ☎842-2337; Union Station Metro. Never has a post office looked so inviting. Burnham's beauty has had a brew-pub plonked inside its cavernous interior, making it a stunning

place for a beer (though don't bother with the food). Mon & Sun 11am–midnight, Tues–Sat 11am–1.30am; kitchen closes at 11pm.

The Dubliner *Phoenix Park Hotel*, 520 N Capitol St NW ☎737-3773; Union Station Metro. A wooden-vaulted, good-time Irish pub, with draft Guinness, boisterous conversation and live Irish music catering to the more refined Hill set. The patio is a popular summer hangout. Mon–Thurs & Sun 11am–1.30am, Fri & Sat 11am–2.30am.

Irish Times 14 F St NW ☎543-5433; Union Station Metro. Louder and livelier than its more buttoned-down neighbor, *The Dubliner,* this Hill staffer and student hangout has a wide range of beers, above average bar food and live sing-along folk from Wednesday to Sunday. Every June there's an overnight read-through of James Joyce's *Ulysses,* when the imperial pints of Guinness go down extra smooth. Mon–Thurs & Sun 11am–2am, Fri & Sat 11am–3am.

Upper Northwest

Aroma 3417 Connecticut Ave NW ☎244-7995; Cleveland Park Metro. For all its swank atmosphere, Cleveland Park's best bar still manages to feel like a neighborhood watering hole. Order a martini and take in the regular exhibits by local artists. Mon–Thurs & Sun 6pm–2am, Fri & Sat 6pm–3am.

Ireland's Four Provinces 3412 Connecticut Ave NW ☎244-0860; Cleveland Park Metro. Rollicking Irish music five nights a week (small cover on weekends) brings in a college crowd. There's a good atmosphere, and outdoor seats in the summer. Mon–Thurs & Sun 5pm–1.30am, Fri & Sat 5pm–2.30am.

Nanny O'Brien's 3319 Connecticut Ave NW ☎686-9189; Cleveland Park Metro. Cleveland Park's other Irish tavern is a smaller, more personable joint but with the same successful mix of heavy drinking and live music (usually no cover). Monday's jam night is good fun. Mon–Thurs 5pm–2am, Fri 4pm–3am, Sat 11am–3am, Sun 11am–2am.

Zoo Bar (Oxford Tavern) 3000 Connecticut Ave NW ☎232-4225; Woodley Park–Zoo Metro. Timeless suburban saloon across from the zoo, with occasional performances by blues and rock bands. Mon–Thurs & Sun 11.30am–2am, Fri & Sat 11.30am–3am.

⑬

DRINKING AND NIGHTLIFE

14

Arts and entertainment

ashington may come a cultural second-best to New York, and a fairly distant one at that, but there are still plenty of choices if you want to take in a play or comedy show, see a movie or attend a concert or recital.

The prime mover in cultural and artistic matters in the capital is the **John F. Kennedy Center for the Performing Arts** (Ⓦ www.kennedy-center.org) – hereafter known as the Kennedy Center – encompassing Concert Hall, Opera House, three theaters and the American Film Institute. It's home to the National Symphony Orchestra and stages seasonal productions by the city's top opera and ballet companies, and also has a full program of visiting national and international artists, companies and ensembles. In September, the Kennedy Center Annual Open House offers free concerts, drama and film for all comers. The other main promoter in town is the **Washington Performing Arts Society** (WPAS), which sponsors music, ballet and dance productions across the city.

The city also boasts a host of **smaller theaters and performance spaces** dedicated to contemporary, experimental, ethnic or left-field productions, where ticket prices (and availability) tend to be more realistic. And then there are DC's many **art galleries**, **movie houses**, **comedy** and **music clubs**, and big-name **concert venues** – all guaranteeing that you need never face a Saturday night or a Sunday afternoon without some sort of cultural stimulation and entertainment.

There's even plenty that you can **see for free**: the **Smithsonian Institution**, in particular, has a year-round program of events and concerts.

To find out **what's on**, consult the Friday edition of the *Washington Post*, the monthly *Washingtonian*, or the free weekly *CityPaper*. The Washington DC WCTC (see p.20) publishes a quarterly *Calendar of Events*. Other sources are flyers and posters in bookstores and cafés.

> All telephone numbers in this chapter are area code ☏202, unless otherwise stated.

Tickets

Obviously, ticket prices vary considerably according to the event or production. You can expect to shell out a lot for the high-profile events at the Kennedy Center, National Theatre, Arena Stage and the like, and in the case of major opera and ballet productions tickets at any price will be hard to come by unless you book well in advance. But many places, the Kennedy Center included, offer half- or cut-price tickets on the day if there's space. In all instances it's worth a call to the box office: students (with ID), senior citizens, military personnel and people with disabilities qualify for discounts in most theaters and concert halls.

You can also buy many tickets over the phone from various **ticket agencies**, which on the whole sell advance-reserved, full-price tickets (plus surcharge). Usually no changes or refunds are available.

Ticket agencies

Tickets.com ☎703/218-6500 or 1-800/955-5566, ⊛www.tickets.com. Full-price tickets for performing arts, music and sports events, by phone, online or at Olsson's Books and Records outlets.
TicketMaster ☎432-7328 or 1-800/551-7328, ⊛www.ticketmaster.com. Full-price tickets for performing arts, music and sports events, by phone, online or at Tower Records and Hecht's department stores.

TicketPlace, Old Post Office Pavilion, 1100 Pennsylvania Ave NW, Old Downtown ☎842-5387, ⊛www.cultural-alliance.org/tickets. On-the-day (Sun and Mon tickets sold on Sat), **half-price** (plus ten percent surcharge) cash-only tickets for theater and music performances; credit-card bookings for full-price advance tickets. Tues–Sat 11am–6pm.

Box office numbers

Arena Stage ☎488-3300
DAR Constitution Hall ☎628-4780
Kennedy Center ☎467-4600
Lisner Auditorium ☎994-1500
National Theatre ☎628-6161
Shakespeare Theatre ☎547-1122
Smithsonian Institution ☎357-2700
Warner Theatre ☎628-1818

Washington Ballet ☎362-3606
Washington Opera ☎295-2420 or 1-800/876-7372
Washington Performing Arts Society ☎785-9727
Wolf Trap Farm ☎703/255-1860 (Filene Center), ☎703/938-2404 (Barns)

Cinema

The **movie houses** listed below cover every genre, from art films to the latest blockbuster. The Loews Cineplex Odeons are the city's main commercial screens; the best of these is the stately Uptown Theatre, though the Union Station movie house often proves to be the handiest for visitors. The huge stadium-seated megaplexes are all firmly ensconced out in the Virginia and Maryland suburbs and are inaccessible unless you have your own transportation.

Movie tickets everywhere run about $8–9, with many matinees coming in a couple of dollars cheaper – cheapest of all are the bargain daily rates at Georgetown's Odeon Foundry. Check **listings** in *CityPaper* or the *Washington Post*, which also detail the free films on show in some of the city's **museums and galleries**. Don't forget the IMAX screens at the National Air and Space Museum (see p.69) and the National Museum of Natural History (see p.93), especially if you've got kids to entertain. And if you happen to be in DC in April, be on the lookout for screenings tied to the city's annual Filmfest, which premieres national and international movies in theaters across the city.

AMC Union Station 9 50 Massachusetts Ave NE, Capitol Hill ☎703/998-4262; Union Station Metro. Mainstream nine-screen complex inside Union Station.

American Film Institute Kennedy Center, 2700 F St NW, Foggy Bottom ☎785-4600; Foggy Bottom–GWU Metro. America's national film theater, showing two to four movies a day: classic, contemporary, national and foreign, often with associated lectures and seminars.

Arlington Cinema 'n' Drafthouse 2903 Columbia Pike, Arlington, VA ☎703/486-2345. Popular suburban venue for cheap movies, great beers and food. You'll need transportation – it's a quarter-mile east of Glebe Road.

Bethesda Theatre Café 7719 Wisconsin Ave NW, Bethesda, MD ☎301/656-3337; Bethesda Metro. Great retro cinema in suburban Maryland serving food and drink at tables while the movie is screened; minimum age 21.

Loews Cineplex Odeon Screenings of mainstream movies. Branches include Dupont Circle (1350 19th St NW), Dupont Circle Janus (1660 Connecticut Ave NW), Georgetown Foundry (M St at Thomas Jefferson St NW), Inner Circle (2301 M St NW), Outer Circle (4849 Wisconsin Ave NW, Tenleytown), and Uptown (3426 Connecticut Ave NW) – this last an Art Deco classic with massive screen and balcony. For times, reviews and information, call ☎333-3456.

Mary Pickford Theater Madison Building, Library of Congress, 1st St and Independence Ave SE, Capitol Hill ☎707-5677; Capitol South Metro. Free classic and foreign historic movies from the library's archives.

Visions Cinema Bistro Lounge 1927 Florida Ave NW, Dupont Circle ☎667-0090; Dupont Circle Metro. One of the few places in DC showing independent and foreign films; the attached bistro serves good food and drinks, which can be taken into the theater.

Comedy

A couple of central clubs offer the usual mix of big-name **stand-up comedy** acts, **improv**, local/regional circuit appearances and **open-mike** nights. These apart, there are occasional stand-up nights at spots as diverse as Adams–Morgan bars like *Madame's Organ* (see "Blues and country, p.288) and *Chief Ike's Mambo Room* (see p.276) or the Arena Stage and the Kennedy Center; local listings papers have all the latest details.

Keep an eye out, too, for comedy troupes that appear in **cabaret** or improv shows at various venues around town, including major hotels like the *Four Seasons*, the *Mayflower* and the *Washington Hilton*. Capitol Steps is the best-known (and most permanent) of these troupes, but there are also regular shows by ensemble groups like ComedySportz and Gross National Product.

Cabaret performances can be expensive, since there's often a drinks-and-food minimum charge on top of the **ticket** price. A big weekend show can cost as much as $40, though tickets for basic stand-up and improv nights are more like $10–15. **Reservations** are essential.

Capitol Steps Ronald Reagan Building and International Trade Center, 1300 Pennsylvania Ave NW, Old Downtown ☎408-8736; Metro Center Metro. Well-established political satire by a group of Capitol Hill staffers on Friday and Saturday nights at 7.30pm ($30).

Improv 1140 Connecticut Ave NW, New Downtown ☎296-7008; Farragut North Metro. DC's main comedy showcase, mixing big names with local and regional acts and open-mike nights.

Dance

Ballet is fairly limited in DC, though what there is – provided principally by Washington Ballet – is of the highest quality. There's more scope to the modern and **contemporary dance** scene, with performances at the Kennedy

Center, the other main theaters and The Dance Place, which, as its name suggests, specializes in dance performances.

The Dance Place 3225 8th St NE, Brookland ☏269-1600; Brookland–CUA Metro. Contemporary and modern dance productions, mainstream and experimental. Hosts the Dance Africa festival every June.

Washington Ballet ☏362-3606 or 467-4600. Classical and contemporary ballet performed in rep by the city's major ballet company at the Kennedy Center. Every December *The Nutcracker* is performed at the Warner Theatre. Tickets $30–45.

Galleries

Quite apart from the public art galleries and museums, DC has a massive range of **commerical art galleries** that often host changing exhibitions (usually free) of paintings, prints, sculpture, photography, applied art and folk art. The galleries listed below are some of the more reliable; call for details of current shows or check *CityPaper* or the *Washington Post*'s "Weekend" section. There's also a monthly guide available in bookstores with comprehensive listings of DC's art galleries called, appropriately enough, *Galleries* (Ⓦwww.artline.com/plus/gallerymagazine).

The venues themselves are grouped in several distinct city areas. Downtown, those along **7th Street NW** specialize in the works of contemporary DC-area artists, though the major concentration of galleries is in **Dupont Circle**, where more than thirty congregate in a defined Gallery District (mainly **R Street** between 21st and 22nd). Georgetown has a number of art galleries as well. Most are **closed** on Monday and many are also closed on Tuesday.

Downtown

406 7th Street NW Archives–Navy Memorial or Gallery Place–Chinatown Metro. A grouping of galleries featuring the work of DC-area artists – mixed-media, contemporary sculpture, painting and photography. Artists' Museum ☏638-7001, Numark ☏628-3810, and Touchstone ☏347-2787.

Arts Club of Washington 2017 I St NW ☏331-7282; Foggy Bottom–GWU or Farragut West Metro. Changing exhibits of works by local artists.

George Washington University Colonnade Gallery, Marvin Center, 800 21st St NW ☏994-6555; and Dimock Gallery, Lower Lisner Auditorium, 730 21st St NW ☏994-1525; Foggy Bottom–GWU Metro. Regular changing shows by local, student, national and international artists.

Signal 66 926 N St NW (entrance in Blagden Alley) ☏842-3436; Mount Vernon Square-UDC Metro. Hard-to-find insiders' alternative space run by local artists. Open Friday evenings and Saturday afternoons.

Zenith Gallery 413 7th St NW ☏783-2963; Archives–Navy Memorial or Gallery Place–Chinatown Metro. Prints, paintings and sculpture, a good portion of which is by city-based artists.

Dupont Circle

Affrica 2010 R St NW ☏745-7272; Dupont Circle Metro. African masks, figurines, ceramics, textiles and jewelry.

Fondo del Sol Visual Arts Center 2112 R St NW ☏483-2777; Dupont Circle Metro. Nonprofit museum of Latino-Caribbean art, which also features lectures, poetry and performance art and sponsors a summer outdoor Caribbean festival.

Kathleen Ewing Gallery 1609 Connecticut Ave NW ☏328-0955; Dupont Circle Metro. Highly regarded gallery featuring nineteenth- and twentieth-century photography.

Marsha Mateyka Gallery 2012 R St NW ☏328-0088; Dupont Circle Metro. Contemporary painting and sculpture by American and European artists.

Tartt Gallery 2023 Q St NW ☏332-5652; Dupont Circle Metro. Nineteenth- and early twentieth-century photography, plus American folk art. By appointment.

Troyer Fitzpatrick Lassman Gallery 1710 Connecticut Ave NW ☏328-7189; Dupont Circle Metro. Contemporary photography, paintings and sculpture.

Washington Printmakers' Gallery 1732
Connecticut Ave NW ☎332-7757; Dupont
Circle Metro. Original prints by
contemporary artists.

Georgetown

Addison/Ripley Gallery 1670 Wisconsin Ave
NW ☎333-5180. Contemporary fine art.

Atlantic Gallery The Foundry Building, 1055
Thomas Jefferson St NW ☎337-2299.
Traditional paintings and prints –
landscapes, hunting scenes and seascapes.
Fine Art & Artists 2920 M St NW ☎965-0780.
Pop and contemporary art.
Spectrum Gallery 1132 29th St NW ☎333-
0954. Local artists' co-op with regular
exhibitions.

Music

Washington DC has a pretty good **live music** scene. Classical music is performed at Kennedy Center and a half-dozen other concert halls, while

Major concert venues

For details of concerts at the following venues, call the box office numbers, or
TicketMaster or Tickets.com (see p.284).

In the city
Carter Barron Amphitheater, 16th St
and Colorado Ave NW, Rock Creek Park
☎426-0486. Outdoor pop, jazz and R&B
concerts are held at this 4250-seat
theater on summer weekends.
DAR Constitution Hall, 1776 D St NW,
Foggy Bottom ☎628-4780; Farragut
West Metro. Historic 4000-seat indoor
auditorium hosts major pop, jazz and
C&W acts.
Lincoln Theatre, 1215 U St NW, U
Street/Shaw ☎328-6000; U Street–
Cardozo Metro. The 1200-seat theater
features black pop, jazz, soul and
gospel performances.
Lisner Auditorium, George
Washington University, 730 21st St NW,
Foggy Bottom ☎994-1500; Foggy
Bottom–GWU Metro. Rock, pop and
indie acts take the stage at the1500-
seat auditorium on the GWU campus.
MCI Center, 601 F St NW, Old
Downtown ☎628-3200; Gallery
Place–Chinatown Metro. Downtown
20,000-seater hosts big-name rock,
pop and C&W gigs.
RFK Stadium, 2400 E Capitol St SE
☎547-9077; Stadium–Armory Metro.
The 55,000-seater stadium pulls in the
mega-stars.
Warner Theatre, 1299 Pennsylvania
Ave NW, Old Downtown ☎783-4000;
Metro Center Metro. Jazz, Latin,
Broadway and Vegas stars appear here.

Outside the city
FedEx Field, Landover, MD ☎301/276-
6050. The Redskins stadium hosts
occasional summer pop and rock
concerts.
Merriweather Post Pavilion, off Rte
29, Columbia, MD ☎301/982-1800.
Mid-league and major pop, jazz,
country and MOR acts perform in
spring and summer only. There's
pavilion and open-air seating.
Nissan Pavilion at Stone Ridge,
Bristow, VA ☎1-800/455-8999 or
703/754-6400. Outdoor summer
stadium (25,000 seats) plays host to
many of the major summer tours.
Patriot Center, George Mason
University Campus, Fairfax, VA
☎703/993-3000. Big-name concerts
and family entertainment.
USAir Arena, 1 Harry S Truman Dr,
Landover, MD ☎301/350-3400; exits
15A or 17A off the Beltway. Pop, rock,
dance and country stars appear at the
20,000-seat stadium.
Wolf Trap Farm Park, Filene Center and
The Barns, 1624 Trap Rd, Vienna, VA
☎703/255-1860 (Filene Center), 703/938-
2404 (Barns), 703/218-6500 (tickets). US
Park Service gem plays host to a variety
of jazz, country, folk, zydeco and pop
acts. See p.291 for details.

ARTS & ENTERTAINMENT

Acoustic, Irish and folk

There are regular Irish, acoustic and folk sessions in the following bars.

The Dubliner, Union Station, p.281
IOTA, Arlington, p.291
Ireland's Four Courts, Arlington, p.277
Ireland's Four Provinces, Cleveland Park, p.281

Irish Times, Union Station, p.281
Murphy's Grand Irish Pub, Alexandria, p.277
Nanny O'Brien's, Cleveland Park, p.281

concerts by popular performers and bands take place in a variety of **major venues** (see box on previous page) in and outside the city. **Tickets** for these big-name concerts tend to be pricey ($20–80) and need to be booked in advance, either direct from the venues or from one of the major ticket agencies (see "Tickets" on p.284).

Less expensive concerts are staged by the various museums of the **Smithsonian Institution** (☎357-2700). Jazz and folk performances are scheduled throughout the year; they're often free and sometimes open-air. (For an overview of free open-air concerts in the District, see the box opposite.)

For smaller **gigs**, check the music-club schedules, where ticket prices run from $5 to $20. Several of the places listed below are also bars or dance clubs, and are reviewed separately in Chapter 13. We've also listed restaurants where you can catch live bands (see p.290). Take **ID** with you wherever you go: in many clubs you have to be 21 to get in, and in those where the age limit is 18, under-21s still won't be able to drink alcohol.

Blues and country

Birchmere 3701 Mount Vernon Ave, Alexandria, VA ☎703/549-7500. Longstanding country, blues and folk club with an A-list of current and retro acoustic performers. Nightly gigs. Ticket prices vary depending on the act ($15–50).

Cowboy Café 2421 Columbia Pike, Arlington, VA ☎703/486-3467. The region's favorite for C&W, rockabilly and cowboy blues. No cover.

Madame Organ 2461 18th St NW, Adams-Morgan ☎667-5370; Woodley Park–Zoo or Dupont Circle Metro. Unsophisticated Adams-Morgan hangout featuring live blues, raw R&B and bluegrass; small cover. Upstairs, there's a pool table and a rooftop bar.

New Vegas Lounge 1415 P St NW, Dupont East ☎483-3971; Dupont Circle Metro. Raunchy Chicago R&B Monday through Saturday in a decidedly dingy setting. Small cover.

Classical music

The Kennedy Center's Concert Hall is the most prestigious in town for classical music; it's also the home of the

National Symphony Orchestra. Tickets to symphony performances run from $25 to $50 (though the orchestra also performs free outside the US Capitol on the West Terrace on Memorial Day, July 4 and Labor Day). In addition to the regular concerts at the venues listed below, classical music performances are often held at museums (particularly the National Gallery of Art and the Corcoran Gallery of Art), historic houses (such as Dumbarton House, see p.222), churches (including the National Cathedral, see p.208) and embassies. For details about **Smithsonian Institution** concerts, call ☎357-2700.

Coolidge Auditorium Madison Building, Library of Congress, 1st St and Independence Ave SE, Capitol Hill ☎707-5502; Capitol South Metro. Chamber music concerts in a historic venue. Sept–May season.

DAR Constitution Hall 1776 D St NW, Foggy Bottom ☎628-4780; Farragut West Metro. Stately (3700-seat) auditorium hosts major concerts and recitals.

Folger Shakespeare Library 201 E Capitol St SE, Capitol Hill ☎544-7077; Capitol South Metro. Medieval and Renaissance music from the Folger Consort ensemble. Oct–May season.

John Philip Sousa Band Hall Marine Barracks, 8th and I St SE, Eastern Market ☎433-4011; Navy Yard Metro. Free fall and winter chamber recitals by the marine band ensemble, and other occasional concerts.

Kennedy Center 2700 F St NW, at Virginia and New Hampshire aves ☎467-4600; Foggy Bottom–GWU Metro. The National Symphony Orchestra performs in the 2800-seat Concert Hall (Sept–June); there are less expensive chamber recitals in the Terrace Theater, and free concerts in the Grand Foyer.

Lisner Auditorium George Washington University, 730 21st St NW, Foggy Bottom ☎994-1500; Foggy Bottom–GWU Metro. Regular classical and choral concerts, occasionally free.

National Academy of Sciences 2101 Constitution Ave NW, Foggy Bottom ☎334-2436; Foggy Bottom–GWU Metro. Pleasing 700-seat auditorium with occasional free chamber recitals.

National Gallery of Art West Building, West Garden Court, Constitution Ave NW, on the Mall ☎842-6941; Archives–Navy Memorial Metro. Free concerts every Sunday at 7pm (Oct–June) in the lovely West Garden Court. First-come-first-served basis; doors open at 6pm.

The Phillips Collection 1600 21st St NW; Dupont Circle ☎387-2151; Dupont Circle Metro. Classical music concerts in the museum's Music Room (Sept–May Sun 5pm); free with museum admission (see p.194). Arrive early.

Society of the Cincinnati at Anderson House 2118 Massachusetts Ave NW, Dupont Circle ☎785-2040; Dupont Circle Metro. Free chamber recitals once or twice a week in fine mansion surroundings (see p.193).

Free open-air concerts

Summer is a good time to catch a free open-air concert in Washington, though certain locations host events all year round. Check the following places and see DC's festival calendar (p.315) for more information.

C&O Canal, Georgetown. Varied Sunday afternoon summer concerts take place between 30th and Thomas Jefferson St.

Freedom Plaza, Pennsylvania Ave NW. Year-round venue for folk events and music festivals.

National Zoological Park, Connecticut Ave NW. "Sunset serenades" in July, featuring a variety of musical performances.

Netherlands Carillon, Marine Corps (Iwo Jima) War Memorial, Arlington, VA. Carillon concerts every Saturday and on national holidays May through September.

Sylvan Theatre, Washington Monument Grounds, the Mall. Army, Air Force, Navy and Marine Corps bands perform four nights a week June through August (including annual *1812 Overture* performance in August). Other musical events throughout the year, too.

US Capitol. Armed forces bands perform four nights a week (June–Aug) on the East Terrace. National Symphony Orchestra concerts on the West Terrace on Memorial Day, July 4 and Labor Day.

US Navy Memorial, 701 Pennsylvania Ave NW. Spring and summer concert series featuring Navy, Marine Corps, Coast Guard and high-school bands. Regular performances Tues 8pm June–Aug.

Hip-hop and reggae

State of the Union 1357 U St NW, Shaw ☎588-8910; U Street–Cardozo Metro. Funky bar with wide variety of acts, ranging from progressive and acid jazz bands to reggae, go-go and hip-hop acts, several nights a week. Small cover.

Jazz

Blues Alley 1073 Rear Wisconsin Ave NW, Georgetown ☎337-4141. Small, celebrated Georgetown jazz bar, in business for over thirty years, attracts top names. Shows usually at 8pm and 10pm, plus midnight some weekends; cover can run to $40. Book in advance.

The following restaurants and bars all feature regular live performances, from jazz to R&B; there's usually no charge other than the price of the meal or drink. See the individual reviews for details about the places themselves.

Afterwords Café (jazz/blues), Dupont Circle, p.264
Bukom Café (African), Adams-Morgan, p.256
Café des Artistes at the Corcoran (gospel), Foggy Bottom, p. 268
Café Toulouse (jazz/blues), Adams-Morgan, p.276
Chi-Cha Lounge (Latin), U Street, p.282
Columbia Station (jazz), Adams-Morgan, p.276
Kinkead's (jazz), Foggy Bottom, p.269

Mr Henry's (jazz), Capitol Hill, p.260
Mr Smith's (rock/piano bar), Georgetown, p.280
Polly's Café (eclectic), U Street, p.282
Rumba Cafe (Latin), Adams-Morgan, p.277
U-topia (jazz/blues/Brazilian), U Street, p.272
Whitlow's on Wilson (rock/jazz), Arlington, p.277
Zanzibar on the Waterfront (jazz/reggae), Southwest, p.281

Bohemian Caverns 2003 11th St NW, Shaw ☏299-0800. U Street–Cardozo Metro. Legendary DC jazz supper club, recently reopened after three decades. The jazz happens in a basement grotto, below the stylish ground-level restaurant. Cover runs to $15, with a limited number of reserved tickets for bigger acts available online at ☸www.bohemiancaverns.com.
HR 57 1610 14th St NW, Dupont East ☏667-3700; Dupont Circle Metro. Small club dedicated to the preservation of jazz and blues, hosting amateur and professional musicians alike. Small cover.
The Saloun 3239 M St NW, Georgetown ☏965-4900. Cozy bar with nightly jazz trios or bands, and 75 bottled beers. Free admission Monday and before 8pm, otherwise small cover charge.
Takoma Station Tavern 6914 4th St NW, Takoma Park ☏829-1999; Takoma Metro. Laid-back club with jazz several nights a week, featuring mostly local acts, plus decent food. On some evenings reggae acts, comedians or poetry slams take the spotlight. No cover.
Twins Lounge 1344 U St NW, Shaw ☏234-0072; U Steet–Cardozo Metro. Celebrated neighborhood jazz haunt drawing talented musicians Tues–Sun. Cover runs to $15, with a limited number of reserved tickets for certain acts available online at ☸www.twinsjazz.com.

Opera

Summer Opera Theater Company Hartke Theater, Catholic University, Michigan Ave and 4th St NE, Brookland ☏526-1669; Brookland–CUA Metro. Independent company staging two operas each summer, usually July and August.
Washington Opera ☏295-2400 or 1-800/876-7372. Tickets for one of the country's finest resident opera companies (artistic director: Placido Domingo) sell out well in advance, though you may get standing-room tickets at the box office. Performances are in the Opera House and the other Kennedy Center theaters. Sept–June season.

Rock and pop

9:30 Club 815 V St NW, Shaw ☏393-0930; U St–Cardozo Metro. Famous DC venue for indie rock and pop, local, national and foreign. Separate no-cover bar, too. Book in advance for well-known names. It's not in a great part of town – getting there by Metro is okay (two blocks from the Metro; use Vermont Ave exit), but take a cab home.
The Black Cat 1811 14th St NW, Dupont East ☏667-7960; U Street–Cardozo Metro. Part-owned by Foo Fighter Dave Grohl, this indie institution provides a showcase for up-and-coming bands and veteran alternative acts alike.
Galaxy Hut 2711 Wilson Blvd, Arlington, VA ☏703/525-8646; Clarendon Metro. Regular line-up of local indie talent takes the stage

Wolf Trap Farm Park

Wolf Trap Farm Park (1551 Trap Rd, Vienna, VA; ⌐www.wolftrap.org), about forty minutes' drive from downtown DC, is the country's first national park for the performing arts, with three performance venues. Set on 130 acres, the park's **Filene Center** (☏703/255-1860) has indoor and outdoor seating for seven thousand people. It hosts jazz, pop and C&W concerts from June through September, as well as opera, ballet and dance performances. The **Theatre-in-the-Woods** (☏703/255-1827) stages free performances for children during July and August. The rest of the year the action takes place in the indoor **Barns at Wolf Trap** (☏703/938-2404), a 350-seat concert hall hosting jazz, blues, folk, world music and zydeco.

Wolf Trap Farm Park is outside the Beltway, between Route 7 and Route 267 (Dulles Toll Road). For directions on how to get there by public transportation, call ☏703/255-1860 – there's Metro shuttle-bus service for most performances. Call the **box office** numbers for details about the program and tickets, which you can buy over the phone through Tickets.com (☏703/218-6500 or 1-800/955-5566). The park has concession stands and a restaurant, but in summer it's nicer to bring a **picnic** and eat on the grass. **Parking** is free.

---

in this tiny neighborhood hangout, with a bevy of beers on tap.

IOTA 2832 Wilson Blvd, Arlington, VA ☏703/522-8340; Clarendon Metro. Warehouse-style music club with nightly performances by local and national indie, folk and blues bands. A great bar and attached restaurant, too.

Metro Café 1522 14th St NW, Dupont East ☏588-9118; Dupont Circle Metro. A good mix of touring and local bands appears at

this club, which also hosts improv, theater and film events.

Nation 1015 Half St SE, Southeast ☏554-1500; Navy Yard Metro. Mid-sized warehouse concert venue with a state-of-the-art sound system. It doubles as a popular dance club (see *Buzz*, p.281 and *Velvet Nation*, p.296) boasting an assortment of star guest DJs from around the globe. Take a cab home.

Theater

Most **Broadway productions** either preview or tour in Washington; the city also has an enclave of **alternative venues** in the Shaw (14th St NW) district, where relatively low ticket prices reward the adventurous. Travel (or at least leave) by taxi, since the area isn't the most salubrious in town.

African Continuum Theater Company ☏529-5763. Specializes in productions reflecting the African-American experience. Call for schedules and venues.

Arena Stage 6th St and Maine Ave SW, Southwest ☏488-3300; Waterfront Metro. The most respected theatrical institution in the city, with three stages (Arena Stage, Kreeger Theater and Old Vat Room) showing contemporary plays and performance pieces, classics, musicals, comedies and experimental works.

DC Arts Center 2438 18th St NW, Adams-Morgan ☏462-7833; Woodley Park–Zoo Metro. Performance art, drama, poetry, dance and a whole range of multicultural

activities are held in this small northern Adams-Morgan space. Tickets prices are low.

Discovery Theater Arts and Industries Building, 900 Jefferson Dr SW, on the Mall ☏357-1500; Smithsonian Metro. Year-round daytime children's theater, offering musicals and puppet shows at budget prices.

Folger Shakespeare Library 201 E Capitol St SE, Capitol Hill ☏544-7077; Capitol South Metro. A full program is presented at the Elizabethan library-theater (Sept–June), not solely Shakespeare.

Ford's Theatre 511 10th St NW, Old Downtown ☏426-6924; Metro Center Metro. Site of Lincoln's assassination (see pp.180–181), this restored nineteenth-century theater stages mainstream musicals and dramas.

Gala Hispanic Theatre Warehouse Theatre, 1021 7th St NW, New Downtown ☏234-7174; Mount Vernon Square–UDC Metro. Specializes in works by Spanish/Latin American playwrights, performed in Spanish or English, as well as performance art and poetry.

Kennedy Center 2700 F St NW, at Virginia and New Hampshire Ave, Foggy Bottom ☏467-4600; Foggy Bottom–GWU Metro. Site of three theaters: the Eisenhower (drama and Broadway productions), the Terrace (experimental/contemporary works) and the Theater Lab (almost permanently home to the long-running *Shear Madness*, a comedy-whodunnit). The Opera House also hosts musicals.

Lincoln Theatre 1215 U St NW, Shaw ☏328-6000; U Street–Cardozo Metro. Renovated movie/vaudeville house features touring stage shows, concerts and dance.

Metro Café 1522 14th St NW, Dupont East ☏588-9118; Dupont Circle Metro. A whole gamut of cultural events, from film and music to theater and improv, is found here.

National Theatre 1321 Pennsylvania Ave NW, Old Downtown ☏628-6161; Metro Center Metro. One of the country's oldest theaters, it's been on this site (if not in this building) since 1835. Premieres, pre- and post-Broadway productions and musicals.

Shakespeare Theatre *The Lansburgh*, 450 7th St NW, Old Downtown ☏547-1122; Archives–Navy Memorial or Gallery Place–Chinatown Metro. Four (often star-studded) plays a year by Shakespeare and his contemporaries. Each June the company stages free, outdoor Shakespeare performances at the Carter Barron Amphitheater in Rock Creek Park (see p.287).

Source Theatre 1835 14th St NW, Dupont East ☏462-1073; U Street–Cardozo Metro. New and contemporary works and classic reinterpretations. Promotes the Washington Theater Festival, a showcase for new works, every summer.

Studio Theatre 1333 P St NW, Dupont East ☏332-3300; Dupont Circle Metro. Independent theater with two stages presenting classic and contemporary drama and comedy.

Warner Theatre 1299 Pennsylvania Ave NW, Old Downtown ☏628-1818; Metro Center Metro. Erstwhile movie palace now staging post-Broadway productions and big concerts.

Woolly Mammoth Theatre 1401 Church St NW, Dupont Circle ☏393-3939; Dupont Circle Metro. Budget-ticket productions of contemporary, experimental and just plain off-the-wall plays.

Gay and lesbian DC

or a smallish East Coast city better known for its policy prattle than its Pride parades, the District's **gay and lesbian scene** is surprisingly vibrant – although you'll find it a bit more buttoned-down than either New York or San Francisco. But times have certainly changed in the nation's capital since 1975, when gay federal employees risked being fired from their government jobs for engaging in "immoral conduct." Just in the past decade, the first openly gay elected city official took office, *The Washington Blade* grew to more than one hundred pages, and hundreds of thousands descended upon the city to attend the Millennium March on Washington for Equality in April 2000.

The heart of DC's gay community is **Dupont Circle**, where the greatest concentration of shops, bars and restaurants catering to a gay clientele can be found. Most of the action takes place along P Street, just west of the Circle between 21st and 22nd streets, and on 17th Street, where gay and gay-friendly establishments, many with sidewalk patios, form a lively strip between P and R streets. It's here that high-heeled sprinters in drag line up each October for the annual **High-Heel Race**, a sporting event-cum-street carnival.

But the scene is hardly limited to Dupont. Across town in **Capitol Hill**, a handful of spots are clustered in the vicinity of the Eastern Market Metro station, near the intersection of Pennsylvania Avenue and 8th Street, while the somewhat dodgy quadrant of **Southeast** is home to the popular dance club *Velvet* in addition to a few more risqué clubs – take care to come and go by cab when partying in this part of town.

As you'd expect from a city of this size, gay couples will find themselves welcome at most DC **hotels**. Nonetheless many visitors prefer to stay in Dupont Circle, where gay-friendly accommodation abounds. As only a few spots cater specifically to gay travelers, we've also recommended a selection of gay-friendly hotels and B&Bs. Listed below, too, are the restaurants, bars and clubs that are staples of the District's gay scene.

To get a reading on the local pulse, you'll also want to grab a copy of the *Washington Blade* (Ⓦwww.washblade.com), a weekly featuring news, listings and classified ads. For an insider's heads-up on DC's gay nightlife, turn to *Metro Weekly*, a comic-book-size rag that runs up-to-date listings of dining and partying hot spots – including special events, DJs and happy hours – accompanied by a map. Both publications are free and can be picked up at *Lambda Rising* on Connecticut Avenue or at various restaurants and clubs in Dupont and Capitol Hill. A list of other gay resources and organizations in DC appears below.

All telephone numbers in this chapter are area code ℡202, unless otherwise stated.

Accommodation

The following properties cater exclusively to a gay and lesbian clientele. For information on gay-friendly hotels and B&Bs in DC, see the box below; for an explanation of the price codes, see p.244 or the inside front cover.

The Brenton 1708 16th St NW, Dupont Circle ☎332-5550 or 1/800-673-9042, ℱ462-5872, ⓦwww.thebrenton.com;Dupont Circle Metro. Brick-and-stone Victorian B&B, well located near Dupont's 17th Street scene, with eight rooms with shared bath, plus a suite (with private bath and kitchen). Extras include happy hours and free continental breakfast. ❸–❹

The–William Lewis House 1309 R St NW, Logan Circle ☎462-7574 or 1-800/465-7574, ℱ462-1608, ⓦwww.wlewishous.com; U Street–Cardozo Metro. Elegantly decorated B&B set in two century-old townhouses near Logan Circle, with ten antique-filled rooms (all with shared bath). Out back there's a roomy porch and a hot tub set in a garden. Rates include continental breakfast on weekdays and a full American breakfast on weekends. Reservations essential. ❸

Gay-friendly lodging

While only a handful of spots in DC bill themselves exclusively as gay hotels or B&Bs, gay-friendly accommodation is scattered throughout the city. You can count on feeling welcome at most of the Dupont Circle area hotels listed in Chapter 00 (see pp.248–249). A few recommended spots in Dupont and elsewhere in the city are:

Bull Moose B&B 101 Fifth St NE, Capitol Hill ☎547-1050 or 1-800/261-2768, ℱ548-9741, ⓦwww.bullmoose-b-and-b.com. See p.245.
Carlyle Suites 1731 New Hampshire Ave NW, Dupont Circle ☎234-3200 or 1-866/468-3532, ℱ387-0085, ⓦwww.carlylesuites.com. See p.248.
The Dupont at the Circle 1604 19th St NW, Dupont Circle ☎332-5251 or 1-888/412-0100, ℱ332-3244, ⓦwww

.dupontatthecircle.com. See p.248.
Embassy Inn 1627 16th St NW, Dupont Circle ☎234-7800 or 1-800/423-9111, ℱ234-3309. See p.248.
Kalorama Guest House at Woodley Park 2700 Cathedral Ave NW, Upper Northwest ☎328-0860, ℱ328-8730. See p.251.
Tabard Inn 1739 N St NW, New Downtown ☎785-1277, ℱ785-6173, ⓦwww.tabardinn.com. See p.247.

Cafés and restaurants

While more than a few spots reviewed in the main cafés and restaurants chapter (see p.253) have won loyal gay followings – including *Pizzeria Paradiso* and *Afterwords* in Dupont Circle, *Two Quail* in Capitol Hill and *The Diner* and *Perry's* in Adams–Morgan – the handful of spots listed below have become fixtures on the capital's gay and lesbian scene.

Annie's Paramount Steakhouse 1609 17th St NW, Dupont Circle ☎232-0395; Dupont Circle Metro. A Dupont institution, in business since the 1940s, serving inexpensive steaks, good burgers and brunch – including a midnight brunch on weekends – to a loyal crowd. Mon–Thurs & Sun 6am–1.30am, Fri & Sat 24hrs. Moderate.

Banana Café & Piano Bar 500 8th St SE, Capitol Hill ☏543-5906; Eastern Market Metro. A tropical trip serving Tex-Mex staples alongside a few Puerto Rican and Cuban standouts, such as ropa vieja (a hearty shredded-beef delight), cod-fish fritters and plantain soup, the house speciality. Stop by the upstairs *Piano Bar* on weekdays for happy hour, when the celebrated margaritas go for $2 and a piano man is in the house. Mon–Thurs 11.30am–2.30pm & 5–10.30pm, Fri 11.30am–2.30pm & 5–11pm, Sat 5–11pm, Sun 11am–3pm & 5–10.30pm. Moderate.

Franklyn's Coffeehouse Café 2000 18th St NW, Adams-Morgan ☏319-1800; Dupont Circle Metro. Cute corner coffee shop serving hearty, healthy fare such as soup, omelets and sandwiches as well as a selection of coffee that spans the globe. Mon & Tues 7am–10pm, Wed–Fri 7am–midnight, Sat 8am–midnight, Sun 9am–midnight. Budget.

Hamburger Mary's 1337 14th St NW, Dupont East ☏232-7010; Dupont Circle Metro. The gay-owned California chain's first East Coast branch lives up to its name, serving juicy burgers in all guises along with very good spicy fries in a converted garage decked out with kitschy memorabilia and a very long bar. There's also *Titan* bar upstairs, where DJs spin tunes for a cruising crowd (daily 5pm–2am). Mon–Thurs 11am–11pm, Fri & Sat 11am–midnight, Sun 10am–11pm. Budget–Inexpensive.

Jolt 'n' Bolt 1918 18th St NW, Dupont Circle ☏232-0077; Dupont Circle Metro. Townhouse tea- and coffeehouse with side-alley patio tucked away up 18th. Wraps and sandwiches, pastries and fresh juices are served. Daily 7.30am–midnight. Budget.

Sheridan's 713 8th St SE, Capitol Hill ☏546-6955; Eastern Market Metro. Fun and tasty steak house stylishly done up as an Old West saloon, with nightly drink and dinner specials, including a three-course "pre-theater menu" ($18.74) that's served from 5.30–6.30pm. Wed, Thurs & Sun 5.30–9.30pm, Fri & Sat 5.30–10.30pm. Moderate.

SoHo Tea & Coffee 2150 P St NW, Dupont Circle ☏463-7646; Dupont Circle Metro. Trendy, late-night hangout for P Street clubbers refueling on coffee, cakes and sandwiches. Occasional drag and open-mike nights, plus a computer terminal with internet access. Mon–Wed & Sun 7.30am–3am, Thurs & Fri 7.30am–4am, Sat 7am–4.30am. Budget.

Festivals and events

Cherry (April): Weekend dance party with top DJs benefiting various gay and AIDS organizations. ⊛www.cherryfund.com.

Capital Pride (early June): Weeklong festival held annually in early June comprising cultural, political and community events, including films, pageants, a parade, and a street festival along Pennsylvania Avenue NW. ⊜info@capitalpride.org, ⊛www.capitalpride.org.

Atlantic Stampede (September): The East Coast's largest gay rodeo, sponsored by the Atlantic States Gay Rodeo Association,

the weekend-long affair features two days of rodeo plus evening dinner and dance events. ⊛www.asgra.org.

Reel Affirmations (October): One of the nation's largest gay and lesbian film festivals, held annually in October at various venues. ☏986-1119, ⊛www.reelaffirmations.org.

High-Heel Race (late October): Street festival of sorts featuring a carnival-like atmosphere, mind-blowing outfits and a mad dash down 17th Street in three-inch heels.

Bars and clubs

There's no cover charge at the places listed below unless otherwise indicated.

Capitol Hill

Phase 1 525 8th St SE ☏ 544-6831; Eastern Market Metro. Longstanding neighborhood lesbian bar with dancing, DJs and pool table. Mon–Thurs & Sun 8pm–2am, Fri & Sat 8pm–3am.

Remington's 639 Pennsylvania Ave SE ☏ 543-3113; Eastern Market Metro. Slip on the cowboy boots and hit the C&W disco nights. Small cover on weekends. Mostly men. Mon, Wed, Thurs & Sun 4pm–2am, Fri 4pm–3am, Sat 8pm–3am.

Sheridan's Dance Hall and Saloon 713 8th St SE ☏ 546-6955; Eastern Market Metro. Below the steak house, there's dancing, country & western tunes and a bar with cowhide stools to lean on. Various theme nights, including Bimbo Bingo, Latin Night and a weekly Hoedown with line dancing. Mostly men. Wed, Thurs & Sun 5pm–1am, Fri & Sat 5pm–3am.

Downtown: New

Hung Jury 1819 H St NW ☏ 785-8181; Farragut West Metro. An insider's club tucked away off an alley, this popular women's bar and disco draws a younger crowd. Men must be accompanied by a woman to get in. Small cover charge. Fri & Sat 9pm–3am.

Dupont Circle

Badlands 1415 22nd St NW ☏ 296-0505; Dupont Circle Metro. Well-located dance club, with DJs spinning current hits for a party crowd, at its best on Friday and Saturday nights. Get there early on weekends to beat the $10 cover charge (although it does include a drink ticket). Mostly men. Tues & Thurs 9pm–2am, Fri & Sat 9pm–3am.

Chaos 1603 17th St NW ☏ 232-4141; Dupont Circle Metro. Free-spirited must-visit club at the heart of the 17th Street scene, with inexpensive drinks poured from a finely stocked bar. There's a drag brunch, cabaret show and drag bingo, the latter popular with the straight crowd. Men and women. Tues–Thurs 5pm–2am, Fri & Sat 5pm–3am, Sun 11am–2am.

The Fireplace 2161 P St NW ☏ 293-1293; Dupont Circle Metro. Good-time corner bar with vibrant crowd and a long happy hour. A good staging ground for the cruisey P Street scene. Mostly men. Mon–Thurs & Sun 1pm–2am, Fri & Sat 1pm–3am.

JR's 1519 17th St NW ☏ 328-0090; Dupont Circle Metro. A young professional crowd packs into this narrow saloon-bar, which boasts a great location along the 17th Street cruise strip. Very much the place to be seen for cocktails. Mostly men. Mon–Thurs 11am–2am, Fri & Sat 11am–3am, Sun noon–2am.

Lizard Lounge 1520 14th St NW ☏ 331-4422; Dupont Circle or U Street–Cardozo Metro. Super-popular Sunday evening dance and cruise scene at the *Saint* helps you start your week in style. Mostly men. Sun 8pm–2am.

Mr P's 2147 P St NW ☏ 293-1064; Dupont Circle Metro. Longest-serving gay bar in the neighborhood, which means it has had time to acquire a bit of character and attract loyal regulars – though some say it's seen better days. Mirrored walls and dance tunes downstairs, hustling go-go boys up, plus an outdoor patio with a few pink flamingos out back. Mostly men. Mon–Thurs 2pm–2am, Fri & Sat 2pm–3am.

Omega 2122 P St NW, in the rear alley ☏ 223-4917; Dupont Circle Metro. Not much in the way of dancing, but there are four bars, pool tables and a dark video room upstairs. Stop in for happy hour or for a kickoff drink on the weekends. Mostly men. Mon–Thurs 4pm–2am, Fri 4pm–3am, Sat 8pm–2am, Sun 7pm–2am.

Southeast

The Edge & Wet 56 L St SE ☏ 488-1200; Navy Yard Metro. Frenetic gay club with several bars and special events: dance at the *Edge* but expect a somewhat steamier time at *Wet*, where you'll find go-go boys writhing in the buff. Cover. Mostly men. Mon–Thurs 7pm–2am, Fri & Sat 7pm–6am.

Velvet Nation 1015 Half St SE, between K and L ☏ 554-1500; Navy Yard Metro. Star DJs churn out deep grooves for these Saturday night parties held at *Nation*. $12 cover. Mostly men. Sat 9pm–6am.

Gay organizations and resources

Gay and Lesbian Hotline ☎833-3234.
Information, advice and peer counseling
service for the gay and lesbian community
provided by volunteers under the aegis of
the Whitman-Walker Clinic (see below).
Anonymity of both caller and operator is
respected so that both may speak freely on
any topic; no subject is off-limits. Daily
7–11pm.

**Human Rights Campaign Store and Action
Center 1629 Connecticut Ave NW, Dupont Circle**
☎232-8621, ⊛www.hrc.org; Dupont Circle
Metro. National lesbian and gay political
organization that educates visitors on
political issues affecting gay, lesbian,
bisexual and transgender people and
provides them with the tools to take action
on the spot – either in person or via their
website. The store sells Equality Wear
merchandise to raise funds for HRC
programs.

**Lambda Rising 1625 Connecticut Ave NW,
Dupont Circle** ☎462-6969; Dupont Circle
Metro. The city's best-known gay and
lesbian bookstore, which acts as a
clearinghouse for information and events.

Metro Weekly Free magazine that makes
an excellent guide to DC's nightlife. It's
stuffed with ads and listings about the
latest spots and specials. Available at
Lambda Rising (above) and various Dupont
and Capitol Hill venues.

Rainbow History Project ☎907-9007,
⊛www.rainbowhistory.org. Collects,
preserves and promotes community history
through exhibits, talks and archives;
publishes web-based DC timeline and
database of gay and lesbian "places and
spaces" from the 1920s to the present.

Washington Blade ⊛www.washblade.com.
Weekly paper featuring news, listings and
classified ads, available at bookstores,
restaurants and cafés around town.

Whitman Walker Clinic 1407 S St NW ☎797-
3500, ⊛www.wwc.org, wwcinfo@wwc.org; U
Street–Cardozo Metro. Nonprofit community
health organization established by and for
the gay and lesbian community, providing
accessible health care and community
services, including 24hr AIDS information
line (☎332-2437 or 1-877/939-2437).

Women's Monthly ⊛www.womo.com. An
independent magazine by, for and about
women, with literary works, feature articles
and event listings. Available at Lambda
Rising and select cafés and bars.

Shopping

N o one comes to DC to shop, but the city's arty neighborhood stores, fine range of bookstores and incomparable museum and gallery shops – not to mention the profusion of White House, Capitol, Supreme Court and FBI mugs, key rings, baseball caps, posters and buttons – means no one need go home empty-handed.

The nicest areas for **browsing** are Adams-Morgan, Dupont Circle, Georgetown and around Eastern Market, where art and craft shops coexist with specialty book and music stores and student-oriented clothes-and-accessories hangouts. Adams-Morgan has more ethnic soul, and some good shops to match, while in Shaw a number of hipster shops have begun to crop up amid the funky bars and antique shops in the vicinity of 14th and U streets. Farther out in Upper Northwest, the small liberal enclave of Takoma Park has a range of ethnic design and funky clothes stores along Carroll Avenue. Across the river, Alexandria has its fair share of shops, with many specializing in antiques and arts and crafts. Should you find yourself in Old Town, stop in first at the Ramsay House Visitor Center (p.233), which has reams of shopping guides, flyers and information.

The shopping heart has been ripped out of downtown, however, as all the major **department stores**, with the honorable exception of Hecht's, have given up the ghost. This may change over the next few years – development plans for the revitalized downtown area around the MCI Center include new retail units – but for the forseeable future you're best off at one of the **mega-malls** on the outskirts of the city for clothing and most other day-to-day items.

Usual store **opening hours** are Monday to Saturday 10am to 7pm; some have extended Thursday night hours. In Georgetown, Adams-Morgan and Dupont Circle many stores open on Sunday too (usually noon–5pm).

Arts, crafts and antiques

The only indigenous local craft is politics, but specialist stores in DC let you take home a piece of the Southwest or American Victoriana if you so wish. Richest pickings are in Dupont Circle, Georgetown (which also has a run of big-ticket antique shops), and Old Town Alexandria, this last positively dripping with antique/bric-a-brac places aimed at the weekend visitor market. Another great spot to poke around for arts, crafts and other funky finds is the weekend flea market held on Saturday and Sunday at Eastern Market (see p.117). For works of art, visit the galleries of Dupont Circle and those downtown on 7th Street – see p.286.

All telephone numbers in this chapter are area code ☎202, unless otherwise stated.

African Eye 2134 Wisconsin Ave NW, Georgetown ☎625-2552. African-American clothing, crafts, jewelry and textiles.
Appalachian Spring 1415 Wisconsin Ave NW, Georgetown ☎337-5780; Union Station, 50 Massachusetts Ave NE ☎682-0505. Handmade ceramics, jewelry, rugs, glassware, kitchenware, quilts and toys.
Art & Soul 225 Pennsylvania Ave SE, Capitol Hill ☎548-0105. Handmade clothes and contemporary American ceramics, toys, and crafts by more than 200 regional artists.

Beadazzled 1507 Connecticut Ave NW, Dupont Circle ☎265-2323. Antique and new beads from all over the world, plus ethnic jewelry, folk art and related books.
Indian Craft Shop Department of the Interior, Room 1023, 1849 C St NW, Foggy Bottom ☎208-4056. High-quality Native American arts and crafts – Navajo rugs, Hopi jewelry and assorted ceramics. The shop is inside the department; see p.150.
The Old Print Gallery 1220 31st NW, Georgetown ☎965-1818. Old maps, charts and prints, plus political cartoons, DC scenes and American landscapes.

Bookstores

Washington's array of bookstores is one of its high points: you'll find a place to suit whether you want discounted new novels or political science books, flagship superstores with coffee bars or cozy local secondhand shops. The weekly *CityPaper* and Friday's *Washington Post* list all bookshop lectures, concerts, readings and events.

General

Barnes & Noble 3040 M St NW, Georgetown ☎965-9880; 555 12th St NW, Old Downtown ☎347-0176. Quality chain bookstore on three floors, offering heavy discounts, one of the best crime/mystery sections in the city, and *Starbuck's* coffee.
Borders Books & Music 1801 K St NW, New Downtown ☎466-4999. Huge bookstore (entrance on L St) with good selection of magazines, newspapers and discount books, full CD and tape selection, readings, gigs, events and an espresso bar.
Chapters Literary Bookstore 1512 K St NW, New Downtown ☎347-5495. Downtown bookstore with a high-quality selection and supporting program of readings and events.
Kramerbooks 1517 Connecticut Ave NW, Dupont Circle ☎387-1462. City institution with a good general selection, a great café-restaurant and long hours (around the clock on the weekend). It's where Monica Lewinsky bought her presidential beau a copy of Nicholson Baker's *Vox*, hence the store T-shirts ("Subpoenaed for Book Selling").
Olsson's Books and Records 1239 Wisconsin Ave NW, Georgetown ☎338-6712; 1307 19th St NW, Dupont Circle ☎785-2662; 1200 F St NW,

Old Downtown ☎393-1853; 418 7th St NW, Old Downtown ☎638-7613. Massive range in one of Washington's oldest independent bookstore chains; it's a great spot to browse. Other pluses: tapes and CDs, regular book signings, and a café in the 7th Street branch.
Politics & Prose 5015 Connecticut Ave NW, Tenleytown ☎364-1919. Good independent bookstore/coffee shop, plus one of the best programs of author appearances and readings in the city.

Secondhand

Bryn Mawr Lantern Bookshop 3241 P St NW, Georgetown ☎333-3222. Great general selection of secondhand books, though only open four or five hours a day.
Idle Time Books 2410 18th St NW, Adams-Morgan ☎232-4774. Large, late-opening used bookstore with lots of bargains.
Kulturas 1608 20th St NW, Dupont Circle ☎462-2541. Offbeat secondhand bookstore with an emphasis on philosophy and art but also hawking vintage clothing and hosting art exhibits. A second location is a block away at 1706 Connecticut Avenue.
Second Story Books 2000 P St NW, Dupont Circle ☎659-8884. Large range of used books and records; also a useful spot to find out what's on in the city.

Specialty

ADC Map & Travel Center 1636 I St NW, New Downtown ☎628-2608. Extensive selection of maps, atlases and travel guides.

Big Planet Comics 3145 Dumbarton Ave NW, Georgetown ☎342-1961. A serious comic-book store specializing in alternative comics, manga and graphic novels.

Bridge Street Books 2814 Pennsylvania Ave NW, Georgetown ☎965-5200. Volumes on politics, literature, history, philosophy and film.

Brookings Institution Bookstore 1775 Massachusetts Ave NW, Dupont Circle, ☎797-6258. Political science tomes and policy studies from the prestigious think tank.

InfoShop 18th St and Pennsylvania Ave NW, Foggy Bottom ☎458-5454. Courtesy of the adjacent World Bank, this high-minded development bookstore offers a wide range of country studies, books and reports published by the Bank, Oxfam and the like.

International Language Centre 1803 Connecticut Ave NW, Dupont Circle ☎332-2894. Specializing in foreign-language books and self-instruction cassettes and offering a generous helping of foreign-language magazines.

Lambda Rising 1625 Connecticut Ave NW, Dupont Circle ☎462-6969. Extensively stocked gay and lesbian bookstore.

Lammas Women's Bookstore 1607 17th St NW, Dupont Circle ☎775-8218. Feminist and lesbian bookstore.

Mystery Books 1715 Connecticut Ave NW, Dupont Circle ☎483-1600. The city's specialist in detective, spy and crime fiction.

Reiter's 2021 K St NW, New Downtown ☎223-3327. Books on business, computing, finance, engineering and other scientific and professional topics.

Sisterspace 1515 U St NW, Shaw ☎332-3433. Books by and for African-American women; locally and nationally known authors frequently drop by to promote their work.

Travel Books & Language Center 4437 Wisconsin Ave NW, Tenleytown ☎237-1322. Superb travel bookstore, featuring a comprehensive selection of guides, maps, atlases, software, international cookbooks, magazines, newspapers and a full program of events and lectures.

US Government Bookstore 710 N Capitol St

Malls

Although **malls** are flourishing in revitalized downtown areas, they tend to be showy, tourist-oriented collections of gift shops, novelty stores and food courts. Head for the suburbs for the best malls (and, incidentally, slightly lower local sales taxes); there's direct Metro access to those at Friendship Heights, Crystal City and Pentagon City listed below. Opening hours are usually Monday through Saturday from 10am to 8pm, Sunday from noon to 6pm.

Downtown

Old Post Office Pavilion, 1100 Pennsylvania Ave NW ☎289-4224; Federal Triangle Metro.

The Shops at National Place, 1331 Pennsylvania Ave NW ☎783-9090; Metro Center Metro.

Union Station Mall, 50 Massachusetts Ave NE ☎371-9441; Union Station Metro.

Georgetown

Georgetown Park, 3222 M St NW ☎298-5577; Foggy Bottom–GWU Metro.

Out of town

Chevy Chase Pavilion, 5345 Wisconsin Ave NW ☎686-5335; Friendship Heights Metro.

Crystal City Shops, Crystal Drive, Arlington, VA ☎703/922-4636; Crystal City Metro.

Fashion Center at Pentagon City, 1100 S Hayes St, Arlington, VA ☎703/415-2400; Pentagon City Metro.

Mazza Gallerie, 5300 Wisconsin Ave NW ☎966-6114; Friendship Heights Metro.

Potomac Mills Outlet Mall, 2700 Potomac Mills Circle, Prince William, VA ☎1-800/826-4557; Wed–Sun shuttle from Metro Center, Rosslyn and Pentagon City Metro stations.

Tysons Galleria, 2001 International Drive, McLean, VA ☎703/827-7700; Capital Beltway exit 11B.

White Flint Mall, 11301 Rockville Pike, Bethesda, MD ☎301/231-7467; shuttle from White Flint Metro.

16

SHOPPING

NW, Old Downtown ☎512-0132; 1510 H St NW, New Downtown ☎653-5075. All the official facts and figures you could ever want, from the government's own bookstores. Open Mon–Fri only.

Vertigo Books 1337 Connecticut Ave NW, Dupont Circle ☎429-9272. Washington, American and world politics; black and social studies; and modern literature.

Regular signings and readings, too.

Yawa 2206 18th St NW, Adams-Morgan ☎483-6805. African and African-American books, magazines, crafts and cards.

Yes Bookstore 1035 31st St NW, Georgetown ☎338-7874. Extensive New Age book and music store. Holdings cover everything from Eastern religions and personal development to acupuncture and mythology.

Clothing

The best areas for browsing are in New Downtown (along Connecticut Ave), Dupont Circle (also along Connecticut Ave) and Georgetown. Tucked among the ubiquitous Gaps, you'll find a handful of unique boutiques worth a look. Even rapidly gentrifying Adams-Morgan has begun to get in on the act, with a growing number of ultra-hip clothing shops hanging out their shingles along 18th Street amid the trendy bars and restaurants.

But nearly every serious shopper winds up heading to **Georgetown**, the District's retail epicenter. Here – in particular along M Street and Wisconsin Avenue – you'll find the greatest concentration of the national retail chains, places like J Crew, Nine West and Urban Outfitters, as well as local boutiques and more exclusive shops. There are a few deals to be had here, though, with vendors setting up shop along the sidewalks to sell **knock-off designer handbags** to those shoppers who just can't stand to spend more than $15 on a "Kate Spade" bag.

For still more places to enhance your wardrobe, also see "Malls," p.301, and "Department stores," p.304.

Boutiques

All About Jane 2423 1/2 18th St NW, Adams-Morgan ☎797-8719. With contemporary clothes ranging from the sophisticated to the sexy, Jane spares women-on-the-go the trip to New York. Designers include Alice & Trixie and Tessuto; there are also T-shirts from Custo Barcelona and handbags by Lily Scott. Closed Tuesday.

Betsey Johnson 1319 Wisconsin Ave, Georgetown ☎338-4090. The upscale but whimsical creations of the well-known designer of women's fashions call out from behind a bright yellow facade.

Betsy Fischer 1224 Connecticut Ave, New Downtown ☎785-1975. Sophisticated women's attire, from conservative to hip, comes with sage advice from Betsy herself. Popular with urban professionals on the prowl for Shin Choi, Vivienne Tam and Jenne Maag.

Daisy 1814 Adams Mill Rd, Adams-Morgan ☎797-1777. Across Columbia Rd, this "unique girlie boutique" exudes a West Coast vibe, selling Earl Jeans, Mitzi Baker leather and accessories by London handbag queen Lulu Guinness. Closed Tuesday.

Donna Lewis 309-B Cameron St, Alexandria ☎703/548-2452. Hip-yet-classy clothes for women and a handful of Italian bags and shoes give this store New York flair.

Kaur 2102 18th St NW, Adams-Morgan ☎299-0404. Trendy sophisticated women's boutique featuring designer samples from the likes of Paul&Joe, Trosman Churba, Vivienne Tam and Anna Sui. The back lounge is stocked with vintage accessories. Closed Monday.

Niagara 2423 18th St NW, Adams-Morgan ☎332-7474. Tucked into a corner of an Adams-Morgan CD shop, this hip boutique features hard-to-find styles for men and women, with clothing from Built By Wendy, Milk Fed and Steven Alan. Closed Tuesday.

Nuevo Mundo 313 Cameron St, Alexandria ☎703/549-0040. Globetrotting mother-daughter team offers jewelry, unique "wearable art" from around the world, and easy-care travel clothing for men and women.

Pua Naturally 444 7th St NW, Old Downtown ☎347-4543. Upmarket Third World boutique brings a splash of ethnic color to downtown DC, with hand-woven skirts, jackets and scarves, most of which hail from South Asia.

Saks Jandel at the Watergate 2522 Virginia Ave NW ☎337-4200. Women's formal wear and cocktail dresses – just in case – from the Valentino, Vera Wang and Saks Jandel collections.

Funky clothing

Backstage 545 8th St SE, Capitol Hill ☎544-5744. Whether you're at a loss on Halloween or looking for an elaborate disguise, this Capitol Hill costume shop – teeming with wigs, boas and cat suits – just may be able to help. Buy or rent.

Commander Salamander 1420 Wisconsin Ave NW, Georgetown ☎337-2265. Funky T-shirts, sneakers, sportswear, bags, party gear and gimcrack jewelry. Open late.

Khismet 1800 Belmont Rd NW, Adams-Morgan ☎234-7778. "Wearable art" – meaning hand-crafted jewelry, textiles and clothes with an African flair for men and women.

Leather Rack 1723 Connecticut Ave NW, Dupont Circle ☎797-7401. Chaps, vests, boots and more – it's not just about blue blazers and khakis in DC anymore.

Red River Western Wear 641 Pennsylvania Ave SE, Capitol Hill ☎546-5566. DC's only Western-wear store carries everything from boots and Stetsons to Native American jewelry and Southwestern clothing.

Smash! 3285 1/2 M St NW, Georgetown ☎337-6274. Punks gasping for air amid Georgetown's well-scrubbed shops and restaurants can take refuge among the racks of bondage pants, zebra-stripe Creepers and studded leather belts or select a vinyl classic from the tidy selection of punk records.

Men's clothing

Everett Hall 1230 Connecticut Ave NW, Dupont Circle ☎467-0003. Celebrated local designer outfits *GQ* men with classically designed Italian-made suits, shirts and ties as well as contemporary sportswear. Hall has dressed his share of celebrities, including Nelson Mandela, Maury Povich, Stephen Baldwin and local hoops hero Patrick Ewing.

Universal Gear 1601 17th St NW, Dupont Circle ☎319-1157. Gay men's pit stop for current fashion along the 17th Street strip.

Secondhand and vintage

Meeps & Aunt Neensie's Fashionette 1520 U St NW, Shaw ☎265-6546. Neighborhood favorite offering a cool selection of men's and women's vintage attire that dates as far back as the 1940s.

Rage Clothing 1069 Wisconsin Ave NW, Georgetown ☎333-1069. Vintage clothing shop with jeans galore.

Shoes and accessories

Fleet Feet 1841 Columbia Rd NW, Adams-Morgan ☎387-3888. Fleet's friendly, experienced staff first outfits you in the proper shoes for running, walking, soccer or aerobics, and then lets you take the pair for a test drive outside. An assortment of sports clothes and accessories are also on hand.

Kenneth Cole 1259 Wisconsin Ave NW Georgetown ☎298-0007. Men's and women's shoes, belts and jackets.

Proper Topper 1350 Connecticut Ave NW, New Downtown ☎842-3055. Stuffed with stylish hats as well as bags, jewelry and an eclectic array of knick-knacks that make great gifts, this cozy little shop is a rewarding place to browse. That a few of the store's items have landed on *Sex and the City* attests to its genius. A second, more spacious, location is in Georgetown at 3213 P St NW (☎333-6200).

Shake Your Booty 2324 18th St NW, Adams-Morgan ☎518-8205; 3225 M St NW, Georgetown ☎333-6524. Hip shoes and one-of-a-kind accessories add a kick to the District's limp shoe scene.

Cosmetics and fragrances

Blue Mercury 3059 M St NW, Georgetown ☎965-1300; Dupont Circle at 1745 Connecticut Ave NW ☎462-1300. If you find yourself desperate for fancy face creams, hair products, scents and salves, this is your shop. There's an attached spa for on-the-spot pampering.

Sephora, 3065 M St NW, Georgetown ☎338-5644. French makeup boutique offering fragrances, well-being products and brand-name cosmetics.

Department stores

You'll have to travel if you're looking for the flagship **department stores**. Neiman Marcus, Nordstrom, Saks Fifth Avenue, Lord & Taylor, Bloomingdale's and Macy's are all firmly ensconced in the out-of-town malls (see p.301). Only Hecht's and Filene's Basement have maintained their downtown outposts.

Filene's Basement 1133 Connecticut Ave NW, New Downtown ☎872-8430; The Shops at National Place, 529 14th St NW, Old Downtown ☎638-2519. Famed Boston-based bargain fashion retailer with good deals on men's and women's clothing, shoes and accessories.

Hecht's 1201 G St NW, Old Downtown ☎628-6661, and suburban locations. Classic downtown department store with a full range of clothing and home furnishings. The store is a century old, though this stylish building was put up in 1985.

Museum and gallery stores

Virtually all DC's museums – in particular the Smithsonians – have well-stocked stores. The list below picks out the best; see the relevant pages for transport and museum details. (Smithsonian stores can also be found at National Airport.) Note that every other major attraction – US Capitol to Pentagon – also has its own gift shop, selling enough name-emblazoned souvenirs to satisfy even the most avid collectors of souvenirs and kitsch.

Arthur M. Sackler Gallery 1050 Independence Ave SW ☎357-4880. Jewelry, prints, waistcoats, fabrics, Asian art, ceramics, rugs, beads and calligraphy.

B'nai B'rith Klutznick National Jewish Museum 1640 Rhode Island Ave NW ☎857-6583. Jewelry, goblets, ceramics, T-shirts, arts and crafts, linen and embroidered goods, all with Jewish motifs.

Bureau of Engraving and Printing 14th and C St SW ☎1-800/456-3408. Just the place for that presidential engraving, prints of Washington DC, copies of famous texts, and even bags of shredded cash.

National Air and Space Museum Independence Ave and 7th SW ☎357-1387. Fantastic array of air- and space-related goodies, from books to ray-guns and spaceman ice cream.

National Gallery of Art Constitution Ave, between 3rd and 7th St NW ☎842-6002 or 1-800/697-9350. DC's best art shop – thousands of books, prints, slides, posters and postcards.

National Museum of African Art 950 Independence Ave SW ☎786-2147. Splendid displays of African arts and crafts, including great fabrics and jewelry.

National Museum of American History 14th St and Constitution Ave NW ☎357-2700. The Smithsonian's biggest store is great for souvenirs. Everything about America – music, books, T-shirts, kitchenware, ceramics, posters, toys, crafts, jewelry and repro items from the museum.

Textile Museum 2320 S St NW ☎667-0441. Unique T-shirts, ethnic fabrics, textile books, silks, cushion covers, ties, kimonos and jewelry.

Music stores

CD Warehouse 3001 M St NW, Georgetown ☎625-7101. Good across-the-board selection of used CDs.

DC CD 2423 18th St NW, Adams-Morgan ☎588-1810. New and used CDs and vinyl; late opening hours.

Flying Saucer Discs 2318 18th St NW, Adams-Morgan ☎265-3427. Basement store with good range of used pop, rock, rap, jazz, world and classical CDs.

Kemp Mill Music 12th and F St NW, Old Downtown ☏638-7077; 1900 L St NW, New Downtown ☏223-5310. Local chain for mainstream and chart releases, often with good discount offers.

Smash! 3285 1/2 M St NW, Georgetown ☏337-6274. Punk, hardcore, new wave and indie music, along with T-shirts, boots and clothes.

Tower Records 2000 Pennsylvania Ave NW, Foggy Bottom ☏331-2400. Biggest music store in town, with in-store appearances. Daily until midnight.

Specialty shops

Another Universe 3060 M St, Georgetown ☏333-8651. Sci-fi specialist for games, comics, cards, toys and posters.

Discovery Channel Destination Store 601 F St NW, Old Downtown ☏639-0908. Nifty stuff you never knew you wanted, from African art and flight jackets to spaceship models, teapots, games, jewelry and books.

FAO Schwarz Georgetown Park, 3222 M St NW, Georgetown ☏965-7000. Major toy store with massive amount of merchandise, modern and traditional, dolls to video games.

Ginza 1721 Connecticut Ave NW, Dupont Circle ☏331-7991. All things Japanese, chopsticks to kimonos.

Go Mama Go! 1809 14th St NW, U St/14th St Corridor ☏299-0850. Funky home-furnishings store featuring cool Asian dinnerware, some designed by the store's Thai owner.

Movie Madness 1083 Thomas Jefferson St NW, Georgetown ☏337-7064. Thousands of movie posters, old and new.

Orioles Baseball Store 925 17th St NW, New Downtown ☏296-2473. Stock up on jerseys honoring the legendary Cal Ripken and other O's paraphernalia or buy tickets to see the District's adopted team in Camden Yards.

Political Americana Union Station, 50 Massachusetts Ave NE ☏547-1685; 1333 Pennsylvania Ave NW, Old Downtown ☏547-1871. Everything from historic and topical buttons and bumper stickers to gifts, books and videos on every side of the political divide.

16

SHOPPING

Food and drink

Washington isn't exactly known for the quality of its delis, though a few good places to stock your larder stand out. Good **coffee**, at least, isn't hard to find – many of the coffee bars listed in Chapter 12 can sell you the beans. For quality **tea**, try one of Teaism's branches (p.261, p.266) or Ching Ching Cha (p. 269) in Georgetown.

Old-style **markets** are thin on the ground: **Eastern Market** is your best bet (p.117), while the Waterfront **Fish Wharf** (p.127) has a great selection of Chesapeake Bay seafood. There are weekend **farmer's markets** in Adams-Morgan (p.199), Alexandria (p.234), Dupont Circle, Takoma Park and at Arlington Court House.

For bread, you can't beat the **Breadline** (p.268) or **Firehook** bakery/coffee shops (p.265). Best general deli is the splendid **Dean & Deluca** (p.263) in Georgetown, although Dupont Circle's homespun **Marvelous Market** (p.265) is a great local find. Southwest fanciers should call at the **Red Sage** restaurant's shop (p.264).

Sports and outdoor activities

Visitors to Washington may be surprised to find that the nation's capital is one of America's greenest cities, with easy access to a multitude of woodsy trails. It also boasts a major waterway, the Potomac River. Thanks to these natural attributes, DC is a great place for people who like to cycle, sail, hike, paddle, skate, run or just stroll in the great outdoors – all a welcome relief from pounding the pavement between monuments and museums.

The capital city also has a lot to offer those who prefer to enjoy their sports from the sidelines – or from in front of the TV set. In fact, the **spectator sports** scene in Washington is going through something of a renaissance – much to its own surprise. For years DC has been just a football town, but the new millennium saw sports luminaries Michael Jordan, Jaromir Jagr and Mia Hamm arrive in town, stealing much of the Redskins' thunder.

Outdoor activities

Visitors looking to stretch their legs after a day on a Tourmobile will find plenty to keep them busy. The green expanse of Rock Creek Park – which stretches from the city's northern edge to the Potomac River – and the network of **trails** heading out from the capital to Virginia and Maryland together offer miles of routes for biking, walking and inline skating. Downtown, the **Mall** and the **Ellipse** provide the city with a central playground, particularly in summer when softball season swings into gear, and are good spots to go for a run.

Forming DC's southern boundary, the **Potomac** offers everything from heady Class VI rapids to guided tours for novice paddlers to sunset sails, making it easy to see DC from the water.

Bicycling

For a pleasant outdoor excursion, the nicest option might be to rent a bike for short **rides along the Potomac River** or the **C&O Canal towpath,** something you can do at Big Wheel Bikes' Georgetown branch, Thompson Boat Center, near the Watergate Complex, and Fletcher's Boat House two miles farther up the canal towpath (see details overleaf). Bicycle rentals run anywhere from $4/hour for a plain-vanilla cruiser from Thompson's to $48/day for a flashy Enduro FSR mountain bike at Blazing Saddles.

Among DC's long-distance **cycle paths** are one in Rock Creek Park (see p.213), the 18.5-mile Mount Vernon Trail (see p.231), and the entire 184-mile length of the C&O towpath (see p.218).

The eleven-mile **Capital Crescent Trail**, starting at Thompson Boat Center, branches off the C&O towpath after three miles and follows the course of an old railway line up into Bethesda, Maryland, and on to Silver Spring. Once in Bethesda, riders can turn this trip into a 21-mile loop by returning via Rock Creek Park – follow the signs to the unpaved Georgetown Branch Trail, which cuts across Connecticut Avenue, to find the park. On the southern end, the trail links up with the **Mount Vernon Trail** (via the Key Bridge) and the **Rock Creek Trail** (via K St). Be warned that this trail is extremely popular on weekends; for more information on this trail plus a detailed map, check out ⓦ www.cctrail.org.

Many trails and bicycle paths crisscross the Metrorail system, giving you the option of cutting short a trip or avoiding backtracking. Keep in mind that while bikes are permitted on the Metro at any time during the weekend, they are prohibited during weekday rush hours (7–10am & 4–7pm) and on some major holidays.

Bike rentals

Better Bikes ☎293-2080. Will deliver anywhere in DC.
Big Wheel Bikes 1034 33rd St NW, Georgetown ☎337-0254; 2 Prince St, Alexandria ☎703/739-2300.
Blazing Saddles 445 11th St NW, Old Downtown ☎544-0055.
Fletcher's Boat House 4940 Canal Rd NW, Georgetown ☎244-0461, ⓦ www.fletchersboathouse.com.
Thompson Boat Center 2900 Virginia Ave NW, Georgetown ☎333-4861, ⓦ www.guestservices.com/tbc.
Washington Sailing Marina 1 Marina Dr, George Washington Memorial Pkwy, Alexandria, VA ☎703/548-9027, ⓦ www.guestservices .com/wsm. The marina is located along the Mount Vernon Trail.

Bike shops

Chain Reaction 1701 6th St NW, Shaw ☎265-0179.
City Bikes 2501 Champlain St NW, Adams-Morgan ☎265-1564, ⓦ www.citybikes.com.
Spokes, Etc 1545 N Quaker La, Alexandria, VA ☎703/820-2200, ⓦ www.spokesetc.com.

Bike tours

Bike the Sites Inc 3417 Quesada St NW, Upper Northwest ☎966-8662, ⓦ www.bikethesites.com. Three-hour guided bike tours of the city's major sights ($40, includes bike and helmet), plus tours of Mount Vernon and customized tours throughout the District. Reservations required.

Riding resources

Bike Washington ⓦ www.bikewashington.org. Online recreational bicycling guide loaded with tips on local routes and trails.
Washington Area Bicyclist Association ☎628-2500, ⓦ www.waba.org. Advocacy group

---

Health clubs

If you'd prefer to sweat it out indoors, several area **health clubs** open their doors to nonmembers, although this will cost you. The following clubs have everything you need for a solid workout.

Results the Gym 1612 U St NW, Shaw ☎518-0001. Nonmembers pay $20 per visit. Mon–Fri 5.30am–11pm, Sat & Sun 8am–9pm.
Washington Sports Club 1211 Connecticut Ave NW, New Downtown ☎296-7733; 214 D St SE, Capitol Hill ☎547-2255. The two branches of this upscale club are open to nonmembers for a $25-per-visit fee. New Downtown: Mon–Fri 6am–10pm, Sat & Sun 8.30am–8.30pm. Capitol Hill: Mon–Thurs 6am–11pm, Fri 6am–10pm, Sat & Sun 8.30am-8.30pm.

whose website offers info on trails, gear and local events. The association also publishes *The Greater Washington Area Bicycle Atlas* ($16.95), a 300-page tome detailing 67 rides in Washington and beyond.

Inline skating

The Capital Crescent and Mount Vernon trails are both traveled by skaters as well as cyclers (see "Bicycling", opposite). But one of the best spots for bladers to head on the weekends is forested **Beach Drive** in Rock Creek Park, which is closed to vehicular traffic on weekends from 7am Saturday to 7pm Sunday. Near Parking Lot 6, just north of the intersection of Beach and Military roads and near the Public Golf Course, a gently hilly six-mile stretch is a popular training and cruising ground for local bladers. Skilled city skaters shouldn't have too much trouble getting there from the Van Ness Metro station, though it's probably easier to drive or catch a cab.

Skaters accustomed to slicing through city traffic will find the roads and sidewalks in the vicinity of the Mall hit and miss in terms of pavement quality, though you will feel a bit safer than you would, say, blading down Fifth Avenue in New York. One good area downtown is the strip of Pennsylvania Avenue **in front of the White House**, which is closed to vehicular traffic. Though it's not the longest stretch of road, it is wide and safe from cars whizzing past, making it popular with local rollerhockey aficionados. It's also the meeting point for the **Washington Area Roadskaters** (℡466-5005, @www.skatedc.org), a local club that organizes frequent group skates of varying lengths as well as free weekly inline skate clinics (April–Oct) in Rock Creek Park.

Jogging, running and walking

Of course you can **walk or jog** on any of the trails described under "Bicycling," but many prefer to simply put on their running shoes and hit the **Mall**, where the imperial buildings and monuments of the capital provide an inspiring backdrop for a daily workout. The gravel path circumscribing the mammoth front lawn of the city center provides a surface easier on the knees than your typical city pavement.

Those looking for a quieter place for a constitutional should head to **Roosevelt Island**, a nature park with 2.5 miles of trails that meander through marsh, swamp and forest. Access to the island, which lies at the start of the Mount Vernon Trail, is via a footbridge on the Arlington side of the Potomac.

Water sports

The **Potomac River** provides visitors and locals with plenty of chances to get out on the water. North of the city, twenty minutes beyond the Beltway, lies Seneca Creek State Park, where a flat expanse of river is ideal for canoeing. The current picks up and the crowds emerge a bit farther downstream as the Potomac races through **Great Falls**, where **Class VI rapids** providing ample challenge for experienced white-water kayakers.

Near Georgetown, several boat-rental shops offer the means to explore the calmer waters on either side of the Key Bridge and around Roosevelt Island, a stretch of the river that provides a worthy afternoon retreat. From here, it's easy enough to paddle your way into the **Tidal Basin**, an outing especially pretty in spring, when the cherry blossoms are in bloom.

Landlubbers keen on staying closer to shore can head to the Tidal Basin Boat House near the Jefferson Memorial and rent a **paddleboat** in March through September (℡484-0206; Mon–Fri 10am–6pm, Sat & Sun 10am–7pm; 2-seaters $8/hr, 4-seaters $16/hr).

Continuing downriver, the river widens as it flows past Alexandria toward the **Wilson Bridge**, an area popular with sailors, windsurfers and sea-kayakers. Just south of the bridge on the Virginia side, you can glide into **Dyke Marsh Wildlife Preserve**, a freshwater tidal wetland that's home to osprey, great blue heron and a variety of other birds.

Rentals, as you'd expect, vary in price with the size and type of boat you're after, with discounted rates offered for booking an entire day. Kayaks, canoes and rowboats go for anywhere from $9/hr to $40 for the day. Sailboats range from $9 to $19/hr (though you may find that there's a two-hour minimum rental) to $140 for the whole day. As rental service tends to be seasonal (March–Nov), you'd do well to call in advance in early spring or late fall before heading to the waterfront.

Boat rentals

Fletcher's Boat House 4940 Canal Rd NW, Georgetown ☎244-0461, ⊛www .fletchersboathouse.com. Rents rowboats, canoes and bikes and sells bait and tackle to the fishing crowd.
Jack's Boats 1034 33rd St NW, at K St NW, Georgetown ☎337-9642. Located under the Key Bridge, it rents canoe, kayak and rowboats.
Thompson Boat Center 2900 Virginia Ave NW, Georgetown ☎333-4861, ⊛www .guestservices.com/tbc. Single and double kayaks, canoes and recreational and racing rowing shells (from $13/hr; must be certified) plus bikes.

Canoeing and kayaking tours and instruction

Atlantic Kayak Company 1201 N Royal St, Alexandria, VA ☎703/838-9072,

⊛www.atlantickayak.com. Sunset tours, moonlight outings and daylong excursions (from $39 for a 2.5hr tour) plus sea-kayak instruction ($125 per day) and rentals.
Outdoor Excursions Boonsboro, MD ☎1-800/775-2925, ⊛www.outdoorexcursions.com. Located below Great Falls, with rafting (from $38) and tubing ($22) trips plus white-water kayaking and sea-kayaking instruction (each $85 per day), the latter on the Chesapeake Bay near Annapolis.

Sailing and windsurfing

Alexandria Seaport Foundation Prince St, Alexandria, VA ☎703/549-7078, ⊛www.capaccess.org/snt/alexsea. Sunset sails twice a week aboard a Potomac River dory, a work boat common on the river a century ago. The wooden vessel, a replica launched in 1995 by the foundation, is one of two of this class currently afloat. Reservations required; donations requested.
Belle Haven Marina Alexandria, VA ☎703/768-0018, ⊛www.saildc.com. Boats for rent (8.30am–sunset) include canoes, kayaks and rowboats, plus sailboats – Flying Scots, Hobie Cats and Sunfish – and windsurfers. A 34-foot sloop is available for charter ($90/hour including captain).
Washington Sailing Marina 1 Marina Dr, George Washington Memorial Pkwy, Alexandria, VA ☎703/548-9027, ⊛www.guestservices .com/wsm. Seasonal sailboat rentals (11am–4pm, by reservation only) include Islands, Flying Scot, and Sunfish. Rental bikes, too – the marina is located along the Mount Vernon Trail.

Spectator sports

Although far from a New York or a Philadelphia as far as sports-crazed fans go, DC certainly loves its teams – the **Redskins** have sold out their games for years to come and Washingtonians still pine for the days when baseball season meant something more than Hill staffers swatting at softballs on the Mall. While the city still lacks a baseball team, recent years have brought other new franchises to town: soccer's **Freedom** and **DC United** (already three-time champions) and basketball's **Mystics** have given the capital something new to cheer – or boo, this being the East Coast.

An outing to a sporting event can be expensive, however, once the cost of tickets, snacks and beer are tallied. Tickets to Caps and Wizards games can run as high as $100, though entry to soccer matches and WNBA games tends to be much cheaper. Buy your **tickets** through Ticketmaster (☎432/SEAT, ⊛www.ticketmaster.com) or directly through the team's or stadium's box

△ Banners at the MCI Centre, Old Downtown

Where the pros play

Camden Yards 333 W Camden St, Baltimore, MD ☎410/685-9800, ⓦwww.theorioles.com. Baltimore Orioles baseball.
FedEx Field 1600 Raljon Rd, Landover, MD ☎301/276-6050. Washington Redskins football.
MCI Center 601 F St NW, Old Downtown ☎628-3200,

ⓦwww.mcicenter.com; Gallery Place–Chinatown Metro. Washington Wizards and Washington Mystics basketball, Washington Capitals hockey.
RFK Stadium 2400 E Capitol St SE, Southeast ☎547-9077, ⓦwww.rfkstadium.com; Stadium–Armory Metro. DC United and Washington Freedom soccer.

office. If going to the game in person isn't your thing, you can always head to a downtown **sports bar**, such as *The Rock* (see p.279) or *ESPN Zone* (see p.279), where you can catch your team on television.

Baseball

The capital has been without a baseball team since the Washington Senators packed their bags for Texas in 1971. Local politicians and businessmen have clamored for a team for several years now, most recently seizing upon the terrorist attacks of September 2001 to call for a "national landmark ballpark" in Northern Virginia. With a die-hard baseball fan in the White House – President Bush also happens to be a former owner of the Texas Rangers – such talk just might become reality. Until then locals passionate for America's pastime will continue to root for the **Baltimore Orioles** (☎410/685-9800, ⓦwww.theorioles.com; April–Oct season). If you've never been to a baseball game, Oriole Park at Camden Yards in downtown Baltimore presents a chance to catch a game in a prime setting – although the team's recent struggles may make for a less than riveting outing. Built in 1992, the park is a stylish throwback to the classic baseball stadiums of the early twentieth century and proved so popular that it sparked a nationwide push to relocate local clubs in old-school fields.

Basketball

Basketball legend Michael Jordan dazzled the Washington sports world in January 2000 when he became part owner and president of basketball operations for the chronically mediocre **Washington Wizards** (☎661-5050, ⓦwww.nba.com/wizards; Nov–April season). Jordan's arrival tantalized fans – who have had little to cheer about since the team's lone championship in 1977 – with the hopes that the greatest player to ever play the game would join the Wizards on the court. His Airness put the rumors to rest by coming out of his second retirement in the 2001-02 season. While few expect Michael to notch his seventh championship in DC, his presence has made the team a hot ticket, both at the MCI Center and on the road.

In summers, the focus swings to the **Washington Mystics** (☎661-5050, ⓦwww.wnba.com/mystics; June–Aug season), DC's pro women's team, led by all-stars Nikki McCray and Chamique Holdsclaw. Despite struggling since the inception of the WNBA in 1997, the team draws one of the largest crowds in the league to the MCI Center.

Football

Football's **Washington Redskins** (☎301/276-6050, ⓦwww.redskins.com; Sept–Dec season) are the dominant obsession of the capital's sports fans. One of American football's oldest franchises, the team has also been

SPORTS AND OUTDOOR ACTIVITIES

one of the league's most successful franchises since arriving in the capital in 1937, with a total of five championships under its belt. The fortunes of the team have dimmed in recent years, however, hampered by poor play, salary mismanagement and a meddling new owner, Dan Snyder, a multimillionaire whose antics are routinely lampooned in the local press.

Despite all its recent woes, the team, which plays at 80,000-seat FedEx Field in Landover, Maryland, remains one of DC's hardest tickets to snag – indeed tickets are sold by the season only and the waiting list is years long. So unless you're prepared to pay ridiculous prices to scalpers, agents and newspaper advertisers for an individual game ticket, chances are slim that you'll see the 'Skins in action.

Hockey

The MCI Center's other main tenant, hockey's **Washington Capitals** (℡ 266-2277, ⓦ www.washingtoncaps .com; Oct–April season), has its own major draw, high-scoring wing Jaromir Jagr, brought in before the 2001–02 season and signed for a mint. While the Caps have yet to win the coveted Stanley Cup since they joined the league in the 1970s, the team is generally quite competitive and fun to watch, and new owner Ted Leonsis has been making good on his pledge to plumb his deep pockets for more additions.

Soccer

The city's major league soccer team, **DC United** (℡ 703/478-6600; ⓦ www.dcunited.com; March–Oct season), is one of the most successful in the United States. Since the inaugural MLS season in 1996, the team has won the title three times (last in 1999) and was also the first American club to win the CONCACAF Champions Cup (1998), the major competition for clubs from North and Central America and the Caribbean. The team has fallen off a bit in recent years, though average home attendance is still around 25,000. Two star Bolivians – midfielder Marco Etcheverry ("El Diablo") and forward Jaime Moreno – get most of the plaudits, alongside homegrown players like defender Eddie Pope. If you want to go and cheer the Black-and-Red, the noisiest fans – the self-styled Screaming Eagles – usually occupy sections 133 and 134 at RFK Stadium.

Women's soccer came to DC in April 2001 when the **Washington Freedom** (ⓦ www.washington-freedom.com) took to RFK's pitch in the WUSA's debut season. The team features gold medalist Mia Hamm, the top scorer in the history of international play, who led the US side to victory in the 1999 World Cup.

Festivals and events

The best of DC's major **festivals**, **parades and annual events** are listed below – for a comprehensive list contact the Washington DC Convention and Visitors Association (see p.20) or seek out the events calendar at Ⓦwww.washington.org. Note that the dates of many festivals vary from year to year, while birthday celebrations for famous people generally take place on the nearest weekend; call the numbers given, check with one of the organizations listed below and watch the local press for exact dates.

Open days at museums, galleries and attractions are covered in the relevant parts of the guide. For a list of **national public holidays**, see Basics, p.33.

All telephone area codes in this chapter are ☎202 unless otherwise stated.

January

Dr Martin Luther King Jr's Birthday (15th): wreath-laying at the Lincoln Memorial, reading of the "I have a dream" speech, concerts and speeches. ☎619-7222.
Robert E. Lee's Birthday (19th): celebrations, music and food at Arlington House in Arlington Cemetery; special events in Old Town Alexandria, VA. ☎703/548-1789.

February

African-American History Month (all month): special events, exhibits and cultural programs. Information from the Martin Luther King Memorial Library ☎727-1186 or the Smithsonian or National Park Service (see box below).
Chinese New Year (date varies): dragon dancers, parades and fireworks on H St NW in Chinatown. ☎638-1041.
Abraham Lincoln's Birthday (12th): wreath-laying and reading of the Gettysburg Address at the Lincoln Memorial. ☎619-7222.
Frederick Douglass' Birthday (14th): wreath-laying and other events at Cedar Hill, Anacostia. ☎426-5961.

George Washington's Birthday Parade (22nd): spectacular parade and events in Old Town Alexandria, VA. ☎703/838-9350. Also, events, concerts and wreath-laying at Mount Vernon. ☎703/780-2000.

March

St Patrick's Day (17th): Big parade down Constitution Ave NW on the Sunday before the17th (call ☎637-2474 for grandstand seats) and another through Old Town Alexandria on the first Saturday of the month (☎703/237-2199). There's also a celebration on the17th at Arlington House, Arlington National Cemetery, VA (☎703/557-0614).

Information lines

National Park Service ☎619-7222
Post-Haste ☎334-9000
Smithsonian ☎357-2700
Washington DC CVA ☎789-7000
Washington DC Events Office ☎619-7222

For more details on these organizations, see p.20.

Smithsonian Kite Festival (end of the month): kite-flying competitions for all at the Washington Monument. ☎357-2700.

April

National Cherry Blossom Festival (late March/early April): the famous trees around the Tidal Basin (see p.58) bloom in late March/early April; celebrated by a massive parade down Constitution Ave NW, the crowning of a festival queen, free concerts, lantern-lighting, dances and races. Parade ticket information ☎728-1137; other events ☎547-1500; general info and blooming reports @www
.nationalcherryblossomfestival.org.

Thomas Jefferson's Birthday (13th): wreath-laying and military drills at the Jefferson Memorial. ☎619-7222.

Filmfest DC (mid-month): two-week festival premiering national and international movies in theaters across the city. ☎724-5613, @www.filmfestdc.org.

Blessing of the Fleet (mid-month): nautical celebrations and services at US Navy Memorial. Associated events at Southwest Waterfront marina. ☎737-2300.

Easter Sunrise Service (Easter Sun): sunrise memorial service at Arlington National Cemetery. ☎703/695-3250 or 202/685-2851.

White House Easter Egg Roll (Easter Mon): entertainment and egg rolling (eggs provided) on the White House South Lawn. Special garden tours one weekend after Easter. Call well in advance. ☎456-2200, @www.whitehouse.gov.

Duke Ellington's Birthday (20th): music and events at Freedom Plaza, Pennsylvania Ave NW. ☎331-9404.

Smithsonian Craft Show (late April): craft exhibitions in the National Building Museum. Information ☎357-2700, @www.smithsoniancraftshow.org; tickets ☎1-888/832-9554.

Marvin Gaye/Save the Children Day (end of the month): downtown street festival sponsored by the African-American Music Foundation. ☎678-0503.

May

Flower Mart (first weekend): flowers, booths, children's entertainment and displays at Washington National Cathedral. ☎537-6200.

Asian–Pacific American Heritage Festival (first weekend): cultural displays, food stalls and activities in Freedom Plaza, Pennsylvania Ave NW. ☎659-2311 or 703/354-5036.

Malcolm X Day (mid-month): commemorative concerts, films and speeches in Anacostia Park. ☎724-4093.

Bob Marley Commemorative Day Festival (mid-month): reggae concerts and events at Freedom Plaza, Pennsylvania Ave NW. ☎724-9060.

Worldfest (date varies): two-day outdoor array of ethnic music, food and events on Pennsylvania Ave between 9th and 14th streets. ☎724-5430.

Memorial Day (last Mon): wreath-layings, services and speeches at Arlington Cemetery ☎685-2851, Vietnam Veterans Memorial ☎619-7222 and US Navy Memorial ☎737-2300. The National Symphony Orchestra performs on the Capitol's West Lawn on the Sunday before, and there's a jazz festival in Old Town Alexandria. ☎703/883-4686.

June

Philippine Independence Day Parade (3rd): Pennsylvania Ave parade and a fair on Freedom Plaza. ☎724-4093.

Dance Africa (mid-month): festival of African dance, open-air market and concerts at Dance Place, 3225 8th St NE. ☎269-1600, @www.danceplace.org.

Marvin Gaye Jr Appreciation Day (mid-month): street events and music on Pennsylvania Ave between 13th and 14th streets. ☎724-4093.

DC Caribbean Carnival (mid-month): a Caribbean-style parade, with masqueraders and live music, from Georgia and Missouri avenues to Banneker Park near Howard University. ☎829-1477, @www.dccaribbeancarnival.com.

Smithsonian Festival of American Folklife (usually last week of June to first week of July): one of the country's biggest festivals: American music, crafts, food and folk heritage events on the Mall. ☎357-2700.

July

National Independence Day Celebration (4th): reading of the Declaration of Independence at National Archives, parade along Constitution Ave NW, free concerts at the Sylvan Theatre near the Washington Monument, National Symphony Orchestra performance on west steps of the Capitol, finishing with a superb fireworks display. Get there as early as possible for all events. ☎619-7222.

Mary McLeod Bethune Celebration (date varies): wreath-laying, gospel choir and speakers at Bethune statue, Lincoln Park. ☎673-2402.

Caribbean Summer in the Park (mid-month): outdoor music, food and dancing at RFK Stadium. ☎249-1028.

Latin-American Festival (end of the month): Constitution Ave parade; food, crafts, music, dance and theater in Adams-Morgan and Mount Pleasant. ☎301/588-8719.

August

Arlington County Fair (mid-month): traditional fair with rides, crafts, entertainment, food stalls and concerts at Thomas Jefferson Center, 3501 2nd St, Arlington, VA. ☎703/358-6400.

Georgia Avenue Day (end of the month): parade along Georgia Ave (at Eastern Ave NW), plus carnival rides, music, food and stalls. ☎723-5166.

September

Labor Day Weekend Concert (Sun before Labor Day): National Symphony Orchestra plays on west lawn of the Capitol to mark the end of the summer season. ☎619-7222.

Adams-Morgan Day (first Sun after Labor Day): one of the best of the neighborhood festivals, with live music, crafts and cuisine along 18th St NW – always packed and great fun. ☎789-7000, Ⓦwww.adamsmorganday.org.

Constitution Day Commemoration (17th): US Constitution displayed at the National Archives to celebrate the anniversary of its signing; naturalization ceremonies, parade and concerts. ☎501-5215.

National Frisbee Championships (date varies): Frisbee-related activities – including amazing disk-catching pooches – on the Mall, near the Air and Space Museum. ☎1-800/423-3268.

Black Family Reunion (2nd weekend): Weekend festival on the Mall featuring food, dance performances and music. ☎737-0120.

German-American Day (end of the month):

Teutonic food and entertainment in Freedom Plaza. ☎554-2664.

October

Taste of DC (date varies): restaurant festival mixing tastings with arts and crafts displays, children's shows, and entertainment on Pennsylvania Ave NW. ☎724-5347 or 724-5430 (24hr hotline).

Columbus Day Ceremonies (second Mon): wreath-laying, speeches and music at the Columbus Memorial in front of Union Station. ☎301/434-2332.

White House Fall Garden Tours (mid-month): free garden tours and military band concerts. Call for reservations well in advance. ☎456-2200, Ⓦwww .whitehouse.gov.

Halloween (31st): unofficial block parties, costumed goings-on and fright-nights in Georgetown, Dupont Circle and other middle-class neighborhoods.

November

Annual Seafaring Celebration (date varies): the Navy Museum hosts a family event with maritime activities, food, arts and children's performances. ☎433-4882.

Veteran's Day Ceremonies (11th): solemn services and wreath-laying at 11am at Arlington Cemetery (usually with the president in attendance), Vietnam Veterans Memorial and US Navy Memorial.

December

Christmas Tree Lightings (beginning of the month): separate ceremonies for the lighting of the Capitol (west side) and National (Ellipse) Christmas trees – the latter lit by the president. The entire month on the Ellipse sees Nativity scenes, choral groups and other seasonal displays. ☎619-7222.

Washington National Cathedral Christmas Services (all month): carols, pageants, choral performances and bell-ringing. ☎537-6200, Ⓦwww.cathedral.org/cathedral/.

Pearl Harbor Day (7th): wreath-laying ceremony at the US Navy Memorial to commemorate the attack on Pearl Harbor. ☎737-2300.

White House Candlelight Tours (usually 26th–28th): extremely popular free evening White House tours. Call well in advance for reservations. ☎456-2200 or 619-7222, Ⓦwww.whitehouse.gov.

Directory

Airlines Air Canada ☎1-800/776-3000; Air France ☎1-800/321-4538; Alitalia ☎1-800/223-5730; America West ☎1-800/235-9292; American Airlines ☎1-800/433-7300; British Airways ☎1-800/247-9297; Continental Airlines ☎1-800/525-0280; Delta ☎1-800/221-1212; Finnair ☎1-800/950-5000; Icelandair ☎1-800/223-5500; Japan Airlines ☎1-800/525-3663; KLM ☎1-800/374-7747; Korean Air ☎1-800/438-5000; Lufthansa ☎1-800/645-3880; Midwest Express ☎1-800/452-2022; Northwest ☎1-800/225-2525; SAS ☎1-800/221-2350; Southwest ☎1-800/435-9792; Swissair ☎1-800/221-4750; TWA ☎1-800/221-2000; United Airlines ☎1-800/241-6522; USAir ☎1-800/428-4322; Virgin Atlantic ☎1-800/862-8621.

American Express ☎1-800/528-4800, ⊛www.americanexpress.com; offices at 1150 Connecticut Ave NW ☎457-1300; Pentagon City Mall, Arlington, VA ☎703/415-5400.

Area code All phone numbers are area code ☎202 unless otherwise stated.

Banks Citibank ☎1-800/926-1067, ⊛www.citibank.com; branches at 600 Pennsylvania Ave SE, Capitol Hill; 1000 Connecticut Ave NW, New Downtown; 1901 Wisconsin Ave NW, Georgetown. Riggs ☎301/887-6000, ⊛www.riggsbank.com; branches at 1913 Massachusetts Ave NW, Dupont Circle; 833 7th St NW, Old Downtown; 1920 L St NW, New Downtown. SunTrust ☎1-888/786-8787, ⊛www.suntrust.com; branches at 1369 Connecticut Ave NW, Dupont Circle; 1111 Connecticut Ave NW, New Downtown; 2929 M St NW, Georgetown.

Bus departures Call Greyhound (☎1-800/231-2222, in DC ☎289-5154) or Peter Pan Trailways (☎1-800/343-9999). Departures to Baltimore, Philadelphia, New York, Boston and beyond are from the terminal at 1005 1st St NE.

Doctors and dentists Lists of doctors can be found in the Yellow Pages under "Clinics" or "Physicians and Surgeons." Most large hotels either have a doctor on call or will direct you to a private doctor. For a doctor referral service call Washington Hospital Center (☎877-3627) or George Washington University Hospital (☎1-888/449-3627), or contact your embassy (see below). The basic consultation fee is $50–100, payable in advance. Contact the DC Dental Society ☎547-7615 (Mon–Fri 8am–4pm) for dentist referral.

Electricity 110 volts AC. Plugs are standard two-pins – foreign visitors will need an adaptor and voltage converter for their own electrical appliances.

Embassies and consulates Australia: 1601 Massachusetts Ave NW, 20036 ☎797-3000; Canada: 501 Pennsylvania Ave NW, 20001 ☎682-1740; Ireland: 2234 Massachusetts Ave NW, 20008 ☎462-3939; Netherlands: 4200 Linnean Ave NW, 20008 ☎244-5300; New Zealand: 37 Observatory Circle NW, 20008 ☎328-4800; United Kingdom: 3100 Massachusetts Ave NW, 20008 ☎588-6500.

Floors The first floor in the US is what would be the ground floor in Britain; the second floor would be the first floor and so on. However, the design of some DC buildings and institutions (including various Mall museums and galleries) incorporates underground and mezzanine levels, so on occasion buildings do have a "ground floor" on the level at which you enter. This is never as confusing as it sounds.

Hospital George Washington University Hospital, 901 23rd St NW (☎715-4000, general patient information) has a 24hr-emergency department (☎715-4911) and

DIRECTORY

travelers' clinic (☎994-5400).

Internet access Available at the Martin Luther King Memorial Library, 901 G St NW, Old Downtown ☎727-1186 (Mon–Thurs 10am–9pm, Fri & Sat 9am–5.30pm, Sun 1–5pm) or at one of the following outlets: Cyberlaptops.com, 1636 R St NW, Dupont Circle ☎462-7195 (Mon–Sat 9am–9pm); Cyberstop Café, 1513 17th St NW, Dupont Circle ☎234-2470 (daily 7am–midnight); Kinko's Copies, 317 Pennsylvania Ave SE, Capitol Hill ☎547-0421 (daily 24hr), 1612 K St NW New Downtown ☎466-3777 (daily 24hr), 3329 M St NW, Georgetown ☎965-1415 (daily 24hr); and The Newsroom, 1803 Connecticut Ave NW, Dupont Circle ☎332-1489 (daily 7am–9pm).

Libraries The general public can use the Library of Congress (see p.111 for details), while the main city library is the Martin Luther King Memorial Library, 901 G St NW (see above and p.180).

Pharmacies CVS has forty different locations throughout DC, with convenient downtown and Georgetown sites and 24-hour stores at 1121 Vermont Ave NW, at Thomas Circle ☎628-0720, and 7 Dupont Circle ☎785-1466.

Police In an emergency call ☎911. For nonemergency help, information and the location of local stations call ☎727-1010. The Metro Transit Police can be contacted at ☎962-2121.

Post offices and mail services DC's main downtown post office is across from Union Station at 2 Massachusetts Ave NE, 20002 (Mon–Fri 7am–midnight, Sat & Sun 7am–8pm; ☎523-2628). There are also convenient post office branches at 1800 M St NW, New Downtown ☎523-2506 (Mon–Fri 9am–6pm), and 1200 Pennsylvania Ave NW, 20004 ☎523-2386 (Mon–Fri 9am–6pm, Sat 8.30–2pm). Service counters offering stamps and information are in the Old Post Office building on Pennsylvania Avenue NW (see p.162), in the National Museum of American History (p.86) and in the US Capitol (p.98). Downtown mail boxes can be found on Constitution Avenue NW at 11th, 14th and 21st; on Independence at 14th; and on 15th outside the Bureau of Engraving and Printing.

Tax DC sales tax is 5.75 percent; restaurant tax, 10 percent; hotel tax, 14.5 percent.

Taxis Capitol Cab ☎546-2400, Diamond Cab ☎387-6200, Yellow Cab ☎544-1212.

Thomas Cook ☎1-800/287-7362, ⊛www.fx4travel.com; branches at 1800 K St NW (Mon–Fri 9am–5pm); Union Station, Massachusetts Ave NE (Mon–Sat 9am–5pm, Sun noon–6pm); and at National and Dulles airports (both daily 7am–9pm).

Time Washington DC is in the Eastern zone, which covers the area inland to the Great Lakes and the Appalachian Mountains; this is five hours behind Greenwich Mean Time (-5 GMT). Daylight saving time, when clocks are turned back an hour, operates between April and October (check newspapers for specific dates).

Train departures Amtrak (☎1-800/872-7245 or 484-7540) operates out of Union Station, offering service along the Northeast Corridor and beyond. Tickets are available at either Union Station (ticket office open daily 5.30am–10.30pm) or New Carrollton station in Maryland. Maryland Rail Commuter Service (MARC; ☎1-800/325-7245) connects DC to Baltimore.Tickets can be purchased from self-service ticket machines at Union Station.

Travel agencies American Express, 1150 Connecticut Ave NW ☎457-1300; Council Travel, 3300 M St NW ☎337-6464; STA Travel, 2401 Pennsylvania Ave NW ☎887-0912.

Travelers aid society Useful help, emergency and information desks run by a voluntary, nonprofit agency. Main office is at Union Station (☎371-1937; Mon–Sat 9.30am–5.30pm, Sun 12.30–5.30pm); other offices at National Airport (☎703/417-3972; Mon–Fri 9am–9pm, Sat & Sun 9am–6pm) and Dulles Airport (☎703/572-8296; Mon–Fri 10am–9pm, Sat & Sun 10am–6pm).

Weather For five-day city weather forecasts check the daily *Washington Post* or call ☎334-9000, code 9100.

Western Union ☎1-800/325-6000, ⊛www.westernunion.com; offices at Barmy Wines & Liquor, 1912 L St NW, New Downtown ☎833-8730 (Mon–Sat 10am–9pm); Mail Boxes Etc., 2000 Pennsylvania Ave NW, Foggy Bottom ☎457-8166 (Mon–Fri 9am–5.30pm).

contexts

contexts

CONTEXTS

A history of Washington DC

In the two centuries since Washington DC was founded, it has been at the heart of American government, a showcase city embodying the ideals and aspirations of the United States of America. However, it's also a city where people live and work, a fact that's easy to forget among the mighty monuments and memorials. The history below provides a brief exposition of the main themes in the city's development. For more detail on specific matters – from biographies of famous people to histories of buildings – follow the pointers at the end of each section.

Early settlers

The first white settlers to clap eyes on the Potomac River region – site of modern DC – were the pioneers under Captain John Smith of the Virginia Company in 1608. Sponsored by the English King James I, they had established the first successful **English colony** in America the previous year at Jamestown on the coast, to the south, and lost little time exploring their surroundings. Despite early setbacks, and conflict with the local native population, the colonists flourished on the back of a thriving tobacco trade. Virginia, and then Maryland (created as a haven for Catholics in 1632), expanded as English, Irish and Scottish settlers poured into the region, displacing the indigenous population and introducing **slaves** from Africa to work the plantations. Among these pioneers was one Captain John Washington, George's great-grandfather, who in 1656 arrived from Essex in England and immediately set about establishing a plantation on the river. The Potomac remained an important commercial thoroughfare, and vibrant new towns sprang up alongside it: notably Alexandria in Virginia (1749) and Georgetown in Maryland (1751).

Alexandria, history	p.231	Georgetown, history	p.216

Establishment of the capital

In 1775, in the context of increasing hostilities with the British, the colonies – now calling themselves states – drafted the Declaration of Independence. Following the ensuing **American War of Independence** (1775–83), during which Virginia's George Washington served as commander-in-chief of the Continental Army, came proposals for the establishment of a permanent **capital city**. There was no obvious site: the exigencies of war and conflicting political interests in the new republic meant that early meetings of Congress had gathered in several different cities. The Constitutional Convention of

1787, which devised a permanent system of government for the nation, was held in Philadelphia, while George Washington was elected as first President of the United States in New York City in 1789. Extended political wrangling between the mercantile North and agrarian South, both of which wanted the capital, came to an end when a southern site on the Potomac was chosen (near George Washington's beloved estate at Mount Vernon), with land to be donated by Virginia and Maryland. Washington hired surveyors Andrew Ellicot and Benjamin Banneker, an African-American, to conduct the preliminary survey.

Building the city

In 1791, French engineer Pierre Charles L'Enfant began work on a grand plan for the new city, and though he was fired the following year, his blueprint was largely followed by his successors. The first stone of the Executive Mansion (later known as the **White House**) was laid in 1792, construction of the **US Capitol** followed in 1793, and in 1800 Congress and second president John Adams moved from Philadelphia to the nascent city. The following year, Thomas Jefferson became the first president to be inaugurated in Washington DC. The population of 3500 was then little more than that of a village, based largely around Capitol Hill and the Executive Mansion, overseen by a mayor and council. Its numbers were boosted by over three thousand slaves who labored on the new buildings, wharves and streets and lived in the swamp-ridden reaches near the river. Progress was interrupted by the **War of 1812** with England; in 1814, English occupying forces burned the White House, Capitol and other public buildings to the ground. President Madison was forced to relocate to a private house, known as the Octagon, while Congress met in a hastily assembled Brick Capitol until the US Capitol was fully restored in 1819.

Mid-nineteenth-century malaise

Between the War of 1812 and the Civil War, the new capital struggled to make its mark. **The Mall** – L'Enfant's showpiece thoroughfare – remained a muddy swamp, and construction was slow and piecemeal. Foreign ambassadors collected hardship pay while stationed in this marshy outpost, and criticism was heaped upon the place; early detractors included such notable visitors as Charles Dickens (in the 1840s) and Anthony Trollope (1860s). Despite its critics, however, the capital city was slowly beginning to look the part. Pennsylvania Avenue was spruced up (and the Treasury Building added in 1836) and work started on the Washington Monument in 1848. British gentleman scientist and philanthropist James Smithson made a huge bequest in 1829, which led to the founding of the **Smithsonian Institution**; its first home, the Smithsonian Institution Building (or the "Castle") on the Mall, was completed in 1855.

Though the city's population increased slowly, throughout the first half of the century it never rose above 60,000. The balance of the steadily increasing **black population** shifted, however, as the number of runaway slaves and free blacks (migrants from Southern plantations) increased dramatically. Separate black schools and churches were established as debate intensified between abolitionists and pro-slavery adherents – the so-called Snow Riots (1835) saw intimidation and destruction by white mobs intent on maintaining slavery in the capital.

The Civil War

Following the Confederate attack on Fort Sumter, which finally propelled the country into **civil war**, Abraham Lincoln's call to defend the Union in 1861 brought thousands of volunteer soldiers to Washington, virtually doubling the city's population. Others left to join the Confederate cause, among them Robert E. Lee, who abandoned his home at Arlington and his Union Army post to take command of the Virginian military. Washington DC became the epicenter of the Union effort and the North's main supply depot, surrounded by defensive forts, its public buildings turned over to massive makeshift hospitals. Lincoln determined to continue construction in the capital (symbolically, the Capitol dome was added in 1863), despite fear of imminent attack by Southern forces – the city was never overrun, though several of the bloodiest and most decisive battles (including Bull Run, Antietam and Gettysburg) were fought within ninety miles of it. As Lincoln's war aims became more focused, the Civil War became a war about **slavery**. This was outlawed in DC in 1862, and in 1863 Lincoln signed the Emancipation Proclamation freeing all slaves in the rebel states. Thus defeated by the North's superior strength and economic muscle, and legally stripped of the right to operate a system crucial to its economic survival, the Confederate South was effectively vanquished. The war ended in April 1865 with Lee's surrender to General Ulysses S. Grant. Five days later, President Lincoln was assassinated in the capital while attending a play at Ford's Theatre.

Reconstruction and expansion

The period after the Civil War was an era of tremendous growth in DC as ex-slaves from the South and returned soldiers settled in the city – within thirty years, the population stood at 300,000, and distinct neighborhoods began to emerge. Black residents now constituted forty percent of the population and enjoyed unprecedented rights and privileges in the aftermath of emancipation. Suffrage was extended to all adult men for local DC elections (1866); black public schools became established and the all-black Howard University was founded (1867); segregation was prohibited (1870) and ex-slave, orator and abolitionist Frederick Douglass was appointed marshal (and, later, recorder of deeds) of DC (1877). In 1867, when Congress granted the District of Columbia territorial status, for the first time the city embarked on a coherent public works program under Alexander "Boss" Shepherd – a short-lived exercise in local democracy that ended in 1874, when control of the debt-ridden city passed back to Congress. Washington's cultural profile, however, went from strength to strength, boosted after the 1876 Philadelphia Centennial Exhibition when the Smithsonian Institution built **America's first National Museum** (now the Arts and Industries Building) on the Mall to provide a permanent home for the exhibition's artifacts. The Renwick and Corcoran galleries – two of the earliest public art galleries in the country – both opened during this period. The **Washington Monument**, first of the city's grand presidential memorials, was finally completed in 1884, as DC began to reshape itself as a national showpiece. As its stock rose, place-seekers and lobbyists (a term first coined during Grant's presidency) flooded into the city, seeking attachment to the administration of the day. In 1881, just four months after his inauguration, President James Garfield became the second president to be assassinated in Washington, shot by a man denied a civil service post.

The turn of the century

By the turn of the century, Washington had established itself as a thriving, modern capital city with civic and federal buildings to match: in a flurry of construction, the Patent Office, Post Office, Pension Building and fine new premises for the Library of Congress (1897) were erected, while Theodore Roosevelt carried out the first full-scale expansion and renovation of the White House (1901). Meanwhile, LeDroit Park, Adams-Morgan and Woodley Park became fashionable suburbs, Georgetown was formally merged with DC, and the Smithsonian branched out again with the establishment of the National Zoo. In 1901, a committee under Senator James McMillan proposed the development and extension of the city's park system. Later, the National Commission of Fine Arts was established to coordinate public improvements and new building design: the country's largest train station, Union Station, was completed in the prevailing Beaux Arts style in 1908, and in 1910, height restrictions were imposed on downtown buildings to preserve the cityscape. However, after the high hopes of the Reconstruction years, the city's black population suffered from increasing segregation and loss of civil rights. Housing in black neighborhoods like Foggy Bottom and Georgetown was in poor shape, federal jobs became harder to come by, and the black population actually decreased.

World War I and the Depression

The US entered World War I in 1917, despite President Woodrow Wilson's avowed efforts to remain neutral; after the war, Washington's population increased again as soldiers returned home. The post-war years were as troubled for DC as they were for the rest of the US. Under Wilson (the only president to remain in the city after his term of office), Prohibition was imposed in an attempt to improve the morality of the nation, and a number of strikes were violently broken. **Racial tension** increased in this uneasy climate, which saw segregation entrenched, the Ku Klux Klan parading at the Washington Monument, and race riots, fanned by demobilized white soldiers, breaking out in the city in 1919. Ironically, segregation also worked to boost the fortunes of DC's black neighborhoods: prevented from socializing elsewhere, blacks made Shaw's U Street famous as the "Black Broadway," nurturing stars such as Duke Ellington. Downtown, the Phillips Collection, America's first modern art museum, opened in 1921, while the building of the Lincoln Memorial (1922) and Freer Gallery (1923) represented the last cultural gasps of the McMillan Commission. The capital, with its government agencies and large federal payroll, was not as hard hit as rural or industrial areas by the **Great Depression**; unemployed marchers from the rest of the country descended on the Capitol to register their distress in 1931 and 1932 (the latter march being dispersed by the army). Franklin D. Roosevelt's **New Deal**, and, specifically, the **Works Progress Administration** (WPA), put thousands of jobless men to work – in DC, among other projects, building Federal Triangle and the Supreme Court (1935). If proof were needed that racial prejudice was still institutionalized in America's capital, it came in 1939 with the banning by the Daughters of the American Revolution (DAR) of black contralto Marian Anderson from singing in their building – she subsequently appeared in front of a huge, desegregated crowd at the Lincoln Memorial.

CONTEXTS | History

World War II to 1968

In 1941 the US entered **World War II** and a third great wartime influx boosted the population of Washington DC again. Guards were posted at the White House and Capitol, air defenses installed in case of Japanese attack, and the **Pentagon** built in 1943 to accommodate the expanding War Department. The war years also saw the opening of the National Gallery of Art (1941), the nation's finest art gallery, and the completion of the Jefferson Memorial (1943). Following the war, Washington grew as the federal government expanded under presidents Truman and Eisenhower. By 1960 the population touched 800,000; the White House was completely overhauled; neighboring Foggy Bottom – once a poor, black area – became the seat of various departments and organizations; and new housing proliferated in suburban Maryland and Virginia.

The war had gone some way to changing racial perceptions in America, as black soldiers had again enlisted in droves to fight for freedom, and in the postwar years the **Civil Rights** movement began to gain strength. Segregation of public facilities was finally declared illegal by the Supreme Court ruling on *Brown vs. Topeka Board of Education*, and schools in DC were desegregated in 1954. In the Southern states, however, the ruling was obeyed in name only, leading to an increasingly politicized, nationwide stream of demonstrations, boycotts, sit-ins and marches in the 1950s and early 1960s. A nascent feeling of widespread hope culminated in the close election victory in 1961 of John F. Kennedy – the youngest president ever to take office, and the first Catholic – and was epitomized by Dr Martin Luther King Jr's famous "I have a dream" speech during the March on Washington for Jobs and Freedom at the Lincoln Memorial in August 1963. Just three months later, however, JFK was assassinated in Dallas and buried in Arlington Cemetery. In 1964 DC citizens voted in a presidential election for the first time, following the 23rd Amendment of 1961, which gave them new electoral rights. The contest was won with a huge majority by Lyndon Johnson, who as vice president had been governing the country since Kennedy's death.

By the late 1960s protest had broadened beyond the realm of Civil Rights, and demonstrations in Washington were called against poverty (notably the Poor People's March, in 1968) and the war in Vietnam. Discrimination against blacks forced itself explosively back onto the agenda with the assassination of Dr Martin Luther King Jr in Memphis in 1968. His death sparked off nationwide riots, including the worst in DC's history; Shaw and the Old Downtown neighborhoods were devastated. The white flight to the suburbs began in earnest and DC became predominantly black.

© CONTEXTS | History

The 1970s

The 1970s put politics center stage in DC. In 1970, DC got its first nonvoting delegate to the House of Representatives; three years later, the Home Rule Act paved the way for the city's first elected mayor – Walter Washington – for more than a century; and the Watergate scandal of 1974 led to the resignation of a president. Meanwhile, **divisions within the city** became increasingly stark. Downtown areas continued to reshape themselves – the Kennedy Center opened in 1971, the Hirshhorn Museum (1974) and East Wing of the National Gallery of Art (1979) were added to the Mall, the K Street business district in New Downtown thrived, the new Southwest Waterfront acquired character, and arty Dupont Circle became one of the city's trendiest neighborhoods – while Shaw and areas of southeast and northeast Washington slipped further into degradation, with a drug-and-crime problem that earned DC the enduring tag of "Murder Capital" of America. Such contradictions were largely ignored, however, and in 1976, Bicentennial year, the city celebrated by opening its Metrorail system and the National Air and Space Museum – still the top museum attraction in Washington.

The 1980s

Under Ronald Reagan, the nation's economy boomed and busted as taxes (and welfare and aid programs) were cut, and the federal budget deficit soared. In DC, the souped-up economy paved the way for drastic **downtown renovation projects**: the building of the Convention Center (1980) signaled the revitalization of Old Downtown; Pennsylvania Avenue and its buildings – eyesores for three decades – were restored; and the yuppies moved into Adams-Morgan. Reagan survived an assassination attempt in DC in 1981, but his reputation (and that of his successor, George Bush) were put through the mill by the various Iran-Contra proceedings, whose revelations (in an echo of Watergate) were carried live on TV from hearings in the city. As American military spending increased dramatically, major new patriotic memorials were built to the Vietnam veterans (1982) and US Navy (1987). Culturally, the city went from strength to strength. The Smithsonian expanded its collections on the Mall with the addition of the Sackler Gallery and African Art Museum in 1987; the National Postal Museum opened (1986); and Union Station was restored (1988). City politics took a colorful turn with the successive administrations of Mayor **Marion Barry** (first elected in 1978), whose initial success in attracting investment soon gave way to conflict with Congress that was to become the hallmark of the following decade. The city began its slide into insolvency just as Bill Clinton was elected on promises to turn the economy around and restructure welfare.

CONTEXTS | History

The city today

To the casual eye, it was business as usual in the 1990s in DC – now one of the most touristed cities in America, with almost 20 million visitors a year – as **new attractions** continued to open: the National Law Enforcement Officers Memorial in 1991, the Holocaust Memorial Museum in 1993, the Korean War Veterans Memorial and the White House Visitor Center in 1995, the FDR Memorial and MCI Center in 1997. Behind the scenes, though, Washington lurched into crisis in the first half of the 1990s, as the federal budget deficit spiraled. Amazingly, Marion Barry returned from a drug-related prison sentence to be re-elected as mayor in 1994 – only for Congress to revoke Washington's home rule charter a year later and place a congressionally appointed **financial control board** in charge of the city's affairs.

The city rebounded under the control board, which by virtue of its success put itself out of a job in 2001, **restoring power** to the city council and the mayor, Anthony Williams, a former chief financial officer of the board who won election in 1998 in convincing fashion. The city's **rising fortunes** can be seen in lower crime rates, newly paved roads and a revitalized downtown, where restaurants, cultural happenings and sports events have begun to attract visitors to areas once overrun by drug dealers. Perhaps most tellingly, DC's population appears to have stabilized at last after decades of decline. Washington, it seems, is no longer a place from which residents wish to flee for the suburbs. Yet despite the optimism generated by the reformist Williams, the city still has a long way to go. Away from the Mall, museums and memorials, parts of the city still look more like the Third World than capital of the First. Most pressingly, the government, with its narrow tax base, still needs to figure out how to pay for the basic services that it must provide.

As the city was grappling with its financial woes, the public exposure of President Clinton's affair with intern **Monica Lewinsky** put DC in the national spotlight in a way not seen since the Watergate hearings of the 1970s. As always the cover-up seemed worse than the crime, but President Clinton survived the impeachment hearings of 1999. In April 2000, **anti-globalization protestors** descended on downtown Washington in an effort to shut down meetings of the World Bank and International Monetary Fund; in December hordes of reporters arrived, eagerly awaiting the Supreme Court's decision regarding the muddled **2000 presidential election**.

On **September 11, 2001**, terrorists hijacked a United Airlines jet and crashed it into the Pentagon, killing nearly 200 people, including those on the plane. A second plane, thought to be headed for the White House or the Capitol, crashed in a Pennsylvania field before reaching its target, while two other hijacked planes destroyed New York's World Trade Center, killing thousands. Soon after, **anthrax spores** were found in a letter mailed to Senate leader Tom Daschle, heightening tensions in an already shaken DC. The House suspended its session for a week and several federal buildings were closed pending investigation and fumigation. In the aftermath, **security** was tightened throughout the capital and tourism slowed to a trickle as government leaders and city officials began to grapple with their next challenge: balancing the openness demanded of a democratic capital with the vital needs of public and national security, an issue likely to be at the forefront of the city's concerns for some time.

| White House security | p.135 | DC in decline | p.169 |
| New memorials and museums | p.48 | Downtown development | pp.177–178 |

The American system of government

The American system of government derives squarely from the articles of the **Constitution of the United States**, thrashed out by the original thirteen states at the Constitutional Convention in Philadelphia and signed on September 17, 1787. Deriving its authority from the essential force of popular sovereignty – "We the People" – this gave a federal administration certain designated powers so that it could both resist attack from abroad and prevent the fragmentation of the nascent nation. Two centuries and 27 amendments later, the Constitution's provision of "checks and balances" on the exercise of power still provides the basis for the fundamental democratic stability of a country that has often looked less than united.

In a self-governing republic – good government in some places, dubious in others – three thousand miles wide, eighteen hundred miles long, with fifty separate states which in many important matters have almost absolute powers – with two hundred million people drawn from scores of nations, what is remarkable is not the conflict between them but the truce.
Alistair Cooke, *Letter from America*, 1969

The idea was simple enough. The earlier **Articles of Confederation** (adopted during the Revolution) had joined a loose grouping of independent states together in Congress under a weak central legislature, but by the late 1780s it was clear that the system lacked internal logic. With no separation of executive powers, Congress had to request permission from the states every step of the way; each state retained the right to refuse consent (whether for money, permission for new laws or soldiers) and exercised the power in its own interest. What was needed, according to Federalists like Alexander Hamilton and James Madison, was a strong central government buttressed by a supreme Constitution; the Antifederalists who opposed them, fearing encroachment upon the sovereignty of the individual states, were appeased by the promise of the ratification of various amendments (adopted in 1791 in the ten-point Bill of Rights) that would encompass many of their demands. What was produced at the Constitutional Convention was nothing less than a triumph: eighty percent of the original text of the Constitution remains unchanged today; only seventeen more amendments have been added in the two centuries following the Bill of Rights; and the United States remains, on paper at least, one of the world's most enduring democracies.

As a **federal republic**, the country splits its powers between the government and the fifty individual states, basically protecting the states from unnecessary intrusions from an overbearing central government while allowing federal decisions to be made to benefit (or protect) the whole country: thus the states can police themselves, make local laws and raise taxes, but they can't issue currency, conclude foreign treaties, or maintain armed forces. On the other hand, the Constitution pledges that the federal government shall protect each of the states against invasion or "domestic violence." Moreover, those who framed the Constitution took great pains to emphasize that individual states should retain all powers not specifically removed or curtailed by the Constitution; reinforced by the 10th Amendment, this notion remains a fundamental tenet of American democracy, in which local and national powers are stringently defined within the framework of a federal, and not centralized, republic. Thus each state has a significant amount of autonomy, while the states' political structures duplicate the federal system, with their own legislative chambers, state courts and constitutions.

The branches of federal government

The **federal government** itself comprises three distinct branches: the **legislative**, **executive** and **judiciary**. Each operates as a check and balance on the other, and each directly affects individual liberties and not just those of the states.

Article 1 of the Constitution vests all **legislative** powers in a bicameral **Congress** made up of a House of Representatives and a Senate, both of which meet in the US Capitol. When established in the eighteenth century, the House of Representatives was conceived of as the body whose directly elected members would represent the people; the addition of a Senate, or upper house, would not only be a check on the House's power, but also a way of balancing the interests of the smaller states against the larger, since each state in the Senate has an equal vote. Moreover, the separation of roles between House and Senate was institutionalized from the start – representatives and senators are elected at different times, from differently sized constituencies for different lengths of office.

The **House of Representatives** (or simply the "House") has 435 members (this size was fixed in 1929), with states allocated a number of representatives based on their population (which is reassessed, or "reapportioned," every ten years; each state is entitled to at least one representative). Members are elected from defined congressional districts (each containing about 500,000 people), serve for two years and receive $145,000 per annum (plus the support of up to thirty staff members). The House is the more representative of the two chambers: more frequent elections mean a closer convergence with the general public's mood, while the House always has a significantly higher percentage of women and ethnic minority members than the Senate (though neither remotely reflects the demographic make-up of the modern US). Apart from the fifty states thus represented, there are also nonvoting delegates in the House, representing the territories of Samoa, Guam and the Virgin Islands, and, since 1973, Washington DC itself (see p.168 for more on Washington's peculiar status within the Union). The chief officer of the House is the **Speaker** (chosen from the ranks of the majority party and paid $186,000 a year). Each party also elects a leader in the House, known accordingly as the House Majority or House Minority leader, and a House whip (whose job is to ensure that party members vote).

The **Senate** comprises two senators from each state. At first, in rather aristocratic fashion, senators were chosen by the individual state legislatures, but in 1913, the 17th Amendment allowed for the direct election of senators by state voters. Senators are elected for six years, with one third being elected every two years; like members of the House, they get paid $145,000 a year. The presiding officer in the Senate is the US Vice President (though on a day-to-day basis the Senate Majority Leader takes the chair); the Vice President doesn't have a vote unless it's to break a tie.

In Congress, the House and the Senate share certain **responsibilities**, like assessing and collecting taxes, borrowing money, overseeing commerce, minting currency, maintaining the armed forces, declaring war and, crucially, making "all Laws which shall be necessary and proper for carrying into Execution" these matters. But each separate chamber also has its own responsibilities: all revenue-raising (ie tax) bills originate in the House of Representatives, though the Senate can propose changes to such bills; only the Senate offers advice to the President on foreign treaties or on nominations to presidential appointments; and while the House has the sole power of impeachment of the President or other federal officer, the Senate is the body that decides whether to remove the person from office or not.

The House and Senate have separate chambers in the US Capitol, in which their debates take place. In practice, however, the **bills** that Congress debates as a prelude to making laws are generally put together and taken apart ("marked up," in the jargon) by more than 250 smaller **standing committees** and **subcommittees** (not to mention ad hoc committees and joint committees) that meet in rooms in the Capitol building or in the various relevant House or Senate Office buildings. The committees are made up of members from both parties, in rough accordance with their overall strength, and are usually chaired by senior members of the controlling party.

If a bill survives this process (and many don't), it is "reported" to the full House for consideration; at that point **amendments** may be added before the particular bill is voted upon. If it passes it's sent to the Senate, which can also make amendments before returning it to the House. Any differences are resolved by wrangles in a joint House-Senate **conference committee,** which produces a final bill, acceptable to a majority in Congress. In addition to the standing committees of Congress, on occasion **select committees** are established to deliberate on special congressional investigations or matters of national importance – most famously, perhaps, the unravelings of the Watergate affair.

Voting in Congress doesn't always divide up according to party as it usually does in parliamentary democracies. Although the Speaker and the Rules Committee (which arranges the work of the House) can ensure that the majority party influences the make-up of various committees, the order of debates and the nature of proposed amendments, strict party discipline is becoming less important. In the House, members often vote along state lines on particular issues, while specific matters are increasingly agreed and voted upon by members grouped into caucuses (or interest groups), which can cut across party loyalties.

Once a bill passes Congress it goes to the **executive** branch of government – whose head is the **President**, or Chief Executive – for approval. The President can either sign the bill, at which point it becomes law, or veto it, in which case the bill goes back to the chamber where it originated. With two-thirds majority votes in both houses, Congress can override the President to make the bill law. The powers of the President (whose annual salary is $400,000 plus $50,000 in expenses; the Vice President gets $186,000) are defined in Article 2 of the Constitution. As well as being Chief Executive, the President is also **Commander-in-Chief** of the armed forces; he can make treaties with foreign powers – provided two-thirds of the Senate agrees – and (again if two-thirds of the Senate are in favor) can appoint ambassadors, Supreme Court judges and other federal officers. Lest the Chief Executive get too bold, though, the Constitution provides **parameters** for presidential power: under the terms of the 22nd Amendment, ratified in 1951, the President (and the Vice President) is elected to office for four years and may only serve two terms. The amendment was a direct result of the presidency of Franklin Delano Roosevelt, who, determined to preserve his New Deal program and wary of impending war, served an unheard-of four consecutive terms. Moreover, the President is not above the law and can be removed from office by Congress "on impeachment for, and conviction of, treason, bribery, or other high crimes and misdemeanors."

This, however, is rarely attempted. The **impeachment** of President Clinton in 1999 was only the second such attempt in the country's history (the first was against Andrew Johnson; Nixon resigned before he could be impeached), and its failure was due in part to the nebulous nature of the defined standards of impeachment as laid down by the Constitution. "High crimes and misdemeanors" can essentially mean anything the House wants it to – in the eighteenth century, it probably referred to offenses against the state. However, if the President is removed from office by these means, or dies while in office or resigns, the Vice President gets the job until the next election; the Speaker of the House is third in line in the order of succession, followed by the Senate Majority Leader and then the Secretaries of the various executive departments in order of precedence. For more on the role of the presidency, see the box on p.138.

This entire system is underpinned by the third arm of government, the **judiciary**, whose highest form is manifested in the **Supreme Court**, established by Article 3 of the Constitution. Right from the outset, the Court was designed as the final protector of the Constitution; its task is to uphold its articles and the laws made under it – in effect, to maintain what the Constitution calls "the supreme law of the land." Every Congress member, and all executive and federal officers, are bound by oath to support and uphold the Constitution since they derive their powers from it. Ultimately, this notion of judicial supremacy boils down to the Constitution being what the Supreme Court says it is: the country has an "inferior" federal court system, in which legal decisions are made, and states are empowered to pass their own laws, but the appointed justices of the Supreme Court have the absolute right to throw out any legislation or legal argument that, in their opinion alone, violates the Constitution. Naturally, for this reason, the executive branch in the shape of each president is keen to appoint sympathetic justices to the Supreme Court bench. This, fortunately for the system, is not as easy or as predictable as it might appear. For more on the make-up of the Supreme Court itself, see pp.108–109.

Over the years, constitutional developments have also taken place outside the Constitution – that is, **informal changes** have been introduced to the system of government through custom or historical event. The Constitution makes no mention of political parties, primary elections or the congressional committee system for example, though each is now firmly entrenched in the system.

Real-world politics

That's the theory of American government. In practice, depending on whom you listen to, the entire structure – carefully crafted more than two hundred years ago – is in a state somewhere between bare working order and terminal decline. Political historian David McKay puts his finger on the nub when he says that the "federal system, with its myriad governments and what amounts to fifty-one distinct constitutional structures, is the very essence of fragmentation." The most obvious drawback of the system of "checks and balances" is that it can work both for and against political progress. The Constitution forces the President to work with Congress on policy, and some of the wilder presidential excesses are certainly curtailed by congressional deliberations. But in an entrenched **two-party system** such as exists today, much depends on the prevailing political climate in either House or Senate: stalemate or ineffective compromise tend to be the natural outcome of the checks and balances system.

Real-world congressional politics, as opposed to the theoretical marvel of American democracy, can be an unedifying spectacle, involving the often squalid trading of political favors, known as "logrolling." Moreover, the people are increasingly isolated from their elected representatives by the simple fact that candidates now need to be very rich to stand in the first place. Partly in response to the Watergate revelations, the 1974 Federal Election Campaign Act limited party and corporate contributions to a candidate's campaign, though failed to place a limit on the candidate's own contributions – a **campaign** for a prospective House seat can now cost $250,000, up to ten times that for a Senate seat, and countless millions for the presidency. Hardly surprisingly, becoming a member of Congress is now seen as a career move: having invested the time and money, incumbent members are less likely to stand down whatever their personal or political failings and, statistically, more likely to be re-elected than a challenger (who doesn't have the same access to the media and to the reflected political glories of Congress colleagues).

As both Democrats and Republicans scramble to occupy the increasingly crowded middle ground, the **electorate** it seems is becoming more sophisticated in its intentions. A reasonably high (though ultimately futile) protest vote went to third-party candidate Ross Perot in 1992 and again in 1996 (though in 2000, Ralph Nader got only three percent of the vote). Moreover, the voters are becoming less willing not only to give a president's party control of both houses of Congress at the same time (as they showed in the 1996 and 2000 elections) but also to give a president an overwhelming popular mandate. Since Richard Nixon's landslide in 1972, the presidential victor's share of the popular vote has bobbed under and around fifty percent – the only one to buck the trend was Ronald Reagan in 1984 (who gained almost 59 percent of the vote). In the end, though, the general disdain felt for what happens on Capitol Hill is perhaps best indicated by the fact that the **turnout** for presidential and House elections ranges from only thirty to fifty percent – one of the lowest in any democracy in the world.

Presidents of the USA

Name	Party	Date	State of birth
George Washington	–	1789–97	Virginia
John Adams	Federalist	1797–1801	Massachusetts
Thomas Jefferson	Democratic-Republican	1801–09	Virginia
James Madison	Democratic-Republican	1809–17	Virginia
James Monroe	Democratic-Republican	1817–25	Virginia
John Quincy Adams	Democratic-Republican	1825–29	Massachusetts
Andrew Jackson	Democrat	1829–37	South Carolina
Martin Van Buren	Democrat	1837–41	New York
William H. Harrison	Whig	1841 (died in office)	Virginia
John Tyler	Whig	1841–45	Virginia
James Polk	Democrat	1845–49	North Carolina
Zachary Taylor	Whig	1849–50 (died in office)	Virginia
Millard Fillmore	Whig	1850–53	New York
Franklin Pierce	Democrat	1853–57	New Hampshire
James Buchanan	Democrat	1857–61	Pennsylvania
Abraham Lincoln	Republican	1861–65 (assassinated)	Kentucky
Andrew Johnson	Union	1865–69	North Carolina
Ulysses S. Grant	Republican	1869–77	Ohio
Rutherford B. Hayes	Republican	1877–81	Ohio
James A. Garfield	Republican	1881 (assassinated)	Ohio
Chester A. Arthur	Republican	1881–85	Vermont
Grover Cleveland	Democrat	1885–89	New Jersey
Benjamin Harrison	Republican	1889–93	Ohio
Grover Cleveland	Democrat	1893–97	New Jersey
William McKinley	Republican	1897–1901	Ohio
Theodore Roosevelt	Republican	1901–09	New York
William H. Taft	Republican	1909–13	Ohio
Woodrow Wilson	Democrat	1913–21	Virginia
Warren G. Harding	Republican	1921–23 (died in office)	Ohio
Calvin Coolidge	Republican	1923–29	Vermont
Herbert Hoover	Republican	1929–33	Iowa
Franklin D. Roosevelt	Democrat	1933–45 (died in office)	New York
Harry S. Truman	Democrat	1945–53	Missouri
Dwight D. Eisenhower	Republican	1953–61	Texas
John F. Kennedy	Democrat	1961–63 (assassinated)	Massachusetts
Lyndon B. Johnson	Democrat	1963–69	Texas
Richard M. Nixon	Republican	1969–74 (resigned)	California
Gerald Ford	Republican	1974–77	Nebraska
James (Jimmy) Carter	Democrat	1977–81	Georgia
Ronald Reagan	Republican	1981–89	Illinois
George Bush	Republican	1989–93	Massachusetts
William (Bill) Clinton	Democrat	1993–2001	Arkansas
George W. Bush	Republican	2001–	Connecticut

Books

There are plenty of books that touch upon the history, politics and personalities of Washington DC; the problem is in getting an overall picture of the city. There's no one single straightforward and up-to-date history of DC, while visitors through the ages have tended only to include their observations of the capital as part of wider works about America. However, every book on American history contains at least a few pages about the founding of the capital city; Civil War treatises highlight DC as Lincoln's headquarters (and place of assassination), while presidential autobiographies and biographies, from those of George Washington onwards, necessarily recount the daily experience of political and social life in the capital.

In this chapter we've picked out some of the better, and more widely available, books about Washington DC, including novels set in the city. Many are available in good bookshops everywhere, and most in good **bookstores** in DC itself (see p.300 for a list) – where you'll also find local guides to ethnic restaurants, political trivia, cycling in the city, what to do with kids, and the like. Every major museum, gallery and attraction in DC sells related books, too, and these are a good first stop if you're looking for something arcane or specific – say a *History of Cats in the White House* or *101 Things to Do with a Beltway Journalist*. The selection in the National Museum of American History is perhaps the finest, while the Smithsonian Institution itself produces a wide range of titles on a variety of city-related topics. Finally, the White House Historical Association (740 Jackson Place, DC 20503 ☎202/737-8292, ⊛www.whitehousehistory.org) publishes a series of informative accounts of the White House, its contents and historical occupants.

History

Catherine Allgor *Parlor Politics* (US, University Press of Virginia). As nineteenth-century Washington developed from backwater to capital, the arrival of high society in the shape of the First Ladies and their social circles began to have a growing influence on politics – a thesis encapsulated in the book's subtitle: "In which the ladies of Washington build a city and government."

★ **David Brinkley** *Washington Goes to War* (US, Ballantine/UK, Deutsch). Acclaimed account of the capital during World War II under FDR, charting its emergence onto the international stage.

Francine Curro Cary *Urban Odyssey: A Multicultural History of Washington DC* (US, Smithsonian Institution Press). A readable historical account of settlement (and racial discrimination) in the city.

Alistair Cooke. Over sixty years as a correspondent has left Cooke with a wealth of American stories, personal histories and snapshots of cities, times and crises that adorn everything he writes and broadcasts. Although the capital appears as a bit player in much of his work, its presidents, politicians and people provide substance.

Noel Epstein (ed.) *Redskins: A History of Washington's Team* (US, Washington Post Books). An illustrated history of DC's favorite team.

David L. Lewis *District of Columbia: A History* (US, Norton). Useful – if now rather dated (1976) – history of the District.

Lloyd Lewis *The Assassination of Lincoln: History and Myth* (US, University of Nebraska Press). Lyrical, minute-by-minute account of the city's most notorious assassination and its aftermath, first published in 1929 (as *Myths After Lincoln*).

Anthony S. Pitch *The Burning of Washington: The British Invasion of 1814* (US, Naval Institute Press). Re-creation of the dramatic events of the summer of 1814 as the British set fire to the young capital and Francis Scott Key was inspired to write the "Star-Spangled Banner."

Politics and people

Anonymous *Primary Colors* (US, Warner/UK, Vintage). Highly readable, barely disguised account of a presidential primary campaign by young, charismatic, calculating, philandering, Southern governor Jack Stanton. Published amid great controversy in 1996, the book threw into the public domain the more reprehensible antics of press and politicians – its author was eventually unmasked as journalist and Washington insider Joe Klein. *The Running Mate* (US, Delta/UK, Vintage) was his follow-up satire, a presidential-campaign novel with even more backstabbing and scandal on every page.

★ **Carl Bernstein and Bob Woodward** *All the President's Men* (US & UK, Touchstone); *The Final Days* (US & UK, Touchstone). America's most famous journalistic sleuths tell the gripping story of the unraveling of the Nixon presidency. *All the President's Men* is a great book, later made into a great film; *The Final Days* saw the duo wrapping up the loose ends. Although both men have written investigative books since, none has matched these early classics.

Paul F. Boller, *Presidential Anecdotes*; *Presidential Campaigns*; *Presidential Wives*; *Congressional Anecdotes* (all US & UK, OUP); *Presidential Inaugurations* (US, Harcourt Brace). Amusing, inconsequential political factoids – who did what, where and when, and with whom.

Ben Bradlee *A Good Life* (US & UK, Touchstone). The autobiography of the executive editor of the *Washington Post* covers the years between 1968 and 1991. Watergate made Bradlee famous, and he still lives in DC, offering pertinent political comment.

Nigel Cawthorne *Sex Lives of the Presidents* (US, St Martin's Press/UK, Prion). Cawthorne turns his scurrilous eye to the horizontal pleasures of the world's most powerful men.

Frederick Douglass *The Life and Times of Frederick Douglass* (US & UK, various). The third volume (1881) of statesman, orator and ex-slave Frederick Douglass' autobiography sees him finally living in DC as US marshal and recorder of deeds. But the first volume, *Narrative of the Life of Frederick Douglass: An American Slave*, 1845, which covers part of Douglass' early life before he arrived in Washington, is actually more gripping.

★ **Katherine Graham** *Personal History* (US, Vintage/UK, Phoenix). Acclaimed autobiography of the *Washington Post* owner and Georgetown society hostess lifts the lid on DC's social and political niceties.

Meg Greenfield *Washington* (US, Public Affairs). Posthumously published memoir by long-time columnist, editorial writer and, eventually, editor of the *Washington Post*. Greenfield writes perceptively about the cocoon-like qualities of DC life and the beguiling range of its personalities.

Wesley O. Hagood *Presidential Sex: From the Founding Fathers to Bill Clinton* (US, Citadel Press). Hagood tells you more than you ever wanted to know about illicit presidential nookie.

David McKay *American Politics and Society* (UK, Blackwell). Best general introduction to who does what, why and when in the United States government, with diversions into American beliefs and values, and coverage of social, economic and foreign policy.

Andrew Morton *Monica's Story* (US, St Martin's Press/UK, Michael O' Mara). Biography of DC's most famous intern, telling the warts 'n' all story of Lewinsky and the Pres – by Princess Diana's confidant.

★ **P.J. O'Rourke** *Parliament of Whores* (US, Vintage/UK, Picador). All O'Rourke's demented political insights and raving right-wing prejudices brought together in a scabrous critique of the American political system as practiced in

Washington DC. It's also very, very funny.

Aaron Sorkin *The West Wing Script Book* (US & UK, Newmarket Press). Full scripts from the much-loved TV series present the daily machinations of the Josh Bartlett administration, one that many Americans wish was for real.

Kenneth W. Starr *The Starr Report* (US, various). The findings of independent counsel Ken Starr on Clinton and the Lewinsky affair are required reading for anyone fascinated by the entire sordid spectacle.

George Stephanopoulos (US & UK, Back Bay Books). Political memoir of arch presidential advisor (under Clinton) and master of spin Stephanopoulos, who knows all there is to know about what makes DC, the White House and the presidency tick.

Hunter S. Thompson. Gonzo's at his best taking sideswipes at corrupt politicians full of cant, and any of his books or collected essays feature a Washington villain or twenty – shot down in flames by a man for whom politics isn't the only drug.

Presidential biographies

Any good bookstore can provide a massive range of presidential biographies and memoirs. It's difficult to separate the wheat from the chaff, but standard works and particularly well-received tomes include (in presidential order):

John Adams by David McCullough (US & UK, Simon & Schuster)

Lincoln by David Herbert Donald (US, Touchstone)

Lincoln: A Foreigner's Quest by Jan Morris (US, Da Capo/UK, Penguin)

The Rise of Theodore Roosevelt and *Theodore Rex* by Edmund Morris (both US Random House/UK HarperCollins)

Franklin D. Roosevelt by Frank Friedel (US, Little, Brown)

Truman by Roy Jenkins (US, HarperCollins)

Truman by David McCullough (US & UK, Simon & Schuster)

Eisenhower: Soldier and President by Stephen E. Ambrose (US, Touchstone)

Nixon: A Life by Jonathan Aitken (US, Regnery)

Clinton: The President We/They Deserve by Martin Walker (US, Crown/UK, Vintage).

Guidebooks

Thomas J. Carrier *Washington DC: Historic Walking Tour* (US, Arcadia). Photographic record of the development of DC, incorporating informed walking tours around downtown areas.

Alzina Stone Dale *Mystery Reader's Walking Guide: DC* (US, Passport). Guided walks around the city in the company of the prose of crime and mystery writers.

Kathryn Allamong Jacob *Testament to Union* (US, Johns Hopkins University Press). Exhaustive record of the District's Civil War monuments and memorials, with over 90 photographs by Edwin Harlan Remsberg and accompanying historical text.

Claudia D. and George W. Kousoulas *Contemporary Architecture in Washington DC* (US, Preservation Press). Concentrates on the buildings of contemporary DC which, though no Chicago or New York, has enough to interest architecture buffs.

Christopher Weeks *AIA Guide to the Architecture of Washington DC* (US, Johns Hopkins University Press). Authoritative illustrated guide to the architecture of the city, covering buildings from every period since its founding.

Travel and impressions

David Cutler *Literary Washington* (US, Madison). The words and wisdom of celebrated writers, past and present, who have visited, worked and lived in DC.

★ **Charles Dickens** *American Notes* (US & UK, Penguin). One of the most quoted of all DC visitors, Dickens came in the early 1840s, when it was still, famously, a "City of Magnificent Intentions." Highly enjoyable satirical banter from a British writer at ease with America.

Jan Morris *Destinations* (US & UK, OUP). Typically dry observations of Washington high- and low-life, one of a series of pieces (about international cities) first written in the early 1980s for *Rolling Stone* magazine.

Watergate

If Washington has one domestic scandal it can call its own, it's **Watergate** (see pp.154–155), whose various aspects have been exhaustively covered since Bernstein and Woodward first set the ball rolling with *All the President's Men*. For the full story you could consult Fred Emery's *Watergate: The Corruption of American Politics and the Fall of Richard Nixon* (US, Touchstone) or a host of other eye-witness accounts, including Nixon's own *Memoirs* (US, Simon & Schuster), Robert Haldeman's *Haldeman Diaries: Inside the Nixon White House* (US, Berkley), John Dean's *Blind Ambition* (US, Simon & Schuster) and *Lost Honor* (US, Stratford Press), John Erlichman's *Witness to Power* (US, Simon & Schuster) and Gordon Liddy's *Will: The Autobiography of G. Gordon Liddy* (US & UK, St Martin's Press) – all first-hand (if not completely reliable) testimony from those who were there at the time. Virtually everyone else involved has written about the affair at some time or other, too, from Watergate burglar James McCord to Judge John Sirica, while *Nixon: An Oliver Stone Film* (US, Hyperion) presents the original screenplay of said movie alongside transcripts of taped Watergate conversations, previously classified memos and essays by key protagonists. More of the secret tapes recorded by Nixon, and betraying his deep prejudices, turn up in Stanley Kutler's *Abuse of Power: The New Nixon Tapes* (US & UK, Touchstone).

★ **Anthony Trollope** *North America* (US, Penguin/UK, Granville). Two-volume account of Trollope's visit to the US in the early 1860s. Picking up where his pioneering mother, Fanny, had left off in her contentious *Domestic Manners of the Americans* (1832; Da Capo/ Alan Sutton), Trollope lays about him with ire and verve – in Volume II, the Capitol building, White House, DC's streets and hotels, the Washington Monument and the Smithsonian all come in for undiluted carping and moaning. Great stuff.

DC in fiction

Henry Adams *Democracy* (US & UK, Meridian). A story of election-eering and intrigue set in 1870s DC, written (anonymously) by the historian grandson of John Quincy Adams.

★ **William Peter Blatty** *The Exorcist* (US, HarperCollins/UK, Corgi). Blatty's seminal horror story about the possession of a teenage girl, written in 1971, was set around Georgetown University and made into the scariest film ever produced.

Allen Drury *Advise and Consent* (US, Avon). Blackmail and slippery politics in Washington's upper echelons in the late 1950s; the novel – a great read once you adapt to the measured pace – was turned into a fine film by Otto Preminger starring Henry Fonda.

Sebastian Faulks *On Green Dolphin Street* (US, Random House/UK, Vintage). A British diplomat's wife embarks on an affair with an American reporter during the 1960 presidential election. The Cold War politics of the period act as a chilly backdrop to this taut tale of love and deception.

Ward Just *Echo House* (US, Mariner Books). Elegiac, epic novel of a DC political dynasty, with much to say about the nature of power in the city.

★ **Gore Vidal** *Burr; Lincoln; 1876; Empire; Hollywood; Washington DC; The Golden Age* (all US, Vintage/UK, Abacus). DC's – and America's – most potent, cynical chronicler sustains a terrific burst of form in seven hugely enjoyable novels tracing the history of the US from the Revolution to modern times and relying heavily on Washington set-piece scenes. The moving epic *Lincoln* is the real tour de force. Vidal's other books include *Palimpsest* (US, Penguin/UK, Abacus), a terrific memoir chronicling his life and loves, themes that are developed in his novel, *The Smithsonian Institution* (US, Harvest/UK, Abacus).

Crime and thrillers

Jeffrey Archer *Shall We Tell the President?* (US & UK, HarperCollins); *The Eleventh Commandment* (US & UK, HarperCollins). The "master storyteller" serves up the usual offerings – risible characterization, feeble plot development and leaden prose wrapped around tales of assassination plots and Cold War shenanigans set in DC.

Tom Clancy. One of the best of the blockbuster thriller writers, Clancy weaves DC scenes (or at least the White House, Capitol building, FBI and CIA HQ at Langley in Virginia) into nearly every tale of spook and terrorist intrigue. *Debt of Honor* (US, Berkeley/UK, HarperCollins), in which the President, Cabinet and most of Congress perish in a terrorist attack on the US Capitol, now seems eerily prophetic; *Executive Orders* (US, Berkeley/UK, HarperCollins) sees Jack Ryan (the Harrison Ford character of *Patriot Games*) take over as president of a shattered country.

Richard Timothy Conroy *The India Exhibition; Mr Smithson's Bones; Old Ways in the New World* (all US, St Martin's Press). Murder, mystery and labyrinthine goings-on in a series of engaging thrillers set in the Smithsonian Institution.

John Grisham. DC pops up in most of Grisham's work, notably in *The Pelican Brief* (US, Dell/UK, Arrow), a renowned legal whodunnit starting with the assassination of two Supreme Court judges and delving into dodgy politics and murky land deals, and in *The Street Lawyer* (US, Dell/UK, Arrow), a rather good exposé of city homelessness and poverty.

David Ignatius *A Firing Offense* (US, Ivy Books). Former *Post* journalist puts his newspaper experience to good use in an intelligent espionage thriller that jumps from DC locations to France and China.

★ **Charles McCarry** *Shelley's Heart* (US, Ivy Books). Page-turning thriller detailing stolen elections, secret societies and other political jiggery-pokery. His *Lucky Bastard* (US, Random House) details the rise of a charismatic, liberal, womanizing, presidential hopeful – now who could that be based on?

James Patterson *Along Came A Spider; Kiss The Girls; Cat and Mouse; Pop Goes the Weasel; Jack and Jill; Roses Are Red; Violets Are Blue* (all US, Warner/UK, HarperCollins). High-profile thriller writer whose dreadful prose style and imbecilic characterization do nothing to blunt his success. These seven books all feature black DC homicide detective Alex Cross.

William D. Pease *Playing the Dozens; The Monkey's First; The Rage of Innocence* (all US, Signet). A former Assistant US Attorney in DC, Pease writes legal/police thrillers that range across all the usual city locations and power sites.

★ **George P. Pelecanos.** DC's hippest chronicler, Pelecanos writes pointedly and beautifully about the city in a series of great thrillers, spanning the years and ethnic divide. *A Firing Offense* (his first), *Nick's Trip*, and *Down By the River Where the Dead Men Go* (all US & UK, Serpent's Tail) introduce feisty private eye Nick Stefanos; *King Suckerman* (US, Bantam/UK, Serpent's Tail) is a tour de force of Seventies drugs and racial tension; while *The Sweet Forever* (US, Dell/UK, Serpent's Tail) updates *Suckerman*'s characters to coke-riddled 1980s DC. Later novels, *Right As Rain* (US, Warner/UK, Orion) and *Hell To Pay* (US, Little, Brown/UK, Orion) feature the gritty pairing of black private eye Derek Strange and white ex-cop Terry Quinn, drifting through the murky DC underworld.

Phyllis Richman *The Butter Did It* (US & UK, HarperCollins). The *Washington Post*'s longtime restaurant critic turns her hand to mystery, introducing Chas Wheatley, the – surprise, surprise – *"Washington Examiner"* restaurant reviewer turned detective.

Elliott Roosevelt *Murder in the . . .* (US & UK, St Martin's Press & Avon). White House murder tales (with the dark deed committed in the Blue Room, West Wing, etc) by FDR's son, with the highly improbable First Lady-turned-sleuth Eleanor riding to the rescue every time.

Margaret Truman *Murder . . .* (US & UK, Fawcett). Harry's daughter churns out wooden murder-mystery stories set in various neighborhoods and buildings of DC, from Georgetown to the National Cathedral.

Poetry

★ **Walt Whitman** *Leaves of Grass* (US & UK, various). The first edition of *Leaves of Grass* appeared in 1855, and Whitman added sections to it for the rest of his life. His war poems, *Drum-Taps* (1865), were directly influenced by his work in DC's Civil War hospitals. *Memories of President Lincoln* were added after the assassination – including the famous and affecting *O Captain! My Captain!*.

index

and small print

Index

Map entries are in color

I

INDEX

Twenty years of Rough Guides

In the summer of 1981, Mark Ellingham, Rough Guides' founder, knocked out the first guide on a typewriter, with a group of friends. Mark had been traveling in Greece after university, and couldn't find a guidebook that really answered his needs.There were heavyweight cultural guides on the one hand – good on museums and classical sites but not on beaches and tavernas – and on the other hand student manuals that were so caught up with how to save money that they lost sight of the country's significance beyond its role as a place for a cool vacation. None of the guides began to address Greece as a country, with its natural and human environment, its politics and its contemporary life.

Having no urgent reason to return home, Mark decided to write his own guide. It was a guide to Greece that tried to combine some erudition and insight with a thoroughly practical approach to travelers' needs. Scrupulously researched listings of places to stay, eat and drink were matched by careful attention to detail on everything from Homer to Greek music, from classical sites to national parks and from nude beaches to monasteries. Back in London, Mark and his friends got their Rough Guide accepted by a farsighted commissioning editor at the publisher Routledge and it came out in 1982.

The Rough Guide to Greece was a student scheme that became a publishing phenomenon. The immediate success of the book – shortlisted for the Thomas Cook award – spawned a series that rapidly covered dozens of countries. The Rough Guides found a ready market among backpackers and budget travelers, but soon acquired a much broader readership that included older and less impecunious visitors. Readers relished the guides' wit and inquisitiveness as much as the enthusiastic, critical approach that acknowledges everyone wants value for money – but not at any price.

Rough Guides soon began supplementing the "rougher" information – the hostel and low-budget listings – with the kind of detail that independent-minded travelers on any budget might expect. These days, the guides – distributed worldwide by the Penguin group – include recommendations spanning the range from shoestring to luxury, and cover more than 200 destinations around the globe. Our growing team of authors, many of whom come to Rough Guides initially as outstandingly good letter-writers telling us about their travels, are spread all over the world, particularly in Europe, the USA and Australia. As well as the travel guides, Rough Guides publishes a series of dictionary phrasebooks covering two dozen major languages, an acclaimed series of music guides running the gamut from Classical to World Music, a series of music CDs in association with World Music Network, and a range of reference books on topics as diverse as the Internet, Pregnancy and Unexplained Phenomena. Visit **www.roughguides.com** to see what's cooking.

SMALL PRINT

Rough Guide credits

Text editor: Mary Callahan
Series editor: Mark Ellingham
Editorial: Martin Dunford, Jonathan Buckley, Kate Berens, Ann-Marie Shaw, Helena Smith, Judith Bamber, Orla Duane, Olivia Eccleshall, Ruth Blackmore, Geoff Howard, Claire Saunders, Gavin Thomas, Alexander Mark Rogers, Polly Thomas, Joe Staines, Richard Lim, Duncan Clark, Peter Buckley, Lucy Ratcliffe, Clifton Wilkinson, Alison Murchie, Matthew Teller, Andrew Dickson, Fran Sandham (UK); Andrew Rosenberg, Stephen Timblin, Yuki Takagaki, Richard Koss, Hunter Slaton, Julie Feiner (US)
Production: Susanne Hillen, Andy Hilliard, Link Hall, Helen Prior, Julia Bovis, Michelle Draycott, Katie Pringle, Zoë Nobes, Rachel

Holmes, Andy Turner, Michelle Bhatia
Cartography: Melissa Baker, Maxine Repath, Ed Wright, Katie Lloyd-Jones
Picture research: Louise Boulton, Sharon Martins, Mark Thomas
Online: Kelly Cross, Anja Mutic-Blessing, Jennifer Gold, Audra Epstein, Suzanne Welles, Cree Lawson (US)
Finance: John Fisher, Gary Singh, Edward Downey, Mark Hall, Tim Bill
Marketing & Publicity: Richard Trillo, Niki Smith, David Wearn, Chloë Roberts, Demelza Dallow, Claire Southern (UK); Simon Carloss, David Wechsler, Kathleen Rushforth (US)
Administration: Tania Hummel, Julie Sanderson

Publishing information

This third edition published May 2002 by
Rough Guides Ltd,
62–70 Shorts Gardens, London WC2H 9AH.
Penguin Putnam, Inc., 375 Hudson Street, NY 10014, USA.
Distributed by the Penguin Group
Penguin Books Ltd,
80 Strand, London WC2R 0RL
Penguin Putnam, Inc.,
375 Hudson Street, NY 10014, USA
Penguin Books Australia Ltd,
487 Maroondah Highway, PO Box 257, Ringwood, Victoria 3134, Australia
Penguin Books Canada Ltd,
10 Alcorn Avenue, Toronto, Ontario, Canada M4V 1E4
Penguin Books (NZ) Ltd,
182–190 Wairau Road, Auckland 10, New Zealand
Typeset in Bembo and Helvetica to an original design by Henry Iles.

Printed in Italy by LegoPrint S.p.A

© Jules Brown, 2002

368pp includes index
A catalogue record for this book is available from the British Library

ISBN 1-85828-884-3

The publishers and authors have done their best to ensure the accuracy and currency of all the information in **The Rough Guide to Washington DC**, however, they can accept no responsibility for any loss, injury, or inconvenience sustained by any traveller as a result of information or advice contained in the guide.

Help us update

We've gone to a lot of effort to ensure that the third edition of **The Rough Guide to Washington DC** is accurate and up to date. However, things change – places get "discovered," opening hours are notoriously fickle, restaurants and rooms raise prices or lower standards. If you feel we've got it wrong or left something out, we'd like to know, and if you can remember the address, the price, the time, the phone number, so much the better.

We'll credit all contributions, and send a copy of the next edition (or any other Rough Guide if you prefer) for the best letters. Everyone who writes to us and isn't already a subscriber will receive a copy of our full-color thrice-yearly newsletter. Please mark letters: **"Rough Guide Washington DC Update"** and send to: Rough Guides, 62–70 Shorts Gardens, London WC2H 9AH, or Rough Guides, 4th Floor, 345 Hudson St, New York, NY 10014. Or send an email to:
mail@roughguides.co.uk or
mail@roughguides.com

Acknowledgments

Jules Thanks to Jeff Cranmer for a superb updating job on this edition, and Andrew Rosenberg for helping things run as smoothly as ever.

Jeff Many thanks to Mary for her superb editing and to Jules, Andrew and Richard at the Rough Guides for their guidance (and patience). Hats off to DC nightlife connoisseur Andre Bald, Quentin Hodgson, Susie Park, Dave Peters, Sam Scoles, Katy Vincent and Tim & Tina Wickham – without all of their help this update could not have been completed. A big thank you to everyone else who assisted me along the way, especially: the Alexandria Convention & Visitors Association, Jasmin Chakeri, J.P.

Ferguson, Zack Henry, Sidney Lawrence at the Hirshhorn, Sandi Leavitt, Laura Lipscomb, Nishaya Mangklapruk, Rebecca Pawlowski at the WCTC, Madhavi Swamy, Zoe Vantos and Yao. And to the fine gentlemen of 17th Street Lounge – Whit, Bram, Ole and Kyle – I raise my glass.

Thanks, too, go to Helen Prior and Michelle Bhatia for layout and typesetting; Michelle Draycott for dogged photo research work; Maxine Repath for overseeing maps; Derek Wilde for proofreading; Jeff and Jules for another great guide; and Julia Bovis, Ed Wright, and Hunter Slaton for their various contributions.

SMALL PRINT

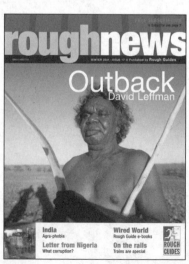

around the world

Alaska ★ Algarve ★ Amsterdam ★ Andalucía ★ Antigua & Barbuda ★ Argentina ★ Auckland Restaurants ★ Australia ★ Austria ★ Bahamas ★ Bali & Lombok ★ Bangkok ★ Barbados ★ Barcelona ★ Beijing ★ Belgium & Luxembourg ★ Belize ★ Berlin ★ Big Island of Hawaii ★ Bolivia ★ Boston ★ Brazil ★ Britain ★ Brittany & Normandy ★ Bruges & Ghent ★ Brussels ★ Budapest ★ Bulgaria ★ California ★ Cambodia ★ Canada ★ Cape Town ★ The Caribbean ★ Central America ★ Chile ★ China ★ Copenhagen ★ Corsica ★ Costa Brava ★ Costa Rica ★ Crete ★ Croatia ★ Cuba ★ Cyprus ★ Czech & Slovak Republics ★ Devon & Cornwall ★ Dodecanese & East Aegean ★ Dominican Republic ★ The Dordogne & the Lot ★ Dublin ★ Ecuador ★ Edinburgh ★ Egypt ★ England ★ Europe ★ First-time Asia ★ First-time Europe ★ Florence ★ Florida ★ France ★ French Hotels & Restaurants ★ Gay & Lesbian Australia ★ Germany ★ Goa ★ Greece ★ Greek Islands ★ Guatemala ★ Hawaii ★ Holland ★ Hong Kong & Macau ★ Honolulu ★ Hungary ★ Ibiza & Formentera ★ Iceland ★ India ★ Indonesia ★ Ionian Islands ★ Ireland ★ Israel & the Palestinian Territories ★ Italy ★ Jamaica ★ Japan ★ Jerusalem ★ Jordan ★ Kenya ★ The Lake District ★ Languedoc & Roussillon ★ Laos ★ Las Vegas ★ Lisbon ★ London ★

in twenty years

London Mini Guide ★ London Restaurants ★ Los Angeles ★ Madeira ★ Madrid ★ Malaysia, Singapore & Brunei ★ Mallorca ★ Malta & Gozo ★ Maui ★ Maya World ★ Melbourne ★ Menorca ★ Mexico ★ Miami & the Florida Keys ★ Montréal ★ Morocco ★ Moscow ★ Nepal ★ New England ★ New Orleans ★ New York City ★ New York Mini Guide ★ New York Restaurants ★ New Zealand ★ Norway ★ Pacific Northwest ★ Paris ★ Paris Mini Guide ★ Peru ★ Poland ★ Portugal ★ Prague ★ Provence & the Côte d'Azur ★ Pyrenees ★ The Rocky Mountains ★ Romania ★ Rome ★ San Francisco ★ San Francisco Restaurants ★ Sardinia ★ Scandinavia ★ Scotland ★ Scottish Highlands & Islands ★ Seattle ★ Sicily ★ Singapore ★ South Africa, Lesotho & Swaziland ★ South India ★ Southeast Asia ★ Southwest USA ★ Spain ★ St Lucia ★ St Petersburg ★ Sweden ★ Switzerland ★ Sydney ★ Syria ★ Tanzania ★ Tenerife and La Gomera ★ Thailand ★ Thailand's Beaches & Islands ★ Tokyo ★ Toronto ★ Travel Health ★ Trinidad & Tobago ★ Tunisia ★ Turkey ★ Tuscany & Umbria ★ USA ★ Vancouver ★ Venice & the Veneto ★ Vienna ★ Vietnam ★ Wales ★ Washington DC ★ West Africa ★ Women Travel ★ Yosemite ★ Zanzibar ★ Zimbabwe

also look out for our maps,
phrasebooks, music guides
and reference books

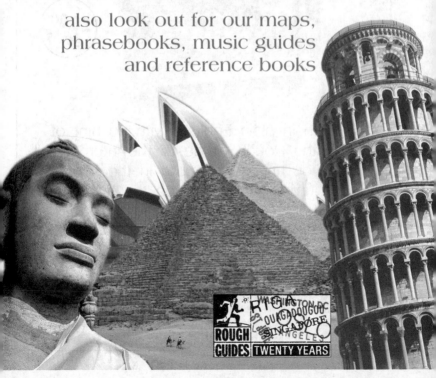

ROUGH GUIDES TWENTY YEARS

Will you have enough stories to tell your grandchildren?

Yahoo! Travel

Do You
YAHOO

The ideas expressed in this code were developed by and for independent travellers.

Learn About The Country You're Visiting

Start enjoying your travels before you leave by tapping into as many sources of information as you can.

The Cost Of Your Holiday

Think about where your money goes - be fair and realistic about how cheaply you travel. Try and put money into local peoples' hands; drink local beer or fruit juice rather than imported brands and stay in locally owned accommodation. Haggle with humour and not aggressively. Pay what something is worth to you and remember how wealthy you are compared to local people.

Embrace The Local Culture

Open your mind to new cultures and traditions - it will transform your experience. Think carefully about what's appropriate in terms of your clothes and the way you behave. You'll earn respect and be more readily welcomed by local people. Respect local laws and attitudes towards drugs and alcohol that vary in different countries and communities. Think about the impact you could have on them.

Exploring The World – The Travellers' Code

Being sensitive to these ideas means getting more out of your travels - and giving more back to the people you meet and the places you visit.

Minimise Your Environmental Impact

Think about what happens to your rubbish - take biodegradable products and a water filter bottle. Be sensitive to limited resources like water, fuel and electricity. Help preserve local wildlife and habitats by respecting local rules and regulations, such as sticking to footpaths and not standing on coral.

Don't Rely On Guidebooks

Use your guidebook as a starting point, not the only source of information. Talk to local people, then discover your own adventure!

Be Discreet With Photography

Don't treat people as part of the landscape, they may not want their picture taken. Ask first and respect their wishes.

We work with people the world over to promote tourism that benefits their communities, but we can only carry on our work with the support of people like you. For membership details or to find out how to make your travels work for local people and the environment, visit our website.

www.tourismconcern.org.uk

TourismConcern
Campaigning for Ethical and Fairly Traded Tourism

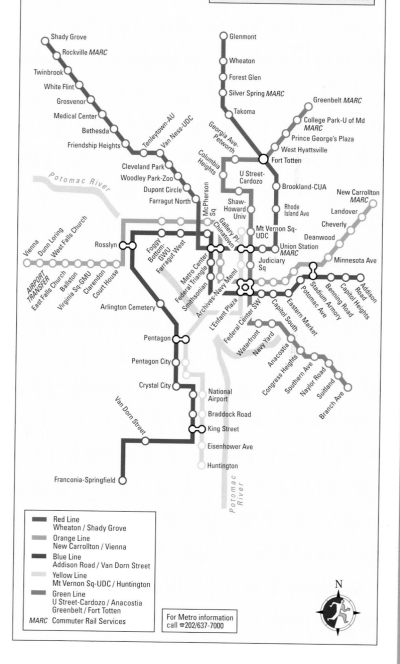

THE METRORAIL SYSTEM

Red Line
Wheaton / Shady Grove

Orange Line
New Carrollton / Vienna

Blue Line
Addison Road / Van Dorn Street

Yellow Line
Mt Vernon Sq-UDC / Huntington

Green Line
U Street-Cardozo / Anacostia
Greenbelt / Fort Totten

MARC Commuter Rail Services

For Metro information
call ☎202/637-7000

N

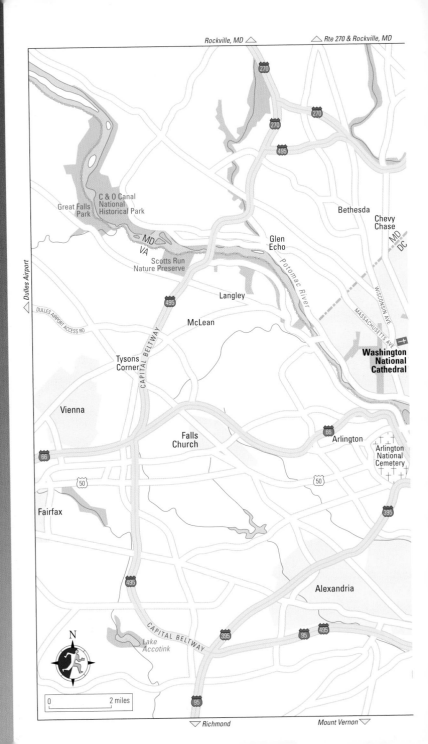

△ Rte 270 & Rockville, MD

△ Dulles Airport

DULLES AIRPORT ACCESS RD

270

270

495

270

495

C & O Canal
National
Historical Park

Great Falls
Park

MD
VA

Scotts Run
Nature Preserve

Langley

McLean

Tysons
Corner

CAPITAL BELTWAY

Vienna

66

66

50

Fairfax

Falls
Church

50

495

Bethesda

Chevy
Chase

MD
DC

Glen
Echo

Potomac River

WISCONSIN AVE

MASSACHUSETTS AVE

**Washington
National
Cathedral**

66

Arlington

Arlington
National
Cemetery

395

Alexandria

495

CAPITAL BELTWAY

Lake
Accotink

395

95

495

N

0   2 miles

95

▽ Richmond

Mount Vernon ▽

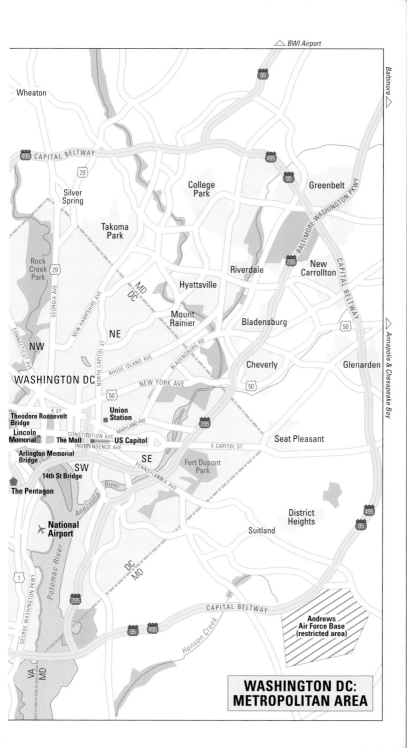

See 'Northwest' map for more detail

Washington National Cathedral ✝

WOODLEY PARK

National Zoological Park

See 'New Downtown, Dupont and Adams-Morgan' map for more detail

See 'Georgetown' map for more detail

NEW MEXICO AVE
MASSACHUSETTS AVE
CLEVELAND AVE
CONNECTICUT AVE
COLUMBIA RD

Woodley Park National Zoo Ⓜ

Rock Creek Park

ADAMS-MORGAN

Meridian Hill Park

FLORIDA AVE

Glover Archbold Park

TUNLAW RD

WISCONSIN AVE

US Naval Observatory

MASSACHUSETTS AVE

ROCK CREEK AND POTOMAC PKWY

FLORIDA AVE

18TH ST

NEW HAMPSHIRE AVE

16TH ST

U ST

14TH ST

SHAW

S ST

Dumbarton Oaks Park

Montrose Park

R ST

SHERIDAN CIRCLE

DUPONT CIRCLE

Georgetown University

37TH ST

35TH ST

RESERVOIR RD

Q ST

30TH ST

28TH ST

Dupont Circle Ⓜ

P ST

LOGAN CIRCLE

GEORGETOWN

PROSPECT ST

M ST

23RD ST

NEW HAMPSHIRE AVE

SCOTT CIRCLE

NEW DOWNTOWN

THOMAS CIRCLE

N.

FOXHALL RD

MACARTHUR BLVD

CANAL RD

CANAL RD

WHITEHURST FREEWAY

Francis Scott Key Memorial Bridge

GEORGE WASHINGTON MEMORIAL PKWY

Potomac River

Foggy Bottom-GWU Ⓜ

WASHINGTON CIRCLE

PENNSYLVANIA AVE

K ST

Farragut North Ⓜ

Farragut West Ⓜ

McPherson Square Ⓜ

H ST

NEW YORK AVE

George Washington University

FOGGY BOTTOM

The White House

17TH ST

15TH ST

14TH ST

Ⓜ

66 CUSTIS MEMORIAL PKWY

Theodore Roosevelt Island

Little River

ROCK CREEK AND POTOMAC PKWY

VIRGINIA AVE

Kennedy Center

E ST

The Ellipse

ⓘ

Rosslyn Ⓜ

66

WILSON BLVD

Court House Ⓜ

ARLINGTON BLVD

Theodore Roosevelt Bridge

50

Department of State

Vietnam Veterans Memorial 🏛

C ST

CONSTITUTION AVE

Federal Triangle

Washington Monument 🏛

Smithsonian Ⓜ

Constitution Gardens

Lincoln Memorial

Holocaust Museum

Arlington Cemetery Ⓜ

Arlington Memorial Bridge

West Potomac Park

Bureau of Engraving & Printing

Tidal Basin

14th St Bridge

ARLINGTON BLVD

Arlington National Cemetery

JEFFERSON DAVIS HWY

Jefferson Memorial 🏛

ARLINGTON BLVD

WASHINGTON BLVD

JEFFERSON DAVIS HWY

GEORGE WASHINGTON

George Mason (14th St) Meml Bridge

East Potomac Park

50

WASHINGTON BLVD

Rochambeau Meml Bridge

MEMORIAL PKWY

Potomac River

Pentagon Ⓜ

Pentagon

ARLINGTON RIDGE ROAD

WASHINGTON BLVD

SHIRLEY HWY

ARMY NAVY DRIVE

COLUMBIA PIKE

Pentagon City Ⓜ

ARLINGTON VILLAGE

395

See 'Arlington' map for more detail

JOYCE STREET

HAYES STREET

SMITH BLVD

Washington National Airport

ADDISON HEIGHTS

△ Silver Spring, MD

WASHINGTON DC

M Brookland CUA

0   500 yds

N

GEORGIA AVE

MICHIGAN AVE

FRANKLIN ST

NORTH CAPITOL ST

18TH ST

RHODE ISLAND AVE

13TH ST

McMillan
Reservoir

**Howard
University**

W ST

M Rhode Island
Avenue

U Street
Cardozo
M

LEDROIT PARK

VERMONT AVE

Shaw-
Howard
University
M

RHODE ISLAND AVE

BLADENSBURG RD

NEW YORK AVE

Brentwood
Park

**US National
Arboretum**

WEST VIRGINIA AVE

See 'Central Washington DC' map for more detail

1ST ST

**New
Convention
Center (site)**

ST

**Gallaudet
University**

FLORIDA AVE

50

M ST

M Mt Vernon
Sq-UDC

NEW JERSEY AVE

M ST

MT VERNON
SQUARE

**Greyhound
Bus Terminal**

NORTH CAPITOL ST

**Convention
Center**

MASSACHUSETTS AVE

K ST

MARYLAND AVE

BENNING RD

Gallery
Place
M

Metro
Center

Judiciary
Square
M
395

Union
Station
M

**Union
Station**

F ST

E ST

M

H ST

**OLD
DOWNTOWN**

PENNSYLVANIA

M
AVE

Archives-Navy Meml

**Senate
Offices**

STANTON
SQUARE

C ST

MADISON DR

CONSTITUTION AVE

**CAPITOL
HILL**

MARYLAND AVE

The Mall

US Capitol

**Library of
Congress**

4TH ST

EAST CAPITOL ST

LINCOLN
PARK

EAST CAPITOL ST

JEFFERSON DR

MASSACHUSETTS AVE

**RFK
Stadium**

Federal
Center SW

INDEPENDENCE AVE

N CAROLINA AVE

M Stadium
Armory

C ST

House Offices

M

KENTUCKY AVE

L'Enfant
Plaza
M

NEW JERSEY AVE

Capitol
South
M

SEWARD
SQUARE

SOUTH CAROLINA AVE

Eastern
Market M

PENNSYLVANIA AVE

M Potomac
Ave

395

VIRGINIA AVE

**SOUTHWEST/
WATERFRONT**

SOUTH CAPITOL ST

M ST

M Navy Yard

**Washington
Navy Yard**

**John Phillip
Sousa Bridge**

295

Washington Channel

Washington

M
Waterfront

■ Navy
Museum

ANACOSTIA DRIVE

ANACOSTIA FREEWAY

MINNESOTA AVE

Anacostia River

11th St
Bridge

**Fort
McNair**

**Frederick
Douglass
Meml Bridge**

Anacostia
M

ANACOSTIA

NAYLOR RD

ROBBINS ROAD

GOOD HOPE RD

MARTIN LUTHER KING JR AVE

**Frederick Douglass
National Historic Site**

Fort Stanton
Park

**Naval District
Washington
Anacostia**

295

ALABAMA AVE

**GARFIELD
HEIGHTS**

SUITLAND PARKWAY

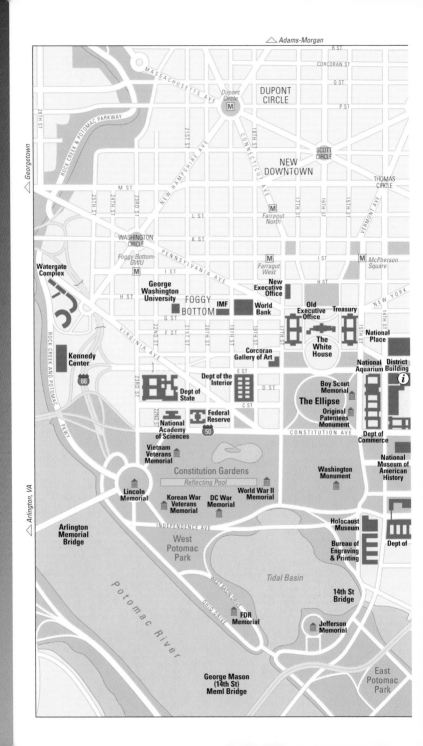

△ Adams-Morgan

R ST
CORCORAN ST
Q ST
P ST

Dupont
Circle M

DUPONT
CIRCLE

28TH ST

MASSACHUSETTS AVE

ROCK CREEK & POTOMAC PARKWAY

△ Georgetown

21ST ST

18TH ST

CONNECTICUT AVE

SCOTT
CIRCLE

NEW
DOWNTOWN

THOMAS
CIRCLE

VERMONT AVE

M ST

25TH ST
24TH ST
23RD ST

NEW HAMPSHIRE AVE

L ST

K ST

CONNECTICUT AVE

17TH ST

16TH ST

15TH ST

M Farragut
North

WASHINGTON
CIRCLE

PENNSYLVANIA AVE

Foggy Bottom-
GWU M

I ST

M
Farragut
West

I ST

M McPherson
Square

Watergate
Complex

George
Washington
University

FOGGY
BOTTOM

IMF

H ST

New
Executive
Office

World
Bank

H ST

Old
Executive
Office

Treasury

NEW YORK

14TH ST

ROCK CREEK AND POTOMAC

VIRGINIA AVE

22ND ST
21ST ST
20TH ST

G ST
F ST

19TH ST

18TH ST

17TH ST

National
Place

Kennedy
Center

66

23RD ST

Corcoran
Gallery of Art

E ST

The
White
House

15TH ST

National
Aquarium

District
Building

i

Dept of the
Interior

D ST

Boy Scout
Memorial

Dept of
State

Federal
Reserve

50

C ST

The Ellipse

National
Academy
of Sciences

22ND ST

Original
Patentees
Monument

Dept of
Commerce

Vietnam
Veterans
Memorial

CONSTITUTION AVE

National
Museum of
American
History

Constitution Gardens

Reflecting Pool

World War II
Memorial

Washington
Monument

Lincoln
Memorial

Korean War
Veterans
Memorial

DC War
Memorial

INDEPENDENCE AVE

Holocaust
Museum

Arlington
Memorial
Bridge

West
Potomac
Park

WEST BASIN DR

Bureau of
Engraving
& Printing

Dept of

△ Arlington, VA

Tidal Basin

14th St
Bridge

Potomac River

OHIO DRIVE

FDR
Memorial

Jefferson
Memorial

George Mason
(14th St)
Meml Bridge

East
Potomac
Park

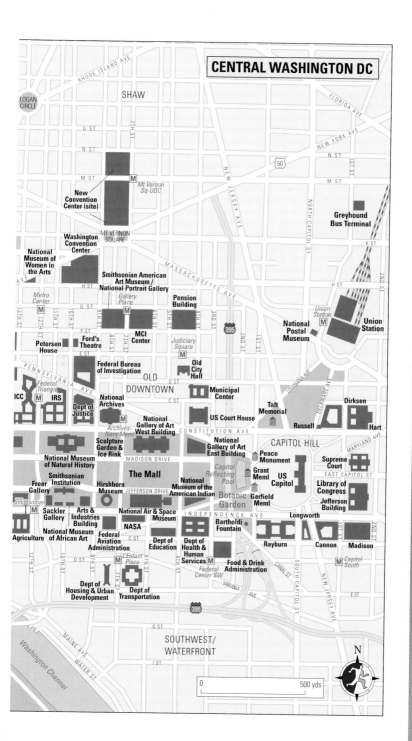

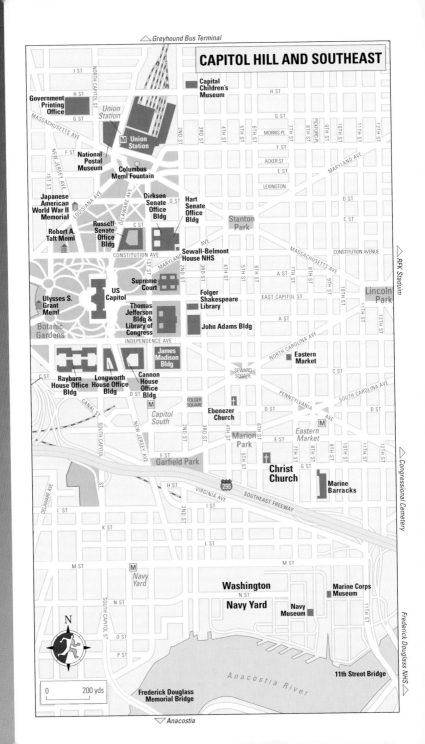

△ Greyhound Bus Terminal

CAPITOL HILL AND SOUTHEAST

Government Printing Office

Capital Children's Museum

Union Station

Ⓜ Union Station

National Postal Museum

Columbus Meml Fountain

Japanese American World War II Memorial

Dirksen Senate Office Bldg

Hart Senate Office Bldg

Russell Senate Office Bldg

Robert A. Taft Meml

Stanton Park

Sewall-Belmont House NHS

Ulysses S. Grant Meml

US Capitol

Supreme Court

Folger Shakespeare Library

Lincoln Park

Botanic Gardens

Thomas Jefferson Bldg & Library of Congress

John Adams Bldg

James Madison Bldg

Eastern Market

Rayburn House Office Bldg

Longworth House Office Bldg

Cannon House Office Bldg

Ⓜ Capitol South

Ebenezer Church

Marion Park

Eastern Market

Garfield Park

Christ Church

Marine Barracks

295 Virginia Ave Southeast Freeway

Ⓜ Navy Yard

Washington

Marine Corps Museum

Navy Yard

Navy Museum

N

0   200 yds

Frederick Douglass Memorial Bridge

Anacostia River

11th Street Bridge

△ RFK Stadium

△ Congressional Cemetery

△ Frederick Douglass NHS

▽ Anacostia

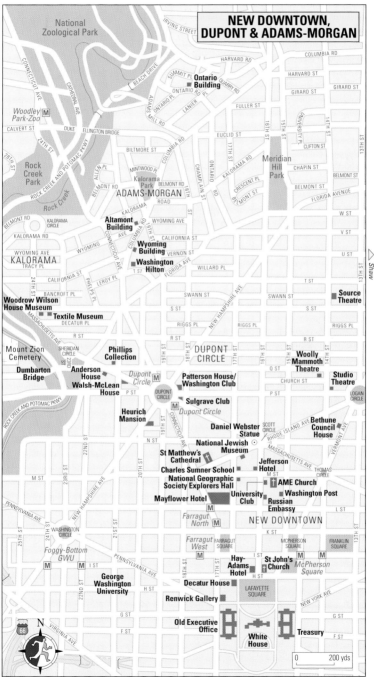

NEW DOWNTOWN, DUPONT & ADAMS-MORGAN

National Zoological Park

IRVING STREET

HARVARD RD

COLUMBIA RD

HARVARD ST

GIRARD ST

SUMMIT PL

ONTARIO PL

Ontario Building

QUARRY RD

GIRARD ST

BEACH DRIVE

ADAMS MILL RD

ONTARIO RD

LANIER

FULLER ST

UNIVERSITY PL

CONNECTICUT AVE

CATHEDRAL AVE

Woodley Park-Zoo M

DUKE

ELLINGTON BRIDGE

CALVERT ST

EUCLID ST

CLIFTON ST

14TH ST

13TH ST

16TH ST

CHAPIN ST

Meridian Hill Park

BELMONT ST

CRESCENT PL

FLORIDA AVENUE

BILTMORE ST

COLUMBIA RD

KALORAMA RD

28TH ST

24TH ST

ROCK CREEK AND POTOMAC PKWY

Rock Creek Park

Rock Creek

BELMONT RD

ALLEN PL

MINTWOOD PL

Kalorama Park

BELMONT RD

ADAMS-MORGAN

ROAD

CHAMPLAIN ST

ONTARIO RD

BELMONT ST

W ST

KALORAMA

Altamont Building

18TH ST

WYOMING AVE

V ST

BELMONT RD

KALORAMA CIRCLE

KALORAMA RD

WYOMING

CONNECTICUT AVE

COLUMBIA RD

CALIFORNIA ST

Wyoming Building

VERNON ST

Washington Hilton

FLORIDA AVE

U ST

13TH ST

KALORAMA

WYOMING AVE

TRACY PL

PHELPS PL

LEROY PL

WILLARD PL

T ST

CALIFORNIA ST

BANCROFT PL

T ST

SWANN ST

SWANN ST

Source Theatre

24TH ST

Shaw

Woodrow Wilson House Museum

Textile Museum

DECATUR PL

S ST

NEW HAMPSHIRE AVE

S ST

MASSACHUSETTS AVE

R ST

RIGGS PL

RIGGS PL

RIGGS PL

Georgetown

Mount Zion Cemetery

SHERIDAN CIRCLE

Phillips Collection

R ST

15TH ST

18TH ST

R ST

DUPONT CIRCLE

17TH ST

16TH ST

Woolly Mammoth Theatre

R ST

Dumbarton Bridge

23RD ST

22ND ST

Anderson House

Dupont Circle M

Patterson House/ Washington Club

CHURCH ST

Q ST

Studio Theatre

LOGAN CIRCLE

Walsh-McLean House

P ST

DUPONT CIRCLE

Dupont Circle

P ST

ROCK CREEK AND POTOMAC PKWY

Heurich Mansion

M

Sulgrave Club

19TH ST

N ST

CONNECTICUT AVE

Daniel Webster Statue

SCOTT CIRCLE

RHODE ISLAND AVE

Bethune Council House

VERMONT AVE

National Jewish Museum

National Jewish Museum

20TH ST

St Matthew's Cathedral

Charles Sumner School

MASSACHUSETTS AVE

Jefferson Hotel

THOMAS CIRCLE

National Geographic Society Explorers Hall

M ST

AME Church

Washington Post

PENNSYLVANIA AVE

Mayflower Hotel

University Club

Russian Embassy

L ST

Farragut North M

NEW DOWNTOWN

25TH ST

24TH ST

WASHINGTON CIRCLE

21ST ST

Farragut West

FARRAGUT SQUARE

K ST

MCPHERSON SQUARE

FRANKLIN SQUARE

13TH ST

Foggy-Bottom GWU

M

M

I ST

PENNSYLVANIA AVE

18TH ST

17TH ST

Hay-Adams Hotel

I ST

St John's Church

M

McPherson Square

M

23RD ST

22ND ST

George Washington University

H ST

Decatur House

H ST

LAFAYETTE SQUARE

Renwick Gallery

N

66

VIRGINIA AVE

G ST

Old Executive Office

White House

NEW YORK AVE

Treasury

G ST

F ST

F ST

0   200 yds

Lincoln Memorial

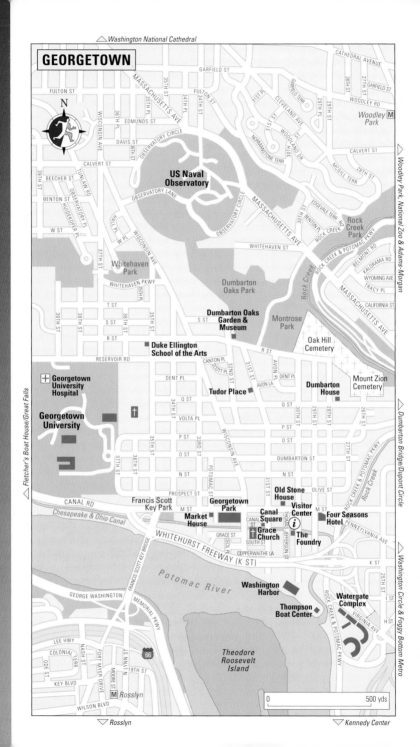

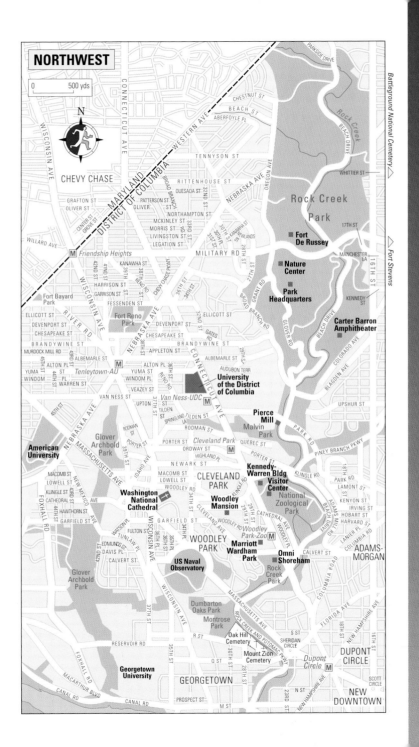

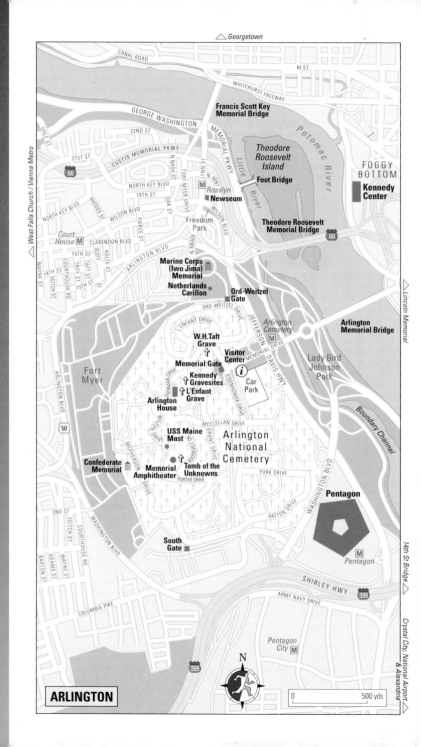

△ *Georgetown*

CANAL ROAD

M ST

WHITEHURST FREEWAY

Francis Scott Key Memorial Bridge

GEORGE WASHINGTON

22ND ST

Potomac River

Theodore Roosevelt Island

21ST ST

66

CUSTIS MEMORIAL PKWY

FOGGY BOTTOM

Kennedy Center

UHLE ST

NORTH KEY BLVD

18TH ST

WILSON BLVD

N NASH ST

FORT MYER DRIVE

N KENT ST

N NASH ST

MEMORIAL PKWY

Little River

M *Rosslyn*
■ **Newseum**

Foot Bridge

△ *West Falls Church / Vienna Metro*

NORTH KEY BLVD

RHODES ST

PIERCE ST

Freedom Park

WILSON BLVD

Theodore Roosevelt Memorial Bridge

66

Court House M

CLARENDON BLVD

15TH ST

SCOTT ST

ROLFE ST

ARLINGTON BLVD

TAFT ST

TROY ST

13TH ST

Marine Corps (Iwo Jima) Memorial 🏛

WAYNE ST

14TH ST

COURTHOUSE RD

Netherlands Carillon ●

Ord-Weitzel Gate ■

ORD-WEITZEL DRIVE

L'ENFANT DRIVE

JEFFERSON

Arlington Cemetery M

DAVIS HWY

Arlington Memorial Bridge

△ *Lincoln Memorial*

W.H.Taft Grave ✝

Visitor Center

MEMORIAL DRIVE

Fort Myer

Memorial Gate ■

SHERMAN DRIVE

Kennedy Gravesites ✝
✝ **L'Enfant Grave**

ⓘ

Lady Bird Johnson Park

EISENHOWER DRIVE

Arlington House

WILSON DRIVE

Car Park

MCCLELLAN DRIVE

ARLINGTON BLVD

50

MCPHERSON DRIVE

USS Maine Mast ●

GRANT DRIVE

Boundary Channel

Confederate Memorial 🏛

Memorial Amphitheater

✝ **Tomb of the Unknowns**

PORTER DRIVE

Arlington National Cemetery

WASHINGTON BLVD

YORK DRIVE

Pentagon

2ND ST

WASHINGTON BLVD

PATTON DRIVE

VEITCH ST

WAYNE ST

ADAMS ST

BARTON ST

COURTHOUSE RD

South Gate ■

M *Pentagon*

COLUMBIA PIKE

SHIRLEY HWY

ARMY NAVY DRIVE

395

14th St Bridge △

Pentagon City M

△ *Crystal City, National Airport & Alexandria*

N

395

ARLINGTON

0 — 500 yds